AMERICAN IMMIGRATION & ETHNICITY

A 20-Volume Series of Distinguished Essays

EDITED BY
George E. Pozzetta

A Garland Series

TITLES IN THE SERIES

VOLUME 19

THE IMMIGRANT RELIGIOUS EXPERIENCE

EDITED BY
George E. Pozzetta

GARLAND PUBLISHING, INC.
New York & London
1991

Introduction Copyright © 1991 by George E. Pozzetta
All Rights Reserved

Library of Congress Cataloging-in-Publication Data

The Immigrant religious experience/ edited by George E. Pozzetta.
p. cm.—(American immigration and ethnicity; v. 19)
ISBN 0-8240-7419-X (alk. paper)
1. United States—Church history—19th century. 2. United States—
Church History—20th century. 3. Ethnicity—United States—
Religious aspects—Christianity. 4. Immigrants—United States,
Religious life. 5. Church work with immigrants—History.
I. Pozzetta, George E. II. Series.
BR525.I66   1990
208'.693—dc20   90-49041

Printed on acid-free, 250-year-life paper
Manufactured in the United States of America

INTRODUCTION

Once I thought to write a history of the immigrants in America. Then I discovered that the immigrants were American history.

Oscar Handlin,
The Uprooted (1951)

When it first appeared forty years ago, Oscar Handlin's startling observation occasioned disbelieving reactions; today, changes in historical scholarship have moved immigrants much closer to the central position posited by Handlin than perhaps even he ever considered possible. Once relegated to the fringes of historical investigation, immigrants now speak to the main themes of American history with an eloquence that belies the lack of attention they received earlier. In large part this is true because of what has happened to the field of immigration studies. Drawing from the momentum of the new social history, with its perspective "from the bottom up" and its insistence on exploring the experiences of ordinary people, the scholarly inquiry into immigration and ethnicity has produced an astounding outpouring of books and articles over the past several decades.

This rich and complex historical literature has drawn heavily from the methodologies and insights of the other social sciences and humanities, and the wider investigation into immigration has criss-crossed disciplinary boundaries at a rapid pace. The major journals of History, Political Science, Anthropology, Sociology, and Geography, for example, regularly carry essays dealing with the immigrant experience, and hundreds of articles appear in the more specialized local, regional, and topical publications of each discipline. Simply finding the relevant essays on any given topic within the general field has become a substantial challenge to researchers. This collection, therefore, represents an effort to bring together a selected cross section of the most significant articles on immigration and ethnicity. It is not definitive, no compilation treating with such broad-ranging and dynamic topics can ever be, but it is indicative of the scholarship that has shaped—and continues to shape—these important subjects. The major themes and issues of the field are discussed below, and each volume contains an individualized listing of supplemental readings for additional guidance. Taken together the collected essays contained within these volumes explore the manifold ways in which "immigrants were American history."

The liberation of immigration studies from its previously marginalized position has flowed from a number of critical interpretive and conceptual advances. One of the most important of these has been the effort to place immigration to America in the context of broader patterns of movement. Alerted by Frank Thistlethwaite's pioneering work, which showed how European migration to America was only part of a much larger transatlantic population and technological exchange, researchers now realize that an American-centered perspective is too restrictive to comprehend the full dimensions of migration. Immigrants from all quarters of the globe often envisioned America as only one destination among many, and then not necessarily a permanent one. Outmoded conceptions of "America fever" and exclusive one-way movement have given way to more complex understandings of the various manners by which America attracted and retained immigrants. The best works have taken into account the ability of multinational labor markets, economic cycles, transportation networks, as well as individual familial strategies, to propel immigrants outward in multi-step journeys.

At the same time as Thistlethwaite called for attention to large scale movements, he also urged that scholars be sensitive to the highly particularized nature of small scale migrations. Instead of studying "an undifferentiated mass movement" of individuals from loosely defined nation states, he insisted that immigrants be seen as emanating from "innumerable particular cells, districts, villages, towns, each with an individual reaction or lack of it to the pull of migration." This perspective necessarily involved linking the homeland with the new land in very precise ways, accounting for the specific influences of such factors as chain migration, kinship networks, travel agents, steamship companies, and repatriation flows, as well as the highly individualized economies of local regions.

Rudolph J. Vecoli's seminal work on Italian peasants in Chicago has pushed the study of premigration backgrounds in new directions. By pointing out that old world cultures survived the ocean crossing and significantly influenced adaptations in America, Vecoli stimulated a broad-based inquiry into the various ways in which immigrant traditions articulated with new world realities. The resulting scholarship has shifted the emphasis of investigation away from attention to the forces of assimilation and cultural break-down to those of cultural persistence and ethnic continuity. Immigrants did not succumb passively to pressures for conformity, but rather followed patterns of resistance and accommodation to the new land by which they turned themselves into something new—ethnic Americans. The ethnic culture that they created has proved to be a dynamic quality that has had influence into the third and fourth generation and beyond.

Such a viewpoint has led to different conceptions of assimilation and acculturation. Less often have scholars viewed these processes as easy, straight-line movements from "foreign" to "American." Nor have they continued to be captivated by
images of a vast "Melting Pot" at work that has thoroughly erased differences.
Rather, newer studies have posited a syncretic outcome in which both immigrants
and the mainstream society have been changed, and the overall process of immigrant
integration has emerged as more contingent and unpredictable than previously
imagined. Attempts to preserve immigrant languages, value structures, and tradition, for example, could not, and did not, result in the exact replication of old-world
ways. In a process of "invention" and "negotiation," immigrants adapted their
ethnic cultures to meet changing historical circumstances and to resolve the
problems of duality inherent in their straddling of Old and New Worlds. At the same
time, the host society was changing, or "reinventing," its own cultural traditions, in
part because of the need to accommodate the presence of diverse clusters of
immigrants.

Much of the most stimulating new research carried out along these lines has
adopted the urban immigrant community as its setting. Community studies have
not only examined the institutional structures of settlements, but have also typically
attempted to penetrate into the "interior worlds" of newcomers to discover the
mentalities, values, and life strategies that shaped immigrant destinies. Such
inquiries have probed deeply into the families, kin groups, and neighborhoods that
formed the core of immigrant districts. Their conclusions have revised older
conceptions of immigrant neighborhoods that emphasized the social pathology of
family breakdown, crime, and deviant behavior. Immigrant communities emerge as
remarkably vibrant and complex entities that provided effective cushions between
the often strange and harsh dominant society and newly arrived residents. They also
were far from the homogenous bodies so often envisioned by outsiders, but rather
were replete with various "subethnic" divisions based upon distinctions of class,
religion, ideology, and local culture. The process of immigrant adaptation to
America, therefore, was as often marked by tension and conflict *within* ethnic
concentrations as it was by friction between the group and the receiving society.

Internal divisions were also features of immigrant communities in rural and
small town locations. However, the distinctive physical and cultural contexts
encountered in such settings meant that immigrants usually experienced different
adjustment patterns from those of their urban-dwelling cousins. More isolated from
mainstream contact and better able to establish a local hegemony, immigrant
settlements in these settings often maintained traditional languages and folkways for
longer periods of time and with less change than was possible in city neighborhoods.
The ethnic culture that rural immigrants crafted correspondingly reflected these
particular conditions.

Eschewing a reliance on sources generated by the host society and utilizing a broad range of foreign language materials, researchers have demonstrated the existence of a remarkable range of civic, labor, religious, recreational, cultural, and fraternal organizations created by immigrants. Each of these played important roles in mediating the difficult adjustment to new-world conditions, and the presence of these institutions points to the need of recognizing immigrants as active agents in determining their own futures. To be sure, they were often circumscribed in their actions by poverty, nativism, discrimination, and limited skills, but they typically responded with imaginative adaptations within the limits imposed upon them. Many formal immigration institutions such as labor unions and mutual aid societies, for example, employed collective strategies to overcome the constraints restricting immigrant lives. Informal familial and kin networks often assisted these initiatives with adjustments of their own to ease the process of insertion into America.

The most fundamental institution of all, the immigrant family, reveals these patterns clearly. Families did not disintegrate under the pressures of immigration, urbanization, and industrialization, but rather proved to be remarkably flexible and resilent. Family structures and values responded to the multiple challenges imposed by migration—both in urban centers and rural spaces—by expanding their roles to accommodate a variety of new demands. Immigrant women, in their capacities as mothers and daughters, played critical functions in these transformations. Recent work, however, has attempted to move the study of immigrant women beyond the family context and to view women as historical actors who were able to influence the larger society in many different ways. The broader challenge has been to reveal how women confronted the multiple dilemmas posed by migration, and, more generally, to insert the issue of gender into the wider interpretations of the immigrant experience.

Since most immigrants entered America in quest of work, and after the 1860s usually industrial work, their relationship to the labor performed assumed a special importance. The vast majority arrived with preindustrial cultural values and confronted a complex urban-industrial economy. This encounter was a crucial factor not only in understanding the patterns of immigrant assimilation and social mobility, but also in comprehending the nature of American industrialization and the processes by which an American working class came into being. Through their collective labor as workers, their actions as union members, and their varied responses to exploitation and insecurity, immigrants were critical elements in the shaping of a modern American economy and labor force. Researchers are continuing to explore the exact nature of this dialectical relationship as they attempt to link immigrant values and expectations with the demands of the workplace.

Just as scholars have pursued the immigrant into the factory, home, and mutual aid society, so too have they entered the doors of immigrant churches in their investigations. The denominational pluralism that has characterized American society is a direct outgrowth of the nation's ethnic pluralism. Older works concentrated on examining the institutional histories of different immigrant religions and on the conflict engendered by such issues as parochial education and the formation of national parishes. More recently scholars have moved the study of America's religious tapestry out of church buildings and diocesan boardrooms and into the streets and neighborhoods. By examining the "popular piety" of immigrants, researchers hope to understand more clearly the ways in which new arrivals integrated the actual practice of religion into their everyday lives.

Investigators have already learned much about the relationships between ethnicity and political behavior. Indeed, one of the most surprising findings of the "new political history" was the discovery that ethnocultural considerations—often in the form of religious indentifications—were critical influences in shaping American voting patterns. Election outcomes in many parts of the nation often hinged on such factors. Indeed, perhaps no aspect of the American political arena has been immune to the force of ethnicity. Currently, researchers have been interested in determining how immigrants shaped a political culture of their own as they adapted to the American environment. Arriving from dissimilar backgrounds and frequently containing within their ranks followers of many different political ideologies, immigrants cannot be neatly classified into simple categories. Whether as supporters of urban machines, leftist critics of American capitalism, or as second and third generation politicians pushing group demands, immigrants and their progeny have been essential ingredients in the American political equation.

The American educational system similarly underwent profound transformation due to the immigrant presence. Many newcomers approached this powerful institution with ambivalent feelings since education in America offered both an opportunity for future progress and a danger to valued traditions. For their part, schools and school officials were forced to cope with unprecedented problems of space, curriculum, rules of discipline, attendance, and staffing. Immigrants ultimately found it necessary to judge the worth of education defined in new-world terms, both in relation to themselves and their children. They reacted in various ways, ranging from the formation of separate educational initiatives that sought to maintaine cherished values to the avoidance of formal educational institutions altogether. One thing was certain: both sides of the equation were changed by the contact.

America responded to the immigrant presence in varied ways. During periods of crisis, the host society often reacted by promoting rigid programs of Americanization that sought to strip away foreign customs and values. Research has shown that even programs of assistance and outreach, such as those offered by settlement houses and philanthropic agencies, often contained strong doses of social control. Immigrants were not unaware of these elements and frequently reacted to these

and such programs as bilingual education and affirmative action have engendered sharp public division. The present collection of essays, therefore, should be seen as providing the first installment of an important research agenda that needs to be open-ended in scope, responsive to new methodologies and interpretations, and cognizant of its relevance to contemporary American society.

The editor wishes to thank Leonard Dinnerstein, Victor Greene, Robert Singerman, Jeffrey Adler, Robert Zieger, and especially Rudolph Vecoli and Donna Gabaccia, for their helpful advice on this project.

GEORGE E. POZZETTA

SUPPLEMENTAL READING

Tomas Almaguer, "Racial Discrimination and Class Conflict in Capitalist Agriculture: The Oxnard Sugar Beet Worker's Strike of 1903," *Labor History*, 25 (Summer 1984), 325–350.

Mie Liang Bickner, "The Forgotten Minority: Asian American Women," *Amerasia Journal*, 11 (Spring 1974), 1–17.

Melvin Dubofsky, "Organized Labor and the Immigrant in New York City, 1900–1918," *Labor History*, 2 (1961), 182–201.

Melvin Dubofsky, "Success and Failure of Socialism in New York City, 1900–1918," *Labor History*, 9 (Fall 1968), 361–375.

Charlotte Erickson, "Emigration from the British Isles to the U.S.A. in 1831," *Population Studies*, 35 (1981), 175–197.

Frances H. Early, "The French Canadian Family Economy and Standard-of-Living in Lowell, Massachusetts, 1870," *Journal of Family History*, 7 (Summer 1982), 180–199.

Howard M. Gitelman, "No Irish Need Apply: Patterns of and Response to Ethnic Discrimination in the Labor Market," *Labor History*, 14 (1973), 56–68.

Philip Gleason, "Confusion Compounded: The Melting Pot in the 1960s and 1970s," *Ethnicity*, 6 (1979), 10–20.

Philip Gleason, "The Melting Pot: Symbol of Fusion or Confusion?" *American Quarterly* SVI (Spring 1974), 20–46.

Bruce C. Levine, "Immigrant Workers, 'Equal Rights,' and Antislavery: The Germans of Newark, New Jersey," *Labor History*, 25 (Winter 1984), 26–52.

Hubert Perrier, "The Socialists and the Working Class in New York, 1890–1896," *Labor History*, 22, No. 4 (Fall 1981), 485–511.

Thaddeus Radzialowski, "Immigrant Nationalism and Feminism: Glos Polek and the Polish Women's Alliance in America, 1898–1980," *Review Journal of Philosophy and Social Science*, 2 (1972), 183–203.

Robert Swierenga, "Dutch Immigrant Demography, 1820–1880," *Journal of Family History*, 5 (Winter 1980), 390–405.

Peter Temin, "Labor Scarcity in America," *Journal of Interdisciplinary History*, 1 (Winter 1971), 251–264.

CONTENTS

HAROLD J. ABRAMSON

ETHNIC DIVERSITY WITHIN CATHOLICISM: A COMPARATIVE ANALYSIS OF CONTEMPORARY AND HISTORICAL RELIGION

The historical and sociological fact of ethnic diversity within religion is well known. Church scholars have often incorporated the phenomenon into discourses on the social history of religion.[1] Historians of nationalism have examined the role of religion in the sociopolitical movements of European peoples, and have pointed out the dissonant or consonant relationships of ethnic minorities with religious institutions.[2] And sociologists have examined different kinds of social systems, in terms of ethnic heterogeneity and religious conflict.[3]

From a comparative point of view, however, the sociological and historical analysis of religion and ethnicity has been neglected. A problem for sociology is the understanding of elements which contribute to the shape of religious behavior, and the search for meaningful social and cultural patterns among the welter of historical facts.[4] The exploration of the roots of ethnic diversity within a shared religion affords such an opportunity for sociological and historical research.

HAROLD J. ABRAMSON is in the Department of Sociology at the University of Connecticut. This is a revised version of a paper read at the meetings of the Society for the Scientific Study of Religion, Boston, October 1969.

1. For example, H. Richard Niebuhr, *The Social Sources of Denominationalism* (New York, 1929); Kenneth Scott Latourette, *Christianity in a Revolutionary Age* (New York, 1958–1962), Vols. 1–5.
2. Salo W. Baron, *Modern Nationalism and Religion* (New York, 1960); Walter Kolarz, *Myths and Realities in Eastern Europe* (London, 1946); Hans Kohn, *Nationalism: Its Meaning and History* (New York, 1956).
3. Louis Wirth, "The Problem of Minority Groups," in *The Science of Man in the World Crisis*, ed. Ralph Linton (New York, 1945), 347–72; Werner J. Cahnman, "Religion and Nationality," in *Sociology and History*, ed. Werner J. Cahnman and Alvin Boskoff (New York, 1964), 271–80.
4. Yinger has raised a number of problems and ideas in this area, most of which are yet to be examined with sustained study. J. Milton Yinger, *Sociology Looks at Religion* (New York, 1963).

1

TABLE 1. FOREIGN-BORN CATHOLIC CHURCH ATTENDANCE AND SUPPORT OF AVAILABLE CATHOLIC ELEMENTARY SCHOOLS, BY ETHNICITY AND SOCIO-ECONOMIC STATUS BACKGROUND (Percent to Mass once a week or more, and percent children to available Catholic schools)

	Mother's church attendance		Father's church attendance		Children with some or all Catholic elementary schooling	
	Low SES (1–2)	High SES (3–10)	Low SES (1–2)	High SES (3–10)	Low SES (1–2)	High SES (3–10)
French-Canadian	97(38)*	95(19)	95(37)	78(18)	97(34)	100(15)
Irish	91(22)	100(24)	82(22)	89(282)	94(16)	96(25)
German	86(29)	78(27)	74(31)	69(29)	60(15)	72(18)
Polish	78(55)	77(26)	78(60)	66(32)	86(51)	92(24)
Italian	67(112)	76(110)	40(125)	39(127)	29(86)	43(96)
Spanish-speaking	56(62)	65(23)	41(66)	31(26)	28(39)	50(16)
TOTAL†	73(390)	79(264)	59(417)	55(297)	59(292)	64(216)

* The numbers in parentheses refer to the case bases from which the percentages are derived.
† Total refers to the sum of the total sample born-Catholics who constitute the cases in each category. It is not the sum of the groups selected in the table.

There has been enough empirical documentation of distinctive ethnic styles in religious behavior in the United States, for example, to warrant an investigation for the sociological and historical background which may help explain this diversity.[5] Table 1 offers recent data from a national sample of white Catholic Americans on ethnic heterogeneity, with regard to such measures of formal religious involvement as church attendance and the support of available Catholic parochial schools.[6]

---

5. For some recent evidence of ethnic heterogeneity within American Catholicism, as well as denominational diversity within American Protestantism, see Harold J. Abramson and C. Edward Noll, "Religion, Ethnicity, and Social Change," *Review of Religious Research* 8 (Fall 1966), 11–26. For a broader discussion of ethnic diversity, see Nathan Glazer and Daniel Patrick Moynihan, *Beyond the Melting Pot* (Cambridge, 1963).
6. The data used in table 1 originate from a National Opinion Research Center study of the effects of parochial school education among Catholic Americans. The universe sampled is the total noninstitutionalized white Catholic population of the United States, 23 to 57 years of age. The sample is limited to those respondents who identified themselves as Catholic, in reply to a question on current religious preference. The total sample size numbers 2,071 respondents, drawn from a standard multistage area probability sample. Questions asking for nationality background of fathers and mothers supply the data on ethnicity. For a fuller description of the survey and the final report, see Andrew M. Greeley and Peter H. Rossi, *The Education of Catholic Americans* (Chicago, 1966). For more extensive analysis of the data used in table 1, see Harold J. Abramson, "The Ethnic Factor in American Catholicism: an Analysis of Inter-Ethnic Marriage and Religious Involvement," doctoral dissertation, University of Chicago, 1969.

The rank orders of associational involvement for the different Catholic ethnic groups show the Irish and the French-Canadians to be the most consistently involved, the German and Polish Catholics at a relatively intermediate position, and the Italians and Spanish-speaking Puerto Ricans and Mexicans among the least involved in the formal requirements of their shared religion.

Only differences in ethnic background can explain such diversity. The data of the table are limited to the foreign-born parents of the survey's born-Catholics—hence excluding generational factors—and come closest to reflecting the state of formal religious involvement for the immigrants and their countries of origin. Mothers and fathers are of ethnically endogamous marriages, so that the presumed influences of intermarriage and of spouses of differing ethnic backgrounds are eliminated.

Finally, it has often been shown that social class plays a role in one's religious behavior; those of higher status tend to go to formal services more regularly and are more supportive of the religious school system.[7] Accordingly, there is a control for household socioeconomic status background in table 1.[8] It is apparent that class background makes no difference in the rank order of these foreign-born ethnic groups, and that ethnicity is the stronger factor. Indeed, the most involved Irish and French-Canadians are just as likely to send their children to the available Catholic school system when they are poor, as when they are of some higher class. The relative position of the Italian and Spanish-speaking Catholics also remains; even the more affluent members of these ethnic groups are among the least supportive of the denominational school program.[9]

Given evidence of ethnic diversity within the Catholic Church, a number of questions need to be raised. What are the structural sources of the religious traditions which the different immigrant groups brought with them to America? What religious and national

---

7. This is as true in the United States as it is in Europe. See Gerhard Lenski, *The Religious Factor* (New York, 1961), chap. 2; also, E. R. Wickham, *Church and People in an Industrial City* (London, 1957); Emile Pin, *Pratique Religieuse et Classes Sociales dans une Paroisse Urbaine Saint-Pothin à Lyon* (Paris, 1956).

8. Social class background is measured by the Duncan scale, based on the respondent's occupation. For explanation, see O. D. Duncan, "A Socio-Economic Index for All Occupations," in *Occupations and Social Status*, ed. Albert J. Reiss, Jr. (New York, 1961).

9. It is also true that socio-economic background has some influence on Italian and Spanish-speaking Catholics. They are considerably more likely to support the parochial school system, when they are of higher status, although not to the extent of their class counterparts from other ethnic groups.

characteristics help explain these distinctive levels of ethnic involvement among the foreign-born Catholics in the United States? Considerable research has been done on individual ethnic backgrounds, and some of this is cited in subsequent sections of this paper, but what comparative analysis can be employed for all six ethnic backgrounds? These are the questions which prompt this inquiry.

Comparison is developed around a model of societal competition, based on the social and political characteristics of national Catholicism in the histories of the six ethnic groups discussed. The research is necessarily limited in a number of different ways. A good deal of religious involvement certainly is to be explained by social psychological factors, such as matters of subjective ethnic identification, cultural and religious value systems, and the nature of national character. This paper will not dwell as much on the psychological determinants of religious association as it will on the more sociological and political factors which contribute to the shape of religioethnicity.

Second, the emphasis is on formal religious association and involvement, and not on "religiosity" or the measure of religious experience, feeling, or piety. The distinction is between that which is public, formal, and integrated into Church requirements, as opposed to that which is private, informal, and at variance with Church norms.

A third point refers to the factor of immigration. The investigation will not probe into the meaning of the change or the persistence of ethnic behavior after immigration to the United States, but will explore the traditional sources of the old country, which are presumed to give rise to traits and values brought to America with immigration. It is assumed that an understanding of the roots of ethnicity is important and basic for subsequent study into the changes brought about by the American experience. Finally, the research is limited by reliance upon the secondary literature. Perhaps future efforts in social history and the sociology of religion and ethnicity will survey original sources in developing explanatory hypotheses for comparative ethnic behavior.

THE NATURE OF SOCIETAL COMPETITION

There may be numerous approaches for explaining the differential religious involvement of Catholic groups, but one of the more common problems is the lack of empirical data with which to make a systematic beginning. In this regard, an important contribution to the comparative study of religious behavior is Michael Fogarty's *Christian Democracy in Western Europe*, for its valuable work on socioreligious movements.[10]

Fogarty is concerned with associational involvement within Protestantism and Catholicism. "Across Western Europe, from Flanders to Venice, there lies a belt of high religious observance, where people are more likely than elsewhere not only to profess a religion but to practice it; a sort of heartland of European Christianity."[11] With due concern for the imperfect statistics of religious practice, Fogarty tentatively argues that this phenomenon might be traced, as in the frequency of Protestant religious observance in Germany, to the nature of religious competition and the proportions of different religions in the population:

One explanation might be that religion thrives on competition, since the areas of low observance tend also to be those where the proportion of Protestants in the total population is highest. Silesia, an eastern territory, but one where the balance between Catholics and Protestants was till the Second World War more equal than elsewhere, showed till then a rather high level of observance among Protestants. But if there is such a rule it should apply also to Catholics, whereas in fact the statistics show that Catholic observance is high in the mainly Catholic west and south, but falls away, like observance among Protestants, toward the mainly Protestant east and north.[12]

Thus, within Germany, the relationship between high observance and the viability of religious competition does not seem to hold for Catholics. Fogarty pursues this further, with an examination of the more specific geographical outlines of the "heartland" of practicing Christianity, both Catholic and Protestant:

High observance . . . is most commonly to be found in the belt, which includes Holland, Belgium, French Flanders, Alsace-Lorraine, Westfalia, the Rhineland, most of south Germany and Austria, Switzerland (although here statistics are lacking), and parts of north Italy. There are large Protestant as well as Catholic populations in this area, and the tendency to high observance applies to both. As the case of Germany shows, competition between religions is probably not by itself enough to explain this. But it may be that competition of a more general kind is at the bottom of it; for this is a land not only of political but also of linguistic and cultural frontiers.[13]

---

10. Michael P. Fogarty, *Christian Democracy in Western Europe 1820–1953* (London, 1957).
11. Ibid., 7.   12. Ibid.   13. Ibid., 8.

Fogarty stops here with this particular hypothesis, but the idea of linguistic and cultural competition might well be developed as a basic dimension of the level of religious involvement. Indeed, had Fogarty considered the cases of Ireland and Quebec (which were excluded from his survey of Western Europe), the argument for the influence of cultural competition on religious observance would have assumed even stronger tones.

The concept of societal competition, whether political-linguistic or political-cultural, is a relevant one for the sociology of religio-ethnic systems. As Fogarty suggests in the case of Germany, mere religious heterogeneity within a society is not sufficient for explaining levels of religious involvement. More to the point is the proximity to and the salience of religious and cultural differences within the ethnic orientation of a people. Thus, the idea of the frontier between competing groups serves as a symbol of competition and diversity, and especially so if the frontier represents a border separating the powerful from the powerless.

The idea of societal competition then embraces at least two specific macro-sociological factors. The first would be the basic presence of religious differences, reinforced by linguistic and cultural competition. The extent of conflict which is generated by the competition may vary, but the sense of competition is the important issue. It is reasonable to suppose that the greater the conflict, the more salient the sense of religious distinctiveness and the higher the level of religious involvement, for the competitively subordinate group.

A second major factor refers to the degree of political autonomy enjoyed by the cultural groups involved. Competition between religio-ethnic systems might be present within the borders of the same geographical area, or the competition might be an expression of distinctiveness across frontiers. Political control by a different religio-ethnic group may be present within the given society (as a kind of internal colonialism), or it may extend across geographical borders (in the classic conventions of external colonialism).[14] In either event, the reality of societal competition is expected to show differences in political power and the probability of controlling behavior.

Following fairly closely from Fogarty's suggestion, the model of societal competition is based on the two dimensions: differences in

14. The distinction is made by Blauner in the context of black-white relations in the United States. Robert Blauner, "Internal Colonialism and Ghetto Revolt," *Social Problems* 16 (Spring 1969): 393–408.

religio-cultural systems and differences in their political power. Other points might well be taken into consideration. Religio-ethnic distinctiveness in the past has often led to nationalist movements, and the institutionalization of religio-ethnic differences under certain conditions may lead to political movements of secession and independence. These movements reinforce religious consciousness, along with other aspects of cultural identity. The converse of this relationship may also be true. Emergent nationalism may stimulate dormant religio-ethnic distinctiveness, and the new consciousness then reinforces the political movement.

Other, more micro-sociological, factors are presumably relevant in the context of societal competition. The extent of religio-communal organization, the relationship of religion to the needs of the people, and the extent to which there is conflict of class interests within the given religio-ethnic group, for example, are important questions, and they will be considered in the subsequent analysis.

It is proposed then that the condition of societal competition, with its characteristics of religio-ethnic differences, conflict, and corresponding levels of power, is a positive correlate of the degree of religio-ethnic activity and consciousness. A review of the state of Catholicity in the background histories of six American ethnic groups will document the degree of societal competition experienced by these peoples and, it is proposed, will help explain their varied levels of involvement within their common religion.[15]

THE IRISH

Perhaps the greatest difficulty which confronts the historian of the Irish is that of differentiating between the specifically Irish and specifically Catholic aspects of their lives. They had emerged into the modern world from a past in which Catholicism had played a stronger role than among any other people of Western Europe. By the end of the seventeenth century, the Irish were a conquered people, their leaders had either fled or been despoiled, and thereafter Gaelic cultural disintegration matched strides with the expansion of English authority. The peasant Irish, therefore, found their securities in the Church and their leadership in the priesthood. Hatred and fear of English Protestantism were part of their cultural heritage.[16]

---

15. The review is presented in the following order of involvement within the Church: highest, the Irish and the French-Canadians; lowest, the Southern Italians and the Spanish-speaking Mexicans and Puerto Ricans; intermediate, the German Catholics and the Polish Catholics.
16. Thomas N. Brown, *Irish-American Nationalism 1870–1890* (Philadelphia, 1966), 34–35.

The fusion of religion and nationality, inherent in the above quotation from Thomas Brown, is perhaps the most recurrent theme in the meaning of Irish ethnicity. The fusion was the consequence of centuries of societal competition with the Protestant English. For the Irish the competition meant conflict, and the conflict itself was virtually institutionalized within the structure of the society. It incorporated every aspect of life, including that of religion.

Irish Catholicism was different from the Church in France, Spain, or Italy. Religion in Ireland did not mean vested interests, the dilemmas of institutionalization, or priorities in whatever established society there happened to be, to the degree that religion on the Continent did. Far longer in history, the Church in Ireland had been poor, landless, and without power. It was more objectively and subjectively an integral part of the peasant's own poverty, and could not be held as responsible for the problems of such poverty. It shared a subordinate status, and this fact facilitated the identification which the individual Irishman made of his struggling religion with his struggling nationality.

Instead of a prevailing class of prosperous clergy to contrast with the poverty of the peasants, many Irish priests were close to and among the people. The closing of the monasteries threw the friars out to beg among the poor. O'Faolain writes of the rebellious strain among the clergy when, in the period from 1805 to 1845, the forces of O'Connellism in the presbytery were fighting and defeating the monarchists and their traditions of Gallicanism in the seminary, or even more actively and in still earlier years, when priests either died with guns in their hands during the 1798 Rebellion or were taken to be hanged after the Rising ended.[17]

Potter notes that the fusion of religion and nationality was so complete in Irish Catholic culture that it extended even to their linguistic view of the English.[18] The Irish word, Sassenach, for example, means both Protestant and Englishman. Apostasy from Catholicism was considered the greatest of crimes in the sight of the Irish peasant; the apostate was thought to be a betrayer, not only of religion, but also of

---

17. Sean O'Faolain, *The Irish: A Character Study* (New York, 1949). This is not to imply that all relations between clergy and laymen were close, or that divisions along ideological lines did not emerge among the Churchmen themselves. See O'Faolain for discussion of these aspects as well. Also, R. E. Burns, "Parsons, Priests, and the People: The Rise of Irish Anti-Clericalism 1785-1789," *Church History* 31 (1962): 151-63.
18. George W. Potter, *To the Golden Door: The Story of the Irish in Ireland and America* (Boston, 1960).

nationality.[19] This is an excellent example of what Fishman, in another context, has called the far-reaching syncretism of ethnic and religious values and traditions: culminating in the "sanctification" of ethnicity and the "ethnization" of religion.[20]

Thus was so much of Irish Catholicism a response to the societal conflict confronting the people. There was always England, identified with contempt and hate, trying to Anglicize Ireland and proscribe everything Irish, including the Irish religion. The persecution fostered the integration of the nationality with the religion, and contributed a great deal to the emergence of the feelings of nationalism.

Glazer has remarked how the Irish Catholic immigrants in the United States were more likely to identify themselves first as being from Ireland, rather than Galway or Cork, as opposed to the Italian Catholics, whose lack of national consciousness had them view their primary origins as Sicily or Calabria (or even villages and communes within these regions), instead of Italy.[21] The choice of local or national identification probably has much to do with the extent of religio-ethnic involvement and degree of societal competition.

The question of national identification should not be confused with the ideology of nationalism. The former sentiment, developed around anti-English themes, was probably much more pervasive than the reality of nationalism, with its complicated sets of opposing issues and directions.[22] The movement for nationalism, however, was based upon the foundation of societal competition and gathered much of its strength and logic from the argument for religio-ethnic distinctiveness.[23]

---

19. Ibid.
20. Vladimir C. Nahirny and Joshua A. Fishman, "Ukrainian Language Maintenance Efforts in the United States," in *Language Loyalty in the United States*, ed. Joshua A. Fishman, et al. (The Hague: 1966), 318–57.
21. Nathan Glazer, "Ethnic Groups in America," in *Freedom and Control in Modern Society*, ed. Morroe Berger, et al. (New York, 1954), 158–73.
22. On the complications in the relations between the movement for nationalism and the institutions of Church and State, see Emmet Larkin, "Church and State in Ireland in the Nineteenth Century," *Church History* 31 (1962): 294–306. For a discussion of the personification of this problem, see Emmet Larkin, *James Larkin: Irish Labour Leader 1876–1947* (Cambridge, 1965).
23. The argument for religio-ethnic distinctiveness may be clearer than the precise nature of the Irish Church or Irish Catholicism. O'Dea has pointed out that religion and nationality came to dominate the Irishman's conception of his self, partly because Catholicism in Ireland seldom assumed the posture of defensiveness. Despite the occasional clashes between religion and nationalism, as illustrated by the problems of Parnell, the norm was more likely to be the militance of the local clergy in support of the peasantry. See Thomas F. O'Dea, "The Catholic Immigrant and the American Scene,"
3

The history of societal competition, with its elements of religio-ethnic conflict and corresponding facts of Irish powerlessness, contributed a good deal to the shape of Irish Catholicity.[24] It was a heritage developed in Ireland and represented quite clearly by the Irish immigrants in the United States, not only in the development of the structure of the Catholic Church in America but also in their high level of association with and involvement in its religious requirements.

THE FRENCH-CANADIANS

The religious element was never absent from the second Hundred Years' War which the French and English waged against each other in America until the downfall of New France. This fact has left its mark on the French-Canadian mentality, which weds the concept of nationality to that of religion and asserts its separateness from English-speaking North America on both counts.[25]

This historical accounting of the French-Canadians by Mason Wade suggests the important similarity shared with the Irish: the interpenetration of religion and nationality in confrontation with the Protestant English-speaking Canadians. The parallels with the Irish in terms of societal competition are striking, especially for the similar end results of extremely close association with the religious and educational requirements of the Catholic Church.

Despite general similarity, the Catholic history of the French-Canadians has some uniqueness, and this has contributed a more tradition-based, parochial social organization to French-Canadian religious life. The French in Canada never experienced the degree of devastation of their society and culture which the Irish did. While party to the political conflicts and different views of the relationship

---

Thought 31 (Summer 1956): 251–70. On the other hand, Larkin argues that competition has created a specific defensiveness: "A hostile English Government in the seventeenth century, a proselytizing Protestantism in the eighteenth century, and a revolutionary Nationalism in the nineteenth century all had put the Irish Church on the defensive. The result was that the Church in Ireland reacted negatively rather than positively to the ways of the world." Emmet Larkin, "Socialism and Catholicism in Ireland," *Church History* 33 (1964): 481. The difference here may be due to confusion between national identification and ideology of nationalism. The former may have been less threatening and more of an asset than the latter.

24.   The historical pattern itself was probably one of increasing religious involvement. After the Great Famine of 1846, ironically, religious and related economic activity increased. Emmet Larkin, "Economic Growth, Capital Investment, and the Roman Catholic Church in Nineteenth-Century Ireland," *American Historical Review* 72 (April 1967): 852–75.

25.   Mason Wade, *The French-Canadian Outlook* (Toronto, 1964), 3–4.

between Church and State, the French-Canadians in Quebec had the geographical insularity and enough ultimate sovereignty for the elaborate development of a parish-dominated social organization.

The problems of conflict and powerlessness, as well as a resultant nationalism, are quite explicit in the bilingual and bicultural consciousness which characterizes contemporary Canada.[26] They are symbolized in the separatist movement in Quebec and have come to prevail in much of the analysis of French-Canadian society and culture. Quoting Marcel Rioux, Dumont offers a summary of the national character:

"The French-Canadian ideology has always rested on three characteristics of the French-Canadian culture—the fact that it is a minority culture, that it is Catholic, and that it is French. It is from these characteristics, first envisaged concretely but, with the passing of time, more and more as a framework, that ideology has formulated its national doctrine and has come to control the thinking of most of the educational and intellectual institutions of Quebec." As can be seen, here again the Conquest has not been forgotten.[27]

The distinctiveness of societal competition rests as much with economic disparity as it does with the question of political power. Much has been written about the conscious and unconscious confinement of French-Canadian resources.[28] The "second-class citizenship" qualities which are perceived to arise from the ethnic division of labor in Canada are not unlike some of the economic and social problems between blacks and whites in the United States.

While similar to the religio-ethnic conflicts of the Irish and the English, if not in intensity then in kind, the Church in Quebec has been able to take advantage of opportunities for its development. In his review of the place of Catholicism in French Canada, Falardeau notes that from the beginning of its settlement, Quebec society has been completely surrounded by and dominated by the influence of Catholicism. "The history of French Canada is the history of the Church in Canada and vice versa."[29]

---

26. In a recent survey, considerable ethnic differences were found in perceptions of Canadian society. See John C. Johnstone, Jean-Claude Willig, and Joseph M. Spina, *Young People's Images of Canadian Society* (Ottawa, Studies of the Royal Commission on Bilingualism and Biculturalism, 1969).
27. Fernand Dumont, "The Systematic Study of the French-Canadian Total Society," in *French-Canadian Society*, vol. 1, ed. Marcel Rioux and Yves Martin (Toronto, 1965), 392.
28. See the numerous essays in Rioux and Martin.
29. Jean-Charles Falardeau, "The Role and Importance of the Church in French Canada," in Rioux and Martin, 342.

Tied to the notions of church and society are the two central themes of language and nationalism. The French language is more than a medium of communication or a carrier of culture in Quebec. It is almost mystically regarded as the "guardian of the faith." As another instance of the "sanctification" of ethnicity, the loss of language is believed frequently to lead to the loss of Catholicism, and the depth of this conviction has led to the elaborate development of the parochial school system, not only in Quebec, but also among the American children of the French-Canadian immigrants in New England.[30]

The politico-religious philosophy of French-Canadian nationalism has also gained explicit and universal support among clergy and laymen alike. "This was the belief in French Canada's fortunate vocation based on one obvious sign—the fact that modern France, in becoming secular and atheistic, had abandoned its mission as the older daughter of the Church, while the French Canadians had remained faithful to the past and to God, and must therefore replace a France who had betrayed its trust."[31] The intensity of this feeling, as exemplified by the involvement and association of French-Canadians with their religion, is evident.

In terms of the more micro-sociological aspects of religion in the French-Canadian community, the pervasive Catholicity stands out still more sharply. In his discussion of the growth of industry and the changes in the economic and social order of French Canada, Hughes points out how the parish persists as the central aspect of the French-Canadian's life: "The parish was historically the first institution of local self-government in rural Quebec; it remains the point of active integration of religious and secular matters. The roles of parishioner and of citizen are scarcely distinguishable."[32]

The role of religion in the daily routine of rural Quebec is so predominant as to comprise in itself the meaning of communality. In his account of St. Denis, Miner observes the Mass to be so important to the social system of the parish that he devotes an entire chapter to the effect it has on village life: "Masses are public religious celebrations whether they are Sunday Masses or Masses for marriages, anniversaries of death, burial, or special supplication. They are prac-

---

30. Ibid.
31. Ibid., 350–51.
32. Everett C. Hughes, *French-Canada in Transition* (Chicago, 1943), 10.

tically the only activity in which the whole parish participates as a group."[33]

The clergy of Quebec are an essential part of this communality. Like the priests of Ireland, they share similar backgrounds and values with their parishioners. The historical pattern is important because it means that the clergy of French Canada has rarely been recruited from a single social class, let alone a dominant status, in contrast to the custom of many European countries. "One seldom finds a French-Canadian family that does not include a member or a relative who is in the clergy or in one of the orders," writes Falardeau.[34] The clergy are within and of all strata of the society.

The traditions of Quebec province were transplanted in New England by the French-Canadians who immigrated, and the transplanting was an easier task because of the proximity to Canada. They concentrated almost exclusively on the reestablishment of the parish-centered social organization.[35] On the communication between the two countries, Ducharme writes: "By visit and by letter a sort of communal life exists. Birth and marriage and death are the interest of all, and the frontier is no barrier, for it merely serves to separate the clans temporarily."[36]

In his fictional representation of French-Canadian life in New England, Ducharme conveys the importance of the religious traditions: "The Church meant a great deal to the French Canadian who had left his country. It was like the hub of a wheel to which he gravitated once a week, and which set his pace. There he could always hear his own language spoken, and there he could find solace in time of trouble. Not yet broken was the spell that the village church had for him when he was on his farm in Quebec."[37]

As with all immigrant groups, there are interests in and attempts at maintaining the traditions of the Old World.[38] The Irish and the French-Canadians each brought their own distinctive views of religion and styles of group involvement. Because of the extent of cultural and religious conflict and competition within their respective

---

33. Horace M. Miner, *St. Denis, a French-Canadian Parish* (Chicago, 1939), 105.
34. Farlardeau in Rioux and Martin, 355.
35. George F. Theriault, "The Franco-Americans of New England," in *Canadian Dualism*, ed. Mason Wade (Toronto, 1960), 392–411.
36. Jacques Ducharme, *The Shadows of the Trees* (New York, 1943), 14.
37. Jacques Ducharme, *The Delusson Family* (New York, 1939), 52.
38. Robert E. Park and Herbert A. Miller, *Old World Traits Transplanted* (New York, 1921).

societies, and helped by well-developed communal organizations, they brought to the United States their own intimate association with formal religion. Other Catholic groups had other kinds of historical experiences, and brought other religious traditions.

THE SOUTHERN ITALIANS

They unfurled a red-white-and-green handkerchief from the church-tower, they rang the bells in a frenzy, and they began to shout in the village square, "Hurray for Liberty!"

Like the sea in storm. The crowd foamed and swayed in front of the club of the gentry, and outside the Town Hall, and on the steps of the church—a sea of white stocking-caps, axes and sickles glittering. Then they burst into the little street.

"Your turn first, baron! You who have had folks cudgelled by your estate-keepers!"

At the head of all the people a witch, with her old hair sticking up, armed with nothing but her nails. "Your turn, priest of the devil! for you've sucked the soul out of us!"

... Then for his Reverence who used to preach Hell for anybody who stole a bit of bread. He was just coming back from saying mass, with the consecrated Host inside his fat belly. "Don't kill me, I am in mortal sin!" Neighbor Lucia being the mortal sin; Neighbor Lucia whose father had sold her to the priest when she was fourteen years old, at the time of the famine winter, and she had ever since been filling the streets and the Refuge with hungry brats. . . .[39]

The stories of Verga, as well as the novels of other Italian writers, are dramatic sources for illustrating the estrangement of the southern Italians from the Catholic Church.[40] Indeed, the quoted episode goes further than suggesting the contempt of these mob-stricken peasants for the Church; it points to the links of anticlericalism with the nationalist mood.

In stark contrast to the Catholicity of the Irish and the French-Canadians, the state of formal church-involved religiousness in Sicily and other regions of southern Italy was in a precarious condition, a legacy of the alliance between the Church and the Old Order.

---

39. Giovanni Verga, *Little Novels of Sicily* (New York, 1953), 197–198.
40. Many novels, especially those by Levi and Silone, illustrate this mood. For example, Carlo Levi, *Christ Stopped at Eboli* (New York, 1947); Ignazio Silone, *A Handful of Blackberries* (New York, 1953).

The idea and reality of societal competition—that network of conflicts between linguistic and religious differences—were nonexistent in southern Italy. There was no identification of a populist religion or church with powerlessness and national identity. The history of the nineteenth century in Italy shows the Catholic Church to be, for the most part, an established force against national consciousness and, directly and indirectly, for maintaining the powerlessness of the poor. In a real sense, the institutional Church itself was the alien religion— the Catholicism of Rome, the North, the upper classes, and the status quo.[41]

From the point of view of the educated classes of the South, the Papacy and the State were one. This helped to produce both anti-clericalism and widespread indifference to formal religion, just as the interlocking of religion and nationality helped to create intense identification with Catholicism among the Irish and the French-Canadians. In the Italy of the nineteenth century, resistance or indifference to the social order would extend to religion.

The fact that cultural distinctions prevailed between the North and the South of Italy did not change with political unification. Latourette notes how important geography was in the structure of the Catholic Church in Italy.[42] It was from the regions north of Rome where most of the active support of the Church could be found. All of the popes of the nineteenth century were born in the North, with the sole exception of Leo XIII.[43] Most of the new congregations had their beginnings in the North. Little activity and even less support could be traced to the *Mezzogiorno*. And it was from the South of Italy that the vast majority of immigrants to the United States had come.[44]

The writings of many scholars, both proclerical and anticlerical in temperament, provide evidence of the popular moods toward religious involvement with formal Catholicism. The struggles between the Church and the movement for unification left their mark, as noted in Henry Browne's survey of the "Italian problem" within American Catholicism: "The comments of an anti-papal Italian traveller to America suggest that almost of necessity the political affairs of Italy, which for years made it practically impossible for a good Catholic

---

41. A. C. Jemolo, *Church and State in Italy 1850–1950* (Oxford, 1960); see also Baron.
42. Latourette, vol. 1 : 415–19.
43. Even Leo XIII was a native of the region only slightly to the south of Rome, ibid.
44. Robert F. Foerster, *The Italian Emigration of Our Times* (Cambridge, 1919).

to be a good citizen of the newly united Italy, had an influence on the religious mentality of Italians even after migration."[45]

In his autobiography, Panunzio describes the memories of his boyhood in Apulia, in a home that can be said to be comfortable, if neither affluent nor impoverished:

While we all received instruction of various kinds, dealing mainly with good manners and proper conduct, our religious education was very limited, almost a negligible factor in our lives. Religion was considered primarily a woman's function, unnecessary to men, and a matter about which they continually joked. . . . We children continuously heard our male relatives speak disparagingly of religion, if religion it could be called. They would speak of the corruption of the Church.[46]

Among the poorest classes, educational and religious instruction in formal Catholicism were even less common and characteristic. Feelings against the Church were widespread, if not always vocal. Banfield describes the lack of both religious and secular influence of the two churches and their priests in Montegrano.[47] Barely more than ten percent of the 3,400 Montegranesi go to hear Mass on a Sunday, and most of these are women:

By tradition the men of Montegrano are anticlerical. The tradition goes back a century or more to a time when the church had vast holdings in Southern Italy and was callous and corrupt. Today it owns only one small farm in Montegrano, and the village priests are both known to be kindly and respectable men. Nevertheless priests in general—so many Montegranesi insist—are money-grubbers, hypocrites, and worse.[48]

The feelings had become a tradition, despite changes in the social system. And the tradition of relative indifference to and contempt for the formal Church was brought to the United States with immigration.

It is ironic that the indifference to the formal doctrines of Catholicism among the southern Italians persisted despite the fact that so many of the *contadini* were fairly isolated in their peasant villages from the currents of anticlericalism and changing political thought

---

45. Henry J. Browne, "The 'Italian Problem' in the Catholic Church of the United States, 1880–1900," *United States Catholic Historical Society, Historical Records and Studies* 35 (1946): 46–72.
46. Constantine M. Panunzio, *The Soul of an Immigrant* (New York, 1921), 18.
47. Montegrano is the fictitiously named commune in Southern Italy which was the location for Banfield's study of the conditions of political and communal organization. Edward C. Banfield, *The Moral Basis of a Backward Society* (New York, 1958).
48. Ibid., 17–18.

abroad throughout Italy.[49] As Vecoli points out, much of this is due to the particularistic folk-ceremonies of the local varieties of religion: "While nominally Roman Catholics, theirs was a folk religion, a fusion of Christianity and pre-Christian elements, of animism, polytheism, and sorcery with the sacraments of the Church. . . . Dominated by a sense of awe, fear, and reverence for the supernatural, the peasants were profoundly religious. However, their beliefs and practices did not conform to the doctrines and liturgy of the Church."[50] This variant of religion, of course, clashed with the more institutional ecclesiasticism of the Vatican, as it clashed after immigration with the Irish style of Catholicism predominant in America.[51] Regardless of the lack of ideological anticlericalism, the poor in southern Italy, in marked contrast to the poor in Ireland and Quebec, often showed contempt for the formal religion. For this they had the justification of their own experience. Vecoli summarizes this orientation:

For the Church as an institution the South Italian peasants had little sense of reverence. Historically it had been allied with the landowning aristocracy and had shown little sympathy for the misery of the *contadini*. Although surrounded by a multitude of clergy, the people by and large were not instructed in the fundamental doctrines of the Catholic faith. Toward their village priests, whom they regarded as parasites living off their labors, the peasants often displayed attitudes of familiar contempt. Clerical immorality and greed figured largely in the folk humor of Italy.[52]

The lack of involvement in the Church in southern Italy, it is proposed, is comparatively explained by the absence of societal competition between distinct cultural and religious systems, and the attendant identification of religion, not with an emerging sense of social and political reform, but with the existing policies of the old order. The characteristics of competition as defined—the extent of religio-ethnic conflict and the salience of powerlessness—which contributed to high Church involvement and religious observance among the Irish and the French-Canadians were absent in southern Italy. Indeed the model of competition worked in reverse because it was the Church

---

49. Rudolph J. Vecoli, "Prelates and Peasants: Italian Immigrants and the Catholic Church," *Journal of Social History* 2 (Spring 1969): 217–68.
50. Ibid., 228.
51. Ibid.
52. Ibid., 229. In contrast again to the Irish, few priests wanted to accompany Italian Catholics during emigration, and few wanted to serve in Italian parishes in the United States. According to Vecoli, this was not due to the desire of Italian clergy to remain in Italy. It was more often explained by outright hostility and disrespect. Ibid., 235.

which was held responsible for social problems and not some foreign cultural system.

THE MEXICANS AND THE PUERTO RICANS

A factor all but universal in Spanish America . . . was the shock brought to the Roman Catholic Church by independence and the inevitably painful adjustments. Crises arose from the disorders which were features of the wars of independence, from the Spanish birth of many of the clergy, from the historic patronage exercised by the crown, from the insistence of new governments on the transfer to them of that authority, from the unwillingness of Madrid to surrender its prerogatives, and from the political situation in Spain which made Rome hesitate to go counter to Spanish claims.[53]

Societal competition between religious and cultural systems was also lacking in Mexico and Puerto Rico, as elsewhere throughout Latin America, and some of the same problems of the history of Church and State in Italy could be seen in the history of Spanish-speaking America. Most notable, as the above quotation suggests, is the universality of Church power and control.

To varying extents, Latin American countries were considered as mission territories by the Church. This led to a number of unique factors which were subsequently seen to contribute to the lack of involvement of Latin Americans in the formal religious system of Catholicism. Both Mexico and Puerto Rico emerged from the Spanish colonial tradition, and the attachments of Mexicans and Puerto Ricans to the Church were founded not so much on the basis of instruction and conviction—both positive values of Catholicism—as on the presence of social and religious customs, artifactual medals, holy pictures, and fiestas.[54]

According to a recent study by Houtart and Pin, data on the low religious observance of Latin American Catholics form a regular pattern which is traced to and explained by the predominance of the colonial tradition itself.[55] The people of Latin America are ascribed Catholics, and subsequently religion becomes a mere social attribute. Religion then becomes nothing more than another characteristic with which one is born.

---

53. Latourette, 3:295.
54. Joseph P. Fitzpatrick, "Mexicans and Puerto Ricans Build a Bridge," *America* 94 (31 December 1955):373–75.
55. Francois Houtart and Emile Pin, *The Church and the Latin American Revolution* (New York, 1965).

18

The state of Catholicity in Latin America is further affected by the underdeveloped conditions of religio-communal organization, data for which will be presented below. The numbers of priests are few, relative to the size of the population in Latin America, and parishes are too large and thus inadequate for religious organization.[56] Above all, the clergy were traditionally recruited from Europe, during early years of colonization, in keeping with the missionary perspective of the areas. This only served to maintain the problem of the social and religious distance between parishioner and Church.

The distance between the clergy and the people mirrors the broader problems of Church and State. As in Italy, there was no competition with alien cultures and religions. Instead, there was conflict with the established powers of Catholicism. Mecham has pointed out how much at odds were the Church and its Spanish-born clergy with the movements for political independence.[57] In the subsequent conflicts in the different countries, the clergy were often divided. With few exceptions, the general division saw the bishops and higher clergy standing for the monarchical form of government, and the lower clergy (increasingly, as the societies grew more populous, native-born to Latin America) on the side of change.

In Mexico, the leadership in the political struggle for independence came at first from local village priests, close to the pressing social problems of the population.[58] In this, as far as the role of the local village priest was concerned, the Mexican struggle was similar to the Irish. The differences for the larger societies, however, are evident. There was less division among the clergy in Ireland, partly because of the overwhelming presence of religious and cultural differences with the English lords. In Mexico, as elsewhere in Latin America, the clergy who did take the side of independence found themselves in a position which the Church hierarchy deplored. It was a classic case of pervasive role conflict. In Spanish America, it was the religiously homogeneous society which was in competition with itself; there was no alien religio-cultural scapegoat, real or imagined.

---

56. Ibid. Countries such as Venezuela, Paraguay, Costa Rica, and Ecuador have concentrations of between 50 and 78 percent of their Catholic clergy in their capital cities. In Uruguay and Cuba, the percentages are even higher. See Carlos M. Rama, "Pasado Y Presente de la Religion En America Latina," *Cuadernos Americanos* 26 (July-August 1967): 25–43.
57. J. Lloyd Mecham, *Church and State in Latin America* (Chapel Hill, 1934).
58. Ibid.

In Puerto Rico too, as throughout much of Latin America, orthodoxy within Catholicism prevailed almost exclusively among the
upper classes. Despite the Church's standardized doctrines and procedures, local communities in Puerto Rico blended formal Catholicism with cults of saints, witchcraft, spiritualism, and later in the
twentieth century, even elements of Protestantism.[59] The fact of
variation from the formal religion of Catholicism is not unlike the
deviations found in the religious life of southern Italy.

Steward draws attention to a number of factors which prevented
the integration of the greater proportion of Puerto Ricans into the
institutionalized life of the Church.[60] Poverty, dispersal of the population, inadequate clergy, missionary attitudes of patronization,
and the inconsistent stands of the Church on social issues (e.g.,
slavery), all contributed to the shape of religion in Puerto Rico. As in
Mexico, there was no historical confrontation for Catholicism in
Puerto Rico, and this fact would influence not only the Church's
view of Latin Americans but also the population's view of the
Church.

After the United States became sovereign over Puerto Rico, there
came a complete separation of religion from the government. The
island was opened, for the first time, to missionary activity by
Protestant groups. Steward argues that these two events introduced
still more heterogeneity to the Catholicism of the island, and even
worked to supplant the traditional religious forms in some areas of
Puerto Rico.[61]

Studies of Mexican and Puerto Rican communities in the United
States document quite consistently the "token bond" with formal
Catholicism which characterizes the Spanish-speaking groups.[62]
Like the Italians, the Mexicans and the Puerto Ricans brought with
them to the United States their ethnic indifference to a religious
system which they, for the most part, either traditionally took for
granted or perceived to be standing in the way of change and pressing

59.   Julian H. Steward, et al., *The People of Puerto Rico* (Champaign, 1956).
60.   Ibid.
61.   Ibid. If Protestantism in Puerto Rico is identified with Anglo-Saxon culture, it
would be interesting to see if higher levels of religious involvement among both Catholics and Protestants on the island result from instances of religio-cultural competition.
62.   For Mexican communities, see Arthur J. Rubel, *Across the Tracks: Mexican-
Americans in a Texas City* (Austin, 1966); Ruth D. Tuck, *Not with the Fist* (New York,
1946). For Puerto Rican communities, see Glazer and Moynihan; C. Wright Mills,
Clarence Senior, and Rose K. Goldsen, *The Puerto Rican Journey* (New York, 1950);
Elena Padilla, *Up from Puerto Rico* (New York, 1958).

reform. They differ quite essentially from the Irish and the French-Canadians, for whom the fights for autonomy in matters of nationality and religion substantially reinforced each other.

THE POLISH CATHOLICS

Religion was . . . in some measure a field of national cooperation, particularly in the southeastern part of Russian Poland, Lithuania, and White Ruthenia, where religious and national interests went hand in hand. . . . But aesthetic and intellectual interests had but little influence upon the large masses of the population and . . . the role of the Catholic Church in Polish national life was limited by its international politics. The most secure and the widest ground of national cooperation lay elsewhere—in the economic domain.[63]

The Polish Catholics, like the German Catholics to be discussed next, show a degree of involvement not exactly like the four backgrounds already presented. The Poles are indeed well involved in their religion, and thus they are decidedly different from the Italians and the Spanish-speaking of Latin America. But given the empirical levels of religious and educational involvement, the Poles do not represent the type of intensity which characterizes the place of the Irish and the French-Canadians in historical and contemporary Catholicism. They reflect a kind of intermediacy.

It is frequently observed that the state of Catholicism in Poland has been historically similar to the religious situation of Ireland and Quebec. Baron offers Polish history as another instance of the coincidence of national interests and religious loyalties.[64] Fishman discusses the presumed consequence of ethnic and political allegiances for the individual peasant in rural Poland.[65] While there is no denial of some historical similarities, certain differences have been overlooked and the above quotation from Thomas and Znaniecki suggests that the history and the role of the Church in Poland, in its bearing on the individual Catholic, may not have been as close to that in Ireland and Quebec as commonly thought.

In terms of the concept of societal competition, cultural and religious differences were not as graphic in Poland as they were in

---

63. W. I. Thomas and Florian Znaniecki, *The Polish Peasant in Europe and America* (New York, 1927), 2:1440.
64. Baron, 96–108.
65. Fishman.

Ireland and Quebec. There was more diffuse heterogeneity within Poland, as a result of the many competing national and religious groups within constantly shifting and arbitrarily drawn boundary lines. Iwanska cites figures which put the Catholic proportion of the Polish territory between World Wars I and II as approximately 65 percent of the total. The remaining 35 percent included Jews, the Eastern Orthodox, Protestants, and Eastern Rite Catholics, all representing different national origins.[66] This kind of heterogeneity blurred the focus of religion and nationality which emerged with so much intensity in overwhelmingly Catholic Ireland and Quebec.

A second point might be made of the fact that Poland was geographically in confrontation with not one major power, but two, flanking her on both sides; in the east there was Orthodox Russia, and in the west there was Protestant Prussia. Both situations, it has been argued, served to sharpen the consciousness of Polish national identity with the Catholic Church.[67] But at the same time, this dual confrontation became a thorn in the side of political compromise. Accommodation with one power at the expense of the other continually created problems, not only for the Church, but for the cause of Polish nationalism as well.[68]

Complicating matters even more, Prussia had her own Catholic minority, and Poland of course had her religious groups. All of these factors did not lead to any measure of unqualified or predictable support by the Vatican or create the kind of symbolic competition that Catholic Ireland or Catholic Quebec experienced with the Protestant English. In both of these cases, the English were the only major problems perceived by the Catholics of Quebec and Ireland, and the energies of religious and national movement were all the more easily channeled in the one direction.

Within Poland too, the Church did not enjoy the same kind of secular support that it did in Ireland and Quebec. Its appreciation and backing by the peasants were limited fairly much to religious affairs. "Polish peasants were never very clear about how to define the role of their priest. They felt uncomfortable about the two overlapping roles of the parish priest, his secular role as the representative of the parish, and his religious role as the representative of God. The

---

66. Alicja Iwanska, ed. *Contemporary Poland: Society, Politics, Economy* (Chicago, Human Relations Area Files, 1955), 189.
67. Kolarz, 103.
68. Baron.

memoirs of Polish peasants of the interwar period reveal great bitterness toward their village priests."[69]

It might well be argued that memoir-writing is an avocation more often associated with the class of intellectuals than with the peasants, and that the above quotation from Iwanska is somewhat biased. But even at the level of the intellectuals and the educated classes, the differences with the view of the Church in Quebec and Ireland are apparent.

One of the reasons for this disparity is the role the Church adopted within Poland toward the forces of social change. Thomas and Znaniecki write of the breakdown of the peasant community and the lack of any vehicle for the reincorporation of Poles into a viable national community:

Religion and the church organization might have been, indeed, powerful means of unifying the peasant primary groups; but they could not be used, partly because of the unwillingness of the central Catholic Church authorities to let the Polish clergy commit itself in national and social struggles, partly because of the suspicion with which the Russian and Prussian governments looked upon the activities of the Polish clergy, partly also because of the undemocratic character of the church hierarchy.[70]

In Poland, very few priests were found among the peasant leaders.[71] The Church and its representatives were based on the existing social order, and they thwarted the drives toward change, especially in the field of popular education.[72] Having little leadership among the clergy in secular affairs, the Polish Catholics did not identify their Church (in distinction to their religion) with a national identity, to the degree evident among the Irish and the French-Canadians. The nature of societal competition was not as clearly expressive to the Poles, in terms of religion and ethnic conflict, as it was to these other two nationalities.

Parish organization itself appears to have been the salient basis of the traditional way of life in Poland, but there was a strong separation in the peasant's view of the role of the Church and the role of society. They did not merge in traditional Poland. Finestone compares the value systems and peasant communities of rural Poland and southern Italy, and finds that the Church has a greater integrative

---

69. Iwanska, 196.
70. Thomas and Znaniecki, 2:1368.
71. Ibid., 1310.
72. Ibid., 1298.

function in Poland than in Italy.[73] In terms of societal competition, the integrative function of the church and society finds still more expression in the history of Ireland and Quebec.

THE GERMAN CATHOLICS

Religiously the complexion of Germany was determined by the rulers of the several states. By the principle of *cuius regio, eius religio* every prince decided which form of Christianity would prevail in his domain. Some states were Catholic, some Lutheran, and some Reformed. Throughout the nineteenth century each state had its established church and sought to control ecclesiastical affairs within its borders. These *Landeskirchen* persisted into the twentieth century. In the empire Roman Catholics were a minority. At the close of the century they constituted about 36 per cent of the population. The North was fairly solidly Protestant. The Catholic Church was strongest in the South.[74]

The sixth and last group to be discussed are the Catholics of Germany. While considered in the United States as among the most active supporters of the Catholic Church, the German Catholics share a kind of intermediacy with the Poles, in terms of the level of religious involvement.

The nature of cultural and religious competition in Germany has been a mixed phenomenon, as the above quotation suggests. On the one hand, religious affiliation tended to predominate by region within the country. On the other hand, religious groups have competed socially as a consequence of the political unification of the late nineteenth century, despite the fact that in all cases the groups are German.[75]

As Fogarty points out, and as cited above, religious observance tends to be higher only in those areas of the country which are close to the frontiers of actual cultural competition. From the societal point of view, Catholicism in Germany is one of several religious affiliations. And from the regional or subsocietal position, Catholicism in Germany is either a majority or minority religion.

---

73. Harold Finestone, "A Comparative Study of Reformation and Recidivism among Italian and Polish Criminal Offenders," doctoral dissertation, University of Chicago, 1963, chap. IV.
74. Latourette, 1:434.
75. Competition, in terms of the "adjustment of multiple loyalties," among German Catholics and German Protestants in America is discussed by Philip Gleason in *The Conservative Reformers: German-American Catholics and the Social Order* (Notre Dame, 1968), 144–71.

The latter fact poses an important qualification to the overall societal pluralism.

For comparative purposes, societal competition in Germany or with cultural systems outside of Germany has been relevant to German history, but not nearly as exclusively as the conflicts between the Catholics of Quebec and Protestant Canada, or the struggles of Catholic Ireland with Anglican England. The presence of such competition is best illustrated by the *Kulturkampf* which Bismarck's Prussia waged with German Catholicism. The conflict between the Church and the forces for nationalist unification of Germany under the leadership of Protestant Prussia led in itself to the emigration of many German Catholics to the United States, for the expressed purpose of greater freedom in religious observance.[76] Latourette associates this religious competition with the high involvement of German Catholics in the Church: "The effort to defeat Bismarck drew German Roman Catholics together and strengthened their loyalty to the Pope and their church."[77]

On the other hand, much of the *Kulturkampf* varied by region, and the efforts of Bismarck to achieve national unity took advantage of regional differences. Accommodations were made with religious distinctions, and national interests seemed to prevail over sectional ones.[78] The conflicts that were endemic between cultures and religions in Ireland and Quebec were not really sustained over time or pitched to the same degree of intensity in Germany.

With regard to religio-communal organization, German Catholicism achieved considerable development. According to Latourette, Roman Catholicism in Germany attained a kind of national solidarity which was in sharp contrast to the divided Catholicism of France, or the indifferent Catholicism of Italy.[79] The solidarity was helped along by the conflicts with statism, but German Catholicism was popularly based on numerous associations organized early in the nineteenth century. Associations with various institutional interests— the Center Party, the Federation of Christian Trade Unions, the religious groups such as the Society of St. Boniface, and the populistic *Volkverein* and *Gesellenverein*—all contributed to the growth and involvement of German Catholics in their religion.

---

76. Colman J. Barry, *The Catholic Church and German-Americans* (Washington, 1953).
77. Latourette, 1:292.
78. Ibid.
79. Ibid.

The twentieth century witnessed still more development. Organizational participation grew during the Weimar Republic. The most well-known Catholic associations were those of the trade unions and employers' groups for lay activity. But there were also "societies of mothers, of rural laborers, of store clerks, of school teachers, of waiters in hotels and restaurants, and to aid discharged prisoners."[80] Latourette documents the extent of activity within the Church at all levels of society. The rise of Nazism brought about the dissolution of most of these Catholic organizations, but involvement within the religion continued with a concentration of activity in the life of the parish.[81]

German Catholicism appears to have been as well developed as the religion of Ireland and Quebec, especially in terms of parish communities and religious association. But it was decidedly communal in its cast. Largely because of regionalism, German Catholicism lacked the nationalist overtones that colored the religion of the Irish and the French-Canadians.

OVERVIEW AND SUMMARY

Comparative data on specific developments in the religious history of each of the areas described are not easily available. By way of summary, however, some comparison may be made from recent data

TABLE 2. RATIOS OF CATHOLIC POPULATION TO NUMBER OF PARISHES, SELECTED COUNTRIES AND PROVINCES, FOR 1949, 1953, 1957, 1961

Country or Province	Parish Ratios* (Number of Catholics per Parish)			
	1949	1953	1957	1961
Quebec	2,168	2,225	2,326	2,421
Germany	2,173	2,179	2,206	2,245
Ireland	3,041	3,078	3,067	3,028
Poland	3,645	3,358	3,658	3,529
Sicily	3,744	3,757	3,640	3,499
Mexico	10,295	11,310	11,768	14,511
Puerto Rico	18,485	20,047	18,468	20,513

SOURCE: *Annuario Pontificio*, 1949, 1953, 1957, 1961. Citta del Vaticano.
* Ratios are calculated to the nearest whole number, from estimates of Catholic population and numbers of parishes, presented by sees and dioceses of each country shown.

80. Ibid., 4:185.
81. Ibid.

on the number of parishes and clergies reported for the different dioceses and sees within the Catholic Church. Tables 2 and 3 offer the ratios of Catholic population to the number of parishes and the number of clergies, respectively. The latter figures refer to the total number of diocesan priests, clergies in religious orders (males only), and seminarians.[82]

For both tables 2 and 3, the ratios are provided for four different years (arbitrarily chosen, every fourth year after the data first were available in published form) for each of the countries or provinces discussed. Table 2 provides parish ratios, or the number of Catholics per parish in the designated area. It is suggested that the fewer numbers of Catholics per parish, the more elaborate the organization of the Church for the given area. This is an indication of parish development, and serves as a clue to the distance between the Church and the religious involvement of the individual Catholics.[83]

The rank orders of these parish ratios for the four years presented in table 2 are very close, and the ratios themselves do not change considerably from one column to the next. If there is any bias in the reporting of these data, it does not seem to be erratic. The rank orders correlate fairly well with the religious behavior documented for the Catholic Americans originating from these countries, and with the state of Catholicity arising from the degree of societal competition and cultural conflict.

There is evidence of greater parish organization for Quebec, Germany, and Ireland. Poland and Sicily are next in order, and Mexico and Puerto Rico are the most underdeveloped. In view of the condition of Catholicity in Latin America, and the factors discussed above, it is not surprising to see these parish ratios for Mexico and Puerto Rico. The ratios for Sicily, however, are higher than one might expect in view of the lack of formal involvement in southern

---

82. The source for these data is the *Annuario Pontificio* (Vatican Yearbook) for 1949, 1953, 1957, and 1961. The problem of reliability is considerable; data are reported by the diocesan curias concerned and are not subject to any controls. Another important problem refers to the shifting boundaries within dioceses and general population movements. I made the effort to include the total populations of the same sees and dioceses for each year shown. Estimates of Catholics include all who are baptized as Catholics and who are not apostatized. A third problem is the gross comparability between these recent years and the historical decades of emigration to the United States. Unfortunately, similar figures are not available for years prior to World War II. As a result, I am leaning on the assumption that these figures represent some continuity and historical pattern, unless otherwise noted.
83. Fitzpatrick; Rama.

27

Italy. This is probably explained by the presence of the Vatican in Rome, and the existence of a formal religious structure throughout Italy which has developed despite generalized indifference.

Table 3 offers the ratios of Catholic population to clergies. Nationalities of the priests are not known, but it is assumed that with some exceptions among religious orders and the missionary groups in Mexico and Puerto Rico most of the clerics and seminarians are native to the areas shown. These ratios may serve to illustrate the extent to which clerical development varies with the different Catholic regions.

TABLE 3. RATIOS OF CATHOLIC POPULATION TO NUMBER OF CLERGIES, SELECTED COUNTRIES AND PROVINCES, 1949, 1953, 1957, 1961

Country or Province	Clergy Ratios* (Number of Catholics per Cleric)			
	1949	1953	1957	1961
Quebec	417	425	436	437
Ireland	423	410	383	356
Sicily	816	849	965	953
Germany	862	844	872	879
Poland	1,666	1,494	1,311	1,307
Mexico	3,501	3,336	3,100	3,657
Puerto Rico	6,512	6,479	5,216	4,948

SOURCE: *Annuario Pontificio*, 1949, 1953, 1957, 1961. Citta del Vaticano.
* Ratios are calculated to the nearest whole number, from estimates of Catholic population and numbers of clergy (defined as diocesan priests, clerics in religious orders, and unordained seminarians), reported by sees and dioceses of each country shown.

For the four years of table 3, the rank orders are again very approximate to each other, and the ratios are fairly constant for the years reported. Ireland and Quebec are both the lands of priests; the prevalence of clergy among the Irish and the French-Canadians confirms the past histories of these peoples.

Sicily is relatively well endowed with clergymen, comparing similarly with Germany. Again, as with the indications of parish development, the traditions of southern Italy and Sicily have produced an indifference to the Church in the face of well organized parish systems and the availability of priests.

For the remaining three areas—Poland, Mexico, and Puerto Rico —the proportions of population to religious functionaries yield ratios of well over one thousand. The ratios for Poland may reflect the newer post-World War II problems of church and state under communism. But the ratios for Mexico and Puerto Rico again confirm the expectation that there is little clerical assistance for the size of the Latin American Catholic population.

ဢ

The comparative analysis of the historical backgrounds of six Catholic ethnic groups in the United States has explored selective facets of the nature of religio-ethnic systems. The major goal has been an explanation of the religious involvement of these ethnic groups primarily in terms of a model of societal competition based on religious and cultural differences.

The highest involvement of the Irish and the French-Canadians in the Catholic Church is a function of the intense societal competition each of these groups experienced throughout history. Catholics in other countries, whose social systems were not subject to the conflicts brought about by different religio-cultural traditions, did not emerge with the same religio-ethnic identification and close association with the Church, which characterizes the Irish and French-Canadians. Correlating with this kind of societal competition is a fairly well-developed parish system and religious communal organization.

The intermediate position of the German and Polish Catholics is explained by the mixture of competition which marked their histories. Catholics in Germany and Poland were subject to qualified degrees of competition and conflict, not equal to the intense variety which prevailed in Quebec and Ireland. Modifying factors, such as regionalism in Germany and the inconsistent role of the Church on social, economic, and political problems in Poland, prevented the complete identification of ethnicity with religion that was so pervasive in Ireland and Quebec.

The low involvement of the Italian and Spanish-speaking Catholics is related to the lack of any societal competition which would have fostered the relevance of religious observance and the Church for these people. The indifference of the Latin Catholics is further traced to the factor of church-state alliances, and the identification of the Church with the established order and against the movements for nationalism, social justice, and change.

As an exploration into the relationship between religion and ethnicity, this paper has attempted to integrate sociological and historical concerns. A good deal more research is needed, not only for an appreciation of the roots of diversity in religion and ethnicity, but also for an understanding of the process of change in these areas of life. The blending of historical and sociological inquiries and styles of research should contribute to these endeavors.

DANIEL S. BUCZEK

POLISH-AMERICANS AND THE ROMAN CATHOLIC CHURCH

There is a pervasive theme that runs through the history of the relations between the Polish immigrants and their children—the parishes and community institutions they created—and the leadership of the Roman Catholic Church, mainly of Irish-German ancestry in the twentieth century. That theme is succinctly expressed by the most recent historian of the Roman Catholic Church in the United States, Rev. Thomas C. McAvoy, C.S.C., thus: "permeating the whole problem of Catholicism in the United States was the internal difficulty of the Americanization of the millions of immigrants who constituted so much of the body of Roman Catholicism...."[1]

The problem of "Americanization" is a problem of definition, viewed from the perspective of a myriad of historical experiences contending with one another for dominance in a majority Anglo-Saxon environment. In this sense, in its basic formulation, it is an example of a "conflict of cultures," with the Irish-American hierarchy of the Church attempting to serve "in the role of mediator between the newer immigrant communities and the larger American society that was native, Protestant, Anglo-Saxon and middle-class...."[2] It is the purpose of this essay to survey the reaction of the Polish immigrant churches and communities in the United States to this purported mediatory stance taken by the episcopal leadership of the Roman Catholic Church in the United States.

There were obvious and profound cultural and religious differences between the Polish immigrants who engulfed the American Catholic Church at the turn of the century and the second generation Irish-Americans who assumed a dominant position in that Church. These differences are immediately obvious to the naked eye, yet much more

---

[1] Thomas C. McAvoy, C.S.C., *A History of the Catholic Church in the United States* (Notre Dame, Ind., 1969), p. 371.
[2] The role of mediator is the opinion expressed by William V. Shannon, *The American Irish* (New York, 1963), pp. 135-136.

39

difficult to specify with any degree of precision.[3] Attitudes toward language are the most obvious. The Irish, after a lengthy struggle, finally succumbed to the anglicizing pressures of the English whereas the Poles in all three partitioned parts were largely successful in resisting the Germanizing and Russifying pressures of their occupiers. Because the Irish immigrants in America found their knowledge of English to be such a distinct advantage, they found it difficult to understand why other immigrant groups found it so important to defend their language, indeed even to link language with nationality and religion. For the Irish immigrant, nationality and religion were inexorably linked; for the Polish immigrant, language and religion defined his nationality.

As bishops, administrators of dioceses, and representatives of a "universal Church" which was by definition identical with no particular culture, a Church whose official language was universal, a Church which officially welcomed the multi-cultural, polyglot peoples of the world, the Irish immigrant leaders of the Roman Catholic Church were unfortunately ill-suited for the role that was thrust upon them.[4] To exercise successfully the role as mediators, then finally as the "Americanizers" of the polyglot immigrant waves that inundated the cities of America in the first half of the twentieth century demanded an ecumenicity that neither the Irish nor the Anglo-Saxon elements in American society possessed. One is tempted to focus attention on the fact that both peoples are island peoples, relatively untouched by the movements of populations and cultures that have been a characteristic feature of the historical experiences of the peoples of East-Central and Southern Europe.[5]

If there is any intelligible clue to an understanding of the Polish immigrant's reaction to the status he acquired in Church and society as

---

[3] No specific comparative studies presently exist which might illuminate this vital problem. Comparative studies of the Polish and Western European religious mentality at the turn of the century are in their infancy, let alone more specifically those related to Polish and Irish Catholicism. However, in Poland, the pioneering study of Karol Górski, *Od religijności do mistyki. Zarys dziejów życia wewnętrznego w Polsce. Część pierwsza, 966-1795* (Lublin, 1962) and the same author's *Dzieje życia wewnętrznego w Polsce* (Lublin, 1969) permit us some license to discuss the character of the Polish Catholicism which the Polish immigrants transported to our land. On the Irish side, we can rely broadly on *A History of Irish Catholicism*, General editor, Patrick J. Corish, Vol. VI, No. 2, *The United States of America*, eds. Thomas P. McAvoy, C.S.C. and Thomas N Brown (Dublin, 1970)

[4] Historically the Roman Catholic Church is a European institution, so closely identified with the culture of western Europe as to lead one of its prominent lay publicists to conclude that "the Faith is Europe and Europe is the Faith." See Hilaire Belloc, *Europe and the Faith* (London, 1920), p. 331.

[5] In this context, one is reminded of the oft-repeated boast that the British Isles have not been successfully invaded since the Norman Conquest of 1066. Edward Wakin and Rev. Joseph F. Scheuer, *The De-Romanization of the American Catholic Church* (New York, 1966), pp. 31-32 assert that "defensiveness, parochialism and inflexibility all stem from the militancy of the immigrant struggling for his place in America . . . ," but they continue that these traits "are most striking in the Irish Catholic milieu."

he arrived in the United States, in search of bread and freedom, it is the perpetuation, in a somewhat different form, of the perennial problem of East-Central Europe in modern history, the conscious nationality deprived of statehood. The Polish immigrant Catholic saw the cleavage between state and nation perpetuated in a new form in his new home: as a Pole and a Roman Catholic, deeply conscious of both in his immigrant community, he felt the same sense of alienation and deprivation that he had felt in his native land in the face of the obedience demanded of him by Russian, Prussian and Austrian autocrats.[6] In America, his cultural adjustment was rendered even more difficult for in Poland, having been deprived of statehood, at least the hierarchy of his Church was in the hands of men who shared the profoundest experiences with him. Here, both political power and control of the one institution which immediately influenced his life, beyond the family, were in the hands of the Anglo-Saxons and the Irish respectively. The history of the participation of the Polish immigrants and their children in civil society and in the Roman Catholic Church in the United States, is, therefore, a determined struggle, as viewed through the eyes of the intelligentsia, lay and clerical, of these immigrant communities to destroy the cleavage between state and nation, between nation and institution, and, to this intelligentsia, the very heart of the solution to that dilemma was full and equal participation, without loss of identity, in a pluralist and polyglot Church and in American society.

That struggle began rather inauspiciously, for the first Polish immigrant settlement in the United States, at Panna Maria, Texas is associated with the name of an intrepid Polish missionary priest of the Order of Friars Minors, Conventuals, the Reverend Leopold Moczygemba who led a group of 100 Polish immigrant families from Silesia to settle in a new farming community in the south of Texas in 1854.[7] This first parish and community of Poles on American soil was the precursor of that massive immigrant wave that would begin after the failure of the Polish insurrection of 1863 and the beginning of the Prussian Chancellor Bismarck's *Kulturkampf* against the Roman Catholic Church and other non-German influences in the new German Empire. The settlers of Panna Maria were peasants, unlike other Poles who settled in the United States up to that time, but the influence and significance of the Texas settlement on the larger panorama of Polish-American life was

---

[6] There is no need to be reminded of the periodic attempts of young Polish patriots to recapture their statehood throughout the nineteenth century.

[7] On the Polish settlement in Panna Maria, Texas, see Rev. Edward J. Dworaczyk, *The Centennial History of Panna Maria, Texas, the Oldest Polish Settlement in America, 1854-1954* (Panna Maria, Texas, 1954); also, Dworaczyk, *Church Records of Panna Maria, Texas* (Chicago, 1945).

minimal because of the remoteness and isolation of that small community from the numerous larger parish-communities forming in the industrial states of the midwest and northeast.[8]

One can subscribe to the proposition that small groups of immigrants,
of a different language and culture, do not pose a threat to the continued
dominance of Church and society by the "in-group" because of their
numerical weakness. The flow of Polish immigrant peasants into the
industrial states and cities along the Great Lakes, in the coal mining
regions of Pennsylvania, and in the industrial cities of the New England
and the Middle Atlantic states between 1870 and 1924 posed tremendous problems for the authorities of the Roman Catholic Church.
Among these problems was the integration of the immigrants into the
life of the American Church.

A fairly consistent pattern emerged which was repeated in many communities where Poles concentrated in large numbers. Initially, the Poles
were forced to worship in the nearest parish church in their neighborhood. Their settlements were often located adjacent to the German
neighborhood because many of them were familiar with the German
language, as immigrants from Prussian Poland.[9] Whether they worshipped in an English-language parish (which they called an "Irish"
parish), or a German-language parish, they felt a sense of alienation, a
feeling that they were "foreign" intruders. It is difficult, at this point,
to determine what the reaction of the clergy and people of the English
or German-speaking parishes was toward these Poles.[10] We may at
least infer that they felt uncomfortable in these surroundings, and, as
soon as a sufficient number of Polish families settled in an area, a group
of its more able leaders gathered to form a mutual aid society under the
patronage of some Polish saint (St. Stanislaus and St. Casimir were the

---

8 Other Polish settlements in Texas were established in San Antonio, Bandera,
Yorktown, and St. Hedwig soon after the founding of Panna Maria, and still later
at Czestochowa, Kosciuszko, Falls City and Polonia. See Joseph A. Wytrwal, *America's
Polish Heritage* (Detroit, 1961), p. 62.

9 The settlements in Detroit, Buffalo, and Philadelphia are cases in point. On
these settlements, see Sr. M. Remigia Napolska, C.S.S.F., "The Polish Immigrant in
Detroit to 1914," *Annals of the Polish Roman Catholic Union Archives and Museum*,
X, (1946), p. 23; Rev. Joseph Swastek, *Detroit's Oldest Polish Parish: St. Albertus,
1872-1973* (Detroit, 1973), pp. 34-42; Sr. M. Donata Slominska, C.S.S.F., "Rev.
John Pitass, Pioneer Priest of Buffalo," *Polish American Studies*, XVII (1960), pp.
28-29; and Sr. M. Theodosetta Lewandowska, H.F.N., "The Polish Immigrant in
Philadelphia to 1914," *Records of the American Catholic Historical Society of Phi-
ladelphia*, LXV (1954), p. 82.

10 This is a subject that needs further study. Scattered references, based on meagre
information, indicate that the Poles were not welcome in these parishes, that they
were held up to ridicule, made to feel inferior, and derisively referred to as "foreigners." However, Victor Greene, *For God and Country. The Rise of Polish and Lithuanian Ethnic Consciousness in America* (Madison, Wisconsin, 1973,) p. 30, claims
that the presence of these earlier Irish and German communities helped to "cushion
the cultural shock" for the newly-arrived immigrants.

most popular) in order to raise money and begin the process of form-ing their own parish and building their own church.[11]

As soon as enough money was gathered, the group applied to the bishop of the diocese for permission to build a church. The bishop meanwhile had either assigned an itinerant priest to minister to their spiritual needs in the English-language parish, or promised to assign one who would then take command of the parish's building and organ-izational activities.[12]

A number of difficulties immediately arose which foreshadowed fu-ture difficulties between the budding Polish congregation on the one hand and the pastor of the English-language parish and the local ordi-nary on the other. For reasons that still need a thorough study, the pastor of the English-language parish sometimes opposed the creation of another Catholic parish within the territorial confines of his own parish.[13] The bishops, on the other hand, feeling pressure from two sides within their own diocese, were not, as a rule, sympathetic to the creation of an ethnic "national parish," but could not, by virtue of the obligations of their office, oppose the request indefinitely. There are a number of examples where bishops pleaded with the immigrant com-munities for forbearance and patience because Polish priests were not available.[14] When a priest was available, at times he was a recently arrived immigrant from Poland, who had hastily gathered his meagre personal belongings to escape tyranny in his native land, but without the necessary identification papers from his bishops in Poland.[15] The risks that a bishop took in accepting such an unknown quantity into

---

[11] As is clear from several studies, the mutual aid society was far more than a parish-building organization. It took care of many of the social needs of the im-migrants. See William I. Thomas and Florian Znaniecki, *The Polish Peasant in Europe and America* (New York, Dover Publications, ed., 1958), II, 1518-1528; Wytrwal, *op. cit.*, pp. 156-157.

[12] Almost every pastor of a fledgling immigrant parish was engaged in such itin-erant activities. Particularly noteworthy in this respect were pastors Jan Pitass of Buffalo, Lucyan Bójnowski of New Britain, Conn., Thomas Misicki of Williamsport, Pa., etc., John Chmielinski of Boston. Rev. Waclaw Kruszka, *Siedem Siedmioleci* (Poznań, 1924), I, 241-252, chronicles his own missionary wanderings in rural Wis-consin at the end of the nineteenth century. Rev. Antoni Klawiter, who later joined the Independent Church movement, was noteworthy for the great distances he tra-velled.

[13] The citations are too numerous to detail here, but the Poles charged the English-language pastor with opposition to their venture because the pastor would be losing a lucrative source of revenue for his parish. Although one may not dis-count this reason, the subject has never been studied from the perspective of the Irish-American pastors.

[14] One such case was Bishop Michael Tierney of Hartford, Conn., who ran afoul of the wrath of the Polish Catholics of his diocese because he was not sending them priests. See Daniel S. Buczek, *Immigrant Pastor: The Life of the Rt. Rev. Msgr. Lucyan Bójnowski of New Britain, Conn.* (Waterbury, Conn., 1974), p. 36.

[15] Two such priests were reported in New Britain, Conn.: Revs. Władysław Ra-kowski and Edward Umiński. See *ibid.*, p. 26.

his diocese were great.[16] The risks that he took in rejecting him were even greater, for he was immediately exposed to the charge that he was unsympathetic to the creation of a new national parish, that he wished to impose on the young congregation a priest of a different language and culure.[17]

The dramatic increase in the number of Polish national parishes in the United States between the years 1870 and 1924 brought the "cultural conflict" between the immigrant parishes and their ordinaries to a head.[18] The Poles followed the ancient adage that "there is strength in numbers," and proposed to attack the problem of their status within the Roman Catholic Church on several fronts. At the very time that the Poles were beginning to move toward a solution to their problem, the American hierarchy was presented with a challenge from the German-language minority in the form of the Abbelen memorial which was sent to the Roman Congregation *De Propaganda Fide* in November, 1886.[19] In this memorial, signed by Archbishop Michael Heiss of Milwaukee, Rev. P. M. Abbelen sought to open for discussion "the question" concerning "the relation of non-English to English parishes...." Father Coleman J. Barry has thoroughly studied this important question in his monograph, a question which in like manner had affected the Poles, yet, for obvious reasons, neither the Germans nor the Poles ever sought to join forces with one another in a common effort for a common end.

The Abbelen memorial and the arguments and sentiments therein

---

16 The "Umiński affair" in New Britain, Conn., chronicled by the pastor of Sacred Heart Church, Father Bójnowski, in his *Historja Parafji Polskich w Djecezji Hartfordskiej w stanie Connecticut w Stanach Zjednoczonych* (New Britain, Conn., 1939), pp. 72-92; and Buczek, *op. cit.*, pp. 26-34.

17 The charges levelled against Bishop William Hoban of Scranton, Penna. in 1898 which eventually led to the organization of the Polish National Catholic Church are the classic example of such misunderstanding. See Rev. John P. Gallagher, *A Century of History: The Diocese of Scranton, 1868-1968* (Scranton, 1968), p. 229. However, two recent studies have challenged the traditional interpretation that the American hierarchy was generally unsympathetic toward the creation of national parishes. See Richard M. Linkh, *American Catholicism and European Immigrants* (New York, Center for Migration Studies, 1975), passim; and Greene, *For God and Country*, p. 60.

18 The number of Poles residing in the United States and the parishes they built is subject to conjecture owing to the inaccuracy of the statistics available which is in turn due to the inability of census takers and parish officials to arrive at an acceptable criterion of who a Pole was. However, if we may trust the calculations of the first historian of Polish America, Rev. Wacław Kruszka, in his *Historya Polska w Ameryce* (Milwaukee, 1905), I, 76, there were in 1870 50,000 Poles in ten parishes with 25 priests, and by 1875 there were about 300 Polish communities in the United States with 50 parishes. By 1942 the number of Polish parishes in the United States had risen to 831. On the latter statistic, see Rev. Stanisław Targosz, *Polonja Katolicka w Stanach Zjednoczonych w przekroju* (Detroit, 1943), pp. 3-5. The largest number of new parishes created came in the first two decades of the twentieth century.

19 This memorial is published in full by Colman J. Barry, O.S.B., *The Catholic Church and the German Americans* (Milwaukee, 1953), appendix III, pp. 289-296.

expressed could well have been written by a Polish clergyman.[20] Both the Abbelen memorial and the reply to it by Bishops John Ireland of St. Paul and John J. Keane of Richmond constitute the positions taken by the German, Polish and other clergy versus the position of the English-speaking clergy, mainly of Irish ancestry, on the important national questions which vexed the Church. The Abbelen memorial's main thrust was pointed against the oft-repeated notion that "the common welfare requires that Catholics shall be one in language and customs. Therefore, when the greater part of them is of English speech, and customs, the lesser part should conform. We are in America, we should be Americans."[21] Almost disarmingly, the memorial declared: "Certainly, and we wish it to be." However, the memorial continues, "experience teaches that the only means by which Catholic Germans (and other foreigners) shall be able to preserve their Catholic faith and morals is that they shall have their own priests who shall instruct them in the language and traditions of their fatherland. Wherever even Bishops have fallen into that most fatal of errors ... of seeking to 'Americanize' Germans as speedily as possible ... wherever that most sad dictum, 'let them learn English,' has prevailed or now prevails, there has been and there will be, a truly deplorable falling away of them from the Church." Concluding the thrust of the main argument, the memorial advised: "Let the 'Americanization' of the Germans be a slow and natural process; let it not be hastened to the prejudice of the religion of the Germans."[22]

How wide a cultural divide existed between the non-English-speaking, "foreign" immigrant peoples, then forming their parishes and organizations, and the English-speaking, "Irish" people, with their parishes, and the predominantly Irish-American hierarchy is apparent from the contents of the reply of Bishops Ireland and Keane to the Prefect of the Congregation *De Propaganda Fide*.[23] Referring to the Abbelen mem-

---

[20] These same sentiments were, indeed, expressed a generation later by Rev. Wacław Kruszka. See below, p. 16.

[21] Quoted from the Abbelen memorial, in Barry, *op. cit.*, p. 292.

[22] *Ibid.*, pp. 292-293. The memorial then concluded that "besides a difference in language, we must not by any means make light of the difference and discrepancy of Catholic customs as they are to be found among Germans and Irish," such as the different "traditions of their fathers, love of the beauty of the church edifice and the pomp of ceremonies ... ," the "administration of ecclesiastical goods and affairs ... ," finally, "even manners and social customs of the two nationalities differ exceedingly."

[23] *Ibid.*, pp. 296-312: letter dated December 6, 1886. It should be noted that the American hierarchy was by no means united in the effort to Americanize or assimilate the immigrant. Linkh, *American Catholicism*, pp. 2-4 defines two contending positions, "liberals" versus "conservatives," with the conservatives, led by Archbishop Corrigan of New York generally favoring the defense of the immigrants' national cultures.

orial and the activities of certain German priests in the United States as "these sinister intrigues," the Bishops' letter clearly established the main line of the argument proposed by the ruling hierarchy of the Church in the twentieth century, thus:

With a German Church in America there is no hope for the conversion of American Protestants .... The Church will never be strong in America; she will never be sure of keeping within her fold the descendants of emigrants, Irish as well as others, until she has gained a decided ascendancy among the Americans themselves.[24]

Thus, the Americanization of the immigrant was linked to the higher goal of proselytization, the Catholicizing of Protestant America. To convert the Protestants, Bishops Ireland and Keane continue, "give her [i.e. the Church] in her exterior forms, an American character...; and above all, choose for her as her principal pastors, and great representatives, men whose sympathies and whose accent show that they understand the country and are devoted to its interests."[25] Any prolonged emphasis on foreign nationalisms harms the task of the Church in the United States which is still looked upon by Americans "as a foreign institution, and that it is consequently, a menace to the existence of the nation."

The challenge of the American nativists is here clearly implied, though one is not sure whether the Bishops' letter was motivated more by fear of nativist reaction or genuine evangelical zeal for conversion of the Protestants. However, almost as if they were totally oblivious of either concern, German and Polish clergy and people continued to work and organize for the preservation of their language and culture in the United States. If there is a shortage of Polish-speaking priests, then a Polish seminary would provide a flow of them. Hence, the idea of a Polish seminary germinated in the mind of several Polish immigrant pastors, but is in fact associated with the name of the priest who actually brought the seminary into being, Rev. Józef Dąbrowski.[26] Further to protect the language, culture and faith of the Polish immigrants, Father Dąbrowski and his confrères prepared schemes for the building of parochial schools attached to the Polish parishes.[27] He was instrumental

---

[24] *Ibid.*, p. 306.
[25] *Ibid.*
[26] The Polish Seminary in Detroit, later Orchard Lake, Michigan, has received a thorough, scholarly treatment by Rev. Joseph Swastek, "The Formative Years of the Polish Seminary in the United States," in *Sacrum Poloniae Millennium* (Rome, 1956), VI, 39-150. Although several biographies of Father Dąbrowski have been written, the popular-scholarly work of Rev. Msgr. Alexander Syski, *Ks. Józef Dąbrowski, Monografia historyczna, 1842-1942* (Orchard Lake, Mich., 1942) is still the best available, though a scholarly study is still needed.
[27] According to Father Swastek, *ibid.*, pp. 53-54, several schemes for the creation of secondary schools and primary schools were considered and dropped for lack of funds.

in negotiating the arrival of the Felician Sisters from Cracow, Poland in November, 1874 to staff the parochial school in Polonia, Wisconsin.[28]

The need for some encompassing national organization of Roman Catholic sponsorship, which would coordinate the many schemes and plans for the defense of the immigrant, became apparent as the Poles in their new land were showing their propensity for proliferating their social and charitable organizations often in wasteful duplication of effort. Because the leadership of the growing Polish communities had initially and naturally devolved on the Catholic clergy and had not yet been challenged, the idea of the national organization was originally broached by Rev. Joseph Gieryk of Detroit, then seconded by another dynamic pastor, the Resurrectionist Father Vincent Barzyński of Chicago. Both combined their efforts and called a meeting of the intelligentsia of the Polish communities to Detroit, Michigan for October 3, 1873. An organization known as the Polish Roman Catholic Union was then founded which defined its objectives at its national congress in Chicago the following year.[29]

These objectives were: the upholding of the national spirit of the Polish-Americans; the preservation of their faith; the maintenance of interest in things Polish by the youth; and support for the Polish parochial schools in the United States. Yet, even as this auspicious organizational effort of America's Poles was underway, dark clouds of unrest and division were beginning to appear which not only tested the mettle of the clergy, but added another challenge to their dominance of the social and cultural development of Polish America. In the very year that Father Gieryk had publicly called for a national organizational meeting of Poles, an "independent" parish was organized in Polonia, Wisconsin which denied the jurisdiction of the local bishop over it. The specific details of that earliest confrontation with ecclesiastical authorities still needs investigation, but the spirit of religious independency, whose antecedents are traced to the struggle of the Irish Catholics in the American South shortly after the War of 1812 against a predominantly French-speaking hierarchy, was increasing among the Catholic Poles.[30]

The second attempt at "independency" is associated with the formation of the Holy Trinity Parish in near-north Chicago, only a short

---

[28] Sr. M. Jeremiah Studniewska, C.S.S.F., "Father Joseph Dąbrowski and the Felicians," *Polish American Studies,* XVI (1959), 12-23.

[29] Much has been written on the two fraternal societies, the Polish Roman Catholic Union and the Polish National Alliance, its rival. On the Union, see Mieczysław Haiman, *Zjednoczenie Polskie Rzymsko-Katolickie w Ameryce* (Chicago, 1948); Wytrwal, *op. cit.,* chapter VIII, pp. 212-226; Dr. Karol Wachtl, *Polonia w Ameryce* (Philadelphia 1944); Thomas & Znaniecki, *op. cit.,* II, 1575-1610.

[30] Peter Guilday, *The Life and Times of John England, first Bishop of Charleston, 1786-1842,* 2 vols. (New York, 1927), I, 31-33. German and French "independent" churches also arose prior to the Polish independent church in Polonia, Wisconsin.

walk from that city's first Polish parish of St. Stanislaus Kostka. Because of its wider repercussions and the larger milieu in which it took
place, the Holy Trinity affair took on the aspect of a *cause célèbre* in
Polish American circles and is, therefore, much better known. Victor
R. Greene has used the controversy betwen the pastor of St. Stanislaus
Kostka Parish and the early founders of Holy Trinity Parish to advance
the dubious thesis that "the Church was not the instrument of purposive
Americanization but rather an association which allowed for cultural
pluralism."[31] Greene further states that, in seeking the causes of the
rise of "Slavic self-consciousness," "forces within these groups were far
more significant in creating and shaping ethnic nationalism than relations without, between Slav and non-Slav."[32]

The issues raised in this important confrontation were, indeed, internal national issues, and the Chicago community was undoubtedly
raising for the first time the question of definition: what is a Pole?
However, it was a question which could only have been raised in the
context of the wider issue of the Polish immigrant's place in his Church
and in American society. As one moves across the panorama of Polish
versus non-Polish relations, and specifically of Polish-Irish relations
at the turn of the century, wherever these relations were marred by
serious confrontations between Polish parishioners and their pastors, in
a number of cases, the pastor had been accused of being given too much
to the "Irish ways," and not enough toward the traditional Polish ways.[33]
Greene is undoubtedly correct in his assertion that "the Church under
Irish control did allow for elements of nationalism by early fostering
and promoting ethnic parishes," and that Irish-American Bishops, like
Foley and Feehan of Chicago, Ryan of Buffalo, and O'Hara of Scranton
were, in fact, solicitous and concerned over the welfare of their immigrant
flocks, exercising great patience and restraint in the handling of volatile
situations like those in Chicago and Scranton. Frequently, this restraint
was translated in the Polish immigrant's mind into indifference, and
indifference into silent hostility. These impressions had some basis in
fact, as Greene himself has pointed out elsewhere, in the social class

---

31 Victor R. Greene, "For God and Country: the Origins of Slavic Catholic Self-
Consciousness in America," *Church History*, XXXV (1966) 459.

32 *Ibid.*, p. 447. Greene has more recently buttressed his thesis with an impressive
monograph, *For God and Country; The Rise of Polish and Lithuanian Ethnic Consciousness in America* (Madison, Wisconsin, 1975).

33 A more thorough study is needed on this important issue. However, the con-
frontations in Scranton, leading to the formation of the Polish National Catholic
Church, 1896-1907, and those in New Britain, Conn. in 1903 clearly do not support
Greene's thesis. On the Scranton situation, see Hieronim Kubiak, *Polski Narodowy
Kościół Katolicki w Stanach Zjednoczonych Ameryki w latach 1897-1965. Jego spo-
łeczne uwarunkowania i społeczne funkcje* (Warsaw, 1970), p. 111; on the New
Britain situation, see Buczek, *op. cit.*, p. 30.

conflict that took place among the unskilled and semi-skilled workers of Polish versus Anglo-Saxon ancestry in America's factories, mills and coal mines.[34] It is a simple progression to subsume under the same rubric all those who speak English, and whose cultural values are different from your own.

The struggle in north-end Chicago between those, like the dynamic Resurrectionist priest-organizer, Father Vincent Barzyński, and his lay compatriots, Antoni Smarszewski-Schermann and Peter Kiołbassa on the one hand, who defined Polishness in religious terms, as the identification of the Pole in America with his Catholic parish, and those of Holy Trinity Parish, led by the layman Władysław Dyniewicz, later joined by the Rev. Casimir Sztuczko, C.S.C., on the other hand, who defined Polishness in national terms, without denying the religious factor, foreshadowed the internal struggles among the Poles in America for several generations.[35] This simplified dichotomy explains the internal struggle within Polish-American communities which was carried on between the two major fraternal societies, the Polish Roman Catholic Union and the Polish National Alliance, whose founding dates to a meeting of some Polish laymen, led by Agaton Giller in Philadelphia on February 15, 1880.[36]

Most of the Catholic clergy of Polish America viewed the organization and growth of the Polish National Alliance and of religious "independency" with profound misgivings as examples of the growth of secularism amongst the Poles. Because the Irish-American bishop would not take an active part in the struggle against the former and was placed in an uneviable and untenable position vis-à-vis the growth of "independency," the Polish clergy, forced to defend their dominant position within the Polish-American community on their own, without the visible support of their hierarchy, experienced stress and division among themselves, as the differing positions of Father Barzyński and Sztuczko in Chicago, Pitass and Chowaniec in Buffalo had shown.[37] The positions of Fathers Barzyński and Pitass, opting for the large, un-

---

[34] Victor R. Greene, *The Slavic Community on Strike: Immigrant Labor in Pennsylvania Anthracite* (Notre Dame, Ind., 1968), p. 148.

[35] Greene, "For God and Country," pp. 449-457; also, *For God and Country*, pp. 66-84.

[36] On the Polish National Alliance, see Adam Olszewski, ed., *Historia Związku Narodowego Polskiego*, 4 vols. (Chicago, 1957); and Wytrwal, *op. cit.*, pp. 173-177 and chapter IX wherein he compares the two fraternal societies.

[37] The controversy between Rev. Dean Jan Pitass and his assistants, Revs. Peter Chowaniec and Anthony Klawiter, is touched upon lightly by Sr. M. Donata Słomińska, C.S.S.F., *op. cit.*, pp. 35-36. Obviously, this important affair still awaits a thorough investigation. Rev. Joseph Swastek, *op. cit.*, pp. 87-88, writes of "two clerical parties" which formed ranks, one supporting the Polish National Alliance, while the other, larger group was called the United Priests, led by Father Barzyński. In the 1890's there were at least four priestly factions in America.

wieldy parish may be explained by the familiar "will to power" argument. However, human motives are often a mixture of the personal, the noble and the practical, and the hypothesis is here offered that the Barzyński-Pitass position may also be interpreted as a desperate attempt by two dynamic priest-titans in the formative period of the Polish-American parish, to strengthen the position of the Polish Catholic clergy and people in their struggle against all the forces in American society they deemed inimical to their faith.[38]

If the challenge of the Polish National Alliance had consumed the energies of Chicago's Polish leaders, the Rev. Dean Jan Pitass of Buffalo watched with ever-growing concern the spread of independency, and particularly that which had developed in Scranton, Pennsylvania under the leadership of the Rev. Francis Hodur. By 1894, the Independent movement, heretofore confined to individual parishes, was beginning to show signs of coalescing into formal churches with bishops.[39] Because one of these unity movements had appeared in his own community, Father Pitass had proposed to his clerical confrères the convening of a first Polish Catholic Congress to deal with the problem of Independency.

Although the first Polish Catholic Congress which met in Buffalo on September 22-25, 1896 was well-prepared as to agenda and well-attended, the results of this first attempt of Polish Catholics to deal with their problems was negative owing to an unfortunate oversight in not establishing an executive committee to implement its resolutions.[40] However, the agenda of this Congress is revealing for the direction in which the Polish clergy and laity were moving. Placed high on the agenda, in addition to the problem of independency, was the issue of Polish representation in the American hierarchy. It is not the first time this issue, which was to consume the passions of the Polish clergy for several generations, was discussed among them. It was the first time that the issue was publicly debated and it indicated both the mood and

---

38 I have already suggested this hypothesis elsewhere. See my *Immigrant Pastor*, p. 144. The large, unwieldy parish thus became a "surrogate diocese," thus strengthening the position and increasing the influence of the pastor in his relations with the lay and ecclesiastical wielders of authority.

39 Before the organization of the Polish National Catholic Church, two attempts to unite independent parishes into formal churches ruled by bishops were made: in Buffalo, by a Rev. Stefan Kamiński, a layman ordained and consecrated to the episcopacy by Archbishop J. R. Vilatte of the Old Catholic Church of America; and by Rev. Anthony Kozłowski of Chicago, who founded the Polish Old Catholic Church of America in 1897. According to Henry R. T. Brandreth, *Episcopi Vagantes and the Anglican Church* (London, 1947), p. 35, the Episcopal Church in 1892 declared all consecrations of Archbishop Vilatte null and void.

40 The proceedings of the first Polish Catholic Congress are in *Polak w Ameryce*, Buffalo, N.Y., September 22-25, 1896. An excellent interpertation of its proceedings in Rev. Joseph Swastek, *op. cit.*, pp. 123-124.

the direction in which the Polish clergy were moving. A reasonable inference may be drawn that the Polish clergy saw the issues of independency and representation in the hierarchy in juxtaposition, i.e. Irish-American bishops were insufficiently aware of the dangers to faith which lurked in the Independent movement, and indeed the entire Independent movement fed on Polish dissatisfaction with Irish bishops and their authoritarian approaches, real or imagined.[41]

It is clear from the foregoing and subsequent events that two branches of American Catholicism were not working in harmony, that a chasm had opened between the hierarchy and the clergy of the Polish parishes. Neither seemed to have appreciated the difficult position of the other. The offensive of the American nativists against all foreign influences in American life had taken a decidedly militant turn with the economic depression of 1893, and much of this militancy was directed against the Roman Catholic Church.[42] On the other hand, the "leakage" from the faith which the Abbelen memorial had alluded to was, in fact, occurring among the Poles, yet the available evidence shows no appreciable concern by the hierarchy of the Church in stemming the tide of independency.[43]

As the Polish clergy watched the growth of independency with increasing concern, they were disturbed by remarks made by the leading episcopal exponent of the Americanization of the immigrant, Archbishop John Ireland of St. Paul. In a speech to the students and faculty of the Polish Seminary on November 28, 1899, he stated: "if you, the future leaders of the Poles, will be able to choose that path [i.e. a median path] wisely and follow it, then we, the ruling Church in America, will confidently entrust into your hands the administration of the Church."[44] Father Swastek has clearly demonstrated the conciliatory nature of Archbishop Ireland's remarks.[45] Yet, the storm of protest which arose in Polish America over the Archbishop's remarks, paraphrased as, "Americanize the Poles for us, and we shall make you bishops," indicated the mood of militancy among the Polish clergy and the

---

[41] Other items on the agenda included: the Polish Seminary, the need of a Polish primary school, the Polish-American press, the Polish National Alliance, the need for Polish labor unions, and a Catholic federation of organizations. See *ibid.*, p. 123.

[42] A brilliant study of American nativism is by John Higham, *Strangers in the Land: Patterns of American Nativism, 1860-1925*, corrected ed. (New York, 1965).

[43] When confronted with a direct challenge to their authority, the bishops were naturally drawn into the fray, as in Detroit, with the so-called "Kołasinski affair," involving factions of that city's first Polish parish, St. Albertus. See the short discussion of this affair in Swastek, *op. cit.*, pp. 68-69. Father Swastek has also published a centennial volume, *Detroit's Oldest Parish: St. Albertus Centennial, 1872-1972*, (Detroit, 1973) which contains a fuller account of the "Kołasinski affair" on pp. 63-88.

[44] As quoed by Rev. Joseph Swastek, "The Formative Years...," p. 127.

[45] *Ibid.*

dangerous impasse to which the Polish clergy and the American hierarchy were proceeding.[46]

The conciliatory remarks of Archbishop Ireland, in which he noticeably softened his earlier position, as expressed in his reply to the Abbelen memorial, may have been occasioned by the admonition of the papal brief *Testem benevolentiae* of January 22, 1899 which, in addition to its warnings against the "phantom heresy" of Americanism, deplored the national contentions in the American Church.[47] The increasing militancy of Polish Catholics, on the other hand, may have been occasioned by the knowledge that the Polish Cardinal Mieczysław Ledóchowski, since 1892 the prefect of the Sacred Congregation *De Propaganda Fide,* had apparently thrown his support toward the Gibbons-Ireland position at a time when the fires of independency were spreading.[48]

If, as now seemed apparent at the turn of the century, the American hierarchy was to leave the problem of independency in the hands of the Polish clergy, greater Polish representation in the ranks of the hierarchy was desirable. Although, as Father Swastek has noted, the origins of this movement go back to 1870 and Father Barzyński's suggestion of gaining a missionary bishop for Slavic immigrants in America, the serious effort in that direction belongs to the early twentieth century.[49] The agitation for Polish bishops now passed into the hands of a fiery young priest-journalist, Rev. Wacław Kruszka, then of Ripon, Wisconsin who challenged the American Catholic hierarchy with a ringing indictment of their linguistic provincialism in an article entitled "Polyglot Bishops for Polyglot Dioceses," originally submitted to the *American Ecclesiastical Review,* rejected for its obvious overstatements, then finally published in the *New York Freeman's Journal* of July 29, 1901.[50]

The tone of the article is fiery, challenging. Its sentiments remind one of the Abbelen memorial of the German Catholics. Taking the theme of "unity in diversity," Father Kruszka lectured his audience that

[46] Ks. Wacław Kruszka, *Siedm Siedmioleci, czyli pół wieku życia,* 2 vols. (Milwaukee, 1924), I, 321.

[47] Barry, *op. cit.,* pp. 237-238; John Tracy Ellis, *The Life of James Cardinal Gibbons, Archbishop of Baltimore, 1834-1921,* 2 vols. (Milwaukee, 1952), II, 68-69.

[48] The important question of Cardinal Ledóchowski's role in the nationality questions which dominated the American Church in the two decades before and after the turn of the century has not been adequately studied. However, see Ks. Józef Swastek, "Kardynał Ledóchowski, 1892-1902," *Sodalis,* XXXVIII (1957), 68-70; 91-93; 154-156, and an excerpt of a letter by Ledóchowski to Cardinal Gibbons, dated Rome, May 15, 1892, as quoted by Barry, *op. cit.,* p. 207.

[49] Swastek, "The Formative Years...," p. 129. Various efforts thereafter were made, both in Rome and in the United States to no avail. See also Greene, *For God and Country,* pp. 122-142.

[50] The article is published in full by Kruszka, *Siedm Siedmioleci,* I, 390-391.

Catholic unity is not based on uniformity of language or culture, rather, the diversity of language and customs strengthens, and does not weaken the Church. The mood of the second Polish Catholic Congress was decidedly militant and apprehensive, as it was held three weeks after President William McKinley had been assassinated by a Polish anarchist in the same city of Buffalo. In spite of the apprehension, the Congress resolutely proceeded to attack the problem of Polish bishops in the hierarchy in a two-fold manner: first, by despatching letters to the Apostolic Delegate, Archbishop Satolli, to Cardinal Gibbons, and to all the bishops assembled in their annual meeting in Washington, on November 21, 1901, asking consideration for the creation of Polish speaking auxiliary bishops in twelve dioceses which had between one-quarter and one-half Polish Catholics in their population.[51] If this tactic failed, the Congress was prepared to finance a three-man committee of Father Pitass and Kruszka and a layman as a delegation to Rome with a petition for considering the appointment of Polish-speaking bishops to the American hierarchy. The hierarchy, in turn, having treated the petition of the Congress as an improper procedure, rejected the Polish Catholic Congress's request; therefore, the wheels were set in motion for the special petitioning committee to leave for Rome. Father Kruszka, in his *apologia,* details the intrigues that finally forced the Venerable Dean Pitass to withdraw from participation in the journey, and a committee of Father Kruszka and the Hon. Rowland B. Mahaney of Buffalo, a former congressman, set sail for Rome in July, 1903.[52]

What transpired in Rome must be viewed through the eyes of Father Kruszka, a well-informed but not an impartial witness. In several audiences with Pope Pius X, Father Kruszka reported that the Holy Father had promised that "something in the near future will be done according to your wishes," but not immediately.[53] His *apologia* gives us glimpses of the political cross-currents which dominated the Roman Curia in these years, a picture which can only be described as unedifying. Apparently, even though Father Kruszka had found the Holy See well-informed about the conditions of the Polish parishes in the United States, and the influence of the American hierarchy substantial in the Curia, he had won a concession.

The visit to the United States of Archbishop Albin Symon, of Polish ancestry, who landed in New York on May 18, 1905 as a papal representative "in at least a semi-official capacity" occasioned an out-

---

[51] The letter is fully reported in *ibid.,* I, 441-444.
[52] Father Kruszka, *ibid.,* I, 488-617 detailed the work of this committee in the Roman congregations.
[53] *Ibid.,* II, 805.

pouring of emotion in Polish parishes throughout the country where
he visited that had seldom been witnessed.[54] The euphoria generated
by the Archbishop's visit was not stilled by rumors that he had been
critical of the low intellectual level of the Polish clergy in America. His
report to Pope Pius X concluded that "a Polish bishop, e.g. a suffragan
in those dioceses where there is a large number of Polish parishes, like
Chicago, Milwaukee, Detroit, Pittsburgh, Buffalo, and Philadelphia, is
badly needed for the ecclesiastical affairs of this people."[55]

The consecration of the Most Rev. Paul W. Rhode as Auxiliary of
Chicago in 1908 was probably the tangible result of Father Kruszka's
efforts.[56] However, Father Kruszka was plainly dissatisfied with this
exercise in tokenism, the more so because Bishop Rhode, in spite of his
non-jurisdictional position, was "intended to have wider responsibilities
in caring for and mediating among Polish Catholics in the entire United
States."[57] This indicated that the American hierarchy viewed the appointment of a Polish representative within its ranks as having solved
the main issue, whereas Father Kruszka "was unable to accept anything
less than full stature for the Polish clergy in America, preferably as
national bishops who would minister exclusively to the Poles."[58] Bishop
Rhode's consecration did still the fires of controversy temporarily as
new and more urgent issues began to encroach upon the consciousness
of American Catholics, not the least of which was the challenge of social radicalism among the immigrants, particularly the beguiling temp-
tations of the Marxist-oriented International Workers of the World.[59]
On this issue, the Polish-American clergy were placed in an extremely
difficult and unenviable position, for their role as pastors embraced the
whole gamut of human experiences in which the Polish immigrants
were engaged. They were by necessity forced into the vortex of political
and economic controversy, whereas their position as Christian pastors
and their oath militated against such activity. However much one might

[54] *Ibid.*, II, 90-162 traces the movements of Archbishop Symon and the reaction
of Polish-American and Irish-American priests and bishops to his visit. Some bishops
did not receive him which raises a doubt as to the official character of his visit. See
Anthony J. Kuzniewski, Jr., *Faith and Fatherland: An Intellecual History of the
Polish Immigrant Community in Wisconsin, 1838-1918* (unpublished Ph.D. dissertation, Harvard University, 1973), p. 250.
[55] Kruszka, *Siedm Siedmioleci*, II, 171-172 contains Archbishop Symon's report
to Pope Pius X.
[56] Greene, *For God and Country*, pp. 141-142 maintains that the immediate antecedents of the nomination of the Rev. Paul W. Rhode lie in renewed Polish Catholic defections to Independency and Archbishop Quigley's consequent alarm and
visit to Rome in 1907. However Father Kruszka's visit and Archbishop Symon's visit
need not be minimized.
[57] Kuzniewski, *op. cit.*, p. 309.
[58] *Ibid.*, p. 241.
[59] The role of the Polish Catholic clergy in the social class conflict between left-
wing and right-wing elements still awaits a study, and indeed, to this day, only
sporadic mention is made of it, perhaps because of the paucity of evidence.

argue that the challenge of the Marxist-oriented I.W.W. was within the purview of a priest's pastoral responsibilities, that, in fact, the I.W.W., by its un-Christian espousal of class struggle, presented a moral and a theological challenge, the charge of meddling in politics *prima facie* seemed to many Americans a valid one.[60] It is perhaps one of several reasons why the Polish Catholic clergy took a conservative "law and order" stance on the great social and political issues in the decade before America's entry into World War I.

The challenge of the I.W.W. did not markedly affect the relations between the Polish clergy and their parishioners because that was a movement instigated outside the parish and community. As early as 1912, when debate began to appear about the future status of Poland, the Polish clergy, along with the rest of Polish America, were seriously divided into ideological camps, the vast majority of the clergy following the lead of Bishop Rhode who, in order to counteract the left-wing Committee of National Defense, founded in 1912 and popularly known as KON (Komitet Obrony Narodowej), founded a rival organization of patriots known as the Polish National Committee which worked in cooperation with the Alliance of Polish Priests in America.[61] The Polish clergy overwhelmingly accepted the challenge of Rev. Edward Kozłowski, later Auxiliary Bishop of Milwaukee, who stated at the organizational meeting of the Alliance of Polish Priests that "the time had come when.. the Polish priest must come from behind the sacristy and work not only in the Lord's vineyards but also in the fields of his mother country."[62] Many priests worked together with Polish relief and recruitment organizations and actually turned their rectories into recruiting stations for the Polish legion of General Joseph Haller.

The unity of purpose and the achievements of Polish America, led by its clerical intelligentsia during World War I, was to be her finest hour. Never before or since have the energies and the monetary generosity of the Poles in the United States reached such unprecedented heights. To be sure, there were many failures along the way, but by the end of 1919, the local Citizens' Committees, frequently attached to the Polish

---

[60] The Lawrence mill strike of 1912, sparked by a group of Polish women, is the most celebrated of the instances of social unrest which involved a Polish community. See Marc Kerson, *American Labor Unions and Politics, 1900-1918* (Carbondale, Ill., 1958), pp. 182-183; and Donald B. Cole, *Immigrant City: Lawrence, Massachusetts, 1845-1921* (Chapel Hill, N.C., 1963), pp. 177-194.

[61] Stanley R. Pliska, *Polish Independence and the Polish-Americans* (unpublished Ed.D. dissertation, Teachers College, Columbia University, 1955), pp. 81-85; Karol Wachtl, *op. cit.*, pp. 291-296.

[62] Stanisław Osada, *Jak się kształtowała polska dusza Wychodźtwa w Ameryce*, 1st ed. (Pittsburgh, 1930 p. 52. Actually, the Association finally accepted a compromise statement that, as "Polish clergy, they were not opposed to any Catholic organization which would work for the good of Poland."

parishes, raised a sum estimated at $1,500,000 for General Haller's army of six full divisions and 108,000 men.[63]

Unfortunately, these magnificent achievements could not be sustained indefinitely, and with the emergence of an independent Polish Republic and the end of the war, the Polish clergy suddenly faced a changed world and two new challenges. For various reasons, the aftermath of war brought a disillusionment with Poland on the part of Polish-Americans, as they began to redirect their energies toward specifically Polish-American problems, a position fostered by the clergy.[64] The political and cultural ties that had once bound these Polish-American communities to their "motherland" were intentionally severed so that these communities and their priest-leaders were left to their own devices to face a new and more dangerous wave of American nativism. Because the Church, as a "foreign" institution, was itself under attack, the possibility that the Church's hierarchy would join forces with its immigrant newcomers to parry the thrusts of this new, convulsive wave of nativism existed at least *in potentia*. The hierarchy's answer to the problem was their pastoral letter of 1919 calling upon all Catholics "to help the immigrants to prepare themselves for the duties of citizenship."[65] How great a fissure had developed between the Polish clergy and the hierarchy of the Church on the issue of Americanization may be visualized from the fact that already in 1919 fifteen states decreed that English must be the language of instruction in all primary schools.[66] Although all of these laws were eventually declared unconstitutional, the hierarchy of the Church did not seem to be concerned with the obvious effects these laws would have on the immigrant parochial schools which instructed bilingually.[67] On the contrary, if the relations between the huge Chicago Polonia and her archbishop, George Cardinal Mundelein, are any barometer, that fissure in 1920 developed into a huge chasm. Stung by a series of reversals in their lengthy struggle to achieve "equality of right" for the clergy, i.e. a proportional number of bishops of Polish ancestry, the Association of Polish Clergy joined the Polish Embassy at the Vatican in presenting to the Holy See a memorial, *I Polacchi negli Stati Uniti dell'America del Nord*.[68] Among the many grievances expressed by the Association of Polish Clergy was the charge

---

63 I rely here on the thorough study of Pliska, *op. cit.*, pp. 213-257.

64 *Ibid.*, p. 440.

65 *The National Pastorals of the American Hierarchy*, ed. Peter Guilday (Westminster, Md., 1954), p. 326.

66 Higham, *op. cit.*, p. 260.

67 No study exists on this vital question.

68 I rely here on the excellent study of Joseph J. Parot, *The American Faith and the Persistence of Chicago Polonia, 1870-1920* (unpublished Ph.D. dissertation, Northern Illinois University, 1971), pp. 327-342. The memorial was dated June, 1920.

that "the Catholic Church through its Bishops [have] become the instruments of Americanization among the Polish immigrants."[69]

Cardinal Mundelein's rebuttal to the memorial of the Association of Polish Clergy is the classic defense of the hierarchy's position. Confidently, almost arrogantly bearing down on the obvious impropriety of involving a foreign government in the affairs of another country, even if they be of a religious character, he stated the American hierarchy's case against ethnic pluralism: "The American people in general, and the government of the United States in particular ... expect the various nationalities ... to become one people, one race, loyal to the government of this country ...." Furthermore, Cardinal Mundelein bluntly stated that "it will be a disaster for the Catholic Church in the United States if it were ever to become known that the Polish Catholics are determined to preserve their Polish nationality and that there is among their clergy and leaders a pronounced movement of Polonization...."[70] There is no doubt that, as Parot has concluded, the memorial of the Polish clergy was a colossal blunder, indefensible from a diplomatic standpoint as well as a *faux pas* in terms of etiquette. There is no doubt that the Polish clergy failed to appreciate the tremendous nativist pressures weighing on the hierarchy. From the hindsight of another generation, however, the American hierarchy seemed to have committed one of those recurring philosophic blunders, the result of a myopic vision, a malady common to nationalist patriots of all lands: they confused uniformity with unity. Not once did it ever occur to the signatories of the memorial, indeed to the clergy of Polish America, that their desire to foster the language and traditions of the motherland of their culture could be considered an act of disloyalty to their adopted land. They, as the German clergy before them, were proposing a pluralistic Church united by bonds of love. Their vision of their Church in America was a microcosm of that which America had in fact become.

The mood of the American hierarchy generally was to uphold the law of the land without questioning the wisdom or propriety of the law. Thus, the unfortunate, matter-of-fact, though not malicious order of the bishops of Buffalo and Brooklyn for all parochial schools of their dioceses to comply with the New York State education law regarding exclusive instruction in the English language during official school hours was particularly galling to the Polish-American clergy.[71]

---

[69] As quoted by *ibid.*, p. 333.

[70] Ibid., pp. 338-339.

[71] Sr. Ellen Marie Kuznicki, *An Ethnic School in American Education: A Study of the Origin, Development, and Merits of the Educational System of the Felician Sisters in the Polish American Catholic Schools of Western New York* (unpublished Ph.D. dissertation, Kansas State University, 1973), pp. 161-166 studied the reaction of one religious teaching body to these episcopal instructions.

The storm of protest generated by these ill-advised orders, particularly in Buffalo, led to demands from numerous clergy for drastic action in the face of the mounting threat to the future of the Polish ethnic parish, both from the nativists as well as from the "Americanizers" in the Church. The Association of Polish Priests in America, at its triennial meeting in Philadelphia on February 26-27, 1924 again placed the dormant issue of "equality of right" and specifically representation of the Polish clergy in the hierarchy as the main item on its agenda, together with the defense of the Polish Catholic parochial school.[72] A perusal of the papers read at this gathering indicates a mood of passion and frustration. The keynote address was delivered by Rev. Louis Grudziński of Chicago who accused the American Catholic hierarchy of attempting to denationalize the immigrant, a policy which had no precedent in human history.[73]

Hanging over this significant gathering of clergy was the mournful truth that since the end of World War I, a new generation of Polish-Americans had arisen whose interest in the policy of cultural pluralism espoused by the older generation was minimal, who were more interested in their social and economic status in American society rather than in the preservation of the language and culture of the Polish community in America. The 250-odd priests who attended this gathering, much less than half of the total of Polish-speaking priests in America, for the most part agreed with the resolutions proposed by the Association, but it was clear that a serious division had invaded the ranks of the Polish-American clergy as they contemplated the future of the ethnic Polish parish. Younger priests, born and educated in America, were losing command of the Polish language, and encouraging the greater use of the English language in church and school.[74]

The threat of the disintegration of the Polish national parish in America was already appearing in the 1920's. A harbinger of this was the increasingly caustic criticism in the Polish-language press of the purported failure of the so-called "Polish school" to educate the children adequately in the English language. Caught in the middle of this debate about the future of Polish America were the teaching sisterhoods, the religious orders of women who had staffed the schools. The decades of

---

72 The papers read at this meeting have been published in the organ of the Association, *Przegląd Kościelny*, XI (1924).

73 Rev. L. Grudziński, "Wydział Narodowy i stosunek jego do kleru i społeczeństwa," *ibid.*, XI (1924), p. 193.

74 Examples of this trend are not yet numerous in the 1920's but see Sr. Ellen Marie Kuznicki, *op. cit.*, pp. 166-167 wherein she points out that Rev. Anthony Majewski, pastor of St. Casimir's Church, Buffalo, took a position that English be encouraged; and *Nowiny Polskie* (Milwaukee), October 13, 1924, p. 3 which reported a protest by 123 children of the parochial school of St. Constance, Chicago, against the teaching of the Polish language in that school. The pastor, Rev. A. Knitter, later admitted that he agreed with the protesters.

yeoman service to both Church and school in America by the various Polish women's religious congregations were somehow forgotten in the midst of the fury of the debate over the effectiveness of the "Polish school."[75]

As the younger generations of Polish-Americans began to question the usefulness of the Polish language in the 1920's, bishops were watchful for any signs of disintegration in the national parishes. The first instance of the transformation of an hitherto national parish into a territorial parish was apparently achieved in Iron City, Michigan at the Parish of the Assumption B.V.M. in 1924.[76] Much better known because it was located in Chicago was the case of St. Thecla's Parish which became a territorial parish in 1929 by order of George Cardinal Mundelein. The case of St. Thecla's reverberated throughout the Polish-American press in that year, yet little, if anything, could have been done to reverse the decision because both the pastor, Rev. Paul Sobota, and the younger parishioners were in agreement with the decision.[77]

The struggle to maintain the "Polishness" of the Polish national parishes continued in the 1930's with unabated fervor in spite of the powerful trend toward Americanization. The subject received increasing emphasis in the pulpit, especially in the radio sermons of the popular preacher of that decade, Father Justin Figas, Franciscan Conventual of Buffalo.[78] However, taking cognizance of the situation developing in the 1930's, the Holy See issued a declaration in 1938 to the effect that "when foreign immigrants and their children speak the English language and do not wish to belong to their own national parishes, they must affiliate with the American territorial parish in which the English language may be spoken."[79] Although this papal declaration guaranteed the individual's freedom of choice, it was widely regarded as a blow to

---

[75] This part of the history of the American Catholic Church as it relates to the Polish women's religious congregations is the most neglected aspect. Although each religious congregation has published a commemorative volume which includes a short history, the value of such volumes is sociological, not historical. The most serious account, limiting itself to the education work of the Felician Sisters in one province is by Sr. Ellen Marie Kuznicki, already cited.

[76] *Nowiny Polskie*, November 20, 1924, p. 4.

[77] The facts as presented in the Polish-language press were confusing and contradictory as to whether the Archdiocese of Chicago had established the status of St. Thecla's originally from its foundation in 1923 as a territorial parish. Two Chicago dailies, *Dziennik Związkowy* and *Dziennik Chicagoski*, could not agree. See *Dziennik dla Wszystkich* (Buffalo, N.Y.), June 3, 1929, p. 4; also *Przewodnik Katolicki* (New Britain, Conn.), July 5, 1929, p. 15 for two different views.

[78] O. Justyn Figas, O.M.C., *Mowy radiowe wygłoszone w latach 1932-1948*, 31 vols. (Milwaukee, 1932-1948). The achievements of the Polish-American clergy in the field of homiletics have received a thorough historical survey by Rev. Dr. Jacek Przygoda, "Szkic historyczny polskiej katolickiej literatury homiletycznej w Stanach Zjednoczonych," *Sacrum Poloniae Millennium* (Rome, 1957), IV, 461-569.

[79] T. Lincoln Bouscaren, S. J., *The Canon Law Digest* (Milwaukee, 2 vols., 1943), pp. 79-80.

the future of the ethnic parishes by the Polish-speaking clergy, and a victory by the English-speaking clergy of America.

Only a temporary reprieve with the flow of the Polish political refugees, the so-called D.P.'s, has saved the Polish national parishes from more rapid disintegration since World War II. That disintegration continues in spite of an apparently changed attitude by the Holy See itself, for on August 1, 1952 the Apostolic Constitution *Exsul Familia* guaranteed "the rights of immigrants to proper pastoral care in their own language and traditions."[80] Furthermore, the Constitution of Vatican Council II on the Church in the Modern World included a chapter on "the proper development of culture" which recommended "increased exchanges between cultures which ought to lead to a true and fruitful dialogue between groups and nations." The Council clearly stated, in the form of a rhetorical question, that absence of such dialogue disturbed the life of communities, destroyed ancestral wisdom, and jeopardized the uniqueness of each people.[81] In the long, at times unedifying, contention between the Polish-American Catholics of America and the predominantly Irish-American ruling hierarchy of the Roman Catholic Church, the position in the "cultural conflict" assumed by the intelligentsia of Polish America—lay and clerical—was precisely that which was counselled by Vatican Council II.

Most of that hierarchy, particularly between the two wars of the twentieth century, followed the admonitions of James Cardinal Gibbons and Archbishop John Ireland, thus: "to Catholicize America we must Americanize the immigrants."[82] If, by this approach, they viewed themselves as "mediators" between the Anglo-Saxon majority culture and people and the Church's immigrant newcomers in the late nineteenth and twentieth centuries, they were not so regarded by the intelligentsia of the Polish emigration.[83] It is difficult to avoid the conclusion of a recent young scholar of Wisconsin's Polish immigrant experience:

Fearful of the nativists and outspoken in their proclamations of loyalty to the United States, many of these prelates [i.e. of the 1920's and 1930's] de-emphasized the universality which their Church professed in the interest of acceptability. More attuned to questions of power and influence and individuals outside the fold, they sacrificed part of the legitimate in-

---

80 A discussion of this apostolic constitution is by Zbigniew Zysnarski, "Parafie etniczne w oczach Papieży i Soborów," *Sodalis,* XLVI (1967), 244-245.
81 Walter M. Abbott, S. J., *The Documents of Vatican II* (New York, 1966), p. 261.
82 The quotation is actually a paraphrase of a statement made by Cardinal Gibbons, as quoted by Ellis, *op. cit.* I, 386: "Ours is the American Church, and not Irish, German, Italian or Polish, and we will keep it American."
83 See Joseph A. Wytrwal, *Poles in American History and Tradition* (Detroit, 1969), pp. 260-274.

terests of those, like the Poles and Italians, whose loyalty could be taken for granted because they had no alternative.[84]

Such a conclusion is buttressed by a recently published letter of the directorate of the newly formed National Catholic Welfare Council to Pope Pius XI protesting the official papal dissolution of that Council.[85] In assigning reasons for the desirability of maintaining a National Catholic Welfare Council, the signatory bishops complained that "the effect of the [papal] decree upon our non-Catholic brethren would, we fear, be particularly unfortunate."[86]

From the perspective of the Polish element in the Roman Catholic Church in the United States in the twentieth century, their Church's policy of Americanization and often of "benign neglect" was particularly unfortunate.

---

[84] Kuzniewski, *op. cit.*, p. 470.

[85] Elizabeth McKeon, "Apologia for an American Catholicism: The Petition and Report of the National Catholic Welfare Council to Pius XI, April 25, 1922," *Church History*, XLIII (1974), pp. 514-528.

[86] *Ibid.*, p. 519.

Mary the Messiah: Polish Immigrant Heresy and the Malleable Ideology of the Roman Catholic Church, 1880-1930

JOHN J. BUKOWCZYK

"IN RELIGION the Poles are predominantly Roman Catholic," Presbyterian minister Paul Fox observed in 1922. And although Rev. Fox lamented that theirs was "a religion of external rites, symbolic forms, servile fear, and magical personal salvation," he nonetheless praised them as "a church-going people." Group writers would not endorse Fox's condescending nativist view, but have nonetheless concurred with his central point, "the earliest and most important institution among Polish immigrants was the church."[1] Immigration historians, too, have accepted this conclusion about Polish immigrant religiosity. Roman Catholicism formed a ponderous proportion of the "cultural baggage" that Poles carried with them when they journeyed to America; they held on to this attachment tightly even after they settled here.[2]

When the social history of immigrant religion is examined however, we find that the Poles' faith did not fall into place quite so automatically as this broad concord of opinion might suggest. In Poland and in the immigrant districts of America, popular belief often diverged from religious orthodoxy, incorporating an assortment of beliefs and practices with magical or pagan connections.[3] In America, dispersal of the Roman Catholic immigrant population and assimilation eroded belief, while assorted radical ideologies spawned in reaction to industrial capitalism became an attractive alternative to the doleful submissiveness counselled by the church.[4]

To be sure, the erosion in traditional religious practice was not the result of immigration alone. Polish sociologists, for example, have observed that marked secularization later in Poland itself was associated with industrialization, urbanization, and the rationalization of agriculture.[5] Yet immigrant and native-born clerics alike often identified loss of faith principally as an immigrant problem. Rev. Wenceslaus Kruszka, Polish America's authoritative early historian, estimated the Poles' resulting "leakage" from the church at the staggering rate of one-third.[6]

55

Though Kruszka's figure was dubiously high, by 1920 denominational statistics did show a total of thirty-one Polish Protestant churches and missions in the United States with nearly four thousand adherents.[7] Other Polish defectors remained apostate or succumbed to the appeal of secular ideologies like socialism, anarchism, syndicalism, positivism, and secular variants of Polish nationalism. Of these, Polish socialists alone numbered up to a few thousand.[8] Clearly, immigration, urbanization, and industrialization were taking their toll, and Roman Catholicism consequently enjoyed far weaker ties to its immigrant parishioners than stereotypes have depicted.

Churchmen and their lay allies could not agree on what strategy would best counter the growing threat posed by popular religious deviations, secularism, disobedience, and heresy. Marching in lock step with the progressive encyclical, *Rerum Novarum* ("On the Condition of Labor"), which Pope Leo XIII issued in 1891, church liberals argued that they could win over those who strayed by becoming more responsive to the needs of their urban industrial flock.[9] As a whole, the American church lay closer to the liberal position, so much so that church liberalism would come to be called "Americanism."[10] But because conservatives led so many heavily immigrant dioceses and archdioceses—e.g., New York, Brooklyn, Cleveland, Philadelphia, Rochester, and Milwaukee, working-class immigrants like the Poles more often encountered conservative strategies to keep them in the church. If the Poles' reputation for religiosity survived, it was thus not the persistence of premigration rural culture alone, but the success of those conservative strategies which reinforced—imposed and extended—habits of religious devotion among them.

Of the strategies that conservative bishops employed in order to retain immigrants within the fold, none was more important than their reliance upon national, i.e., ethnic, parishes.[11] By 1912, six years before a revision in Canon Law froze the number of ethnic parishes in the United States, the *Official Catholic Directory* listed nearly 1600 national parishes in the United States, including 214 Italian, 346 German, and 336 Polish.[12] That figure, however, was vastly undercounted, for by 1900 Polish Roman Catholic parishes alone already had numbered 517.[13]

This multiplication of national parishes gave a distinctive stamp to the church's campaign against unbelief and decisively influenced the shape of American Catholicism during the period. First, by using immigrant priests to serve the foreign-born flock, bishops sacrificed religious uniformity in the interest of more effectively reaching their linguistically and culturally diverse communicants. Sanctioning the creation of national parishes institutionalized the growing ethnic divisions that fractured the American church, but it also insured that Roman Catholicism would remain a powerful force in immigrant life. Secondly, the endorsement of national parishes helped to decentralize power and authority within the American church. While immigrant priests still failed to gain access to positions in the church hierarchy, within their own ethnic parishes they acquired wide de facto autonomy in preserving and defending immigrant faith.[14] In 1871 in Chicago, for example, the Polish missionary Congregation of the Resurrection of Our Lord Jesus Christ negotiated a jurisdictional arrangement with Bishop Thomas Foley under which the Resurrectionists won the right to administer all non-diocesan Polish parishes in the Chicago diocese for ninety-nine years.[15] Yet if Chicago's Resurrectionist Fathers were at all atypical, it was not in kind, but only in degree. Other Polish pastors like Buffalo's Jan Pitass and Connecticut's Lucyan Bójnowski also enjoyed huge power, while scores of lesser Polish clerics wielded more modest though still extensive authority in their own parishes.[16] Many of them were Polish born. But after 1884, Polish born and trained priests' monopoly over Polish-American parishes began slowly to crack. In that year, Bishop Caspar Borgess approved Rev. Joseph Dąbrowski's request to establish a Polish seminary in Detroit, the first in the United States.[17]

The creation of national parishes meant that, henceforth, the day-to-day battle against Polish unbelief would be fought and led by Polish priests. Indeed, the Polish-American clergy pressed its own two-pronged offensive against secularism, apostasy, and deviations from orthodox belief. In the campaign to counter superstition and nagging vestiges of paganism, Polish priests selected a tactic of sapping and strategic retreat. In time-honored ways, they seemed largely to have coexisted with magic, superstition, and the occult—criticizing them when they undercut priestly authority, hoping they would eventually fade, and meanwhile co-opting them through the quasi-magical "theater" of the mass.[18] The fight against secularism was, however, a different matter. Such a direct challenge to religion, the church, and their own pastorates impelled Polish priests to confront irreligion head on. The staunch efforts made by priests like New Britain's Rev. Bójnowski are by now quite familiar, but the campaign these few celebrated Polish pastors waged was hardly unique.[19] Ordinary immigrant priests like Brooklyn's Rev. Leon Wysiecki and Rev. Joseph Lenarkiewicz of Shenandoah, Pennsylvania, pursued their own local efforts against "the socialists" in the 1890s.[20] Of course, it remains difficult to gauge the effect of the Polish clergy's campaign, but at least some priests thought it was working. In 1897, for example, Brooklyn's Rev. Wysiecki proudly informed his bishop that even the socialists had started coming to confession.[21]

However doggedly and successfully immigrant clerics fought against unbelief, their efforts remained largely a holding action. The real locus of the battle to uphold the faith lay not among the adult immigrants, but among their innocent, vulnerable children. In November of 1884, the Third Plenary Council of Roman Catholic prelates in America had met in Baltimore and ordered that all American Catholics—native-born and immigrant alike—should educate their children in parochial schools in order to protect them from Protestant and secular influences.[22] In the next three decades, Polish pastors rose to the challenge, judging by Polish-American education statistics. Between 1887 and 1914, the number of Polish parochial schools rose from fifty to nearly four hundred, while enrollments climbed from 14,150 to 128,540 during the same period. These figures become more impressive when set in context. Before World War One, the ratio of Polish parochial schools to Polish parishes stood at roughly two to three.[23]

In the 1920s, this extensive parochial education system taught approximately two-thirds of the Polish children in the United States;[24] clearly, immigrant parents accepted church-sponsored education as an obligation, in part out of obedience to their clergy, in part as a means to inhibit deculturation of the second generation. But church strategy to educate Catholic youth in parochial schools depended on more than just the compliance of immigrant parents. It also required a corps of religiously reliable teachers to staff the church-run institutions. The centerpiece of that strategy therefore became the burgeoning female religious congregations of teaching nuns, with which the Poles were especially well endowed by the second half of the nineteenth century.

Socially active sisterhoods began to multiply in Poland between the 1850s and 1880s with the formation of congregations like the Sisters of Saint Felix (Felicians) and the Sisters of the Holy Family of Nazareth. During this period of religious renewal, Polish nationalist passions, repeatedly thwarted in a series of failed insurrections, sought a new outlet in religious mysticism, while a growing Polish economy for the first time afforded the daughters of Poland's propertied classes the leisure to translate spiritual piety into a new way of life. The sisterhoods, moreover, grew up at a time when the dislocations of urbanization and industrialization called educated men and women on both sides of the Atlantic into careers of social service and reform. Finally, the female congregations also gave young Polish women an opportunity for achievement largely absent in male-dominated secular society.[25]

Poland's female religious congregations checked dangerous social ferment by counseling that classes should exist in Christian harmony. The Felicians revitalized religious zeal among "the laiety of all classes," for example, by "bringing together humble servants and seamstresses, . . . teachers, public officials, and even women from the aristocracy." They also labored for religious and social reform in the Polish countryside. After the Polish Agricultural Society, an association founded by Count Zamoyski, asked the Felician congregation to perform social service work among the Polish peasantry, the Felicians staffed twenty-seven rural social centers (*ochrony*) in the Polish Congress Kingdom (central and eastern Poland) between 1859 and 1863. When members of the Agricultural Society inspected the centers a year after their opening, according to a Felician historian, "They were astounded by the manifest improvement in morals and in mutual relations between the peasants and their lords."[26] Thus Roman Catholic prelates were able to harness the nuns' religious zeal and keep it as a capable defender of the social status quo, the church's spiritual affairs, and the temporal interests of Poland's propertied classes.

As Polish immigration mounted, it was not long before Polish pastors in the United States also discovered similar uses for the new Polish sisters and invited successive Polish congregations to establish convent houses and take up teaching duties in America. So successful were these efforts that, already before the war, 2180 teaching sisters served the Polish parochial education system in the United States.[27] The addition of nuns to the staff of the urban parish provided the fortunate pastor with a trained corps of assistants who could aid in the administration of religious and temporal affairs in the parish. Sisters performed services for the various parish societies, cared for the altars and decorated the church, drilled the altar boys and looked after their vestments, enlisted immigrant children for service to the parish, and organized "vocation days" to recruit new nuns and priests.[28] Yet the Polish nuns exerted a broader influence on the immigrants' popular religious culture. Teaching in the parochial schools, where they disseminated the articles of faith, the sisters espoused innovative church doctrine: the mystical adoration of the Blessed Virgin Mary.

Of itself, Marianism was not a new idea. In the Middle Ages, mysticism—direct, personal, intuitive relations with the Divine—and Marianism—cultic devotions to the Blessed Virgin Mary—became touchstones

of the Roman Catholic faith.[29] Later, during the Counter Reformation,
Marian mysticism developed as an especially pervasive feature of *Polish*
belief and would remain so into the modern period.[30] Marian influences
were thus a commonplace in Poland's Roman Catholic church and in the
immigrant districts of America where Poles often encountered Resurrectionist Fathers and other priests who were steeped in Marian piety.[31] What
made the Polish nuns a unique fount of Marian mysticism, however, was
the lengths to which they carried their devotion to the Blessed Virgin and
the way they personalized their relationship to her and to Christ. Polish
sisters singlemindedly embraced Marian mysticism as the rule for their
spiritual lives and as the moral dimension of their social activities—
teaching, charity, and social work.

Each Polish female congregation highlighted a different aspect of the
Marian cult, from which it derived its own distinctive character. Under
Felician rule, for example, female religious practiced humility, poverty,
"seraphic love," constant expiation, and, most characteristically, continual self-abnegation in order to atone for the sins of the world. Each
Felician nun was "a Bride of a thorn-crowned Spouse," offering each
year a waxen image of a pierced heart on the Feast of the Immaculate
Heart in order to symbolize "total consecration."[32] The Sisters of the
Holy Family of Nazareth shared the Felicians' main purpose, "total
self-immolation through prayer, work and suffering offered for the intentions of the Vicar of Christ [the Pope] and the Church," but eliminated
many of the austerities practiced by the older sisterhoods. Instead, they
sought to create a Marian "family atmosphere" within their convents.[33]
Sisters of the Holy Family were encouraged to develop "a sound appreciation of Mary's role in the mystery of the Redemption and . . . a filial
confidence in her patronage," and alternatively told to become "a little
Mary," "a true daughter of the immaculate Virgin Mary," "Mary-like,"
"a slave of Mary."[34] Still, like the Felicians, Nazarethan Sisters also embraced "the mysticism of reparation" in order to help souls to salvation.
In the final profession ceremonies of the congregation, Sisters of the Holy
Family of Nazareth therefore received rings to signify them as "spouses
of Christ" as each solemnly pledged, "I renew and confirm it, and again
renounce forever the devil, the world, and myself, in order to live only for
Jesus Christ Our Lord."[35]

This Marian mysticism which the Polish nuns catechized in the parochial schools represented a new development in the religion of rural Polish
immigrants. Though sparse elementary education had sometimes been
provided by village priests in Polish country districts, more usually it was
conducted by literate farmers or male or female lay teachers, not by

teaching sisters.[36] The cult of the Blessed Virgin Mary had been introduced into the Polish countryside by the higher classes, and Polish peasants had adopted Mary as a character in hundreds of parables and stories in the popular religious folklore.[37] But even though Mary had penetrated into local lore, Polish peasants still had not adopted any of the elements that composed Marian *mystical* belief. Religion—like magic—remained a mechanical means to influence practical affairs. Polish peasants saw themselves related to the Roman Catholic God only through the Roman Catholic church.[38] This changed in America. Teaching in the parochial schools, the Polish Roman Catholic sisters now systematically indoctrinated immigrant youth in Marian mysticism—an individual spiritual connection to an esoteric Divinity aided by the intercession of the meek, mild, long-suffering Blessed Virgin.

At a time when churchmen increasingly were relying upon a mystical Mary to counter the rationalist influences of a secular age, obedient Polish female religious who instilled Marian mystical ideals in immigrant youth marched in the church's vanguard to proselytize and defend the faith.[39] But disseminating mystical belief could only counter the rationalist secular threat. Alone it could do little to prevent another problem that confronted the clergy during these years, namely, disobedience *within* the church. Moreover, in some cases, the supposed personal, intuitive link with the Divine that lay at the core of mystical belief itself could become an alternative source of religious legitimacy which could undercut the authority of the clergy. In the 1880s and 1890s, this would create a new and far more subtle problem for the shepherds of the church.

Disobedience to clerical authority issued from several sources during the mass migration years. On the local level, immigrant parishioners reacting against the trend toward greater centralization in ecclesiastical administration often challenged pastoral control over parish finances and management.[40] Frequently, these advocates of lay trusteeism and parishioner democracy were themselves devout yet ambitious members of the rising immigrant middle-class.[41] More serious still, secular Polish nationalists, without disavowing the faith, often objected to clerical domination over immigrant politics. In fact, the Polish National Alliance, the immigrants' most important fraternal benevolent organization, typified this position, to the consternation of the immigrant clergy.[42] Finally, the nuns who worked in the parishes also sometimes collided with pastoral authority over, for example, congregation jurisdictional issues.[43] Not so easily dismissed as outlaws, such assorted internal critics of ecclesiastical policy and practice confounded the church.

Yet immigrant churchmen, however confounded, repeatedly rose to counter disobedience within the flock. Against secular organizations like the Polish National Alliance, Polish priests formed their own organizations, like the Polish Roman Catholic Union, a large religious fraternal which competed for immigrant working-class loyalties in the late nineteenth century.[44] More routinely, they relied upon the sacerdotal traditions of Roman Catholicism to bolster their priestly authority and at once undercut the religious legitimacy of opponents who, as laymen, could not consecrate the Eucharist in the holy sacrifice of the mass. It therefore represented a severe turn of events when disobedient laymen joined with dissident clerics or when renegade priests themselves challenged pastoral or episcopal authority—viz., Rev. Anthony Kozłowski, Rev. Stefan Kamiński, Rev. Dominik Kolasiński, Rev. Francis Kolaszewski [Rademacher], and Rev. Anthony Klawiter.[45] Priestly opposition threatened to sidestep the obstacle of sacerdotalism and create a parallel religious hierarchy, seemingly as legitimate as the pastors it criticized. But the church could still up the ante and did so, disciplining insurgent priests or excommunicating them and thereby nullifying their priestly functions. Discipline and excommunication worked, of course, because all parties in these disputes—pastors and parishioners, bishops and priestly renegades—all operated *within* the same religious system. As historians have recently used the term, that system was "hegemonic" because its symbols and meanings always belonged to Rome, the apex of the hierarchy.[46] But Rome, too, sometimes could be circumvented. In fact, a more dangerous threat to church authority would arise if sacerdotally valid insurgents would intentionally break with the symbols of the church and create an alternative religion which could challenge the authority of the Pope in Rome. In the nineteenth and early twentieth centuries, as Poles on both sides of the Atlantic chose this course of action, in the eyes of the church they opted for heresy and schism.

Two major heresies fractured the unity of Polish Roman Catholicism during the period of the partitions. The first grew up in the 1830s as Polish nationalists came to blows with the Roman Catholic hierarchy over the thorny "Polish question." During that time, Rome's recognition of the Polish partitions inspired nationalist partisans like Poland's great Romantic poet, Adam Mickiewicz, to create a Romantic, radical Polish nationalist tradition, still distinctly Christian but, after the fashion of French liberal Catholic Hugues-Felicité-Robert de Lamennais (1782-1854), decidedly anti-clerical.[47] Called Polish messianism, Mickiewicz's heretical religious nationalism endowed the Polish nation with the mission of a chosen people whose tribulations and sufferings would redeem

Poland and earn its resurrection.[48] The resurrected Poland would herald the moral regeneration of the Universe and thus become the "Christ of Nations."[49]

Polish messianism passed out of vogue between the positivist 1860s and 1880s, but was revived by nationalist publicists late in the century. In an atmosphere of renewed nationalist ferment, it comes as no surprise that Polish messianic writings found a receptive audience among Poles who migrated to the United States during this period. Polish immigrants voraciously read Mickiewicz, Julius Słowacki, and other messianic poets whose works appeared excerpted on fraternal benevolent association calendars and almanacs and filled Polish language libraries. Polish messianism raised the nationalist ardor of working-class immigrants, but parenthetically also offered them a compelling alternative to the ideology of orthodox Roman Catholicism and to the domination of the clergy. Positing a mystical, visionary link between Poles and their God, Polish messianism resembled the Marian mysticism espoused by the Polish sisterhoods. Indeed, Mary held a prominent place in the Polish messianists' devotions.[50] But because Mary so much symbolized long suffering, docility, patience, humility, and above all obedience to the church, the message of Marian mysticism was other-worldly, passive, and escapist—in short, hardly a suitable inspiration for a broader religious or political activism.[51] The Polish messianists' mysticism therefore highlighted Jesus Christ, the Redeemer. Crucified or resurrected, Christ symbolized a religious involvement that was politicized and active. Polish messianism thus added a terrestrial purpose to orthodox Roman Catholic mysticism: Polish national liberation.

Between the 1850s and the 1880s, the church in Poland increasingly had absorbed some of the messianists' concerns—e.g., opposition to the partitions—while some Polish clerics, principally from the Galician lower clergy, began to echo the messianists' calls for social justice.[52] Doctrinally, however, Poland's church remained very conservative and, as noted, developed a pronounced Marian devotionalism—derisively termed "Mariolatry"—which became a dual prop of the first and second estates—the clergy and the aristocracy.[53] Polish churchmen remained thus preoccupied when the Western European church—in such varied countries as France, England, Italy, Germany, and Austria—was subsequently gripped by the diverse and eclectic movement for reform which came to be known as modernism. Peaking around 1900, church modernists challenged ecclesiastical authority as centered in Rome, stressed the importance of revelation over dogma, sympathized with efforts at social re-

form, supported scientific research free from dogmatic constraints, and
sought to have the church come to grips with the undeniable facts of the
modern rational world.[54] Deeply absorbed in their own national religious
affairs, Poles seem to have escaped these modernist influences during this
period.[55] Yet despite the country's reputed theological retardation, it
seems likely that some Polish clerics had to have been familiar with modernist ideas, given Poland's intellectual proximity to France and its geographical proximity to Germany.[56] Immigrant priests might have been
similarly exposed because of the English influences on Christianity in
America.[57] Meanwhile, social and economic change in Poland became an
independent source for modernist-sounding thought.

Though difficult to characterize, the period's second major Polish
heresy, the Mariavite movement, blended together conservative Marian
devotional themes with reformist tendencies which in the West might
have been termed modernist. At the outset, the religious revival that
coalesced into the Mariavite movement differed little from other out-
croppings of Marianism in nineteenth-century Poland. In 1888, a pious
young Pole named Feliksa Kozłowska founded a small religious community, not unlike other female religious congregations which were spawned
in post-insurrectionary Poland. By 1893, however, Kozłowska claimed to
have had a series of relevations in which God showed her "the universal
corruption of the world . . . [and] the laxity of morals among the clergy
and the sins committed by priests." The doomed world's last chance for
rescue was "in the Veneration of the Most Holy Sacrament and in Mary's
help." To spread this doctrine God reportedly directed Kozłowska to help
organize a congregation of priests aptly called the "Mariavites" after
their Marian devotionalism. God allegedly made Kozłowska the "mis-
tress and mother" of the Mariavite congregation. In good Marian
fashion—viz., the Annunciation (Luke 1:26–38)—she replied, "Behold!
the handmaid of the Lord; be it unto me according to thy word."[58]

The sect that Feliksa Kozłowska and Rev. Jan Maria Michał Kowalski,
her later collaborator, founded was piously Marian, but it also explored
themes that paralleled some of the modernists' concerns. Responding to
contemporary social issues, the Mariavites challenged the authority of
Rome, questioned the doctrine of papal infallibility, and criticized the
clergy. They advocated a kind of religious democracy, replaced Latin
with Polish in the liturgy, and—as they watched Poland changing around
them—promoted new social service functions for a changing church that
would cushion ordinary people from the shocks of Poland's social and economic transformation, e.g., mutual aid and savings associations,

schools, commercial and agricultural cooperatives.[59] Finally, they espoused a personal revelatory mysticism that shook dogmatic certitude. Whereas some modernists had reasoned that revelation was a more immediate, direct religious experience than dogma or other intellectual formulations of the faith, the Mariavites practiced what they preached and lived the living faith.[60] Because of the Mariavites' disobedience to episcopal authority and their mystical tendencies (but probably also because of their alleged sexual aberrations) Kozłowska and the Mariavite priests were excommunicated in 1906. Thereupon they opted for schism. At their peak, around 1911, the Mariavites gathered in as many as two hundred thousand adherents. If they were not clearly "modernist" in orientation, in some ways they certainly could claim to be "modern." More a popular movement than an intellectual heresy as was Western European modernism, the socially active Mariavites showed particular strength in industrial centers of Poland like the coal-mining region of Silesia and the textiles city of Łódź, the "Polish Manchester."[61]

No record of direct Mariavite involvement in the United States has surfaced; perhaps there was none. Yet a third heresy did arise among the Polish immigrants in the United States which shared a number of elements in common with the Mariavites, the modernists, and the Polish messianists. That heresy, the Polish National Catholic movement, emerged during the 1890s and early 1900s in the heavily Polish anthracite region of eastern Pennsylvania to produce the only major schism ever to split the Roman Catholic church in the United States.

The roots of schism in eastern Pennsylvania ran as deeply as the region's coal veins. Throughout the 1880s and 1890s, Polish demands for control of parish property and Polish-speaking priests had sparked intermittent local conflicts with Roman Catholic pastors and bishops throughout America, but because so many conservative urban bishops favored an accommodation with the immigrant Catholics, most of these early fights did not result in the formation of schismatic churches, but in the founding of new Roman Catholic parishes led by the dissidents.[62] In 1896, however, Poles in Scranton, Pennsylvania, who sought parishioner representation in the management of parish affairs were sharply rebuked by their pastor and reprimanded by the local Irish bishop. With tensions mounting, dissidents asked Rev. Francis Hodur, pastor of a nearby Polish parish, for aid, and he advised them to build their own church. When the bishop refused to consecrate the new church unless they turned over the deed to the property, the insurgent Poles invited Hodur to defy episcopal authority and establish a dissenting parish.[63] Therewith Scranton's working-class Polish immigrants passed the point of no return. In 1904, the conflict finally climaxed when what had formerly been an "independent" or "people's" church consolidated the evergrowing number of breakaway parishes in the region into the Polish National Catholic church, with Hodur himself eventually serving as bishop.[64]

If Polish National Catholicism articulated working-class immigrant concerns, its success or failure ultimately would depend upon other more practical matters. The Polish National Catholics' insurgency was able to take root and spread because it circumvented the single greatest obstacle that often had thwarted Polish religious dissent, the Poles' religious tradition of sacerdotalism. The defection of legally ordained Polish Roman Catholic priests to the Polish National Catholic church and, more importantly, the legal consecration of Hodur as an Old Cathlic bishop (which thus made him a part of the apostollic succession and empowered him to ordain new priests) now enabled excommunicated schismatics to acquire sacramental mediators who were religiously as valid as Roman Catholic clerics. The structure of the schismatic Polish National Catholic church thus fortuitously accommodated Polish religious tradition and produced a system of authority that conformed to the Poles' religious expectations. As for the underlying religious ideology that could legitimize the antecedent act of schism, Bishop Hodur sought a doctrine which would connect schismatic clerics directly to God, sidestep their episcopal or papal superiors, and command wide popular appeal. In fact, a suitable ideology was not hard to find, for only one such tradition of extra-institutional religious dissent had made a serious mark on nineteenth-century Poland and Polish America—Polish Messianism. As a young seminarian in Cracow, Hodur had read all of Adam Mickiewicz's mystical poetry. With the founding of the schismatic church, he now built an institutional home for the heresy of Polish messianism.[65]

Three major messianic themes formed the centerpiece of Polish National Catholic doctrine. The first theme was a pointed anticlericalism. "The Roman bishops," Hodur wrote in 1928, "greedy for power and domination over the whole world, withdrew from the people and ceased working the way the Apostles worked." In the Polish National Catholic church, Hodur believed, "Our measure of religion is our personal relationship to Jesus Christ, to the Holy Teacher." "The duty of every priest of the national church" is not self-aggrandisement, but "to aspire to a surplus of justice" for the people.[66] The Polish National Catholic priest still retained special authority in the spiritual and moral affairs of the parish and, accordingly, significant influence in its temporal affairs as well. But given the fact that intense struggle between parishioners and their priests had helped spark the schism, that temporal influence was deliberately curtailed. Management and administration of Polish National Catholic parishes passed largely into the hands of laymen, who also had a voice in clergy assignments.[67] Church procedure abolished pew collections and required clerics to perform all sacramental services free of charge "according to Jesus' injunction," unlike their Roman Catholic counterparts. Adult parishioners also were freed from the symbolically submissive act of individual confessions to particular priests, but instead could publicly confess their sins in a group at mass. Finally, the Polish National Catholic church denounced the Roman Catholic dogma of papal infallibility and instead expounded religious law at meetings of the General Synod of the church.[68]

The schismatics' belief that the Roman Catholic clergy oppressed Polish working people revealed a second Polish messianic theme carried over into Polish National Catholic doctrine: progressive social politics. Hodur's political consciousness had been influenced by 1890s Galician populism, a radical agrarian movement which had inherited democratic traditions popularized by Polish Romantic nationalists in the 1830s. During the schismatic ferment in eastern Pennsylvania, the Polish National Catholic church shaped these progressive social concerns around the needs of Polish anthracite miners and incorporated them into church doctrine. Polish National Catholicism sought to become a working-class religion, to provide an active social ministry to Polish laboring people, and "to defend the interests of the oppressed and down-trodden."[69] Church doctrine thus embraced egalitarianism. In it, Christ was "the leader, teacher and friend of the poor, spurned, disinherited . . . masses of the nation." Indeed, the poor formed an integral part of the religion.[70] The Polish National Catholic church's liturgical calendar featured a Feast of the Poor Shepherds, which "signifies, through the visit of the shepherds to the infant Christ, the part played by poor and homeless people . . . in helping to make known God's love to mankind."[71] Not surprisingly, the church also promoted the interests of the downtrodden through temporal activities. For example, unlike the local Roman Catholic parishes, the church sided with Polish working people after the 1897 Lattimer Massacre and during the 1900 and 1902 anthracite strikes.[72]

However central anti-clericalism and social progressivism were in Polish National Catholic ideology, a third theme became the wellspring of legitimacy for the schismatic religion. That theme was messianic Polish nationalism. Like its messianic forbears, the Polish National Catholic movement inverted Roman Catholic symbolism. It shifted symbolic focus away from the crucified Christ or the merciful Mary, with their passive, long-suffering connotations; and it discarded religious devices like pilgrimages, indulgences, relics, and Marian scapular medals which the Roman Catholic church had used to control the faithful.[73] Instead, Polish National Catholics emphasized Christ resurrected and ascendant. By further shifting emphasis to Christ's glorious Second Coming, the apocalyptic Millennium contained in the Book of Revelation, the Polish National Catholic church transformed the text that Roman Catholic theologians had used to promote belief in the Immaculate Conception of Mary into a tract with revolutionary political implications for the Christian person and the Polish people.[74] Drawing on the religious legacy of Roman Catholic mysticism, the Polish National Catholic church envisioned that spiritually reawakened individuals would come "nearer to God" in a personal, direct, unmediated way.[75] But by focusing on Jesus the Messiah, the risen Christ, the Polish National Catholic church, unlike its Roman Catholic counterpart, counseled not passivity, but action; not obedience, but initiative; not denial, but affirmation.

The resurrection allegory and apocalyptic promise contained in Polish National Catholic ideology pointedly applied to Poland, for Polish National Catholicism tried to become the messianic religion of the oppressed Polish nation.[76] Practice throughout the church stressed Polish nationalism. One of Hodur's first acts when he broke completely with Rome in 1900 was to replace Latin with Polish as the language of the mass. In 1904, the church opened a seminary which it named Bartosz Głowacki House, in honor of the Polish peasant hero who fought under Kościuszko at the celebrated Battle of Racławice.[77] In 1914, the Polish National Catholic church synod added a feast to the liturgy, the Feast of the Polish Homeland. Among the Polish national heroes that church holidays honored were the three Polish messianists—Zygmunt Krasinski, Julius Słowacki, and Adam Mickiewicz—and the Polish Romantic nationalist poet, Marja Konopnicka.[78]

Though the Polish National Catholics adopted a religious organization that had a distinctly congregational look, it seems that contact with American Protestantism and exposure to American political institutions exerted little if any influence on this Polish religious and social movement.[79] To the contrary, Polish National Catholicism arose from the circumstances and conditions Polish immigrants faced in industrial America and drew upon intellectual and ideological traditions indigenous to the Polish group. The Polish National Catholics' ties to Polish messianism are palpable. Hodur's theology, however, also evoked some of the concerns of the Roman Catholic modernists—viz., opposition to the doctrine of papal infallibility, commitment to social reform, criticism of the clergy. Moreover, some of the intellectual antecedents of both movements were similar. Both were linked to the French reformer Lamennais, modernism indirectly through liberal Catholicism, Polish National Catholicism directly through the Polish messianists.[80] Also, Hodur had formal ties and the modernists informal connections with the anti-papal Old Catholic church.[81] Still, despite these points of concourse with modernism, Polish National Catholicism in the United States shared more in common with Poland's Mariavite movement. Reflecting late nineteenth-century social change, both movements democratized religious practice, attacked papal authority and Roman Catholic dogma, invoked Polish messianic symbols, promoted social service, and drew their strength in industrial areas.[82] Perhaps it comes as no surprise, then, that the Polish National Catholics and the Mariavites developed some institutional links, however transitory. The Mariavites briefly cooperated with the Polish National Catholics, until a quarrel between Mariavite leader Jan Michał Kowalski and Hodur drove them apart. One Mariavite priest, Szczepan Żebrowski, broke with the sect and emigrated to the United States where he was consecrated as a Polish National Catholic bishop. Finally, it should be recalled, both Hodur and Kowalski themselves were consecrated bishops by Old Catholic bishops in Utrecht.[83]

It is impossible to gauge how quickly—or deeply—adherents to the new church embraced these doctrinal innovations. In terms of sheer numbers, however, the church's partisan stance paid off during the World War period, when Poland was "resurrected." The rising tide of left-wing Polish nationalism boosted church membership in the United States to between sixty thousand and eighty-five thousand members by 1925–26.[84] Even so, the success of Polish National Catholicism fell far short of the leaders' more sanguine expectations, for it never became the official church of Poland nor the majority religion in Polish America. In part this resulted from the church's own institutional limitations. In part, however, it also resulted from popular religious conservatism. Tradition dies hard, and given the nature of Polish peasant religiosity—the centrality of magic, sensualism, and ritual in Polish rural religious practice and the longstanding association between Roman Catholicism and Polish national identity—there are reasons why the Polish National Catholic church might have had only modest appeal despite its attempts to attract working-class communicants.[85]

But Polish National Catholicism also found that it had to reckon with a determined Roman Catholic opposition which likened the heretical Polish nationalist challenge to assorted secular threats it had faced and took decisive steps to outmaneuver it during those turbulent years. Polish Roman Catholic priests branded the nationalist schismatics "pagans," "heathens," "atheists," "revolutionaries," "lawbreakers," and "heretics."[86] Moreover, given the nature of patronage and clientage networks in immigrant settlements, National Catholic dissenters also faced economic and social sanctions because of their religious secession. But Polish National Catholicism threatened the Roman Catholic church, it should be noted, *because* it made a persuasive and compelling ideological argument. The Roman Catholic church therefore also met the schismatics' thrust with an artful ideological parry.

Though Polish National Catholicism attacked the authority of the entire American church hierarchy, it fell to Polish-American priests, who held day-to-day responsibility for Polish immigrant religious affairs, to counter the schismatic insurgency touched off by their immigrant conationals. Many Polish priests themselves had participated in Polish nationalist politics. Shunning heresy but nonetheless attempting to bend Roman Catholic orthodoxy to fit Polish political requirements, they succeeded in fashioning an ideology with such wide appeal in Polish America that it stole the schismatics' rhetorical thunder. Cleverly merging formerly incompatible iconographies, they took the messianic elements of the Polish Romantic nationalist tradition and harnessed them to the Roman Catholic church's hegemonic symbol system, Marianism.[87] The resulting fusion might be called "Marian messianism."

In the history of the church, there was another side to the docile, long-suffering Mary. Mary was a splendidly malleable symbol who elicited submission to the church, but also invoked resistance against its foes. Nowhere was Mary's dual nature more pronounced than in Poland. During the MIddle Ages, Polish knights sang a hymn to the Blessed Virgin Mary before battle, and Mary's miraculous martial role recurred frequently thereafter. Poles defending the monastery at *Jasna Góra* against an invading Swedish Protestant Army in 1655 raised the icon-like image of Our Lady of Częstochowa before the enemy force and, it was claimed, saw the seige miraculously lifted.[88] After that victory, Poland's King John Casimir named the Blessed Virgin Mary as Queen of the Polish Crown. Henceforth, too, the Galician town of Częstochowa became a popular pilgrimage site and patriotic Poles forevermore would associate a feminine Poland with her patroness, the Blessed Mother. Marian martial usages thus continued. At the Polish relief of Vienna in 1683, the battle cry of Jan Sobieski's forces as they charged the Turkish host was Marian, "In the name of Mary, help us, Lord God!"[89] A century later Poles who joined Kościuszko's insurrectionary army to fight for Polish freedom in the 1790s reputedly wore Marian scapular medals, given to them by wives, sisters, and mothers.[90] By the period of the partitions, Mary clearly had become Poland's foremost nationalist emblem.

In all of these instances, perhaps Mary merely functioned as any mother would, protecting her imperilled children. But the Cult of Mary contained elements that went beyond the Blessed Mother's traditional protective, maternal, nurturing role. It contained elements that imputed *redemptive* attributes directly to her. This occurred as early as the Middle Ages when Mary was identified with Jesus through such devices as the doctrine of Mary's compassionate martyrdom and the "cult of sorrows" to which it gave rise. In it, Mary was believed to have felt all the suffering from the tortures that Jesus was to experience.[91] The image of Mary promulgated by the "cult of sorrows" it spawned thus featured many of the same elements attributed to Christ's martyrdom—pierced heart, bloody tears, crown of thorns—and Mary became a redemptive figure in her own right.

The Blessed Virgin Mary's "cooperation with Jesus in redeeming mankind" came to be known as the doctrine of "coredemption." In it, Mary became a coredeemer, wholly dependent upon Christ, but in perfect spiritual union with him. "By her compassion," Roman Catholic theologians granted, "Mary comerited for man all that Christ merited by His Passion."[92] The Polish Resurrectionist Fathers, who dominated immigrant religious affairs in Chicago, embraced the mystery of coredemption in the devotional life of their congregation.[93] Poland's Mariavite sect also celebrated the doctrine of coredemption but carried it to the point of heresy, when the sect's foundress, Feliksa Kozłowska, lost herself in revelatory mysticism, when her followers styled her a second Virgin Mary or Mary reincarnate, and when the Mariavites defied the authority of the Roman pontiff.[94]

Significantly, when Roman Catholic churchmen and their lay partisans plunged into Polish nationalist politics in the late nineteenth century, they too drew upon the doctrine of coredemption and the symbolism of the Cult of Sorrows: a Mary-like Poland compassionately suffered a Christ-like martyrdom. A long address delivered at a Chicago Polish nationalist demonstration in 1895 typified this new ideological genre. Poland, one speaker intoned, is "nailed to a cross"; "its hands and feet tied," it "cannot shed its fetters."

> You, our beloved mother, be glorified the more through your poverty, martyrdom and defamation, for all these will help make a crown [viz., of thorns] for your glorious head.[95]

The Chicago speech once again made it abundantly clear that Marianism could be readily changed from a submissive doctrine into an ideological weapon. Marianism thus became messianic, as Mary shed part of her meekness and acquired active, mystical redemptive powers, similar to Christ's but virtually independent of his. Like the Marianism of the Mariavites, this bordered on heresy. But like the Marianism of the Resurrectionists and the various Polish sisterhoods—that is to say, like orthodox Marianism—it stayed safely on this side of the invisible, indelible line that defined the bounds of acceptable religious belief and practice. Marian messianism, however mystical, did not challenge the authority of the Pope or his bishops, did not undercut the institutional church. To the contrary, Mary the Messiah enabled the church to bridge the gap between piety and modernity. A political redeemer but not a religious one, she allowed the church to extend its ideological influence into the relatively alien sphere of aggressive Polish nationalist politics.

As this turn widened the secular political influence of Polish Roman Catholic churchmen, it also placed them on a collision course with the schismatic Polish National Catholics. With war impending in Europe, in December 1912, Polish immigrant factions patriotically resolved to close ranks in a Committee for National Defense (*Komitet Obrony Narodowej*, abbreviated K.O.N.).[96] While the Polish Roman Catholic clerical leadership pushed to give this body a Roman Catholic cast, Polish National Catholic leaders insisted on an equal role, for not to have done so would have belied the purpose of their schismatic movement.[97] Clearly, K.O.N. could not contain two Polish churches with equal ambitions yet diametrically opposed claims to legitimacy and political programs. When a vote for seating the schismatic Polish National Catholics split evenly, the resolution was moved that representatives of the Roman Catholic Alliance of Polish Priests also be excluded.[98] Incensed, the Roman Catholic clerical faction bolted from the meeting and formed its own organization, the Polish National Council (*Polska Rada Narodowa*).[99] Thus engaged, Polish Roman Catholic prelates and their proclericalist partisans also raised the tempo of ideological warfare against their leftist and schismatic opponents. At their disposal was the entire Marian messianic symbology.

During the next ten years, a messianic Mary became the central ideological symbol of Polish Roman Catholics involved at home and abroad in Polish nationalist politics. A Polish political poster published for a Polish-American convention in Buffalo, New York, in 1914 solidified the image of the 1895 Chicago speech by depicting a seated woman, chained and crowned with thorns, who represented the shackled, martyred, Mary-like Poland.[100] In the Polish Army's training camp at Niagara-on-the-Lake, Canada, at the start of World War One, Polish immigrant troops sang the Polish anthem, *"Boże Coś Polskę"* (God Who Helped Poland), beneath a flag that bore an image of the Blessed Virgin Mary.[101] Donors to the campaign to raise money for the Polish Army in France, a fund drive conducted by the immigrants' proclerical, conservative leadership, received prints of Ladislaus Benda's painting in which the Blessed Virgin of Częstochowa united the three Polish partitions—redeemed them—and blessed Polish-American troops speeding to battle.[102]

In Poland, too, messianic Marian symbols filled Polish Roman Catholics' ideological arsenal. A huge nationalist demonstration in Cracow in 1910, commemorating the five-hundredth anniversary of the victory over the Teutonic Knights at the Battle of Grünwald, featured the mass singing of the medieval hymn to the Blessed Virgin Mary, *"Bogu Rodzica"* (Mother of God).[103] But the best example occurred ten years later when General Joseph Piłsudski, an anticlericalist and moderate socialist, defeated an invading Bolshevik army on the outskirts of Warsaw on the banks of the Vistula River. The battle took place on 15 August 1920, the Roman Catholic Feast of the Assumption of the Blessed Virgin Mary; to counter Bolshevik antireligious propaganda and to neutralize Piłsudski's political gain from the victory, Polish rightists, noting the date, ascribed victory to Mary's miraculous intervention and dubbed the triumph *"Cud Wisły,"* "the miracle on the Vistula."[104] The Pope soon followed suit. By designating May 3 as the Feast of the Queen of Poland, the Pope shrewdly turned the anniversary of Poland's revolutionary Constitution of the Third of May (1791) into a Polish national holiday to honor Mary, Poland's Saviour.[105]

Thereafter, Roman Catholic churchmen—both immigrant and American-born—alternated Marian themes according to circumstances and situation. As the political excitement of the early twenties subsided, Marian messianism easily yielded to the Roman Catholic church's time-honored ideological mainstay, Marian mysticism, which continued to serve a hegemonic function. Here, the highlights of devotional life in one Roman Catholic parish in New York are instructive. In the early 1920s, the Vincentian Fathers, a missionary order devoted to Marian mystical doctrine, assumed control of Brooklyn's Saint Stanislaus Kostka parish. In 1926, the new pastor returned from a visit to Rome with a relic of Saint Theresa of the Infant Jesus, a recently canonized nun, and instituted regular devotions to this Marian figure. With the outbreak of the Depression and amidst the rising tide of Marianism, in autumn of 1930 the parish celebrated the hundredth anniversary of the apparitions of Our Lady of the Miraculous Medal to Catherine Labouré, a Daughter of Charity, while in the same year a Saint Theresa Society was formed there. In 1934, as the Depression deepened, Marian mystical devotions reached a new height when the parish received a gift painting of the popular Saint Theresa from artist Tadeusz Styka.[106] Needless to say, Marianism was not confined to this one parish during the period. Since 1927, New York Poles also encountered Marian radio broadcasts, as Father Justin Figas of Buffalo, New York, began his syndicated "Rosary Hour."[107]

As Marian mysticism helped contain popular ferment in the 1920s and 1930s, Marian messianism once again helped mobilize Polish Roman Catholics during the following decade. In September 1939, over four decades after the female image of a martyred Poland had gained ideological currency in the United States during the Polish nationalist agitation in the 1890s, Poland once again endured an hour of national crisis. As Nazi and Soviet armies overran their homeland, Poles in America rallied anew behind familiar ideological banners—messianic and implicitly Marian. In one newspaper advertisement printed in November 1939, a thorn-crowned, shackled woman, dressed in royal robes bearing the Polish coat-of-arms, sat beside a thorn-framed visionary panorama depicting the devastated Polish countryside.[108] A political cartoon of similar vintage was even more striking. The cartoon showed a blood-stained sword bearing swastika and hammer-and-sickle markings, plunged into a Polish city's smoking ruins. A peasant woman, labelled "Poland," hung from the hilt of the sword: the woman was crucified.[109]

In the nineteenth and early twentieth centuries, Roman Catholic churchmen had tried a variety of approaches to hold on to communicants whose faith they could no longer take for granted. Lacking the support of a devout landed gentry that had sustained it in Europe, the Roman Catholic church still had to seek for new secular allies that would bolster it against the strains of a modern American society locked in the throes of industrial growth and urban change during the period. At the diocesan level, native-born bishops made overtures to industrialists and they in turn reciprocated, recognizing, as William Howard Taft remarked, that the church formed "one of the bulwarks against socialism and anarchy in this country.''[110] At the parochial level, meanwhile, immigrant pastors courted local factory managers and eventually worked out a *modus operandi* with middle-class parishioners who became pillars of their communities and mainstays of the ethnic parishes.[111]

But despite these secular props, in American factory districts religious practice simply could no longer be coerced as it could in manorial Europe. To be sure, religion could still serve a powerful function in working-class lives, but in order to do so that religion necessarily had to change to accommodate the needs of men and women who had entered the urban, industrial world. Meanwhile, changing pastoral and clerical style also tried to conform to the changing sensitivities and identities of working-class parishioners.[112] The changing composition of the clergy also fitted working-class parishes more closely, as peasant, working-class, and lower middle-class sons began to enter the priesthood on both sides of the Atlantic.[113] Yet perhaps most important were the political moves that churchmen undertook to keep the allegiance of working-class immigrants. The malleable Marian symbols which they used fired immigrant hearts, excited their minds, and preserved their souls in the bargain. Marian ideology operated as a mechanism of control. But it also worked as a militant engine. In both roles, it powerfully countered erosive secular ideologies and dangerous heresies wielded by anticlericalists of all political persuasions.

NOTES

Versions of this article were presented at the 1980 meeting of the Organization of American Historians in San Francisco and the History Workshop on Religion and Society, held during July 1983, in London. I wish to thank Ronald Bayor, Stanley Blejwas, Christa Walck, Christopher Clark, Stephan Thernstrom, Mark Stolarik, Victor Greene, Christopher Johnson, Daniel Buczek, and the members of the conference panels for their helpful discussion, suggestions, and comments at various stages in its preparation.

1. Paul Fox, *The Poles in America* (New York, 1922), pp. 107, 109, 110; Sr. M. Liguori, "Parish Records as Source Material for a History of American Poles," *Polish American Studies*, 1 (1944): 15–16, quoted in Theresita Polzin, *The Polish Americans: Whence and Whither* (Pulaski, Wis., 1973), p. 88.

2. See, for example, Leonard Dinnerstein, Roger L. Nichols, and David M. Reimers, *Natives and Strangers: Ethnic Groups and the Building of America* (New York, 1979), p. 168.

3. On popular religion in rural Poland, see William I. Thomas and Florian Znaniecki, *The Polish Peasant in Europe and America*, 2 vols. (New York, 1927), 1: 205–288; Sula Benet, *Songs, Dance, and Customs of Peasant Poland* (New York, 1951); Jan Stanisław Bystrob, *Kultura Ludowa*, 2d. ed. (Warsaw, 1947). Examples of immigrant popular belief that departed from religious orthodoxy are plentiful. See, for example, Mary Adele Dąbrowska, "A History and Survey of the Polish Community in Brooklyn" (M.A. thesis, Fordham University, 1946), pp. 120–121; Arthur Evans Wood, *Hamtramck, Then and*

Now: A Sociological Study of a Polish American Community (New York, 1955), pp. 40–42; Murray Godwin, "Motor City Witchcraft," *North American Review*, 233 (June 1932): 530; Jan L. Perkowski, *Vampires, Dwarves, and Witches Among the Ontario Kashubs*, Canadian Centre for Folk Culture Studies, Paper No. 1 (Ottawa, 1980). For an Italian immigrant comparison, cf. Rulolph J. Vecoli, "Cult and Occult in Italian-American Culture: The Persistence of a Religious Heritage," in *Immigrants and Religion in Urban America*, eds. Randall M. Miller and Thomas D. Marzik (Philadelphia, 1977), pp. 25–47.

4. See Richard M. Linkh, *American Catholicism and European Immigrants (1900–1924)* (Staten Island, N.Y., 1975), pp. 35–48; and for the larger European context, Lillian Parker Wallace, *Leo XIII and the Rise of Socialism* (n.p., 1966). On radicalism *within* the American church, cf. Mel Piehl, *Breaking Bread: The Catholic Worker and the Origin of Catholic Radicalism in America* (Philadelphia, 1982).

5. See Władysław Piwowarski, *Religijność Wiejska w Warunkach Urbanizacji: Studium Socjologiczne* (Warsaw, 1971), 31ff.; idem, "La Pratique Religieuse dan les Villes Polonaises au Cours des Vingt Dernieres Annees," Social Compass: International Review of Socio-Religious Studies, 15 (1968): 277–284; idem, "L'influence de l'industrialisation sur la religiosité populaire en Pologne," *Changement Sociale et Religion, Conference Internationale de Sociologie Religieuse, Actes de la 13e Conference, Lloret de Mar, Espagne, 31 Aout-4 Septembre 1975* (Lille, France, n.d.), pp. 425–431.

6. This estimate was probably too high, as Kruszka presented the threat of high and increasing Polish "leakage" from the faith as an argument for the appointment of a Polish bishop in America. See Fox, *Poles in America*, p. 112. I have been unable to locate Fox's source for Kruszka's estimate; none is given in the text.

7. Fox, *Poles in America*, pp. 114–116. Cf. Barbara Leś, *Kościół w Procesie Asymilacji Polonii Amerikańskiej: Przemiany Funkcji Polonijnych Instytucji i Organizacji Religijnych w Środowisku Polonii Chicagoski*, Biblioteka Polonijna, no. 9 (Wrocław, 1981), pp. 243–266.

8. Victor Greene, "Poles," in *Harvard Encyclopedia of American Ethnic Groups*, ed. Stephan Thernstrom (Cambridge, Mass., 1980), p. 795. Also see Wiktor Tylewski, "Materiały do Dziejów Polskiego Socjalizmu w Stanach Zjednoczonych," *Problemy Polonii Zagraniczwej*, 2 (1961): 210–216.

9. Robert D. Cross, *The Emergence of Liberal Catholicism in America* (Cambridge, Mass., 1967), pp. 23, 38, 47, 109–110, 113. For a representative example of Church liberalism, see Bishop J.L. Spalding, *Socialism and Labor, and other arguments social, political, and patriotic* (Chicago, 1902).

10. See Thomas T. McAvoy, *The Great Crisis in American Catholic History, 1895–1900* (Chicago, 1957).

11. See Joseph E. Ciesluk, *National Parishes in the United States* (Washington, D.C., 1947).

12. Linkh, *American Catholicism and European Immigrants*, p. 108. These figures were obtained by counting the parishes identified in the 1912 *Directory*. See *The Official Catholic Directory and Clergy List . . . 1912* (New York, 1912), p. 16–763.

13. Wacław Kruszka, *Historya Polska w Ameryce*, 13 vols. (Milwaukee, 1905–1908), 1: 90–139, 2: 6–10. The *Directory*, for example, fails to identify the largest Polish parish in the United States, Chicago's Saint Stanislaus Kostka, as Polish. See *Official Catholic Directory . . . 1912*, p. 60.

14. On the fight for Polish representation in the church hierarchy, see Victor Greene, *For God and Country: The Rise of Polish and Lithuanian Ethnic Consciousness in America, 1860–1910* (Madison Wis., 1975); Anthony J. Kuzniewski, *Faith and Fatherland: The Polish Church War in Wisconsin, 1896–1918*, Notre Dame Studies in American Catholicism, no. 3 (Notre Dame, Ind., 1980); Wacław Kruszka, *Siedm Siedmioleci czyli*

Pół Wieku Życia: Pamiętniki i Przyczynek do Historji Polskiej w Ameryce, 2 vols. (Milwaukee, 1924), 1: 389–397. On the broader issue of immigrant representation in the hierarchy, also cf. Colman J. Barry, O.S.B., *The Catholic Church and the German Americans* (Milwaukee, 1953); John Meng, "Cahenslyism: The First Stage, 1883–1891," *Catholic Historical Review*, 31 (January 1946): 389–413; idem "Cahenslyism: The Second Chapter, 1891–1910," *Catholic Historical Review*, 32 (October 1946): 302–340.

15. Joseph John Parot, *Polish Catholics in Chicago, 1850–1920* (DeKalb, Ill., 1981), pp. 49–51, 227–228.

16. There is still no satisfactory study of Buffalo Polonia or of Rev. Jan Pitass, but one may consult M. Donata Slominska, "Rev. John Pitass, Pioneer Priest of Buffalo," *Polish American Studies*, 17 (1960): 28–41. For treatments of Rev. Lucyan Bójnowski, see Daniel S. Buczek, *Immigrant Pastor: The Life of Right Reverend Monsignor Lucyan Bójnowski of New Britain, Connecticut* (Waterbury, Conn., 1974); Stanislaus A. Blejwas, "A Polish Community in Transition: The Origins of Holy Cross Parish, New Britain, Connecticut," *Polish American Studies*, 34 (Spring, 1977): 26–69.

17. See Joseph Swastek, "The Formative Years of the Polish Seminary in the United States," *Sacrum Poloniae Millennium*, 13 vols. (Rome, 1959), 6: 39–150; Lawrence D. Orton, *Polish Detroit and the Kolasiński Affair* (Detroit, Mich., 1981), p. 57.

18. Fragments describing early Polish immigrant religious practices can be found in parish commemorative journals, masters theses, folklore and oral history interviews, and fileopietistic accounts. See, for example, *St. Stanislaus Kostka, Brooklyn/Greenpoint-New York, 1896–1971* (South Hackensack, N.J., 1972), pp. 42–44; Dąbrowska, "Polish Community in Brooklyn"; Polish and Polish American Folklore Collections, 1953 (42), 1959 (12), 1964 (99), 1967 (102), Wayne State University Folklore Archive, Detroit, Michigan; Joseph A. Wytrwal, *Behold! The Polish-Americans* (Detroit, 1977), pp. 288–301. Also cf. E.P. Thompson, "Patrician Society, Plebian Culture," *Journal of Social History*, 7 (Summer 1974): 382–405; James Obelkevich, *Religion and Rural Society: South Lindsey, 1825–1875* (Oxford, 1976).

19. Buczek, *Immigrant Pastor*, pp. 39, 55–56, 75, 91; Blejwas, "Polish Community in Transition," p. 34. See *Przewodnik Katolicki* (New Britain, Conn.), 14 January, 15 April 1921, for examples of Bójnowski's approach.

20. Rev. Leon Wysiecki to Bishop Charles E. McDonnell, 30 April 1897, Chancery Archives, Roman Catholic Diocese of Brooklyn, N.Y.; Victor R. Greene, *The Slavic Community on Strike: Immigrant Labor in Pennsylvania Anthracite* (Notre Dame, Ind., 1968), p. 248.

21. Rev. Leon Wysiecki to Bishop Charles E. McDonnell, 1 February 1897, Chancery Archives, Roman Catholic Diocese of Brooklyn, Brooklyn, N.Y.

22. John Tracy Ellis, *American Catholicism*, 2d. ed. rev. (Chicago, 1969), p. 104. Also see Peter Guilday, *A History of the Councils of Baltimore* (New York, 1932), pp. 221–249; Rev. James A. Burns, *The Growth and Development of the Catholic School System in the United States* (New York, 1912).

23. Józef Miąso, *The History of the Education of Polish Immigrants in the United States*, trans. Ludwik Krzyżanowski, Library of Polish Studies, vol. 6 (New York, 1977), pp. 47, 103, 117.

24. Ibid., p. 230.

25. Sr. M. DeChantal, *Out of Nazareth: A Centenary of the Holy Family of Nazareth in the Service of the Church* (New York, 1974), p. ix; Sr. Mary Tullia Doman, *Mother Mary Angela Truszkowska, Foundress of the Felician Sisters* (Livonia, Mich., 1954), p. 14; Marina Warner, *Alone of All Her Sex: The Myth and the Cult of the Virgin Mary* (New York, 1976), p. 185; Thaddeus C. Radzialowski, "Reflections on the History of the Felicians in America," *Polish American Studies*, 32 (Spring 1975): 19–28. On religious revi-

val and renewal in the United States during the same period, see Jay P. Dolan, *Catholic Revivalism: The American Experience, 1830–1900* (Notre Dame, Ind., 1978).

26. Doman, *Mother Mary Angela Truszkowska*, pp. 16–17.

27. Kuzniewski, "The Catholic Church in the Life of the Polish Americans," p. 411. Also see Sr. Mary Tullia, C.S.S.F., "Polish American Sisterhoods and their Contribution to the Catholic Church in the United States," *Sacrum Poloniae Millennium* 13 vols. (Rome, 1959), 6: 371–612.

28. *Saint Stanislaus Kostka Parish Golden Jubilee, 1896–1946* (Brooklyn, n.d.), pp. 54, 81; *St. Stanislaus Kostka . . . 1896–1971*, pp. 119–120.

29. See Warner, *Alone of All Her Sex*, pp. 147, 214, 218, 247, 301, 306–308, 328, 390–391.

30. See Marian Helm-Pirgo, *Virgin Mary Queen of Poland (Historical Essay)* (New York, 1966); Maria Winowska, "Le Culte Marial en Pologne," in *Maria: Études sur la Sainte Vierge*, ed. Hubert du Manoir, 7 vols. (Paris, 1956), 4: 683–710.

31. On the history of the Resurrectionists in America, see Rev. John Iwicki, *The First One Hundred Years: A Study of the Congregation of the Resurrection in the United States, 1866–1966* (Rome, 1966).

32. Doman, *Mother Mary Angela Truszkowska*, pp. 9, 13; *Magnificat: A Centennial Record of the Congregation of the Sisters of Saint Felix (The Felician Sisters), 1855 Nov. - 1955* (n.p., n.d.), pp. 16, 47–49.

33. DeChantal, *Out of Nazareth*, pp. 26, 39; Rev. Francis A. Cegielka, "*Nazareth*" *Spirituality*, trans. Sr. M. Theophame [sic] and Mother M. Laurence (Milwaukee, Wis., 1966), p. 65.

34. DeChantal, *Out of Nazareth*, pp. 14, 22–23, 41; Rev. Francis A. Cegielka, *Reparatory Mysticism of "Nazareth"*, trans. A Sister of the Holy Family of Nazareth (Philadelphia, 1951), pp. 100–102.

35. Cegielka, *Reparatory Mysticism*, pp. xvi, 8, 12, 13, 19; DeChantal, *Out of Nazareth*, p. 52.

36. Louis E. Van Norman, *Poland: The Knight Among Nations* (New York, 1907), pp. 243–244; Jan Słomka, *From Serfdom to Self-Government: Memoirs of a Polish Village Mayor, 1842–1927*, trans. William John Rose, shortened Engl. ed. (London, 1941), pp. 5, 167–168.

37. Thomas and Znaniecki, *Polish Peasant*, 1: 286–287; Van Norman, *Poland*, pp. 245–246.

38. Thomas and Znaniecki, *Polish Peasant*, 1: 286–287.

39. On 8 December 1854, Pope Pius IX proclaimed the Immaculate Conception of the Blessed Virgin Mary—her freedom from original sin—and four years later the Virgin reportedly appeared to a local shepherdess at Lourdes. These events set the stage for what was to follow. In an 1883 encyclical, Pope Leo XIII urged daily recitation of the rosary and the Litany of the Blessed Virgin in all churches during the month of October and, in particular, stressed the efficacy of the former in combatting modern evils. Two years later, the Pope fixed March as the month to honor St. Joseph, the foster father of Christ. The Pope commended Mary's husband as "a model of all laboring classes and of the poor," presumably for his role as the good, humble, and faithful worker. In 1919, the crescendo of Marian mysticism culminated in the visions at Fatima, Portugal. See Warner, *Alone of All Her Sex*, pp. 52, 236, 259; DeChantal, *Out of Nazareth*, pp. 30, 81, 153.

40. On the early history of trusteeism, see Msgr. Peter Keenan Guilday, *Trusteeism (1814–1821* (New York, 1928). Also see David Gerber, "Trusteeism and the Survival of European Communal Traditions?—The Case for a New Perspective: Notes Based on the Experience of Buffalo's St. Louis Church, 1829–1856," *American Catholic Studies Newsletter*, 6 (Spring 1980); Patrick Carey, "Two Episcopal Views of Lay-Clerical Conflicts: 1785–1860," *Records of the American Catholic Historical Society*, 87 (March-

December, 1976): 85–98; idem, "The Laity's Understanding of the Trustee System, 1785–1855," *Catholic Historical Review*, 64 (July 1978): 357–376; idem, *A National Church: Catholic Search for Identity, 1820–1829*, Center for the Study of American Catholicism, Working Paper Series, no. 3 (Fall 1977); idem, "Trusteeism: American Catholic Search for Identity, 1785–1860," *American Catholic Studies Newsletter*, 3 (Fall 1977).

41. See John J. Bukowczyk, "The Immigrant 'Community' Re-examined: Political and Economic Tensions in a Brooklyn Polish Settlement, 1888–1894," *Polish American Studies*, 37 (Autumn 1980): 5–16.

42. See Stanisław Osada, *Historya Związku Narodowego Polskiego i Rozwój Ruchu Narodowego Polskiego w Ameryce Północnej* (Chicago, 1905); Victor Greene, *For God and Country*; Joseph A. Wytrwal, *America's Polish Heritage: A Social History of the Poles in America* (Detroit, 1961), ch. 9.

43. John J. Bukowczyk, "Steeples and Smokestacks: Class, Religion, and Ideology in the Polish Immigrant Settlements in Greenpoint and Williamsburg, Brooklyn, 1880–1929" (Ph.D. diss., Harvard University, 1980), pp.205–206.

44. For a history of the P.R.C.U., see Mieczysław Haiman, *Zjednoczenie Polskie Rzymsko-Katolickie w Ameryce, 1873–1948* (Chicago, 1948).

45. See John J. Bukowczyk, "Factionalism and the Composition of the Polish Immigrant Clergy," p. 41; Orton, *Polish Detroit*; Greene, *For God and Country*, pp. 102, 111.

46. See Alan Dawley, "E.P. Thompson and the Peculiarities of the Americans," *Radical History Review*, 19 (Winter 1978–79): 43.

47. DeChantal, *Out of Nazareth*, pp. 6, 9; Peter Brock, "The Socialists of the Polish 'Great Emigration,'" in *Essays in Labour History in Memory of G.D.H. Cole 25 September 1889–14 January 1959*, eds. Asa Briggs and John Saville (New York and London, 1960), p. 148.

48. Nikolai Onufrievich Losskii, *Three Chapters from the History of Polish Messianism*, International Philosophical Library Periodical Publication, vol. 2, no. 9 (Prague, 1936), pp. 20–21.

49. Monica Gardner, "The Great Emigration and Polish Romanticism," in *The Cambridge History of Poland*, eds. William F. Reddaway et. al., 2 vols. (New York and London, 1941), 2: 326; Brock, "Socialists," p. 157.

50. Jerzy Peterkiewicz, *The Third Adam* (London, 1975), pp. 64–65.

51. Cf. Guenter Lewy, *Religion and Revolution* (New York, 1974), pp. 253–254.

52. Piotr S. Wandycz, *The Lands of Partitioned Poland, 1795–1918* (Seattle, Wash., 1974), pp. 136, 196, 226, 234.

53. See Winowska, "Le Culte Marial en Pologne," passim.

54. On modernism in the church, see J.J. Heaney, "Modernism," *New Catholic Encyclopedia*, 17 vols. (New York, 1967), 9: 991–995; Roger Aubert, *The Church in a Secularised Society*, trans. Janet Sondheimer (New York, 1978), pp. 186–203; Alec R. Vidler, *The Modernist Movement in the Roman Church: Its Origins & Outcome* (Cambridge, 1934); Bernard M.G. Reardon, ed., *Roman Catholic Modernism* (Stanford, Calif., 1970), pp. 9–67.

55. Vidler, *The Modernist Movement in the Roman Church*, p. 213.

56. Wilfried Daim, *The Vatican and Eastern Europe*, trans. Alexander Gode (New York, 1970), p. 81.

57. Of course, George Tyrrell, Irish by birth and English by upbringing, was a chief exponent of religious modernism within the church. See Vidler, *The Modernist Movement in the Roman Church*, pp. 143–181. On other English modernists, cf. Alec R. Vidler, *A Variety of Catholic Modernists* (Cambridge, 1970), pp. 109–133.

58. Peterkiewicz, *The Third Adam*, pp. 10ff. On the development of the Mariavite sect, also see Émile Appolis, "Une Église des Derniers Temps: L'Église Mariavite," *Archives*

de Sociologie des Religion, 10 (1965): 51–67; B. Stasiewski, "Mariavites," *New Catholic Encyclopedia*, 9: 217–218.

59. Peterkiewicz, *The Third Adam*, pp. 36–37, 61, 119; Appolis, "Une Énglise des Derniers Temps," p. 53.

60. Peterkiewicz, *The Third Adam*, pp. 12–13. Cf. Aubert, *The Church in a Secularised Society*, p. 193; Michele Ranchetti, *The Catholic Modernists: A Study of the Religious Reform Movement, 1864–1907*, trans. Isabel Quigly (London, 1969), pp. 157–158; Vidler, *The Modernist Movement in the Roman Church*, p. 142.

61. Stasiewski, "Mariavites," p. 217–218; Peterkiewicz, *The Third Adam*, pp. 35, 119.

62. In New York City, for example, cf. Theodore F. Abel, "The Poles in New York: A Study of the Polish Communities in Greater New York" (M.A. thesis, Columbia University, 1924), p. 19.

63. Theodore Andrews, *The Polish National Catholic Church in America and Poland* (London, 1953), pp. 17–19, 26–29; Rev. Stephen Wlodarski, *The Origin and Growth of the Polish National Catholic Church* (Scranton, Pa., 1974), pp. 21–23, 25; Greene, *For God and Country*, p. 113.

64. Andrews, *Polish National Catholic Church*, pp. 19–20, 31; Wlodarski, *Origin and Growth*, p. 181; Greene, *For God and Country*, pp. 98, 113; Paul Fox, *The Polish National Catholic Church* (Scranton, Pa., 1961), p. 28.

65. Wlodarski, *Origin and Growth*, p. 39.

66. Francis Hodur, "Doctrines of Faith of the National Church," (lecture given at the Warsaw Synod, 1928), typewritten translation, ms. pp. 3–4.

67. Fox, *Polish National Catholic Church*, pp. 24, 117; Andrews, *Polish National Catholic Church*, pp. 39, 69–70.

68. Wlodarski, *Origin and Growth*, pp. 109, 177, 188; Fox, *Polish National Catholic Church*, p. 82; Andrews, *Polish National Catholic Church*, pp. 42, 48.

69. Wlodarski, *Origin and Growth*, pp. 40–41; 50.

70. Franciszek Hodur, *Our Faith*, trans. Theodore L. Zawistowski and Joseph C. Zawistowski, mimeographed (n.p., 1966), [p. 13].

71. Andrews, *Polish National Catholic Church*, p. 60.

72. Greene, *Slavic Community on Strike*, pp. 141, 155, 183; Buczek, *Immigrant Pastor*, p. 154. On Hodur's socialist connections, see Joseph W. Wieczerzak, "Bishop Francis Hodur and the Socialists: Associations and Disassociations," *Polish American Studies*, 40 (Autumn, 1983): 5–35.

73. Wlodarski, *Origin and Growth*, pp. 187–188; Fox, *Polish National Catholic Church*, p. 49.

74. Cf. Lewy, *Religion and Revolution*, pp. 39–41; Rev. 12:1.

75. Hodur, *Our Faith*, [pp. 7–9].

76. Fox, *Polish National Catholic Church*, p. 90; Hodur, *Our Faith*", [p. 13].

77. Wlodarski, *Origin and Growth*, pp. 71–72, 90. In the Battle of Racławice in 1794, a small Polish force defeated an invading Russian army. The victory marked the highpoint of Polish resistance to the Second Partition.

78. Wlodarski, *Origin and Growth*, p. 103; Andrews, *Polish National Catholic Church*, pp. 60, 74.

79. See Timothy L. Smith, "Lay Initiative in the Religious Life of American Immigrants, 1880–1950," in *Anonymous Americans*, ed. Tamara Hareven (Englewood Cliffs, N.J., 1971), pp. 214–249.

80. Vidler, *The Modernist Movement in the Roman Church*, pp. 22–23. Also see Oskar Schroeder, *Aufbruch und Misverständnis: Zur Geschichte der Reformkatolischen Bewegung* (Vienna, 1969), pp. 13–46.

81. Vidler, *The Modernist Movement in the Roman Church*, pp. 235–236.

82. On the messianism of the Mariavites, see Appolis, "Une Église des Derniers Temps," p. 58.

83. Peterkiewicz, *The Third Adam*, pp. 39, 44–45, 164n; Appolis, "Une Église des Derniers Temps," pp. 53, 59; Greene, *For God and Country*, p. 113.

84. Wlodarski, *Origin and Growth*, p. 117; Fox, *Polish National Catholic Church*, pp. 62–63; Hieronim Kubiak, *Polski Narodowy Kościół Katolicki w Stanach Zjednoczonych Ameryki w Latach 1897–1965; Jego Społeczne Uwarunkowania i Społeczne Funkcje* (Kraków, 1970), p. 134.

85. Cf. the interesting discussion of religious decline, persistence, and change under more recent conditions of urbanization in Władysław Piwowarski, *Religijność Wiejska w Warunkach Urbanizacji*, passim.

86. *Nowy Świat* (New York), 21 September 1922, 19 October 1922.

87. See above, pp. 10, 35.

88. Helen Laura Bilda, "The Influence of Częstochowa on Polish Nationalism" (M.A. thesis, St. John's University, 1948), pp. 17–18, 20, 22–23, 25–26, 123–124; Walter J. Slowiak, "A Comparative Study of the Social Organization of the Family in Poland and the Polish Immigrant Family in Chicago" (M.A. thesis, Loyola University, 1950), p. 63; Helm-Pirgo, *Virgin Mary Queen of Poland*, p. 27; Stanley Bruno Stefan, "The Preparation of the American Poles for Polish Independence, 1880–1918" (M.A. thesis, University of Detroit, 1939), pp. 100–101; Dąbrowska, "Polish Community in Brooklyn," p. 129.

89. Winowska, "Le Culte Marial en Pologne," p. 696.

90. Bilda, "Influence of Częstochowa," p. 58; *Dziennik Chicagoski* (Chicago), 4 April 1894, Reel 56, IIIB3a, IIH, IG, Chicago Foreign Language Press Survey.

91. Warner, *Alone of All Her Sex*, p. 218.

92. See M.J. Horak, "Coredemption," *New Catholic Encyclopedia*, 4: 323–324.

93. Winowska, "Le Culte Marial en Pologne," p. 704.

94. Appolis, "Une Église des Derniers Temps," pp. 57, 59.

95. *Dziennik Chicagoski*, 2 December 1895, Reel 56, IIIB3a, Chicago Foreign Language Press Survey.

96. Stefan, "Preparation," pp. 58, 100; Buczek, *Immigrant Pastor*, p. 48; Frank Renkiewicz, *The Poles in America, 1608–1972: A Chronology and Fact Book* (Dobbs Ferry, N.Y., 1973), p. 16.

97. William Galush, "American Poles and the New Poland: An Example of Change in Ethnic Orientation," *Ethnicity*, 1 (October 1974): 211.

98. Ibid.; Stefan, "Preparation," pp. 63–64.

99. Stanley R. Pliska, "Polish Independence and the Polish Americans" (Ed.D. diss., Columbia University, 1955), p. 82; Galush, "American Poles," pp. 211–212; Stefan, "Preparation," p. 63; Buczek, *Immigrant Pastor*, p. 48; idem, "Polish-Americans and the Roman Catholic Church," *Polish Review*, 21 (1976): 55.

100. Arthur L. Waldo, *Sokolstwo, Przednia Straż Narodu: Dzieje Idei i Organizacji w Ameryce*, 4 vols. (Pittsburgh, 1953, 1956, 1972, 1974), 4: 184.

101. Stefan, "Preparation," pp. 138–139. The flag that flew over the troops, which were trained by the Polish Falcons, a paramilitary nationalist fraternal, might have been a Falcon Banner. The standard of the Łwów Falcon Nest, for example, depicted the Queen of the Polish Crown, Our Lady of Częstochowa. See Waldo, *Sokolstwo*, 1: 187.

102. Pliska, "Polish Independence," p. 248.

103. Stefan, "Preparation," pp. 100–101.

104. Piotr S. Wandycz, *Soviet-Polish Relations, 1917–1921* (Cambridge, Mass., 1969), p. 241.

105. Bilda, "Influence of Częstochowa," pp. 58, 131.

106. *Saint Stanislaus Kostka, 1896–1971*, p. 42–43, 84.

107. Buczek, *Immigrant Pastor*, p. 111; Justyn [M. Figas], *Mowy Radiowe, 1931–1934–1944–1946*, 8 vols. (Milwaukee, Wis., 1934–1947).

108. *Czas* (Brooklyn), 24 November 1939.

109. Waldo, *Sokolstwo*, 1: 242. I would like to extend warmest thanks to Arthur Waldo for his long and thorough reply to my query about dating the illustration.

110. Cross, *Emergence of Liberal Catholicism*, pp. 34–35.

111. This is discussed at length in Bukowczyk, "Steeples and Smokestacks," pp. 239–256, 270–277.

112. Consideration of these changes is beyond the scope of this article, but the reader may wish to consult Daniel S. Buczek, "Three Generations of the Polish Immigrant Church: Changing Styles of Pastoral Leadership," in *Pastor of the Poles: Polish American Essays*, eds. S. Blejwas and M. Biskupski, Polish Studies Program Monographs, no. 1 (New Britain, Conn., 1982), pp. 20–36.

113. Bukowczyk, "Factionalism and the Composition of the Polish Immigrant Clergy," pp. 45–46; Edward Ciupak, *Kult Religijny i Jego Społeczne Podłoże: Studia nad Katolicyzmem Polskim* (Warsaw, 1965), p. 401.

The Transforming Power of the Machine:
Popular Religion, Ideology, and Secularization among Polish Immigrant Workers in the United States, 1880–1940

John J. Bukowczyk
Wayne State University

In the last fifteen years or so, a generation of European social historians, armed with an integrated understanding of society, class, culture, and politics, has demystified the history of religion. In particular, they have probed the complicated relationship between institutional and popular belief in the time when Roman Catholicism formed the ideological mainstay of landed power in the precapitalist European countryside. Even apart from the Reformation, they have shown that orthodox religion faced a raft of powerful popular challenges. Superstition, magic, and other "pagan"—or folk— carryovers still survived. Even when accepted, orthodox religion often underwent subversive transmutation at the hands of supposedly docile and devout underclasses who reinvested its practices with new meanings, reappropriated its symbols for their own ends, and sometimes thereby used it as a resource against the predations of society's rulers. In the process, they transformed the Church's own religion from a theology of subjugation into an arena for popular struggle, resistance, expression, and assertion.[1]

The mass migration that brought rural Europeans to urban, industrial America in the late nineteenth century did not eliminate religion as a theater of conflict. Yet while historians of nineteenth-century Europe have examined the tensions between orthodoxy and popular religion that often punctuated rural Europe's passage to commercial and industrial capitalism,[2] American social historians have largely ignored this conflict, especially insofar as it involved working-class immigrants who experienced that passage while coming to America.[3] This may not be surprising, given that a penchant for institutional history and a predilection for functionalist sociological models generally have colored scholarly treatments of immigrant religion in America. But the immigrants' extrainstitutional popular religious beliefs found no ready place in immigration historiography also because, like most histories, the history of immigrant religion has focused not on the losers but on the winners. In America, religious orthodoxy largely triumphed in its battle against popular religion.

Despite this outcome, it is the contention of this article that the struggle between popular belief and orthodoxy nonetheless represents an important moment in immigrant social history as it opens a window on class and power relations within the immigrant world and also between that world and the larger American society, which immigrants entered or, at least, abraded against. Accordingly the article will explore

International Labor and Working-Class History
No. 34, Fall 1988, pp. 22–38

three hypotheses. First and most documentably, it will argue that while the Church survived transplanting to the North American continent with altered but largely undiminished ideological ambitions, several million European migrants also carried extrainstitutional "popular" beliefs with them when they traversed Europe and journeyed to America. The second proposition remains more tentative because, in absolute terms, sources for it simply are less forthcoming. It is, namely, that immigrants used popular religious belief to meliorate situations of relative powerlessness in which they found themselves in America. In the realm of the personal, immigrants sometimes deployed popular religious devices against one another. In the realm of the political, popular religious belief and practice sometimes became a resource—and often provided a framework—through which and by which they expressed the class antagonisms they experienced in the workplace. Similarly, popular religion offered a means to sidestep the authority of the clergy, while religious heresy presented a potent ideological alternative to the hegemony of the Roman Catholic Church.

It is, however, the third proposition that is most intriguing and, in large measure, still eludes us here. It cannot be denied that the Church defeated the popular challenges it faced in the factory districts of industrial America, but even as the Church won, arguably it also lost. While more research needs to be done to buttress this proposition, it can be suggested that the antecedent social and cultural changes associated with secularization, which had sapped the vitality of popular belief and thereby enabled the Church's triumph, also undercut orthodox belief. Both orthodoxy and popular religion in the end thus succumbed to this third force which, in metaphorical terms, we might call "the transforming power of the machine."

In considering these three propositions, it is convenient to examine migrants from rural Poland who came to the United States in the late nineteenth and early twentieth centuries, for they strikingly illustrate both the persistence of popular religious forms and the conflict between orthodoxy and popular belief. In premigration Poland, their religious belief system had been an elaborate syncretism of Roman Catholic symbols, Christianized "pagan" or folk beliefs, animism, naturalism, spiritualism, and pre-Christian magic.[4] Although immigrant Poles quickly dropped many such popular religious forms pertaining to the Polish agrarian cycle, ostensibly because they seemed out of place in urban America,[5] they held onto others to a remarkable extent.

Perhaps most common was their retention of Christianized "pagan" practices, testimony not only to the fact that most such practices seem not to have provoked much opposition from the Church in Poland (and, judging by the Italian immigrant experience, perhaps only mild derision from the Irish-dominated Church hierarchy here),[6] but also that Roman Catholicism in Europe itself had coopted—and thereby helped to perpetuate—so many of the time-honored rituals from the agrarian world. In early-twentieth-century Brooklyn and Detroit, for example, while Poles placed symbolic bits of straw beneath the table cloth at Christmas Eve supper, an evocation of the straw-filled manger, they also shared Christmas wafers and Easter eggs for good

luck and dragged Judas figures through the streets during the pre-Easter Holy Week—
both practices with magical or "pagan" connections.[7] For Polish immigrants there and
elsewhere, the Sunday before Easter was still "switching day," when the first one
awake aroused other family members with symbolic lashes from a willow switch,
while Easter Monday remained "spilling day" (Dyngus), when young men doused
young women with water or sprinkled them with perfume.[8] Both folk customs recalled
ancient fertility rites. American Poles, meanwhile, continued to invest Roman
Catholic objects with magical properties and to use Roman Catholic symbols in
unorthodox ways. As late as the 1950s, for example, one second-generation working-
class Polish-American in New Jersey carried a piece of palm, obtained at church on Palm
Sunday, in his wallet in the belief that, as a result, he would always have money there.[9]

Drawing on both Roman Catholic and "pagan" traditions, spiritualist beliefs
similarly survived the transatlantic crossing. These centered on death and the dead.
While Brooklyn Poles placed consecrated candles in the hands of the dying[10]—a
practice compatible with religious orthodoxy—Polish immigrants also departed from
"acceptable" beliefs. Poles in New Jersey believed the superstition that cutting down a
fruit tree would cause or predict death and that a dog howling all night would prophesy
sickness or death.[11] Some beliefs verged on the macabre: if a person had a double row
of teeth, he would return after death unless turned face-down in the coffin before
internment. But belief in spirit-return was commonplace among the Poles here. In
order to stop visits by the spirits of the dead, funeral processions passed the church
and surrounding neighborhood as many as three times before heading to the cemetery,
while pallbearers customarily carried a casket from a house so that the corpse's feet
would leave first. Immigrant Poles clearly populated a dense spirit-world and behaved
circumspectly toward the unknown. Each All Saint's Day (November 1), for example,
they gave food to beggars, who, they believed, communicated with the spirits of the
dead.[12] Some spiritualistic beliefs overlapped naturalism and animism. Thus a Polish
folksong one immigrant learned from friends in Buffalo in the early twentieth century
told the story of an orphan who died and was buried on the other side of the church
from where her mother's grave lay:

> Lo, on that grave, on the mother's,
> Sprang a little lime tree.
> And somehow, upon the orphan's,
> A birch tree was seeded.
> Though the mother and the daughter
> Did not lie together,
> High above the church, the branches
> Of the two trees joined hands.[13]

The eerie image contained in this one folksong suggests how much popular
belief—a blend of animism and reincarnation—sometimes departed from orthodox
Christianity. Other immigrant folksongs featured talking trees, birds, and animals that
dispensed lessons about innocence, mortality, and love.[14] Still another folksong figure

was the talking raven that brought news to a Polish mother of her son's death in battle:

Black your skin and black your feathers;
Evil omen that.
Heartbreak you bring, pain and sorrow
Wing their way to me.

The raven, "the embodiment of evil prophecy,"[15] opens a window to the darker side of Polish immigrant belief, the survival of a panoply of "pagan" magical beliefs and practices. Polish immigrants purchased a popular liniment called *Zmijecznik*, on whose label the picture of a snake presumably invoked popular religious belief in the curative powers of snake ointment.[16] Poles consulted books on magic, devils, and dreams so avidly that even Anthony Paryski, the highly reputable Toledo publisher, included these subjects among the titles his firm carried.[17] In Detroit in the 1930s, meanwhile, one Polish woman attributed the death of a friend's child, obviously a victim of infantile paralysis, to a malady she described as "tangled hair." "Tangled hair" resulted from bewitchment and could be countered by clipping the matted locks off and placing them beneath the sufferer's pillow.[18] Bewitchment, Poles believed, was carried out by the power of the "evil eye" possessed by magicians, witches, other persons considered malevolent, and sometimes even by animals.[19] It is not hard to speculate what benefits Polish immigrants continued to derive from these magical beliefs. A belief in magic gave immigrant Poles a resource for explaining—and thereby coming to psychological terms with—the stresses and losses they daily faced in an often hostile alien world they could not control.[20]

In their shared belief in witchcraft, however, the powerless also found a tool they might use against one another within the immigrant enclave. In this regard, a Polish folksong, learned in Passaic, New Jersey, in the early twentieth century, underscores an association familiar to Polish immigrants: the aged person as witch (*czarownica stara*).[21] As late as the 1950s, members of one working-class Polish-American family in New Jersey still suggested that a certain neighbor, an elderly widow, could give the "evil eye."[22] Arguably, the Polish elderly—and especially elderly women—found themselves particularly open to such aggressive allegations and speculations in both Poland and in America.[23] In Poland, while the aged were shown respect, typically they passed on property and authority to their children when the latter married, a cause for considerable intergenerational conflict, tension, and resentment.[24] In America, if elderly immigrants clung to property and social authority after their own economic role had declined, they elicited a similar effect.[25] Those conversant with Polish-American social history are familiar with the tensions between superannuated immigrant parents and their American-born adult offspring over a range of social and economic issues, including education, occupation, assimilation, and the choice of marriage partners. Accusation—or suspicion—of witchcraft directed against the elderly—and particularly elderly women who typically survived their older husbands—might have expressed, by transference, the open conflict between wives and mothers-in-law or, even more likely, the concealed tensions between daughters (and sons) and their mothers.[26] It should come as no surprise if at least a few elderly immigrant women did try to summon forth magical forces at times. Whereas elderly immigrant men might have found an outlet for psychological and social stress in strong drink or domestic violence, elderly immigrant women enjoyed fewer options. For such an especially vulnerable segment of immigrant society, magic might have offered a special hope and solace. It was, according to one rural informant in Canada, "those old people" who told tales about spirit visits in the night and, as if to inflate their own social authority, dispensed advice on how to ward them off. Outside one Canadian church, meanwhile, immigrant women from Poland, believing themselves hexed by a tap upon the shoulder from one of their peers, answered blow for blow in the hope that the devil would return to its owner.[27]

As America's Polish immigrants lodged occasional allegations of witchcraft, they also may have harbored other suspicions about the "unnatural" in their midst. Although evidence for American factory towns is still lacking, perhaps Polish immigrants there shared some beliefs held by one group of rural Ontario Kashubs, an ethnic minority from northern Poland. The latter believed a night spirit called the succuba, the wandering soul of a sleeping, usually unbaptized girl, tried to suffocate sleeping victims.[28] They saw mischievous domestic demons called dwarves, whose nocturnal dances caused grass to wither in mysterious circular patches.[29] And they feared the nighttime return of marauding vampires.[30] Immigrants like the Kashubs used their belief in "unnatural" beings to single out—and stigmatize—those who seemed out of the ordinary—people who had a "restless, excitable nature" or a "bloated, blood-red face" or those who refused "to take the Eucharist in the hour of their death and reject[ed] consolation of a priest."[31] Significantly, they also used "unnatural" beings to explain unusual events—like the child born with a piece of placenta on its head[32]—or calamitous ones—like the deformed newborn.[33] In a period of high infant mortality—Polish-American rates exceeded those for Black Americans during the years before World War I—the uncertainty of birth beckoned forth the same species of explanation as the certainty of death.

The occasional recourse immigrant Poles might have had to popular religious beliefs like vampires, dream and natural prophecy, bad luck, or the evil eye, or to practices like magical cures by themselves did not seem either to upset or inconvenience Roman Catholic pastors, who often blinked at the existence of harmless folk traditions among their otherwise faithful parishioners. Some might have encouraged a belief in magic, so as to lend credibility, by inference, to orthodox belief. Some priests of rural background themselves might even have half-believed in a few superstitions that, considered objectively, were fairly harmless after all. Something else, however, was not. Black magicians and other professional practitioners and purveyors of the magical arts sometimes directly challenged the Church by desecrating—and thereby appropriating for their own uses—the Church's own symbols. For example, one witch described in an immigrant folksong, learned in Passaic, New Jersey, in the early twentieth century, cast a spell by taking a lock of her intended victim's hair and burying it " 'neath the cross."[35] More generally, however, those with magical expertise threatened the monopoly that Roman Catholic clerics otherwise might have held on religious authority within America's immigrant settlements.

Paradoxically, of all the professional practitioners and purveyors of the magical arts, witches themselves posed the smallest threat to the Church. Although in rural Ontario, Kashubian immigrants believed one "witch" murdered their priest, a Father Słominski, by "implanting" the devil in a batch of dumplings she made that the hapless priest ate before his death,[36] this was a rare case. Since Poles did not seek out the counsel of witches, whom they feared, but avoided them and recoiled from their evil magic, witches hardly could attract a following, and therefore offered scant real challenge to immigrant priests. And so it was not witches, but specialists in "white" magic who competed for the religious loyalties of immigrant Poles. Publishers of magic books, like Toledo's Anthony Paryski, reached a wide audience with their brand of practical advice, and thereby rendered many immigrant readers less dependent on the guidance of their clergy. When criticized for the nature of his literary offering, Paryski reportedly defended the magic books, "saying they were only meant to awaken interest in reading." Ecclesiastical critics might have countered that this was a threat in its own right.[37] Of considerably greater danger, because they served as local opinion-leaders, in competition with the priests, were the assortment of "white magicians" — medicine-women and fortune-tellers — whom immigrants also feared but nonetheless periodically consulted.[38] Immigrant folksongs learned in the early twentieth century in Buffalo, New York, and Passaic, New Jersey, made reference to Poles visiting astrologers and fortune-tellers.[39]

Apparently Poles also practiced what they sang. In the early 1900s Polish immigrants patronized various traffickers in the occult, like "the renowned Egyptian crystal-gazer Aguliapert L. Nebiros" of New York City and "Madame Elba" of Brooklyn, "genuine clairvoyant and fortune-teller," who dispensed advice and "knowledge," sometimes in direct competition with the conventional Roman Catholic clergy.[40] Disregarding "the most solemn admonitions by the priest," for example, in the early 1930s some Polish women in Michigan sought advice on contraception from a "gypsy sorcerer." For the appreciable sum of ten dollars, they procured "a garterlike circlet" to wear about the knee, which allegedly would exert "a magic-magnetic influence on the male principle."[41] While Poles often seem to have consulted non-Poles for magical services, perhaps in the belief that strangers also commanded strange powers,[42] one person typically conversant in magical beliefs and practices was the Polish midwife. In most immigrant settlements, while these women presided over countless immigrant childbirths, it is likely that they also monitored them for appearances of the "unnatural" and could call upon a storehouse of popular religious "folk" practices to neutralize the baneful effects when infants appeared to have been hexed.[43]

The practice of "white" magic may have been fairly widespread in Polish America throughout the 1930s, even if invoked only occasionally. Yet because it was so scattered and unorganized, as an alternative activity it remained prepolitical, a loose set of private acts performed by disconnected individuals that never coalesced into an oppositional movement. Moreover, because not all immigrants shared a belief—or a belief of like intensity—in magic in the same way that most had come to share a belief in Roman Catholicism,[44] it is hard to imagine how magic could have been politicized. When working-class Poles joined together to challenge the relations of power that ribbed their world, they therefore seem to have eschewed magic and turned to another element that composed immigrant popular religion. They wrested Roman Catholic doctrine and symbols away from their ecclesiastical proprietors and bent them toward popular oppositional ends.

At the same time that their Roman Catholicism gave Polish immigrant workers the reputation for obedience and docility in the workplace, it also gave them a powerful resource on which they too could draw, in order to blunt the exploitative excesses of their capitalist employers.[45] Their religion, for example, reinforced preindustrial work rhythms. In ethnically mixed Eastern Galicia, where both Roman Catholic and Orthodox holidays interrupted work, thirty-four districts had 100 to 120 nonworking days, twenty-two districts had 120 to 150 nonworking days, and sixteen districts had a staggering 150 to 200 nonworking days per year.[46] Similarly, in America Polish immigrants' understanding of their religion forced the operators of one coal mine in Glen Lyon, Pennsylvania, to close on three Polish holidays—Three Kings' Day, St. Joseph's Day, and Christmas—presumably to avoid heavy absenteeism among their labor force,[47] and impelled Polish laborers at the American Sugar Refining Company's giant Brooklyn plant to stage a strike in 1910 in protest of a company order that required them to work on Easter Sunday, the holiest day of the liturgical year.[48] Polish immigrant working people also made more pointedly extra-institutional applications of elements of Roman Catholicism. In 1902, for example, striking Polish, Ruthenian, Lithuanian, and Slavic anthracite miners in Pennsylvania directed a eulogy to United Mine Workers president John Mitchell, which borrowed heavily from the liturgical style of the Roman Catholic mass.[49] Poles also demon-strated more militant borrowings. They were doubtless present in 1910, for example, when Slavic workers in Hammond, Indiana, knelt before a crucifix and lighted candles as each swore in turn not to scab, and when Slavic coal miners in Avelia, Pennsylvania, reportedly crucified a despised foreman during another strike that year.[50] These creative—if sometimes brutal—applications of elements taken from their shared religious culture buttressed the militance of working-class Polish immigrants.

In these cases, Poles appropriated Roman Catholic symbols to challenge secular, capitalist power. Insofar as they struck despite urgings to the contrary by conservative priests, and insofar as their secularized use of Roman Catholic symbols represented a theft of the Church's ideological property, Polish immigrant workers collided with ecclesiastical power as well. Their most serious and extensive excursion into insurrec-tionary popular religious forms, however, did not involve the extrainstitutional use of Roman Catholic elements—or perhaps it marked a culmination of extrainstitutional activity: the articulation of a full-fledged heresy, Polish messianism. Polish messia-nism had repercussions for the power relations Poles experienced in industrial America, but, more importantly, it represented a serious challenge to the Roman

Catholic Church. It did so because this heresy, in modified form, became the official doctrine of the only major schism ever to fracture Roman Catholicism in the United States, the Polish National Catholic movement.[51]

In fact, Polish messianism did not begin as a popular religious deviation at all, but as an intellectual outgrowth of nineteenth-century Polish nationalism. Developed in the 1830s by nationalist partisans like Romantic poet Adam Mickiewicz, the anticlerical doctrine criticized the Church in Rome for complicity in Poland's political subjugation and endowed the Polish Nation with the mission of a chosen people. According to Polish messianic belief, Poland's tribulations and sufferings would redeem Poland and earn its resurrection. Poland, the "Christ of Nations," would in turn herald the moral regeneration of the universe.[52] Though an intellectual doctrine, Polish messianism seems to have found a receptive audience among America's Polish immigrants in the late nineteenth century. Polish-language libraries stocked books by Mickiewicz, Julius Słowacki, and other messianic poets, and immigrant readers devoured their prose. The writings of Poland's messianists also were excerpted on fraternal benevolent association calendars and almanacs. When immigrant Poles in the anthracite fields of Scranton, Pennsylvania, found themselves in conflict with ecclesiastical authorities in the 1890s and early 1900s, they did not have far to look for an alternative religious ideology in order to legitimize their incipient insurgency. They turned to an already established strain of belief, Polish messianism.

Led by the Reverend Francis Hodur, a Galician-born cleric who had been steeped in the writings of the Polish messianists and the politics of Polish populism and nationalism, the Scranton Poles collided with the Church hierarchy. Demanding control over Polish property and Polish-speaking priests, they came to espouse a new theology that sought to deliver Poles from their political thralldom and to comfort them in their economic subjugation. The Polish National Catholic Church, which they formed by uniting the growing number of "independent" or "national"—that is to say, schismatic—Polish parishes in America, elaborated the messianists' three central themes.[53] First, Polish National Catholic doctrine was pointedly anticlerical. Writing in 1928, Hodur denounced the "Roman bishops" as "greedy for power and domination over the whole world. . . ." According to Hodur, they "withdrew from the people and ceased working the way the Apostles worked." "The duty of every priest of the national church," Hodur continued, "is not self-aggrandizement" but "to aspire to a surplus of justice" for the people.[54] Second, the Polish National Catholics also embraced progressive social politics. Seeking to create an active social ministry to Polish laboring people and "to defend the interests of the oppressed and down-trodden," Hodur and his followers espoused egalitarianism.[55] The liturgical calendar of the Polish National Catholic Church featured a Feast of the Poor Shepherds, meant to mark "the part played by poor and homeless people . . . in helping to make known God's love to mankind."[56] In contrast with local Roman Catholic parishes, the Church sided with striking Polish workers in Pennsylvania after the 1897 Lattimer Massacre and during the 1900 and 1902 anthracite strikes.[57] Third, the Polish National Catholic Church sought to embody messianic Polish nationalism. After breaking with Rome completely in 1900, the Church replaced Latin with Polish as the language of the mass. In 1904 it named its new seminary Bartosz Głowacki House after the Polish peasant hero of the Battle of Racławicè, highpoint in the Poles' valiant—yet futile—struggle to resist the Second Partition of 1793. Finally, while Church holidays honored Poland's three great messianists—Zygmunt Krasinski, Słowacki, and Mickiewicz—and Romantic nationalist poet Maria Konopnicka, in 1914 the Church synod also added the Feast of the Polish Homeland to the Church's liturgy.[58] Stressing the resurrection allegory and apocalyptic promise drawn from the Bible's book of Revelation, Polish National Catholicism tried to become the messianic religion of the oppressed Polish Nation.[59]

Although the Polish National Catholics adopted a religious organizational form that had a distinctly congregational look and although their church maintained a relationship with the Episcopalians, another "national" church, their links to Protestantism ended there. Millenarian in rhetoric and militantly nationalistic, Hodur and his followers drew upon—and refashioned—intellectual and ideological traditions indigenous to Polish culture. They represented an aspect of popular religion, one that did not try to preserve old ways in the face of change but to synthesize a new approach to national identity, to religion, and to politics. Polish National Catholicism never became the official church of Poland nor the majority religion among Poles in the United States. In fact, its membership never accounted for more than one or two percent of the Poles in America. But the Church's growth was nonetheless impressive and, in the eyes of Polish Roman Catholic prelates, threatening. Riding the rising tide of left-wing Polish nationalism that accompanied Poland's reemergence after World War I as an independent nation-state, by 1925–26, at its height, Polish National Catholicism boasted between sixty thousand and eighty-five thousand adherents in the United States.[60]

Polish clerics in the United States did not fail to respond to the challenge posed by the persistence of popular religious forms, the invention of the messianic, nationalist heresy, and, for that matter, the spread of assorted secular ideologies—notably secular Polish nationalism and socialism—among Poles here. The success of the Church's counterattack depended basically on its superior resources, including bureaucratic cadres of ideologically reliable priests and nuns, but it also rested upon earlier victories. However incomplete or syncretized, Roman Catholicism had penetrated deeply into Polish culture and life. Thus while the battle for immigrant hearts and minds would still include backsliding, when immigrant priests mounted their own counteroffensive they encountered a populace well prepared to receive the sparks of the faith.

Unfortunately, we do not have a very good record of the content of sermons preached in Polish immigrant parishes in the early twentieth century, but fragmentary evidence suggests that pastors used the pulpit and the confessional to rail against the enemies of the Church. One priest in rural Ontario preached against witches, calling them "goats," an odd epithet, or perhaps a pointed one given the symbolic association between goats and the devil.[61] Polish Roman Catholic priests also attacked "socialists,"[62] and branded the Polish National Catholics "pagans," "heathens," "atheists," "revolutionaries," "lawbreakers," and "heretics."[63] But the Church's arsenal contained more powerful arrows than this quiver of insults. In their combat with unbelief in its various guises, Roman Catholic prelates mobilized the rich and complicated ideology of Marianism.[64]

In fact, the Church's stance toward "pagan" and folk religious practices had been, by implication, far more ambiguous and complicated than appears at first glance. In a sense, the Church needed the popular credulity that affirmed the existence of the magical and spiritual worlds, for that same credulity, redirected, also might serve to bolster belief in the "one, true faith." Thus clergymen and nuns desired less to obliterate the panoply of magical objects and practices than to substitute institutionally controlled devices—holy water, medals, scapulars, religious statues, crucifixes, holy pictures, consecrated candles, and rosary beads[65]—that had quasi-magical properties. Arguably Mary herself was one such device whom rural Poles considered—and churchmen encouraged them to consider—a "white magician" in her own right. As such, Mary appeared, alongside talking birds and animals, in hundreds of parables and stories in the popular religious lore.[66] In answer to nineteenth-century unbelief, however, the doctrinal innovation developed by the Church was a mystical Mary, comforting mother, and divine mediatrice. Marian mysticism provided the faithful with a direct spiritual connection to an esoteric God. Yet while this long-suffering Mary counselled immigrant Poles and others to emulate her meekness and mildness, Polish priests also revived another image of Mary for more combative purposes: a Mary who, as messiah, warrior, and Poland's patroness, would deliver the Poles' motherland from bondage, defend the pope's honor from stain, and vanquish the foes of her church.[67] In short, this Mary would fight for church and homeland but not for an improvement of the day-to-day lives of the faithful.

The methods and strategies employed by the Church in its fight—Polish Roman Catholic sisterhoods, parochial education, special missions, Marian devotions, newspaper pieces, and, later, radio broadcasts—have been described elsewhere and need not be reviewed at length here.[68] But what of the outcome? Apparently the Church fared well in its campaign against heretics, devils, and unbelievers. Some pastors, like the Reverend Leon Wysiecki of Brooklyn, could report by the late 1890s that even the socialists had started coming to confession.[69] The Polish National Catholic schism, though it had made many a parish into a battleground (Wysiecki himself lost his pastorate after a nationalist-led split about twenty-five years later), had been contained by the late 1920s.[70] Thereafter few new national parishes were established. Meanwhile, by the 1940s a local writer contended that "the Pole in Brooklyn does not believe in superstitions. . . ."[71] Against popular religion, the Church therefore also appears to have won, even though, as we have seen from some of our examples here, throughout the 1950s superstitious belief had not been entirely stamped out.

Embedded in the Church's extensive victory over popular religious deviations, however, lay an unsettling paradox, the unraveling of which reveals how much—or how little—Roman Catholic prelates actually had won. While the Church had tried to suppress popular religion among Polish immigrant working people, its triumph left their religious attachment to Roman Catholicism not stronger, but weaker. In part all "traditional" religion suffered for the simple fact that one of the major intergenerational "culture carriers," the aged, were virtually absent in America's Polish immigrant settlements.[72] Among the households of Poles in the sugar refining industry in the early nineteenth century, for which complete data were obtained, for example, a scant 4.6 percent of household members were forty-five years of age or older. In contrast, the comparable figure in German refinery employer households was 28.3 percent.[73] Moreover, Roman Catholic religious attachments may have weakened because another force in immigrant society in the factory districts of industrial America tended to loosen the ties of *all* forms of religion—both popular and orthodox. That force was secularization.

Both orthodox belief and popular religion succumbed to the world Polish immigrants had entered, a world in which, while much was new, fewer and fewer elements were mysterious. Walking the grimy streets of American industrial cities, immigrant working people might have feared chance encounters with men who meant to harm them but probably did not worry about "unnatural" beings and evil spirits. Strongly associated with Polish rural culture, most of the Poles' ghosts and goblins had been left behind. In the new world familiar rites of passage also were transferred outside the home, and strangers now tended to become the masters of immigrant life and death. Thus undertakers and mortuaries now buried the immigrant dead while increasingly doctors and hospitals attended to childbirth. Science, the civic authorities, and improved standards of living thus combined to demystify the two major life events in which magic had been worked. Developments among rural Ontario Kashubs were probably magnified for urban-dwelling immigrants. The former began to equate black magicians with evangelistic faith healers. They started to seek occult advice less for the breaking of spells than for medical cures. They remembered less and less about witches and witchcraft, which they presumably found out of place.[74] As a result, by today elderly Polish-Americans are more likely to turn to pseudoscientific, commodified forms of popular medicine, like chiropractors, health foods, and medical-advice radio programs than to consider the "black arts." Like most other working-class Americans, they thus have slipped comfortably into a particular niche in the mass-consumption market, even while seeking alternatives to an institutional medical system that apparently has failed to fill their needs.

The factory, meanwhile, also pulled immigrants away from a belief in non-material causes, spiritual happenings, and "unnatural" events, all strangely out of place in the "dark, satanic mill." Machines and other manufactured objects lacked mystery. Assimilation and forcible Americanization conducted by civic leaders, factory managers, and middle-class immigrants made "superstition" seem silly and even tended to dismiss orthodox religion. Thus whereas in 1910 Polish immigrants in one Brooklyn factory struck against having to work on Easter Sunday, fifty years later working-class Polish-Americans coveted work on Sundays and holidays for it now paid "time-and-a-half" or "double-time." In sharp contrast to their parents or grandparents who had left rural Poland, religion — both orthodox and popular — had much less to do with them and they with it.

In dialectical fashion, however, the Church's successful control over religious belief and, in turn, its reassertion of proprietorship over its own symbols, also may have caused Polish immigrants to look elsewhere for ideologies and a language through which they could express their aspirations and articulate their grievances. If religion was, in the final accounting, the property of the priests with whom immigrants did not always agree, the latter had a reason to abandon it and to embrace the secularized world of city, factory, mass-consumption market, and also of ideas. In the 1920s when middle-class Polish immigrants sought to assert their own primacy over the immigrant pastors whose social authority derived from the place they occupied in a sacerdotal religion, those middle-class immigrants had to step outside the clerics' world. In the hyphenate secular ideology of "Polish-Americanism" they found a terrain in which their priests did not automatically hold the high ground.[75] Working-class Poles also came to embrace this secular Polish-American identity promoted by their own middle class, but found other secular ideologies that more closely addressed their concerns and expressed their interest as workers in American factories. Except for cases cited earlier, we have no examples of Polish immigrant workers organizing strikes in the United States around the ideology or iconography of Roman Catholicism. They needed a set of symbols shared by a religiously diverse work force, and Roman Catholicism therefore would not do. In short, a set of beliefs the Church so clearly controlled was not very salient to them as they marched on the picket line.

What was? On the one hand, Polish-American workers came to imbibe the republican ideology of rights of the late-nineteenth- and early-twentieth-century labor movement. In 1897, for example, striking Polish miners in Lattimer, Pennsylvania, did not shoulder the cross but instead marched behind two American flags.[76] Similarly, according to one observer, Polish and Lithuanian workers who struck a Brooklyn jute mill in 1910 "counted themselves Americans."[77] One of them, Agnes Teviskevitski [sic], when brought before a local magistrate who lectured her "as to the 'good' qualities of a lady," replied indignantly that, "she was an American citizen and had the right to walk along the streets and persuade others from taking her job."[78] While some workers thus drew upon republican ideas in order to reject middle-class notions about class, politics, and, in this case, femininity, others reached more broadly into secular popular culture for points of agreement with other workers. When striking women sugar refinery workers walked out of a heavily Polish plant in Brooklyn in 1921, they did not sing either peasant folk tunes or religious or patriotic hymns but popular jazz songs.[79] This borrowing typified the increasingly derivative nature of the consumer's cultural world.

In light of the secularization of working-class Polish immigrants, the recent strikes staged by members of the Solidarity union in People's Poland may seem strange indeed. From them came "photographs of Gdansk shipyard workers kneeling to the Madonna and taking communion"[80] and of the televised image of Lech Wałesa, the redoubtable Solidarity leader, wearing a Virgin Mary lapel pin. What was witnessed in Poland, however, may be less a European variant of liberation theology than, more simply, the power of outlawed religion, that is to say, religion as an alternative to the repressive power of the state. In the United States we see few if any similar displays, not just because the diversity of the American workforce does not allow religion to emerge as the common cultural denominator of a class. By the 1950s some Polish working people in the United States increasingly may have found Roman Catholicism to be a conservative, bureaucratic institution with its own special interest, not something they could easily redirect toward popular ends. They and other Roman Catholic workers therefore might have had good cause to turn toward ideologies of the secular world, for in them they might have found independence from the dictates of the Church, dictates that became increasingly out of step with the social realities of the so-called "modern world." They shed the talismans of popular religion and Roman Catholic orthodoxy and found security in the purchase of commercial commodities. The trinity to which they now turned, however, represented a new hegemony: Americanism, mass consumption, and mass culture became the new Father, Son, and Holy Ghost.

NOTES

An earlier version of this article was presented at the 1980 meeting of the Organization of American Historians in San Francisco. I wish to thank Christopher Clark, Nora Faires, Christopher Johnson, Ewa Morawska, Stephan Thernstrom, Robert Zieger, and the editors of *ILWCH* for their helpful discussion, suggestions, and comments at various stages of its development. I would also like to thank Lisa Popham for typing the manuscript.

1. See Keith Thomas, *Religion and the Decline of Magic* (New York, 1971); E. P. Thompson, "Patrician Society, Plebeian Culture," *Journal of Social History* 7 (1974): 382–405; Natalie Zemon Davis, *Society and Culture in Early Modern France* (Stanford, 1975); Emmanuel LeRoy Ladurie, *Montaillou: The Promised Land of Error*, trans. Barbara Bray (New York, 1978); Carlo Ginzburg, *The Cheese and the Worms: The Cosmos of a Sixteenth-Century Miller*, trans. John and Anne Tedeschi (Baltimore, 1980); David Warren Sabean, *Power in the Blood: Popular Culture and Village Discourse in Early Modern Germany* (Cambridge, 1984); Steven L. Kaplan, ed., *Understanding Popular Culture: Europe from the Middle Ages to the Nineteenth Century* (Berlin, 1984); Robert Muchembled, *Popular Culture and Elite Culture in France, 1400–1750*, trans. Lydia Cochrane (Baton Rouge, 1985).

2. After James Obelkevich, this article uses the term "popular religion" to mean "non-institutional religious beliefs and practices, including unorthodox conceptions of Christian doctrine and ritual. . . ." See James Obelkevich, *Religion in Rural Society: South Lindsey, 1825–1875* (Oxford, 1976), 261. Also see, for example, E. P. Thompson, "The Transforming Power of the Cross," in his *The Making of the English Working Class* (New York, 1963), 350–400; J. F. C. Harrison, *The Second Coming: Popular Millenarianism, 1780–1850* (London, 1979); Edward Berenson, *Populist Religion and Left-Wing Politics in France, 1830–1852* (Princeton, 1984).

3. On popular religion in immigrant America, see Rudolph Vecoli, "Prelates and Peasants: Italian Immigrants and the Catholic Church," *Journal of Social History* 2 (Spring 1969): 217–68, and "Cult and Occult in Italian-American Culture: The Persistence of a Religious Heritage," in *Immigrants and Religion in Urban America*, ed. Randall M. Miller and Thomas D. Marzik (Philadelphia, 1977), 25–47; Alixa Naff, "Belief in the Evil Eye among the Christian Syrian-Lebanese in America," *Journal of American Folklore* 78 (January–March 1965): 45–51.

4. See William I. Thomas and Florian Znaniecki, *The Polish Peasant in Europe and America* (New York, 1958), 1:205–87; Sula Benet, *Song, Dance, and Customs of Peasant Poland* (New York, 1951); Jan Bystroń, *Kultura Ludowa*, 2d ed. (Warsaw, 1974).

5. Polish sociologists observed an erosion of traditional religious practice in Poland, too, owing to industrialization, urbanization, and the rationalization of agriculture. See Władysław Piwowarski, *Religijność Wiejska w Warunkach Urbanizacji: Studium Socjologiczne* (Warsaw, 1971), 31ff.; "La Pratique religieuse dans les villes polonaises au cours des vingt dernières années," *Social Compass: International Review of Socio-Religious Studies* 15 (1968): 277–84; and "L'influence de l'industrialisation sur la religiosité populaire en Pologne," *Changement Sociale et Religion, Conference Internationale de Sociologie Religieuse, Actes de la 13e Conference Lloret de Mar, Espagne, 31 Aout-4 Septembre 1975* (Lille, n.d.), 425–31.

6. Compare Richard M. Linkh, *American Catholicism and European Immigrants (1900–1924)* (Staten Island, 1975), 40.

7. Mary Adele Dabrowska, "A History and Survey of the Polish Community in Brooklyn" (M.A. thesis, Fordham University, 1946), 120–21; Arthur Evans Wood, *Hamtramck, Then and Now: A Sociological Study of a Polish American Community* (New York, 1955), 40–42.

8. Dabrowska, "History and Survey of the Polish Community in Brooklyn," 125. According to Sula Benet, among "peasants who have risen in the social scale and acquired 'genteel' manners, and among cityfolk," the dousing with water was replaced by the sprinkling with perfume or cologne. Polish immigrants also seem to have made this substitution. See Benet, *Song, Dance, and Customs*, 48–49, 56–57.

9. This example comes from a childhood recollection of the author.

10. Dabrowska, "History and Survey of the Polish Community in Brooklyn," 120–21.

11. The author also heard these beliefs expressed as late as the 1960s.

12. Irene Stella Pyszkowski, "The Polish Communities in Brooklyn: Their History and Development" (Ph.D. diss., Ottawa University, 1950), 176; "Religion and Churches," Folder 26, Box 3584, WPA Federal Writers Project Historical Records Survey, Municipal Archives, New York City; Wood, *Hamtramck*, 40–42; Dabrowska, "History and Survey of the Polish Community in Brooklyn," 120–21.

13. This song, of course, recalls the story of Tristan and Isolde. There is some debate whether many Polish folksongs originated among "the folk" or whether they had upper-class origins and were disseminated downward to the lower ranks of society. See Harriet M. Pawlowska, ed., *Merrily We Sing: 105 Polish Folksongs* (Detroit, 1961), 138–39, 229.

14. Ibid., 68–69, 90–91.

15. Ibid., 146–47, 232.

16. Thomas and Znaniecki, *The Polish Peasant*, 1:219. *Zmiecznik* could always be found, for example, in the bathroom medicine cabinet of the author's grandmother.

17. Józef Miąso, *The History of the Education of Polish Immigrants in the United States*, trans. Ludwik Krzyżanowski, vol. 6, Library of Polish Studies (New York, 1977), 86–87.

18. Murray Godwin, "Motor City Witchcraft," *North American Review* 233 (June 1932): 529–30.

19. Benet, *Song, Dance, and Customs*, 41. Also see Jan Perkowski, *Vampires, Dwarves and Witches among the Ontario Kashubs*, Canadian Centre for Folk Culture Studies Paper No. 1 (Ottawa, 1972). The Kashubs are a Polonized ethnic minority resident in northern Poland. While it is hard to generalize immigrant Kashubian data from rural Canada to the factory districts of the industrial United States, the Perkowski study does nonetheless show that a wide range of popular beliefs survived immigration. If they were carried to and perpetuated in a rural setting, they probably also were carried to and—in some measure—perpetuated in urban settings. Several studies have suggested that urban and rural assimilation patterns were similar. See Irwin T. Sanders and Ewa T. Morawska, *Polish-American Community Life: A Survey of Research*, Community Sociology Monograph Series, vol. 2 (New York, 1975), 210–11. I would like to thank Mark Stolarik for calling the Perkowski study to my attention.

20. See Perkowski, *Vampires*, 54.

21. Pawlowska, *Merrily We Sing*, 45.

22. Recollection of the author.

23. See Benet, *Song, Dance, and Customs*, 40–41.

24. Ibid., 228–30. Also see Thomas and Znaniecki, *The Polish Peasant*.

25. Compare Roman L. Haremski, *The Unattached, Aged Immigrant: A Descriptive Analysis of the Problems Experienced in Old Age by Three Groups of Poles Living Apart from Their Families in Baltimore* (Washington, D.C., 1940).

26. On the former, see Benet, *Song, Dance, and Customs*, 178; on the latter, compare Paul Boyer and Stephen Nissenbaum, *Salem Possessed: The Social Origins of Witchcraft* (Cambridge, Mass., 1974).

27. Perkowski, *Vampires*, 30–31, 49.

28. Ibid., 49.

29. Ibid., 43–45. The withering could be attributable to a grass fungus. I would like to thank Phil Schmidt for calling this regional botanical malady to my attention.

30. According to one Ontario Kashub interviewed in the late 1960s: "There was a lot of that at Wilno in the graves. They opened the graves. They cut the heads off. When those who were born vampires are not seen to, then they have to dig up the graves. First he [the vampire] carries off his relatives and then those as far as the bell rings. It happened at Wilno [Ontario]. They have dug up many, but it was not told, never revealed. They had to dig it [the vampire's body] up and cut off the head while he sat in the coffin." Postmortem decapitation with a spade was only the last resort for "seeing to" vampires. Among other practices, Kashubs in Europe placed a rosary or crucifix in the coffin of the suspected vampire, but this cultural practice was modified in rural Ontario. There Kashubs employed crosses constructed of poplar. See Perkowski, *Vampires*, 2, 27–29.

31. Ibid., 21–22, quoting Friedrich Lorentz, *The Cassubian Civilization* (London, 1935), 132–34. Interestingly, atheists and socialists fell into this last category.

32. For the child born with the "little cap," Kashubs believed that the antidote to the vampire's fate was to remove the placenta, dry it, grind it to dust when the child was seven years old, and administer it in the child's drink. Burning it was an alternative. See Perkowski, *Vampires*, 21–22, 26. In other cultures, the "little cap" appears to have signified positive talents and gifts. Compare Ole Rölvaag, *Peder Victorious: A Tale of the Pioneers Twenty Years Later*, trans. Nora O. Solum and O. E. Rölvaag (New York, 1929). Among Eastern Europeans, it is interesting how much it resembled the yarmulke and may shed some light on cultural attitudes toward Jews.

33. Among Ontario Kashubs, dwarves were believed to substitute their own malformed children for healthy infants. See Perkowski, *Vampires*, 46.

34. John J. Bukowczyk, *And My Children Did Not Know Me: A History of the Polish-Americans* (Bloomington, Ind., 1987), 24.

35. Pawlowska, *Merrily We Sing*, 44–45. Desecration of Christian sacred objects was a time-honored technique of witches in Polish lore. See Thomas and Znaniecki, *The Polish Peasant*, 1:267–68.

36. Perkowski, *Vampires*, 33–34.

37. Mią̨so, *The History of the Education of Polish Immigrants*, 86–87.

38. Benet, *Song, Dance, and Customs*, 40–41. One medicine woman who administered to Ontario Kashubs insisted that if her client did not follow her instructions and pay her, her client would die. See Perkowski, *Vampires*, 37.

39. Pawlowska, *Merrily We Sing*, 20–21, 150–51.

40. *Czas* (Brooklyn), 3 March 1906, 2 January 1914.

41. Godwin, "Motor City Witchcraft," 530.

42. See Perkowski, *Vampires*, 36.

43. Though the following story from the study of Ontario Kashubs does not specifically identify the protagonist as a midwife, we can well imagine the kind of activities described in it taking place during a childbirth. The Ontario informant reported:

[A] vampire . . . was born to some people. The child was fine, baptized. Everything was good and he died. I was there. It was forty years ago [1920s]. And my neighbor was there. They said that I was to sew a garment for the child and I took it and was sewing the garment, but I said to Mrs. Martin Etmanski, "Come here. The child is alive. The child is coming to life, but the mother is dying." And then Mrs. Etmanski said, "Yes, but I will put it straight." She took a needle. From the ring finger, but I can't say whether it was two drops or three, she drew blood. The blood was alive and she administered it. When she gave it from the girl to the mother, the mother got better and began to sit up. The child grew cold and they buried it. . . .

This vignette also reveals the delicate ambiguity of episodes of alleged witchcraft or whose life immigrants considered more important. Under other circumstances, Mrs. Etmanski or the informant might have been accused of hexing the birth. See Perkowski, *Vampires*, 25.

44. In some cases, of course, magic has been politicized. See Tristan Platt, "Notes on the Devil's Cult among South Andean Miners," and Terence Ranger, "Religion in the Zimbabwe Guerilla War," in *Disciplines of Faith: Studies in Religion, Politics and Patriarchy*, ed. Jim Obelkevich, Lyndal Roper, and Raphael Samuel (London, 1987), 245–58 and 259–79, respectively.

45. For a longer discussion of the way this related to immigrant working-class formation, see John J. Bukowczyk, "Polish Rural Culture and Immigrant Working Class Formation, 1880–1914," *Polish American Studies* 41 (Autumn 1984): 23–44.

46. Johann Chmelar, "The Austrian Emigration, 1900–1914," trans. Thomas C. Childers, *Perspectives in American History* 7 (1973): 327.

47. John Bodnar, *Workers' World: Kinship, Community, and Protest in an Industrial Society, 1900–1940*, Studies in Industry and Society, No. 2 (Baltimore, 1982), 85.

48. Lithuanian firemen at the plant also walked out. The men's other grievance protested a company order that banned the consumption of alcohol during the working day and inside the plant. See *Brooklyn Daily Times*, 29 March 1910.

49. Bukowczyk, "Polish Rural Culture," 35–36.

50. Herbert G. Gutman, "Work, Culture, and Society in Industrializing America, 1815–1919," *American Historical Review* 78 (June 1973): 578.

51. For a lengthier discussion of Polish messianism, the Polish National Catholic Church, and Roman Catholic responses to the schismatic movement, see John J. Bukowczyk, "Mary the Messiah: Polish Immigrant Heresy and the Malleable Ideology of the Roman Catholic Church, 1880–1930," *Journal of American Ethnic History* 4 (Spring 1985): 5–32.

52. See Nikolai Onufrievich Losskii, *Three Chapters from the History of Polish Messianism*, International Philosophical Library Periodical Publication, vol. 2 (Prague, 1936), 20–21; Monica Gardner, "The Great Emigration and Polish Romanticism," in *The Cambridge History of Poland*, ed. William F. Reddaway, et al., 2 vols. (New York, 1941), 2:326; Peter Brock, "The Socialists of the Polish 'Great Emigration,' " in *Essays in Labor History in Memory of G. D. H. Cole, 25 September 1889–14 January 1959*, ed. Asa Briggs and John Saville (New York, 1960), 148.

53. In addition to its direct connection with Polish messianism, the church also had doctrinal links with Roman Catholic modernism and with Poland's Mariavite movement. On the former, see J. J. Heaney, "Modernism," *New Catholic Encyclopedia* (New York, 1967), 9:991–95; Roger Aubert, *The Church in a Secularised Society*, trans. Janet Sondheimer (New York, 1978), 186–203; Alec R. Vidler, *The Modernist Movement in the Roman Church: Its Origins and Outcome* (Cambridge, 1934); and Bernard M. G. Reardon, ed., *Roman Catholic Modernism* (Stanford, 1970), 9–67. On the latter, see Jerzy Peterkiewicz, *The Third Adam* (London, 1975), 10ff.; Émile Appolis, "Une Église des derniérs temps: l'eglise Mariavite," *Archives de Sociologie des Religions* 10 (1965): 51–67; B. Stasiewski, "Mariavites," *New Catholic Encyclopedia*, 9:217–18.

54. Francis Hodur, "Doctrines of Faith of the National Church" (Lecture given at the Warsaw Synod, 1928, typewritten translation), ms. pp. 3–4.

55. Rev. Stephen Wlodarski, *The Origin and Growth of the Polish National Catholic Church* (Scranton, Pa., 1974), 40–41, 50.

56. Theodore Andrews, *The Polish National Catholic Church in America and Poland* (London, 1953), 60.

57. Victor R. Greene, *Slavic Community on Strike: Immigrant Labor in Pennsylvania Anthracite* (Notre Dame, 1968), 141, 155, 183; Daniel S. Buczek, *Immigrant Pastor: The Life of Right Reverend Monsignor Lucyan Bójnowski of New Britain, Connecticut* (Waterbury, Conn., 1974), 154. On Hodur's socialist connections, see Joseph W. Wieczerzak, "Bishop Francis Hodur and the Socialists: Associations and Disassociations," *Polish American Studies* 40 (Autumn 1983): 5–35.

58. Wlodarski, *Origin and Growth*, 71–72, 90, 103; Andrews, *Polish National Catholic Church*, 60, 74.

59. Paul Fox, *The Polish National Catholic Church* (Scranton, Pa., 1961), 90; Franciszek Hodur, *Our Faith*, trans. Theodore L. Zawistowski and Joseph C. Zawistowski (mimeographed, n.p., 1966), 13.

60. Of these, we cannot know how many embraced the church's doctrinal innovations fully. Wlodarski, *Origin and Growth*, 117; Fox, *Polish National Catholic Church*, 62–63; Hieronim Kubiak, *Polski Narodowy Kościół Katolicki w Stanach Zjednoczonych Ameryki w Latach 1897–1965; Jego Spoleczne Uwarunkowania i Spoleczne Funkcje* (Kraków, 1970), 134.

61. Perkowski, *Vampires*, 30.

62. Rev. Leon Wysiecki to Bishop Charles E. McDonnell, 30 April 1897, Chancery Archives, Roman Catholic Diocese of Brooklyn, New York; Greene, *Slavic Community on Strike*, 248.

63. *Nowy Świat* (New York), 21 September 1922, 19 October 1922.

64. See Bukowczyk, "Mary the Messiah."

65. All were typically in the possession of immigrant Poles. See Godwin, "Motor City Witchcraft," 527.

66. Thomas and Znaniecki, *The Polish Peasant*, 1:286–87; Louis E. Van Norman, *Poland, the Knight Among Nations* (New York, 1908), 245–46.

67. Bukowczyk, "Mary the Messiah," 8ff.

68. Ibid.

69. Letter from Rev. Leon Wysiecki to Bishop Charles E. McDonnell, 1 February 1897, Chancery Archives, Roman Catholic Diocese of Brooklyn, New York.

70. See John Joseph Bukowczyk, "Steeples and Smokestacks: Class, Religion, and Ideology in the Polish Immigrant Settlements in Greenpoint and Williamsburg, Brooklyn, 1880–1929" (Ph.D. diss., Harvard University, 1980), chap. 6.

71. Dabrowska, "History and Survey of the Polish Community in Brooklyn," 120–21.

72. Jan Slomka, *From Serfdom to Self-Government: Memoirs of a Polish Village Mayor, 1842–1927*, trans. William John Rose, shortened English ed. (London, 1941), 98.

73. U. S. Congress, Senate Immigration Commission, *Immigrants in Industries*, Document 633, 61st Congress, 2d session, 1911, 15:661.

74. See Perkowski, *Vampires*, 29, 40–41.

75. For a discussion of middle-class Polish immigrants' involvement in Americanization work and their evolution of a "Polish-American" identity, see John J. Bukowczyk, "The Transformation of Working-Class Ethnicity: Corporate Control, Americanization, and the Polish Immigrant Middle Class in Bayonne, New Jersey, 1915–1925," *Labor History* 25 (Winter 1984), 76ff.; Bukowczyk, *And My Children Did Not Know Me*, 70.

76. Edward Pinkowski, *Lattimer Massacre* (Philadelphia, 1950), 11.

77. [Lyman Abbott], "A Case of Industrial Autocracy," *The Outlook* 95 (1910): 543.

78. *New York Call*, 22 April 1910.

79. *Brooklyn Daily Times*, 5 July 1921.

80. Jim Obelkevich, Lyndal Roper, and Raphael Samuel, eds., *Disciplines of Faith*, 6.

The Immigrants and Their Gods: A New Perspective in American Religious History

JAY P. DOLAN

Twenty years ago Jerald Brauer wrote an essay on the writing of American church history entitled, "Changing Perspectives on Religion in America." In this essay he noted that "change in perspective marks the writing of the history of religion in America." After discussing the work of Robert Baird and William Warren Sweet, the two historians whose perspectives most influenced the writing of American church history in the nineteenth and twentieth centuries respectively, Brauer then directed his attention to a third and new perspective. This new perspective had developed in the post-World War II era and was the result of the work of Sidney E. Mead, Sydney E. Ahlstrom, Winthrop S. Hudson, and others. Brauer described the new perspective by pointing out how it differed from the work of Sweet. It was clear to Brauer, however, that no one historian or school of historians had yet emerged whose perspective was able to dominate the landscape in the manner that Baird and Sweet had. There really was no new single perspective, but a variety of approaches and interpretations. In other words, in the late 1960s the discipline of American church history was in a state of flux, and "a number of young historians" were, in Brauer's words, "anxious to develop a new perspective through which to view the development and nature of Christianity in America."[1] Twenty years have passed since Brauer wrote those words, and since then a great amount of work has been done in American religious history and a new generation of historians has emerged. Nonetheless, the discipline is still in a state of flux and no one has been able to present a perspective or interpretation that commands the landscape.

I do not pretend to claim that I have found the magical interpretive key of church history past. In fact, no single interpretation or theory can explain adequately the more than three hundred years of American religious history.

---

1. Jerald C. Brauer, "Changing Perspectives on Religion in America," in *Reinterpretation in American Church History*, ed. Jerald C. Brauer (Chicago, 1968), p. 19.

Mr. Dolan is professor of church history and director of the Cushwa Center for the Study of American Catholicism in the University of Notre Dame, Notre Dame, Indiana. This is his presidential address delivered at the annual meeting of the American Society of Church History, 29 December 1987.

61

Nonetheless, I want to suggest a new perspective through which historians can view the historical development of religion in the United States. In order to appreciate the usefulness of this perspective some general remarks about the present state of American religious history are in order.

In the past twenty years an explosion of historical information has taken place. So many articles and books have been published that it has become virtually impossible for any one person to keep up with this information explosion. The positive side of this development is that we know a great deal more about the history of religion in the United States than we did twenty years ago. Moreover, historians have developed new approaches to the study of religious history which have challenged our assumptions and provided new models for doing history. New questions are being asked about the past and new trends in the study of religious history are evident.[2] This situation is as true of the historical study of religion in Europe as it is of American religious history, perhaps even more so. But there is also a dark side to this explosion of historical information. Because of this explosion any hope for synthesis or coherence has vanished. Thus, a central problem for historians is how to organize and integrate all this new information with the canon of American religious history.

This problem of the whole and its parts, or the one and the many, is common to all areas of history and has been discussed by many historians. Bernard Bailyn summed up one aspect of the problem in the following manner. "Modern historiography in general," he wrote, "seems to be in a stage of enormous elaboration. Historical inquiries are ramifying in a hundred directions at once, and there is no coordination among them. Even if one reduces the mass of new writings in the early modern period to the American field, and still further to the publications of card-carrying historians, the sheer amount of the writing now available is overwhelming." He then went on to note that "the one thing above all else that this outpouring of historical writings lacks is coherence."[3] For Bailyn and numerous others, defining the relationship between the whole and its parts is a major issue for historians. How then can we achieve coherence in the writing of history?

One way that historians of American religion can move toward a more coherent synthesis is to avoid a narrow, parochial approach to history. This faulty approach is found in all areas of history when such issues as nationalism and religious sectarianism motivate historians. The myopic vision of sectarian church history was commonplace not too long ago. It was

---

2. See Jay P. Dolan, "The New Religious History," *Reviews in American History* 15 (1987): 449–454; and Jon Butler, "The Future of American Religious History: Prospectus, Agenda, Transatlantic *Problematique*," *William and Mary Quarterly*, 3d ser., 42 (1985): 167–183.
3. Bernard Bailyn, "The Challenge of Modern Historiography," *American Historical Review* 87 (1982): 2–3; see also the essay by Carl N. Degler, "In Pursuit of an American History," *American Historical Review* 92 (1987): 1–12.

divisive, narrow, and unappealing except to the zealot. Though it has not disappeared entirely, such an understanding of history is much less common today.

Denominational history is still very much in vogue and will remain so as long as the need exists for a more complete understanding of a specific religious tradition. Such histories are the building blocks from which any future synthesis will be constructed. But denominational history does not have to be parochial, and above all it should not be sectarian and apologetical. One way to avoid the intrinsically narrow nature of denominational history is to integrate such studies into the larger framework of American history in such a manner that they become central to the American experience.

To move toward more coherence in the writing of American religious history requires more than just avoiding narrow denominational history and sectarian myopia. It requires the grand vision. Historians must use a wide-angle lens when they look back at the past and seek to discover the dominant themes that shaped historical development. Such grand themes by their very nature clear away the debris of history and bring clarity and coherence to the past. They also transcend denominational boundaries and for this reason become more central to the American experience and thus more important to historians in search of a usable past.

Puritanism has become one of the grand themes of American colonial history. This theme served to organize that period of history, and the more Puritan studies progressed, the more understandable the past became. In fact, the theme of Puritanism unified colonial historiography to such an extent that it eventually dominated the field. At about the same time, however, historians began to look beyond Puritanism and the region of New England in order to understand colonial history more fully. Nonetheless, the study of Puritanism continues to have a unifying effect on the writing of colonial religious history.

More recently, the theme of evangelicalism has emerged as a grand theme in the study of nineteenth-century America. Books and articles on American evangelicalism continue to drop off the press in heaps. Like the grand theme of Puritanism, evangelicalism cuts across denominational boundaries and tends to unify the mass of historical information pertaining to the nineteenth century.[4] The study of evangelicalism, like the study of Puritanism, concentrates on the Protestant expression of this religious tradition. But this exclusive focus on Protestantism does not have to be. The evangelical tradition also found a home among Roman Catholics, and Puritanism was rooted in Augustine as well as Calvin.

Fundamentalism is another case in point. The study of religious funda-

---

4. See the bibliographic essay by Leonard I. Sweet, "The Evangelical Tradition in America," in *The Evangelical Tradition in America*, ed. Leonard I. Sweet (Macon, Ga., 1984), pp. 1–84, where he discusses this abundant literature.

mentalism necessarily must move beyond the trials and debates of the 1920s in the Protestant community and include manifestations of fundamentalism in other religious traditions. Fundamentalism, like Puritanism and evangelicalism, is not just a Protestant phenomenon. Jews, Muslims, and Catholics also possess fundamentalist inclinations. Historians of American religion, the majority of whom are Protestant, must move beyond the boundaries of the Protestant tradition and begin to write history that is reflective of the ecumenical climate of the late twentieth century. The same can be said for historians of American Catholicism and American Judaism. Denominational history is needed, but if we ever are going to achieve some measure of coherence in American religious historiography, we will need histories that are conceptually more inclusive, more ecumenical.[5]

The popularity of Puritan studies and evangelical studies reflects the dominance of intellectual history among historians of American religion. One reason for this is the long-standing bond between church history and theology; in fact, in some institutions church history really translates into the history of theology. Another reason is the intrinsic appeal of intellectual history and the ability it affords scholars to limit their focus to the thought of prominent clergy or laypersons. Such a focus, however, necessarily restricts the value of these studies since it excludes the vast numbers of laypeople who make up the religious population of the United States. In recent years scholars have sought to move beyond the pulpit to the pew in order to probe more thoroughly the rich complexities of American religious history. The major reason for this trend has been the emergence of social history.

In the past quarter century, social history has bulled its way in the marketplace and now occupies a very prominent position in the historical academy. This statement is as true for the study of European history as it is for American history. The impact of social history on European history has been significant. An explosion of historical information has occurred, but along with this explosion has come the grand synthesis, the major interpretive work. One stunning example is John Bossy's book, *The English Catholic Community 1570–1870*. Not only is this book a fine example of the social history of religion, but it also has offered an entirely new interpretation of English Catholicism in the post-Reformation period. The French historian Jean Delumeau has achieved something similar in his work, *Catholicism Between Luther and Voltaire*. A leading member of the *Annales* school of historical studies, Delumeau has combined the long view of history with the thematic approach and has written a book that offers a major reinterpretation

---

5. See Jay P. Dolan, *Catholic Revivalism: The American Experience 1830–1900* (Notre Dame, Ind., 1978), for the Catholic side of evangelicalism in the nineteenth century; and Charles Hambrick-Stowe, *The Practice of Piety: Puritan Devotional Disciplines in Seventeenth Century New England* (Chapel Hill, N.C., 1982), for a broader understanding of Puritanism.

of the Counter-Reformation period. As the work of Bossy and Delumeau suggests, the social history of religion, with its focus on the religious life of the laity, brings coherence and synthesis to historical studies.[6]

The influence of social history on American religious history has not been as significant as in European studies. Nonetheless, the impact is noticeable. Its influence is seen especially in colonial history, where community studies and other types of social histories of colonial religion have enhanced our understanding of the role of religion in American life. Social history also has made its mark in nineteenth-century historiography in such areas as the study of revivalism. The new history of American Catholicism also mirrors the influence of social history.[7] Another major development in recent years has been the emergence of women's studies. Though significant cultural changes help to account for this development, the inclusive nature of social history has encouraged historians to examine the place of women and the role of gender in American society. Historians of American religion have not been as quick to follow this development, but every indication is that the issue of women and religion is moving from the periphery to the center in American religious historiography.[8]

Another area that has benefitted from the renaissance in social history is immigration history. In the past quarter century immigration history has come into its own, and in the United States it now has its own journal and professional organization, as well as several research centers that concentrate on immigration studies. The number of published works in this area is most impressive, and the implications of these studies for American religious history cannot be overlooked.[9]

Immigration has never attracted very much attention from American religious historians. In fact, until recently the historical study of immigration attracted the attention of only a handful of scholars. This lack of attention is illustrated very dramatically in the following statistic: of all the dissertations written on immigration between 1899 and 1972, 50 percent were done in one decade, 1962-1972.[10] Thus the increased interest in immigration history

6. John Bossy, *The English Catholic Community 1570–1870* (New York, 1976); and Jean Delumeau, *Catholicism Between Luther and Voltaire: A New View of the Counter-Reformation*, trans. Jeremy Moiser (Philadelphia, 1977).
7. See Butler, "Future of American Religious History," for a discussion of some of these studies.
8. A major reason for this movement is the three-volume work, Rosemary Radford Ruether and Rosemary Skinner Keller, eds., *Women and Religion in America* (San Francisco, 1982-1986), which includes essays and primary documents related to American religious history from colonial times to the mid-twentieth century.
9. See Rudolph J. Vecoli, "The Resurgence of American Immigration History," *American Studies International* 17 (1979): 49–66; and Thomas J. Archdeacon, "Problems and Possibilities in the Study of American Immigrations and Ethnic History," *International Migration Review* 19 (1985): 112–134.
10. Edward Kasinec, "Resources in Research Centers," in *Harvard Encyclopedia of American Ethnic Groups*, ed. Stephan Thernstrom (Cambridge, Mass., 1980), p. 876.

clearly is linked to the recent renaissance in social history as well as to other social developments. Even with this renewed interest in the study of the immigrants, historians of American religion have remained reluctant to turn their attention in this direction. A search of books reviewed in the four major historical journals between 1965 and 1985 revealed a total of fifty-eight books that treated both immigration and religion or immigration and the church. That is a meager number indeed. The bulk of those books that treated both immigration and religion were published in the 1965–1975 period, and since then a noticeable decrease has occurred. Another statistic further illustrates the meager attention given to the study of religion and immigration: of the 3,534 dissertations written in immigration history between 1885 and 1983, only 128, or 3.6 percent, treated the theme of religion.[11] Such neglect is understandable given the past history of American religious historiography. But to continue such neglect is inexcusable.[12] It would mean that historians would be overlooking not only a very valuable area of study, but one that brings greater coherence and understanding to the field of American religious history.

Even though immigration was an important aspect of colonial history and remains very much a part of contemporary American life, I want to focus on the nineteenth century, pointing out how the study of the immigrant experience not only will enrich our understanding of that era of American religious history, but also will bring greater coherence to the study of religion in the nineteenth century. Puritanism, evangelicalism, and fundamentalism are intellectual or theological principles, systems of belief, and for this reason they are able to provide coherence or synthesis for a particular period of study. As a theme or organizing principle of study, immigration can function in a similar manner and provide historians with a perspective through which they can view the development of American religion.

First, immigration was a phenomenon that cut across denominational boundaries. It was not limited to Italian Catholics, Russian Jews, or Norwegian Lutherans. It was a typically American experience. The 1916 census of religious bodies points this out very clearly. Of the 200 denominations studied, 132 reported a part or all of their congregations using a foreign language—a remarkably high percentage. Equally striking is the revelation that forty-two languages were in use in these churches. Among Roman Catholics, twenty-eight foreign languages were spoken; the Methodists

---

11. My thanks to Susan White for searching the following journals: *American Historical Review, Journal of American History, Church History,* and *Catholic Historical Review;* A. William Hoglund, *Immigrants and Their Children in the United States: A Bibliography of Doctoral Dissertations, 1885–1982* (New York, 1986), p. viii.
12. See Jay P. Dolan, "Immigration and American Christianity: A History of Their Histories," in *A Century of Church History: The Legacy of Philip Schaff,* ed. Henry Warner Bowden (Carbondale, Ill., 1988), for an examination of the treatment of immigration in American church history during the past century.

reported twenty-two different languages in use. Clearly, immigration affected all religious traditions in nineteenth-century America.[13] Because it transcends denominational boundaries, the theme of immigration provides historians with a perspective that enables them to examine issues that are common to many religious traditions. For this reason it brings greater coherence and synthesis to the historical study of American religion.[14]

Second, studying the immigrant experience in the United States will force historians to acquire a comparative perspective. Religion is such a distinguishing feature of American life, and yet rarely is it studied comparatively. Immigration can provide that comparative perspective for the nineteenth century and force historians to look beyond the American scene and ask if what happened in America may have differed from what went on in the Old World. Did the establishment of the Dutch Reformed tradition in the United States differ significantly from developments in the Netherlands, and if so, why? Did the American environment alter the folk religion of Italian Catholics, and if so, how? Questions like these and countless others will enlarge our vision and force us, as Carl Degler noted, to "emphasize aspects of our past that may have gone unnoticed," and "call for explanations where none was thought necessary before."[15] Only through such a comparative perspective will we find out how distinctive the American religious experience was. And in discovering this distinctiveness, historians will better understand the development of religion in the United States.

By studying the immigrant experience American religious historians also will be able to draw on the vast amount of published material produced by immigration historians in the past twenty years. Not only will this lead church historians beyond the confines of their own field, but it also will provide them with a rich source of historical information pertinent to the study of religion in American life. Historians of immigration have examined the old-world background of the newcomers, their patterns of settlement in the United States, and their efforts to adjust to American society and the stresses and strains this adjustment caused. The issues of language and Americanization also have attracted the attention of immigration historians.

All of these issues have relevance for religious history. Realizing this, many historians of immigration have incorporated the theme of religion into their work. Some historians have focused on the issue of conflict in the immigrant community. Not surprisingly, a good deal of attention in such studies centers on religious conflict. In recent years historians have begun to examine the persistence of old-world cultures in the New World. One of the major keepers of culture was the church; this role was manifested in architecture, theology,

---

13. *Religious Bodies 1916* (Washington, D.C., 1919), pt. 1, pp. 76, 85, and pt. 2, p. 457.
14. Timothy L. Smith demonstrated this in his essay "Religion and Ethnicity in America," *American Historical Review* 83 (1978): 1155–85.
15. Degler, "In Pursuit of an American History," p. 7.

and devotional practices. The relationship between religion and politics in the immigrant community also has attracted the attention of scholars, and their work has demonstrated how influential religion was in shaping politics in the immigrant community. These are just some of the issues pertinent to American religious history which historians of immigration have studied. A survey of these studies clearly reveals that religion was central to the immigrant experience. It was especially important in rural areas where community was essential to the survival of immigrant culture. If there was no church, there was no colony; and without a colony, the culture of the immigrants would have disappeared.[16]

Because the issues immigration historians study transcend denominational boundaries, they have a unifying influence on religious history. The persistence of religion in the New World is not something unique to Polish or Italian Catholics. Norwegian Lutherans and English Methodists experienced it as well. By examining this issue within various denominations, historians will be able to study an experience common to all immigrant communities. In this manner historians can bring more unity to a field that of its nature tends to be very splintered. This is what I have tried to do in my own work in American Catholic history. Not only have I relied on the writings of historians of immigration, but I have used immigration as an organizing theme in my work. This method has enabled me to bring a greater measure of synthesis and coherence to the history of nineteenth-century American Catholicism.[17] I believe that if a similar approach is used in the study of nineteenth-century American religious history, scholars will gain a richer understanding of the field and religion will become more central to the study of American history.

Convinced of the need for more coherence in American religious historiography and the value of immigration as an organizing principle, I have begun a long-range project which will study the immigrants and their gods. This project will focus on Catholics, Protestants, and Jews and will seek to understand the role and meaning of religion in the lives of the immigrants. The expanding body of literature in immigration history will help to make such a study feasible. Much of this literature, however, is limited to the social history of the institutional church. Equally important is the religious behavior of the people, a topic of special interest for me. I am eager to discover the religious world of the people, not just the institutional nature of the church. In other words, I am in search of the religious mentality of nineteenth-century immigrants.

---

16. The *Journal of American Ethnic History* and the *Immigration History Newsletter* are publications of the Immigration History Society and provide information on recent publications in this field of study.
17. Jay P. Dolan, *The American Catholic Experience: A History From Colonial Times to the Present* (New York, 1985).

In order to understand the religion of the people, historians have examined prayer books, sermons, rituals, hymns, diaries, and an array of other sources. For historians of nineteenth-century immigration, another resource exists which can be most helpful in opening up the religious world of the people: the letters that the immigrants wrote to their family and friends in the old country.

For the past two years I have been reading immigrant letters, both published and unpublished, in an effort to understand the religious world of the immigrants. Though I am still in the midst of this research, I have read enough letters from a variety of people that I can make some observations about the immigrants and their gods.

God-talk was an integral part of the immigrant letter. The God of the immigrants was always present, watching over the people, and many letters refer to God in this manner. Some groups were more inclined to God-talk than others. Irish Catholics and Jews were reticent when it came to God-talk. Norwegian Lutherans, Dutch Reformed, and English Methodists liked to talk about God in their letters. Among the Irish, God-talk was more a decorative feature of their letters, with "thanks be to God" often being about as effusive as they could get. Among Norwegian Lutherans, however, it was common for a letter writer to speak about God in a lengthy sentence or two. Only rarely does a letter writer discourse at length about God or religion; those so inclined tended to be individuals of an evangelical persuasion who often would write at length about a conversion experience.

The God of the immigrants was very busy. The divinity watched over the people at all times, protecting them from all types of adversity. A Dutch Reformed traveller recounted his experience on board a sailing vessel and the fear that gripped him and his wife as the ship began to roll on its side during a storm. Then, he wrote, "most likely, in answer to the prayer of one or other pious passenger, the Lord God spared us and caused the storm to abate." For a Norwegian Lutheran in Texas, God was always arranging "everything so well."[18] In a letter to his family in Ireland a young Irish immigrant, Denis Hurley, noted the historic importance of the new year of 1876 and then wrote the following prayerful remark: "May Almighty God be equally propitious to us with his favors in the New as He has been in the old. May he preserve us from family broils, bitterness and contention, and enable us to live in unity, peace and harmony to the end of our lives."[19] At first glance Hurley's remarks appear innocuous, the pious thoughts of a lonely young man. Nonetheless,

18. Henry S. Lucas, ed., *Dutch Immigrant Memoirs and Related Writings*, 2 vols. (Seattle, 1955), 2:89; Theodore C. Blegen, ed., *Land of Their Choice: The Immigrants Write Home* (St. Paul, Minn., 1955), p. 348. My thanks to Michael Hamilton, who greatly assisted me in the study of published collections of immigrant letters.
19. Correspondence of Denis and Michael Hurley, Carson, Nevada, to parents in Clonakilty, Ireland, 6 January 1876, Archives of City of Cork, Ireland.

they paint a portrait of the divinity that was common among all the people whose letters I have read. The God of nineteenth-century immigrants was a personal God who was in close touch with the people. The divinity was not remote, but was a constant companion, guide, and savior in whom the immigrants learned to trust "for everything." The God of the immigrants was not a stern Calvinist who stirred up fear in the people, nor did the divinity resemble the Roman Catholic God of judgment who was ready to pounce on people because of their sins.

The immigrants were not immune to suffering and hardship. Disillusionment with the New World, loss of the harvest, sickness, and death itself were frequent themes in their letters. Despite the harshness of these experiences, the immigrants put such suffering in a religious context. A Dutch Catholic writing from Wisconsin to his mother, brothers, and sisters talked about the misfortunes that had struck his family. "Of the four children which we brought from Holland," he wrote, "Johanna is the only one left." He continued, "misfortunes in our family have been too many and too severe. But it is God's will, and we must carry our Cross no matter how heavy it is." A Norwegian woman spoke of the suffering she had to endure and then stated that "God often sends us sufferings and tribulations to test our faith if we have patience both in good fortune and adversity."[20] The immigrants shared a common understanding of suffering and it was obvious that they had learned this teaching very well. In the good times they thanked God for many blessings; in the bad times they also saw the hand of God at work.

Another common concern reflected in these letters is the immigrants' belief in the afterlife. Moreover, they had a distinctive understanding of what life would be like beyond the grave; the most frequent comparison was to a place of reunion. An Irish letter writer who held a strong belief in the afterlife as well as in God's providence assured his mother that they would meet again in heaven. A Norwegian immigrant ended his letter with greetings to his mother, daughter, and "all my relatives, acquaintances, and friends." He then prayed that "we sometime with gladness may assemble with God in the eternal mansions where there will be no more partings, sorrows, no more trials, but everlasting joy and gladness."[21] This understanding of the afterlife as a place of reunion mirrored the social experience of the immigrants and the sense of separation inherent in the immigrant experience.

One of the most striking features in these letters is the absence of Jesus. For the vast majority of letter writers he seemed not to exist and thus he was rarely mentioned. The letter writers did not talk about sin either. Another striking omission is the absence among Catholic writers of any reference to Mary or individual saints or any devotions thought to be so central to

20. Lucas, *Dutch Immigrant Memoirs*, 2:168; Blegen, *Land of Their Choice*, p. 187.
21. Unidentified letter, 7 March 1876, Schrier Collection, Ms. 8347, National Library, Dublin, Ireland; Blegen, *Land of Their Choice*, p. 430.

Catholic belief. In fact, in many instances it would be difficult to determine the religious affiliation of the letter writers based on their references to religion. Denominational distinctiveness seldom appears, and because of this absence the belief systems of these people appear to be remarkably similar. They are spartan in their simplicity, with God, suffering, and the afterlife forming the major religious themes. The immigrants manifested a strong belief in a personal God who was very involved in their lives.

The one noticeable denominational difference that does appear in the letters that I read was the preoccupation of some writers from the more hierarchically structured churches (the Episcopal and Roman Catholic in particular) with clergy, ritual, and church. Irish Catholics frequently talked about the clergy, and in very positive terms. On occasion they also mentioned some Catholic rituals, mostly the mass and the parish mission. Both Episcopalians and Roman Catholics talked about the absence of church and clergy. When they did so, however, it was not in a religious or spiritual manner. It was more a statement of fact than an expression of belief. Methodists seldom commented on church and clergy. Good evangelicals that they were, Methodist letter writers were more inclined to talk about revivals and conversion. They met God at revivals and in a conversion experience, whereas Roman Catholics and Lutherans met God when they encountered suffering and the providential hand of the divinity.[22]

One striking observation that emerges from this study is the difference between the religion of Roman Catholic immigrants articulated in prayer books and rituals, and that found in their letters. The letters reveal a very plain religion centered around a God who cares about people. The prayer books and rituals reveal what I have called the Catholic ethos—a belief system grounded in sin, authority, ritual, and the miraculous.[23] These four marks of the Catholic ethos are found in prayer books and rituals developed by the clergy, whereas the letters of the people articulated a more plain religion or ethos. In the people's writings the emphasis was on simplicity, and especially on the miraculous or transcendent aspect of religion. They were not preoccupied with sin in their letters, whereas the clergy emphasized conversion from sin. This striking difference leads to at least two conclusions: as valuable as they are, immigrant letters cannot be the only resource used in searching for the religious world of people; and, as revealing as it might be, the behavior of people at church-sponsored rituals does not completely express the religion of the people. They practiced their religion in other settings, and oftentimes the beliefs professed on these occasions—in this case in the course of reflection and writing—were more plain and uncomplicated.

22. See Charlotte Erickson, *Invisible Immigrants: The Adaptation of English and Scottish Immigrants in Nineteenth-Century America* (Coral Gables, Fla., 1972), pp. 87–92, 127–128.
23. Dolan, *American Catholic Experience*, pp. 221–240.

The churches and their clergy emphasized certain aspects of religion, whereas the people emphasized other features of their belief. But these different expressions of religion did not contradict one another; rather, one complemented the other.

For too long historians of American religion have neglected the study of the immigrant experience. There is no reason to continue this neglect. Now is the time for the recovery of immigration as a theme and organizing principle in the writing of American religious history. Social historians of immigration have provided us with a substantial amount of historical information pertinent to the study of American religious history, and we cannot afford to overlook this work. Moreover, historians of American religion are desirous of writing a more representative history, one that incorporates the laity as well as the clergy. The study of immigration encourages this development by focusing the attention of historians on the religious world of the people. Its helpfulness is especially clear when the focus is on immigrant letters, but is also true when the historian studies the social history of the immigrant community and church. The study of immigration also provides historians with a grand view of history, for it enables them to study themes that transcend denominational boundaries and can readily be extended over long periods of time. In addition, the study of immigration provides scholars with a comparative perspective, not only between the Old World and the New, but between various immigrant groups and religious traditions as well. Such a perspective will enable scholars to understand more completely the uniqueness and complexity of religion in American life. Finally, the use of immigration as an organizing theme of study can bring greater coherence to a field which, because of its denominational traditions, is inclined to splinter into disconnected phenomena.

Immigrants in the City: New York's Irish and German Catholics

JAY P. DOLAN

In the 1860s Walt Whitman described New York as a "city of spires and masts" with "the flags of all nations . . . duly lowered at sunset."[1] To this celebrator or urban life New York was a "city of the world! For all races are here; all the lands of the earth make contributions here."[2] The cosmopolitan character of New York was especially reflected in the city's Roman Catholic community. In the words of John Hughes, the Roman Catholic Archbishop of New York at mid-century, his "people were composed of representatives from almost all nations."[3] There were Italian and French Catholics, German and Irish Catholics as well as white and black American-born Catholics. And if one looked long enough, he would come across Catholic merchants from Spain and Catholic chefs from Switzerland. But within this polyglot community the two most significant ethnic groups in ante-bellum New York were the Irish and German immigrants.

The Irish immigrants, like most groups, tended to settle in distinct neighborhoods. One such distinctively Irish district in New York was located south of Canal Street in the general vicinity of City Hall. In 1840 one-third of the city's population was concentrated south of Canal Street, and the most densely populated section of this area was a strip of land that stretched from the Hudson River to the East River and was designated as the Fourth, Fifth and Sixth Wards of the city.[4] By 1855 thirty-seven percent of the population in these three wards were foreign-born Irish and ten years later, despite a decrease in total population, one of three people living in the area had been born in Ireland.[5] If one adds to this percentage the second-generation Irish "immigrants", then the Irish dominance in the area becomes even more evident.[6]

The concentration of the Irish in this district of the lower city is also reflected in the relative Catholic population in New York in the year 1840. Basing the relative size of a parish on the frequency with which the sacraments of baptism and marriage are administered in a given year, that is, the sacramental index, the two parishes located in the central belt of the lower city constituted thirty-six percent of the Catholic population in New York.[7] Based on this same sacra-

---

1. Walt Whitman, *Leaves of Grass*, ed. John Kouwenhoven (New York: The Modern Library, 1950), "Mannahatta," p. 370 and "Crossing Brooklyn Ferry," p. 132.
2. *Ibid.*, "City of Ships," p. 233.
3. Rev. Henry J. Browne, "The Archdiocese of New York a Century Ago: A Memoir of Archbishop Hughes, 1838-1858," *U. S. Catholic Historical Society Records and Studies*, 39-40 (1952), 183.
4. The density of the city wards is given in New York State Assembly, *Report of the Tenement House Committee of 1894* (Albany, 1895), p. 273; also the *New York State Census 1865* (Albany, 1867), pp. xxiv-xxv.
5. *New York State Census 1855* (Albany, 1857), p. 110; *New York State Census 1865*, p. 130 and p. xxv.
6. See Stephan Thernstrom, "Immigrants and Wasps: Ethnic Differences in Occupational Mobility in Boston, 1890-1940," *Nineteenth Century Cities*, ed. Stephan Thernstrom and Richard Sennett (New Haven: Yale University Press, 1969), pp. 132ff., for a discussion of the immigrant character of second-generation immigrants.
7. The use of the sacramental index as a measure of relative population has been made by Francois Houtart in his work, *Aspects Sociologiques du Catholicisme Américain* (Paris: Les Editions Ouvrières Economie et Humanisme, 1957), pp. 227ff.

Mr. Dolan is assistant professor of history in the University of Notre Dame.

354

---

mental index, Transfiguration Church, located in the Irish Sixth Ward was the largest Catholic parish in the city in 1840. Though Transfiguration Church lost its first-place position by 1865 to another Irish parish, St. Peter's Church, it still remained one of the larger city parishes and retained its dominant Irish character throughout the period.

By the 1830s the principal German settlement in the city was already being formed on the Lower East Side of New York. Along the Bowery Road, German bakeries, grocery stores and butcher shops with their German signs and their German-speaking clientele gave the area a distinctively European character. This district along the Bowery Road and overflowing into the neighborhoods east of the Bowery came to be known as "Little Germany".[8] Life in Little Germany was so distinctively German that one contemporary claimed that it had "very little in common with the other parts of New York."[9]

In 1845 more than half of the city's foreign-born German population (24,-416) lived in the four wards of the Lower East Side—Wards Ten, Eleven, Thirteen and Seventeen. As immigration increased in the following decades so did the German presence on the Lower East Side, and by 1865, 57,796 foreign-born Germans were living in the four wards of the area.[10] If one would add to this number the second-generation German immigrants, then the concentration of Germans on the Lower East Side of New York would be even more clearly illustrated. The population of the Tenth Ward was thirty-four percent German born, and in the Seventeenth Ward, where the Germans numbered thirty percent of the total population in 1865, there were 24,227 German-born residents. The German population of this ward alone was more than the total number of foreign-born Irish living in the three wards in the central belt of the lower city.[11]

The principal German Catholic parish in this district of the city was Most Holy Redeemer Church. The original church of Most Holy Redeemer was a small wooden structure built in 1844. By 1851 immigrant pride and immigrant needs had outgrown this humble structure, and a more pretentious church was built. The new church, its original structure still standing today on Third Street on New York's Lower East Side, was one of the largest churches in the city, and German Catholics affectionately referred to it as the German Cathedral.[12] Most Holy Redeemer Church, together with the only other German Catholic church in the area, St. Nicholas, ministered to the needs of approximately 35,000 German-speaking Catholics.[13] Such a large parish population was not unusual for New York at that time. Irish churches in the area, for example, were judged

---

8. Robert Ernst, *Immigrant Life in New York City 1825-1863* (Port Washington, N.Y.: Ira J. Friedman, Inc., 1965), pp. 41-42; Bayrd Still, *Mirror for Gotham: New York Seen by Contemporaries from Dutch Days to the Present* (New York: New York University Press, 1956), pp. 161-63.
9. Quoted in Still, *Mirror for Gotham*, p. 161.
10. *Census of State of New York 1845* (Albany, 1846), not numbered; *Census of the State of New York 1865*, p. 130; the Lower East Side generally includes the Seventh Ward, but this ward was not included in the description since it was predominantly Irish, while the other four wards were very German with some mixture of Irish.
11. *Census of the State of New York 1865*, p. 130.
12. John L. Obendorfer, C.SS.R., *Portrait of a Mother: Church of Most Holy Redeemer* (New York: Church of Most Holy Redeemer, n.d.), pp. 16ff.; *Katholische Kirchenzeitung*, June 10, 1858.
13. This figure was arrived at by a study of the relative sacramental index of the New York Catholic parishes, the estimated Catholic population of 350,000 in 1865 as well as other measurements of the relative German Catholic population in New York. See Jay P. Dolan, "Urban Catholicism: New York, 1815-1865," (Unpublished Ph.D. dissertation, University of Chicago, 1970), pp. 152-55.

to include as many as 20,000 people in their respective communities.[14]

It was not unusual for Irish and German churches to be located within a stone's throw of one another, and this feature of urban Catholicism illustrates a basic characteristic of the nineteenth-century city—the coexistence of diverse communities within the same neighborhood. Louis Wirth described this aspect of urban life in his essay "Urbanism as a Way of Life," and more recently Richard Sennett has pointed out its significance in his work, *The Uses of Disorder*.[15] In nineteenth-century New York, Irish children often had to walk by the German parochial school to get to their own English-speaking school. The same was often true for German Catholic children. Irish and German immigrants lived on the same streets and not infrequently in the same tenements. There is no question that certain streets and certain tenements were distinguished by a concentration of a particular immigrant group. First Avenue on the Lower East Side provides a good example of this concentration in 1865. The Germans were concentrated along the avenue between Second and Sixth Street, while the Irish dominated the avenue between Eleventh and Fourteenth Street. But equally significant was the fact that between Sixth Street and Eleventh Street the population along First Avenue was a mixture of Irish, German and American natives.[16]

The diversity of the urban neighborhood becomes even more evident when one studies the land maps of the city. Living in a tenement house often meant competing for space with slaughter houses, stables, coal yards, back yard shops and retail stores. This was as true for the Irish in the Sixth Ward as it was for the Germans in the Eleventh Ward. The only difference might have been that the East Side breweries and slaughter houses, indiscriminately tucked behind the tenement houses, gave that area a unique aroma.[17]

The coexistence of diverse communities in the same neighborhood also meant that they shared similar characteristics. This similarity was equally true in areas where one immigrant group was heavily concentrated, such as the Irish Sixth Ward or the German Eleventh Ward. Both Irish and German immigrants had firsthand experience with the tenement-house culture of New York. When an investigator or a reporter wanted to visit the worst of New York's tenements, he invariably chose the Irish Sixth Ward, notorious for its "tenements, yards, and sinks" in a "filthy and most disgusting condition."[18] Father, mother and children lodged together in crowded quarters, and in one block 1,562 people were packed together in old, worn-out buildings.[19] When the cholera struck New York in 1849, it inevitably chose a Baxter Street tenement in the Sixth Ward as its breeding ground and an Irish laborer as its first victim.[20] Living conditions in

14. Archives of the Archdiocese of New York, (hereafter referred to as AANY), Diary of Rev. Richard L. Burtsell, June 22, 1865.
15. Louis Wirth, "Urbanism as a Way of Life," *The American Journal of Sociology*, 44 (July 1938), 1-24; Richard Sennett, *The Uses of Disorder* (New York: Alfred A. Knopf, 1970).
16. *The Citizens' Association of New York. Report of the Council of Hygiene and Public Health* (New York: D. Appleton and Co., 1865), p. 148.
17. The maps used in the study were drawn up under the direction of William Perris, *Maps of the City of New York Surveyed Under Directions of Insurance Companies of Said City*, Vols. 1-4 (1852-53); see also *Report of the Council of Hygiene*, p. 160.
18. *New York Association for Improving the Condition of the Poor, First Report of a Committee on the Sanitary Conditions of the Laboring Classes in the City of New York* (New York: 1853), p. 10.
19. *Ibid.*
20. *Report of the Council of Hygiene*, p. 84; Charles E. Rosenberg, *The Cholera Years* (Chicago: University of Chicago Press, 1962), pp. 104-107.

the German Eleventh Ward were not much better. "Folsom's Barracks" was the most familiar name of a tenement in the Eleventh Ward and it was considered by a state investigating committee in 1857 as "one of the worst places they had seen."[21] Close by was a section called "Rag Pickers Paradise." In 1864 it was a rambling row of tenements housing 120 Germans, fifty dogs, thirty cats and piles of dirty rags and bones.[22]

Another characteristic which Irish and German immigrants had in common was their poverty. Archbishop John Hughes described the Irish in New York as "the poorest and most wretched population that can be found in the world" —"the scattered·debris of the Irish nation."[23] During the depression of 1837 the Irish poor of Transfiguration Church, who had loaned their money to the church in the hope of seeing it increased annually at a rate of seven percent, began "to besiege the door of the trustees' room, on evenings when they are in session, demanding from them the whole or parts of money they so generously and confidingly lent" to the church.[24] They came telling tales of woe describing how their few pieces of furniture were being seized as payment for rent and how they had been out of work for months and "in the utmost distress."[25] Others sent messages "from their bed of sickness begging a small portion of their money to procure necessary food and care."[26] The deprivation of poverty was also characteristic of the Catholics in the German Church of Most Holy Redeemer on the Lower East Side. The priests of the parish readily acknowledged that many parishioners belonged to the poorer classes of society.[27] And, when the depression of 1857 struck, many more of the German Catholics were reduced to poverty, and not a few of them longed for the old country.[28]

Although the poor stood out because they were so plentiful, both the Irish and German Catholic communities were represented in the middle and upper levels of society. A scientific random sampling of the baptismal registers of the respective churches for the year 1850 indicates this distribution within the occupational hierarchy. The German sample group had twenty percent employed in non-manual occupations while the Irish had nineteen percent. The trades in which they were engaged reflected the ethnic predilection for specific types of work, but the general distribution of both sample groups was remarkably similar. This similarity was very clearly indicated by the fact that among the Germans eighty percent of the sample group were employed in unskilled, semi-skilled and skilled occupations while the corresponding figure for the Irish was eighty-one percent. Neither sample group had any professionals numbered among them, and the percentage of unskilled occupations in each group was remarkably similar, twenty-one percent for the Irish and twenty-five percent for the Germans.[29]

21. New York State Assembly, *Report of a Select Committee Appointed to Examine into the Condition of Tenant Houses in New York and Brooklyn*, 1857, Vol. 3, No. 205, p. 28.
22. *Report of the Council of Hygiene*, pp. 177-79.
23. Archives of the University of Notre Dame, (hereafter referred to as AUND), Bishop John Hughes to Society for the Propagation of the Faith, Paris, June 26, 1849, f. 104; Browne, "The Archdiocese of New York a Century Ago," p. 165.
24. Archives of Transfiguration Church, Trustees' Minutes, October 8, 1840.
25. *Ibid.*
26. *Ibid.*
27. Joseph Wuest, C.SS.R., *Annales Congregationis S.S. Redemptoris Provinciae Americae* (Ilchestriae, Md.: Typis Congregationis S.S. Redemptoris, 1893), 2, p. 35.
28. Archives of Most Holy Redeemer Church, Chronicle of Most Holy Redeemer Church, p. 115.
29. The random sample was taken according to the principles of random sampling explained in W. Allen Willis and Harry V. Roberts, *Statistics: A New Approach* (New York: The

The trustee system in Transfiguration Church reflected this distinction of classes within the Catholic community. The trustees were not the day laborers or the stage drivers, but they were men representative of the upper levels of the occupational hierarchy—professional men, proprietors of small neighborhood businesses and skilled artisans.[30] The leading laymen in Most Holy Redeemer Church reflected a similar class distinction. The pew-rent system, adopted by both parishes, was another indication of the social distinction within the community. The price of rental was not insignificant, and the pews in the front of the church were rented at what was regarded as a "sufficiently high price."[31] Some parishes auctioned off front seats at rentals as high as $100 and $150 a year, and it was said that they met with "no opposition."[32] The custom of renting pews did come in for criticism from some Catholics precisely because it excluded "those who are too poor to have pews."[33]

Recent studies have emphasized the mobility of the urban population both within the city and out of the city, to other frontiers.[34] Such mobility was char- strom, *Poverty and Progress.* acteristic of nineteenth-century New York, and the Irish and German Catholics were not immune to it. The traditional moving day for New Yorkers was May 1. One observer remarked that on May 1 the city "turned topsy-turvy, thousands of persons being in the act of removal, the streets filled with carts laden with furniture, porters, servants, children, all carrying their respective movables. . . ."[35] To John Dubois, the Catholic bishop of New York from 1826 to 1842, it appeared that every year "at the first of May half of the inhabitants of the city moved from one district of the city to another."[36] Less noticeable, but no less real, was the movement of people out of the city. This pattern of mobility in New York becomes even more evident when the residential mobility of individual families is studied.

In order to determine the degree of residential mobility among Catholics in New York, I selected a random sample group of families from the baptismal registers of Transfiguration Church and Most Holy Redeemer Church for the year 1850. I then traced these families through the City Directories for a twenty year period to determine their frequency and patterns of mobility. The results indicated that both the Irish and German Catholics were on the move.[37]

Within a twenty-year period fifty-five percent of the sample group of Irish in Transfiguration Church moved out of the city. The rate of mobility out of the city for the Germans was fifty-eight percent. For those people who remained in the city the pattern of mobility was even more striking. Among the Irish sample

Free Press, 1956), pp. 334-39; the occupational categories were derived from Stephan Thernstrom, *Poverty and Progress* (Cambridge: Harvard University Press, 1964), pp. 90-94.
30. The trustees were listed in the minutes of the board of trustees of the parish, and their occupations were derived from the City Directory.
31. Wuest, *Annales,* 2, p. 161.
32. AANY, Burtsell Diary, Dec. 27, 1866 and Jan. 7, 1867.
33. *Freeman's Journal,* July 25, 1857.
34. See, for example, Thernstrom and Sennett, eds., *Nineteenth Century Cities* and Thern-
35. Still, *Mirror for Gotham,* p. 114.
36. AUND, Bishop John Dubois to Society for the Propagation of the Faith, Paris, May 9, 1836, f. 104.
37. The random sample was taken according to the principles explained in Willis and Roberts, *Statistics.* The Irish sample group involved fifty-three heads of families of male children baptised in the year 1850, or thirteen percent of the total of 393 families. The German sample involved fifty-three heads of families of male children baptised in 1850, or twenty percent of the total of 264 families.

group seventy-one percent of these families made at least one move, and of those who moved two out of five changed their place of residence more than once. Among the Germans the patterns were very similar with seventy-five percent moving at least once, and of those who moved two out of three made more than one move. One significant difference between the mobility patterns of the Irish and German Catholics was that the German immigrants who remained in the city for any length of time seldom moved out of the Lower East Side to another section of the city. However, when an Irishman sought a new address in the city, he had many more options open to him. He could leave the Irish Sixth Ward and move to one of the many Irish neighborhoods in the city. Since there were relatively few German districts in New York at this time, the German Catholics had fewer options open to them and they tended to remain within their distinctively German neighborhoods. The conclusions of this particular mobility study challenge the thesis that the ethnic neighborhood was a stable community. Further studies for successive years would have to be made to strengthen this conclusion, but the indications from this study, as well as from other mobility studies, point to the fact that the city was made up of very mobile ethnic communities. The continuity was maintained in Little Germany by German newcomers taking the place of the German transients, but the Germans who lived there in 1860 were to a large degree not the same people who had lived there in 1850.[38]

The mobility of the population, together with the poverty and the grim living conditions of the people, presented a formidable challenge to the church in the city. Established in the midst of tenement houses and surrounded by poverty, the church in the city had to adapt its mission to the new frontier. As the center of the church's pastoral, educational and apostolic life, the neighborhood parish faced the challenge of making religion viable in the city. If the local parish could not do it, then it was just not done. As the vital center of religion, the neighborhood parish was where the beliefs, the worship and the concerns of the immigrant church were evidenced. And if they were not manifest in the parish, then they could hardly have existed at all.

The urban frontier was a shared experience for Irish and German Catholics. Despite this common bond both groups manifested a tendency to forge distinct communities in the midst of the city. As one observer remarked, the newcomers "create for themselves distinct communities almost as impervious to American sentiments and influences as the inhabitants of Dublin and Hamburg."[39] This tendency illustrated the group consciousness of the immigrants and it was particularly evident in the organization of neighborhood parishes.

The neighborhood church of the immigrant has been characterized as a "transplanted church" and as a "national parish." Both descriptions identify the same phenomenon—the institutionalized attempt of an immigrant group to preserve the religious life of the old country.[40] Traditionally the American Catholic parish was organized on a territorial basis with the pastor of the parish having jurisdiction and responsibility for a particular area.[41] However, the large influx

38. See Richard C. Wade, "Urbanization," *The Comparative Approach to American History*, ed. C. Vann Woodward (New York: Basic Books, 1968), pp. 193-94.
39. *Annual Report of the New York Association for Improving the Conditions of the Poor*, 1867, p. 42.
40. Robert D. Cross, ed., *The Church and the City* (New York: Bobbs Merrill Co., 1967), pp. xx-xxi; see Houtart, *Aspects Sociologiques*, pp. 49ff.
41. For example, *Synodus Dioecesana Neo-Eboracensis Prima* 1842 (Neo-Eboraci: Typis Georgii Mitchell, 1842), pp. 11-12.

of immigrants from different nations speaking different languages necessitated the adoption of the national parish to satisfy the religious needs of the various foreign groups.[42] As a result the national parish emerged as a solution to a language problem and was more identified with a foreign language than with a single nationality.

Religion and ethnicity were intimately bound up together in the national parish, and one supported the other. Among the Germans this close association between religion and ethnicity was especially evident. Before long the two were so inextricably joined together that the loss of language was tantamount to the loss of faith. And faith, it was alleged, would be preserved only through the preservation of the German language and German religious traditions. As one historian of German American Catholicism has observed, the German immigrants desired to have separate churches "in which their traditional religious observances and customs would be carried out, where they could hear sermons in their mother tongue, go to confession as they had learned to confess from early childhood, and take an active part in parish life through their beloved societies."[43] Archbishop Gaetano Bedini, a papal visitor to the United States in 1853, made a similar observation. In his opinion the German priest was "too zealously nationalistic. He tries, unfortunately, to develop this national feeling as much as possible in a land where there are more Irishmen than Germans."[44] Archbishop Bedini added that the priests found support for such enthusiasm among the people who wanted "everything in German, and if they are ever obliged to have Irish or American priests, they complain loudly about this insult. . . ."[45]

This group consciousness was not peculiar to the Germans alone. Despite the ideal of an assimilated and unified Catholic-American Church, the reality of a polyglot community was only too evident. A New York priest, Father Jeremiah Cummings, described the situation in the following manner: ". . . the Irish find it difficult to discard their affection for everything that concerns Old Hybernia and thus would like to establish here an Irish Catholic Church. Germans stay on their own and do not want to have anything to do with the Irish. Frenchmen, in many instances would like indeed a Roman, Apostolic Catholic Church, but would like to dress her up à la française."[46]

The tendency of the immigrant Catholics to form distinct communities was also manifest in the organizational activities of the parish. This was particularly true of the German Catholics for whom the local parish appeared to be more of a rallying point than among the Irish. There is no question that the local parish was the center of religious life for the Irish, but the social experience of the Irish was not centered on the local Catholic parish to the degree that it was in the German neighborhood. Both Catholic communities were participants in many aspects of city life as workers, as voters and as members of a particular ethnic community, but among the German Catholics, more so than among the Irish, the

42. François Houtart, ''A Sociological Study of the Evolution of the American Catholics,''
    Social Kompass, January/April, 1955, pp. 189-216; C. J. Nuesse and Thomas J. Harte,
    eds., *The Sociology of the Parish* (Milwaukee: Bruce Publishing Co., 1951).
43. Colman J. Barry, *The Catholic Church and German Americans* (Washington, D.C.:
    Catholic University of America Press, 1953), p. 9.
44. James F. Connelly, *The Visit of Archbishop Gaetano Bedini to the United States of
    America* (Rome: Libreria Editrice dell' Università Gregoriana, 1960), p. 241.
45. *Ibid.*
46. AUND, *Scritture Riferite nei Congressi: America Centrale dal Canada all'istmo di
    Panama*, Vol. 14, letter 226, Rev. Jeremiah Cummings to Prefect of Propaganda Fide,
    Nov. 24, 1847, f. 639.

local parish was the center around which much of their community activities revolved. As a religious center it was the setting for the traditional German pomp and splendor of the liturgy, and as a social center it provided the nucleus around which many voluntary associations were clustered.

The parochial phenomena of associational life, called the *Vereinwesen*, was peculiar to the German Catholic experience, and it served to reinforce the religious nationalism of this immigrant community.[47] In Little Germany there were many German "vereins," but Catholics were urged to form their own associations.[48] Such a separatist mentality defined by religious affiliation was a heritage of post-Reformation German Catholicism. In the Protestant environment of the United States this attitude endured for many years among German Catholics.

For German Catholics a "verein" without religion was not judged very favorably. The German Catholic press urged Catholics to belong to Catholic vereins since such associations were religious and contributed towards one's spiritual end and the good of the church.[49] One of the more popular vereins among the Germans was the *Turn-Verein*. But the *Turn-Verein* was not Catholic and it was thus judged to be "not good for young Catholic blood [since] the right spirit does not prevail there."[50] There was a fear that if a Catholic joined the *Turn-Verein*, such association might "turn him out" of the church.[51] This attitude of the German Catholics toward non-Catholic German vereins illustrated the distinctive consciousness which they had as Catholics in Little Germany. Such a mentality was concretized in an elaborate parochial *vereinwesen*.

The most numerous type of verein in the parish was the society which provided relief to the sick and dying, appropriately called the *Unterstützungs-Verein*.[52] By 1863 there were five such vereins in Holy Redeemer parish. The purpose of all these associations was relief for the sick and dying members of the association and occasionally for non-members. The concept behind the verein was fundamentally that of a savings bank, and the vereins were called such by the people. They provided insurance money for their members when it was most needed. A truly Catholic verein was judged to be one that supported "poor and sick without distinction of nationality," and such an association not only cared for dues-paying members, but for anyone in need. Anything less was considered to be merely a "savings bank verein."[53] These parish associations had their flags and banners, they took part in the liturgical celebrations of the parish and they enjoyed frequent outings together.[54]

In addition to the mutual-relief societies, Holy Redeemer parish also supported the *Jägercompagnie*. The "Jaegers," as they were commonly known, were organized about 1852 and they were initially a militia-type group which was organized to protect the church property during the disorders of the Know Nothing era. The Jaegers also functioned as honor guards at liturgical ceremonies, and by 1869 the group had become a mutual relief society.[55] Like the other parish

47. See Philip Gleason, *The Conservative Reformers* (Notre Dame, Ind.: University of Notre Dame Press, 1968), pp. 9-10.
48. *Katholische Kirchenzeitung*, September 17, 1857 and September 2, 1858.
49. *Ibid.*
50. *Ibid.*, September 2, 1858.
51. *Ibid.*
52. Georg Dusold, C.SS.R., *Goldenes Jubiläum der Kirche zum Allerheiligsten Erlöser* (New York, 1894), p. 58.
53. *Katholische Kirchenzeitung*, September 7, 1857.
54. *Ibid.*
55. Dusold, *Goldenes Jubiläum*, p. 60.

vereins the *Jäegercompagnie* also had their outings, and on such occasions the parish school often closed down so the children could join in the celebration. In Little Germany there were many other militia-type organizations. One such group was the Henry Henning Guards, an organization made up of Catholics, which like the *Jäegercompagnie*, featured attractive uniforms, sharpshooting contests, parades and frequent picnics.[56] Such picnics were often held on Sundays, a day regarded by the Germans as their recreation day, and a favorite spot for such outings was Jones Woods, located near Seventy-First Street along the East River.[57] In addition to such social and relief societies, there were also several societies devoted to more strictly spiritual purposes, as well as a parish "reading verein" to encourage a taste for good Catholic literature among the German youth.[58]

Such group solidarity also extended to extra-parochial organizations. Both the Irish and the German Catholics in New York supported their own Catholic newspaper. They also established separate hospitals, orphanages and secondary schools. Even at the moment of death the diversity of the community showed itself, and German Catholics were most eager to have their own cemeteries, separate from the Irish. Archbishop Hughes, however, was against such separation, and at the moment of death the Germans and Irish were united in a common burying ground.[59]

The controversy over separate cemeteries, insignificant as it first might appear, demonstrated the potential conflicts present in the pluralistic Catholic community in the city. The German Catholics claimed that the Irish administrators of the Catholic cemetery discriminated against them, and it was only after the threat of interdict was hurled against the dissident Germans that they acquiesced.[60] Such conflict was even more apparent in parishes made up of both Irish and German Catholics. One church in New York, St. Alphonsus, experienced such tension because of its mixed community. The Germans in the parish did not favor sermons in English and they sought to exclude the Irish from the church.[61] Because of such opposition English sermons were suspended in the church for a few years. The conflict became serious enough that the Redemptorist priests momentarily thought of abandoning the mission. As the Irish presence in the neighborhood became more pervasive the tension subsided, and the priests were finally able to preach and hear confessions "in all those languages which they believed to be beneficial to the faithful."[62] The conflict that arose in St. Alphonsus Church was precisely what the national parish sought to avoid. When the church ignored the ethnicity of its people and failed to recognize their peculiar religious traditions, conflict inevitably arose. This was true in the middle decades of the century and became more pronounced in later decades as new Catholic immigrants arrived in the United States.

The diversity of the two Catholic communities was also visible in the religious life of the respective parishes. One of the most obvious differences was

56. *Katholische Kirchenzeitung*, October 1, 1857.
57. *Ibid.*; Charles D. Shanly, ''Germany in New York,'' *Atlantic Monthly*, 19 (May 1867), 560.
58. Dusold, *Goldenes Jubiläum*, pp. 61-64.
59. AANY, Archbishop John Hughes to Pastor and Congregation of Most Holy Redeemer Church, August 5, 1849; Wuest, *Annales*, II, 35-37.
60. *Ibid.*
61. Francis X. Murphy, C.SS.R., *The Centennial History of St. Alphonsus Parish* (New York, 1947), pp. 15ff.
62. Wuest, *Annales*, 5, part I, 163.

the use of language in the liturgy. While Latin was the official language of the liturgy in both communities, sermons were preached in English in the Irish churches and German was the language of preaching in Redeemer parish. German hymns were sung in Redeemer Church, but by the 1860s it was not unusual to hear the children sing hymns in English while at the same Mass the Sisters would lead the congregation in German hymns.[63] This bilingual approach, also present in the German parochial school, illustrated the German Catholic dilemma in America. As Germans the people wanted to preserve the bonds with the religious traditions of the fatherland, but at the same time they were confronted with the inevitable Americanization of their children.

The Irish wake has become legendary, and nothing similar took place in the German community. The boisterous tradition of the Irish wake of the dead brought forth frequent condemnations from their bishops, but to no apparent avail. Bishop John Dubois said that funerals among the Irish were more like festivals with "frequent drinking instead of holy water, distasteful conversation instead of prayers."[64] In 1861 the New York Provincial Council of Bishops spoke out against abuses at funerals which, in their opinion, had "degraded into an exhibition of ostentatious and unseemly display, sometimes even into an occasion of revelry and rioting."[65]

The Irish loved their whiskey and the Germans enjoyed their beer. Among the Irish, however, temperance became a crusading issue and intemperance was regarded as one of the principal causes of poverty.[66] The German Catholics did not support intemperance and their preachers spoke out against it.[67] But at the same time, German Catholics in New York were encouraged to support the good taverns and *biergartens* of Little Germany. One such healthy locale was situated directly opposite Holy Redeemer Church on Third Street, and its proprietor was a German Catholic. The crowd that gathered there, in distinction to those in other types of taverns, was "always a sober group, mostly people from the community, orderly people," and it was a place "where one can have a good glass of beer or wine and also carry on a Christian discourse."[68] To the Germans beer was regarded "as healthy and nourishing"[69] and not something to be avoided, but enjoyed. Unlike the Irish press the German Catholic newspaper always printed advertisements for beer and wine as well as for specific German *biergartens*.[70]

This degree of difference between the religious life styles of Irish and German Catholics was well summarized by a German American priest in the following manner:

> . . . we must not by any means make light of the difference and discrepancy of Catholic customs as they are to be found among Germans and Irish. The Irish . . . love simplicity in divine service, and in all the practice of religion, and do not care much for pomp and splendor. But the Germans . . . love the beauty of the church edifice and the pomp of ceremonies, belfries and bells, organs and sacred music, processions, feast days, sodalities, and the most solemn celebra-

63. Archives of Most Holy Redeemer Church, Chronicle of Most Holy Redeemer Convent, p. 48.
64. AUND, *Scritture Riferite nei Congressi: America Centrale dal Canada all'istmo di Panama*, Vol. 9, letter 1015, Pastoral Letter of Bishop John Dubois, July 6, 1827, f. 25.
65. *Metropolitan Record*, June 8, 1861.
66. *Freeman's Journal*, March 6, 1847.
67. Joseph Wissel, C.SS.R., *The Redemptorist on the American Missions* (3rd. rev. ed., privately printed, 1920), 1, pp. 230-40.
68. *Katholische Kirchenzeitung*, September 23, 1858.
69. *Ibid.*, May 7, 1863.
70. *Ibid.*, and many other issues of the newspaper.

tion of First Communion and weddings. These and other like things, although not essential to Catholic faith and life, foster piety and are so dear and sacred to the faithful that not without great danger could they be taken away from them.[71]

Despite their diversity in those practices "not essential to Catholic faith and life," the Irish and German Catholics shared a common religion and exhibited a similar spirituality. This spirituality may be briefly summed up in the axiom of the Tridentine Counter-Reform period: the salvation of souls is the supreme law.[72] In both communities great stress was placed on the salvation of the individual, and there was little trace of the social gospel at this time. One aspect of their spirituality which clearly highlighted the salvation of the individual was the extraordinary emphasis placed on the sacrament of penance and the confession of sins. In a description of one sermon given in a New York church it was said that the preacher stressed the suffering of Christ in his passion and death, and "he portrayed with such practical conclusions the Scourging, the Crowning with thorns, the Crucifixion; and he dwelt especially on the desolation of Christ, 'My God, why hast thou forsaken me'; . . . He drew as conclusions: (1.) That we must never commit another mortal sin which would alone crucify Jesus. (2.) We must suffer patiently as Christ suffered."[73] The sermon was delivered to a packed church in such a way that "one woman began to cry aloud, twenty others joined in as a chorus; and the whole congregation showed similar symptoms when the preacher said: 'Don't cry now but cry at your confession: then bewail your sins.' . . ."[74]

More than anything else this emphasis on confession stands out as a dominant feature of religious life among the Catholics, and especially among the Irish. They conceived themselves to be sinners in the sight of God, and each serious sin only added to their own misery. Confession was a momentary relief from this consciousness of guilt and its practice was widely encouraged. Such a spirituality of personal misery over sin as well as a patient endurance of suffering in imitation of the suffering Jesus did not conflict with the style of life in the urban neighborhood. On the contrary, for the immigrant Catholic miserable living conditions were more a state of life than a gross injustice to the pilgrim sinner, and such poverty and misery were a condition to be endured patiently in imitation of the suffering Jesus.[75]

Preaching was highly esteemed by both groups and the principal sermon on Sunday was delivered at the Solemn Mass at 10:30 A.M. The sermons not only emphasized the necessity of personal conversion from sin, but they also tended to be heavily apologetical. They would often focus on the antiquity of the Roman Catholic Church and its progress through the centuries as well as its contributions to ages past. A quotation from Scripture frequently opened the sermon, and other quotations from the Scriptures and the Church Fathers were scattered throughout the talk.[76] The sermons were long, sometimes an hour or more, and it was said that "the people . . . seem to be accustomed to long sermons; one

71. Barry, *The Catholic Church*, p. 294.
72. Pier G. Camiani, "Interpretazioni della Riforma Cattolica e della Controriforma," *Grande Antologia Filosofica* (Milan, 1964), 6, pp. 452-53.
73. AANY, Burtsell Diary, November 18, 1867.
74. *Ibid.*
75. James E. Roohan discusses the attitude of Catholics toward poverty in his work "American Catholics and the Social Question," (Unpublished Ph.D. dissertation, Yale University, 1952).
76. Examples of such sermons may be found in *Truth Teller*, February 22, 1834, December 21, 1839, and October 1, 1842.

can hardly be long enough."[77] A twenty-minute sermon was considered a short sermon.[78]

Indicative of the type of spirituality encouraged at this time were the sermon books used by priests. One such book, available to the New York priests, was written by William Gahan (1730-1804), an Irish Augustinian priest, in the last quarter of the eighteenth century. By 1847 the book had gone through six editions in Ireland, and its popularity necessitated an American edition.[79] Another source book used by some New York priests was the collection of sermons delivered by the Italian Bishop, Cornelio Musso (1511-1574), in the reform period of the sixteenth century.[80] Both books were remarkably similar in their content and style, and both collections reflected a spirituality very much in harmony with the Counter-Reform motto that the salvation of souls was the highest law. In the words of Father Gahan,

To save your souls, my brethren, is the capital point for you. As for the rest, though you should be reduced to the lowest condition; though you should live here in sufferings, in misery, and contempt; though you should be stripped of all your worldly possessions; though you should be without succors, without friends, accused, condemned and persecuted as the scorn and outcast of men —all this is nothing if you arrive at length at the happy term of salvation, because you will then find a glory that will amply idemnify you for all the disgraces of the world, a glory infinite, a glory immortal, a glory without end. You will then find a treasure which will amply indemify you for all the miseries of the world; for you will possess God Himself, who will be your treasure—an inexhaustible treasure in the kingdom of heaven.[81]

With the promise of such rewards, life in the tenement-house culture took on an entirely different meaning.

Despite the lofty ideals offered by the preachers in their sermons, both groups were vulnerable to a degree of religious indifference. A modern novelist's description of Sunday morning in an Irish apartment in nineteenth-century New York included the following dialogue between a mother and her rebellious son:

"Ye coming with me to mass?" his mother said.

"I was to mass Easter."

"An' won't be again till Easter next," she said.[82]

The mother lost the contest and the son did not go to church that Sunday. This attitude of indifference towards the church, fictionalized in the novel Casey, was present among both the Irish and German Catholics in New York. It is difficult, and perhaps impossible, to assess accurately the religious indifference of the Catholic immigrants in the city. Archbishop Hughes, along with many of his contemporaries, readily acknowledged that the church did not reach the entire Catholic community.[83] The Catholic press publicly admitted that "thousands of Catholics seldom if ever attend Mass,"[84] and a New York priest stated that nine-

77. Thomas Meehan, "Notes and Comments," *U. S. Catholic Historical Society Records and Studies*, 10 (January 1917), 184-85.
78. AANY, Burtsell Diary, June 17, 1866.
79. William Gahan, O.S.A., *Sermons for Every Sunday in the Year and for the Leading Holidays of Obligation*. Rev. ed. (New York: P. J. Kenedy, 1895); see also Leslie Stephen and Sidney Lee, eds., *The Dictionary of National Biography* (London: Oxford University Press, 1917), 7, p. 800.
80. *Prediche del Reverendiss. Monsig. Cornelio Musso* (Vinegia: Gabriel Giolito de Ferrari, 1560); see also *Enciclopedia Cattolica* (Citta del Vaticano, 1952), 8, col. 1564-65; reference to both sermon books was made in the Burtsell Diary, March 4, 1866.
81. Gahan, *Sermons*, p. 254.
82. Ramona Stewart, *Casey* (Boston: Little, Brown and Co., 1968), p. 37.
83. Lawrence Kehoe, ed., *Complete Works of the Most Rev. John Hughes D.D.* (New York: Lawrence Kehoe, 1865), 2, p. 693.
84. *Freeman's Journal*, April 5, 1851.

teen out of twenty of his sick calls involved people "who, for years, have been away from the church."[85]

One of the principal causes given for this low level of church attendance was the lack of a sufficient number of churches in the city. The United States Census in 1860 listed sittings for 54,426 people in the city's thirty Roman Catholic churches.[86] This was an average capacity of 1,814 people for each church which appears to be highly unlikely given the small size of most churches at this time. Taking into consideration the scheduled number of Masses offered in the city on a given Sunday and the average seating capacity of the churches as estimated by the census, as well as the estimated Catholic population of 250,000 people, the best conclusion one can arrive at is that approximately sixty-five percent of the Catholics in New York would have been able to attend church on a given Sunday in 1860.[87] This was the maximum possibility which is based on two very fragile hypotheses—that each Mass was filled to capacity and that there were 54,426 sittings in the Catholic churches.

This figure of approximately sixty-five percent of the community attending church on Sunday is very close to an estimate of sixty-six percent given in 1865 by the religious journal, *Catholic World*.[88] Both estimates were based on the maximum possible attendance, and for this reason the real figure would have been considerably lower. In 1867 a New York priest, Father Richard Burtsell, estimated that the Catholic churches in New York could accommodate 160,000 people at Sunday Mass.[89] If one takes as the size of the Catholic population at this time the conservative figure of 350,000, then the churches under the best of circumstances could accommodate about forty-six percent of the community.

From these figures one conclusion stands out. Under the best of circumstances only forty-six to sixty-six percent of the Catholic population were able to attend church on Sunday. These figures not only minimize the level of religious practice in the 1860s, but they also illustrate the inability of the church to keep up with the rapid increase in population. The important fact is not, as it is always mentioned, that the churches were always crowded, but that they were so inadequate to the needs of the large Catholic population. This situation was convincingly described by Father Burtsell who stated that no more than six thousand out of an estimated 20,000 Catholics (that is, thirty percent) in the parish of Immaculate Conception on East Fourteenth Street were able to squeeze into the church on Sunday at the five Masses offered that day.[90]

Another cause given for the low level of church attendance, and one which was less frequently noted, was the infidelity of the people. Not a few Catholics agreed with the opinion of one New York Catholic that religion had "little influence on the lower classes of the Catholic Church."[91] To overcome this situation more than church buildings was needed, and one attempt at evangelizing the unchurched population of New York was the parish mission. The parish mission

85. *Freeman's Journal*, April 14, 1866.
86. *U. S. Census, Statistics of the U. S. in 1860*, Part II, p. 433.
87. Browne, "The Archdiocese of New York a Century Ago," p. 157; the number of Masses on Sunday in each parish varied from as many as five to as few as two and the average number was three. See *Metropolitan Catholic Almanac and Laity's Directory 1860* (Baltimore: John Murphy and Co., 1860), pp. 136-38.
88. "Religion . . . in New York," *Catholic World*, 3 (June 1866), 386-87.
89. AANY, Burtsell Diary, January 14, 1867.
90. *Ibid.*, June 22, 1865.
91. *Ibid.*, February 22, 1865.

had long been a tradition in Europe and its use was encouraged in the United States. Even though the parish mission was both a rural and an urban phenomenon, it was thought to have a special relevance to the city. In the opinion of one Catholic revivalist "the great need for missions lay in the cities and large towns, where dense masses of Catholics were gathered, and where churches, clergy and religious organizations of all kinds were inadequate to the spiritual wants of the people."[92]

The mission was primarily intended for those least influenced by the ordinary ministry of the parish clergy, and it was stated that "more than one-half of the people at a mission would be persons who had not been at confession for five, ten, or twenty years, and of these a great number had seldom been at church, and still more rarely heard a sermon."[93] The parish mission was conducted by a special group of intinerant preachers, generally belonging to one of the religious orders. One priest described them as "independent revival preachers,"[94] and their similarity to the Protestant revivalists was not unfounded. The missions were held in both Irish and German parishes and lasted anywhere from eight to sixteen days depending on the size of the parish. They began early in the morning and ended early in the evening.[95]

The selection of topics treated in the mission sermons illustrate the three main purposes of the revival—conversion, perseverance and instruction. In one handbook on parish missions, written by one of the outstanding Redemptorist preachers at mid-century, the list of sermons offered for a short mission indicates the issues that were emphasized by the preachers.[96] After an introductory sermon, the preacher treated the following topics in order: the importance of salvation, mortal sin, sacrilegious confession, the sinner's death, general judgment, hell, the passion and death of Christ, protection of the Blessed Virgin Mary, delay of conversion, drunkenness and impurity, and finally the chief means of perseverance. In conducting these parish missions it was advised that unlike the custom in Europe, theatrical performances should be avoided.[97] The reason given was that such performances "would only excite the ridicule of the people."[98]

Despite this admonition some preachers were known for their flamboyance and theatrical display. One such occasion was the sermon on death, at which time a catafalque, surrounded by lighted candles, was placed in a conspicuous spot in the church to dramatize the theme of the sermon. The atmosphere was further enhanced by a mournful rendition of the *De Profundis*.[99] How successful the missions were in reaching the unchurched population is difficult to determine, but the judgment of the chronicler of Holy Redeemer parish sheds some light on the question. Speaking about the 600 youths who attended a parish mission in 1853, he sadly noted that many "were not found among the sheep of Christ" a few years later.[100]

92. A. S. Hewit, *Sermons of the Rev. Francis A. Baker, C.P.S. with a Memoir of His Life.* 6th ed. (New York: The Catholic Publication House, 1865), p. 122.
93. *Ibid.*, p. 125.
94. AANY, Burtsell Diary, November 24, 1867.
95. Wissel, *The Redemptorist on the American Mission*, Vol. I, is devoted entirely to a description of parish missions; see also AUND, *Scritture Riferite nei Congressi: America Centrale dal Canada all'istmo di Panama*, Vol. 19, letter 1841, Rev. Isaac Hecker to Prefect of Propaganda Fide, June 26, 1861, f. 229-230.
96. Wissel, *The Redemptorist on the American Mission*, 1, p. 58; 1, pp. 323-403.
97. *Ibid.*, 1, p. 53.
98. *Ibid.*, 1, p. 114.
99. *Ibid.*
100. Wuest, *Annales*, 2, p. 262.

There is no doubt that the parish missions attracted many people, and such success, however temporary it might have been, manifested the vitality of urban Catholicism. The active parochial life, the establishment of a parochial school system, the building of numerous churches and the organization of hospitals and orphanages all exhibited a vibrant church life. Within one generation the German Catholics had founded eight churches in the city, an orphanage, a hospital, a newspaper, numerous vereins, several parochial schools, a high school for boys and an academy for girls. Such achievements were not the result of failure, but signs of successful adaptation to the urban frontier. The accomplishments of the Irish were no less extraordinary. Protestant ministers recognized this achievement and praised the Catholic Church for its ability to minister to the rich and poor alike.[101] The low percentage of Catholics attending church on Sunday in the 1860s compared very favorably with twentieth-century figures.[102] And despite the unknown numbers of those who abandoned the church, without the persistent efforts of the church in New York the loss would undoubtedly have been greater.

The one institution that in large part enabled the Roman Catholic religion to be maintained in the city was the parish. For the immigrant Catholics the ethnic parish, in the words of a Catholic newcomer, gave them the opportunity "to unite to pray and worship the Lord and preserve . . . intact the rites as transmitted to them by their ancestors."[103] This was the genius of Catholicism in America. It was able to meet the religious needs of various ethnic groups and from this variety it forged a unity which enabled the church to survive in its new environment. The diversity of city life and a common religious heritage furnished the hammer and anvil by which the unity of American Catholicism was forged, and the success of the church in the city was the measure of its achievement in the nation.

101. AANY, Burtsell Diary, November 24, 1867; "Religion in New York," *Catholic World*, 8, pp. 381-85.
102. Houtart, "A Sociological Study . . . ," pp. 81ff., discusses the question of attendance at Sunday Mass in the U.S. and a report for the Diocese of New York in 1954 which concludes that about thirty percent of the Catholic population attended Mass on a given Sunday.
103. AUND, *Scritture Riferite nei Congressi: America Centrale dal Canada all'istmo di Panama*, Vol. 18, letter 1701, Petition of Italians to Archbishop John Hughes, August 16, 1860, f. 1522.

BOTH POLISH AND CATHOLIC:
IMMIGRANT CLERGY IN THE AMERICAN CHURCH

BY

WILLIAM GALUSH*

In 1902 Father Stanislaus Nawrocki wrote of his peers in America: "In addition to their heavy clerical obligations, [they] must function as collectors, builders, contractors, bankers, judges, teachers, accountants, organizers, etc. . . . "[1] Busy men in burgeoning parishes, they found America as novel as did their lay countrymen. Dwelling in ethnic enclaves lacking the accustomed secular leadership provided at home by the nobility and intelligentsia, immigrant clergy went beyond their spiritual role to assist the largely peasant newcomers in other aspects of existence.[2] Persons of high status in the old country observed this process with some regret, seeing it as giving a clerical cast to the Polish-American community.[3] The slow growth of a better-educated and more assertive lay elite, including some articulate anticlericals, came to offer alternative

---

*Mr. Galush is an assistant professor of history in Loyola University of Chicago.

[1] *Naród Polski* [*Polish Nation*, Chicago], April 30, 1902, p. 1; see also January 20, 1904, p. 2.

[2] The clergy always figure in any broad study of Poles in America, as well as works focused on religion among these immigrants. There is a common perception of the centrality of the priests in the homeland village and in the new land, often including examples of enlarged roles here. The tendency has been to examine individuals, or clergy acting together on specific issues, rather than their efforts at organizational formation and the mechanisms to attain it. This essay is an effort to initiate such an investigation.

For representative comments on clerical roles, see Daniel Buczek, *Immigrant Pastor: The Life of the Right Reverend Monsignor Lucyan Bójnowski of New Britain, Connecticut* (Waterbury, Connecticut, 1974), pp. i, 141; Victor Greene, *For God and Country: The Rise of Polish and Lithuanian Ethnic Consciousness in America, 1860-1910* (Madison, 1975), pp. 26-27; Edward Kantowicz, *Polish-American Politics in Chicago, 1888-1940* (Chicago, 1975), pp. 30-31; and Anthony Kuzniewski, S.J., *Faith and Fatherland: The Polish Church War in Wisconsin, 1896-1918* (Notre Dame, Indiana, 1980), p. 13.

[3] *Przegląd Emigracyjny* [*Emigration Review*, Lwów], July 1, 1982, pp. 3-4. Cf. Charles Morley (ed.), *Portrait of America: Letters of Henry Sienkiewicz* (New York, 1959), pp. 272, 282 and passim for similar observations in the late 1870's.

sources of information and leadership to the masses. Simultaneously the priests had to deal with unfamiliar non-Polish religious superiors whose concerns were indifferent or even hostile to ethnicity.[4] Challenges from different sides, as well as a natural inclination for companionship and support from persons of similar calling, prompted the scattered missionaries to form clerical associations, which in turn formulated and promoted common goals. Inevitably this process included conflict as well as co-operation.[5] But the priests successfully combined loyalty to Roman Catholicism in the new land with a strong retention of Polishness (*Polskość*) to pursue religious and ethnic goals. Before World War I they pragmatically allied with either bishops or laity as specific issues dictated, in the process developing greater group consciousness and organizational solidarity.

The background of the immigrant clergy conditioned their interaction with American Catholicism. As Oscar Handlin has observed, Roman Catholicism is "... universal rather than national in organization, and catholic in essential dogma, [yet] it nevertheless partook of the quality of men who professed it . . . ."[6] Poles accepted Latin Christianity near the beginning of their national existence, and after the partitions of the late eighteenth century the Church was the only institution transcending the borders of the conquering powers. The Polish clergy nurtured a rudimentary national consciousness through persistent use of their native tongue for preaching and teaching. In the Russian and German partitions official efforts to stifle Polishness prompted many clergymen to defend their cultural and national as well as religious heritage.[7] Austria-Hungary, a Catholic power, combined Josephinist state control and demands for dynastic loyalty with increasing toleration of nationalistic activity by the late nineteenth century. Some

---

[4]See Richard Linkh, *American Catholicism and European Immigrants, 1900-1924* (New York, 1975), pp. 4-8, 22-28, 44; James Moynihan, *The Life of Archbishop John Ireland* (New York, 1953), pp. 54-78.

[5]Conflict need not be viewed solely as a negative phenomenon. Lewis Coser argues persuasively that some conflict can aid the formation and persistence of groups, with struggle for a supra-individual cause conferring a respectability of acting in a representative role rather than simply promoting self-interest. In the end conflict might modify or create new rules of behavior, form new structures, or at least make the participants conscious of rules dormant before the conflict. These observations have relevance to such issues as trusteeism and the quest for a Polish-American bishop. See Lewis Coser, *The Functions of Social Conflict* (New York, 1964), pp. 31, 114-115, 121-128.

[6]Oscar Handlin, *Boston's Immigrants* (New York, 1968), p. 128.

[7]Aleksander Gieysztor, *History of Poland* (Warsaw, 1968), pp. 533-540; Norman Davies, *God's Playground: A History of Poland* (New York, 1982), II, 209-217.

priests here felt their Galician brethren were seduced into support for the Hapsburgs by subsidy and permissiveness.[8] With some variation the priesthood was an object of official pressure in all the Polish lands.

In addition to the state, there were three other sources of influence upon the priest. A declining but long-standing one was the patron, often a noble, whose familial generosity had purchased certain privileges in the endowed parish.[9] Another factor was the general laity, traditionally passive and ill-organized, but occasionally aroused and clamorous.[10] Finally there was the religious superior, usually a bishop and in any case a Polish-speaker.[11] This pattern of pressures changed significantly in the American environment, the locale for increasing numbers of clerics after the Civil War.

Movement of Poles to the United States in numbers sufficient to hinder rapid assimilation began in the 1850's but reached the scale of thousands per year only in the 1870's.[12] The newcomers were overwhelmingly peasants, whose lives took meaning from the soil, family, and faith. Seeking familiarity amidst strangeness, they clustered in colonies, first rural but increasingly in urban settings. The first settlement was Panna

[8]*Ibid.*, p. 209; *Polak w Ameryce* [*The Pole in America*, Buffalo], March 1, 1897, p. 1; March 4, 1897, p. 1.

[9]Patronage *(patronat)* in Poland was a traditional and canonically sanctioned arrangement, as elsewhere in Catholic Europe, but subject to varying state regulation in the partition period. See "Poland," *Catholic Encyclopedia* (New York, 1913), XII, 187-192; "Patronage," *ibid.*, XI, 560-562; "Patronat w Polsce" ["Patronage in Poland"], *Encyklopedja Kościelna* [Church Encyclopedia] (Warsaw, 1892), XVIII, 380-399. Patrons could still exercise the right of presentation of candidates in Galicia at the turn of the century, but the government could reject the nominee. See *Polak w Ameryce*, March 4, 1897, p. 1. By the eve of the war the authorities were allegedly considering widening the right of presentation to include the generality of parishioners. *Kuryer Polski* [*The Polish Courier*, Milwaukee], September 26, 1913, p. 4.

[10]William I. Thomas and Florian Znaniecki, *The Polish Peasant in Europe and America* (New York, 1958), I, 143 and 275.

[11]The religious authority structure in Poland was more elaborate than in the contemporary United States. In addition to bishops, secular clergy were subordinate to active "deans," priests with limited supervisory power over others in their vicinity. Moreover, the proportionately greater number of clergy meant that more were assistants, unlike America where the shortage of Polish priests meant a rapid rise to a pastorate. For comparative comments, see *Naród Polski* [*The Polish Nation*, Chicago], May 14, 1902, p. 1.

[12]Victor Greene," Pre-World War I Polish Emigration to the United States: Motives and Statistics," *Polish Review*, VI (Summer, 1961), 46-47; Jerzy Zubrycki, "Emigration from Poland in the Nineteenth and Twentieth Centuries," *Population Studies*, VI (March, 1953), 248-272.

Maria in Texas, led by Father Leopold Moczygemba. Beginning in 1854, he drew entire families from Silesia into a very different rural environment. The unsuccessful uprising of 1863, the *Kulturkampf* of the next decade in German Poland, and poverty in general drove swelling thousands to seek a new life in America, where most settled in the industrializing northeast quarter of the nation.[13] With them came a few men in black: Polish priests going to the missions across the sea.

The United States offered several novelties of particular interest to these immigrant clerics. Here the state stood aloof from religion, protecting a *laissez-faire* competition which seemed to foster denominational anarchy but gave a greater boon—no government control. A necessary consequence was less easily assimilated: solicitation of voluntary contributions from the laity. Priests accustomed to endowments and government subsidies were unfamiliar with stimulating many small donations. In the course of years they developed the necessary skills and instilled the appropriate habits in their parishioners. Prior to World War I, however, there was an annual assessment or pew rental which constituted the largest single source of income in many parishes. While in Chicago and perhaps elsewhere the collector was a priest, laymen often performed this function.[14] They easily equated this with collection of dues for fraternal insurance societies, and the aid from laity with basic business experience fostered the proliferation of parish committees. Assistance in parochial administration implied to some laymen that they might have rights as well as obligations.

In terms of the schema noted above, the sources of pressure on the clergy were halved. Bishops and laity alone remained. Yet there was novelty here as well. Intellectually the priests had realized that their new superiors would be non-Poles, but the actual experience too often was unhappy. They found some bishops of German extraction, whose background was familiar if not beloved. New were the ubiquitous Irish-Americans, whose intense Catholicism became less attractive as closer contact revealed many to be assimilationists. Multi-lingual Polish priests found them insular, and difficulties of communication fostered some mistrust on both sides. The

[13]Caroline Golab offers a useful discussion of the settlement patterns of Poles and other European immigrants in *Immigrant Destinations* (Philadelphia, 1977).

[14]For Chicago, the largest Polish-American center, see Edward Kantowicz, *Corporation Sole: Cardinal Mundelein and Chicago Catholicism* (Notre Dame, Indiana, 1983), p. 69; for the lay role in several cities, see William Galush, "Forming Polonia: A Study of Four Polish-American Communities, 1890-1940" (unpublished Ph.D. dissertation, University of Minnesota, 1975), pp. 95-97, 156-158; *Zgoda,* January 19, 1905, p. 2.

outcome, while not inevitable, was ethnic segregation in a Church reluctant to acknowledge its pluralism, with a tiny fraction passing into outright rebellion.[15]

The Polish-American laity was surprising as well. They were mainly ex-peasants, with the rustic manners and speech of their relatives at home; yet they were different. They had removed themselves from the stultifying grip of village society, with its conservatism and fatalism. Though they participated in America overwhelmingly at its lower levels, they were absorbing new values of optimism, activism, and individualism.[16] They joined these to the thrift and fortitude of their ancestral culture to begin a slow but steady improvement of their material condition.[17] These immigrants formed a more familiar environment through residential concentration, and within these urban villages they wove a dense web of supportive institutions. The most widespread form of voluntary association was the fraternal insurance society, probably patterned after similar bodies seen among neighboring older ethnic groups. Most newcomers retained their Catholicism, but worship among Irish, Germans, or even Bohemians was less comforting than the ways of home. They sought the familiar forms of Polish Catholicism, and for that they needed a Polish priest. An immigrant cleric found a warm welcome in a developing colony.

Central to the enclave was a Polish parish. Congregational formation was common here, a striking difference from the homeland where parishioners worshiped in a church whose existence seemed to transcend time. Most often concerned laymen democratically chose a committee to collect funds, buy land, and construct an edifice. At the inception, or sometimes later, a Polish priest entered the process, and ultimately the bishop had to designate a pastor and dedicate the church.[18] The participation in the foundation, and usually in subsequent administration, inflated lay aspirations regarding control of the parish.

[15] Anthony Kuzniewski offers a suggestive interpretation of the alternatives for Poles and the American Catholic Church in "Wenceslaus Kruszka and the Fight for a Polish Bishop," Working Paper — Notre Dame Seminar, 1977; also *Faith and Fatherland*, pp. 124-128 and passim.

[16] Thomas and Znaniecki, *op. cit.*, I, 89-97 on Poland, pp. 98-104 on attitudinal changes in the United States; Father Anthony Gorski also noted the greater independence of Poles here. See *Naród Polski*, May 14, 1902, p. 1.

[17] Galush, *op. cit.*, pp. 106-136 and 267-280 for occupational and other mobility.

[18] *Ibid.*, pp. 82-105; see also John Gallagher, *A Century of History: The Diocese of Scranton, 1868-1968* (Scranton, 1968), pp. 156-171 for occasionally more extreme examples of lay assertiveness in the anthracite region, and the representative contemporary account of a New York parish in *Naród Polski*, January 20, 1904, p. 2.

The parish was the largest and most important local institution, but it was just that — local. Immigrant clergy saw themselves as nurturing Polishness, but the formulation and promotion of ethnicity could be more efficiently sponsored at a level above the congregation. Since the diocese was indisputably in non-Polish hands, clerical patriots sought a vehicle which could foster religion and ethnicity while remaining under Polish control. They chose the fraternal aid federation. In so choosing, they created a means for exceptional priests to exercise influence far beyond their parochial borders.

The process began in the 1870's, when Poles were yet relatively few in number and uninclined to make demands on the American episcopate, The concrete expression of this desire for supra-parochial organization was the Polish Roman Catholic Union (Zjednoczenie Polskie Rzymsko-Katolickie), initiated by Father Theodore Gieryk, a secular priest, in 1873. He was soon joined by the Resurrectionist Vincent Barzynski and his lay brother John, editor of *Pielgrzym (The Pilgrim)*, who ardently supported the project in his newspaper. The involvement of the energetic and assertive Father Barzynski significantly altered the membership philosophy of the proposed federation. While Gieryk wanted the Union open to all who felt themselves Polish, Barzynski successfully pressed for a narrower basis: Poles who professed the Roman Catholic faith. The Resurrectionist triumphed and the PRCU emerged under the slogan "Bóg i Ojczyzna" (God and Fatherland).[19]

The constitution of the Union called for the maintenance of the holy faith, mutual aid, and cultural improvement.[20] Article III required members to revere their priests and obey their bishops, among other items on religion and discipline. Article XI enjoined commemoration of two nationalistic holidays. Religion and patriotism went hand in hand, and prior to 1880 several priests served as presidents, while Barzynski cast his shadow over PRCU headquarters from his immense parish a few blocks away.[21]

Despite the clerical presence, the PRCU was mainly lay in leadership and overwhelmingly so in membership, and as a democratic organization necessarily catered to its major constituency. Clerical contacts had

---

[19]Mieczysław Haiman, *Zjednoczenie Polskie Rzymsko-Katolickie w Ameryce, 1873-1948 [The Polish Roman Catholic Union of America]* (Chicago, 1948), pp. 23-42.

[20]*Gazeta Polska Katolicka [The Polish Catholic Gazette*, Chicago], May 20, 1875, p. 3.

[21]Haiman, *op. cit.*, pp. 54-55; Greene, *For God and Country*, pp. 75-77, 85-89.

increased through the formation of the Union, and with it the perception that their distinctive status would be best served by an exclusive society. In 1875, under the leadership of Father Barzynski, some priests in Illinois and states east formed the Association of Polish Roman Catholic Priests in the United States (Tow. Księży Rzymsko-Katolickich Polskich w Stanach Zjednoczonych). Its stated goals were the fostering of clerical unity, assisting American bishops, avoiding giving scandal to the faithful, and guiding the laity.[22] The aims indicated both difficulties and aspirations. Scattered widely and as yet few in number, these clerical immigrants consciously sought to promote discipline and concord amidst strangeness and heavy burdens. The passage of years brought increasing confidence and other aims, though the original goals proved difficult to meet. By 1887 the group numbered thirty, and Barzynski brought it into the Polish Roman Catholic Union as a member lodge, symbolic of priestly approval of the federation.[23]

Barzynski might well have felt the need to strengthen the Union, for the 1880's opened with a challenge to the clerical definition of ethnicity.[24] A well-publicized plea from the noted patriot in Swiss exile, Agaton Giller, catalyzed discontent with the PRCU and led several prominent laymen to form the Polish National Alliance (Związek Narodowy Polski) in 1880. This new fraternal federation took in all who declared themselves Poles, regardless of religion. Non-believers and Jews thus could join, though the vast majority of members were Roman Catholics. The Alliance was exclusively lay-led, but despite Catholic criticism its alleged anticlericalism was occasional rather than consistent, varying largely by the personal inclinations of national officers. It soon attracted some priests, notably Fathers Dominic Majer of St. Paul and Constantine Domagalski of Cincinnati, with most from Minnesota and Wisconsin. Perhaps more significantly, all were diocesan clergy, unlike the mixture of seculars and

[22]John Iwicki, C.R., *The First Hundred Years: A Study of the Apostolate of the Congregation of the Resurrection in the United States, 1866-1966* (Rome, 1966), p. 239. For regional origins, see Haiman, *op. cit.,* pp. 83-84.

[23]Iwicki, *op. cit.,* p. 240. The clerical association's constitution also called for support of Polish parochial education and the encouragement of a Polish Catholic press. The former was so generally accepted by the laity that it never became an issue before 1914, while the latter was vague and in practice was left almost entirely to lay initiative.

[24]For perceptive comments on the role of the ethnic elite in formulating group goals, see Philip Gleason, "The Crisis of Americanization" in Gleason (ed.) *Contemporary Catholicism in the United States* (Notre Dame, Indiana, 1969), pp. 3-32.

Resurrectionists in the PRCU lodge.[25] They were more sympathetic to the Jagiellonian spirit of the PNA, hearkening back to a Polish state of many nations and creeds. Soon Father Barzynski led what came to be termed the "Union" priests in denunciations of the so-called "Alliance" clergy.[26] In March of 1887 the Alliance priests were driven to a collective affirmation:

> ... we, the undersigned, all have Alliance groups in our parishes, and they are truly ornaments of our parishes, and the same as church brotherhoods. They are practicing Catholics . . . .
> ... We see the Polish National Alliance as a very noble institution for our nationality and our people.[27]

The pro-Catholic editor of *Zgoda (Harmony)*, the PNA organ, supported the Alliance priests through articles affirming the federation's essential Catholicism and cited approval by various bishops.[28] Not only did this avail nothing with the Unionist critics, but the clerics in the Alliance were conditional in their support. Their commitment was contingent on a continuing perception of the PNA as basically Catholic.

The national Alliance convention of 1889 shattered clerical confidence. In an atmosphere of episcopal fears of secret societies and radicalism, the priests had successfully demanded the expulsion of a socialist-inclined lodge the year before. Now Fathers Majer and Domagalski led an effort to oust socialists and other undesirables throughout the federation. The attempt failed in a stormy confrontation, and the clergy and some laymen quit the PNA, opening the way for the election of anticlerical officers and editor.[29] Rivalries of personality more than principle disinclined the

---

[25]The PNA-affiliated priests called themselves the Society of Polish Priests (Stowarzyszenie Księży Polskich) and their membership included no regulars. See *Zgoda* [*Harmony*, Chicago], March 2, 1887, p. 2. The Resurrectionists then and later were portrayed by their lay and clerical critics as aggressive, intriguing, or at least pursuing interests specific to their order. These perceptions, coupled with other factors operating after 1890, led to a decline in their influence among the clergy. Cf. *Zgoda*, February 9, 1887, p. 4; February 20, 1889, p. 1; August 6, 1896, p. 4; *Wiarus* [*The Veteran*, Winona, Minnesota], September 3, 1896, p. 1; Wenceslaus Kruszka, *Historja Polska w Ameryce od czasów najdawnejszych aż do najnowszych* [*A History of Poles in America from the Earliest to the Most Recent Times*] (Milwaukee, 1937), I, 720-722, 767-769.

[26]*Wiarus*, December 30, 1886, p. 1; *Zgoda*, February 9, 1887, p. 1; Haiman, *op. cit.*, pp. 79-84.

[27]*Zgoda*, March 2, 1887, p. 4.

[28]*Ibid.*, January 19, 1887, p. 4; February 20, 1889, p. 1; April 18, 1889, p. 1.

[29]*Ibid.*, September 18, 1889, p. 1; *Wiarus*, September 19, 1889, p. 1; see also Stanisław Osada, *Historia Związku Narodowego Polskiego* [*A History of the Polish National Alliance*] (Chicago, 1957), I, 285-296; Haiman, *op. cit.*, pp. 93-99.

former Alliance clergy from joining Barzynski's association, and after Father Majer established a new fraternal federation, the Polish Union of America (Unja Polska w Ameryce), most joined it in a clerical lodge.[30]

The 1890's saw a continuation of clerical division, much lamented by priests of the day.[31] In reality, they did come together for particular purposes, such as the Polish Emigration Society (Polskie Towarzysztwo Emigracyjny) to aid new immigrants or to organize the first Polish Catholic Congress in 1896.[32] Clergymen such as John Pitass of Buffalo, Vincent Barzynski of Chicago, and Jacob Pacholski of Minnesota might be in competing clerical societies, but they could co-operate in and even lead such special projects.[33] Yet being elected to a post in a Polish society did not have the same significance as priestly participation in their primary institutional affiliation: the Roman Catholic Church. As the Church was an authoritarian organization, with its major leaders being bishops consecrated in the apostolic succession, no elective office could equal the episcopate. This conception of rank gives added meaning to the quest for and subsequent role of Polish-American bishops.

[30] *Wiarus*, September 5, 1889, p. 7; *Naród Polski*, July 27, 1904, p. 5.

[31] E.g., Father Stanisław Radziejewski in *Kuryer Polski*, June 16, 1894, p. 3; "Father Marek" (pseud.) in *Gazeta Katolicka* [*The Catholic Gazette*, Chicago], February 2, 1899, p. 1.

[32] "Z Ameryki" ["In America"], *Niedziela* [*Sunday*, Detroit], January 23, 1896, pp. 61-62; "Sprawozdanie z przedkongresowej konferencyi odbytej dnia 11 czerwca b. r. w Detroit, Mich., w plebanii wielebnego ks. P. Gutowskiego" ["Report of the Pre-Congress Conference of June 11 in Detroit, Mich., in the Rectory of Father P. Gutowski"], *ibid.*, June 18, 1896, pp. 399-400.

[33] The first example refers to the effort to establish an immigrant home in New York City, and reasonably enough all priests save one were from seaboard states. While five were present or past members of the "Alliance" priests or its successor organization in the Polish Union of America, the affiliation status of the others is uncertain. It may be that the Alliance-Union conflict was seen by eastern priests as having a regional character in which they felt no need to choose sides.

The pre-congress conference is more significant since it involved issues of concern to all clergy. Excluding the few laymen, the fourteen clerics were evenly divided between seaboard and inland states, indicating an effort at regional balance. More importantly, at least four, including the chairman, John Pitass, and Dominic Majer, were of "Alliance" background while at least three, among them Vincent Barzynski, had "Union" roots.

For members of various clerical organizations, see Haiman, *op. cit.*, p. 83 ("Union"); *Zgoda*, March 2, 1887, p. 4 ("Alliance"); "Z Ameryki," *Niedziela*, September 24, 1893, p. 623 (Polish Union of America). While a suspicion of the Resurrectionists among many secular clergy may have given a vague ideological content to affiliation, I believe that most priests were moved by such factors as personal acquaintance, perceptions of relative status of competing societies or other idiosyncratic factors in choosing (or not choosing) to join.

The best example of lay-clerical alliance was the drive for representation in the American episcopate. In this instance religious desires for a proper leader were interwoven with ethnic concerns for recognition, but lay-oriented publicity was largely in the latter terms. The general (but not universal) desire of the clerics for bishops was the most important factor in consolidating them in a single dominant association.

Ironically in view of later developments, Father Barzynski seems to have been the first to write of the need for a Polish bishop. In 1870 he envisioned a Slavic Vicariate Apostolic whose bishop would be able to "speak, write, listen, and judge in Polish" and complained bitterly of neglect of these new immigrants.[34] Such concerns remained within clerical ranks for many years, but their saliency grew with the tide of Polish newcomers. In April of 1886 Father Ignatius Barszcz, a diocesan priest from New Jersey, brought it to the attention of the hierarchy in a letter to Bishop Richard Gilmour of Cleveland. He urged the desirability of a national leader of the Poles, though he ingenuously asserted that such a man would be a suffragan to Gilmour. Already suspicious of German-American Catholic efforts to alter their ecclesiastical status, the bishop was not sympathetic.[35] Submission of the Abbelen Memorial later that year and the subsequent Cahenslyist movement for ethnic hierarchies drew some Polish support. But the hostile reaction of the American bishops gave them pause, and Polish priests largely recast their hopes in terms of auxiliary bishops for existing dioceses. They also realized that priestly pressure was insufficient and began to enlist lay support.

The priests made adroit use of the ethnic press and techniques of organization honed as leaders of young and growing parishes. In 1888 Father Barszcz was able to advocate the creation of a separate diocese of SS. Cyril and Methodius in the secularist weekly *Gazeta Polska (The Polish Gazette)*, alerting the laity to the matter.[36] In 1891 Father John Machinowski sent a petition allegedly signed by 100,000 Poles to the Holy See advocating Polish-American bishops.[37] The public movement for

---

[34]Kruszka, *op. cit.*, I, 516.

[35]Father Ignatius Barszcz to Bishop Richard Gilmour, April 8, 1886, Archives of the Diocese of Cleveland; see also Colman J. Barry, O.S.B., *The Catholic Church and German-Americans* (Milwaukee, 1953), pp. 56-68.

[36]*Gazeta Polska [The Polish Gazette*, Chicago], March 1, 1888, p. 2.

[37]Joseph Swastek, "The Formative Years of the Polish Seminary in the United States," in *The Contribution of the Poles to the Growth of Catholicism in the United States,* edd. F. Domanski *et al. (Sacrum Poloniae Millennium,* Vol. VI [Rome, 1959]), p. 130.

bishops was promoted under the catchword "equality" *(równouprawnienie)*, a much more evocative term than possible alternatives such as "representation" *(representacja)*. Poles proud of their ethnicity but acutely conscious of their inferior status in the multi-national American Church found demands for parity rather than tokenism satisfying.

Priests leading the movement for an episcopal presence used the device of mixed lay-clerical conventions to publicize and co-ordinate the effort. The upsurge of independentism, embodied in several small but noisy "Polish Catholic" denominations, led loyal clergy to link equality with the fight against schism from about 1895.[38] The first Polish Catholic Congress was held in Buffalo in 1896, the stronghold of the redoubtable Father John Pitass. Reflecting clerical intent to involve the laity, topics included education and workers' concerns, but the main item was equality. Barzynski, reversing his position of 1870, moved for requesting a Polish advisor to the Apostolic Delegate.[39] As the second congress was to show more clearly, the clerics were dividing. The Resurrectionists were losing their enthusiasm for Polish-American bishops, while Pitass and other seculars, both "Union" and "Alliance," became increasingly supportive. Non-participants in the 1896 congress criticized it as unrepresentative and a vehicle for the ambitions of Pitass and Barzynski.[40] The lack of a mechanism to implement convention resolutions meant there was little concrete effect, but equality received much publicity in the ethnic press.

The next Polish Catholic Congress convened in a different environment. Father Vincent Barzynski had died in 1899, and with him passed much of the Resurrectionists' influence. Father Pitass, even more active than before, promoted Buffalo as the site and functioned as president of the congress. As an Ohio priest noted, planning and representation this time included the local PNA as well as Catholic fraternal lodges and parishes, with a wide range of topics for discussion.[41] Clerics chaired all seven

[38] Daniel Buczek, "Polish-Americans and the Roman Catholic Church," *Polish Review*, XXI, esp. 50-52; also *Naród Polski*, April 30, 1902, p. 1; for a general history of independentism, see Hieronim Kubiak, *The Polish National Catholic Church in the United States of America from 1897 to 1980* (Cracow, 1982).

[39] *Niedziela*, March 26, 1896, p. 208.

[40] As Joseph Parot notes, the congress movement has not yet been adequately studied, but he and others have information on it in works which have sections on the quest for bishops. See Joseph Parot, *Polish Catholics in Chicago, 1850-1920* (Dekalb, Illinois, 1981), pp. 133-160; Greene, *For God and Country*, pp. 122-142; Buczek, "Polish-Americans," pp. 50-54.

[41] *Dziennik Chicagoski* [*Chicago Daily News*, Chicago], April 21, 1901, p. 2. See also *ibid.*, September 30, 1901, p. 2.

committees save that on business.[42] Equality headed the agenda, but while laymen proved highly supportive, the clergy were divided. The "Union" priests were split since the Resurrectionists now openly opposed pressing for bishops. In an interview shortly before the congress convened, their Superior General, Paul Smolikowski, termed equality a challenge to the American hierarchy which would produce polemical ammunition for antireligious persons to set diocesan clergy against regulars and then against the bishops. He then went on to accuse Pitass of conniving to keep the Resurrectionists out of the congress.[43] Whatever the validity of the Resurrectionist's remarks, they were out of step with the desires of most priests and laity, and clerical societies thereafter were under secular domination. Naród Polski, organ of the PRCU, contended that the order was cool to equality since they already had a bishop in their general, and the congress went on to strongly urge the appointment of Polish-American bishops.[44] An executive committee was set up to implement convention resolutions and the congress voted to send a delegation to the Vatican to lobby for the cause.[45] In this context the leading promoter of the episcopal cause became Father Wenceslaus Kruszka of Wisconsin, a prolific author and independent and original thinker. After considerable difficulty, he went to Rome and pressed the pope on the matter, returning in 1904 in a mood of high optimism, which in the event proved premature.[46]

Improved clerical organization accompanied efforts for equality. In addition to the cleric-dominated executive committee, the diocesan clergy established the Secular Priests Society (Tow. Księży Świeckich) in 1902 in "defense of Polish clerical interests" and pointedly excluded the Resurrectionists.[47] Pleas to bishops for support for Polish episcopal

---

[42] Ibid., April 23, 1901, p. 2.; Wenceslaus Kruszka, Siedem siedmioleci czyli pół wieku życia [Forty-nine Years or a Half-Century of Life] (Milwaukee, 1924), I, 423-424.

[43] Dziennik Chicagoski, September 30, 1901, p. 2. So distressed was the editor of the paper, Resurrectionist in origin, that he appended a long statement asserting his independence from the congregation. Congress coverage was in fact extensive and reasonably objective.

[44] Naród Polski, May 7, 1902, p. 4.

[45] Dziennik Chicagoski, September 30, 1901, p. 2; October 1, 1901, p. 2; Naród Polski, January 8, 1902, p. 1.

[46] The career of this fascinating and maverick cleric has been best studied by A. Kuzniewski for the period of this essay. Kuzniewski rightly stresses the theological basis of Kruszka's call for polyglot bishops over Greene's more secular interpretation. See Kuzniewski, Faith and Fatherland, esp. pp. 45-46; Greene, For God and Country, esp. pp. 133-134.

[47] Dziennik Chicagoski, February 7, 1902, p. 2; Greene, For God and Country, p. 132.

representation aroused little interest or ineffective agreement prior to the last congress in 1904.[48]

The third and last Polish Catholic Congress was held in 1904 and imitated its predecessor. It originated through the secular clergy and convened in Pittsburgh to discuss a wide variety of topics. Father Kruszka, having recently returned from Rome, gave an optimistic report on prospects for at least one bishop.[49] Press coverage was again generous, and clerics and supportive laymen looked with hope to the future, but action did not soon follow words. The arrival of a papal investigator, Archbishop Albin Symon, in mid-1905 aroused expectations once more. This was an ethnic event of the first magnitude, as the head of the third convention's executive committee, Father Casimir Truszynski, led Symon on a tour orchestrated by the Secular Priests Society.[50] Symon made his sympathy plain and once again hopes rose, only to subside with no concrete result.[51] Finally, in 1907 Archbishop James F. Quigley of Chicago, convinced of the necessity for a Polish auxiliary in the ethnic capital, applied successfully to Rome. He further earned the gratitude of his Chicago Polish priests by requesting them to nominate a candidate from their own ranks. They chose Paul Rhode, soft-spoken but determined and in accord with their view of the role of a Polish bishop in America.[52]

Rhode proved to be an excellent choice for the post. While maintaining good relations with his superior, he traveled widely and established himself in the long-awaited role of "moral guide to Poles in America."[53] If one bishop was hardly "equality," the immense publicity surrounding his installation and his subsequent active leadership satisfied most Poles. The clergy had successfully interested the religionist and even many secularist laity in an issue remote to them by framing the matter largely in ethnic terms. The long-divided priests had a more immediate interest in a leader of their own ancestry from a mixture of religious and ethnic motives. The

---

[48]*Naród Polski,* January 22, 1902, p. 1; May 22, 1902, p. 1.

[49]*Ibid.,* April 20, 1904, p. 2; April 27, 1904, p. 2 on clerical initiatives for a third congress; October 12, 1904, p. 4 for topics; Greene, *For God and Country,* pp. 136-138; Parot, *op. cit.,* pp. 152-153.

[50]*Naród Polski,* June 7, 1905, p. 1; June 14, 1905, p. 1.

[51]*Ibid.,* June 28, 1905, p. 5; July 12, 1905, p. 4.

[52]Greene, *For God and Country,* pp. 141-142; Parot, *op. cit.,* p. 158.

[53]Buczek, *Immigrant Pastor,* p. 72 for this description of Rhode in the 1920's. Numerous earlier references by clerics and Catholic laymen exist in the religionist Polish press. E.g., *Polak w Ameryce,* April 6, 1894, p. 1; *Dziennik Chicagoski,* September 13, 1901, p. 2; *Naród Polski,* September 10, 1902, p. 1.

incomparable status of the episcopal office conferred an authority unmatched by secular elections and brought with it the hope of unity and order long sought but hitherto unattainable. Recalling Rhode's installation, Edward Kozlowski, himself the second Polish auxiliary (1914-1915), put this perception of the new bishop's leadership role clearly:

> And I whispered to my colleagues seated around me: 'At long last we have a leader — we are assigned to him as a staff and officer corps and we owe him military obedience — and he will lead American Polonia to victory.'[54]

For the priests, and indirectly the laity, his national leadership took concrete shape with the formation of the Union of Polish Priests (Zjednoczenie Kapłanów Polskich) about 1911. Bishop Rhode became president by acclamation, and this was the largest of clerical societies, with some three hundred members spread across the nation.[55] It served as a forum to discuss issues of ethnic and religious importance and to frame common policy under Rhode's direction. While it depended on moral suasion rather than the force of canon law, it was the framework for a quasi-denomination for Poles in America.[56]

The quest for bishops coincided with a less dramatic effort to undergird an ethnic Catholicism: establishment and maintenance of a Polish

---

[54]Bishop Edward Kozlowski, "Postulaty naszego społczeństwa pod względem zachowania wiary św. naszego ludu" ["Postulates of our Society with Regard to the Preservation of the Holy Faith among our People"], Przegląd Kościelny [The Church Review, Chicago], II (May-June, 1915), 150.

[55]Ibid., p. 151 for membership. The article is a very suggestive survey of the quest for leadership and the nature of clerical and episcopal authority for the Polish clergy and for the generality of Poles in America.

[56]Kantowicz insightfully discusses the role of various ethnic "quasi-denominations" in his recent work, Corporation Sole, esp. pp. 71-72. See also Timothy Smith, "Religious Denominations as Ethnic Communities: A Regional Case Study," Church History, XXXV (June, 1966), 217-222 for such among Slovenes.

Listings of officials of the U.P.P. c. 1914 show how Rhode sought inclusivity for the new society. The sixteen directors were all seculars and evenly split between seaboard and inland states. While the officers were mainly from inland states, two of the six were Resurrectionists, including Joseph Weber of Chicago, who was named honorary president. Weber was titular Archbishop of Darnis and high in a society mistrusted by many secular priests. Already in his sixties, he arrived in Chicago only months before Rhode's selection as episcopal candidate, all of which seems to have prevented his assuming the role of national Polish religious leader. Given Parot's suggestion of Resurrectionist efforts to block Kruszka's mission, Weber's inclusion in the high council of the U.P.P. is a tribute to Rhode's diplomacy. See Parot, op. cit., pp. 154-155; "Zarząd Glowny Zjednoczenia Kaplanów Polskich w Ameryce Północnej" ["Central Board of the Union of Polish Priests in North America"], Przegląd Kościelny, II (January-February, 1915), 1.

seminary. This lacked the glamor of mitres, but many priests saw such an institution as essential for fostering Polish Catholicism here. In the face of episcopal apathy or hostility, and occasionally divided clerical ranks, concerned clergy mobilized the support of their colleagues and laity for the project.

The idea of an ethnic seminary was broached in 1869 by Father Joseph Dąbrowski (Dombrowski), a Polish missionary, who urged the Resurrectionists to undertake its foundation. Not only did they not do so, but Dąbrowski himself promoted it and became its first rector when it opened in 1886 as SS. Cyril and Methodius Seminary.[57] He and other advocates of the institution made a significant choice. They forsook the establishment of Polish programs at existing diocesan seminaries, an option open and even practiced occasionally in the eighties and nineties, to tread the path of separate development.[58] The ethnic advantage lay in greater control, and the promoters wanted a religionist institution — both Polish and Catholic. Bishop Caspar Borgess of Detroit was hospitable to the idea and the seminary was begun there.[59]

The seminary's early experience reflected the stresses of contemporary Polish-American society. Hardly was it founded when Union and Alliance priests contended for clerical and lay support, while Father Dąbrowski sought to maintain neutrality and to keep all sources of income open for the struggling institution.[60] For some years the secularist Polish National Alliance proved more willing to donate funds and scholarships than the religionist Polish Roman Catholic Union, and even after the 1889 PNA convention, money flowed to what Dąbrowski successfully portrayed as an ethnic as well as religious institution.[61] While the first Polish Catholic Congress included the seminary on its agenda, the school as an issue lacked

---

[57]Swastek, *op. cit.*, pp. 48-59, 72. His is the best work on the school.

[58]For examples of Polish student groups or special courses at diocesan seminaries, see *ibid.*, p. 95; *Wiarus*, November 9, 1906, p. 4. Clubs had irregular existence while courses depended on permission of local ordinaries.

[59]Swastek, *op. cit.*, pp. 59-60.

[60]*Ibid.*, pp. 88-89.

[61]*Ibid.*, pp. 95-99. Dąbrowski publicly thanked the Alliance for its support in *Zgoda*, February 22, 1893, p. 1. For general comments in 1911 in an official Alliance publication, see "Pamiętnik wzniesienia i odsłonięcia pomników Tadeusza Kościuski i Kazimierza Pułaskiego tudzież połączonego z tą uroczystocią pierwszego Kongresu Narodowego Polskiego" ["Memorial Book of the Erection and Unveiling of the Thaddeus Kosciuszko and Casimir Pulaski Monuments as well as the Occasion of the First Polish National Congress"] (Chicago, 1911), p. 22.

the breadth of clerical constituency enjoyed by equality, and its continuation was due to the persistence of a small number of concerned clergy.[62]

To improve its financial position and to enlarge the student body, there were curriculum innovations unthinkable in Poland: extensive business courses along with the theological program. In 1905 a skeptical Archbishop Symon criticized the seminary as "half-secular," but the faculty realized that it broadened its constituency.[63] Moreover, the lack of homeland support lent a carping tone to Symon's comments. Seminary advocates wanted to ensure a domestic supply of clergy educated in their vision of group identity and were flexible about means.

One other departure from homeland practice stood out. About 1900 Erazm Jerzmanowski, reputedly the first Polish-American millionaire, offered to endow the institution. This gesture, in the classic tradition of the old country patron, presented a painful choice to the perennially underfunded school. After some debate, the trustees refused. The clergy would not dilute their independence. The seminary continued to rely on fees, donations from sympathetic persons or organizations, and profits from its print shop.[64] By publicly portraying the school as a bastion of Polishness, its clerical supporters ensured its existence and in effect provided the quasi-denomination headed by Bishop Rhode with its own training center.

Thus far we have shown priests pursuing "Polish" concerns through coalitions with the laity. But on some important issues the clergy had to stress their "Catholicism." Here the pattern of alliance was reversed: they sought support from their religious superiors against assertive laymen.

The outstanding example of clerical-episcopal co-operation was the common stance on parish polity. Disputes with laymen occurred over parochial title, administration, and priestly tenure. Conflict over one usually led to arguments about all, and the legal structure of American Catholicism meant episcopal involvement. The intensity of these struggles drew from sources beyond the points at issue. Timothy Smith has described

---

[62]Buczek, "Polish-Americans," p. 51n. Priests associated with the Polish Union, for example, voted $1000 for the seminary in 1893, but such support was irregular. See "Z Ameryki," *Niedziela*, December 24, 1893, p. 831.

[63]*Polonia w Ameryce* [*Polonia in America*, Cleveland], November 23, 1905, p. 1. For a similar combination of theological and business training in the new land among Finns, see Smith, "Religious Denominations as Ethnic Communities," pp. 212-214.

[64]Swastek, *op. cit.*, pp. 84-85, 96, 120 and passim.

migration as a theologizing experience" in which religious concerns took on heightened meaning in the new land.[65] Here a characteristically devout laity developed intense interest in the congregations which they were instrumental in establishing. On their part, priests here even more than at home saw themselves as the true guides of the "helpless immigrants" and thus could interpret lay initiative and demands as undermining their proper paternalistic role.[66]

As canonical issues, these had been settled long before the postbellum influx of Poles. In the early republic Irish or German congregations occasionally had incorporated themselves, administered affairs through elected parish committees, and even hired or discharged priests.[67] Stern papal and episcopal action presumably squelched such pretensions. In 1829 the First Provincial Council of Baltimore decreed that title was "to be assigned by a written document to the bishop in whose diocese it [the parish] was to be erected." Regarding tenure, the council affirmed that "... a right of appointing or dismissing pastors assumed by laymen is entirely repugnant to the doctrine and discipline of the church."[68] Subsequent councils elaborated on episcopal and clerical power in the Amercian Church but did nothing to weaken the earlier assertion of authority.[69]

Poles more than most post-Civil War Catholic immigrants reopened the issue of parish governance. Their background combined with their American experience inclined some laymen to challenge established Catholic practice here. At home they were acquainted with the concept, if

---

[65]Timothy L. Smith, "Religion and Ethnicity in America," *American Historical Review*, LXXXIII (December, 1978), esp. 1174-1179. This rich article summarizes his extensive research and reflection on these themes.

[66]This common clerical theme was strongly stressed at the first Union of Polish Priests convention. See Lucjan Redmer, "Wiec Księży Polskich w Ameryce Północnej" ["Convention of the Polish Clergy of North America"], *Przegląd Polsko-Amerykański* [*Polish-American Review*, Chicago], II (January-March, 1912), 3-5. Lay religionist papers echoed such views. Cf. *Naród Polski*, January 13, 1904, p. 1; April 13, 1904, p. 2 for examples.

[67]Patrick Carey, "A National Church: Catholic Search for Identity, 1820-1829" (Notre Dame - Working Paper Series, 1977); Jay P. Dolan, *The Immigrant Church: New York's Irish and German Catholics, 1815-1865* (Baltimore, 1975); Thomas T. McAvoy, C.S.C., *A History of the Catholic Church in the United States* (Notre Dame, Indiana, 1969), pp. 92-122.

[68]Patrick J. Dignan, *A History of the Legal Incorporation of Catholic Church Property in the United States, 1784-1932* (Washington, D.C., 1933), pp. 145-146.

[69]Kuzniewski, *op. cit.*, pp. 7-8.

not the practice, of patronage, which was occasionally collective.[70] In the United States conditions not only encouraged lay initiative, but frequently required it. Bishops were inclined to wait for organized lay requests, and promoters of a new congregation customarily drew upon experience gained as leaders of fraternal societies. These were democratic structures led by men of ambition, persuasiveness, and ability, and in turn they admired American representative government.[71]

Parochial conflicts tended to follow a pattern. The dissatisfied members necessarily took the initiative, criticizing the pastor for "tyranny" and occasionally for immorality as well. Upon refusal of the pastor to mend his ways, the dissenters went to the bishop or even to the Apostolic Delegate, list of grievances in hand.[72] The quarrel received publicity, both positive and negative, as both sides sought to express their positions through sympathetic newspapers. On the eve of World War I advocacy of "lay rights" achieved institutional form in the Milwaukee-based Federation of Polish Catholic Laymen (Federacja Świeckich Polaków Katolików w Ameryce), sponsored by Michael Kruszka's *Kuryer Polski* in 1911. The following editorial drew upon traditional acquaintance with patronage:

> In the old country the founders and benefactors [of a parish — the patron(s)] had a voice not only in the running of church affairs, but in the selection of the pastor. Here in America, the founders and benefactors of the Polish churches, the Polish people, should certainly have the same rights and privileges.[73]

The Federation imitated the popular fraternal society structure with local lodges, pressing for a more democratic polity while trying for a time to distinguish its goals from the schismatic Polish National Catholic

---

[70]A "collegium" of patrons was an accepted variant of patronage. See "Patronat" ["Patronage"], *Encykopedja Kościelna*, XVIII, 378-379. In a random selection of ten Galician parishes, at least three had multiple patrons, usually delegates of villages within the parish. See Józef P. Chodkiewicz, *Kościół katolicki na ziemiach polskich przed wojną europejską* [*The Catholic Church on Polish Soil Before the European War*] (Pulaski, Wisconisn, 1914).

[71]See Galush, *op. cit.*, pp. 82-100 for examples of lay activity in the formation of four congregations.

[72]Examples of parish conflict may be found *ibid.*, pp. 217-241; Gallagher, *op. cit.*, pp. 210-223; Greene, *For God and Country*, pp. 70-78 and passim.

[73]*Kuryer Polski*, January 25, 1912, p. 4; also August 17, 1912, p. 4.

Church.[74] The untenability of this limited form of rebellion led some to use the movement as a transition to independency, and the Federation itself evolved into another fraternal insurance organization.[75]

The Polish-American clergy saw such agitation, whether home-grown or Federation-assisted, as a challenge to their legitimate authority, and implicitly to their paternalistic role. In their adversity they appealed to their bishops, who supported clerical prerogatives even when they transferred or disciplined priests for improprieties.[76] Both bishops and priests shared common perceptions of authority in parish affairs, and so there was usually no difficulty in obtaining episcopal assistance.

Lay attacks were also an occasion for manifesting clerical solidarity, and beleaguered priests received moral support from fellow members of clerical associations.[77] The religionist press was encouraged to condemn rebellion.

The very real possibility of schism resulting from parish conflict offers a more complex example of clerical concern for their Catholicity. More than other Roman Catholics, Poles were inclined to set up independent denominations claiming to be Catholic, which by 1907 consolidated into the Polish National Catholic Church. The leader was Father Francis Hodur, a dissenting priest whose episcopal consecration by the Old Catholic Archbishop of Utrecht testified both to his regard for the apostolic succession and to his feeling that Polishness could only be preserved outside the Roman obedience.[78] Though ardent evangelists, the "independents" (niezależnicy) attracted less than five percent of Polish-

[74]Ibid., September 6, 1912, p. 4. The Federation established chapters in Wisconsin, Minnesota, Indiana, Ohio, and elsewhere, utilizing the services of an itinerant organizer as well as local initiative stimulated through the Kuryer. Many of these branches were probably short-lived. See Kuryer Polski, January 29, 1912, p. 2; March 4, 1912, p. 2; August 13, 1912, p. 4 and passim.

[75]The Federation began offering insurance about a year after its founding and then changed its name to the less provocative "Federation of Poles in America" (Federacja Polaków w Ameryce) in late 1913.

[76]E.g., Kubiak, op. cit., pp. 102-106; Galush, op. cit., pp. 221-222, 236-237; idem, "The Polish National Catholic Church: A Survey of Its Origins, Development and Missions," Records of the American Catholic Historical Society of Philadelphia, LXXXIII (September-December, 1972), 135-136.

[77]Wiarus, August 13, 1914, p. 4 for an example of a clerical society meeting at the rectory of a church during a bitter parish controversy.

[78]"Po drodze życia w 25-ta rocznice powstania Polskiego Narodowego Kosciofa" ["On the Road of Life — The 25th Anniversary of the Birth of the Polish National Catholic Church"] (Scranton, 1922), p. 135.

Americans, who overwhelmingly maintained their loyalty to the ancestral faith.[79] The challenge of independency provided an opportunity for loyal clerics to pursue two disparate goals under the banner of Roman Catholicism.

Their first and more overt aim was to identify "lay rights" with schism or heresy. Since Hodur and similar dissenters advocated the holding of title by the congregation, lay administration in non-spiritual affairs, and a popular voice in selection of pastors, such demands from any source were anti-Roman Catholic. This identification was both strategic and realistic. It tarnished lay-rights demands with disloyalty and reflected the fact that association with such groups as the FPCL was often a stage on the road to the Polish National Catholic Church.[80] Prelates such as Sebastian Messmer, Archbishop of Milwaukee, co-operated in issuing condemnations of the Federation "since the aim of this association is to encourage confusion and even schism...."[81] Clerics also sought to mobilize lay opinion by discussing the dangers of independency at the Polish Catholic Congresses.[82] Uncompromising rejection of lay demands and incessant attack on the PNCC testified to the loyalty of Polish priests to the Roman Catholic Church.

A second aspect of this stalwart defense of Roman Catholicism was that loyalty should be rewarded. The priests linked the fight against independency with their pleas for Polish bishops, who would be unifiers and defenders of the faith.[83] Less dramatically, ordinaries could publicly demonstrate their regard for faithful Polish-American clergy by naming them as diocesan consultors or permanent rectors, and in fact promotion

---

[79]Kubiak (op. cit., p. 121) notes about 15,000 members in 1906 and only about 20,000 by 1916, a tiny fraction of the over two million Poles in the United States by then. For causes of parish quarrels, ibid., pp. 91-93.

[80]This can be seen in at least two instances — Minneapolis and Cleveland in 1914. As the Federation became less concerned with parochial reform, this relationship probably disappeared. See Galush, "Forming Polonia," pp. 217-241.

[81]Wiarus, February 22, 1912, p. 4.

[82]Parot, op. cit., pp. 144-147; Naród Polski, October 12, 1904, p. 4.

[83]Ibid., p. 146.

increased significantly from 1895 to 1910.[84] While a tie between public marks of favor and the fight against the PNCC can only be inferred, bishops were aware of Polish loyalist difficulties and the favorable publicity surrounding such appointments.

The collective story of the Polish clergy was thus a struggle for cohesion and status in a novel and challenging environment. Their inclination to form clerical societies was stimulated by several factors. They saw themselves as distinct from lay immigrants both in their paternalistic role and in having interests specific to their calling. Yet their non-Polish clerical brethren monopolized the episcopate and were apathetic or hostile to Polish ethnic concerns. Holding to a more pluralistic vision of Catholicism, but unable to promote it effectively within the larger American Church, the ethnic clergy segregated themselves in Polish parishes and various societies. Fortunately for them, lay-run ethnic organizations were usually more pragmatic than ideological, which allowed them to mobilize the immigrant masses and leaders in causes the clerics advocated. They facilitated this by portraying their concerns to the laity mainly in ethnic terms, making support of such causes a proof of Polishness. Yet they also liked the enhanced authority of the pastor in American Catholicism and co-operated with the non-Polish bishops in defense of their prerogatives and legitimate polity.

The result of this successful effort to appear both Polish and Catholic made them the most influential group of their size in Polish America and won them increasing recognition from the bishops. They were well placed to play a major role in the great testing time of World War I.

[84] The representation of Poles in diocesan posts of honor where the ethnic group was numerically strong increased significantly, but not in proportion to their numbers. Figures are taken from the *Official Catholic Directory* for 1895 and 1910.

DIOCESE	1895				1910			
	DC	PR	VG	BP	DC	PR	VG	BP
Buffalo		(na)			1	1		
Chicago		(na)			1	2	1	1
Cleveland		(na)						
Detroit					1			
Milwaukee	1	(na)			1	(na)		
New York		(na)				(na)		

DC - diocesan consultor/council; PR - permanent rector; VG - vicar general; BP - bishop; (na) - not available.

MODERNITY IN THE SERVICE OF TRADITION: CATHOLIC LAY TRUSTEES AT BUFFALO'S ST. LOUIS CHURCH AND THE TRANSFORMATION OF EUROPEAN COMMUNAL TRADITIONS, 1829-1855

In 1852, a substantial majority of the male parishioners of Buffalo's immigrant St. Louis Church petitioned Pope Pius IX for support in pressing grievances against diocesan bishop, Rev. John Timon.[1] This 414-signature petition was a consequence of over a decade of efforts by the parish's predominantly German and Alsatian laymen and their elected trustees to achieve control over the parish's property and the hiring of its secular employees.[2] At the time of the petition, St. Louis Church had been without a priest for 15 months because of the parish's refusal to allow Timon to disband an uncooperative trustee board and replace it with one of his own choosing. The bases of the parish's claim to these prerogatives were complex, involving legalities and customs which spanned old and new worlds. But whatever those bases were, such lay power was not, in the minds of the nation's Catholic hierarchy, supported by Catholic tradition. Increasingly after the 1829 Baltimore Council, the American hierarchy demanded that diocesan property be held in the name of and subject to direct control by the diocesan bishop.[3] (Many bishops remained willing, as a practical matter, to allow for daily self-management.)

Other parishes had fought with their bishops about such matters, but the St. Louis affair was unique in one important way: it reached a climax in the 1850s, during an era of intense anti-Catholicism. It received ample coverage not only in the daily newspapers, but also in the nativist press, which saw it as a struggle between republican ideals and Papal despotism. In consequence, the Pope gave serious attention to the petition, for he was conscious that the public controversy born of the parish's struggle not only threatened the internal unity of the American Church, but bolstered the forces which jeopardized its very existence. He sent a personal emissary, Archbishop Gaetano Bedini, to America in 1853 to mediate.[4] But neither Bedini's emphatic judgment that the parish must obey Timon, nor the excommunication of the trustees because of their refusal to accept that judgment, nor the continuing of the interdict denying the parish a priest, led the laymen to surrender. Indeed, the lengths the trustees and their lay supporters soon went in carrying their fight beyond the Church probably are unique in the annals of American Catholicism. Through petitioning and lobbying, they won the cooperation of anti-Catholic, New York State legislators in obtaining passage of a law making legal ownership and inheritance of church property by members of an episcopal hierarchy impossible.[5] Yet but a few months after the passage of the Putnam Law,[6] the parish accepted a compromise, which though preserving some unique law powers, gave its bishop substantial oversight of parish affairs.

This essay analyses the social and ideological forces and the aspirations and fears which led St. Louis parish's laymen first to a strikingly bitter opposition to their Church, and then to an equally striking, sudden reconciliation with it.

The St. Louis conflict is an example of "trusteeism" — the struggle between the American Catholic episcopacy and laity, as represented by democratically elected parish trustees, over control of ecclesiastical properties and/or investitures. (The latter was not at issue in Buffalo, and will not be discussed here.) In the early nineteenth century, elected trustees exercising various powers over properties and employees were quite common. Trustees had existed at St. Louis from the time of its founding in 1829. Legal incorporation of trustee bodies, which had existed since 1838 at St. Louis and provided the legal basis for its claims, was less common, though easily accomplished under New York State Law. Even in New York, however, incorporated trusteeship was not necessarily coterminous with legal ownership; as at St. Louis, trustees often had their property titles state that property was being held in trust for the diocesan bishop. In still other parishes, a number of *ad hoc* arrangements governed both property ownership and management.[7] The diversity of early nineteenth-century arrangements was a consequence of two factors. First, Catholic population grew rapidly and spread over a vast territory, while the expansion of episcopal authority, in the form of new dioceses, was much slower to occur and to spread beyond the eastern seaboard. Second, and relatedly, the ever-present Protestant pattern of church governance surrounded, and suggested models for, American Catholics establishing their parishes in this episcopal vacuum.[8] But all arrangements, *ad hoc* or formal, depended on the willingness of both clergy and laity to cooperate in the creation and maintenance of well-defined principles of lay management and clerical oversight. When such cooperation broke down, as at St. Louis Church and a significant number of other parishes at the time, the result was often intense controversy.

One of the most abiding concerns of American Catholic historiography, trusteeism has had two explanations. Dating from the nineteenth century, the first may be associated largely with the clergymen and small group of eminent Catholic laymen, most notably John Gilmary Shea, who were Catholic America's pioneer historians. Their position was hardly different from that of the episcopal participants in these conflicts, who were their contemporaries. They were horrified by the disunity and well-publicized quarreling, both to the satisfaction of Catholicism's many enemies, which lay assertiveness always seemed to bring with it. Moreover, they found little value in the usual justifications for lay assertiveness, such as ethnic rivalries and mistrust between Irish and continental Catholic immigrants. Instead, they returned always to the belief that laymen had the unquestionable duty to obey priestly authority in church matters. All else was insubordination.[9] Bent on condemnation, and utilizing sources of reflecting the hierarchy's view, this episcopal perspective was unable to conceive of trusteeism as an historical phenomenon, with complex antecedents and contemporary influences, let alone take lay trustees on their own terms, examining their motives and goals as the laymen themselves articulated them. Nor could it explain why such wayward Catholics fought so singlehandedly for prerogatives within a Church they might easily have left.

Recently a new perspective, with faint echoes of the antebellum nativist interpretation, has emerged in the work of Patrick Carey.[10] While acknowledging that trusteeism correlates with class and particularly with ethnic divisions among Catholics, Carey has located the roots of trusteeism in ideology. He contends that trusteeism developed out of the gradual absorption by American and immigrant Catholics of the native republican tradition (with its emphasis on citizens rights, individual conscience, anti-elitism, restriction of the secular power of organized religion, and local self-government) and the subsequent, conscious struggle of laymen to change European-fashioned, hierarchical, and bureaucratic, formal church practice as defended by intransigent bishops, to meet American ideological requirements.[11]

This challenging view demands close inspection on a number of fronts. Its assertion of the centrality of republicanism leads us to ask for a deeper exploration of this secular political ideology than Carey provides. After all, republicanism was hardly a monolithic ideology in ante-bellum America: Whig, Democrat, and Republican; northerner and southerner; abolitionist and slaveowner — all paid obeisance to republican values in their diverse, contradictory, and at times deeply ambivalent, ways. So, too, did anti-Catholic nativists.[12] And so, too, did the nineteenth-century hierarchy in frequent efforts to demonstrate the Americanness of Catholicism in order to counteract nativist claims to the contrary.[13] The point is not the irrelevance of republicanism, but rather its complexity as revealed in its many formulations, and the consequent difficulties involved in using this ideological tradition as a general causality. If there was no single republican tradition in America, we must ask ourselves which one rebellious Catholic laymen appropriated? Or did they formulate their own? As we shall see, the St. Louis laymen were deeply but ambivalently engaged by republican values, and their ambivalence will ultimately tell us more about them and their conflict with the Church than their republicanism.

Furthermore, the new perspective on trusteeism may well claim an explanatory universality it cannot sustain. Much of Carey's work up to this time has been on the formative period of American Catholicism — from the ascendence of Bishop Carroll in 1780 to the Baltimore Council of 1829. Perhaps this is the reason his views do not seem applicable to the St. Louis parish conflict. The controversies he examined almost entirely involved Catholic laymen who were native-born Anglo-Americans or, in a minority of cases, relatively assimilated, pre-Famine Irish-Americans. For these groups, the ideological influences posited may well have been at work. Both groups were in a position to be directly engaged by American political and social values. Though of recent immigration, the Irish had been prepared (perhaps uniquely so in American immigration history) to assimilate native republicanism through development in the Old World of vital, popular traditions of both prepolitical and political opposition to British colonialism. Yet this very colonial subjugation, the brutalities of which reached a zenith in the mid-nineteenth century, thrust the Church and clergy into the forefront of the Irish struggle for national survival. Both Church and clergy gained in authority because they provided bastions of stability, continuity, and cultural coherence in a society of improverished near-powerless peasants who lived amidst increasingly desperate circumstances.[14] We should not be surprised tha, outside of a few, isolated examples, nineteenth-century Irish-American laymen were rarely (and, at that, decreasingly) involved in conflict with their Church.[15]

The lay trustee conflicts of the four decades before the Civil War, however, often involved recent, continental immigrants, particularly German-speakers of various regional and national backgrounds.[16] At the center of the St. Louis struggle, for example, were Alsatians and Germans, principally Rhinelanders. At a time when social historians have frequently pointed out the resilience of European folk and communal traditions in American ethnic cultures, one may question a view of trusteeism which asks us to see recently arrived German immigrants as self-conscious forwarders of American republican ideology. Political history invites the same conclusion. The large majority of ante-bellum German-speaking immigrants, who came from Bavaria and the Rhine Valley states, lacked experience with democratic politics based on popular participation.

Self-evident in the case of the peasants, this is also true of the substantial number of town dwellers among the immigrants. With their cooptive offices and strong deference to (and functional reinforcement of) traditional status hierarchies, town governments of Bavaria and Rhenish Bavaria, Baden, Rhenish Prussia, and Würtemburg hardly prepared their residents to step easily into the role of American republican.[17] The St. Louis conflict establishes good reason to take seriously the importance of both tradition and customary status hierarchies in immigrant political life. For, as we shall also see, even though a frequent, public theme of the parish's dissent was its legal right under state law, by virtue of incorporation, the laymen also spoke of wishing to continue to enjoy prerogatives in chruch governance known in Europe.[18] Their dissent expressed alongside their concern with democratic rights and republican freedom from coercive control, a preoccupation with obedience to legitimate authority, suggesting they had not broken with the deeper political concerns of the Catholic tradition. Finally, their own, formally democratic parish government was informally structured to give functional support to emergent ethnic status hierarchies within their parish.

It is hardly desirable, however, to deny that republican ideology had any role to play in influencing rebellious Catholic laymen. What is doubtful is not the salience of ideological conflict, but rather an interpretation of such conflict lacking a firm foundation in a theory of immigrant adjustment. If we are to understand the origins and social meanings of trusteeism among ante-bellum continental immigrants, we must have a view of cultural change among immigrants which departs from a notion of lock-step, unilinear movement. Instead we must have a perspective which allows for an interplay of communal and folk tradition, modernity and democracy as experienced in America, and practical responses to the exigencies daily presented by resettlement in another society.[19]

Proceeding from these remarks, and based on the admittedly limited, single case of St. Louis parish, the present analysis will advance this framework for interpreting trusteeism among ante-bellum continental immigrants:

(1) The impetus to lay assertiveness originated in the desire to preserve European communal traditions of lay management of parish temporal affairs. Over time, in America, these traditions were consciously and unconsciously altered, as immigrants met the challenges of resettlement and absorbed a new culture.

(2) The desire to pres rve such traditions was based upon the felt-necessity of maintaining group identity and cultural coherence admist the potentially disorganizing circumstances of resettlement. The defense of old, though altered forms of lay involvement may have appropriated American republican ideas and such modern republican civil procedures as church incorporation. But republicanism was less the inspiration for lay assertiveness than one of its subsequent justifications. Though this justification would itself come to have a life of its own in the consciousness of the laymen, its formulation in the context of the immigrant's commitment to an Old World, Catholic ethnoreligious tradition always sharply limited its ability to emerge as an ideology comfortable with modern conceptions of liberty.

(3) Interethnic mistrust, cultural misunderstanding, and rivalries for resources and power within the American Catholic Church, which took their most acute form at the time in Irish-German relations, did not determine the direction of trusteeism, but rather exacerbated it by reinforcing ideological and cultural conflict with objective social divisions.

This perspective sees lay Catholic assertiveness not as a battle between the modern (i.e., republican trustees) and the traditional (i.e., unyielding bishops) but as a conflict of two traditions, both responding to and appropriating American influences during a formative period of ethnic and institutional assimilation.

Indeed, at St. Louis parish, it was the modern, in the form of republican ideas and republican politics and government, which served the traditional, as represented by communal customs of lay governance.

In the next section this essay will establish the social bases of trusteeism in Buffalo by analyzing structural patterns of authority and power among the various social groups comprising Catholicism in the city and in St. Louis parish. Then we will proceed to an analysis of the ideological and cultural foundations of lay assertiveness, examining both European and American political and religious attitudes and practices. Here we will discover that the Alsatian and German immigrants who were the parish's most influential members had brought with them from Europe a centuries-old tradition of lay management of parish temporal affairs. This tradition, which was itself being transformed by contact with American institutions and ideologies, was at the heart of the conflict between parish and hierarchy.

Founded in 1829, St. Louis was Buffalo's first parish. It was created in response to the religious needs of a rapidly growing Catholic population, much of which was very recently settled in the strategically located boom-town at the terminus of the Erie Canal. At its inception, the parish was totally ethnic, and at that heterogeneous, in a pattern which increasingly reflected the sociology of Catholicism in the North. However, German-speakers were dominant in the parish, outnumbering the Irish and few Canadian and continental French-speakers approximately three to one in the first years. The German-speakers were a mixed lot, composed of a few Swiss (soon to travel further West as a group), many more Bavarians, and still a larger number of Alsatian and German Rhinelanders. Sacramental records, various printed sources, and oral tradition indicate that Alsatians were the most numerous of the German-speakers, though not necessarily a majority. The impression of Alsatian numerical predominance is reinforced by the Alsatian origin of a number of early trustees and the Alsatian or Lorrainian birth of the parish's first several priests. Alsatian *social* predominance was enhanced by the fact that the parish's beloved benefactor, Louis LeCouteulx, who donated land on which the church was built, looked upon them with favor as fellow countrymen. Under any circumstance, Rhinelanders, principally French-born, but also German, would dominate the parish population and provide leadership throughout the ante-bellum period. This leadership carried considerable prestige: throughout the ante-bellum years, St. Louis was Buffalo's largest church and its most populous and affluent parish.[20]

During the '30s and '40s a number of social processes changed the parish's ethnic and class composition, and consequently influenced its attitudes and behavior in the conflict with its bishops. First, until 1843 when a larger structure was completed, the church's physical space proved more and more inadequate to accommodate a Catholic population constantly supplemented through immigration.[21] Second, ethnocultural differences of language, identity, and traditions of worship, which were doubltess exacerbated by pressures on physical space, began to become sources of division. Furthermore, the emergence of such ethnocultural divisions was hastened by differing orientations within the parish on the trustee conflict.[22] Third, the emergence of new neighborhoods, far from St. Louis Church, necessitated the building of new churches. These new residential areas were the product of the settling in Buffalo of growing numbers of recently arrived, poor Irish and German immigrants, who carved out neighborhoods on land which was, relative to that adjacent to St. Louis Church, more low-lying and unhealthy and less valuable. Moreover, the new working class neighborhoods, which were located east and south of the central business district, were within short walking distance of the location of many of the industrial, commercial, and transport jobs held by the recent immigrants. By contrast, St. Louis parish lay on high ground, considerably north of the central business district, in an area which became one of Buffalo's more affluent residential neighborhoods.[23]

The net result of the simultaneous evolution of these segmenting processes was the creation of new parishes. The movement of the Irish out of St. Louis Church began in 1837, when, charging harrassment by the German-speakers, a few Irish withdrew to worship in rented rooms. The remaining Irish left over the next decade, particularly because of their opposition to the disobedience of the German-speakers to hierarchical (and it must be noted, *Irish*) authority in the persons of the second and third bishops, John Hughes and Timon.[24] The refusal of St. Louis trustees in 1848 to allow just-appointed Bishop Timon, the first bishop of the new Buffalo diocese, to make the church his cathedral surely must have led the last Irish to leave.[25] A similar process of detachment, marked by intercultural misunderstanding and charges of harassment, led to the bitter exodus of the small French-speaking population from St. Louis parish in the late '40s.[26] Finally, beginning in the late '40s with the creation of St. Mary's, which the more affluent congregants of St. Louis Church derisively called "the woodchoppers' church" because so many poor sawyers and wood haulers worshipped here, there was the rise of a number of working-class German parishes in the city's expanding, "Deutschen Dörfchen" on the east side.[27] Contentions over trusteeism also influenced the development of German parishes. The city's second-largest German-speaking parish, St. Michael's, was founded in 1851 by German Jesuits in an only partly successful effort to break the solidarity of St. Louis's ranks.[28]

Just as St. Louis's affluence gave it a singular position among local parishes, so did its ethnic composition. No doubt it appeared to Buffalonians by 1850 that the parish was exclusively German — which was certainly true in regard to *language*. But the parish also contained the overwhelming majority of the city's nearly 700 Alsatian Catholics,[29] whose national origin was French and whose ethnic identity was the product of a unique history.

Though Alsatians played a crucial role in the parish's governance, and hence in its conflict with the hierarchy, there is little evidence that they were ever recognized as a distinct people, neither French nor German, by the bishops who dealt with them. This lack of intercultural awareness was only in part a result of the lamentable lack of practical knowledge of the parish held by its various bishops. It is also true that Alsatian immigrants were not readily identifiable, and were easily lost among other German-speaking immigrants. In contrast to the approximately two million Germans migrating here between 1820-1860, only some 20,000 Alsatians came, and while German immigration continued after the Civil War, Alsatian immigration declined rapidly after the late '40s. Moreover, typically the Alsatian immigrants, who were largely from Catholic Upper Alsace, migrated up the Rhine to Rotterdam and across the Atlantic accompanied by much large numbers of Bavarians, Swiss, and German Rhinelanders, among whom Alsatians often settled in America, and from whom they appeared indistinguishable to outsiders.[30]

Alsatian immigrants were culturally as well as physically elusive. Toward the close of the ante-bellum Alsatian migrations to America, almost two centuries had passed since the conquest of 1648, which had resulted in Alsace's annexation by France. Yet there had still been no conclusive resolution of the province's cultural identity. Though politically integrated into France, Alsace had always rejected French language, education, and high culture, and, due in large part to the province's territorial isolation, little French-Alsatian intermarriage had taken place. Under Louis Philippe (1830-1848) determined efforts were made to draw Alsatians to French culture through education and propagation of the French language. But this effort failed. Alsatians clung tenaciously to their folk traditions and their singular German dialect (in Upper Alsace, a Franconian speech, like Palatine German across the Rhine), and continued to send their children to German-language schools. Because German remained the language of almost all daily business and social relations, few vital inducements existed to change languages. But at the same time a more self-conscious, ethnic rejection of French was taking shape, and it was rejuvenating Alsatian identity. In response to French assimilationist policies, cultural nationalism swept the province, manifesting itself, for example, in increased identification with German and Alsatian art, music, and literature.[31] St. Louis Church's Alsatian immigrant parishioners were the legates of this cultural nationalism, and it is not difficult to imagine that, however invisible as a people they might have been to those around them, they came to America with a heightened sense of their cultural identity.

Yet distinctive as Alsatian identity was, ample bases existed for communal feeling and collective action among the parish's Alsatians and Germans. The differences among all the German dialects present in the parish were hardly great enough to inhibit communication among Alsatians, Swiss, Swabians, and Rhinelanders.[32] There are other indications as well of the Germanness of the Alsatians. Alsatians with European schooling (and the signatures themselves on the 1853 petition suggest most of the Alsatians, and other parishioners, too, had some schooling) had received a German educaton, probably in parish schools. The likelihood of a German education, if any at all, among the Alsatians was testified to by the fact that the trustees of the '50s, the large majority of whom were Alsatian, seem not to have been able to write in French. (It is possible, of course, that they refused to.) They never communicated parish business, even with the Vatican, in French, which was, along with Latin, the language of Church diplomacy. In fact, they were represented in dealings with the Vatican by a French ethnic parishioner. Further testimony to the German education of the Alsatians was their frequent recording of their signatures in the same old-style German handwriting used by their co-parishioners from across the Rhine.[33] Above all else perhaps, Alsatians and Germans in the parish shared a particularly devout Catholicism. All came from the region of western Europe where, as Michael Fogarty has observed, the results of the Reformation remained indeterminate. In an arc descending from Holland in the northwest to northern Italy in the southeast, the numbers of Protestants and Catholics were more likely to be approximately equal then elsewhere in western Europe, a situation which lent itself to intense religious competition, and, Fogarty argues, to greater religious concern and observance.[34] Such intense concern, when fused with a tradition of lay management of temporal affairs shared, as we shall see in the next section, among many parishioners, across national lines, was at the heart of the conflict between parish and hierarchy.

St. Louis parish Alsatians and Germans also shared many common elements of an American way of life, which formed the vessel in which their common cultural background was contained. St. Louis parish had a singular social structure which contrasted markedly with other local German-speaking parishes. But within St. Louis parish, social differences between Alsatians and non-Alsatians and between residential persisters and more recently settled parishioners were also pronounced. These differences help greatly to account for patterns of authority and power both in parish government and in the trustee controversy.

We may more fully grasp social patterns within and among parishes by analyzing the social bases of German-speaking Catholicism in Buffalo in the early '50s. From population samples drawn from sacramental records (and, for St. Louis parish, from the 1852 petition), we may begin by comparing the church-going populations of St. Louis and St. Michael's.[35] The latter provides the best comparison not only because it was then the city's second-largest German-speaking parish, but also because it was established for the purpose of attracting St. Louis parishioners loyal to Bishop Timon. Consequently, a comparison of the two may also provide insight into the social bases of trusteeism itself.

In point of fact, the early character of St. Michael's appears not to have been determined by the exodus of St. Louis Catholics, though some 19 families left the older parish in protest against its trustees.[36] Instead St. Michael's in the early '50s was shaped largely by the recency of arrival in Buffalo (and most probably in America) of the majority of its parishioners, whose collective portrait, as revealed in the samples, suggests a typical immigrant social demography. Thus (Table I) relative to St. Louis, the newer parish had many more males who were under age 40; who had more recently arrived in Buffalo; and who were not naturalized citizens. Furthermore, sacramental records reveal that, in proportion to its total population, St. Michael's had fewer burials of adults than St. Louis.[37] These patterns are easily explained: located in a neighborhood convenient to Buffalo's less affluent eastern sector, where the large majority of recent German immigrants were settling, the newer parish attracted larger numbers of recent arrivals than the less convenient St. Louis. (Reinforcing this choice of parish was the interdict which closed St. Louis between mid-1851 and mid-1855, and made access of its parishioners to the sacraments unsure.)[38] One consequence of relative youthfulness and recency of arrival was that St. Michael's parishioners, in comparison with those at St. Louis, were lower in factors making for civic influence — age, citizenship, and significant length of residence. Another consequence was that (Table I) St. Michael's parishioners had lower socio-economic status: relative to St. Louis, there were fewer owners of land among them; fewer of them were in white collar occupations (business ownership, professions, management); fewer lived in residences with high value; and more lived in Buffalo's poorer residential wards. Reflecting the fact that the city's German-speakers either dominated or were overrepresented in many crafts,[39] both parishes had large, similar percentages of men employed in craft occupations (58% St. Louis; 50% St. Michael's). But the newer parish had a much greater percentage in lower status occupations (unskilled labor/domestic service/teamsters) — 20% for St. Louis and 37% for St. Michael's.

St. Louis parishioners themselves did not show uniformity in the same civil and socio-economic attributes. The parish's probable "charter group," the Alsatians (42% of the St. Louis sample, while but 10% of the St. Michael's), registered higher than others in a considerable number of them. In contrast to the non-French-born (Table II), they were much more likely to be American citizens and to have spent over a decade in Buffalo. Alsatians were also more likely to be among the oldest men in the parish, a reflection perhaps of the slowing down of Alsatian immigration to the U.S. after the late '40s. While some of the differences in socio-economic position (ownership of property; presence in lower status

TABLE I
INTERPARISH SOCIAL PATTERNS:
ST. LOUIS AND ST. MICHAEL'S

		St. Louis[1]		St. Michael's[2]	
		% of sample	N	% of sample	N
Age	(40+)	43%	(55)	13%	(11)
Years in	0-15	17%	(20)	48%	(27)
Buffalo	6-10	25%	(29)	27%	(15)
(as of 1855)	11-	58%	(65)	25%	(14)
Citizenship	Alien	24%	(26)	59%	(30)
	Naturalized	74%	(81)	39%	(20)
		>77%		>41%	
	Native	3%	(4)	2%	(1)
Occupation[3]	Unskilled	12%	(23)	18%	(14)
	Craft	62%	(116)	63%	(44)
	Owns Business	16%	(30)	6%	(5)
		>19%		>10%	
	Managerial-Professional	3%	(5)	4%	(3)
	Domestic/Service	2%	(3)	1%	(1)
	Transportation	2%	(4)[A]	5%	(4)
	Miscellaneous	1%	(2)	2%	(2)
	No occupation	3%	(5)[B]	0%	(0)
"Owns Land"[4]		39%	(47)	20%	(12)
Values of	0$999	37%	(44)	61%	(34)
Residential	$1000-2999	47%	(56)	32%	(18)
Property[C]		>63%		>39%	
	3000-	16%	(20)	7%	(4)
Residence in Higher Valuated, Primarily Residential Wards[5]		62%	(204)	56%	(80)

SOURCES AND NOTES

[1,2]Samples based on: 1852 parish petition (St. Louis); sacramental records of baptism, marriage, and death (St. Michael's); *Buffalo City Directory* (1852-1855); 1855 New York State Census (alphabetized, coded, compiled by Laurence Glasco).

[3]Occupational classification based (with some modifications) on Laurence Glasco, "Ethnicity and Social Structure: Irish, Germans, and Native-Born in Buffalo, New York, 1850-1860" (unpublished Ph.D. dissertation, SUNY/Buffalo, 1973).

[4]Category used by 1855 New York State Census.

[5]Based valuations in Buffalo *Commercial-Advertiser*, 9/2/1855, 2/2/1856.

[A]All teamsters.

[B]All but one of five, over 65 yrs. of age and presumed retired.

[C]No boarders or lodgers in samples.

TABLE II
INTRAPARISH SOCIAL PATTERNS:
ST. LOUIS CHURCH BY NATIVITY[1]

		French-born [2] % of sample	N	Others[3] % of sample	N
Age 40+	40-49	40%	(8)	37%	(13)
Years in	0-15	11%	(5)	22%	(15)
Buffalo	6-10	21%	(10)	27%	(19)
(as of 1855)	11-	68%	(30)	51%	(35)
Citizenship	Alien	15%	(6)	69%	(45)
	Naturalized	85%	(34)	29%	(20)
		>85%		>33%	
	Native	0%	(0)	4%	(3)
Occupation[3]	Unskilled	14%	(7)	15%	(10)
	Craft	45%	(23)	57%	(38)
	Owns Business	20%	(10)	14%	(9)
		>24%		>17%	
	Managerial-Professional	4%	(2)	3%	(2)
	Domestic/Service	2%	(1)	6%	(4)
	Transportation	4%	(2) [4]	3%	(2)
	Miscellaneous	2%	(2)	1%	(1)
	No occupation	9%	(5)[5]	1%	(1)
"Owns Land"[4]		40%	(17)	37%	(30)
Values of	0$999	29%	(12)	42%	(31)
Residential	$1000-2999	46%	(21)	47%	(35)
Property[6]		>71%		>58%	
	3000-	25%	(11)	11%	(8)
Residence in Higher Valuated, Primarily Residential Wards		80%	(31)	63%	(46)

SOURCES AND NOTES

[1]Sources for this table are the same as for Table I. However sizes for ward and occupation are smaller than for I, because city directories, which do not provide nativity data, could be used to identify individuals for I, but not II.

[2]"French-born" is the closest category to "Alsatian" the census will allow us; the German names of the "French-born," in every case but one of the petition signers, combine with other impressionistic evidence, to establish that the overwhelmingly majority (c.98%) were Alsatians. The total sample of French-born=55. Data could not always be found for every category for each of 55, so sample sizes for individual categories of information differ.

[3]Others: total sample=74 (63/Germany; 4/USA; 7/Etc.), but data not always found for every category for each of 74.

[4]All teamsters.

[5]All but one of five over 65, and presumed retired.

[6]No boarders or lodgers in samples.

occupations) are not large, and while there were actually fewer Alsatians in craft occupations, Alsatians were significantly more likely to be in white collar employment; to be able to retire at an advanced age in an era when few could afford to do so; to have the most valuable residences; and to live in the more affluent wards.

Because, as we shall see soon, Alsatians were, relative to their numbers in the parish population, overrepresented — indeed always a majority — on trustee boards in the '50s, we must keep these sources of their influence in mind. But it is also necessary to find other perspectives on intraparish stratification. The most important reason for doing so is that Alsatians were a minority, if sizeable, in the parish in the '50s, and could not have exercised dominance in a democratic polity unless able to forge alliances and share power with those having the same vision of parish governance. Length of residence in Buffalo provides an important foundation for such a process of cohesion, and hence it provides another perspective from which to view intraparish stratification. (If projected back far enough into the past, length of residence also is a measure of years of attendance at St. Louis; there were no alternatives for German-speakers until the mid-'40s). Other parishioners likely to share the Alsatians' views would have demonstrated their agreement in no better way than by remaining loyal to the church from its earliest years, through such critical decisions as the adoption of the trustee format and of incorporation, and through the parish's various crises. Moreover, to the extent that length of residence correlates with the attainment of other attributes of civil influence and socio-economic status, there would be a yet broader basis for intergroup cohesion.

Specifically we may compare the relative position in regard to these civil and socio-economic attributes of those parishioners who in 1855, the climax of the crisis, had lived in Buffalo 18 or more, or less than 18, years. Eighteen years has been chosen because it represents the median number of years spent in Buffalo of the French-born sample of signers of the 1852 petition. Coincidentally, this takes us back to the years just prior to the parish's incorporation, and thus draws in those who participated in that decision and remained to defend it.

Table III contains data on St. Louis parishioners by length of residence. It establishes a very pronounced, comparative residential persistence for the group of 49 parishioners (59% Alsatian; 39% German; 2% other) who had been in the city 18 or more years. This is clear when we contrast the 23.5 years median of the 49 not only with the median years residence (13) of the remaining 70 parishioners in the sample, but with all Buffalo's male household heads (8.8) and with Buffalo's oldest males (35-44 years, 9.2; 45-54, 11.4; and 55 and over, 13.4). The 49 were unusual both for a parish with high persistence even for its *less* persistent members and for the city-at-large. These findings point to the opportunities the 49 parishioners had to gain influence simply by having become rooted in a nineteenth-century American community with characteristically high population turnover.[40] This civic influence was increased by the greater likelihood that these laymen were of mature age and were naturalized American citizens. Moreover their persistence also interlocked with attributes of high socio-economic status, providing additional bases for influence: more white collar and less low status employment; residence in more affluent wards; and greater likelihood of living in higher valued residences. Of course, these attributes were sources of cohesion as well as influence, and cohesion was itself increased by the presence of family relations among the 49. On the basis of comparison of names, ages, length of residence, and birthplace, as well as the contiguity of signatures on the 1852 petition, it appears that at least 27% (13) were related.

TABLE III
INTRAPARISH SOCIAL PATTERNS:
ST. LOUIS, BY LENGTH OF RESIDENCE[1]

		18 or more years residence % of sample	N	less than 18 years residence % of sample	N
Nativity	France	59%	(29)	33%	(26)
	German Rhineland[2]	18%	(9)	18%	(14)
	"Germany" unspecified	17%	(7)	13%	(10)
	Bavaria	6%	(3)	26%	(21)
	Etc.	2%	(1)	10%	(8)
Age	(40-)	61%	(30)	32%	(25)
Years in Buffalo (as of 1855)	Average	23.5	(N=49)	13	(N=79)
	Median	22.5	(N=49)	6	(N=79)
Citizenship	Alien	2%	(1))	33%	(22)
	Naturalized	91%	(30)	64%	(43)
		>98%		>67%	
	Native	7%	(3)	3%	(2)
Occupation[3]	Unskilled	4%	(2)	16%	(10)
	Craft	56%	(27)	60%	(39)
	Owns Business	21%	(10)	12%	(9)
		>23%		>15%	
	Managerial-Professional	2%	(2)	16%	(10)
	Domestic/Service	2%	(1)	4%	(3)
	Transportation	4%	(2)[3]	3%	(2)
	Miscellaneous	0%	(0)	1%	(1)
	No occupation	10%	(4)[4]	1%	(1)
"Owns Land"[4]		38%	(18)	40%	(29)
Values of Residential Property[5]	0-$999	31%	(15)	42%	(29)
	$1000-2999	51%	(25)	41%	(28)
		>69%		>17%	
	$3000+	18%	(9)	17%	(12)
Residence in Higher Valuated, Primarily Residential Wards		86%	(42)	55%	(39)

SOURCES AND NOTES

[1]Same sources as Table I, with some limitations upon the use of city directories because of need to identify nativity.

[2]Rhenish Prussia, Baden, Würtemberg

[3]All teamsters.

[4]All but one over 65 years and presumed retired.

[5]No boarders or lodgers in samples.

There are two significant implications of these patterns — one, having to do with authority and power within the parish; the other, concerning the nature of cultural change among St. Louis's immigrant parishioners. Examining the first, we are now able to understand the nature of political relations among the parishioners. Authority flowed outward into the general population of parishioners from a small, higher status group, members of which had been rooted in the city and probably the parish for many years. Within this group was an Alsatian majority. The numerical prominence of the Alsatians within this minority, combined with their position as the parish's largest individual ethnic group in its early years and their favored relationship with the parish's founder, explain how it was that they continued to play a considerable role in church governance in spite of declining numbers (as revealed in the data on the origin of those living in Buffalo less than 18 years). Furthermore, within the group of the most residentially persistent, we can see the possibility of an especially strong, though not necessarily exclusive, community of feeling between Alsatian and German Rhinelanders (at least 18% of those with 18 or more years residence). In contrast to Bavarians, the other large group of the parish's Germans, the Rhinelanders were more likely to have been in Buffalo many years; and their homeland was close to Alsace, their dialect much like Upper Alsatian.

The key political manifestation of these patterns of authority and cohesion lay in their translation into power in the composition of the annually elected boards of trustees. Trustee boards of 1850, '51, '52, and '54 have been analyzed in Table IV.[41] In each of these years, seven men were elected to serve as trustees. (Since nine of them were elected two or three times, there is need only to discover information about 19 of them; of this number, data of at least some sort were found for 16.) The majority of the sixteen trustees show high socio-economic status and rank high in attributes of civic influence. Moreover, the majority, and hence successive trustee boards of the crucial '50s, were French-born: at least 5 of 7 of two boards and fully 4 of 7 of the other two were French-born. The non-French-born were in three cases Rhinelanders (all from Baden); in two other cases, Bavarians; and in the two remaining, were said by the census to be from "Germany, unspecified."[*] Though ages varied (while usually over 40), the trustees showed a pronounced residential persistence: the median years resident in the city for the 1850 board was 18; the 1851 board, 21; the 1852 board, 19; and the 1854 board, 20. Apparently the approximately 400 adult males in the parish in the '50s were of one mind on the requirements for membership on trustee boards: Members had to share a common commitment to lay control of church temporal affairs; nothing seemed more likely to ensure this commitment, in the minds of parish voters, than being born in France or the German Rhineland, and having roots in the parish from it earliest years.

---

*Whether the census category "Germany, unspecified" was a consequence of a general answer individuals gave to the question of their origin, or of the censustakers's inability to understand more precise answers, it is likely that the actual origin of those in this category reflected the proportions of the specific German subgroups around them. Thus, given the origins of the non-French German-speakers revealed in Table III, it is probable that those here described as "Germany, unspecified" were also Rhinelanders, with some, but less likelihood of their being Bavarian. The census category "Bavarian" probably applied to both Bavarians and residents of the small Rhenish Bavarian province. I believe our knowledge of German immigration allows us to assume, as I have done here, that a very large majority of those in this category were from Bavaria itself.

TABLE IV
SOCIAL CHARACTERISTICS: ST. LOUIS CHURCH TRUSTEES
1850, 1851, 1852, 1854.[1]

Nativity	French-born	56%	(9)
	German Rhineland	5%	(3)
	Bavaria	12.5%	(2)
	"Germany" (unspecified)	12.5%	(2)
Age	40 or over =	58%	(7)
	Median = 49 years		N=12)
Years in Buffalo *(as of 1855)[2]*	Average = 21.5 years		(N=14)
	Median = 23 years		(N=14)
Citizenship	Alien	0%	(0)
	Naturalized	100%	(10)
	Native	0%	(0)
Occupation	Craft	23%	(3)
	Owns business	61%	(8)
	Miscellaneous	8%	(1)
	No occupation	8%	(1)
	Unskilled, domestic/ service; transportation; managerial/professional	0%	(0)
"Owns Land"		61%	(8)
Values of *residential property[3]*	$0-999	9%	(1)
	$1000-2999	36%	(4)
	$3000-	55%	(6)
	Median = $3000		
Residence in higher *primarily residential ward*		75%	(9)

[1]Same sources as Tables I and III, with same limitations.
[2]All were still residents in 1855.
[3]No boarders or lodgers in sample.

Trustees with this commitment were not new at St. Louis. In 1843, for example, during the parish's first confrontration with the hierarchy (Bishop Hughes), 292 adult males cast ballots for two contested seats on the board. Of the three candidates, the one against lay control got four votes; the other two split the remaining 288.[42] But the 1843 election was held when the parish was still young, and a relatively few years separated established parishioners from newcomers. By the 1850s, however, the gap could be decades, not years. In fact, of the 79 parishioners in the sample with less than 18 years residence, 22 (28%) had been in the city five years or less in 1855. This group of pro-trustee newcomers poses, in sharp relief, the problem of the political relations between trustee and voter. We must assume that a continual pattern of election of the same sort of individual, and a backing — even by the most recent newcomers — of the struggle waged by those individuals, suggests the existence within the parish of well-rooted deference relations, not merely of simple collective agreement. This, in turn, suggests strongly that in St. Louis parish the formal mechanisms of democracy and formal principles of republican self-government masked communal loyalties and commitment to emergent status hierarchies.[43] Thus, St. Louis parish was busy creating its own traditions of governance and leadership, which may only superficially be described as "republican." Then, too, the backing of newcomers for trustees standing for lay control may also suggest the extent to which lay control was part of the cultural baggage of many of the immigrants. In fact, as the next section will demonstrate, the notion of lay control of church temporalities did have roots in the Old World, so that the issues in the American parish were translatable into terms which even most of the most recently immigrated parishioners could understand.

The second implication of the findings derived from the parish sample is more far-reaching. On the face of it, the notion advanced by this essay — that European communal tradition in an emergent American form (i.e., parish trusteeism) played a role in the defiance of the hierarchy — is puzzling in light of the social profile of the petition signers. According to several common civil and socio-economic indicators of assimilation, the parishioners and trustees registered high for Buffalo's German Catholics, and thus would appear to be in lock-step movement toward becoming "American." Such a conclusion, however, would not help us understand the ethnic culture of the parish. Whatever theorems might have been developed at a later day to dichotomize "old" and "new" in the lives of immigrants, St. Louis parishioners were creating a more complex reality, combining effectiveness in coming to terms with the American social and economic systems with a desire to uphold those European traditions they continued to believe culturally significant. Yet they did not defend tradition without ambivalence and even confusion, for inevitably, while engaged in the defense of tradition, they acted in the changed circumstances of American life in a manner which transformed tradition. In order to understand this situation, we must now investigate the parish's defense of its position, analyzing the European roots of St. Louis's belief in lay prerogatives, and exploring the limits of the parish's dissent inherent in its complex relation to tradition.

Over approximately a dozen years of conflict, the defense of trustee prerogatives at St. Louis Church involved two distinct arguments. As stated, for example, in the 1852 petition and in the parish's memorial to Bedini during his 1853 mediation, the first held that through its articles of incorporation the parish had obtained rights to the management and control of its property. In addition, the parish had incurred a legal obligation to abide by the terms of its incorporation — in other words, through their trustees, the laymen had no legal choice but to exercise the powers legally granted them.[44] Both aspects of the first argument held that the law mandated implicitly that the Catholic clergy must play only a secondary role, largely consultative, in managing such property. The second argument, also stated in the petition, held that the parish's first church-goers and its subsequent members had enjoyed privileges of lay management of church property in their European villages, and simply wished to exercise the same prerogatives, in partnership with the clergy, in their new, American homes. It was the obstinacy of its bishops alone which forced the parish into conflict with the Church.[45]

These arguments appear quite different. The first is based on political and ideological concerns arising from life in a modernizing republican polity, in which citizens wished to rule themselves, and in which there was widespread desire to limit the political power and secular activity of organized religion. The second harkens back to European communal traditions. The first would lead us to see lay assertiveness as a hopeful reaching out for self-government and new, American liberties, a natural course of events for citizens eagerly assimilating into republican society. The second, however, would lead us to see lay assertiveness as based upon a desire to reestablish Old World tradition without particular regard for, or perhaps in spite of, New World ideals and realities.

Yet, while distinctive, these arguments are not mutually exclusive. The key to resolving this paradox lies in the parish's decision in 1838 to incorporate — a voluntary, and for Catholic parishes not common, step taken under a state law which did not force religious institutions to take advantage of its provisions.[46] Analyzed in the context of the parish's previous and subsequent history, incorporation emerges as an act undertaken to safeguard an Old World tradition of lay management which had become institutionalized in 1829, at the time of the parish's establishment, but was perceived a decade later to be threatened. The situation was not static, however, for the act of incorporation set the parish's laymen on the path of a civil acculturation which they did not intend and which created contradictory impulses in their relationship to their church and its leadership.

Unfortunately, this "key" is not as easily grasped as one searching for neat explanations would prefer. There is a gnawing evidentiary gap in reconstructing the history of the parish prior to the point in the early '40s when the laity clashed with Bishop Hughes, and generated a large number of printed documents in defense of its position. Much has to be inferred from the sparse record of the parish's earliest years, or read backward from statements made in the heat of later events.

A further problem is the "voice" with which the parish spoke. Much of the parish's defense, in print and in interviews before the Catholic hierarchy, was put forward by its most prominent laymen, William LeCouteulx, the elderly, intellectual son of the church's founder. (He also had the virtue of being able to address the Vatican in decorous French.) His father, Louis, the scion of a titled Norman family who had come to America during the Terror and accumulated considerable wealth speculating in western New York land, had donated the property on which St. Louis Church and its school and cemetery were established. The 1852 petition bears the mark of William LeCouteulx's influence. It repeats his careful, considered arguments, and was written in his hand. Since we often must depend on his view of the parish's early years, it is necessary to sort out the problem that his advocacy poses in reconstructing events.[47]

The problem lies in the fact that he often wrote about the early years of the parish as if the majority of its members were, in his words, "French," as were he and his father.[48] Though perhaps natural for a French ethnic used to thinking of the homeland as homogeneous, his use of "French" obscured both the distinct nature of Alsatian identity and the very great probability that, even though the largest ethnic group was probably Alsatian, the majority of the parish was composed of Germans from the various states of the south and west. This description of the parish's early population, which he sometimes extended into its present, must have created confusion in the minds of the parish's chief antagonists, its second and third bishops, the Irishmen Hughes and Timon. After all, their tenures post-dated St. Louis parish's early years, so they were not intimately aware of its history. Moreover, *their* descriptions of the parish as "German,"[49] in both its past and present, suggest that they did not understand the nice distinctions between "Alsatian" and "German," just as LeCouteulx neglected the difference between "French" and "Alsatian." In consequence, the two bishops were never prepared to entertain seriously LeCouteulx's claim that the *French* laymen of the parish, with his father's consent, were instrumental in its incorporation, desirous as they then were said to be to protect their customary privileges in managing the church temporalities. At other times, the claim simply infuriated the bishops, for when they bothered at all to take it on its own terms, they were quick to point out that nothing in the French Catholic tradition allowed for the veritable and legalized control they believed the laymen demanded, let alone the insubordination they displayed. On both counts the clerical position was the stronger,[50] but, as we shall now see, the chaotic situation of ethnic Catholicism in the mid-nineteenth century, which is suggested by the jumble of misconstrued ethnicities complicating the parish's relations with its bishops, led an accepted Old World religious tradition to become the circumstance for New World disobedience.

While the legally sanctioned control the trustees sought bore little resemblance to the episcopally controlled parish governance of Alsace or of France, a tradition of lay management was well-entrenched in both places from the early Middle Ages[51] to the very eve of the era of mass migration, and over long centuries had weathered and indeed been strengthened by the vicissitudes of history. The Reformation and Counter Reformation brought no change, and indeed actually reinforced, communal traditions of lay management. The Council of Trent specifically approved of such parish arrangements, because, in its enhanced concern for the spiritual welfare and religious involvement of the laity, it wished to reorient Catholicism so that the Church might become more parish-centered.[52] Moreover, reinforcement also came from the new rivalry between Protestant and Catholic, which strengthened the two faiths in contested areas like Alsace by increasing individual religious involvement.[53] Nor for Alsatians was the situation changed in the 17th century by annexation into France, for Alsatians carried their own parish traditions into the new episcopal structure whose traditions, in this regard, were complementary. While the repression suffered by institutional Catholicism during the French Revolution did briefly lead to a degeneration of lay management traditions, they were reinstitutionalized, with guarantees added in the civil law, at the time in 1801 of the restoration of episcopal structure and authority under Napoleon.[54]

In France and in Alsace there were parish management bodies (called "fabrique"*) on which sat both lay trustees (called "marguilliers"), who were appointed from among prominent parishioners by the Bishop and the parish priest. Toward the modern era, secular influences entered into the appointment of the *fabrique,* so that one finds the civil authority now appointing a minority of its members and itself represented in the person of the mayor. The criteria for appointment usually were the exercise of religious obligations; residence convenient to the church; and freedom from indebtedness.[55] Canon law defined little of the daily responsibilities of the *fabrique.* In the individual diocese, these were usually established by the bishop, though over many centuries countless local customs initiated by the laity came to supplement episcopal principles. The duties of the *fabrique* usually included not only providing for maintenance of parish buildings and religious objects and art, but also paying parish employees. Once a year, the financial records of the parish were opened to the bishop, who visited the *marguilliers* at their church, examining the books and the maintenance of the church. Bishops found, and routinely complained over many centuries, that the *marguilliers* were squandering funds, complaints reappearing many centuries later in the judgments of American bishops about trustee bodies in their dioceses. But, as in many American dioceses, Old World episcopal authorities had little choice but to accept the system of lay management with clerical oversight. The alternatives were impossible: total control by an already overworked priest, or the

---

*Alsatians used this French term; see below.

centralization of all parish finances, down to the pettiest expenditures, in the hands of a distant bishop. After centuries, too, it would have been very difficult to end the system, for what bishops might regard as an unfortunate expedient, parishioners doubtless had come to regard as a legitimate prerogative. So the system lumbered on from century to century, with the *fabrique* alternately entreated to do better and threatened when it failed, but largely undisturbed in its role.[56]

The tradition of *fabrique* and *marguillier* took root in French North American communities (Quebec,[57] Detroit[58] and Louisiana[59]) and then began its own local processes of evolution, adding, for example, trustee election to replace episcopal nomination. In these French areas, the legitimacy of trusteeship, even when combined with such a democratic apparatus as election, is attested to in each case by the fact that it was established under conditions of episcopal oversight.[60] In contrast, late 18th- and 19th-century Anglo-American or (in many fewer instances) Irish-American trusteeship lacked such legitimacy: it was without the sanction of custom, and had taken root in an episcopal vacuum, in which Catholicism was influenced by the Protestant practice which surrounded it. And, as we have noted, historical circumstances unique to 19th-century Ireland rendered the possibility of conflict between Irish immigrant laymen in America and the Church increasingly unlikely.

These ethnic differences in religious tradition suggest the difficulties St. Louis parish's Alsatians, in contrast to their French countrymen elsewhere in North America, were likely to experience preserving their customary mehtods of conducting parish affairs.[61] At first, the Alsatians were numerically significant, and influenced perhaps by the intensification of cultural nationalism in their homeland at the time of their emigration, firmly committed to preserving their customs. Moreover, their influence was enhanced by the favor accorded them by the parish's French benefactor. For his part, too, the elder LeCouteulx approved of lay management, and may also have approved of incorporation, though the point was hotly contested for many years.[62] Moreover, because of his own French background and the problems the aging, increasingly ineffectual prelate had administering a diocese then as large as New York State, their first bishop, Jean DuBois, had accepted trustees as a necessary evil. He had even consented both to their election, which was certainly easier for him than appointing them from 360 miles away, and apparently to the parish's incorporation, though here too the matter was contested.[63] But after DuBois came Hughes and Timon, both of whom had little personal experience with or cultural heritage of lay management, and seemed confused about the very identity of the Alsatians. They were unlikely either to understand the Alsatians' cultural imperatives or to see the prerogatives St. Louis laymen sought as anything but evil. The consequences were predictable, and went beyond the fact that it was difficult for either bishop to give the parish a sympathetic hearing. As important, there was no common frame of reference through which the parish and its bishops could work out the carefully defined division of lay and clerical duties on which the *fabrique* in Alsace had depended for the maintenance of its moral integrity within the Church.

Once we consider that the defense of trustee prerogatives may well have involved the defense of an Old World tradition, crucial, but at the time inadequately explained, aspects of the struggle became clear. First, the 1838 decision to incorporate may be seen as a defensive reaction. On the one hand, the parish may have been responding to the decision of the 1829 Baltimore Council to curb trustee power in American parishes,[64] and even more immediately to the prospect of a local implementation of the decision. Earlier in 1838 tough-minded

John Hughes became bishop of the diocese of New York. As DuBois' coadjutor, he had recently established a reputation for opposing lay trustees at the New York City cathedral and was almost certain, as Bishop, to be more insistent on the universal application of the council's resolve than DuBois had been. Hughes soon proved these likely fears correct, promulgating an anti-trustee *Pastoral Letter* and acting to discipline the trustees of New York City parishes, before eventually, in 1843, turning his attention to Buffalo.[65]

On the other hand, within a pluralistic institution like the parish, ethnic diversity itself might have been perceived to be as great a threat to one group's tradition as the Irish hierarchy. There may well have been a feeling among the Alsatians of a need to consolidate or freeze their influence through incorporation, because of the threat beginning to be posed by the growing number of newly immigrated Catholics in Buffalo. Recall that at the time of incorporation St. Louis was still the city's only Catholic Church. Though one year before a small number of Irish had left St. Louis, claiming they had been, in the words of the diocesan historian, "forced out"[66] they did not have their own church until 1841. The increasing pressure they felt to leave St. Louis may well point to new anxieties among the St. Louis Alsatians.

Amidst perceived threats to Alsatian predominance, it was probably at this point in the parish's history that a less conscious process of development than the public act of incorporation took shape: a hardening of lines of cooperation, influence, and authority. The parish was increasingly not Alsatian. But its leadership, both informal and trustee, was probably composed of residentially persistent, mature (if not in some cases already aging) Alsatian men, who enjoyed power under minority circumstances, but felt threatened in its future exercise. An outstanding fact of the struggle in the parish is that this minority convinced others, non-Alsatian German-speakers, to follow its lead — German Rhinelanders particularly, who also had a tradition of lay management among the cultural baggage they brought to America. It is known that the institution of *kirchenraten* (church councils), which functioned like *fabrique*, existed in the Rhineland.[67] No doubt both the Alsatian *fabrique* and the Rhineland *kirchenrat* had a common origin in a distant, prenational past, though after the French conquest of Alsace, customs of lay management of church temporalities on each side of the Rhine had ceased their simultaneous development.[68]

Of course, self-conscious disobedience to clerical authority, even in temporal affairs, was not an accepted tradition west or east of the Rhine. There can be little doubt that the parishioners felt the weight of the burden they had created for themselves in struggling, against their own priests, to organize their communities in familiar ways. The laymen's dilemma is constantly highlighted by the complex rhetoric they marshaled when explaining their position. There is, for example, the elaborately deferential language employed when addressing the hierarchy, particularly Archbishop Bedini, even after he abruptly set aside their claims.[69] But even more, their division against themselves is revealed in a defense which shifts in ways revealing ambivalence about disobedience in the name of reaching out after new freedoms. Thus, though they do speak increasingly of "rights" and "freedoms" which are theirs as citizens and by virtue of incorporation,[70] they also speak to Bedini of their obligation to the legitimate authority of the law under which they incorporated.[71] Furthermore, they promise at times that if their claims are recognized they can better obey their priests;[72] and they announce, too, that they are loyal Catholics and that their disobedience is reluctant, a consequence of unfortunate circumstance or of their bishop's misuse of power (thus disavowing any intention to break with the bishop over his *legitimate* powers).[73] They did not seem able to convince themselves that rights were the sole or best basis for establishing a view of what was good or moral. This ambivalence suggests both an inability to break with the abiding concern of the Catholic tradition for obedience to legitimate authority, and a refusal to embrace comfortably the individualistic and democratic-republican formulations of American political ideology. Critics like Bedini, who saw as wholly disingenuous insistence upon obedience to a law one need not have chosen to obey in the first place, failed to see the terrible choice the parish embraced in incorporating. It had to balance off the demands of two legitimate, competing authorities, *both* with compelling claims to its obedience: the Church, which exacted obedience as the price of salvation; and the State, which exacted self-government as the price of liberty.

Certainly St. Louis parish's situation may have been more complex than most cases of trusteeism, particularly because of its incorporation. But the parish's larger dilemma, the battle of the claims of two respected traditions — a communal form and a religious doctrine of obedience — between which the state might be asked to interpose itself, may well have been a problem more common to Catholic laymen than has previously been recognized. Other parishes may not have been as articulate in stating the Old World roots of trusteeism, assuming perhaps that what seemed so natural needed no historical justification. In St. Louis's case, it took William LeCouteulx, as an engaged intellectual, to make explicit what others around him saw as self-evident.

But the dilemma remained, and with their church closed by an interdict and their trustees excommunicated, the parish had to choose.

In the end, it opted for the Church. Nothing proves its commitment to tradition more than the way in which the conflict ended. Within a mere two months after seeking the eager embrace of nativist politicians and hence successfully obtaining legislation to make Timon's claims on their property and polity impossible,[74] the parish's resistance completely collapsed. It accepted the mediation of the eminent Jesuit missionary, Father F.X. Weninger. He achieved a compromise which allowed the parish some autonomy, but gave Timon a good deal of power in its affairs. Thus, while not allowed to hand-pick the slate of nominees for trustee, as he had wished, Timon was now able to examine the parish's books and consult with it on all major expenditures and the hiring of church employees; for its part, the parish was granted the right to remain incorporated, and generally henceforth to enjoy a greater degree of practical self-government, through its trustees, than any other Buffalo parish.[75] The most telling aspect of the process of conciliation was the underlying reason why the trustees consented, in the first place, to Weninger's mediation. Simply stated: the parish hungered for its religion, for the ritual and sacraments of the Church. The signs had been present for some time. Their church closed by an interdict (and thus all parishioners' access to the sacraments unsure to the extent they must now be accepted at another church), and their trustees, in June, 1854, excommunicated, the parishioners worried about the fate of their souls. Since 1852, there had been a steady barrage of complaints that the interdict "deprived [them] of religious succor;" that they suffered "spiritual deprivations," and "the greatest spiritual privations;" and they wrote the Pope in 1852 of their "spiritual suffering."[76] The exact nature of this suffering is unclear, for there is no evidence that rank-and-file St. Louis loyalists were denied the sacraments when they presented themselves at other churches.[77] The situation of the trustees (prior to excommunication) many well, of course, have been different, though the evidence even here is not substantial.

It is not clear how common was the situation implied by the marriage of a trustee's son and the daughter of a long-time, pro-trustee parishioner, which had to be solemnized by a Protestant minister for want of an obliging priest.[78] Perhaps more powerful than anything else was the intense anxiety bred of the *possibility* (and eventually, for the trustees, the certainty) of being denied the sacraments, particularly the last rites — which may well have been on the minds of the approximately one-quarter of the parish over 50.[79]

By September, 1854, the signs of a spiritual crisis were manifest. At that time, with Timon's permission, the interdict and excommunication were temporarily lifted, and Father Weninger gave a "mission" (i.e., revival), which a number of parishioners attended. But the trustees appear to have stayed away. Moreover, they and the parish's male voters unanimously rejected the efforts toward mediation of the conflict which Timon proposed at that time. A year later, not long after the passage of the Putnam Law, Timon again temporarily lifted the interdict and the excommunication to enable Weninger to conduct a mission. The event was a huge success. Perhaps having risked so much in allying with the Church's enemies, the parishioners' spiritual anxieties had reached intolerable proportions. Three of the trustees, said Timon, were "converted" on the spot. It is unclear whether Timon used "converted" here in a spiritual or political sense. It is clear, however, that Weninger's mediation, a political act with immediate spiritual consequences, came very soon after the mission. And after the drafting of an agreement, the church was reopened.[80]

In the charged religious atmosphere of the mid-'50s, the collapse of St. Louis's resistance was a great disappointment to Buffalo's Protestant politicians and opinion leaders. In encouraging the parish over the years, they had apparently looked to the controversy to check Timon's power and to provide a local vindication of the Reformation.[81] Perhaps they hoped that, like Buffalo's small, German "Free Catholic" congregation, which had broken with institutional Catholicism,[82] St. Louis would leave the Church. (This hope was probably strengthened in 1851 when the parish briefly held services without a priest, and in 1855 when it publicly allied with nativists.) But there is no record of any individual St. Louis parishioner, including the excommunicated trustees, leaving the Church. Indeed, the excommunication was soon lifted, and the trustees reentered the fold.[83] So did William LeCouteulx, who, it was well-known in Buffalo, called for and received the last rites from Timon himself when mortally ill in 1859.[84] Doubtless the parishioners were changed by the conflict, at the end perhaps more deeply involved with American ideology, and thus more self-consciously "American" in their conception of themselves. But their ambivalence remained. In the end they settled for the prerogatives (to some extent themselves transformed, it was true) they and their ancestors had enjoyed in the European Church, and they eschewed any antagonistic relation to Catholicism based on new rights and liberties.

But while St. Louis parish failed to fulfill the hopes of many Buffalo Protestants, the Catholic Church failed to fulfill their worst fears — and this perhaps helps to explain why political, as opposed to cultural, anti-Catholicism collapsed in Buffalo in the mid-'50s. To be sure, locally as nationally the issue of the expansion of slavery overwhelmed fears of Papal subversion. As elsewhere, the Republican Party drew the votes of the large majority of Buffalo Protestants who had once backed the nativist American Party.[85] But it was also true that even while marshaling local Protestants against Catholicism and encouraging the St. Louis laity, local Protestant opinion leaders, such as the editor of the prestigious

Commercial Advertiser, had been forced to acknowledge that the Church was proving itself a socially stabilizing force. Publicly this was granted because of the charitable, educational, and hospital work of the diocese among impoverished or working class German and particularly Irish immigrants.[86]

But less evident to the public eye, as the St. Louis struggle established and as many thoughtful Protestants may have sensed, the Church was proving a fortress of moral order in the midst of the fragmenting, custom-smashing forces unleashed by democracy and capitalism. However great remained Protestant doubts about Catholic ritual and doctrine, the social meaning of the St. Louis conflict for them may well have been that the Church had the authority to make men question liberating but potentially disorganizing actions taken in response to the social opportunities presented in a liberal and democratic republic. In the battle within ante-bellum American Protestantism between the imperatives of moral freedom and those of moral order, between conservative evangelical reformers bent on the perfection of the individual and radical evangelical liberationists bent on the perfection of society, most higher status Buffalo Protestants had chosen order. They had crusaded against liquor and the desecration of the Sabbath; proposed the development of custodial, penal, and educational institutions; and opposed abolitionism. So also had the majority of middle class American Protestants elsewhere, all responding to the frightening pace of seemingly inchoate social change around them.[87] In opting for order, they found the Catholic Church and socially respectable Catholics like the St. Louis laymen logical, it not entirely acceptable, allies.

SUNY/Buffalo   David A. Gerber

FOOTNOTES

The author gratefully acknowledges the assistance of the American Philosophical Society, the Center for the Study of American Catholicism and the Research Foundation of the State University of New York in providing funds for the support of research.

1. "A Notre Saint Père, le Pape Pie IX . . .," (petition dated) Sept. 1, 1852, folio 176, *Scritture Riferite nei Congressi: America Centrale* (hereafter as, *Scritture*), Congregation of Propaganda Fide (hereafter as, CPF), Rome, microfilms at Archives of the University of Notre Dame (hereafter as, AUND).

2. A summary of the conflict can be found in Rev. Thomas Donahue, D.D., *History of The Catholic Church in Western New York* (Buffalo, 1904), pp. 141-189. Also, see, [author unknown] *Belege und Berichte über Angelegenheiten der St. Louis Kirche* (Buffalo, 1852), Canisius College Archives, Buffalo (hereafter as, CCA).

3. Rev. Peter Guilday, *A History of the Councils of Baltimore, 1791-1884* (New York, 1932), pp. 87, 90-91; R.F. McNamara, "Trusteeism in The Atlantic States, 1785-1863," *Catholic Historical Review* XXX (1944): 146-147.

4. Rev. James F. Connelly, *The Visit of Archbishop Gaetano Bedini to The United States of America (June, 1853-February, 1854)* (Rome, 1960), pp. 3, 13, 50, 73. New York *Journal of Commerce,* Sept. 17, Oct. 22, Nov. 19, 1842; Boston *Congregationalist,* Apr. 2, 1852, July 22, 1853, New York *Observer,* June 30, 1853; Cincinnati *Gazette,* Nov. 9, 1853.

5. Other parishes, in Philadelphia (1812, 1821) and New Orleans (1828, 1838), had gone to state legislatures in battles against their bishops, but none of these had allied with anti-Catholic politicians nor sought legislation putting general constraints upon the Church. See, John Gilmary Shea, *The History of The Catholic Church in The United States*, 4 vol. (New York, 1886-1892), III, pp. 215, 242, 403, 672-679.

6. On St. Louis parish's brief alliance with nativist politicians and the drafting and passage of the Putnam Law, see, Donohue, *History of The Catholic Church in Western New York*, p. 179; W.S. Tisdale, ed., *The Controversy between Senator Brooks and John, Archbishop of New York* . . . . (New York, 1855); Rev. Joseph P. Murphy, *The laws of The State of New York Affecting Church Property* (Washington, D.C., 1957), pp. 46-49; John, Cardinal Farley, *The Life of John, Cardinal McCloskey: First Prince of The Church in America, 1810-1885* (New York, 1918), pp. 184-194. Richard Shaw, *Dagger John: The Unquiet Life and Times of Archbishop John Hughes of New York* (New York, 1977), pp. 294-297.

7. On the related problems of church property ownership, incorporation, and church governance, see, Patrick J. Dignan, *A History of the Legal Incorporation of Church Property in The United States, 1784-1932* (Washington, D.C., 1933); Martin Joseph Becker, *A History of Catholic Life in The Diocese of Albany, 1609-1864* (New York, 1975), pp. 116-119, 122-130, 132-162, 169-202; Rev. Joseph P. Murphy, *The Laws of New York Affecting Church Property*. For other relevant citations of a more specific and empirical nature, see, notes 9 and 10, *infra*.

8. Rev. Thomas T. McAvoy, *A History of the Catholic Church in The United States* (Notre Dame, 1969), pp. 93-94.

9. E.g.: Shea, *History of the Catholic Church* . . . ., III, pp. 214-216, 229-251, 399-400, 495-496, 672-680; McNamara, "Trusteeism in the Atlantic States . . . ."; Rev. Gerald C. Tracey, "Evils of Trusteeism," *Historical Studies and Records* VIII (1915): 137; Donohue, *History of the Catholic Church in Western New York*, pp. 141-142; C.J. Nuesse, *The Social Thought of American Catholics, 1634-1829* (Westminster, Md., 1945), pp. 175-178; Rev. Peter Guilday, "Trusteeism," *Catholic Historical Records and Studies* (XVIII (1928): 7-13. Written in this vein, to the extent it continues to see trusteeism as a "problem" not a phenomenon to be analyzed, but considerably more dispassionate and subtle, is Rev. John Tracey Ellis, *Catholics in Colonial America* (Baltimore, 1965), pp. 443-445.

10. Patrick Carey, "Two Episcopal Views of Lay-Clerical Conflicts: 1785-1860," *Records of the American Catholic Historical Society* LLXXXVII (1976): 85-114; *A National Church: Catholic Search for Identity, 1820-1829*, Center for The Study of American Catholicism, Working Paper Series, No. 3 (Fall, 1977); "The Laity's Understanding of The Trustee System, 1785-1855," *Catholic Historical Review* LXIV (July, 1978): 357-376; and "Trusteeism: American Catholic Search for Identity, 1785-1860" (a research note) *American Catholic Studies Newsletter* III (Fall, 1977): 4-6.

11. Carey's interpretation leads him to conclusions with which the more thoughtful, less phobic nativists might not have been ill at ease. He contends that the almost total failure of the American hierarchy to respond creatively and flexibly to republican culture has added significantly to American Catholicism's problems. By refusing to make peace with a new world of democratic ideas and republican political practice through, for example, compromise with trustee demands for greater parish self-government, Carey believes that an uncompromising hierarchy exiled American Catholicism to the margins of a liberal, pluralist society. See Carey, *A National Church* . . . ., pp. 21-24; and "The Laity's Understanding . . . .," 373-376.

12. For an extensive and brilliant exposition of the various formulations of ante-bellum republicanism, see, Michael F. Holt, *The Political Crisis of the 1850s* (New York, 1978). Also, Rush Welter, *The Mind of America, 1820-1860* (New York, 1975).

13. Nuesse, *The Social Thought of American Catholics* . . . ., pp. 179-180, 281-286.

14. Emmet Larkin, "The Devotional Revolution in Ireland, 1850-1875," *American Historical Review* 77 (1962): 625-652; David W. Miller, "Irish Catholicism and The Great Famine," *Journal of Social History* IX (Fall, 1975-6): 81-98. William V. Shannon, *The American Irish: A Political and Social Portrait* (New York, 1963), pp. 15-19; Edward M. Levine, *The Irish and Irish Politicians* (Notre Dame, 1966), pp. 31-51. Thomas N. Brown, "The Origins and Character of Irish-American Nationalism," *Review of Politics* XVIII (1956): 346-348.

15. Indeed, as is very well known, Irish-Americans were not only for many decades the Church's principal defender against various varieties of nativism but came early in the nation's history to control its episcopacy. Conflicts between Irish priests and laymen and the hierarchy seem limited exclusively to a brief period in the early nineteenth century when the Irish and French battled for prominence within the Church; see, John Tracey Ellis, *American Catholicism* (Chicago, 1969), pp. 47-50; McAvoy, *A History of the American Catholic Church* . . . ., Chapters 4, 5, 6, 7, 8, passim.

16. Alfred G. Stritch, "Trusteeism in The Old Northwest," *Catholic Historical Review* XXX (July, 1944): 156-164; McNamara, "Trusteeism in The Atlantic States," 144-149; Becker, *A History of Catholic Life in The Diocese of Albany* . . . .," pp. 169-202 passim; Jay Dolan, *The Immigrant Church: New York's Irish and German Catholics, 1815-1865* (Baltimore, 1975), pp. 89-91; Rev. Emmet H. Rothan, *The German Catholic Immigrant in The United States (1830-1860)* (Washington, D.C., 1946), p. 59; Bishop John Timon to Bishop Peter Paul Lefevere, September 7, 1851, Collection: Detroit Diocese, 1843-1852, III-2-h, AUND.

17. Mack Walker, *German Hometowns: Community, State, and General Estate, 1648-1871* (Ithaca, 1971), Chapters 2, 4, 5, 7, 8, and 10 passim.

18. Both Ellis, *Catholics in Colonial America*, pp. 443-444 (regarding the Old World origins of the trustees invoking *jus patronatus*), and Carey, "The Laity's Understanding of the Trustee System," 368-376 (in ways at odds, I believe, with his larger thesis on republican origins of trustee conflict) have suggested the possible relevance of European roots of trusteeism. But only Rev. V.J. Fecher, *A Study of The Movement for German National Parishes in Philadelphia and Baltimore, 1787-1802* (Rome, 1955), pp. 254-279 has sought seriously to uncover those roots and discuss their significance and meanings. This essay, which develops the relevance of those European roots, is greatly indebted to Rev. Fecher, though he was less concerned with trusteeism as such than with ethnic rivalries and conflicts wihtin Catholicism.

19. A conceptualization of immigrant experience derives from Herbert Gutman's now class, "Work, Culture, and Society in Industrializing America, 1815-1919," *American Historical Review* 78 (1973): 531-588, and is suggested in his *The Black Family in Slavery and Freedom, 1750-1920* (New York, 1976), Chapter I and passim. Also, see, Timothy L. Smith, "Religious Denominations as Ethnic Communities: A Regional Case Study," *Church History* 35 (1966): 207-226, and "Religion and Ethnicity in America," *American Historical Review*, 83 (1978): 1155-1185.

20. Buffalo, *Die Weltbürger*, January 29, 1839; Rev. Joseph Salzbacher, *Meine Reise nach Nord-Amerika* (Vienna, 1845), p. 260; Donohue, *History of the Catholic Church in Western New York*, pp. 114-127, 253-254; Anita Louise Beaudette, *A Man and A Church Named Louis* (undated typescript at St. Louis Church, Buffalo), pp. 2, 15-16, 25, 28-29; Paul Batt, "The Enduring Spirit of St. Louis Church," Buffalo *News Magazine*, Nov. 19, 1978, 6-9; Martha J.F. Murray, "Memoir of Stephen Louis Le Couteulx de Caumont," *Publications of The Buffalo Historical Society*, IX (1906), 449; St. Louis Church, *Matrimonial Register, 1829-1836*, and *Baptismorum Registrum, 1829-1836*, at St. Louis Church, Buffalo. (One can get little more from sacramental records than impressions of nationality revealed by names; only occasionally is place of birth recorded. For these early years, it is also very difficult to find

other sources for the sake of crosschecking the names recorded.) Employing François Houtart's "Sacramental index" (see his *Aspects Sociologiques du Catholicisme Américain* [Paris, 1957], pp. 227 ff.), St. Louis, before 1860, registers much higher than other, comparably sized German-speaking parishes (St. Ann's and St. Michael's) in number of congregants. No non-German parish was anywhere near to equal in size to these three before 1860.

21. Rev. Robert T. Bapst, "A Brief History of St. Louis Church," in Bapst, ed., *125th Anniversary, 1829-1954, St. Louis Church, Buffalo* (Buffalo, 1954), 13-14.

22. Rev. John Timon, *Missions in Western New York and Church History of the Diocese of Buffalo* (Buffalo, 1862), pp. 215-216, CCA; Donohue, *History of The Catholic Church in Western New York*, pp. 229-257 passim.

23. Buffalo *Commercial Advertiser*, February 10, 1854, February 2, 1856; [no author], "The Health of The City of Buffalo: Past, Present, and Prospective," *Buffalo Medical Journal*, X (1854-1855), 373-381; *Buffalo Medical Journal*, IXX (1852-1853), 333 [cholera statistics]; Laurence Glascoe, "Ethnicity and Social Structure: Irish, Germans, and Native-Born in Buffalo, New York, 1850-1860" (unpublished Ph.D. dissertation, SUNY/Buffalo, 1973), pp. 5, 9-10, 13, 16-17, and Chapters 2 and 3, *passim*.

24. Timon, *Missions in Western New York* . . . ., p. 216; Donohue, *History of The Catholic Church in Western New York*, pp. 245-246, 250-251, 258-260; Buffalo *Commercial Advertiser*, February 10, 1854. St. Louis Church, *Matrimonial Register, 1829-1836, Baptismorum Registrum, 1829-1836,* and *Liber Defunctorium,* at St. Louis Church, Buffalo, all trace the gradual decline of Irish names in the parish.

25. Charles G. Deuther, *The Life and Times of Right Rev. John Timon, D.D., First Roman Catholic Bishop of The Diocese of Buffalo* (Buffalo, 1870), p. 113.

26. Donohue, *History of The Catholic Church in Western New York*, pp. 260-261; Pierre Alphonse Le Couteulx [draft, legal documents about property gift to French who who left St. Louis], July 26, 1851, at Our Lady of Lourdes Church, Buffalo; Rev. N.J. Perche to Rev. S. Rousselon, October 6, 1850, Collection: New Orleans, 1850, V-5-n, AUND.

27. H. Perry Smith, *History of The City of Buffalo and Erie County*, 2 vol. (Syracuse, 1884), II, pp. 150-154; Deutsch-Amerikanische Historische und Biographische Gesellschaft, *Buffalo und Sein Deutschtum* (Buffalo, 1912), pp. 51-52; Donohue, *The History of The Catholic Church in Western New York*, pp. 242-245, 254-257, 261-262; [no author], *The Centenary of St. Mary's Church, 1844-1944* (Buffalo, 1944), p. 17; [no author], Die Geschichte der St. Anna Gemeinde, 1858-1908," *St. Anna Bote* Buffalo, 1908), pp. 101-103.

28. Donohue, *History of The Catholic Church in Western New York*, pp. 256-257; *St. Michael's Bazar* [sic] *Papers, July 22-August 14, 1889* (typescript, no pagination, at St. Michael's Church, Buffalo).

29. Estimate based on figures on French and French Canadians found in Glascoe, "Ethnicity and Social Structure . . . ," p. 21; Shea, *History of the Catholic Church* . . . ., IV, p. 121; St. Peter's Church, *Sepulturae, 1851-1858, Liber Mortuorim,* and *Marriages, 1850-1858, a L'eglise francaise St. Pierre,* at Our Lady of Lourdes Church, Buffalo. There does not appear to have been a community of German-speaking Lorrainians in Buffalo, so I have adopted the premise that all German-speaking French were Alsatian.

30. P. Leuilliot, "L'Émigration Alsacienne sous L'Empire et au Début de la Restauration," *Revue Historique* CLXV (1930): 254-279, and *L'Alsace au Début du XIXe Siecle: Essais d'Historie politique, économique, et religieuse, 1815-1830* (Paris, 1959), II, pp. 32-40; L. Chevalier, "L'Emigration française au XIXe Siecle," *Etudes d'Histoire moderne et contemporaine* I (1947): 130-132, 143-148, 150, 156-158, 160-162; Heinrich Neu, "Elsasser

und Lothringer als Anseidler in Nordamerika," *Elsass-Lothringische Wissenshaftliche Gesellschaft für Strassberg*, III (1930): 98-129. Like the German immigration at the time, the Alsatian was a consequence of the socio-economic dislocations which, beginning in the 1820s, accompanied industrialization and the commercialization of agriculture. France's 1847 annexation of Algeria, however, ended the convergence of these two streams of mass migration, for many Alsatians bent on migrating were quickly diverted by the lure of French North Africa; Chevalier, *"L'Émigration française...,"* 160-161.

31. Leuilliot, *L'Alsace au Début du XIXe Siècle,* III, pp. 318-329; Buffalo, *Die Weltbürger,* Jan. 26, 1839; Franklin Ford, *Strasbourg in Transition, 1648-1789* (Cambridge, 1958), pp. 170-173, 190 (suggesting Strasbourg was an exception to certain of the generalizations here, but confirming others); Frederick C. Luebke, "Alsatians," *Harvard Encyclopedia of American Ethnic Groups* (Cambridge, 1980), pp. 30. In 1839, an Alsatian correspondent of the German press remarked, with evident surprise, "how powerfully and determinedly the German type and nature continues to make itself valuable in Alsace," after so many years of French rule. Quoted in Buffalo, *Wie Weltbürger,* Jan. 26, 1839.

32. I wish to thank Professor Wilma Iggers of the German Department, Canisius College, for clarifying this linguistic situation for me.

33. Although the French-born did so less often than the German-born, an appreciable 43% (23) of them (in contrast to 69%, or 247 of the latter) used the old Germanic-style handwriting in signing the petition.

34. Michael P. Fogarty, *Christian Democracy in Western Europe, 1820-1953* (London, 1957), p. 7. Also, see, David Martin, *A General Theory of Secularization* (New York, 1978), pp. 19, 79, 142.

35. Supplementing parish records were city directories and the Buffalo manuscripts of the 1855 New York State Census. An alphabetized print-out derived from the 1855 New York State Census for Buffalo is located at the University Archives, SUNY at Buffalo. The St. Michael's sample was generated from names of males appearing in the years 1851-1855 in: *Burials from 1851-1868; Part I Marriages, from 1851-1873;* and *Baptisms from 1851 to 1882,* at St. Michael's Church, Buffalo.

36. *Supra,* note 28.

37. Based on the ratio of adults (age 16 and over) buried to the total of parishioners buried, as revealed in the parish's sacramental index (See, *supra,* note 20) for both parishes: St. Michael's (1854 = .037; 1855 = .008; 1856 = .019); St. Louis (1850 = .021; 1855 = .020; 1856 = .024). When children's burials are included, the ratios are usually the inverse, again suggesting a younger age structure at St. Michael's: St. Michael's (1851 = .150; 1852 = .397; 1858 = .100); St. Louis (1851 = .047; 1856 = .165; 1858 = .124). Unfortunately, it wasn't possible consistently to compare the same years.

38. Donohue, *History of The Catholic Church in Western New York,* pp. 156-189.

39. Glascoe, "Ethnicity and Social Structure ....," Chapter II.

40. Michael Katz, Michael Doucet, and Mark Stern, "Migration and The Social Order in Erie County, New York: 1855," *Journal of Interdisciplinary History* (1978): 679-682.

41. Lists of the names of those comprising the four boards came from: [no author] *Documents and History of The Affairs of St. Louis Church* (n.p., n.d.), p. 4, CCA; [no author], *Belege und Berichte ....,* p. 16, CCA; "A Notre Saint Père ...." (petition, 1852); Buffalo *Commercial Advertiser,* June 27, 1854.

42. Buffalo *Daily Gazette*, Oct. 19, 1843. This board also had an Alsatian majority: of its 7 members, 4 could be traced; all 4 were born in France; Buffalo *Commercial Advertiser*, Aug. 10, 1844.

43. Cf., Kenneth A. Lockridge, *A New England Town: The First Hundred Years* (New York, 1970), pp. 37-56; Kenneth A. Lockridge and Alan Kreider, "The Evolution of Massachusetts Town Government, 1640 to 1740," *William and Mary Quarterly*, XXIII (1966), 549-574.

44. "A Notre Saint Père . . . ." (petition, 1852); [no author], *Affairs of St. Louis Church* (Buffalo, 1853), pp. 3-11 (memorial to Bedini); W.B. Le Couteulx (public letter), Buffalo *Morning Express*, June 28, 1851.

45. "A Notre Saint Père . . . ." (petition, 1852). Also,W.B. LeCouteulx, "To the Right Reverence John Hughes . . . . 31 March, A.D., 1852" (Buffalo, 1852), in folios 73 and 74, *Scritture*, CPF, Rome, AUND; and W.B. LeCouteulx to CPF, Feb. 2, 1853, folios 503 and 504, *Scritture*, CPF, Rome, AUND; and Buffalo *Morning Express*, June 28, 1851.

46. Church incorporation legislation passed in New York State in 1784 and, superseding the former, in 1813. On these laws, see, John Webb Pratt, *Religion, Politics, and Diversity: The Church-State Theme in New York History* (Ithaca, 1967), pp. 100-101; Dignan, *A History of Legal Incorporation . . . .,* pp. 52-54, 64-67.

47. Murray, "Memoir of Stephen Louis LeCouteulx de Caumont," 431-483; "Le Couteulx, Rouen, Juillet 1764 . . . . Lettres de leur Annoblissement," Bibliotheque Nationale, Paris. In addition to frequent letter writing, William LeCouteulx journeyed to Rome late in 1852 and again in 1853 to present the parish's case before the Congregation of the Propaganda Fide; Buffalo *Courier*, Oct. 8, 1852; Sept. 22, 1853. As Bishop Timon frequently complained (e.g., Timon to Archbishop Kenrick, Sept. 27, 1853, Kenrick Papers, Archives of the Archdiocese of Balitmore — hereafter, AAB), William LeCouteulx had "friends in power" within the Church in Europe, probably as a consequence of ties created through branches of the family remaining in France. It is clear, for example, that he knew Cardinal Fornari of Paris, and influenced him to intervene on the parish's behalf during a dispute with Bishop Hughes in the early '40s; see, Donohue, *History of the Catholic Church in Western New York*, p. 181. He also knew Count A. de Reyneval, French Ambassador to the Holy See, who wrote a letter of introduction for him in 1853; see, de Reyneval to CPF, Jan. 27, 1853, folio 598, *Scritture*, CPF, Rome, AUND. The traditional explanation of William LeCouteulx's involvement (Donohue, *The History of the Catholic Church in Western New York*, p. 153) is that he wished through the trustees to get back valuable property his father had deeded to the parish. There is no evidence, however, to sustain such a view, and the great wealth of the family rather firmly militates against it.

48. See citations, *supra*, note 45, for example.

49. *E.g.*, Timon, *Missions in Western New York* . . . ., pp. 214-215, 224-226; Bishop Timon to Bishop Peter Lefevre, September 7, 1851, Collection: Detroit, 1843-1852, III-2-n, AUND; Archbishop John Huges to W.B. LeCouteulx, no date, in Boston *Pilot*, Apr. 21, 1855. Under the circumstances, it was to be expected that authorities in Rome would come to see the parish the same way; see, "Instructions for Mon. Bedini . . . . Special Envoy of the Holy Father in the U.S.A.," Apr. 4, 1853, folios 315-317, *Lettere e Decreti della S. Congregazione*, CPF, Rome AUND, which proves that the Vatican saw St. Louis parish in the same manner.

50. Both Hughes and Timon (and their supporters) proved adept at pointing out the gap between French law and practice and the prerogatives St. Louis parish claimed for itself; see, [no author], *Belege und Berichte* . . . ., pp. 20-21; CCA; Donohue, *The History of the Catholic Church in Western New York*, pp. 184-188.

51. L. Pfleger, "Untersuchungen zur Geschicte des Pfarrei-Institute in Elsass," 3 parts, "Die Einkommensquellen, i. Das Kirchenvermögen," part 3, *Archiv für Elsassiche Kirchengeschicte* VIII (1932): 14; Andre Schaer, "Le Chapitre Rural Ultra Colles Ottinis en Haute-Alsac, Après La Guerre de Trente Ans Jusque à La Révolution. La Vie Paroissale dans Un Doyen Alsacien D'Ancien Régime (1648-1789)," *Archiv de L'Eglise D'Alsace*, XVI (new series) (1967-68): 200.

52. Rev. H.J. Schroeder, *Canons and Decrees of the Council of Trent* (St. Louis, 1941), pp. 157, 429; John Bossy, "The Counter-Reformation and The Catholic People of Europe," *Past and Present* (1970): 51-70.

53. Fogarty, *Christian Democracy in Western Europe* . . . ., p. 7.

54. Schaer, "Le Chapitre Rural Ultra Colles Ottinis . . . .," Part 1, 168, 197, 299-205; Georg Fritz, "Zur Kirchengeschicte der Jahre, 1790-1810," *Archiv für elsassischen Kirchengeschicte*, XVI (1943), 384-387; Leuilliot, *L'Alsace au Début du XIXe Siècle* . . . ., III, pp. 1-17; "Fabrique," *Le Grand Larousse Encyclopédie*, IV, 875-876.

55. Pierre Basile Mignault, *Le Droit Paroissial - Etant Une Etude Historique et Légale de La Paroisse Catholique, de Sa Création, de Son Gouvernment, et de Ses Biens* (Montreal, 1893), pp. 210-215. "Fabrique" is descended from the Latin "Fabrica," which, in its meaning in canon law, referred to both the church as a physical structure and the maintenance of local churches by their congregants through diverse arrangements; see Schaer, "Le Chapitre Rural Ultra Colles Ottinis . . . .," Part 1, 200.

56. Schaer, "Le Chapitre Rural Ultra Colles Ottinis . . . .," Part 1, 200-206, and Part 3 in *Archiv de L'Eglise D'Alsace* XVIII (1970): 174-175.

57. Mignault, *Le Droit Paroissial* . . . ., pp. vi-viii, 44, 214,-225, 234-246, 260-264, 272-273, 308-311.

58. George Pare, *The Catholic Church in Detroit, 1701-1888* (Detroit, 1951), pp. 199-200, 339-340, 443-444.

59. Roger Baudier, *The Catholic Church in Louisiana* (New Orleans, 1939), pp. 91, 121, 158, 255-258, 335, 344-348.

60. *Ibid.*; the Louisiana situation is complicated by the fact that the *fabrique* existed before the diocese was created (when the Church was administered from metropolitan France), and then during the first years of the diocese from 1793 to 1801 with no apparent problems between the *marguilliers* and the episcopacy. Between 1801-1815, however, the diocese had no bishop and the delicate balance on which the system of lay management depended broke down, particularly at the New Orleans cathedral where there were consequently years of struggle. Under more stable parish circumstances, however, the *fabrique* system worked well — from the French hierarchy's point of view. The latter would, therefore, have agreed with Pare's assessment of the contrast between Anglo-American and French trusteeship. In evaluating the *fabriques* of Detroit, Pare said, "[This] parish organization is not to be compared with the lawless trustee system that disgraced the beginnings of the Church in the United States. In the French system there was never any doubt concerning the scope of the bishop's or the pastor's authority and the rights and the extent of the laity's participation were minutely regulated." Pare, *The Catholic Church in Detroit* . . .. ., p. 199, note 54.

61. The same difficulties, in fact, befell Alsatian Catholics in a rural parish, just outside Buffalo, in the 1840s; they clashed with German priests, assigned to their church, over trustee prerogatives. See, Glenn R. Atwell and Ronald E. Batt, *The Chapel: A Comprehensive History of the Chapel and Pilgrimmage of Our Lady Help of Cheektowaga, New York and of the Alsatian Immigrant Community at Williamsville, New York* (Buffalo, 1979), pp. 1-7. And *French*

Catholics at Buffalo briefly clashed with Bishop Timon over the same issues; see, Buffalo *Commercial Advertiser*, Aug. 6, 8, 1855.

62. His sons, William and Pierre (who sided with the bishops) disagreed for many years about their father's wishes regarding incorporation, and hence established the lines of argument for all those wishing to claim the deceased, elder LeCouteulx's authority for their views. See, P.A. LeCouteulx to Bishop Timon, August   , 1851, in Donohue, *The History of the Catholic Church in Western New York*, pp. 175-176; William LeCouteulx, "Exposition of The Deplorable Conditions . . . . of the Buffalo Church of St. Louis," Feb. 2, 1853, folios 503-504, *Scritture*, CPF, Rome, AUND.

63. Shaw, *Dagger John . . . .*, pp. 115-137; William LeCouteulx, "Exposition of The Deplorable Conditions . . . .;" N. Ottenot to Archibishop Bedini, October 23, 1853, folio 742, *Scritturi*, CPF, Rome, AUND. Such consent would certainly have had precedent in 1838. See Dignan, *A History of Legal Incorporation . . . .*, pp. 91, 129-132, 148.

64. Guilday, *A History of The Councils of Baltimore*, pp. 87, 90-91.

65. Bishop John Hughes, "In Regard to . . . . Church Property," (*Pastoral Letter*, Sept. 8, 1842) in Lawrence Kehoe, ed., *Complete Works of The Most Reverend John Hughes . . . .*, 2 vol. (New York, 1864), I, pp. 314-327 and III, pp. 555-559; Shaw, *Dagger John . . . .*, pp. 129-132, 177, 181; Dolan, *The Immigrant Church*, pp. 47-48, 90-91. For the best summary of the brief (1843-1844) but bitter controversy, which ended in indecisive compromise, between Hughes and St. Louis parish, see, Donohue, *History of The Catholic Church in Western New York*, pp. 144-155.

66. Donohue, *A History of The Catholic Church in Western New York*, p. 250.

67. Fecher, *A Study of The Movement for German National Parishes . . . .*, pp. 254-279; R.F. McNamara, "Trusteeism," *New Catholic Encylcopedia*, v. XIV, p. 324.

68. Pfleger, "Untersuchungen zur Geschicte . . . .," 13.

69. [No author], *Belege und Berichte . . . .*, pp. 10-16; CCA; [no author], *Affairs of St. Louis Church*, p. 12; "A Notre Saint Père . . . ." (petition, 1852).

70. William LeCouteulx, "To The Right Rev. John Hughes . . . .," folios 73-74; [letter] to CPF, Apr. 20, 1853, folio 573; [letter] to CPF, Dec. 18, 1853, folios 860-861, *Scritture*, CPF, Rome, AUND; and Buffalo *Courier*, Aug. 27, 1853; Buffalo *Commercial Advertiser*, Jan. 11, Apr. 5, 16, 1855.

71. [No author], *Affairs of St. Louis Church*, p. 8. Also, see [public letter] signed, "A Layman," Buffalo *Commercial Advertiser*, June 29, 1854.

72. [No author], *Belege und Berichte . . . .*, p. 4; CCAA; Buffalo *Commercial Advertiser*, June 19, 1854, Apr. 5, 1855.

73. [No author], *Belege und Berichte . . . .*, p. 16; CCA; Buffalo *Commercial Advertiser*, July 12, 1854, Apr. 13, 1855.

74. From the start, however, the Putnam Law was neither utilized by parishes against their bishops nor enforced by state authorities, justifying the contention made at the time of its passage that its purpose was more symbolic (to appease anti-Catholic prejudice) than practical. It was repealed in 1863, and replaced by a statute accommodating Catholic practice. See, note 6, *supra*.

75. Buffalo *Commercial Advertiser*, June 23, 27, 29, 1855. Trustees retained major powers at St. Louis, alone among Buffalo parishes, until 1979 when these were surrendered to the diocese by the trustees; Buffalo *Evening News*, Oct. 2, 3, 1979.

76. "A Notre Saint Père . . . ." (petition, 1852); Buffalo *Courier*, Aug. 27, 1853; Buffalo *Commercial Advertiser*, June 24, 1854, June 23, 1855; W.P. LeCouteulx to CPF, Mar. 31, 1852, folios 73-74, W.B. LeCouteulx, "To The Right Reverend John Hughes . . . . 1852," foliors 73-74, W.B. LeCouteulx to CPF, Feb. 2, 1853, folios 489-490, *Scritture*, CPF, Rome, AUND.

77. Bishop Timon to Archbishop Francis Kenrick, July 10, 1852, Kenrich Papers, AAB; Archbishop Bedini to CPF, Apr. 2, 1854, folios 967-972, *Scritture*, CPF, Rome, AUND.

78. William LeCouteulx to Congregation of the Propaganda Fide, September 20, 1854, folios 1119-1126, *Scritture*, CPF, Rome, AUND.

79. No one feared more that the prospect of death outside the Church would exert pressure to compromise than Protestant nativist politicians who publicly aligned with the trustees. Wrote George R. Babcock, an American Party State Senator and a cosponsor of the Putnam Law, in a letter to nativist politician James W. Beekman, "The St. Louis Trustees still hold out against Bishop Timon. I fear they will not always be sustained by their congregation. In the process of time, unless there is a revolution in the Church they must be undermined by the gradual falling off of those who dare not die under the curses of the Vatican." (July 10, 1855 in Box 2, Beekman Papers, New York Historical Society.)

80. Deuther, *The Life and Times of Rt. Rev. John Timon . . . .*, pp. 208-212; Bishop Timon to CPF, July 5, 1855, folios 366-367, *Scritturi*, CPF, Rome, AUND; "Proclamation, John, Bishop of Buffalo," Sept. 28, 1854, at St. Michael's Church, Buffalo; Buffalo *Commercial Advertiser*, Sept. 12, 1854, June 23, 1855.

81. Buffalo, *Morning Express*, June 21, 1851; Buffalo *Courier*, Feb. 23, Oct. 8, 1852, June 30, Sept. 14, Oct. 31, Nov. 19, 1853; Buffalo Christian *Advocate*, July 6, 20, 1853; Buffalo *Commercial Advertiser*, June 27, 30, July 5, 12, Aug. 28, Sept. 12, Oct. 3, 1843, Feb. 2, Mar. 5, May 24, 29, June 23, 1855. For expressions of Protestant support from the press outside Buffalo, see Boston *Congregationalist*, Apr. 2, 1852, July 22, 1853, Apr. 27, 1855; Cincinnati *Gazette*, Nov. 9, 1853; *American and Foreign Christian Union*, V (June, 1854), 9-16.

82. [No author], "Missionary Intelligence: The Mission among The German Catholics at Buffalo," *The American Protestant*, V (1849): 49-50; [no author], "Free German Catholics at Buffalo," *Ibid.*, V (1849): 172-173.

83. Deuther, *The Life and Times of Rt. Rev. John Timon . . . .*, p. 210.

84. Donohue, *A History of The Catholic Church in Western New York*, p. 189.

85. Glascoe, "Ethnicity and Social Structure . . . .," Chapter IV, passim.

86. Buffalo *Commercial Advertiser*, e.g., Nov. 23, 28, 1853; June 7, Dec. 30, 1854, Aug. 23, 1855. Also, see, e.g., Buffalo *Courier*, Jan. 4, Apr. 28, Aug. 22, 1851, Jan. 30, 1852. This praise grew more frequent and fullsome in the later '50s, though it remained balanced by criticism of Catholic ritual; see, *Ibid.*, e.g., Jan. 22, 30, Mar. 19, 26, June 7, Sept. 21 1858.

87. Clifford S. Griffen, *Their Brother's Keepers: Moral Stewardship in the United States, 1800-1865* (New Brunswick, 1960); William G. McLoughlin, "Pietism and The American Character," *American Quarterly* XIII (1965): 163-186; David J. Rothman, *The Discovery of The Asylum* (Boston, 1971); Anthony F.C. Wallace, *Rockdale* (New York, 1978), pp. 243-474.

CONFLICT AND COMMUNITY
A CASE STUDY OF THE IMMIGRANT CHURCH IN
THE UNITED STATES

"Go. . . out in the congregations, and look on the schism where the scornful laugh of Satan mixes with the death cries of the people as the billows of party strife dash the people against the rock of salvation only to have them fall again into the sea of their own agitation. . . . Go into into the community, and see the glances of Cain exchanged; see the people pass each other on their way to church, and hear the church bells ring strife into the air. . . .

Norwegian-American clergyman, 1887[1]

Scholars of immigrants in America have consistantly stressed the centrality of religion in the evolution of the immigrant communities.[2] Religion and the church, according to earlier historians and sociologists, provided emotional and material resources which enabled ultimate assimilation. The uncertainties of migration and relocation created the psychological need for solace during a difficult transition. The environment in America, Oscar Handlin argued, was "so new and dangerous," that immigrants were induced to feel "more need than ever for the support of their faith."[3] Moreover, religious institutions performed social services such as providing food, shelter, and even life insurance ultimately to help "settle the immigrants in America."[4] Even when historians in the 1970s began to view ethnic institutions as a contributor to the maintenance of cultural distinctiveness, they considered the role of the church pivotal. Religion remained the "very bone and sinew" of immigrants' ethnicity, "the focal point of immigrant life."[5]

Yet in spite of the emphasis on church centered ethnic communities, historians have also underscored the presence of ethnic conflict focused around the church itself. Scholars have usually perceived religious structure and organization or inter-ethnic group strife as the root of the conflict. Leslie Woodcock Tentler, for example, stressed "conflicting visions" of church and church authority that developed within a Polish Roman Catholic parish.[6] Whereas one segment of the laity felt it should have some control over the priest, Church law stated that priests were to remain independent of the wishes of the congregation. Differing interpretations of the extent of lay initiative and clerical authority, democratic tendencies and hierarchical traditions, led the congregation into a long, agonizing spiritual crisis. Historians have cited conflict around nationality group or inter-regional group rivalries more frequently. As national or regional traditions confronted one another under the aegis of a single church structure, strife often was the result. Such divisions were a frequent source of tension, and schism often occurred even within more monolithic organizations such as the Roman Catholic church.[7]

That there would have been religious conflict within immigrant communities is not surprising. After all, the American society into which European immigrants were arriving in the nineteenth and early twentieth centuries was one of striking flux reflected both in religious organization and ethnic allegiance. Cut away from the state churches of Europe, immigrants were forced to forge new religious organizations in a society which had consciously separated church and state. The result was the American denomination, a voluntary organization based on common beliefs attempting to achieve common objectives.[8] Likewise, the immigrants' perceptions of peoplehood also underwent a continual process of change. Carrying local or regional allegiances to the United States, the immigrants' sense of peoplehood had to be forged in relation to localistic ties as well as national allegiances to their former country and to the United States, both of which were often developed and certainly elaborated upon in America.[9] Moreover, within this matrix of institutional development, immigrant religion and ethnic identification were often intimately tied to one another. Changes in the sense of peoplehood, for example, were often reflected in modifications in religious identification.[10]

Whereas scholars have emphasized religious conflict based on ethnicity or eclesiastical structure, theological schism within ethnic churches has been largely ignored. This neglect is due in part to the mistaken perception that there were few divisions based on theological issues. Jay P. Dolan, in his study of German and Irish Catholics, argued that the infrequency of severe schism within the American Catholic Church was because disagreements rarely were based on theological foundations.[11] Marcus Lee Hansen, citing both Protestant and Catholic traditions, gave a similar assessment. When congregations were organized, "the theological creed created little interest." The church was a place where the mother tongue was spoken and customs were familiar.[12]

Yet throughout the nineteenth century schism based on doctrine was widespread within native American religious denominations.[13] Were European immigrant church bodies so different or have scholars failed to stress theological division? This case study suggests the latter, that theological issues could be of utmost importance in creating social and religious conflict. During this theological schism within a Norwegian-American congregation in rural Minnesota, religious conflict played a central role in the development of an ethnic community resulting in restructured community relationships and more fully articulated theological constructs. Whereas questions of theological interpretation were central to the conflict, they were intertwined with issues of religious organization and friction between different sociocultural groups in the congregation. The result was acrimonious debate ending in schism much like that encountered by many American communities. Conflict as well as community, therefore, were central components of social, religious, and theological development among immigrant settlements which helped redefine social relationships and reorient central beliefs. The structure of the community, which will be examined first, was rife with cleavages that might have resulted in conflict, but that potential was actuated by theological and ecclesiastical issues that arose as a European religious organization was transplanted to the United States and reoriented to American society. It was the synergism of these elements working together that created a situation where the "church bells [rang] strife into the air."

Community Structure

Rural immigrant settlements in the United States obviously did not spring forth full-blown; they had to be created over time. Colonists had to enter a region, obtain land, and build farms. As settlement continued and land became increasingly scarce, some ethnic settlements expanded, while others contracted. The order of entrance into a settlement colored a family's opportunity for land and social interaction. While the earliest households had ample land from which to choose, their opportunities for primary group ties usually were more limited than those households which followed. Such was the case of the Crow River settlement in central Minnesota. Located primarily in Colfax and Burbank townships of northern Kandiyohi county, its first colonists arrived in 1859 after living for eight years in Norwegian settlements in Wisconsin. As initial settlers in the first wave of colonization, two brothers scouted out the region in the fall of 1858 and returned with their families the following spring. While they plowed their newly claimed land and began the arduous process of farm-building, additional immigrants soon arrived, and by the fall of 1860, 13 households lived in the embryonic settlement.[14] The settlement's growth was a classic case of chain migration; nine of the 15 household heads formerly had lived in the Scandinavia settlement in Waupaca County, Wisconsin while three others wed women from Waupaca. Moreover, those early marriages united people from different Norwegian regions, a pattern that would be reversed in later years.[15]

The households in the initial wave of settlement at Crow River were at a clear advantage when compared with those that followed. Not only could they choose from the large expanses of open land, but they paid a lower price for it than would later migrants. Enjoying greater possibilities for material success, the pioneers formed a distinct group as the settlement grew. As late as 1890, although many of the pioneers had retired from active farming, all but one of the ten households still actively farming were among the upper half of the society in landed wealth. Four of the six wealthiest households were descended from these pioneers.[16] The children of these pioneers often wed one another; and when they did not, they rarely married someone from their own region in Norway. Indeed, only one of the group's ten marriages through the 1880s wed a couple of the same regional background (see Table 2). Unlike later immigrants, then, the early arrivals based their sense of peoplehood not so much on former ties in Norway as on shared backgrounds in the United States such as similar residences in Wisconsin and common migration to Minnesota. The basis for this peoplehood did not lose its saliency as settlement progressed, but persisted as marriages continued to cement endogamous bonds of kinship.

The early migrants, however, founded what became distinct subcommunities based on region of origin in Norway. In spite of unique patterns of wealth and intermarriage, the first settlers usually claimed land that ultimately would be part of a spatially defined subcommunity. The earliest immigrant household, for example, originated from the parish of Drangedal, a mountainous area in the region of Telemark in southern Norway. Those who followed in 1859 or 1860 had been born in Bygland, Setesdal near Drangedal, in the central community of Gausdal, Gulbrandsdal, or in the western coastal district of Moster and Stord, Sunnhordland. The sub-communities took form as settlement accelerated. A violent Dakota Indian rebellion which occurred in 1862 halted new in-migration and frightened away those already present. But as old residents began to return in the mid-1860s, so did new households. Thirty-seven Norwegian immigrant households arrived in 1867 and 1868, for example, 24.3 percent of all households which would settle in the Crow River community. Likewise, over half (53 percent) of the households that moved to the settlement arrived between 1865 and 1871.[17]

The settlers of the mid-1860s came overwhelmingly from regions already represented by households in the pioneer wave. Migrants originating in Drangedal, Telemark were the earliest group, arriving on the average about 2½ years before the members of the next community, those from Bygland, Setesdal (see Table 1).[18] Likewise, households from Stord and Gausdal followed early settlers and soon they were joined by people from Melø, Helgeland and Naustdal, Sunnfjord as well as others from Sweden, Denmark, and other Norwegian regions. Members of the earliest sub-communities had often lived in other settlements to the east — those from Drangedal for an average of 6.4 years — while the later arrivals tended to move directly from Norway.

Table 1
ARRIVAL DATES IN THE UNITED STATES AND CROW RIVER SETTLEMENT
OF NORWEGIAN IMMIGRANT HOUSEHOLDS

	United States		Arrival Dates Crow River		Difference	
Sub-community	Mean	S.D.	Mean	S.D.	Years	N
1. Drangedal, Telemark	1858.2	9.1	1864.6	4.4	6.4	16
2. Bygland, Setesdal	1862.0	8.1	1867.2	6.2	4.2	9
3. Stord, Sunnhordland	1864.6	10.1	1867.0	8.3	2.4	25
4. Gausdal, Gudbrands.	1871.8	8.8	1872.7	7.7	.9	44
5. Other	1871.8	9.4	1873.8	8.7	2.0	23
6. Naustdal, Sunnfjord	1872.3	8.0	1873.5	5.7	1.2	14
7. Meló, Helgeland	1877.9	9.3	1877.9	8.8	.0	9

As migration from different regional backgrounds swelled in the 1860s and early 1870s, the regional groups formed spatially distinct subcommunities in the Crow River settlement (see Fig. 1).[19] Settlers From Drangedal, reflecting their early arrival, concentrated in northwestern Burbank township and tended to drift towards the west into Colfax township as colonization continued. Those originating in Gausdal congregated around the first such settler in western Burbank township. Immigrants from the western coastal area of Stord and Moster dominated central Colfax township, those from Moster primarily concentrated in the western portion of the township. The smaller subcommunities of Bygland, Meló, and Naustdal tended to congregate in regions to the north of the two townships not mapped here, although some outliers lived in Colfax and Burbank.

In addition to sociospatial differentiation, developing ties of kinship reflected in marriage patterns indicate increasingly cohesive sub-communities. Rather than marrying outside of the regional subgroup, as earlier immigrants had done, youth increasingly tended to wed others of similar backgrounds. Immigrants and their children from the Stord sub-community, for example, celebrated marriages 55 times between 1862 and the turn of the century. Forty-six of those participants, or 23 couples, wed partners of Stord background while only nine married people outside the sub-community. While this is the most striking example, each sub-community exhibited patterns of intermarriage well above their expected incidences if in- and out-marriage were random. (See Table 2). Clearly, not only were members of the sub-communities settling together, but they were marrying one another as well.

The chain migration that created the sub-communities and the patterns of intermarriage and spatial differentiation that sustained them indicate the advantages that community membership provided. Moving to a strange area, immigrants undoubtedly benefitted from close ties of kith and kin. Social adjustments were eased and the formation of farms was facilitated by exchange of labor and trade of land, implements, and crops.[20] Moreover, as the sub-communities grew, political advantages that were to be had by their leaders within local government or in the church increased.

While sub-communities in the Crow River settlement were formed in America, they carried very real cultural differences from Norway. For although Norway was a political unit with a state Lutheran church, its peasantry practiced diverse customs of courtship, marriage, fertility, use of alcohol and religiosity. One example might suffice. Eilert Sundt, in his monumental work on Norway's peasantry in the mid-nineteenth century, noted the striking variations in "bundling," a pattern of courtship which often involved premarital sex as a couple became more intimate. Not

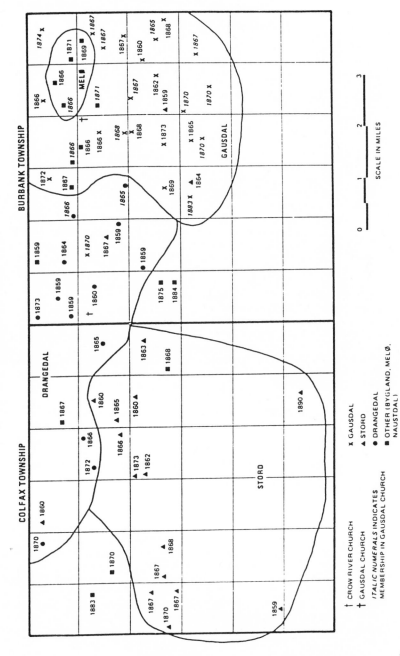

FIGURE 1
NORWEGIAN SETTLERS IN THE CROW RIVER SETTLEMENT BY
REGION OF ORIGIN AND TIME OF ARRIVAL

Table 2
PATTERNS OF INTERMARRIAGE WITHIN CROW RIVER'S REGIONAL
SUB-COMMUNITIES, 1858-1899. EXPECTED NUMBER OF ENDOGAMOUS
MARRIAGES BASED ON INDIFFERENT IN/OUT MARRIAGE
IN RELATION TO ACTUAL EXPERIENCE

Sub-community	Actual marriages Endogamous/Exogamous		Expected marriages Endogamous/Exogamous	
Early settlers	1	9	.3	9.7
Gausdal	16	18	5.5	28.5
Stord	23	9	6.9	25.1
Naustdal	11	7	1.9	16.1
Smaller sub-communities*	8	6	1.1	12.9

*Melö, Bygland, and Drangedal

surprisingly, it also resulted in an increased incidence of prenuptial conceptions and births.[21] While "bundling" was anathema in some areas particularly along Norway's west and south coast (Sundt pronounced their subsequent "morality" good) Norway's central mountain communities regularly practiced the custom. Courtship differences were not an isolated instance of varying cultural patterns. Coastal regions with low rates of prenuptial births remained areas affected heavily by pietist movements and temperance movements; they tended to contribute to Christian missions and as late as 1953 they were the stronghold of Christian political parties. Depicted as the "dark coastal strip," the area remains typified by its conservative moral behavior.[22]

The sub-communities of Crow River originated from areas with strikingly different cultural patterns. Those households emigrating from Gausdal, for example, had lived in a mountainous region with widespread "bundling" and high rates of prenuptial births (see Figure 2). Likewise, those from Melö in extreme north Norway had been exposed to practices resulting in a rate of illegitimacy just below that of Gudbrandsdal (see Table 3). Immigrants from Bygland, Drangedal, Naustdal and Stord, on the other hand, emigrated from the dark coastal strip which reflected its puritanical mores in low rates of prenuptial births. Fragmentary evidence indicates that such patterns were replicated in Crow River through the 1880s. Although prenuptial births were rare, the incidence of prenuptial conceptions in a small sample reiterates patterns observed in Norway. Youth from Gausdal practiced a courtship similar to that of their parents in Norway and at odds with other sub-communities in the settlement and their cultural background (see Table 3).

Norwegian settlements throughout the Upper Middle West composed of regionally based sub-communities encountered conflict based on dissimilar patterns of behavior carried from Norway. One settlement in Wisconsin was divided between people from the region of Hardanger and other areas to the south known in the settlement for their piety. After a house had been built by a "Southerner," four Hardanger-born brothers who were skilled fiddlers asked permission to hold a housewarming dance. "But the Southerner didn't like this," one man remembered; "He looked at [the fiddlers] awhile and then he answered, 'No,' he said, 'we're not like the Hardanger people with dancing every evening!'" And morality often was translated into religiosity. Religious dissension existed between the more easy-going Hardanger people and the immigrants from the region of Sogn in another Wisconsin settlement. The Sognings viewed the Hardanger community as undevout — they drank and swore and then went to church, one said — while Hardanger people regarded their counterparts as hypocrites for no matter who they were, "the minister declared them blessed!"[23]

Table 3
ILLEGITIMACY RATES IN NORWAY COMPARED TO PRENUPTIAL
CONCEPTION RATES IN THE CROW RIVER SETTLEMENT
BY NORWEGIAN REGION

	In Norway 1855*		in Crow River 1859-1889	
	Rank among 63 districts	*Illegitimate births per 100 marriages*	*prenuptial conceptions** per 100 births*	*N*
Bygland, Robygdelaget	5	13.7	.0	6
Drangedal, Nedre Telemark	13	20.9	–	0
Naustdal, Sunnfjord	14	21.8	14.3	7
Stord, Sunnhordland	20	25.5	11.1	9
Melö, Sundre Helgeland	56	67.8	–	0
Gausdal, Gudbrandsdal	61	70.4	66.7	11
Other			.0	2
Mixed Marriages			27.8	18
Total			24.5	53

*Source: Sundt, pp. 427-8 (according to district)
**Child born seven months or less after date of marriage.

The changing community composition thus created cleavages not in the earliest stages of settlement but as the colony developed. Initially peopled by those living in Norwegian settlements to the east where stronger cross-regional ties had developed, the Crow River settlement soon fragmented into regional sub-communities as immigration increased and as land was taken. In settling around a Norwegian Lutheran church community, immigrants were able to form sub-communities at the same time that they satisfied their spiritual needs. In so doing, they also settled near others with dissimilar backgrounds and cultural patterns. Such a setting could result in conflict, often within the confines of the major rural Norwegian-American institution — the Lutheran Church.

The Church Controversy

"After the pioneers built their log cabins and sod houses," according to the Crow River church historian, "their first thought was religion."[24] Religious services were first held in June of 1860 and a church that became the Crow River Evangelical Lutheran Church was organized on All Saints' Day, 1861 under the leadership of B.J. Muus, a pioneer pastor who held services among unchurched Norwegians on the frontier. The church was Lutheran, its ministry had been trained in Norway, and its liturgy was celebrated in Norwegian, but its structure developed into something radically different from the church in Norway. Instead of a state church with involuntary membership, Crow River church, like other Norwegian Lutheran churches in the United States, depended on voluntary membership. Instead of an upper-class pastor who often disdained the peasant congregations he was sent to serve, the Crow River clergyman depended on his congregation for his very job. And instead of a rather narrow range of discussion of church issues, Norwegian-American church congregations, Crow River among them, actively pursued answers to questions inside and out of doctrinal issues.

FIGURE 2
NORWEGIAN ORIGINS OF CROW RIVER SUB—COMMUNITIES

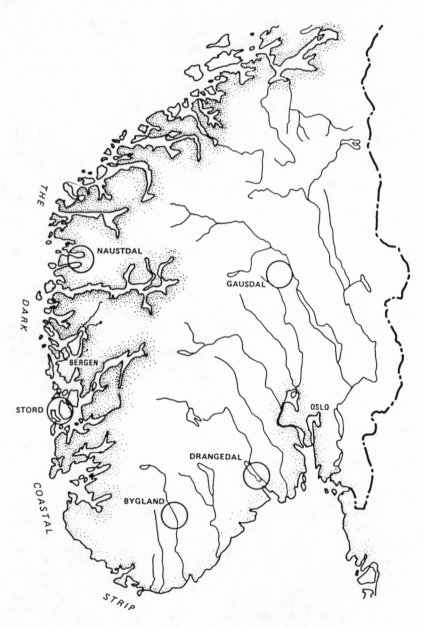

The Crow River church joined the Norwegian Evangelical Lutheran Church in America, known more simply as the Norwegian Synod, of which Muus was also a member. Characterized as the "high church" alternative of Norwegian Lutheranism in the United States, the Synod from its inception tied itself closely to the conservative German-American Missouri Synod.[25] Not only were Norwegian Synod pastors trained at the German-American Concordia Seminary well into the 1860s, but they often accepted the conservative political stands that were consistent with those of their Missouri Synod counterparts and at odds with their parishioners. In 1861, for example, the Norwegian Synod laity discovered that its clergy offered theological justifications for slavery. Amidst the Civil War, parishioners allied with a minority of the clergy to oppose the Norwegian Synod's official neutrality on the slavery issue. The majority of clergymen remained firm on the question, however, in spite of the loss of a few congregations over the stand.

Minor conflicts continued to plague the Synod, but it was the schism in the 1880s arising out of the question of election that eventually tore apart the Norwegian Synod. The orthodox view, again associated with the Missouri Synod, argued that election or predestination was based solely on God's grace. The competing theory, based on the theology of the Lutheran church in Norway, gave men and women a greater role in their salvation, a role that the Missouri Synod and its Norwegian Synod allies argued made faith the cause of election which ultimately repudiated the sovereign activity of divine grace in salvation. In short, the powers that were within the Norwegian Synod, by accepting the former view, seemed to be advocating doctrine that affirmed Calvinistic determinism. The opposition group that developed, which became known as the Anti-Missourians, was appalled at this Calvinism and placed greater regenerative emphasis in the individual himself.

As the conflict spread, the religious press became filled with tendentious debate and soon a schism appeared inevitable. In 1884, the Anti-Missourians encouraged their congregations to bypass the the synodical treasury. Instead the churches were to make contributions to an Anti-Missourian auxiliary treasury which would in effect give financial support to the continuance of the schism. Three years later, the group now known as Anti-Missourian "Brotherhood," established its own seminary in Northfield, Minnesota. The Brotherhood then left the Norwegian Synod after they had been accused by the Synod of being schismatics. Given the alternative by the Synod to withdraw or compromise their convictions, they chose the former course.

The controversy began among the clergy, but it quickly spread to the laity. Church members vehemently discussed the theological questions, according to one participant, "on the streets and in the alleys, in stores and in saloons, and through a continuous flow of agitating articles [in newspapers and periodicals]." Sometimes words led to fights. "They argued predestination in the saloons, with their tongues," said one, "and settled in the alley with their fists."[26] While fisticuffs might have been rare, certain Norwegian congregations suffered wrenching internal strife. "The ties of old friendships broke," remembered a man. "Neighbor did not speak to neighbor. The daughter who was married to a member of the other party became a stranger in her father's house. Man and wife turned into dog and cat. Brothers and sisters were sundered from one another. On the other hand, old enemies became friends and were reconciled only when they found themselves on the same side of the insurmountable fence which had been raised between the [Anti-Missouri] and [Norwegian] Synods."[27] This dissension within congregations was not an isolated instance. One third of the pastors and congregations withdrew from the Synod as a result of the conflict. In Minnesota alone, 69 congregations left the Synod. More tumultuous conflict occurred in 23 additional Minnesota congregations which ultimately split apart, one faction remaining in the Norwegian Synod while the other joined the new Anti-Missourian Brotherhood.[28]

The Crow River congregation was among those 23 churches in Minnesota that split over the Election Controversy. The congregation avoided the conflict until 1890 when a majority of the 114 voting members decided in favor of retaining Norwegian Synod allegience. The minority in response declared they would withdraw and form their own church. Since the seceding households demanded a division of church property, a meeting was held at which an agreement was reached that would permit division if those leaving the church equalled one-fourth of the membership. On November 12, the declaration of secession was signed and delivered by 33 voting members. Although the seceders believed they comprised the necessary one-quarter of the membership, the leaders of the Crow River church determined that only 25 were members in good standing. This lesser number, which did not constitute one-fourth of church membership, permitted the Crow River membership to argue that the seceders were not entitled to the division of church property.[29] Not surprisingly, the minority was not satisfied with the decision. Meetings continued to be held and the majority of Crow River voting members remained adamant about their doctrinal stand. The question went to an outside board of arbitration which finally negotiated a division of the property among the contending parties by late 1893, over two years after a new church had been formed based on Anti-Missourian doctrine on February 14, 1891.[30]

While the litigation dragged on, the members of the new church, like the Crow River church members before them, quickly set about to build their place of worship. The new church building, smaller in size than the Crow River church, was situated within the Gausdal subcommunity. Moreover, its name, the Gausdal Norwegian Lutheran Church, indicated the regional background of the majority of its members. Of the 33 households that formed the new church, 29 originated in Gausdal (see Figure 2).[31] Households in the Gausdal sub-community, clustered in an enclave and practicing customs at odds with the other regional communities, were likely candidates for dissatisfaction within the Crow River church. Statistical tests confirm that background in Norway, rather than time of arrival or wealth, was the overriding reason for membership in the new church.[32] Thus, while the theological discord was based on intellectual disputes, the lines of conflict were closely linked to social relationships within and between the sub-communities in the settlement.

Fourteen Gausdal households, however, chose not to withdraw from the Crow River church although they continued to live in the Gausdal sub-community. While place of birth was of overriding importance in inducing secession, those from Gausdal who remained in the Crow River church were more acculturated and had closer ties to other sub-communities. The earliest settlers, such as the pioneer Gausdal household that entered the region in 1860, tended not to secede from the Crow River church. The average Gausdal household that remained in the church arrived in the settlement nearly three years earlier than the average that left. Likewise, while the wealth profile of the Gausdal sub-community was similar to that of other regional sub-communities, it was clearly the less wealthy who tended to leave the church (see Table 4).[33] Finally, ties of kinship differed among those who remained and those who left the church. Whereas 13 couples among Gausdal church members married within the sub-community between earliest settlement and 1889, only four wed outside the regional group. Conversely, only three children within those Gausdal households that remained in the Crow River church had wed others from Gausdal compared to 14 who married outside the fold.[34] The process of community formation thus continued. On the one hand, a large segment of the Gausdal sub-community removed itself even further from interaction among Norwegians in the settlement by forming its own church. Meanwhile, by remaining within the church, the other portion of the sub-community moved closer to other Norwegian communities. The result was continued societal change and periodic cultural conflict wherein larger theological questions and moral precepts were intricately tied to local patterns of interaction.

Table 4
WEALTH ACCORDING TO GAUSDAL ORIGIN AND GAUSDAL OR CROW
RIVER MEMBERSHIP BY QUARTILES, 1890

	Poor				Wealthy			
	First		Second		Third		Fourth	
Gausdal origin	11	34.4	5	15.6	9	28.1	7	21.9
Crow River membership	1	10.0	2	20.0	2	20.0	5	50.0
Gausdal membership	10	45.4	3	13.6	7	21.9	2	9.1

The spiritual issues that set the community schism in motion were translated into numerous temporal divisions. The cultural contrasts between sub-communities were central to setting groups apart while wealth and time of arrival were salient in creating factions within the seceding Gausdal sub-community. Conversely, the significance of such worldly differences as wealth and time of arrival aid in explaining seemingly paradoxical intellectual positions and the expression of religious freedom in the United States. The Gausdal seceders curiously joined a more revivalistic, antinomian, pietistic church body even if they did not reflect a pietistic attitude towards courtship and use of alcohol. The sub-communities from the "dark coastal strip," on the other hand, did not maintain a pietistic stance on the question of predestination. One might argue that the paradox was simply that, a paradox that is impossible to decipher in this particularistic situation. Yet the incongruities between the social structure and the cultural symbols provide keys for some attempt at explanation. The Gausdal seceders, many of whom were newer arrivals, were prone to accept the older Norwegian interpretation of predestination. The pietistic church leaders of the Crow River church, on the other hand, were now tied into pastoral coalitions that also created inconsistencies, but they followed the voice of their leader.[35]

The symbolic relationships between wealth, election and religious freedom in the United States were even more significant in precipitating social and theological schism. For not only did religious freedom in the United States facilitate the division and creation of new religious communities, but symbols of freedom and democracy in America had to be made consistent with theological positions and clerical authority carried from Europe.

Greater freedom in the United States − religious or otherwise − was one symbol repeatedly celebrated by the immigrants as American. "Freedom is here an element which is drawn in, as it were, with mother milk," wrote an early Norwegian immigrant, "and seems as essential to every citizen of the United States as the air he breathes."[36] Like freedom, democracy was another concept to which the church was forced to respond. The Norwegian Lutheran church was different in America according to an 1879 Norwegian-American novel for it was "an institution which stood in need of patronage and support." Since the congregation paid the pastor's salary, it could censure him.[37]

The church thus acted as an American body − formed on American principles of voluntary membership and democratic representation − even though its rituals, language, and canon had been carried from Norway. Such a circumstance was not without its incongruities. During an intense debate, a Missourian pastor threw up his arms when a vote was called on the election question. "How could a majority determine what was God's law?" he argued. The vote was held, however, since church members contended that the ministry did not necessarily have the sole power to interpret the law either and perhaps a democratic solution would come as close to the truth as possible. One member was so bold as to suggest that the pastor, who was not only a Missourian but who opposed the vote, was a "false teacher."[38]

The Election Controversy created contradictory impulses in relation to democracy and freedom. Ironically, the church in a more democratic environment had been shifted theologically toward a less egalitarian stance in regard to salvation. Structural differences in the community probably made this paradox especially objectionable to the poorer Gausdal sub-community. Through a new form of tyranny, a majority of culturally distinct people now determined church policy, a cruel twist of fate in the supposedly freer environment of the United States. The powers in the congregation were in a sense worse than the upper class pastors in Norway who had held their parishioners in contempt. For the majority in America advocated an interpretation of election which not only contradicted age-old Norwegian Lutheran doctrine, but was antidemocratic to believers in the most profound sense: it denied that all who believed had the possibility of eternal salvation. Religious freedom, however, also provided members of the Gausdal sub-community the means to redress their grievances. They could accept a pietistic intellectual position that did not necessarily reflect their moral behavior, but proclaimed their allegience to new found religious freedom and old-world doctrine. And by so doing, they could free themselves from the subordinate status in their church community.

Conclusion

The Election Controversy within the Crow River settlement was a dramatic instance of a rural immigrant 'community that faced religious controversy. One essential component of that conflict was the changing social configuration of the community. As the area was settled, sub-communities developed, based on regional backgrounds. The regional sub-communities became even more self-contained as endogamous patterns of marriage further tied together increasingly large and spatially distinct regional subgroups. Contrary to linear models of acculturation, the sub-communities became more cohesive only after an enlarged chain migration permitted segmentation into individual regional communities while at the same time reduced land resources constrained them.

Remarkable conflict between the sub-communities did not occur, however, until a theological schism divided the church congregation. Centered on the relatively abstract spiritual issue of predestination and election, the conflict split the community into warring camps based on worldly backgrounds. The motivations of the actors in this drama are impossible to determine given the surviving evidence. But it does appear that the significance of the theological divisions were very real and exacerbated socioeconomic cleavages already present. The church was a focal point for the community and the interpretation of its canon was of central importance to its parishioners. Beyond this, dislikes and disagreements could be expressed through the symbolic language of the conflict. The synergistic relationship that developed between latent community differences and a church controversy which permitted their expression in theological language created the basis for schism.

Most Norwegian Synod congregations probably escaped so dramatic a schism because settlement patterns had not resulted in the juxtaposition of sub-communities so culturally distinct as those of Gausdal and the "dark coastal strip." Likewise, earlier debates over synodical stands such as the neutral position on slavery prior to and during the Civil War had led to debate and conflict within congregations, but nothing on the scale that occurred 30 years later. It was rather the combination of latent social divisions on the congregational level interacting with a new meaning of religious doctrine that provided a flash point ignited by the election controversy. As a minority, members of the Gausdal sub-community in Crow river were not only denied access to power in their own congregation but forced to accept an interpretation of election that was ostensibly un-Norwegian and un-American as well as an example of what the seceders called "unChristian exclusivism." In the end, members of the Gausdal sub-community decided to secede, to form a church where the theological cleavages would be shifted to their favor.

In spite of the vituperative debate and schism, the election controversy in Crow River was an example of cultural conflict rather than disintegration.[39] Certainly the Norwegian Synod declined in power, but it was replaced by new church bodies that reflected greater belief in antinominism and greater lay control which ultimately induced increased lay involvement. Ironically the Anti-Missourian group later played a significant role in the movement to unite all Norwegian Lutherans in a single church body. Likewise, although schisms did result in smaller congregations, the new churches were more culturally cohesive than in the past. Whereas conflict in immigrant communities created bitterness, it worked to redefine cultural and theological meaning in the new American environment.

Notions of sectarianism, voluntarism and revivalism were pervasive in the Norwegian Lutheran church in the United States especially when compared with the State Church of Norway. Certainly questions of theology did influence the Norwegian peasantry especially in the periods of lay revivals, but they were not as prominent as those which occurred among Norwegian immigrants in America. The denominationalism of the Norwegian-American Lutherans, like their American-born Protestant counterparts, resulted in a church more responsive to the neeeds of its parishioners, but for the very same reason also more prone to schism and conflict. The church bells could "ring strife into the air" because of a complex transplantation and adaptation of an institution that defined not orthodoxy but ethnicity. And that strife was made all the more likely by the fluid, dynamic nature of the society of which the combatants were now a part.

University of California
Department of History
Berkeley, CA 94720

Jon Gjerde

FOOTNOTES

An earlier version of this paper was presented at the "Luther and the City of Man" conference in Minneapolis on November 12, 1983. The author would like to thank Nicholas B. Dirks, Phillip Hoffman, J. Morgan Kousser, James Lee, John Modell, Hilton Root, and Rudolph J. Vecoli for helpful comments and criticisms in the reformulation of this draft.

1. Cited in Laila Nilsen, "The Genesis and Organization of the Norwegian Lutheran Church of America," unpublished master's thesis, University of Minnesota, 1933, pp. 46-47.

2. See, for example, Martin Marty, "Ethnicity: The Skeleton of Religion in America," *Church History* 41 (1972): 5-21; and Timothy L. Smith, "Religion and Ethnicity in America," *American Historical Review* 83 (1978): 1155-85.

3. Oscar Handlin, *The Uprooted* (Boston, 1951): 127; Andrew M. Greeley, *The Catholic Experience* (Garden City, NY, 1969): 196. See Kathleen Neils Conzen, "Quantification and the New Urban History," *Journal of Interdisciplinary History* 13 (1983): 671-72.

4. Randall M. Miller, "Introduction," in Randall M. Miller and Thomas D. Marzik, eds., *Immigrants and Religion in Urban America* (Philadelphia, 1977): xv.

5. Ibid. See also John Bodnar, *Immigration and Industrialization: Ethnicity in an American Mill Town. 1870-1940*, (Pittsburgh, 1977): 103-08; Bodnar, "Immigration and Modernization: The Case of Slavic Peasants in Industrial America," *Journal of Social History* 10 (1976): 47; John Rice, *Patterns of Ethnicity in a Minnesota County*, (Umea, Sweden, 1973): 37; Jon Gjerde, "The Effect of Community on Migration: Three Minnesota Townships 1885-1905," *Journal of Historical Geography*, 5 (1979): 407; Robert C. Ostergren, "A Community Transplanted: The Formative Experience of a Swedish Immigrant Community in the Upper Middle West," *Journal of Historical Geography*, 5 (1979).

6. Leslie Woodcock Tentler, "Who is the Church? Conflict in a Polish Immigrant Parish in Late Nineteenth-Century Detroit," *Comparativ: Studies of Society and History* 25 (1983): 247, 258.

7. Timothy L. Smith, "Lay Initiative in the Religious Life of American Immigrants, 1880-1950," in Tamara K. Hareven, (ed.) *Anonymous Americans: Explorations in Nineteenth Century Social History* (Englewood Cliffs, N.J., 1971): 216; Victor R. Greene, "For God and Country: The Origins of Slavic Catholic Self-Consciousness in America," *Church History* 35 (1966): 446-460; Timothy L. Smith, "Religious Denominations as Ethnic Communities: A Regional Case Study," *Church History* 35 (1966): 207-226; Jay P. Dolan, *The Immigrant Church: New York's Irish and German Catholics 1815-1865* (Baltimore, 1975); Peter A. Munch, "Authority and Freedom: Controversy in Norwegian-American Congregations," *Norwegian-American Studies* 28 (1979): 3-34. See also Abner Cohen, *Custom and Politics in Urban Africa: A Study of Hansa Migrants in Yoruba Towns* (Berkeley, 1969); Abner Cohen, ed., *Urban Ethnicity* (London, 1974); and Robert H. Bates, "Ethnic Competition and Modernization in Contemporary Africa," *Comparative Political Studies* 6 (1974): 457-84 for examples of religious and ethnic conflict in other regions of rapid change.

8. See Sidney E. Mead, "Denominationalism: The Shape of Protestantism in America," *Church History* 23 (1955): 291-320; L.A. Loetscher, "The Problem of Christian Unity in Early Nineteenth Century America," *Church History* 32 (1963): 3-16; and Robert C. Ostergren, "The Immigrant Church as a Symbol of Community and Place in the Upper Midwest," *Great Plains Quarterly* 1 (1981): 225-38.

9. Marcus Lee Hansen, "Immigration and Puritanism" in *The Immigrant in American History* (Cambridge, 1940): 114-21; Smith, "Religious Denominations as Ethnic Communities," *passim*.

10. Bodnar, "Immigration and Modernization," 51.

11. Dolan, *The Immigrant Church*: 88.

12. Hansen, "Immigration and American Culture,"in *Immigrant in American History*: 136-37. Some basic religious histories have adumbrated the existence of theological schism within immigrant denominations. See, for example, Sydney E. Ahlstrom, *A Religious History of the American People* (New Haven, 1972): 749-62; William Warren Sweet, *The Story of Religion in America* (New York, 1939): 542. Nevertheless, few recent monographs or articles have specifically addressed the issue.

13. Studies from the Halfway Covenent and the Salem Witch Trials through religious schism arising out of the Second Great Awakening have analyzed in depth the relationships between theology and social change. See, for example, Paul Boyer and Stephen Nissenbaum, *Salem Possessed: The Social Origins of Witchcraft* (Cambridge, 1974); Paul R. Lucas, *Valley of Discord: Church and Society along the Connecticut River, 1636-1725* (Hanover, NH, 1976); Richard L. Bushman, *From Puritan to Yankee: Character and the Social Order in Connecticut, 1690-1765* (Cambridge, 1967); Robert A. Gross, *The Minutemen and Their World* (New York, 1976); and Robert W. Doherty, "Social Bases for the Presbyterian Schism of 1837-38: The Philadelphia Case," *Journal of Social History* 2 (1968): 69. See also William G. McLoughlin, *Revivals, Awakenings, and Reform: An Essay on Religion and Social Change in America, 1607-1977* (Chicago, 1978) for a broader essay on socio-religious change.

14. Victor E. Lawson, *Illustrative History and Descriptive and Biographical Review of Kandiyohi County, Minnesota* (Willmar, MN, 1905): 124-5; Carl M. Gunderson, *Crow River Evangelical Lutheran Church 1861-1961* (n.p., 1961): 7-10.

15. Hjalmar Holand, *De Norske Settlementers Historie: En Oversigt over den Norske Invandring til og Bebyggelse af Amerikas Nordvesten fra Amerikas Opdagelse til Indiankrigen in Nordvesten med Bygde og Navneregister* (Ephraim, WI, 1909): 199-207; Martin Ulvestad, *Norge i Amerika* (Minneapolis, 1902): 18. See Robert C. Ostergren, "Kinship Networks and Migration: A Nineteenth-Century Swedish Example," *Social Science History* 6 (1982): 293-320 for an analysis of the importance of kin in facilitating migration.

16. Kandiyohi County Tax Records, 1890; Crow River Lutheran Church records; Gunderson, *op. cit.*: 7.

17. Crow River Lutheran Church records; Gunderson, *op. cit., passim.*

18. Crow River Lutheran Church records; Gunderson, *op. cit.*

19. Figure 1 was constructed using the county plat book of 1886, plat maps in Lawson, *op. cit.*, the Crow River Lutheran Church records, and Gunderson, *op. cit.* Gunderson was particularly valuable since it indicated place of residence as well as time of arrival in the community.

20. Benefits derived from ties of kinship and neighborhood provided utilities, both pecuniary and non-pecuniary, that tended to reduce the incidence of migration from an immigrant community according to another rural case study. See Gjerde, "The Effect of Community on Migration": 302-22; and John S. MacDonald and Latrice D. MacDonald, "Chain Migration, Ethnic Neighborhood Formation, and Social Networks," *Milbank Memorial Fund Quarterly* 42 (1964): 82-97.

21. Eilert Sundt, *Om Saedeligheds-Tilstanden i Norge* (Christiania, 1857); Eilert Sundt, *Fortsatt Bidrag Angaaende Saedeligheds-Tilstanden i Norge* (Christiania, 1864); Eilert Sundt, *Om Saedeligheds-Tilstanden i Norge. Tredie Beretning* (Christiania, 1866). See also Jon Gjerde, *From Peasants to Farmers: The Migration from Balestrand, Norway to the Upper Middle West* (New York, 1985) for an analysis of courtship patterns in Norway and their alterations among immigrants in the United States.

22. See Gabriel Øidne, "Litt om Motsetninga Mellom Austlandet og Vestlandet," *Syn og Segn* 63 (1957): 97-114.

23. Quoted in Einar Haugen, *The Norwegian Language in America: A Study in Bilingual Behavior* (Philadelphia, 1956), Volume 2: 358-359.

24. This paragraph is based on Lawson, *op. cit.* and Gunderson, *op. cit.* Lay initiative in founding church congregations was a significant factor in facilitating immigrant religious organization. See Smith, "Lay Initiative": 225.

25. The best description of the election controversy, on which this and the following paragraph are based, is E. Clifford Nelson and Eugene L. Fevold, *The Lutheran Church Among Norwegian Americans: A History of the Evangelical Lutheran Church* (Minneapolis, 1960): Volume 1: 253-70. For an earlier description, see Th. Eggen, "Oversigt over den Norsk-Lutherske Kirkes Historie i Amerika" in Johs. B. Wist, ed., *Norske-Amerikanernes Festskrift 1914* (Decorah, IA, 1914): 228-32.

26. U.V. Koren, "Hvad Den Norske Synods Har Villet og Fremdeles Vil," *Samlede Skrifter* 3 (1890): 444.

27. J.A. Erikson, "Større end det Storste," *Ved Arnen* (1939) cited in Dorothy Burton Skardal *The Divided Heart: Scandinavian Immigrant Experience through Literary Sources* (Oslo, 1974): 180.

28. Nelson and Fevold, *op. cit.*, Vol. 1, p. 254. Minnesota figures were derived from congregational histories in O.M. Nordlie, *Den Norske Lutherske Menigheter i Amerika 1843-1916* (Minneapolis, 1918): 436-80.

29. Crow River Lutheran Church records; Gunderson, *op. cit.* Minutes of meetings from church records often indicate how very passionate the theological divisions were. Pastors on the opposite side of the fence were called "false teachers" [see below] or worse. Church histories written years after the event were more circumspect. The Crow River historian argued that travelling ministers "stirred up trouble, and one thing led to another." In spite of the division, however, the majority decided to stay within the Synod because "the only right stand to take was to stay with the old established Church." Gundersen, *op. cit.*: 21-22.

30. Lawson, *op. cit.*: 128; Gunderson, *op. cit.*: 21-22; *History of the Charter and Early Members of the Gausdal Lutheran Church: Ringville Prairie and Georgeville, Minnesota* (n.p., n.d.): 1.

31. *History of the Charter and Early Members of the Gausdal Lutheran Church: Ringville Prairie and Georgeville, Minnesota* (n.p., n.d.).

32. A statistical technique known as logit analysis was employed to determine the effect of sub-community membership, wealth, and arrival time in Crow River on secession from the church. Similar to regression analysis, logit analysis is designed for instances where the dependant variable (in this case, secession from the church) is dichotomous and hence unsuited for ordinary linear regression. Three independent variables were used to explain secession from the church: sub-community membership, wealth (measured in real and personal wealth valuated for tax purposes by Kandiyohi County in 1890), and time of arrival in Crow River (derived from church records). Sub-community membership boosted the chances of secession enormously (t = 4.289 with 74 degrees of freedom) indicating that its effect on secession was no statistical fluke. Wealth and arrival time, on the other hand, did not affect secession significantly (t = 0.854 and 0.377, respectively, with 74 degrees of freedom). Testing for the effect of sub-community membership and wealth alone led to similar results, as did a trial with membership and time of arrival alone. For an explanation of logit analysis by a historian, see J. Morgan Kousser, "Making Separate Equal: Integration of Black and White School Funds in Kentucky," *Journal of Interdisciplinary History* 10 (1980): 399-428.

33. Although wealth did not directly affect secession from the Crow River Church, logit analysis also suggests the tendency of wealthier members within the Gausdal sub-community to remain in the church (t = 4.423 with 75 degrees of freedom for a wealth-subcommunity interaction variable, which measured the effect wealth had on secession for members of the Gausdal subcommunity only).

34. The varying expected as opposed to actual endogamous patterns were striking. The Gausdal households that remained in the Crow River Church had an expected incidence of .8 endogamous marriages compared to three that actually occurred. Those households that seceded had an expected value of 2.1 marriages, yet its members celebrated 13 endogamous marriages.

35. In the continuing tension between religion, ethnicity, cultural symbols and social strucutre, it would be interesting to determine if the new Gausdal church innovated changing patterns of behavior which made it consistant with the new theological pietism while the old pietists from the dark coastal strip became more adamant participants in a high church liturgy. Such analysis, however, is beyond the scope of this essay.

36. Peter A. Munch and Helene Munch, *The Strange American Way* (Carbondale, IL, 1970): 205. For other examples of such Tocqueville-like expressions from Norwegian immigrants, see Johan Reinert Reiersen, *Veiviser for Norske Emigranter* (Christiania, 1844) translated by Frank G. Nelson, *Pathfinder for Norwegian Emigrants* (Northfield, MN, 1981); Theodore C. Blegen, ed., *Land of Their Choice: The Immigrants Write Home* (St. Paul, 1955); and Gunnar Urtegaard, "Og Huen Tages Ikke av Hovedet for Noget Menneske," *Tidsskrift Utgjeve av Historielaget for*

Sogn 27 (1981). For an excellent fictional account of the different uses of "democracy" and "freedom" to justify the stands of contending parties in a church schism, see O.E. Rolvaag, *Peder Victorious: A Tale of the Pioneers Twenty Years Later* (New York, 1929): 44-62.

37. Hjalmar Hjorth Boyesen, *Falconberg* (New York, 1879): 99, cited in Skardal, *op. cit.*, p. 131. Other church organizations and congregations grappled with the question of democracy in the church. See Tentler, "Who is the Church?": 247; and Smith, "Lay Initiative": 215.

38. Ft. Ridgely and Dale Lutheran Church records. This congregation, located to the south of the Crow River settlement, also experienced strife between localized sub-communities and also split, this time into three congregations, in 1885.

39. The conflict and schism constituted a period of rapid change and redefinition of community organization, theological values, and the meaning that underlay them. Some observers have argued that this conflict occurring in societies experiencing widespread change illustrates the occasional disintegrative character of religion in society. See, for example, Thomas F. O'Dea, *The Sociology of Religion* (Englewood Cliffs, N.J., 1966): 13-18; J. Milton Yinger, *Religion, Society and the Individual* (New York, 1957): 56-72. Geertz, on the other hand, has constructed a counter-model which attempts to integrate change and serves as a better design for the Crow River conflict. When scholars deny the independent roles of culture and social structure, they see the discontinuities between them as instances of cultural and social disintegration. Geertz argues instead that discontinuities in a dynamic society are the result of a disharmony in the relationship between culture and social or cultural disintegration. See Clifford Geertz, "Ritual and Social Change: A Javanese Example" in *The Interpretation of Cultures* (New York, 1973): 142-69.

At a time when scholars are beginning to understand the historical importance of studying ethnicity and immigration, it is tragic to realize that the sources required for such research are often discarded or destroyed. The result of this loss may be that, in our enthusiasm to bring immigrants, ethnic groups and cultural minorities themselves to the centre of study, we run the risk of what one immigration specialist has described as, "not reconstructing the past, but rather, imagining how the immigrant would have reacted." The historian, with the help of each community, must instead find and preserve a variety of sources which will enable him to see in its entirety the past and present of each ethnic group.

Paradoxically, if we do not work to save such material, the next generation, regardless of its interest in its ethnic heritage, will not be able to frame the questions necessary to writing ethnocultural history. Although external records such as city directories, immigration reports, the census, and public school records may survive, the attitudes of the immigrants, the records of the institutions they created and the reality of their daily life will be lost to history and to the immigrants' descendants. This would be the final victory of the melting pot over those who have struggled with dignity and resourcefulness to embrace North America while cherishing their own cultural roots.

To avoid such retrospective falsification of our heritage, the Multicultural History Society, along with other similar organizations in Canada and the United States, must make certain that, while encouraging research scholarship, the first priority of immigrant and ethnic history programmes, projects and agencies remains the systematic gathering and preserving of written and oral sources. When collections of research material are available, scholars and communities will have the opportunity to study properly the immigrant and ethnic fact in North American history.

The Multicultural History Society of Ontario hopes that, by viewing immigrant settlements, ethnic groups and minority communities as clusters of formal and informal institutions and by describing the types of manuscript and documentary records that these institutions generate, we can help researchers to study immigration and ethnicity in the context of these historical sources. Obviously, the importance of a given institution varies from community to community, and we can make no pretence to describing fully in these pages the institutions of all those peoples who have contributed to the province's rich history. Nonetheless, each issue of *Polyphony* will offer a general statement on an institution and its role in ethnic communities, and provide some examples of the historical sources created by a variety of ethnic groups.

Some of the institutions we will examine in future issues in order to indicate the avenues of research in ethnocultural history they open will include mutual aid societies, fraternal organizations, business enterprises such as boardinghouses, travel agencies and stores, the ethnic newspaper press, trade union locals, and the family. In this issue, we begin the effort with a discussion of religious institutions, of their role in immigrant and ethnic communities and of the research that they generate.

R.F.H.

1

Religion and Ethnocultural Communities

Whether immigrants had taken religion for granted before the ocean crossing or had fought hard and long to maintain it against oppressors, most asserted their ancestral faith once they arrived in North America. The parish, the congregation and the shul became the places where people with similar backgrounds regrouped after immigrating, the clergy often serving as intermediaries between newcomers and the sometimes frightening civil authorities. Thus, church records contained information about ritual, as well as about ethnic and civil matters.

The church building itself, or an attached hall or school, became both the rallying point for the community and the main physical manifestation of new fellow-feeling. When employment and housing conditions permitted, the church emerged as the geographical and pyschic core of the immigrant or ethnic neighbourhood. In fact, even those who chose to go their own way toward secularism or who joined one of the "North American" faiths often lived near to the very religious or parish authorities whom they opposed. Whether seen as a friend or an enemy, the church was a part of immigrants' ethnic heritage, and scholars have begun to think of the parish not just as a religious entity, but also, in the sociological sense, as a neighbourhood or gathering place.

The clergy often saw their role as maintaining not just the faith of the people but the community's ethnoculture as well. Indeed, for many of the oppressed nations who sent immigrants abroad, clergymen had always served that kind of cultural role. "To maintain and preserve the Polish ethnicity in the urban centres I believe that the Church has a very important responsibility and role to play," a Polish Oblate wrote recently. After the Lateran Pact between Rome and the Italian government, Italy's consular officials guarded against the decline of *Italianità* in certain Canadian parishes. When the local bishop seemed about to put Irish or other non-Italian priests into what had been *de facto* Italian national parishes, the consulate worked to find curates for them who were Italian or who could speak Italian.

The nineteenth century dictum of the German Catholics who successfully resisted Irish American attempts to form a single English-speaking church was that "language saves faith." The historian is learning that, in a very real sense, the reverse is equally true, that is, religious practice often preserves language and culture. A hymn or a sermon in German, Korean, Welsh — a prayer in a mother tongue — carries much the same cultural impact, the same appeal to nostalgia, as the more secular, or profane, use of the mother

tongue in a sport's club or a saloon. The proselytizing churches of North America, committed to the importance of the vernacular in religious services anyway, understood this. The first Italian religious service in Toronto was Anglican. Shortly after that the Casa Metodista came into being in order to minister to the Italian immigrants in their own tongue. Any city walker can see that the effort continues: signs announcing services in Finnish, Chinese or Korean appear on United Churches in the inner city, and other denominations reach out to bring solace to newcomers through ritual spoken in the mother tongue.

Even before a church actually existed to become the focus of revived immigrant or ethnic life, the role of religion and the clergy in the survival of the group often proved critical. In fact, sometimes a clergyman in a rented hall or a floating congregation dominated by a few active, devout laymen provided the only trace of cultural continuity which men and women, uprooted from their homeland, desired.

```
EXPLANATION

OUR LADY HELP OF CHRISTIANS SLOVENIAN  PARISH
PARISH ESTABLISHED Y·1953
CHURCH SOLEMNY BLESSED       BY HIS
EMINENCE  J· C CARDINAL  Mc· GUIGAN
DECEMBER 19ᵗʰ 1954
FAMILIES :  285
PARISHIONERS :  1290
HOLY NAME SOCIETY  ESTABLISHED Y. 1949
MEMBERS :  76
CATHOLIC WOMEN'S LEAGUE
ESTABLISHED  Y· 1950 – MEMBERS :   65
SODALITY  OF MARY ESTABLISHED Y  1955
MEMBERS :  20
SOCIETY OF ST· VINCENT DE PAUL
ESTABLISHED   Y·1955  MEMBERS :   12
SLOVENIAN  CULTURAL SOCIETY OF BISHOP
BARAGA "  ESTABLISHED Y·1955
MEMBERS :  45
PARISH CATHOLIC ACTION AND YOUNG
CHRISTIAN WORKERS ESTABLISHED Y·1954
MEMBERS :  24
BARAGA'S  MISSION SOCIETY ESTABLISHED 1953
CHURCH CHOIR ESTABLISHED  Y·1955
```

3

National identity itself might slumber until a church was organized, but an important and direct relationship existed between religion and ethnicity at all times. In Toronto, for example, the Polish population at the turn of the century went to a separate Sunday mass in the back of the Roman Catholic cathedral. Their obvious commitment to a liturgy of their own led the philanthropic O'Keefe family to buy them the church building that became St. Stanislaus' parish. At about the same time, several hundred Maltese worshipped at the Italian national parish, Our Lady of Mt. Carmel. When they had the necessary strength of numbers, they resolved to build their own church, St. Paul the Apostle, in the Junction area of the city. Many of them spoke Italian, but few, if any, gave up their sense of being Maltese, and one must ask if the practice of their faith reinforced or threatened their ethnic identity in those early years. Parish records should help to find the answer to that question and to many others posed by the social historian.

Lithuanians, worshipping first at St. Stanislaus Polish Church, formed their own Lithuanian Catholic benevolent society before they were numerous enough to build a Toronto parish of their own. At about the same time, Father Antanas Staniukynas and other clergy were forming a Lithuanian Roman Catholic priests' league in the United States to minister to their people and to help them maintain their separate ethnic identity. All this occurred before Lithuania was a free nation. Moreover, lay initiative was so effective that distinctions between local efforts at autonomy and the national cause throughout North America are now lost to the collective memory.

In Ontario, Syrian Melkites and Lebanese Maronites resented both assimilationist thought — "it might be advisable to let them go on without a Maronite priest," wrote one Catholic spokesman, who then went on to explain that "this might help to assimilate the Maronites more effectively than otherwise would be the case" — as well as the attempt to force them into a single Arab American rite: "We don't suppose Your Grace would never advise us to disobey and transgress the Order of the Holy See by giving our spiritual affairs to a Melkite priest. . ." Their English might have been a bit faulty; their ecclesiastical point was exact. At such times, religion became the most important variable in the definition of ethnicity itself, and group survival might depend on the energy of a single clergyman or the courage of laymen. Naturally, the church then became the deposit of a variety of records and manuscript sources which illuminate the ethnocultural life of the group and the efforts of society to integrate newcomers and minorities.

Helen Znaniecki Lopata has described ethnicity as "a gradually emerging fabric." At the heart of the evolution was religious practice, for the cultural and social penumbra which spread from the effort to maintain one's religion affected the whole ethnic group. Historians, sociologists or ethnologists who wish to study and understand ethnicity, or grandchildren who wish to comprehend the ways of thought of their *baba*, grandpa or *nona*, should preserve the materials which bear the traces of that process and the clues to its logic.

No one among the immigrants was really able to practice the faith of his fathers exactly as he had in the

4

Old World. The changes were subtle and barely discernible to outsiders, but what had been traditional faith and form in the Old Country had to be maintained purposefully in the new one, or cease to exist. Ritual, like every other aspect of folk culture and language, was a living thing which borrowed from both the environment and the frame of mind of those who enacted it. Whether it was two Italian *paese* groups bickering over the right to carry San Rocco's statue on his feast day or the young and gifted Jewish violinist who played "God Save the King" at that saint's feast, things were happening in the new country which had not happened in the old. Religious ritual and ethnic identity were subtly changing.

For the Orthodox Christians and the Armenian Apostolic Christians who came to North America, religious life was freer than it had ever been. They could openly and aggressively identify their ethnic survival with their religious beliefs. If they needed to, they could rid themselves of entanglements with patriarchs, exarchs and bishops without fear of reprisal from the state or the dominant religious authority. Although historians have paid little attention to the phenomenon, the public meetings, correspondence, petitions, and evidence of lay initiative that burst forth because of this new freedom should be celebrated as one of the great efflorescences of popular religion.

Men reared in a village church created an urban church embracing parishoners from many different villages. Therefore, no matter how traditional the architecture or how much Canadians might see the immigrant's religious practice as continuous with his old world religion, this was only partially true in the new environment. Linked as ritual was with the seasons, topography and moods of the homeland, it could not be transplanted unscathed, anymore than ethnic identity could remain static. The older immigrants found the little changes in sacramentals, liturgy and religious habits — even the very accents and manners of the clergy — to be nagging proof of change and of traditions endangered by an ocean crossing.

For those who adjusted to these changes, ethnic churches helped to define their identity in North America. Very often the associations in and around the church brought people a larger sense of their nationality than they had ever had in the narrowly circumscribed society they left behind. With the thorough study of church records and the use of oral testimony, it should be possible to learn how religious institutions formed, and why many passed from representing the ethnic parochialism of the *paese*, *heimat*, *selo*, *shtetl*, or *bygd* to serving whole nationalities. In other words, a key to the transition from village or family loyalties to the integral North American ethnic consciousness may lie in the study of religious sources.

Out of the effort of churches, mosques and synagogues to serve their people, a guide to the continuum and the conflict from migration to ethnic self-awareness to acculturation emerges. Churches hold an involved and richly contradictory place in the study of ethnicity. It is obvious that the sources which reflect the role of religion in ethnoculture need to be preserved and studied.

One can picture the religious life of an ethnocultural community as a series of rings — circles of activity and organization — surrounding a main institutional, pastoral and ritual core. At that core is the church itself, as a physical presence and a moral and theological entity. Around the core are rings of activity of many kinds — educational, social, and cultural, those which affect work, housing and business. From the church hall to the parochial school to the credit union to the undertakers, caterers, florists, and printers — these institutions revolve around the church and produce sources important to the historian and archivist.

An archivist's description of St. Vladimir's Ukrainian Greek Orthodox Cathedral in Toronto will show the variety of material found in a well organized religious institution. The archivist's headings include: the church protocols, statutes, membership lists, financial records, minutes of the building committee, circulars, pastoral letters, records of a theatrical

5

group, records of the Ukrainian language school, and an enormous number of occasional publications listed simply as miscellany. When we learn how to analyze this last category of material, it may prove the richest source of all for the study of the *élan* and health of ethnic groups in North America.

Let us then begin at the core and try to describe the church sources which we should help to preserve. The by-law of the priest's duties in a Russian Orthodox church will give us a senses of the range of existing sources:

Besides his pastoral and liturgical duties. . . is the duty of the rector and other members of the parish clergy to look after the decoration in the church, the beauty of the edifice, the establishment of the parish library, the organization of the church school, and to take an active part in the work of the parish council.

It is the duty of the clergy to keep exact metrical records and such other records as may be required by the civil authorities and to report to the diocesan authority with respect to the matters at the times and on the forms indicated.

Thus the primary sources of a church fall into three categories: 1) the actual church registers; 2) those that deal with liturgy, theology and moral education; and 3) those which involve the dealings of the local church with higher church authorities. The value of maintaining and saving the church registers themselves should be obvious to everyone. They are a record of the church's official religious life. Birth, baptismal, marriage, and death records — often other records such as those of first communion, confirmation, tithing, Easter duties, altar boy rosters, and funds for flowers — can lead the scholar to a total picture of piety and practice. At a time when too much of the writing of ethnic history depends on external sources such as city directories, assessment rolls or the census tract, we could draw a truer picture of the ethnic neighbourhood and its people; for instance, the fact that baptismal and marriage registers were often kept in both English and the language of the group may indicate changes in the group's sense of its identity.

Since any sacrament received beyond baptism usually has prerequisite sacraments, the church register forms more than a simple statistical base. It can, in fact, become a way of measuring many things that concern the historian such as the permanence or transience of the church membership, and a sacramental index provides at least a partial insight into the importance of religion in daily life. Most clergy were very careful in the matter of recording the original parish of a bride and groom, the home town of the parents of a child to be baptized, and birth and death data. Much sophisticated historical analysis is possible with such sources. For example, by looking at the membership in specific devotional societies or sodalities, by cross-referencing those who served as sponsors and godparents at weddings, at baptisms, and at first communions, historians can discover how sub-ethnic groups or networks survived within the larger church. Using such sources and methods in conjunction with external records like city directories, the historian will be

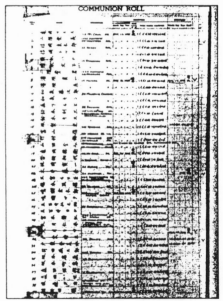

6

able to come closer to recreating the role of the sacred cosmos in ethnocultural life.

If we really wish to know about the attitudes of the "people in the pews" and to understand the choices they made about North America, about occupational mobility, about neighbours, and about social values, then we need to know more about religion's moral, educational and ritual effect upon them. Secular scholars ignore the liturgical, theological and educational aspects of religion at their own peril, and thorough salvaging of the archival materials may finally enable us to evaluate fully the impact of faith on daily life. A valuable literature has gone uncollected and unstudied; many unique collections of prayer books, missals, parochial school books, books of instruction for children, catechisms, descriptions of ritual and parish bulletins have been lost. Combined with oral testimony, this literature comprises an important record of popular religious beliefs and practices, and the folklore that surrounds them.

We have already seen the way in which scholars have been able to recreate the attitudes of people in the Middle Ages or in the Reformation and Counter-Reformation from a very small number of surviving devotional sources. In the future, dialectologists, historians and ethnologists who wish to study the evolution of ethnocultures, who wish to understand levels of piety and people's commitment in time, money, heart and mind will no doubt have to turn to such sources. Although reform in some denominations may seem glacially slow to those involved, the special role of sodalities, devotional societies, and certain aspects of ritual vanish all too quickly for the scholar attempting to trace continuities in ethnic and immigrant religious life.

Correspondence with a higher religious authority such as a diocese, a synod or a religious order's mother house forms a third important source. Reports of pastoral visits, diaries of the clergy or a *codex historicus*, and records of the parish council are very important sources for the study of both local ethnocultural polities and their encounters with North American authorities. The image of newcomers and minorities struggling against Wasp hegemony is too simple; for a much more subtle battle was waged within each denomination, a battle often reflecting the differences between traditions of clerical authority and lay initiative; the pamphlets, minutes and memoirs that were weapons in the struggle form a vibrant part of the ethnocultural religious tradition. Traces of the passion provoked by the conflict can still be found in jubilee volumes and souvenir books as well.

The kinds of associations connected with a church can be varied. They range from those which meet the cultural, social and educational goals of a denomination or of an ethnocultural group to those which show the interweaving of entrepreneurship and ritual in community activity. Here is a list of eighteen distinct organizations from one Polish parish. They included the Altar Boy Society, the Blessed Sacrament Sodality, the Catholic Youth Organization, St. Edward's Sodality, Holy Name Society, the Ladies of

8

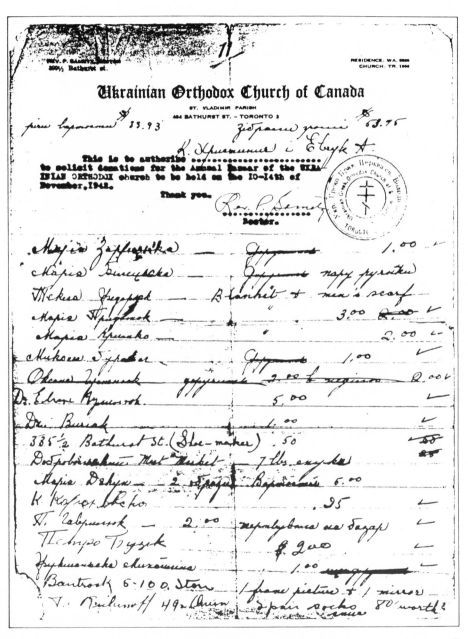

Ukrainian Orthodox Church of Canada

ST. VLADIMIR PARISH
404 BATHURST ST. – TORONTO 3

This is to authorize ....
to solicit donations for the Annual Bazaar of the UKRA-
INIAN ORTHODOX church to be held on the 10-14th of
November, 1942.

Thank you.

Rev. P. Sam...
Rector.

Charity, Holy Rosary Mothers' Club, the *Rosarian* (bulletin), the Sacred Heart of Mary Sodality, the Holy Rosary Sodality, the Third Order of St. Francis, the ushers, the Pulaski Brigade, the Confraternity of Christian Doctrine, the Polish Women's Alliance, Polish War Mothers of Holy Rosary, Polish Roman Catholic Union, and St. Joseph Auxiliary Club. The same parish had a school and a credit union with dependent clubs and societies. Each of these entities has a separate historical existence, officers, records, and a place in the thought and life of the ethnocultural group.

A struggle within a drum and bugle corps may affect the solidarity of a group as much as a scandal within a credit union. A choice as to how a choir will sing the liturgy may lead some people to move to a different parish. All such things affect not just the religious life of the group, and not just incidental associations, but are part of the total community network of an ethnoculture. The illustrations give only a slight idea of the variety of material and its research potential.

The scholar and archivist seeking to preserve material should start at the house of worship itself. As the most salient cultural presence in the community, the building was apt to become the deposit for material from dependent societies, such as choirs, language schools, sports clubs, drama groups, dance and folklore groups, old age or senior citizens organizations, burial societies, benevolent and mutual aid societies, and building and loan societies. And, as we have noted, the club or hall of those opposed to religious influence may very well be nearby.

Religious practice and the church as an institution also affected the business life of the ethnocultural community. Some businesses were and are dependent on the ritual or pastoral activities of the church. The role of the undertaker as sexton in some churches was a direct one. On the corner of the Madonna di Loretto, the first Sicilian parish in New York City, there is a brass plaque attached to the church which describes Provenzano Lanza as both the sexton and funeral director of that church, and his address and phone number are etched there. The effect of church life extended from the undertaker to those who provided baptismal clothing, catered matrimonial feasts, sold flowers or religious articles, to those whose insurance business prospered because they were recognized as good church members, to artisans respected by a building and loan association, to doctors approved by a mutual aid society, and to those who received contracts to build or paint religious properties.

In some cases it would be almost possible for the historian to reconstruct the neighbourhood outward from the church, past the undertaking parlour, the food provisioning store, the church hall, the school, the caterer, the small shops, and reconstruct a community as cohesive as the little village parishes of the Old Country. Even after neighbourhoods decline, memories of a liturgy, familiar hymns and prayers, habits of mind, moral lessons, and faith remain to form part of the ethnocultural heritage.

R.F.H.

Sometimes the effort to create a full archival record and the right to privacy and peace of those who made that record can seem to conflict. In saving church material, one encounters suspicion from the clergy. This distrust stems from three problems. First, the clergy legitimately see themselves as custodians of personal and confidential information. The historian who asks to see marriage registers has no call for righteous indignation if he is mistaken for a private investigator prying into a potential heir's legitimacy. Also, a specific problem exists in that confidential details about the parents of adopted children are held by the parish so that accidental incest will not occur.

The second problem stems from the origins of some of our province's new immigrants. The Christian churches of Eastern Europe and their followers in North America, as well as synagogues concerned with Soviet Jewry, fear that what appears to be scholarly research may be a cover for efforts to stifle dissent and punish relatives of immigrants. The historian may begin by making light of such 'Cold War' preoccupations and end by questioning his own confident North American naivety. Finally, all ethnic clergy, like most leaders, have been compromised either by the inaccurate and insouciant forays of popular journalists or historical researchers less concerned with how church sources might be used to enhance ethnic and immigrant studies and more concerned with recounting specific struggles and factional strife within various congregations.

In recent years, the tendency of dioceses, synods and other large ecclesiastical jurisdictions to microfilm church registers has led to further confusion. Denied access at the Rectory, the researcher finds the source material at the Diocesan Archives or Synod Archives. The result is satisfactory to no one. Ancillary parish records are lost: individual clergy move on with parish records: the whole cluster of sources which are generated by an ethnic religious institution become dangerously attenuated. Also, where religious orders or mission organizations are involved, the question of provenance and deposit are difficult.

Honest negotiation and explanation with provision for closure of truly sensitive material is the only way to show that clergy and scholar are not at cross purposes. Clearly, the gathering and preserving must go on while a satisfactory formula is worked out, for, although in the more hierarchically structured denominations, parish register material survives, every student of the cityscape sees church buildings passing from one group to another, and every archivist or historian hears tales of horror about records lost or destroyed.

German Immigrants and Churches in Nebraska, 1889-1915

As immigration studies have emerged from the morass of filio-pietism and romantic parochialism, historians have made increasing use of the insights and concepts developed by psychologists, sociologists, and other social scientists. A particularly valuable by-product of this orientation has been an increased awareness of the need for analytical and comparative approaches to historical data.[1] One technique which has been used profitably by historians is the systematic tabulation of data extracted from the biographies of persons who were representative of a particular group. First developed by the sociologist, C. Wright Mills, more than two decades ago, this method reveals relationships among various social, cultural, political, and other characteristics of the group being studied.[2]

Immigration history is a field of inquiry which is especially well-suited for this collective approach since it is concerned primarily with groups rather than with persons as individuals. Group problems, group developments, group responses, and group characteristics are often more important to the historian of immigration than are the individual records of prominent members of the group. To illustrate, students of German immigration are more interested in the relationship of Carl Schurz or Karl Heinzen to the German element in the United States than they are in their personal histories as such. Indeed, one of the most serious hazards connected with research in immigration history is to attribute evidence drawn from the leaders of a group to the rank and file members of that group. Excessive reliance on such elite-type evidence may easily distort perceptions of group attitudes and behavior.

Editor's Note: Mr. Luebke acknowledges the assistance of a grant by the National Endowment for the Humanities in the preparation of this article.

1 William O. Aydelotte, "Quantification in History," *American Historical Review*, LXXI (April, 1966), 803-25; Lee Benson, "Research Problems in American Historiography," in Mirra Komarovsky, ed., *Common Frontiers in the Social Sciences*, Glencoe: The Free Press, 1957, 113-83.

2 Mills drew his data from the *Dictionary of American Biography*. He was able to make important discoveries about the origins, education, church affiliation, etc., of American business leaders of the Gilded Age. See "The American Business Elite: A Collective Portrait," *Journal of Economic History*, V (Supplemental issue, 1945), 20-44.

116

In many instances the findings of the collective biography technique substantiate traditionally held views based on impressionistic evidence. In such cases our understanding of the past is strengthened by empirical evidence. Sometimes, however, the results suggest that our views have been out of focus, that they have lacked proper proportions, or that they have been in error. In any case, however, statistics must be used cautiously, for the proof they offer is frequently more apparent than real. Moreover, as Theodore Blegen has warned, historians must realize that "immigrants are people, not nicely tabulated statistics, and that to understand people . . . sources as varied and far-reaching as their interests and activities, their minds and emotions, their work and ambitions" must be used.[3]

Fortunately, the biographies of many German immigrants in Nebraska are available for the latter part of the nineteenth century and early decades of the twentieth. During those years several publishing companies produced massive histories of counties and regions. These compilations were largely financed through a subscription policy. If a potential buyer agreed in advance to purchase a copy of the forthcoming book, he would be assured that his personal history would find a place in the biographical section reserved for representative residents of the area. Standard information was then compiled regarding the subject's birth, education, occupation, family, church affiliation, political activity, land ownership, and so on. Though poorly written, these brief sketches provide more readily accessible information about more ordinary people than any other source.

Certain limitations regarding the use of these biographies must be recognized. The first of these involves socio-economic status. A balanced cross-section of the population is not offered since most of the subjects were middle class persons. Successful farmers dominate the pages, but their hired hands are absent; small town merchants and bankers are listed, but their clerks are not; professional people and craftsmen appear, but not their helpers. Another limitation lies in the fact that the subjects were quite free to withhold information as they saw fit. No doubt many half-truths slipped in. A person may have wanted it recorded for posterity that he was religious, even though the local clergyman would have disputed his alleged status as a churchman. Obviously, exact percentages should

---

[3] Theodore C. Blegen, "The Saga of the Immigrant," in Henry S. Commager, ed., *Immigration and American History,* University of Minnesota Press, 1961, 140.

be accepted with skepticism.   They reveal trends and tendencies, but not with precision.

For the purposes of this study, data were drawn from the biographies of 653 first and second generation Germans living in Nebraska near the end of the nineteenth century.   They constituted all of the members of this ethnic group who were included in four selected county and regional histories.[4]   The earliest group includes 124 German residents in 1889 of Otoe County, located on the Missouri River in the oldest section of the state; the second panel consists of 230 persons who, in 1892, inhabited the Elkhorn River Valley (chiefly in Dodge, Cuming, and Stanton counties), a region with a heavy concentration of German immigrants; the third group, numbering 108 persons, were residents in 1899 of five contiguous counties south of the Platte River, mostly in Seward and York counties; the fourth sampling, which totaled 191 persons, was taken from the heavily Catholic Platte County in 1915.[5]   Since the data for the final group were gathered more than a decade after the other three, potential distortions resulting from this lack of synchrony were compensated for by eliminating all biographees who were born after 1875.   In the tables which follow, percentages are recorded separately for each panel rather than for all subjects combined.   This is done so that regional differences within the state may be revealed.

In order to make the categories employed in the tables meaningful some explanation of them is necessary.   Generational data were tabulated in accordance with the generally accepted definition of *ethnic stock,* that is, European birth, or one or both parents of European birth.   With respect to occupations, it was discovered that with the exception of farmers, the numbers of other occupations were too small for meaningful tabulations.   Hence, all urban or small town occupations are lumped together as "business and professional" persons.   Blacksmiths, harnessmakers, shoemakers, and other craftsmen were included in this group because their activity was also commercially oriented.   Although this broad category lumps such antipathetic occupations as pastor and saloonkeeper, it offers the advantage of separating the subjects on an urban-rural basis.

---

    [4] The sources were as follows: *Portrait and Biographical Album of Otoe and Cass Counties, Nebraska,* Chicago, 1889; *Memorial and Biographical Record and Illustrated Compendium of Biography of Butler, Polk, Seward, York and Fillmore Counties, Nebraska,* Chicago, 1899; G. W. Phillips, ed., *Past and Present of Platte County, Nebraska,* 2 vols., Chicago, 1915; and C. H. Scoville, ed., *History of the Elkhorn Valley, Nebraska,* Chicago, 1892.
    [5] See Map.

All varieties of church affiliation were discovered among the German immigrants. Lutherans, followed by Catholics, were most numerous. The numbers of the non-Lutheran Protestants were so small, however, that they were grouped as one. This created a problem in that ideally a distinction should be made between immigrant and American churches. It was found, however, that the subjects did not consistently distinguish between the English-speaking and German versions of those Protestant denominations which had German conferences, notably the Methodists, Congregationalists, and Baptists. These churches functioned as immigrant institutions in much the same way as the Catholic or Lutheran denominations. Nevertheless, the category of "Other Protestant" may be justified. Such German conferences were almost indistinguishable from their English-speaking equivalents in terms of theological emphases. For example, the German Methodist differed from the mainstream of American Protestantism only in language while the German Lutheran, by contrast, differed in language and ritual, as well as theological heritage. Thus, a prohibitionist could be found as readily in a German Methodist congregation as in an American one.

If no church affiliation was indicated in a given biography, the subject was recorded in the "Not Stated" category. No doubt most persons in this classification were unchurched people although the grouping necessarily includes those who did not wish to reveal their church connections.

Some attempt was made to record the evidence of activity in social organizations. This was done on the assumption that memberships in formal groups increased the number of interpersonal contacts and therefore resulted in a more rapid assimilation into American society. It was found that the only kind of social activity that was consistent enough or frequent enough to warrant tabulation was lodge membership. Distinctively German or religious lodges or their equivalents like the Sons of Herman or the Knights of Columbus were not included. Perhaps the most important lodges in terms of impact on the assimilation process were the Masonic orders, the Independent Order of Odd Fellows, and the Knights of Pythias, although the last named sometimes chartered local lodges organized on an ethnic basis. The strong opposition which the secret societies encountered from Catholics, Lutherans, and Mennonites adds significance to lodge membership as an index to rates of assimilation.

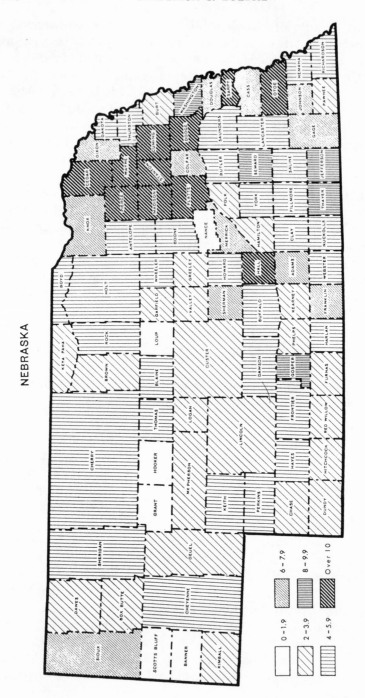

NEBRASKA

MAP DISTRIBUTION OF GERMAN-BORN INHABITANTS IN 1900 BY PERCENT.

0 - 1.9
2 - 3.9
4 - 5.9
6 - 7.9
8 - 9.9
Over 10

Table 1 reveals the general characteristics of the 653 adult males of German ethnic stock who were included in the tabulations. Approximately 75% were born in Europe. The occupational figures show that about two-thirds of the total group were farmers. While approximately one half of Nebraska's population held church memberships at the time,[6] Table 1 reveals that about 80% of the Germans in the survey claimed to be affiliated with some church. About 15% were Catholic, 40% Lutheran, and 20% members of other Protestant churches. The Catholic percentage for Otoe County seems to be low because there were no less than three predominantly German Catholic parishes in the county. The high percentage of Catholics in Platte County (36.1%) is accounted for by a strong Catholic settlement in the north central part of the county. The "Other Protestant" category is remarkably uniform except for the 7.8% recorded for the Elkhorn Valley. This divergence may be partially explained by the relatively higher percentage of first generation Germans in the population of that region. Of those who did not indicate church membership, the unusually high figure of 37.4% in the Elkhorn Valley group is not readily explained. According to assimilation theory, the highest levels of church membership could be expected in the communities with the heaviest concentration of foreign-born inhabitants.[7]

The data in Table 1 on political party identification provide convincing support for the thesis, first advanced by Andreas Dorpalen, that the Germans tended to conform to established community or regional patterns of political behavior.[8] In the counties south of the Platte River, where the Republican party traditionally was strongest, the Germans clearly preferred the GOP. In Otoe County the ratio was two German Republicans for each Democrat. But the relationship was exactly reversed in the Democratic territory north of the Platte. There the German Democrats more than doubled the number of Republicans. The data also demonstrate that the

---

6 U. S. Bureau of the Census, *Religious Bodies: 1906*, 2 vols., Washington, 1910, I, 335–7. The tables record communicant members only. They must be augmented by estimates of the number of children thereby excluded.

7 For a summary of assimilation theory as it pertains to the historical process see Frederick C. Luebke, "The Political Behavior of an Immigrant Group: The Germans of Nebraska, 1880–1900," unpublished Ph.D. thesis, University of Nebraska, 1966, 67–111.

8 See Andreas Dorpalen, "The German Element and the Issues of the Civil War," *Mississippi Valley Historical Review*, XXIX (June, 1942), 55–76.

TABLE I

PERCENTAGE DISTRIBUTION OF CHARACTERISTICS OF 653 GERMAN-AMERICAN ADULT MALES

Date:	1889	1892	1899	1915
County or region:	Otoe County	Elkhorn Valley	Seward-York Area	Platte County
No. of persons:	124	230	108	191
CHURCH AFFILIATION				
Catholic	6.4	16.5	13.9	36.1
Lutheran	49.2	38.3	45.4	35.6
Other Protestant	22.6	7.8	22.2	19.9
Not stated	21.8	37.4	18.5	8.4
Total	100.0	100.0	100.0	100.0
PLACE OF BIRTH				
Europe	75.8	83.0	77.8	67.0
America	24.2	17.0	22.2	33.0
Total	100.0	100.0	100.0	100.0
OCCUPATION				
Farmer	62.9	70.0	80.6	60.2
Business and professional	37.1	30.0	19.4	39.8
Total	100.0	100.0	100.0	100.0
PERSONS WHO INDICATE LODGE MEMBERSHIP				
Yes	14.7	15.2	17.6	24.1
No	85.3	84.8	82.4	75.9
Total	100.0	100.0	100.0	100.0
POLITICAL PARTY IDENTIFICATION				
Republican	58.1	21.3	33.3	21.5
Democratic	25.8	56.1	28.7	53.4
Populist	—	7.0	8.3	—
Prohibition	2.4	.4	.0	.5
Socialist	.0	.0	.9	.0
Independent	3.2	2.6	6.5	9.9
Not stated	10.5	12.6	22.2	14.7
Total	100.0	100.0	99.9	100.0

Germans of Nebraska were not attracted by the Populist party.[9] Since they tended to associate nativism, prohibition, and sabbatarianism with the Populists as well as with the Republicans,[10] it is likely that the small Populist identification came from formerly Republican Germans of reformist sentiments, a characteristic readily associated with immigrants who were inclined to assimilate rapidly. In any case, figures of seven and eight percent for the Populist party are remarkably low, considering the fact that in 1892, the Populist share of the total vote for president in Nebraska was 42.3%.[11]

None of the figures presented so far reveal any comparative relationship between church affiliation and place of birth, occupation, political party identification, or lodge membership. The data merely describe quantitatively what the sample of the German population in Nebraska was like at the time. Not until the four separate groups of immigrants are classified on a percentage scale can the relationships between religion and other characteristics be estimated. For this purpose, four tables follow which present statistical breakdowns for the several religious groupings. In order to facilitate comparisons, percentage distributions for the total German immigrant population of the county or region are also given.

Table 2 shows the relationship between church affiliation and place of birth. The most significant fact which may be drawn from the data is that Lutheran Germans consistently included a significantly larger proportion of foreign-born persons than did the total group.[12] More than the others, the Lutheran church was preeminently an immigrant church. It served best as the institution around which the immigrants could organize their lives and which could symbolize the sentiments and values that had suffered erosion through transfer to the new world.[13]

---

9 This finding runs counter to one of the main thrusts of Walter T. K. Nugent's excellent study, *The Tolerant Populists: Kansas Populism and Nativism*, University of Chicago Press, 1963. Although significant exceptions may be found, Nebraska voting statistics show that generally German voters were less inclined toward the Populist ticket than the total voting population. See Luebke, "Political Behavior," 254–89.

10 This is an impression based upon a reading of the German-language newspapers in Nebraska published during the 1890s.

11 *Nebraska Blue Book for 1901 and 1902*, Lincoln, 1901, 177.

12 Since Lutherans constituted the largest number (266) within the total group of 653 persons, it may be assumed that the data pertaining to them has the highest level of reliability.

13 See Oscar Handlin, *The Uprooted*, Boston, 1952, Chapter V, "Religion as a Way of Life"; H. Richard Niebuhr, *The Social Sources of Denominationalism*, New York, [1929] 1957, 200–35; Frederick C. Luebke, "The Immigrant Condition as a Factor Contributing to the Conservatism of the Lutheran Church-Missouri Synod," *Concordia Historical Institute Quarterly*, XXXVIII (April, 1965), 19–28.

Conversely, the data of Table 2 also demonstrate that non-Lutheran Protestant churches usually enrolled proportionately fewer European-born Germans than the total group. This suggests that a significant number of the children of the immigrants drifted away from the churches of their fathers. The statistics seem to support the conclusions of Marcus L. Hansen, Irvin L. Child, and others who have observed the sense of alienation experienced by the second generation. Frequently the American-born Germans sought to dissociate themselves from immigrant institutions and to identify with churches which seemed more American to them.[14]

TABLE 2

PERCENTAGE DISTRIBUTION OF CHURCH AFFILIATION OF 653 GERMAN-AMERICAN ADULT MALES AS RELATED TO PLACE OF BIRTH

Date:	1889	1892	1899	1915
County or region:	Otoe County	Elkhorn Valley	Seward-York Area	Platte County
No. of persons:	124	230	108	191
BORN IN EUROPE	75.8	83.0	77.8	67.0
Lutheran	83.6	87.8	87.8	77.9
Other Protestant	60.7	55.6*	58.3	86.8
Catholic	75.0*	92.1	100.0*	67.0
Not stated	74.1	84.9	60.0	62.5*
BORN IN AMERICA	24.2	17.0	22.2	33.0
Lutheran	16.4	12.2	12.2	22.1
Other Protestant	39.3	44.4*	41.7	13.2
Catholic	25.0*	7.9	.0*	33.0
Not stated	25.9	15.1	40.0	37.5*

* Category includes less than twenty persons.

The data derived from the Platte County panel deviates from that of the other three groups in several ways. The relatively low figure of European-born for the total group (67.0%) is the consequence of many first generation immigrants having died by 1915 when the data were gathered and that German immigration to

---

14 Marcus L. Hansen, "The Third-Generation American," reprinted in Edward N. Saveth, ed., *Understanding the American Past*, 2nd ed., 1965, 470f.; Irvin L. Child, *Italian or American? The Second Generation Conflict*, Yale University Press, 1943; Will Herberg, *Protestant-Catholic-Jew*, rev. ed., Garden City: Anchor Books, 1960.

America was long past the peak it had reached during the 1880s. The unusually high proportion of non-Lutheran Protestants (86.8%) who were born in Europe reflects the existence of a large colony of Swiss Germans, many of which were members of the German Reformed church.[15] The low percentage of foreign-born Catholics in Platte County (67.0%) is due to the fact that most of them migrated to Nebraska from states of the old Northwest rather than from Europe.[16]

The relationships between church affiliation and urban or rural occupations are revealed in Table 3. The value of the figures lies in the way in which they validate the assumptions of assimilation theory, which, when applied to the historical setting, may read as follows: upon his arrival in Nebraska, the typical German immigrant (who was most often of North German peasant stock and who normally idealized land ownership) moved as soon as he was financially able to an area in which he could establish himself on

TABLE 3

PERCENTAGE DISTRIBUTION OF CHURCH AFFILIATION OF 653
GERMAN-AMERICAN ADULT MALES AS RELATED
TO OCCUPATION

Date: County or region: No. of persons:	1889 Otoe County 124	1892 Elkhorn Valley 230	1899 Seward- York Area 108	1915 Platte County 191
FARMERS	62.9	70.0	80.6	60.2
Lutherans	68.9	79.5	79.6	75.0
Other Protestants	60.7	66.7*	87.5	50.0
Catholics	87.5*	89.5	93.3*	56.5
Not stated	44.4	52.3	65.0	62.5*
BUSINESS AND PROFESSIONAL	37.1	30.0	19.4	39.8
Lutherans	31.1	20.5	20.4	25.0
Other Protestants	39.3	33.3*	12.5	50.0
Catholics	12.5*	10.5	6.7*	43.5
Not stated	55.6	47.7	35.0	37.5*

* Category included less than twenty persons.

15 *Schedules of the Nebraska State Census of 1885*, National Archives Microfilm Publications, Washington, 1961.

16 *Ibid.;* Eugene Hagedorn, *The Franciscans in Nebraska*, Humphrey and Norfolk, Nebr., 1931, 357.

the land. There, in conjunction with his fellow ethnics, he sought to recreate familiar institutions and customs and to sustain old-world languages, values, and attitudes. He was a farmer and a Lutheran, a Catholic, or a Mennonite. Less typical was the German businessman or professional person who lived in the towns and small cities. Experiencing many more interpersonal contacts with native Americans, such persons were assimilated into the host society more rapidly than their rural brethren. Social pressure to conform was keenly felt, and hence the urban German was more inclined to abandon his father's church and to join an American denomination. Thus, Table 3 indicates that Catholics and Lutherans were in most instances proportionately more numerous among the farmers; on the other hand, non-Lutheran Protestants, as well as those who revealed no church connections, formed a significantly larger proportion of the business and professional people.[17]

TABLE 4

PERCENTAGE DISTRIBUTION OF CHURCH AFFILIATION OF 653 GERMAN-AMERICAN ADULT MALES AS RELATED TO LODGE MEMBERSHIP

Date:	1889	1892	1899	1915
County or region:	Otoe County	Elkhorn Valley	Seward-York Area	Platte County
No. of persons:	124	230	108	191
LODGE MEMBERSHIP INDICATED	14.7	15.2	17.2	24.1
Lutherans	4.9	13.6	8.2	16.2
Other Protestants	10.7	27.8*	37.5	57.9
Catholics	.0*	5.3	13.3*	7.2
Not stated	40.7	18.6	25.0	50.0*
LODGE MEMBERSHIP NOT INDICATED	85.3	84.8	82.4	75.9
Lutherans	95.1	86.4	91.8	83.8
Other Protestants	89.3	72.2*	62.5	42.1
Catholics	100.0*	94.7	86.7*	92.8
Not stated	59.3	81.4	75.0	50.0*

* Category includes less than twenty persons.

17 The figures for Platte County diverge from the other groups because of atypical characteristics of the German immigrant population. Catholics were normally more recent arrivals than non-Lutheran Protestants, but the reverse situation pertained in Platte County. Hence the data actually support the hypothesis.

The same relationships are verified in Table 4 which associates church affiliation with lodge membership. To have been a Mason or an Odd Fellow usually meant having a high level of social interaction with native Americans. It may be argued, of course, that lodge membership was merely a concomitant of urban residence and that therefore the data reveal nothing new. Yet the well-known opposition of the Catholic and Lutheran churches, especially the Missouri Synod, adds another dimension to the statistics. The independent impact of church affiliation is substantiated by a comparison of Table 4 with Table 3. For example, while 31.1% of the Lutherans in Otoe County were urban residents, only 4.9% were members of a lodge; similarly, 43.5% of the Catholics of the Platte County group were urban while 7.2% were affiliated with a lodge. The significance of church membership is revealed by a further breakdown of the statistics: of the German lodge members in the Seward-York group (among which the Missouri Synod was strongly represented), 21.0% were Lutheran and 42.1% were members of other Protestant churches; at the same time, 47.6% of the Germans living in towns were Lutherans while only 14.3% were members of other Protestant churches. Another example may be seen in the heavily Catholic Platte County panel. In this case 10.7% of the lodge members were Catholics compared to 47.8% who were non-Lutheran Protestant; conversely, 39.5% of the urban residents were Catholic as opposed to the 25.0% who were members of other Protestant denominations.[18] The data therefore seem to verify the conclusion that the immigrant churches (Catholic and Lutheran) significantly retarded the assimilation process through their opposition to the secret societies.[19]

Table 5 relates church affiliation among Nebraska Germans with political party identification. Because of the comparative complexity of the table, some direction for its reading may be helpful. Otoe County may be used as an example. Of the 124 persons in the panel, 58.1% were Republican, 25.8% were Democratic, 3.2% declared themselves independent of political partisanship, and 10.5% were politically apathetic or, for some reason, refused to reveal their political associations. Moving to the Lutheran sub-group in Otoe County (which numbered 61 persons), we find its party identifi-

---

18 The latter group of percentages are not derived from tables included in this article.

19 For an interesting parallel, see O. Fritiof Ander, "The Immigrant Church and the Patrons of Husbandry," *Agricultural History*, VIII (Oct., 1934), 155–68.

TABLE 5

PERCENTAGE DISTRIBUTION OF CHURCH AFFILIATION OF 653 GERMAN-AMERICAN ADULT MALES AS RELATED TO POLITICAL PARTY IDENTIFICATION

Date:	1889	1892	1899	1915
County or region:	Otoe County	Elkhorn Valley	Seward-York Area	Platte County
No. of persons:	124	230	108	191
REPUBLICANS	58.1	21.3	33.3	21.5
Lutherans	59.0	18.2	42.9	17.6
Other Protestants	71.4	38.9*	33.3	47.4
Catholics	37.5*	5.3	.0*	7.2
Not stated	48.1	27.9	35.0	37.5*
DEMOCRATS	25.8	56.1	28.7	53.4
Lutherans	27.9	71.6	24.5	53.4
Other Protestants	14.3	44.4*	33.3	26.3
Catholics	50.0*	76.3	40.0*	78.3
Not stated	25.9	33.7	25.0	25.0*
POPULISTS	——	7.0	8.3	——
Lutherans	——	5.7	10.2	——
Other Protestants	——	11.1*	8.3	——
Catholics	——	2.6	6.7*	——
Not stated	——	9.3	8.3	——
INDEPENDENT	3.2	2.6	6.5	9.9
Lutherans	3.3	3.4	6.1	19.1
Other Protestants	3.6	.0*	4.2	7.9
Catholics	12.5*	2.6	13.3*	5.8
Not stated	.0	2.3	5.0	18.8*
NO POLITICAL PARTY INDICATED	10.5	12.6	22.2	14.7
Lutherans	8.2	1.1	16.3	13.2
Other Protestants	3.6	5.6*	16.7	15.8
Catholics	.0*	13.2	40.0*	8.7
Not stated	25.9	25.6	30.0	18.8*

* Category includes less than twenty persons. A few Socialists and Prohibitionists have been omitted from the table.

cations corresponded closely to those of the total group: 59.0% Republican, 27.9% Democratic, 3.2% independent, and 8.2% with partisanship not indicated. The percentages for the other religious groups may be read similarly.

The data for the several panels assume importance when they are compared to each other. Following the lines of the thesis that German-American voters tended to follow the patterns of local or regional political behavior, wide variations within one group may be observed, especially among the Lutherans, whose identification with the Republicans, for example, ranged from 59.0% in Otoe County to 17.6% in Platte County, while Lutheran loyalty to the Democatic party ranged from 71.6% in the Elkhorn Valley to 24.5% in the Seward-York area. Yet the data also reveal important consistencies. Catholic tendencies toward the Democratic party were always strong, just as non-Lutheran Protestants were much more inclined to identify with the Republican party. Moreover, while Lutherans may have included large percentages of Republicans, they normally were less inclined to support that party than were members of other Protestant denominations. It is apparent also that the Republican party was also the favorite of those Germans who revealed no church connections.

To summarize, the data of this study indicate that Catholic German immigrants in Nebraska were proportionately very numerous among the European-born and among the farm population. Least likely to hold lodge memberships, the Catholics were the strongest of the groups in identification with the Democratic party.

The Lutherans generally occupied an intermediate position between the Catholics and non-Lutheran Protestants. Like the Catholics, the Lutherans regularly formed a larger proportion of the foreign-born and of the rural residents than the total sampling. Similarly, they were less inclined to hold lodge memberships. Lutherans tended to identify with the major political parties in approximately the same proportions as the entire group. Although wide regional variations in political identification were apparent, the Lutherans were decidedly more Republican than the Catholics and more Democratic than other Protestants.

Persons in the sample who were members of non-Lutheran Protestant denominations were proportionately more numerous among the American-born, the business and professional people, and lodge members. Politically there was less regional variation among them than among the Lutherans. Of all the groups, they were the most inclined toward identification with the Republican party.

Those persons in the study who indicated no church affiliation generally displayed characteristics which were similar to those of the non-Lutheran Protestants. Clearly the most urban of the four groups, they were also the least inclined to reveal their political party preferences.

In conclusion, the data provide a statistical basis for an interpretation of the assimilation of German immigrants into American society. The more recent arrivals (and presumably those psychologically inclined toward a slower assimilation) tended to prefer the cultural isolation which often accompanied rural living. Immigrant churches, chiefly the Lutheran and Catholic, gave them many of their social contacts and served to limit their associations with native Americans. Political involvement was often an early component of their American experience, but their tendency was to identify with the Democratic party which they perceived as the friend of the immigrant and as the champion of the largest measure of personal liberty consistent with law and order. The Republican party, by contrast, often appeared progressive and aggressive, a nativistic party of prohibition, woman suffrage, and sabbatarianism, a party of exploitation and of the centralization of power.[20]

The longer the immigrant lived in this country, however, the more inclined was he to adjust his loyalties and his values to an American standard. Especially if he was an urban resident, he was led by his more frequent associations with native Americans to quit his immigrant church and to join an American Protestant denomination or no church at all. In many cases he was induced to become a member of American social organizations, such as the lodge, just as his tendency to identify with the Republican party also increased. Thus a positive relationship existed (with due allowance for local variations) among membership in the Lutheran and Catholic churches, European birth, rural residence, and identification with the Democratic party; conversely, membership in non-Lutheran Protestant churches or in no church tended to be found among those of American birth, urban residence, lodge membership, and identification with the Republican party.

FREDERICK C. LUEBKE

Concordia Teachers College, Nebraska

---

[20] The relationship of immigrant perceptions of reform measures to partisan politics is treated by Alan P. Grimes, *The Puritan Ethics and Woman Suffrage*, Oxford University Press, 1967, 86f. and *passim*.

Ethnicity: The Skeleton of Religion in America'

MARTIN E. MARTY

"The story of the peopling of America has not yet been written. We do not understand ourselves," complained Frederick Jackson Turner in 1891.[1] Subsequent immigration history contributed to national self-understanding. Eighty years later historians have turned their attention to a second chapter in the half-told tale of the peopling of America. They have begun to concentrate on the story of the regrouping of citizens along racial, ethnic and religious lines, and of their relations to each other in movements of what have come to be called "peoplehood."[2]

PEOPLEHOOD AND TRIBALISM

First, the realities of black power, black religion, black theology and black churchmanship inspired historians of religion in the 1960s to explore hitherto neglected elements in the make-up of spiritual America. The murder of integrationist leader Martin Luther King and the publication of separationist Albert Cleage, Jr.'s *The Black Messiah* in 1968 were signs of a developing sense of "peoplehood" among blacks as well as of what Cleage called the "religiocification" of a black revolution. Ties to the African religious past and to other spiritual forces outside America were regularly stressed: "We must seek out our brothers in all of Asia and Africa."[3]

The black revolution triggered or was concurrent with other expressions of peoplehood. The American Indian frequently stated his case in religious terms and even provided a metaphor for understanding all the movements: people came to speak of the presence of "a new tribalism."[4] Meanwhile, many Jews resisted

1. Quoted in Lee Benson, *Turner and Beard: American Historical Writing Reconsidered* (Glencoe, Illinois: The Free Press, 1960), p. 82.
2. Milton M. Gordon, *Assimilation in American Life* (New York: Oxford University Press, 1964), popularized the concept of "peoplehood," which is the "sense" of an ethnic, racial, or religious group. The word turns up frequently in literature on ethnicity and new movements. Sometimes these movements, among them Women's Liberation, the New Left, "the counter culture," and the like, speak of themselves in the terms of "peoplehood," but this essay restricts itself to study of those groups which have at least a minimal claim on some sort of common ethnic origin and orientation. Significantly, the term worked its way into *Webster's New International Dictionary* during the 1960s; it did not appear in the second edition (1960) but is present in the third (1969): "Peoplehood: the quality or state of constituting a people; also: awareness of the underlying unity that makes the individual a part of the people."
3. The literature on black religion is rapidly expanding; Hart M. Nelsen, Raytha L. Yokley, and Anne K. Nelsen, *The Black Church in America* (New York: Basic Books, Inc., 1971) is an excellent anthology on every major aspect of the subject. The suggestion that 1968 was a watershed year in black religious consciousness appears in this book, pp. 17ff. Cleage is quoted on p. 18 and Bishop Herbert B. Shaw, speaking of ties to Asia and Africa, on p. 21. James H. Cone, *A Black Theology of Liberation* (Philadelphia: J. B. Lippincott, 1970) is a representative charge that most of what had previously been seen to be a generalized and universal theology in America is actually an expression of "whiteness." See also James J. Gardiner, S. A. and J. Deotis Roberts, Sr., *Quest for a Black Theology* (Philadelphia: Pilgrim Press, 1971).
4. Vine Deloria, *We Talk, You Listen* (New York: Macmillan, 1970) was a widely noticed expression of new American Indian assertiveness; it included an explicit suggestion that our impersonal, homogenized America should relearn the tribal model from the original Americans.

Mr. Marty, Associate Dean and professor of the history of Christianity in the Divinity School, University of Chicago, first delivered this paper as the Presidential Address at the dinner meeting of The American Society of Church History on December 29, 1971.

5

being blended into the American mixture. They reinterpreted their community around two particular historical events, the Holocaust and the formation of modern Israel; their new self-consciousness resulted in "the retribalization of the Jew."[5] This change was accompanied in America by some retreat from inter-faith conversation on the part of Jews and some questioning as to whether the common "Judeo-Christian tradition" was anything more than a contrivance.[6] The ghetto walls had largely fallen, but the suburban Jew had not fully resolved his questions of identity and mission.

"Peoplehood" movements brought to view the 9.2 million Americans of Spanish descent, including the newly assertive Chicanos, chiefly in the southwest. "Chicano describes a beautiful people. Chicano has a power of its own. Chicano is a unique confluence of histories, cultures, languages, and traditions. . . . Chicano is a unique people. Chicano is a prophecy of a new day and a new world."[7] In the northeast, particularly in New York City, almost a million Puerto Ricans, representing the first airborne migration of a people, stamped their distinctive claims on the consciousness of a nation.[8]

Americans of Eastern Orthodox descent made moves to recover their heri-tages. Orientals in San Francisco protested school busing because integration might threaten their people's heritage. Chinese and Japanese all across the coun-try became subjects of curiosity by their non-Oriental contemporaries who showed interest in Eastern religion, in Yoga or Zen. Nationalist separatist groups in Quebec gathered around French culture and Catholic faith in neighboring Canada and provided local examples of a world-wide neo-nationalism.

The racial and ethnic self-consciousness of what had been called the 'minority groups' led to a new sense of peoplehood among the two groups which together made up the American majority. One of these clusters came to be called "white ethnic," its members, "ethnics." They took on new group power at a moment when paradoxically, as students of *The Real Majority* pointed out, "ethnics are dying out in America and becoming a smaller percentage of the total population."[9] The actual decline was from 26 percent of the population ("foreign stock") in 1940 down to an estimated 15 percent in 1970. Austrians, "Baltics," Czecho-slovakians, German Catholics, Hungarians, Italians, Poles and other heirs of

5. Richard L. Rubenstein, "Homeland and Holocaust" in Donald R. Cutler, *The Re-ligious Situation: 1968* (Boston: Beacon, 1968), p. 45.
6. Arthur A. Cohen, *The Myth of the Judeo-Christian Tradition* (New York: Harper and Row, 1970), was written to help "break through the crust of harmony and con-cord which exists between Judaism and Christianity" and to help "destroy that in both communities which depends upon the other for authentication" (p. vii). Cohen be-lieves that the myth of the common tradition was largely devised in America in the face of a secular religiosity; it induced two faiths to "join together to reinforce them-selves in the face of a common disaster" (p. xix).
7. Armando B. Rendon, *Chicano Manifesto* (New York: Macmillan, 1971), uses figures (p. 38) from a survey taken in November, 1969: 9.2 million persons claiming Spanish descent would represent 4.7 percent of the population. Three quarters of this number were native born; the rest were immigrants, with half coming from Mexico. See also p. 325.
8. Joseph P. Fitzpatrick, *Puerto Rican Americans: The Meaning of a Migration* (Engle-wood Cliffs, New Jersey: Prentice-Hall, 1971) is a brief but comprehensive survey of the situation of this minority.
9. Richard M. Scammon and Ben J. Wattenberg, *The Real Majority* (New York: Coward-McCann, 1970), p. 66. Andrew M. Greeley, *Why Can't They Be Like Us? America's White Ethnic Groups* (New York: E. P. Dutton, 1971) introduces this conglomeration of hitherto separate ethnic forces. He also points to the fact that in part because its members spoke English and were Catholic the large Irish immigrant group does not fit easily into "the white ethnic/white Anglo-Saxon" Protestant combination. Nor, it might be added, did Germans and Scandinavian Protestants, who did not speak English.

earlier immigration from Europe were often led to see a common destiny despite their past histories of separation and often of mutual suspicion or hostility. Most of them were of Roman Catholic backgrounds, members of a church which in its Second Vatican Council taught its adherents to think of themselves in the image of "The New People of God."[10] In America they wanted also to be a people with identity, a people of power.

Finally, there is "One of America's greatest and most colorful minority groups."

They came here on crowded ships, were resented by the natives and had to struggle mightily for every advance they made against a hostile environment. Despite these handicaps, despite even a skin color different from the native Americans, this hardy group prospered and, in prospering, helped build the nation. They fought in her wars, guided her commerce, developed her transportation, built her buildings. The debt that the country owes to this particular group of immigrants can never be over-estimated. In short, like most American minority groups, they made good citizens.

"The only thing different about the group is that it is the one traditionally viewed as the 'American majority.'" The minority group just described by Ben J. Wattenberg and Richard M. Scammon is "White Anglo-Saxon Protestant," further qualified today as "native-born of native parentage."[11] The acronym and designation WASP-NN in the 1960s represented only about 30 percent of the population. It was divided into 60 percent urban and 40 percent rural, 35 percent southern and 65 percent non-southern communities and included great inner variety. But its critics tended to lump all WASPs together, and increasing numbers of Americans accepted membership in this "people." Among them are large numbers "who happen to be both Anglo-Saxon and white, but whom none would think to describe in terms of WASP power structures. For these particular Protestants (in rural Appalachia, for example) also happen to be exploitable and as invisible as any of America's other dispossessed minorities," and are sometimes themselves referred to as a separate people."[12]

Despite internal variety, at least as late as the 1960s, "the white, Anglo-Saxon Protestant remains the typical American, the model to which other Americans are expected and encouraged to conform."[13] One of the most significant

10. References to the Church as "the new people of God" can be found throughout Walter M. Abbott, S.J., ed., *The Documents of Vatican II* (New York: Guild Press, American Press, Association Press, 1966). In actual practice, ethnocentrism, competing ethnic sub-communities, and isolated or rival "national" groups throughout American history have blurred the vision of their being a single "people of God."

11. Ben J. Wattenberg and Richard M. Scammon, *This U.S.A.: An Unexpected Family Portrait of 194,067,296 Americans Drawn from the Census* (New York: Doubleday, 1965), pp. 45f.

12. David Edwin Harrell, Jr., *White Sects and Black Men in the Recent South* (Nashville, Tennessee: Vanderbilt University Press, 1971), p. viii.

13. Lewis M. Killian, *The Impossible Revolution* (New York: Random House, 1968), p. 18. Richard L. Means, in *The Christian Century*, 78 (Aug. 16, 1961), pp. 979-80, began to discuss the significance of *Anti-Protestant Prejudice*, a theme which subsequently received increasing attention, and which may serve to cause more WASPs to affirm the self-designation they had once shunned—if the experience of other more obvious victims of group prejudice is to be repeated in this instance. See also Peter Schrag, "The Decline of the Wasp," in *Harper's* Magazine, April 1970. While the WASPs "still hold power, they hold it with less assurance and with less legitimacy than at any time in history. . . . One can almost define their domains by locating the people and institutions that are chronically on the defense. . . . For the first time, any sort of settlement among competing interests is going to have to do more than pay lip service to minorities and to the pluralism of styles, beliefs, and cultures. . . . America is not on the verge of becoming two separate societies, one rich and white, the other poor and black. It is becoming, in all its dreams and anxieties, a nation of outsiders for whom no single style

events in the recent study of the peopling of America has been the growing
sense, however, that WASPs are a minority themselves. They have at least lost
statistical bases for providing a national norm for ethnic self-understanding.

RACE, ETHNICITY AND RELIGIOUS HISTORY

These good years for peoplehood have given rise to whole new historical
and social inquiries concerning "ethnicity." The term ('*obs.*, *rare*') once meant
"heathendom," "heathen superstition."[14] Today it is coming to refer to participation in "an ethnic group—racial, religious, or national" in origin.[15] In this
essay, "racial" is a species of the genus "ethnic." People may have authentic or
only imaginary ties to a common place of origin, as Max Weber noted.[16] Thus
when a non-churchgoing American of Swedish descent is listed as a WASP and
accepts that designation, his part in an "Anglo-Saxon" people relates only to an
imagined common origin with some Englishmen.[17] Two American Italians who
share actual ties to common birthplaces in Europe present a more obvious case
for membership in an ethnic group. Yet in practical life and in the world of the
politicians or analysts the Swedish WASP and the Italian will tend to be treated
as equally legitimate participants in the lives of their people.

The new movements of peoplehood and the expressions of ethnic and racial
consciousness—almost all of them marked by claims of "chosenness"—caught
many Americans off guard. I shall argue that professional students of religion
in America for the most part had become committed after the middle of the
twentieth century to theories of interpretation, models and paradigms of inquiry
which led them to neglect, gloss over, or deliberately obscure the durable sense
of peoplehood in the larger American community. This also left many members of the fraternity ill-prepared to tell the stories of those who shared new
styles of ethnic consciousness.

If that argument can be established, we may properly speak of ethnicity as

or ethic remains possible. . . . We will now have to devise ways of recognizing and
assessing the alternatives. The mainstream is running thin.''
14. This definition and two subsequent definitions of ''skeleton'' are from the Oxford
English Dictionary.
15. Charles H. Anderson, *White Protestant Americans: From National Origins to Religious
Group* (Englewood Cliffs, N.J.: Prentice-Hall, 1971), p. viii. ''Every American, as we
shall use the term, is a member or potential member of an ethnic group—racial, religious, or national in origin.''
16. See Max Weber, ''Ethnic Groups,'' translated by Ferdinand Kolegar, in Talcott Parsons, *et al.*, *Theories of Society*, Vol. 1 (Glencoe, Ill., The Free Press, 1961), pp. 305ff.
''Any aspect or cultural trait, no matter how superficial, can serve as a starting point for
the familiar tendency to monopolistic closure.'' ''Almost any kind of similarity or contrast of physical type and of habits can induce the belief that a tribal affinity or dis-
affinity exists between groups that attract or repel each other.'' ''The belief in
tribal kinship, regardless of whether it has any objective foundation, can have important consequences especially for the formation of a political community. Those
human groups that entertain a subjective belief in their common descent—because of
similarities of physical type or of customs or both, or because of memories of colonization and migration—in such a way that this belief is important for the continuation
of non-kinship communal relationship, we shall call 'ethnic' groups, regardless of
whether an objective blood relationship exists or not.'' ''Behind all ethnic diversities
there is somehow naturally the notion of the 'chosen people,' which is nothing else
but a counterpart of status differentiation translated into the plane of horizontal coexistence. The idea of a chosen people derives its popularity from the fact that it can
be claimed to an equal degree by any and every member of the mutually despising
groups.''
17. Charles H. Anderson, *op. cit.*, pp. 43ff. locates Swedes with WASPs. ''They have been
granted WASP status on the basis of their successful adaptation to Anglo-Saxon
America. In a sense even today Scandinavians are second-class WASPs; nevertheless,
Scandinavians know that it is better to be a second-class WASP than a non-WASP in
American society.''

the skeleton of religion in America. In a plea for historically-informed ethnic studies and in an account of the history of the neglect of ethnic groups, Rudolph J. Vecoli says: "Ethnicity in American historiography has remained something of a family scandal, to be kept a dark secret or explained away."[18] This suggests two dictionary images. One is that of "a skeleton in the closet," which is "a secret source of shame or pain to a family or person." The other is that of "a skeleton at the banquet," a "reminder of serious or saddening things in the midst of enjoyment." Equally seriously, ethnicity is the skeleton of religion in America because it provides "the supporting framework," "the bare outlines or main features," of American religion.

When the new particularism was first asserted in the 1960s, students had been enjoying their realization that consensus-minded America no longer seemed to be "tribal." (Tribes, as Lord Bryce pointed out long ago, possessed distinctive and localized religions. "Religion appeared to them a matter purely local; and as there were gods of the hills and gods of the valleys, of the land and of the sea, so each tribe rejoiced in its peculiar deities, looking on the natives of other countries who worshipped other gods as Gentiles, natural foes, unclean beings.")[19] In the midst of the enjoyment, tribalism reappeared. Black messiahs, black madonnas, the black Jesus, "the Great Spirit," the Jewish identification with the land and soil of Israel and charges that white Gentile America had been worshipping a localized self-created deity suddenly disturbed the peace. The issues of ethnicity and racism began to serve as the new occasions for a re-examination of the assumptions and often hidden biases of students of American religion.

OBSERVERS AND ADVOCATES OF A COMMON RELIGION

For the sake of convenience, these students can be divided into two broadly-defined schools. Members of the first seek some sort of spiritual "sameness," if not for the whole family of man, then at least for the whole American people. In the Protestant historical community this search is a kind of enlargement of the nineteenth-century evangelical vision typified by the words of Lyman Beecher in 1820:

> The integrity of the Union demands special exertions to produce in the nation a more homogeneous character and bind us together with firmer bonds. . . . Schools, and academies, and colleges, and habits, and institutions of homogeneous influence . . . would produce a *sameness* of views, and feelings, and interests, which would lay the foundation of our empire upon a rock. Religion is the central attraction which must supply the deficiency of political affinity and interest. [20] [emphasis mine]

Another spokesman of this tradition was theologian Charles Hodge, who in 1829 claimed that Americans were overcoming Europe's problem of disunity by becoming one people, "having one language, one literature, essentially one religion, and one common soul."[21]

In the course of time that vision had to be enlarged so that it could accommo-

18. Rudolph J. Vecoli, "Ethnicity: A Neglected Dimension of American History," in Herbert J. Bass, *The State of American History* (Chicago: Quadrangle, 1970), pp. 70ff. sets the stage for the present essay on religious historiography.
19. Quoted in Carlton J. H. Hayes, *Nationalism: A Religion* (New York: Macmillan, 1960), pp. 20f. Hayes provides one of the best analyses of the dimensions of national cultural religions in Chapter XII. pp. 154ff.
20. Lyman Beecher, *Address of the Charitable Society for the Education of Indigent Pious Young Men for the Ministry of the Gospel* (Concord, Mass., 1820), p. 20.
21. Charles Hodge, "Anniversary Address," in *The Home Missionary*, Vol. II (New York, 1829), p. 18.

date other Americans though many of these others have regularly complained ever since that Protestant views of "sameness" and "essentially one religion, and one common soul" were superimposed on non-Protestants. Many Roman Catholics, on a somewhat different set of terms, also affirmed a religious nationalism that transcended their particular creed.[22]

Philip Schaff in 1855 observed continuing immigration and looked ahead to see that a

> process of national amalgamation is now also going on before our eyes in America; but peacefully, under more favorable conditions, and on a far grander scale than ever before in the history of the world. America is *the grave of all European nationalities;* but a *Phenix grave,* from which they shall rise to new life and new activity. . . .

Then he added, in a still rather ethnocentric line not often quoted with the rest of the paragraph, that this would be "in a new and essentially Anglo-Germanic form."[23] Later, Frederick Jackson Turner, the historian who had wanted the "peopling of America" to be studied for the purposes of national self-understanding, chose to concentrate on the frontier. He argued that "in the crucible of the frontier the immigrants were Americanized, liberated, and fused into a mixed race, English in neither nationality or characteristics."[24] His successors came to expect that a spiritual fusion would accompany the amalgamation of peoples.

Through the years the seekers of spiritual sameness or oneness and ethnic fusion or assimilation had to include the physical presence and spiritual strivings of ever more varied peoples. Those who advocated what John Dewey in 1934 had called *A Common Faith*[25] made little secret of their desire to overcome particularisms of religion, race and class. For some this desire may have been born of weariness over all tribal-religious warfare; for others, it grew out of conscious philosophical choices about reality, religion and nation.

In this spirit at the beginning of this period sociologist Robin M. Williams, Jr., wrote during 1951 that "Every functioning society has, to an important degree, a *common* religion. The possession of a common set of ideas, rituals, and symbols can supply an overarching sense of unity even in a society riddled with conflict."[26] A year later, at the end of a long book on denominational varieties in American religion, J. Paul Williams moved beyond Robin Williams in the quest for a common national faith. He spoke of it as a "societal religion." Williams favored teaching democracy as a religious ultimate, mildly criticized men like Walter Lippmann for having been content to describe it merely as a "public philosophy" when it ought to have been termed a religion, and called moreover for "spiritual integration."[27]

The dean of American church historians throughout this period, Sidney E. Mead, gave a generally positive interpretation of "the religion of the democratic

22. Dorothy Dohen, *Nationalism and American Catholicism* (New York: Sheed and Ward, 1967) brings testimony of numerous nineteenth-century Roman Catholic leaders on this subject.
23. Philip Schaff, *America: A Sketch of Its Political, Social, and Religious Character* (Cambridge, Mass.: The Belknap Press of Harvard University Press, 1961), p. 51.
24. Quoted by Vecoli, *op. cit.*, p. 75.
25. John Dewey, *A Common Faith* (New Haven, Conn.: Yale University Press, 1934). While the book uses the term "God," it is non-theistic and advocates an imaginatively-based synthesis or unification of values in which the many take part.
26. Robin M. Williams, Jr., *American Society: A Sociological Interpretation* (New York: Knopf, 1951), p. 312.
27. J. Paul Williams, *What Americans Believe and How They Worship* (New York: Harper and Row, 1962), 477-592. The first edition appeared in 1952.

society and nation" (over against "the religion of the denominations"). While he clearly retained a Lincolnian sense of judgment over against idolization of the nation, he also agreed with G. K. Chesterton's observation that America is the "nation with the soul of a church," and that it was "protected by religious and not racial selection."[28] The question of racial or ethnic selection played only a very small part in Mead's thought. He was critical of those who stressed religious and theological particularity at the expense of the idea of the nation's "spiritual core." Mead promoted Ronald Osborn's suggestion that "a common type of faith and life . . . common convictions, a common sense of mission . . . could and should be the goal for Americans."[29]

One did not have to be a promoter of the search for "sameness," "oneness," or a "common faith" or religion in order to point to their development after midcentury. Mead singled out Winthrop Hudson, Will Herberg and Martin Marty as three definers of societal religion who withheld consent from it because of interests in religious and theological particularity. It was true that during the Eisenhower era many had been critical about a national "Piety along the Potomac" just as during the Nixon era there are complaints against a "Religion of the East Room of the White House." These referred to the new, currently-sanctioned expressions of common national faiths that were perhaps adhered to by a national majority,[30] but which many members of the liberal academic community rejected.

Most of the intellectuals' affirmations of a generalized American religion came during and shortly after the brief era when John F. Kennedy seemed to be portraying a new spiritual style for America. It was in this mood and at this moment that Robert N. Bellah in 1966 attracted a latter-day market for the term "Civil Religion in America." This was "at its best a genuine apprehension of universal and transcendent religious reality as seen in or, one could almost say, as revealed through the experience of the American people."[31]

The defenses of the common vision as against the particular contention were based on historical observations of good moments in past American expressions of religious "sameness." They also revealed philosophical commitments toward the higher unity. Most of the defenders overlooked ethnic and racial factors because these usually reinforced senses of difference. Rudolf J. Vecoli believes that "the prevailing ideology of the academic profession" which has been the

28. See especially Sidney E. Mead. "The Nation with the Soul of a Church," *Church History*, Vol. 36, No. 3 (September 1967), pp. 262ff. Williams quotes Mead with favor, *op. cit.*, p. 479, in reference to the religion of the democratic society *versus* the religion of the denominations.
29. Sidney E. Mead, "The Post-Protestant Concept and America's Two Religions," in Robert L. Ferm, *Issues in American Protestantism: A Documentary History from the Puritans to the Present* (Garden City, New York: Doubleday, 1969), pp. 387f. Following Paul Tillich's distinction, it might be said that Mead affirmed "the catholic substance" in a common national religion because he trusted the presence of "the protestant principle" of prophetic protest. Those Mead criticized tended to stress "the protestant principle" even where they affirmed the common faith because they feared that its "catholic substance" could be idolized or imposed on people.
30. William Lee Miller. *Piety Along the Potomac: Notes on Politics and Morals in the Fifties* (Boston: Houghton Mifflin, 1964); Stephen C. Rose, *Sermons Not Preached in the White House* (New York: Baron, 1970).
31. Robert N. Bellah, "Civil Religion in America" reprinted by Cutler, *op. cit.*, pp. 331ff., especially p. 346. The paper was first presented at a conference in May, 1966, before the liberal academic community had largely turned its back on the Johnson administration. After the escalation of the Vietnamese war, the rise of the New Left and the intensification of black power movements, this community was somewhat less congenial to the expressions of a national religion once again.

"prime article of the American creed" has been a "profound confidence in the power of the New World to transform human nature." Vecoli related this to Hector St. John Crévecoeur's eighteenth-century discernment of a "new race of men," a "new man," this American, who, "leaving behind him all his ancient prejudices and manners, receives new ones from the new mode of life he has embraced, the new government he obeys, and the new rank he holds. Here individuals of all nations are melted into a new race of men. . . ." The result of this faith has been an "assimilationist ideology."[32] In the nineteenth century Ralph Waldo Emerson, among others, kept this faith alive. Let immigrants come:

> The energy of Irish, Germans, Swedes, Poles, and Cossacks, and all the European tribes—and of the Africans, and of the Polynesians,—will construct a new race, *a new religion*, a new state, a new literature. . . .[33]

Regularly throughout American history, those who failed to be assimilated or who stressed separate racial, ethnic, or religious identities were embarrassments. Ethnicity became the skeleton in the closet and had to be prematurely pushed aside and hidden from view.

THE ANALYSTS AND DEFENDERS OF PARTICULARITY

The other line of interpretation has been dedicated to the love of what the philosopher Leibnitz and the historian Marc Bloch spoke of as "singular things."[34] Some representatives of this approach may have shared a concern for or belief in ultimate unity, but at least they recognized that pluralist terms for life in the civil order must be found. Thus in 1958 Father John Courtney Murray S.J., classically summarized the matter: "Religious pluralism is against the will of God. But it is the human condition; it is written into the script of history. It will not somehow marvelously cease to trouble the City."[35]

The historians and analysts who dealt more critically with "sameness," "oneness," and "common" religion in America after mid-century ordinarily devoted themselves to the religious shape of this pluralism. Only as the result of the racial upheavals and the new ethnic consciousnesses which were manifested during the 1960s have some of them begun to perceive again that ethnicity has been the skeleton, "the supporting framework" of American religion. These historians and other observers have seen that racial, ethnic, class, partisan, religious and ideological conflicts in America have countered or qualified the homogenizing ideals that earlier held together the "consensus" schools of history. Some of them have begun to try to cope specifically with the ethnic pluralism that is also part of "the human condition."

Sometimes spokesmen for ethnic or racial pluralism and separatism have attached ideological commitments to their observations. Out of myriad possibilities the word of Thomas H. Clancy can be regarded as representative. Clancy quoted Daniel Patrick Moynihan, who was one of the first to speak of the failure of

32. Vecoli, *op. cit.*, pp. 74f. Crévecoeur first published his *Letters from an American Farmer* in 1782.
33. Quoted by Stuart P. Sherman in *Essays and Poems of Emerson* (New York, 1921), p. xxxiv.
34. Marc Bloch, *The Historian's Craft* (New York: Vintage, 1964), p. 8. Such a "thrill of learning singular things" was not characteristic of Leibnitz, who tried to transcend variety and pluralism. Over against this, William James posed *A Pluralistic Universe* (New York: Longmans, Green, 1909), which may be seen as the philosophical grandfather of the American schools which tolerate or encourage particularisms.
35. John Courtney Murray, S.J., *We Hold These Truths: Catholic Reflections on the American Proposition* (New York: Sheed and Ward, 1960), p. 23.

assimilationist or "melting pot" theories to explain the American situation. Wrote Moynihan:

The sense of general community is eroding, and with it the authority of existing relationships, while, simultaneously, a powerful quest for specific community is emerging in the form of ever more intensive assertions of racial and ethnic identities.

Adds Clancy: "Black nationalism caused the white ethnics to remember what they had been taught to forget, their own origins." Then came his own theology of "unlikeness":

The year 1970 is the date when the drive for group rights became more important than the struggle for individual rights. (In the demonstrations and rallies of the future, most signs will bear an ethnic adjective.). . . . For a long time now we have been exhorted to love all men. We have finally realized that for sinful man this is an unrealistic goal. The saints and heroes among us will still face the challenge in a spirit of unyielding despair. The rest of us will try first to love our own kind. This is the year when 'brother' and 'sister' began to have *a less universal and hence truer meaning.*[36] [emphasis mine]

Of course not all historians who tried to make sense of racial and ethnic particularism have shared this creed, but it is the common affirmation of many spokesmen for "differences" over against "sameness" in civil and religious life.

The two general approaches just described can be best studied by reference to several prevailing models—many of them defined by sociologists—which are regularly used for historical explorations and contemporary analyses of the shape of American religion.

SAMENESS THROUGH COMMON SECULARITY

First, some advocates of "sameness" have chosen a *secular* interpretation of American religious life. In this view the belief is expressed that there will be progressively less religion in society. Secular men will unite on the basis of some sort of emergent godless, homogenizing, technological and political scheme. The result will be a global village marked by non-religious synthesis for world integration.[37] The "secular theologians" of the 1960s shared this creed, as did many working historians[38] In the view of British sociologist Bryan Wilson, participation in American church life could itself be called secularization, because on the legal basis of the nation's formal secularity "religious commitment and Church allegiance *have become* elements in the American value system." Wilson presupposed or observed that "the common values" embodied in religious institutions and the secular American Way of Life were rather simply congruent with each other.[39]

Seymour Martin Lipset, also writing in this frame of mind, dealt in passing with racial and ethnic groups and explained their continuing appearance in terms of cultural lag: "American religious denominations, like ethnic groups, have experienced collective upward mobility. . . ." On these terms, contemporary

36. In *America*, January 9, 1971, pp. 10f.
37. Secular and religious approaches to world integration are sketched by W. Warren Wagar, *The City of Man: Prophecies of a World Civilization in Twentieth-Century Thought* (Boston: Houghton Mifflin, 1963).
38. For a review of secular theologians' positions, see Martin E. Marty, "Secularization in the American Public Order," in Donald A. Giannella, *Religion and the Public Order,* Number Five (Ithaca: Cornell University Press, 1969), pp. 33f. and "Secular Theology as a Search for the Future," in Albert Schlitzer, C.S.C., ed., *The Spirit and Power of Christian Secularity* (Notre Dame, Ind.: University of Notre Dame Press, 1969), pp. 1ff.
39. Bryan Wilson, *Religion in Secular Society: A Sociological Comment* (Baltimore, Maryland: Penguin, 1966), pp. 40ff. and 181.

Negro religious behavior resembles that of the nineteenth-century lower status migrant white population. The Catholics have taken on the coloration of a fundamentalist orthodox religion comparable in tone and style, if not in theology, to the nineteenth-century evangelical Protestant sects.[40]

Because distinctive religious symbols have been connected with almost all the recently recovered movements of peoplehood, racial and ethnic, their spokesmen would not have been content to see themselves on Lipset's escalator. They would resist and stress their distinctive symbols ("Afro-American," "Amerindian," "Chicano," and the like) rather than accommodate themselves to the secular trend of "the common values" of American life or simply be an element in the scheme of "upward collective mobility."

CIVIL UNITY, RELIGIOUS PRIVACY

A second line of interpretation is close to the secular one. It simply says that a man's beliefs are *private* affairs and that these have little common or civic consequence. Ideological support for this view is deep in the American tradition. While Thomas Jefferson supported the idea that those moral precepts "in which all religions agree" could be supportive of civil order, he believed differing private religions to be a societal luxury: "It does me no injury for my neighbor to say that there are twenty gods, or no God."[41] One could be for sameness and for a common faith independent of private religious opinions. Religion, said philosopher Alfred North Whitehead in 1926, is "what the individual does with his own solitariness."[42] Religion, for William James in 1903, had meant *"the feelings, acts, and experiences of individual men in their solitude. . . ."*[43]

These views find support in the conditions of modern urban and industrial life, says social theorist Thomas Luckmann. He claims that "the most revolutionary trait of modern society" is the fact that "personal identity becomes, essentially, a private phenomenon." Religion, now housed in specialized institutions and religious opinions, has become "a private affair." Each person selects a world of significance from a variety of choices. "The selection is based on consumer preference, which is determined by the social biography of the individual, and similar social biographies will result in similar choices." "Individual religiosity in modern society receives no massive support and confirmation from the primary institutions."[44] Families, sect participation and the like are of some help, but cannot provide much support for community. Luckmann, unfortunately, does not dwell on ethnicity or race as religious factors in this context.

The new advocates of peoplehood, however, would contradict these pictures. "The new tribalism" accuses the American majority of having forced people to lose their identities by throwing all into the private sphere. One Indian summed it up long ago: "You are each a one-man tribe." Another said: "The question

40. Seymour Martin Lipset, *The First New Nation: The United States in Historical and Comparative Perspective* (New York: Basic Books, 1963), pp. 151f.
41. Jefferson to J. Fishback, Sept. 27, 1809, in Albert Ellery Bergh, *The Writings of Thomas Jefferson* (Washington, 1905), XII, 314-316; the second reference is quoted by Anson Phelps Stokes, *Church and State in the United States* (New York: Harper and Brothers, 1950), Vol. I, 335.
42. Alfred North Whitehead, *Religion in the Making* (New York: Macmillan, 1926), p. 58.
43. William James, *The Varieties of Religious Experience: A Study in Human Nature* (New York: Longmans, Green, 1903), p. 31.
44. Thomas Luckmann, *The Invisible Religion: The Problem of Religion in Modern Society* (New York: Macmillan, 1967), pp. 97f., 105f. While Jefferson, Whitehead and James often advocated private limitations of religion, Luckmann merely observes it and regards it as a burden for moderns seeking an identity.

is not how you can Americanize us but how we can Americanize you."[45] Whether or not they succeed in the effort, the new ethnic and racial recoveries are designed to supplant the private interpretation of identity and religion, and historians at the very least have to explore these claims at a time when, as Luckmann and others point out, denominational and sectarian involvement supply little of either.

RELIGIOUS, NOT ETHNIC, PLURALISM

The third model for religion in America, the *pluralist*, moves the discussion to the center of the debate over "sameness" versus "unlikeness" on national *versus* ethnic-racial and religious lines.

The religious pluralist interpretation was born in the face of the problem of identity and power which increased as ethnic origins of Americans became progressively more remote and vague. In a sense, it served to push the skeleton of ethnicity into the closet. Thus Gerhard Lenski in 1961 condensed the thought of Will Herberg, the best-known representative of this view at mid-century:

> Earlier in American history ethnic groups [provided community and identity] and individuals were able to enjoy this sense of communal identification and participation as members of the German, Polish, Italian, and other ethnic colonies established in this country. Today such groups have largely disintegrated, but many of the needs they served continue to be felt. In this situation, Herberg argues, Americans are turning increasingly to their religious groups, especially the three major faiths, for the satisfaction of their need for communal identification and belongingness.[46]

Herberg himself in 1955 had deplored the "sameness" or "common religion" schools, but he recognized the presence of a common faith in the "American Way of Life" as the ultimate. Identification with Protestant, Catholic, or Jewish religions were paths for reaching it.[47] E. Digby Baltzell, a student of the WASP establishment, observed in 1964 that "religious pluralism is replacing the ethnic pluralism of the earlier era."[48] Historian Arthur Mann, ten years earlier, had seen that in the matter of pluralism and a single religion of democracy "American Catholicism, American Protestantism, and American Judaism appear like parallel shoots on a common stock."[49] John Cogley, after hosting a tri-faith conference on pluralism in relation to common religion in 1958, reported with favor on the response of one participant. This man had learned "that the free society of America

45. Quoted in Edgar S. Cahn, ed., *Our Brother's Keeper: The Indian in White America* (New York and Cleveland: World, 1969), pp. 184, 175.
46. Gerhard Lenski, *The Religious Factor: A Sociological Study of Religion's Impact on Politics, Economics, and Family Life* (Garden City, New York: Doubleday, 1961), p. 11.
47. Will Herberg, *Protestant-Catholic-Jew: An Essay in American Religious Sociology* (Garden City, New York: Doubleday, 1955), pp. 88-102. Lenski and Herberg did not regard the common religion of America with favor. Among those who did were Horace M. Kallen, in *Secularism Is the Will of God* (New York: Twayne, 1954) and Duncan J. Howlett, though they treated secularism or humanism as *The Fourth American Faith* (New York: Harper and Row, 1964) which still had to contend for place with Protestantism, Catholicism and Judaism. Samuel A. Mueller, "The New Triple Melting Pot: Herberg Revisited," in *Review of Religious Research*, Vol. 13, No. 1 (Fall 1971), suggests that a new set of categories should be "white Christian, white non-Christian, and black." He bases this on a sociological study of lines between these and Herberg's three groups in the matters of "marriage, friendship, residence, occupations, and politics."
48. E. Digby Baltzell, *The Protestant Establishment* (New York: Random House, 1964), p. 53.
49. Arthur Mann, "Charles Fleischer's Religion of Democracy," in *Commentary*, June 1954, p. 557.

means more than an agreement to disagree; it is posited, rather, on the idea that Americans will disagree in order to agree."[50]

Ethnic and racial pluralism, however, did not go away just because religious pluralism was able to serve some social purposes during the religious revival of the 1950s. Religionists themselves could not agree on the three-faith interpretation. Thus, Orthodox theologian John Meyendorff overstated the case somewhat when he said in 1960 that the Orthodox had later come to be recognized as a fourth "official" American faith.[51] Lenski, who asked no ethnic questions when he studied Detroit religion, did find that Herberg's single "Protestantism" had had to be divided and understood on black/white lines, at least. The religious revival eventually waned, and many people in a new generation no longer found it possible or desirable to define themselves in terms of one of three religions. Most of all, ethnic and racial reassertion did provide identification and community for the "different," who were dissenters against a common faith for all Americans.

MANY DENOMINATIONS, ONE RELIGION

The fourth interpretation has to be taken more seriously because of its obvious appropriateness on so many levels. This is an application to the whole of American Christianity by others of Sidney E. Mead's classic statement that *denominationalism* is the shape of Protestantism in America. "Denominationalism is the new American way in Christianity," wrote Karl Hertz.[52] Catholicism is also regarded as a denomination by historians. Judaism, too, is formally denominationalized.

At first glance it may seem to make little sense to say that the denominational interpretation tended to be favored by those who looked for a common religion. After all, denominations had been invented in order that they might protect peoples' differing ways of looking at religious ultimates without permitting society to disintegrate. It turns out that they seem to have been clever but almost accidental inventions. They served to channel potential conflict out of possibly violent racial or ethnic spheres into harmless and irrelevant religious areas. Where are the dead bodies as the result of persistent denominational conflict?

In effect, argue the viewers of a single American community, denominationalism works just the opposite way. Two illustrations, one from a man who favors a secular and the other a religious scheme for seeing America, in that order, will serve. British sociologist Bryan Wilson, as we noted above, posited "secularization as the experience of Christianity" in America. In a long chapter he then discussed "Denominationalism and Secularization." Denominationalism is "an aspect of secularization." Using an interpretation which stressed class distinctions, Wilson saw "the diversity of denominations . . . as the successive stages in the accommodation of life-practice and ethos of new social classes as they emerged in the national life." And denominational diversity "has in itself promoted a process of secularization." The religious choices offered people effectively

50. John Cogley, ed., *Religion in America: Original Essays on Religion in a Free Society* (New York: Meridian, 1958), p. 9.
51. John Meyendorff, *The Orthodox Church: Its Past and Its Role in the World Today* (New York: Pantheon, 1960), p. 107.
52. Mead's essay is reprinted in Sidney E. Mead, *The Lively Experiment: The Shaping of Christianity in America* (New York: Harper and Row), 103ff. Karl Hertz writes on denominationalism in "Some Suggestions for a Sociology of American Protestantism" in Herbert T. Neve and Benjamin A. Johnson, *The Maturing of American Lutheranism* (Minneapolis, Minnesota: Augsburg, 1968), pp. 36, 42.

cancel out each other. Denominations exist and even thrive, but when people accept the ground rules of denominational civility they telegraph to others that society's ultimate values are being bartered outside the sects, if anywhere.[53]

Sidney E. Mead's religious interpretation works to similar effect. While the churches accepted denominationalism as a pattern which would guarantee their own integrity and relevance, in practice the opposite has happened. The competitive element in sectarian life has worked against the truth claims and the plausibility of the denominations. Those who seek religious affiliation of any sort cannot avoid denominations, though it is true that they need not necessarily repose their ultimate concerns in denominational formulations. In this context Mead includes one of his rare references to nationality and racial backgrounds:

[There has been] a general erosion of interest in the historical distinction and definable theological differences between the religious sects. Increasingly the competition among them seems to stem from such non-theological concerns as nationality or racial background, social status, and convenient accessibility of a local church. Finally what appears to be emerging as of primary distinctive importance in the pluralistic culture is the general traditional ethos of the large families, Protestant, Roman Catholic, and Jewish. If this trend continues, the competition inherent in the system of church and state separation, which served to divide the religious groups in the first place, may work eventually to their greater unity.[54]

By the end of the paragraph, then, the ethnic skeleton has been placed back in the closet, and trends toward higher unity prevail in Mead's world.

The matter was not resolved so easily, however. Denominational distinctiveness remained durable, as Charles Y. Glock in 1965 showed in an essay on "The New Denominationalism."[55] Glock, basing his assertions on his findings of a population sample in California, disagreed with both Will Herberg on the theme of a "common religion" and with Robert Lee on there being a "common core Protestantism." Glock is probably correct: great numbers of Americans *do* want to be loyal to their denominations. The interdenominational Consultation on Church Union, which would cluster and merge denominations, attracts little support. Non- and inter-and para-and counter-denominational, ecumenical ventures do not prosper. Despite this, it would be easy to overstress the importance of denominational pluralism.

For one thing, the denominations are divided down the center in a kind of two-party system. The differences on vital issues (such as racial and ethnic matters) are expressed within and not between denominations, as Jeffrey Hadden demonstrated in 1969.[56] What is more, on matters of deepest significance, even where denominational names have been useful, denominational designations reveal little. For example, black religion was denominationalized, but sectarian bonds have meant almost nothing across racial lines. Millions of southern blacks have been Baptist, but there was until recently almost no contact between them and southern Baptists, the largest white Protestant group in America. The racist has looked at the Negro as a black, not as a Methodist or a Protestant. The black American has had little choice between church bodies when he wished to look

53. Bryan Wilson, *op. cit.*, pp. 47, 51.
54. Sidney E. Mead, *The Lively Experiment*, pp. 132 f.
55. Charles Y. Glock and Rodney Stark, *Religion and Society in Tension* (Chicago: Rand McNally, 1965), pp. 86f.
56. Jeffrey K. Hadden, *The Gathering Storm in the Churches: The Widening Gap Between Clergy and Laymen* (Garden City, New York, 1969), especially Chapter IV, ''Clergy and Laity View the Civil Rights Issue.''

for differences in attitudes among them. "Denomination mattered little, for support of the racist creed ran the gamut from urban Episcopalians to country Baptists," wrote David Reimers concerning the late nineteenth-century situation.[57]

Even among whites, ethnic lines usually undercut denominational interests. WASPs, for instance, once established a line-crossing mission to "Catholic Immigrants." Theodore Abel wrote in 1933 that "in general the work among Catholic immigrants is carried on with the aim of promoting Americanization and breaking down the isolation of immigrants from American society by bringing them into the fellowship of the Protestant Church." In the fifty years before 1933 between fifty and one-hundred million dollars had been spent on the cause. But:

The mission enterprise has failed to realize the main purpose for which it was instituted. It has failed to accomplish to any significant degree the evangelization of Catholic immigrants and their descendants, and it has not achieved the control that it sought of directing the process of their adaptation to American life. No movement toward Protestantism has taken place as a result of these missionary efforts.[58]

That report dealt with a half-century during which Protestants had been notably missionary, expansionist and devoted toward transforming remote churches. But at home, ethnic factors served to frustrate such motives or achievements. Black, Indian, Chicano, white ethnic and other movements of peoplehood found neither the denominational shape nor the nation's soul to be as effective for promoting identity and power as they found race or ethnicity, which was still—or again— the skeleton or supporting framework for their religion.

A COMMON RELIGION

The fifth major line of interpretation has been implied throughout. In it "sameness," "oneness," and a "common faith" found their home in a societal or civil religion that informed, infused and inspired virtually the whole population. How does it fare in a time of new peoplehood or "new tribalism"? Its expression is complicated and compromised. At the very least it must be said that the racial or ethnic group "refracts the national cultural patterns of behavior and values through the prism of its own cultural heritage," as Milton Gordon put it.[59] The black child in the ghetto or the Amerindian youngster may engage in ceremonies of civil religion. But they may think of something quite different from the world of the white child's Pilgrims or Founders when they sing of a "land where my fathers died." This is the land where their fathers were enslaved or killed. The symbols of societal religion can be used in more ways than one by separate groups.

Most of the movements of racial and ethnic consciousness have found it important to oppose militantly the symbols of civil religion. Historian Vincent Harding in 1968 defined Black Power itself as "a repudiation of the American culture-religion that helped to create it and a quest for a religious reality more faithful to our own experience."[60] An Indian does not want the white man's religion. The Chicano detects the Protestant work-ethic in the calls for his participation in a common civil religion. The white ethnic at his American Legion

57. David Reimers, *White Protestantism and the Negro* (New York: Oxford University Press, 1965), p. 29.
58. Quoted in Benson Y. Landis, *Protestant Experience with United States Immigration, 1910-1960* (New York: Church World Service, 1961), pp. 12f.
59. Gordon, *op. cit.*, p. 38.
60. Vincent Harding, "Black Power and the American Christ," in Floyd B. Barbour, *The Black Power Revolt: A Collection of Essays* (New York: Collier, 1968), p. 97.

hall relates to civil religious symbols in a different way than does the Jewish member of the Americans for Democratic Action. The young WASP counter-cultural devotee rejects all American civil religion. The delineations of civil religion themselves are never universal in origin, content, ethos, or scope; they are informed by the experience of the delineators' own ethnic subcommunities. Robert N. Bellah's and Sidney E. Mead's views are unexplainable except as expressions of particular WASP traditions. Orientals, Africans, Latin Americans ordinarily would neither bring Bellah's and Mead's kinds of questions nor find their kinds of answers in civil religion. As British observer Denis Brogan wrote concerning Bellah's essay, "The emblems, the metaphors, the 'note' (as Newman might have put it) of public civil religion is Protestant, even when those symbols are used by Catholics, Jews, Greek Orthodox, . . ."[61] It is precisely this feature that has led to attempts at rejection of civil religion and "common faith" on the part of so many ethnic and racial groups.

In summary, it would appear that the five main models for interpreting American religious "sameness"—the secular, the private, the pluralist, the denominational, and the common-religious—apply appropriately only to the white and largely generalized Protestant academic circles where they originated. Other ethnic-racial-religious complexes can be only occasionally and partially interpreted through these.

ETHNIC AND RACIAL THEMES REINTRODUCED

To suggest that ethnic and racial themes have to be reintegrated into the schemes for posing historians' questions is *not* to say that these should displace the others. The secular tendencies in America will probably not be successfully countered by the new religious practices of minority groups. Many people can find identity in the private sphere without explicit reference to ethnic and racial religious motifs. Protestantism, Catholicism, Judaism may long serve to identify practitioners of a common American religion. Denominationalism may indeed be the shape, and civil religion the soul, of American religion—just as ethnicity is its skeleton or supporting framework. But as the most neglected theme until recently, racial and ethnic particularity deserves compensatory interest and inquiry.

Numerous benefits could result from such an effort. Concentration on religious dimensions of peoplehood could lead to a more accurate portraying of the way things have been—that is always the first goal of the historian. Historians in the once-majority traditions, WASP and white ethnic combined, can re-explore their own assumptions and may be able to discern the ethnic aspects in what they had earlier regarded as their universal points of view. The theories seeking "sameness" and "oneness" tended to be based on a kind of optimistic and voluntaryistic spirit. Ethnic-racial recovery should help historians deal more adequately with the fated, predestined, tragic and even violent elements in religion in America.

WASP HISTORIES AS ETHNIC EXPRESSIONS

In any case, WASP and white ethnic American historians would be able critically to revisit their own older traditions, traditions which were once racially and ethnically self-conscious, for better and for worse. When WASP is seen not as the norm but as an ethnic minority among minorities, the racial special

61. Denis W. Brogan, "Commentary," in Cutler, *op. cit.*, p. 357.

pleading of the fathers appears in a different light. Robert Baird, whom many regard as the first historian of American religion, in 1843 insisted that "our national character is that of the Anglo-Saxon race," and he ranked other ethnic groups downward from Anglo-Saxon.[62] Baird began his history with reference to the differences of Indian, Negro and other non-Anglo-Saxon peoples and kept them in mind consistently as he measured them in the light of his own racial norm.

Not only WASPs were particularists. Baird's counterpart, John Gilmary Shea, the father of American Catholic historiography, was a spokesman for the Irish minority, and Catholic history has been consistently marked by ethnic distinctives.[63] Philip Schaff, a continental "outsider," had to invent artificial ways to blend his German-Swiss background with the Anglo-American dominant strain. Daniel Dorchester in 1890 criticized the German and Irish influx as people of "low habits and ideas, retaining supreme allegiance to a foreign pontiff, or controlled by radical, rationalistic, materialistic, or communistic theories. . . . Can Old World subjects be transformed into New World citizens?"[64] Even Leonard Woolsey Bacon, a man of ecumenical temperament and a devotee of religious "sameness," spoke during 1898 in terms of "masterful races" in American white Protestantism.[65]

Josiah Strong—shall the historians' fraternity claim him?—was explicitly racist in his accounting of American religion in the 1880s and 1890s. For Strong, the Anglo-Saxon's religion was "more vigorous, more spiritual, more Christian than that of any other." It was destined to "dispossess many weaker races, assimilate others, and mold the remainder, until, in a very true and important sense, it has Anglo-Saxonized mankind."

If I do not read amiss, this powerful race will move down into Mexico, down upon Central and South America, out upon the islands of the sea, over upon Africa and beyond. And can anyone doubt that the result of this competition will be the 'survival of the fittest'?[66]

The themes of WASP ethnicity and superiority which had been explicit in the nineteenth century became implicit and taken for granted in the twentieth. The assimilationist ideal took over. In 1923 Peter Mode could write that "American Christianity has . . . no racial coloring and its Americanization as yet has been a process void of racialism," a suggestion about America that would be incomprehensible to most of the world. Instead, said Mode, American Christianity has taken its character by having been "frontierized."[67] Joining the frontierizing-

62. Robert Baird, *Religion in the United States of America* (Glasgow, 1843); see Chapter VI, p. 35ff.
63. John Gilmary Shea, *The History of the Catholic Church in the United States* (New York, 1886-92), four volumes.
64. Daniel Dorchester, *Christianity in the United States* (New York: Hunt and Eaton, 1890), p. 765.
65. Leonard Woolsey Bacon, *A History of American Christianity* (New York: Scribners, 1898), p. 292.
66. Josiah Strong, *The New Era; or The Coming Kingdom* (New York, 1893), pp. 54-55; *Our Country: Its Possible Future and Its Present Crisis* (New York, 1885), pp. 178, 174-175.
67. Peter Mode, *The Frontier Spirit in American Christianity* (New York: Macmillan, 1923), pp. 6, 7, 14. Mode-Sweet-Mead represent a University of Chicago succession which is most familiar to me. See also William Warren Sweet, *The Story of Religion in America* (New York: Harper and Brothers, 1930); another student in this tradition, along with Robert T. Handy (see note 68), is Winthrop J. Hudson, whose *Religion in America* (New York: Scribner's, 1965) pioneered at least in its sense of proportion, since it devoted much attention to black Protestantism, Judaism and other non-WASP religious groups.

sameness school was William Warren Sweet, who dealt at length with slavery, but most of whose energies were devoted to the white Protestant mainline churches as normal and normative. Sidney E. Mead changed the topic to denominationalism and a common national religion without picking up much interest in non-WASP religion.

On the other hand, Robert Handy's recent *A Christian America: Protestant Hopes and Historical Realities*[68] is one of the first important attempts by a WASP to come to terms with the WASP particularism which once had paraded itself as universalism. Handy stresses ethnic, racial and other conflict-inducing questions over against the interpretations which derived from the mid-century "sameness" and "oneness" schools.

THE FUTURE OF TRIBAL CONFEDERATION

Even though the future is not the historian's province, it is sometimes asked whether it is worth scholars' efforts to re-tool so that they can henceforth include the ethnic and racial questions. The assimilating, blending, melting processes do remain and are accelerating. There are few new immigrants. The children of old ones intermarry and expose themselves to common value systems in education and through the media or by travel; they move out of vestigial ghettos. Perhaps the attention to the quest for identity through ethnic and racial communities will pass again as soon as certain needs have been met. The political and psychological use of WASP terms such as "white ethnics" and "WASPs" may soon be exposed as inauthentic, and the new and artifical ethnic coalitions may break apart. Maybe the focus on peoplehood has been only a fashion, a passing fancy, one which can be a partial setback in the quest for expressions of a common humanity.

If the ethnic factor remains strong, certainly there will be times of crisis when a sort of "tribal confederation" will be instinctively and informally convoked so various peoples can get together and affirm their common, not their separate, symbols. The historians can then stand ready to interpret both the past interplay between conflicting particularities and homogenizing concordant elements in national life and the considerable assets and liabilities of each.

Whatever happens, however, it seems clear that not all of men's needs can be met by secular interpretation and private faith, by tri-faith or conventional denominational life or by a common national religion. New particularisms will no doubt continue to arise, to embody the hopes of this "people of peoples." Meanwhile, when spokesmen for the oldest of American peoples, the American Indian, assert that they wish to Americanize the rest of the nation and that they would like to teach their fellow citizens the merits of life in tribes, these other citizens could appropriately reply: "In some senses, we never left home."

68. New York: Oxford University Press, 1971. For another attempt to isolate WASP history and to treat WASPs as an ethnic group, see Martin E. Marty, *Righteous Empire: The Protestant Experience in America* (New York: Dial, 1970).

The Catholic Historical Review

| Volume XXXI | JANUARY, 1946 | No. 4 |

CAHENSLYISM: THE FIRST STAGE, 1883-1891*

THE coming-of-age of the Catholic Church in the United States was marked by internal difficulties characteristic of that stage in human development in which the uncertainties of adolescence are put aside and the more responsible and independent attitudes of manhood are assumed. The transition period covered a span of approximately twenty-eight years, beginning around 1880, and concluding in 1908. Such dates are, of course, arbitrary and approximate only. The terminal point of the period is more clearly marked than is its beginning. It was in 1908 that the Congregation of the Propaganda officially put an end to the missionary status of the Church in this country.

The twenty-five years immediately preceding that date constituted without doubt the most significant quarter-century thus far in the life of the organized Church in the United States. No truly adequate history of this period has yet been written, nor is it perhaps possible to do that job at this comparatively early date. Some preliminary work has been completed by investigators who have discussed in considerable detail individual phases of the multiple inter-related problems of the period. This paper can pretend to do no more than add another stone to the pile of building materials from which a well-constructed, true, and comprehensive history of the Church for these years may be written.

If any one descriptive term may be applied to the fermentations of this period it is "Americanism." But, as has been recently pointed

* Presidential Address delivered at the Twenty-Sixth Annual Meeting of the American Catholic Historical Association, Washington, December 15, 1945.

389

out,[1] by Thomas T. McAvoy of the University of Notre Dame, "Americanism" possessed a number of different aspects which are frequently confused one with the other. As a generic term, therefore, "Americanism" is wanting in certain important respects. Be that as it may, one thing is certain. No single individual problem that confronted the Church in the United States during these years was totally unrelated to its companion problems. There were essentially three main branches to the one great problem of "Americanism." There were the doctrinal question, the political question, and the administrative question—and these three were in essence one.

The doctrinal problem came to a head in Europe, where a sharp controversy over the alleged heretical character of certain American teachings in matters of faith called finally for the definitive intervention of the Holy Father.[2] The political problem centered in the United States upon the relationship of State and Church, particularly with reference to the school question. There were significant matters of faith and administration, as well as of politics, involved in the school question and its settlement.[3] The third phase of the problem, the administrative question, was never far removed from other aspects of Church life at this period.. In a very real sense, there is a certain degree of inaccuracy implicit in treating it as a phenomenon of Church life separate and distinct from the doctrinal and political discussions which accompanied it. A still more risky business is the segregation for special attention of one minor phase of the larger administrative problem. For purposes of brevity and close analysis, however, that risk must be taken.

The purpose of this paper is to look more closely into the background and early development of the demand for a greater degree of ecclesiastical autonomy by foreign language groups within the American Church. This was the movement that became known eventually as "Cahenslyism." There were those in the Church who saw "Ca-

---

[1] "Americanism and Frontier Catholicism," *Review of Politics*, V (July, 1943), 275-301; "Americanism, Fact and Fiction," *Catholic Historical Review*, XXXI (July, 1945), 133-153.

[2] For bibliographical items on this phase of the subject, cf. McAvoy, *op. cit.*

[3] The most adequate survey of the school question published to date is Daniel F. Reilly's *The School Controversy (1891-1893)* (Washington, 1943).

henslyism" as a definite conspiracy to make of the American Church another cog in the machine of Prussian political Pan-Germanism. Others considered it a well-meant but impolitic attempt to strengthen the Catholic faith of the thousands of central European immigrants coming to these shores. The proponents of the demand for autonomy professed nothing more than a deep concern for the spiritual welfare of the foreign language groups in this country, and defended their demands as being necessitated by the administrative weaknesses of Church organization in the United States. There were other shades of opinion on the subject held in various quarters.

It is not possible at the present time to pass authoritative judgment upon any one of these claims. The future historian, for whom this present "footnote" is intended, may have at his disposal the facts necessary to arrive at such a judgment. All that can be done at this juncture is to echo the statement of Father McAvoy which appeared in his discussion of "Americanism" in the last volume of this REVIEW: "Nothing can be gained today by taking one side or the other of the controversy, and the critical searcher for truth will be content to uncover the facts of the case and let the honor or guilt fall where it may."[4]

Peter Paul Cahensly (1838-1923), whose name figured so prominently in American ecclesiastical politics during 1891 and 1892, was a German Catholic merchant, a resident of Limburg am Lahn. Between 1862 and 1868, while employed in his father's exporting business at Le Havre, the great port of departure for emigrants to the New World, he was struck by the lack of provision for the spiritual welfare of Catholic emigrants. A later result of this experience was the establishment of the St. Raphaelsverein zum Schutze katholischer deutscher Auswanderer, which he served as general secretary from 1883 to 1900, and as president from 1900 until his death. Cahensly was also a member of the Prussian Diet from 1888 until the outbreak of the first World War, and of the German Reichstag between 1898 and 1903.[5] These latter facts possess a sinister significance for those who view "Cahenslyism" as a German political conspiracy.

German Catholics in the United States, like Germans of other re-

[4] *Op. cit.*, XXI (July, 1945), 134.
[5] Cf. *Wer Ist's?* (Leipzig, 1908), p. 199.

ligious beliefs, demonstrated at an early date a certain tenaciousness of their traditional culture patterns. From time to time their hesitancy in adopting American ways of life led to ecclesiastical difficulties.[6] It is impossible here to detail the earlier experiences of the American Church in this regard. For present purposes the date 1883 may be taken as the point of departure for an intensified campaign on the part of German-American Catholics to achieve a greater degree of autonomy in affairs ecclesiastical.

The first proper name which appears in a chronological study of the problem is that of Cahensly himself, even though it was considerably later that he emerged as the presiding spirit of the movement that came to bear his name. Cahensly landed in New York on August 17, 1883, as official representative of the German St. Raphael's Society. He visited the principal centers of German settlement in this country, conferring with members of the clergy on the problems of Catholics newly-arrived from the Fatherland. During a stay of "more than a month," he recorded visits to Evansville, Indiana, St. Louis, Arkansas, Kansas, Minnesota, Milwaukee, Cincinnati, Baltimore, and Philadelphia. In New York he visited Archbishop Corrigan and recommended to his care the newly-established American branch of the St. Raphael's Society.[7]

Neither the tenor of Cahensly's conversations nor the character of his recommendations appears in available records. Whether the first public move in the demand for greater ecclesiastical autonomy for German-American Catholics came as a result of Cahensly's visits, or whether the juxtaposition of dates was purely coincidental, this author cannot state. Certain it is that less than two months after Cahensly's departure from St. Louis there appeared in the *Pastoral-Blatt*, German-Catholic newspaper of that city, an article on "Clerical Know-Nothingism" in the American Church. In St. Louis there was a

---

[6] Cf. Reilly, *School Controversy*, pp. 57-58.

[7] Peter Paul Cahensly, *Der St. Raphaelsverein zum Schutze katholischer deutscher Auswanderer. Sein Werden, Wirken und Kämpfen während des 30. jährigen Bestehens erzählt von dessen derzeitigen Präsidenten* (Freiburg im Breisgau, 1900) [*Charitas-Schriften*, Heft 5], pp. 27-29. Cf. also a number of letters from Cahensly to Corrigan, in New York Archdiocesan Archives, E—c. These archives will be noted hereafter as NYAA.

large number of German churches which were under the ecclesiastical jurisdiction of English-speaking parishes. They were, in effect, German chapels lacking canonical autonomy. The article in the *Pastoral-Blatt* condemned this nationalistic discrimination and urged the granting of independence to the German churches. The demand met a receptive audience in the large number of German priests in the archdiocese, led by the vicar general for German, Bohemian, and Polish Catholics, the Reverend Henry Muehlsiepen.[8]

John Gilmary Shea, that learned student of American Catholicism, was quick to recognize some of the implications behind the general movement for German national self-expression which was making itself felt in a number of ways. The undue fostering of national feelings is a great mistake, he held, for it breeds animosity. The rising generation will be American, and if it comes to consider religion a matter of nationality, it will lose its religion along with its nationality. Shea believed that this was happening as he wrote, toward the end of 1883. It is "a canker eating away the life of the Church in the United States."[9]

What was presumably the first attempt to bring the German problem to the attention of the Holy See is said to have taken place in 1884. The Reverend John Conway is authority for the statement that in that year eighty-two German-American priests submitted a petition to Rome asking for a "redress of grievances," particularly in St. Louis.[10] They were entirely unsuccessful. The difficulty here is that Conway, who is the sole authority for this statement, was not a disinterested witness, since he was the editor of the *Northwestern Chronicle* of St. Paul, and stood in violent opposition to "Cahenslyism."

---

[8] John Rothensteiner, *History of the Archdiocese of St. Louis in Its Various Stages of Development from A.D. 1673 to A.D. 1928* (St. Louis, 1928), II, 562-564. Cf. also Frederick J. Zwierlein, *The Life and Letters of Bishop McQuaid* (Rochester, 1927), III, 44-45. This article, and two other pertinent writings, were separately published by their authors, Fathers William Faerber and Innocent Wapelhorst, under the title *The Future of Foreign-born Catholics . . .* (St. Louis, 1884).

[9] "Converts—Their Influence and Work in this Country," *American Catholic Quarterly Review*, VIII (July, 1883), 525.

[10] " 'Cahenslyism' versus Americanism," *Review of Reviews*, VI (August, 1892), 43.

There is little doubt, of course, that adequate archival investigation would uncover the truth of the matter. Were such a petition actually delivered, it is quite possible that Father Conway should know of it because of his close association with Archbishop John Ireland of St. Paul—the determined foe of all movements that seemed to him to hinder in any way the "Americanization" of the Church.

Such a petition might also explain more adequately the reason for a memorial on the German question which Bishops Richard Gilmour of Cleveland and John Moore of St. Augustine submitted to Propaganda on October 2, 1885. Egoism was a characteristic of German-Americans, they claimed. Particularly did this egoism become apparent when Germans were required to attend the same church with peoples of other nationalities. It promised a conflict between German and Irish Catholics, with a consequent scandal to religion and harm to souls. In conclusion, the memorial set forth the belief that the German-Americans were responsible for establishing, if not an organized movement, at least a mutual understanding directed at promoting the spirit of nationalism and at Germanizing the Church in the United States.[11]

On one count at least, Gilmour and Moore were correct. The German question in the United States was formally presented to the Holy See in the guise of a German-Irish conflict. One year later, in the month of November, 1886, the Reverend P. M. Abbelen, later Vicar-General of the Archdiocese of Milwaukee, with the approval of his ordinary, Archbishop Heiss, submitted to Propaganda a long statement which purported to lay bare the unjust restrictions imposed upon the German Catholic minority in the United States by the Irish Catholic majority. In conclusion the memorial petitioned the Holy See to do a number of things to reform Church administration in the United States. German churches, and those of all other nationalities

> shall be placed on an equal footing with the English (Irish) and shall be entirely independent of them. . . . All immigrants from Europe to be assigned to the church of their own language. . . . Let bishops and priests be admonished . . . not . . . to seek to suppress and root out the

---

[11] *Memoriale sulla questione dei Tedeschi nella Chiesa di America (Denkschrift über die deutsche Frage in der Kirche Amerikas)* (N.p., 1885). The Italian and German texts appear on facing pages.

language, the manners, the customs, the usages and the devotional practices of the Germans. . . . Let bishops who are ignorant of the German language, and who govern mixed dioceses, be obliged besides an Irish vicar-general, to nominate also a German.

Abbelen's petition undoubtedly contained a number of justified complaints, but it erred on one serious point. The identification of "Irish" with American called forth a searing blast of criticism from two members of the American hierarchy who happened to be in Rome at the time the petition was presented. Bishops John Ireland of St. Paul and John J. Keane of Richmond were negotiating with Propaganda concerning problems involved in the establishment of the Catholic University of America. Upon hearing of the German manoeuver they delivered, on December 6, 1886, a long memorial to Cardinal Simeoni, Prefect of Propaganda, in which they scored as untrue the claim that there existed any serious problem between German and Irish Catholics in the United States. "The only question that can be considered," they wrote, "is . . . the question between the English language, which is the language of the United States, and the German language, which emigrants from Germany have brought to the United States." They further asserted that the Abbelen petition was engineered in secrecy, without the knowledge of any but a few of the German-American members of the hierarchy. It was an understatement for Ireland and Keane to write: "When the knowledge of this secret movement shall have come to them, the Bishops of the United States will be exceedingly indignant." In another portion of the memorial they added: "We have evidence to prove that among certain German bishops and priests there is a conspiracy followed up by systematic plans and efforts incessantly made, to extend the German episcopate over the entire United States."[12]

---

[12] An extremely limited edition of the Abbelen memorial, together with the objections of Ireland, Keane, and other American prelates, was published in pamphlet form under the title *Relatio de quaestione Germanica in Statibus Foedratis a Rev. P. M. Abbelen, Sac. Milw. conscripta, a Rmo. et Illmo. M. Heiss, Archiep. Milwauk., approbata, et Sacrae Congr. de Propaganda Fide mense Novembri 1886, submissa. Sequuntur objectiones plurimorum Rvmorum Praesulum eidem S. Congr. propositae, e lingua Gallica in Anglicam translatae.* Copies of this rare item are almost non-existent. A complete reprinting of the pamphlet, with the addition of an English translation of the Abbe-

Members of the American hierarchy were, indeed, incensed when they learned by cable from Ireland and Keane of the action taken in Rome by Father Abbelen. The archbishops of Baltimore, Philadelphia, New York, and Boston met at Philadelphia on December 16, 1886, and instructed Archbishop Corrigan of New York to send off a refutation of the German statements "by the morrow's steamer."[13] Archbishop William H. Elder of Cincinnati, Bishop McQuaid of Rochester, Bishop Gilmour of Cleveland, and others cabled or wrote their opposition to Propaganda.[14] Bishop Gilmour's letter, dated December 26, 1886, was typical of their reaction. He wrote, in part:

> The efforts made to obtain special favors for the Germans appear to us as a very serious menace; their being made without the knowledge of the bishops . . . furnishes us with the proof that they dare not discuss openly in America their preposterous claims. . . . it is false to say they have been neglected. . . . Germans receive far more favors than their talents or their number warrant. . . . Certain German ecclesiastics, with narrow and egotistical views, are the instigators of all this turmoil; the German laity are far from nourishing such a fatuous spirit of nationalism as is found among their priests and prelates.[15]

Although the foes of German nationalism have claimed that Abbelen's position resulted in a severe rebuke for the petitioners,[16] the facts of the case indicate that certain of their demands were met.[17]

At this point the problem of ecclesiastical nationalism seemed comparatively clear-cut and simple. The desire of the German ecclesiastics for autonomy was envisioned as a threat to the administrative

---

len memorial was included in the New York *Freeman's Journal and Catholic Register*, LIII (Dec. 24, 31, 1892). First public reference to the pamphlet was a summary of its contents printed in the *Catholic Review* of New York, XL, (July 11, 1891), 18, 31. The New York *Times* likewise printed a summary of it on December 12, 1892. A large portion of Ireland's and Keane's letter was printed in English translation in *The Independent* for January 14, 1897.

[18] Allen Sinclair Will, *The Life of Cardinal Gibbons* (New York, 1922), I, 521, quoting Cardinal Gibbons' diary.

[14] Zwierlein, *op. cit.*, III, 41-42; Reilly, *School Controversy*, pp. 61-62.

[15] *The Independent*, January 14, 1897. Bishop Gilmour was a Scotsman, and had been trained for the Presbyterian ministry.

[16] Cf. Conway, *op. cit.*, p. 43.

[17] Zwierlein, *op. cit.*, III, 42-45.

unity of the Church in the United States. As such, it was opposed in common by prelates who later differed sharply among themselves as this particular issue became less well-defined and intricately enmeshed with other aspects of ecclesiastical politics.

Neither was the German group lacking in unity. The petition to Rome seems to have encouraged common action. If they were rebuked, they showed little evidence of the fact. Propaganda was still receiving indignant letters from American prelates dealing with the Abbelen petition when the first conference of the Deutsch-Amerikanischer Priester-Verein was called to order in Chicago on February 16, 1887. The moving spirits of the organization were the St. Louis priests who had financed Abbelen's trip to Rome. Among the items discussed at this first meeting of German-American clerics were plans for establishing a national German-American Catholic Congress.[18] On the sixth of the following September such a national meeting took place in Chicago. Both conferences, although brief, were successful enough to encourage the organizers to make them yearly affairs, and to enlarge the scope of their operations.[19]

Such effective and open organization as this indicated to the opposite camp that the struggle for Americanization of the Church could not be fought behind closed doors. The first of a long series of polemical pamphlets and articles attacked the Germans as a stubborn foreign group which refused to accept American customs, and threatened to bring another wave of prejudice upon the Church in the United States. The Reverend John Gmeiner, a priest of Archbishop Ireland's diocese, was its author. With considerable heat, and a number of telling arguments, he endeavored to explode the claim that German Catholics were unfairly treated in the United States.[20]

Attacks of this sort were annoying, to be sure, but they seemed to intensify rather than to lessen the desire of the German-Americans for autonomy. The second annual conference of the Priester-Verein met

[18] *Bericht über die Verhandlungen der amerikanisch-deutschen Priester-Versammlung in Chicago am. 16. Februar 1887* (Chicago, 1887).

[19] *Verhandlungen der ersten allgemeinen amerikanisch-deutschen Katholiken-Versammlung in Chicago, Ill.* (Chicago, 1887).

[20] *The Church and the Various Nationalities in the United States. Are German Catholics Unfairly Treated?* (Milwaukee, 1887).

in January, 1888, and was followed in September by another national congress, held this time in Cincinnati. There the assembled German-American Catholics heard read to them a paper on the work of the St. Raphaelsverein, and a letter of encouragement from its German sponsor, Peter Paul Cahensly.[21] It might be well to note here that the proceedings of the various clerical and lay German-American conferences were reported *in toto* by practically all the German Catholic newspapers of the period, so that wide circulation was given to the ideas of unity expressed at these meetings.

The German answer to Gmeiner's pamphlet of 1887 was provided by the Reverend Anton H. Walburg of Cincinnati in 1889.[22] His approach to the problem of nationality seemed fairly mild and reasonable, although his arguments at times appeared to "cut two ways." "Nationalism in the Church has always proved disastrous," he wrote.[23]

The nationalism to which he referred was, of course, an American nationalism. The antidote to its development was untrammeled freedom for the various national groups in the maintenance of their own churches and schools. He bestowed some kind words on the Irish contribution to the American Church, but he saved his choicest encomiums for bestowal upon the Germans. Having outlined the great contribution of the German schools of Cincinnati to the faith, he asked rhetorically: "Can any Catholic say, Cut down this tree laden with the richest fruit and engraft on it the withered sprig of Americanism? Great God! and Mr. Shea calls this 'the canker eating away the life of the Church.' . . . Denationalization is demoralization. It degrades and debases human nature. A foreigner who loses his nationality is in danger of losing his faith and character."[24] Walburg's strictures on the American way of life were intemperate; his defense of German culture was warm and at the same time odd in view of the

---

[21] The full texts of these documents were printed in *Verhandlungen der zweiten allgemeinen deutsch-amerikanischen Katholiken-Versammlung zu Cincinnati, O. am 3. und 4. September 1888* (St. Louis, 1888).

[22] *The Question of Nationality in its Relations to the Catholic Church in the United States* (Cincinnati, 1889).

[23] *Ibid.*, p. 18.

[24] *Ibid.*, pp. 27, 45.

Kulturkampf from which German Catholics under Bismarck had suffered so much. "The cultivation and exercise of military genius," he wrote, "develops the moral and physical health of a nation, reinvigorates its manhood, and is favorable to greatness. So Germany today bears aloft the torch of learning, and stands foremost in the ranks of civilized nations."[25] Surprisingly mild was his conclusion when read at the end of his exposé of foreign contributions to America and the Church:

> No foreign nationality can permanently maintain itself in this country. . . . Immigrants will Americanize in spite of themselves. The American nationality will finally prevail. . . . However, the transition from one nationality to another, is always a dangerous process, and it will not do to hasten it and to force foreigners to Americanize.[26]

The work of German unity continued throughout 1889 and 1890. Opposition to it also built up. The annual conferences attracted an ever larger attendance, so that the two-day congress at Cleveland in September, 1889, was enlarged to a four-day conference at Pittsburgh in the same month of 1890. By the latter year the Priester-Verein had joined its meeting to that of the larger Congress.[27] One of the principal problems discussed at Pittsburgh was the school question, which had a special importance for the German language groups. At the time the storm center was Wisconsin, where a newly-adopted educational measure, the so-called Bennett Law, required the use of English in teaching standard elementary school subjects. The German parochial schools of that state, both Lutheran and Catholic, were directly affected by the law. It called forth a strong protest from the German members of the Wisconsin hierarchy, Archbishop Michael

25 *Ibid.*, p. 37.

26 *Ibid.*, p. 61.

27 Proceedings of these meetings were published as follows:

Verhandlungen der dritten allgemeiner Versammlung der Katholiken deutscher Zunge der Vereinigten Staaten in Cleveland, Ohio (Cleveland, 1889).

Verhandlungen der dritten allgemeinen Versammlung der Katholiken deutscher Zunge der Vereinigten Staaten von Nord-Amerika in Pittsburg, Pa., am 22., 23., 24., und 25. September, 1890 (Pittsburg, 1890).

Bericht über der Verhandlungen der vierten general-Versammlung des deutsch-amerikanischen Priester-Vereins in Pittsburg, Pa. 23. bis 25. September 1890 . . . (Pittsburg, 1890).

Heiss of Milwaukee, Bishop Kilian C. Flasch of La Crosse, and Bishop Francis X. Katzer of Green Bay.[28] Public debate on the law became intense. According again to Father John Conway of St. Paul, who was no friendly critic of the Germans, this whole discussion was an outcome of the foreign movement, and part of the conspiracy to Germanize the Church. The real aim of the "conspirators," according to Conway, was to prevent the development of the English language in parochial schools. They dragged the Catholic Church into an ugly controversy over a law that had some objectionable features, but which did not warrant church interference.[29]

Whether or not Conway was correct, German-Americans generally were among the strongest supporters of the parochial schools, partly at least because in them they might exercise the privilege of teaching in the mother-tongue. Monsignor Joseph Schroeder, professor of dogmatic theology at the recently-founded Catholic University of America, spoke at Pittsburgh on "The Church and the Republic," and later, in the *Catholic World,* described the purposes and conduct of the congress.[30] His account of the congress and of the spirit which animated it does not accord with the veiled and open charges of conspiratorial activity.

The problem of national differences had, by the fall of 1890, become a keg of ecclesiastical gunpowder. Harsh words had been used privately by highly-placed prelates against their colleagues in the hierarchy. Priests had bandied implied insults in the public prints. Back of it all was not only the jurisdictional problem of how best to administer the American Church organization, but also the more important problem which deeply and sincerely concerned men of both "parties"—how best to serve the needs of the Catholic laity in order that losses to the faith should be as small as possible.

A train was being laid to this keg of gunpowder even as the German-Americans met in fraternal amity at Pittsburgh. It was a long

---

[28] Reilly, *School Controversy,* pp. 55-57. The texts of the law and of the bishops' protest are printed in Harry H. Heming, *The Catholic Church in Wisconsin* (Milwaukee, 1895-98), pp. 281-286.

[29] *Op. cit.,* p. 47.

[30] "The Catholic German Congress at Pittsburgh," LII (November, 1890), 263-272.

train, but nonetheless effective. Conway believed that it stretched from St. Louis to Europe, and back again—although he did not use the metaphor. Whether it was a deliberately-laid train, or was simply one of those careless accidents that bring on dire results, need not concern us here.

At Liège, Belgium, in September, 1890, a general European Catholic Congress was being held. During a session devoted to problems of the European emigrant to America, one Abbé Villeneuve of Canada quoted a set of figures. Proof that mathematics is dangerous was quickly forthcoming. The good abbé claimed that twenty-five million Catholics had entered the United States as immigrants, that the Catholic population of this country in 1890 was slightly over five million, and that the other twenty million Catholics "have turned Protestant or have become indifferent."[31]

This charge provided the excuse for consideration of the problem of losses to the faith among emigrants going to the United States at a conference held in Lucerne, Switzerland, on December 9-10, 1890. That meeting brought together the representatives of the various national branches of the European St. Raphael's Society. The result of their deliberations was a direct appeal to Rome for an amelioration of those conditions in Church administration in the United States which they considered responsible for the tremendous loss of faith by immigrants to this country. The Marchese Battista G. Volpe-Landi, president of the Italian St. Raphael's Society, and Peter Paul Cahensly, secretary-general of the German central office of the Society, were instructed to submit to the Pope the representations of the conference. The so-called "Lucerne Memorial," destined to be the spark which eventually detonated the ecclesiastical powder-keg in the United States, was the outcome of these appointments. The memorial was drawn up, dated "February, 1891," and taken to Rome by the two appointed delegates of the conference. Cahensly and Volpe-Landi were delayed somewhat in receiving an audience with

[31] Gerald Shaughnessy, *Has the Immigrant Kept the Faith?* . . . (New York, 1925), p. 233. These figures were totally inaccurate. In the controversy over "Cahenslyism" there was much ado about the correct figures for Catholic immigration and Catholic "losses." That phase of the problem has been disposed of in Bishop Shaughnessy's volume.

Leo XIII, but arrangements were finally made for an interview with the Pontiff on April 16. Two days before, on April 14, Volpe-Landi was called away by a death in his family, so that when the date of the audience arrived, Cahensly alone took the memorial to the Vatican.[32] The document was signed by ten members of the German St. Raphael's Society, by nine Austrians, seven Belgians, one Swiss, and eight Italians, all men of considerable reputation. It was also approved, through a separate communication, by Premier Mercier of Quebec.

The document itself was based upon the premise that "The losses which the Church has sustained in the United States of North America amount to more than ten millions," a reduction by fifty percent of the total of losses asserted at Liège. In view of this fact, the memorial stated, certain steps were essentially necessary in the United States. These included the establishment of separate churches for each nationality; the appointment to these churches of "priests of the same nationality as the faithful;" the teaching of religion in the national language, even where the numbers of immigrants did not justify separate parishes; the setting up of separate parochial schools "for every nationality;" equal privileges for the "priests of every nationality;" the foundation of various Catholic mutual aid associations; wherever possible, inclusion in the American episcopate of bishops of every nationality; and papal encouragement of the training of missionary priests for the United States and of the establishment of branches of the St. Raphael's Society in the various European countries.[33]

Until the end of the first week in May, 1891, the American public

[32] This chronology of the memorial is taken from Cahensly's own account, in Heft 5, *Charitas-Schriften*, of the St. Raphael's Society, *op. cit.*, pp. 33-34. With regard to the general aims of the society cf. also: P. P. Cahensly, *Die deutschen Auswanderer und der St. Raphael-Verein* (Frankfurt a. M. und Luzern, 1887) [Band VIII, Heft 11, *Frankfurter zeitgemässe Broschuren*].

[33] The German text of the memorial, with the names and titles of its signers, is in Cahensly, *Charitas-Schriften*, pp. 34-39. An English translation lacking the signatures, was published in the New York *Herald*, May 28, 1891. John T. Reily, *Collections in the Life and Times of J. Card. Gibbons* (McSherrystown, Pennsylvania, 1895), III, is said to contain the texts of the Cahensly memorials as well as considerable additional material on "Cahenslyism" in general. The writer has been unable to consult this volume. The researcher should be warned

and the Catholic laity of the United States remained in ignorance of the impending controversy over ecclesiastical jurisdiction. This did not permit the larger problem of nationalism in the Church to be forgotten. At the moment, the great success of the *"Katholiken Tag"* at Pittsburgh the preceding September, had encouraged a public exchange of views on the subject of clerical unions. In the Archdiocese of Milwaukee, one of the strongholds of the Deutsch-Amerikanischer Priester-Verein, opposition to the policies of that body had led to the establishment of the American Catholic Clerical Union. Typical editorial comment on the situation which had developed was contained in the *Catholic Review* of New York:

> Priests . . . ought not to be allowed to organize, as priests, into national bodies. There is here a very grave danger. . . . What a check, embarrassment, almost insuperable obstacle those Unions may be to the administration of a bishop! . . . this is America and . . . within the American Church there must be no nationalism.[34]

Sebastian G. Messmer, professor of canon law at the Catholic University of America, riposted with a long and scathing letter in defense of the unions, and particularly of the Priester-Verein. He levelled the charge of calculated prejudice against the *Review*, and concluded with the opinion that "this matter of Clerical Unions is not a subject proper for papers written for the Catholic public at large. . . . there are other appointed watchmen upon the walls of Jerusalem."[35]

First news of the Lucerne Memorial to the Vatican reached the American public through the columns of the New York *Herald* on May 9, 1891. A brief cable dispatch from Rome stated inaccurately that the document requested the Pope to appoint American bishops representative of the nationalities of the immigrants because "the Irish bishops in the United States only nominate Irish priests, who do not know the languages spoken by the immigrants." The memorial actually contained no such assertion. The *Catholic Review* of

---

that the titles and imprints of Reily's volumes vary. They are not easily located, but when found, supply a fund of contemporaneous (and sometimes unrelated) information for this period of United States Catholic history.

[34] XXXIX (March 7, 1891), 152.

[35] *Ibid.* (March 21, 1891), 182. Cf. C. Schaus to editor, *ibid.*, (March 28, 1891), 199.

May 16 printed a shorter, but more accurate cabled account of Cahensly's visit to the Vatican.[36] Excited comment did not begin until a week later, at which time the *Review* devoted its lead editorial to "The Conspiracy of Luzerne." Violent exception was taken to the aspersions which the memorial reputedly cast upon the Irish in America, and to the claim that millions of immigrants had lost the faith. "The statements are entirely false, and the memorial is a piece of brazen impudence. . . . The special malice of the memorial is its design of interference with the American hierarchy. . . . The conspiracy of Luzerne has its roots in the United States."[37]

It was May 28 before the complete text of the memorial was available in this country. On that date the New York *Herald* published it in full, except for the names of the signatories. The *Northwestern Chronicle,* Catholic newspaper of St. Paul, protested "solemnly . . . as Catholics and as Americans against such work. . . . Where the Catholics of this country are most concerned is that a clique in the United States inspired this petition. . . . It is high time for the *Deutscher-Verein* to subside. . . . Its members have done a grave injury to the Church in this country by making Catholics mere foreigners."[38] The question of episcopal jurisdiction they left for future treatment, of which there was more than enough. It was around these two issues that discussion of the whole matter in the Catholic and secular press revolved. Was the Lucerne Memorial the result of an American-German plot and, if its recommendations were followed by the Holy See, would there be created in the United States a double episcopal jurisdiction? The *Catholic Review* concentrated upon the problem of double jurisdiction, printing, for example, Leo XIII's brief *Studio et Vigilante,* of August 26, 1884, condemning double jurisdiction in India under the headline "Official Opinion of Pope Leo XIII on the System Which the Conspirators of Luzerne Would Fasten Upon the United States."[39]

The New York *Times,* under a St. Louis date-line of May 31,

---

[36] *Ibid.,* p. 311.   [37] *Ibid.* (May 23, 1891), 328.   [38] May 29, 1891.

[39] XXXIX (May 30, 1891), 338. Cf. also *ibid.,* pp. 344, 345. In the following number, June 6, the *Review* printed a letter of Cardinal Jacobini's on the same subject, using a similar headline suggesting the relationship to the Lucerne proposals. Cf. p. 354.

printed an interview with Father Phelan, editor of the *Western Watchman* in which the priest was quoted as saying: "The letter was the product of the Deutsch-Amerikanischer Priester Verein. . . . Who wrote it would be hard to determine . . . it is likely they all had a hand in it."[40] So the comments ran. There is little question that the opponents of the Lucerne Memorial followed the lead of Archbishop John Ireland, the "consecrated blizzard" from St. Paul. The objective of Cahensly and his friends, Ireland told a reporter of the New York *Herald* on May 31, in his usual blunt manner,

> is to harness the Church in America into the service of recently arrived immigrants from Germany. . . . We have to note here the actual or assumed ignorance of Mr. Cahensly as to the condition of German speaking Catholics in America. In asserting that they are neglected he does most positive injustice to the bishops of the country. . . . The bishops of America have no more idea of making the Church Irish than they have of allowing it to be made German. . . . What is the most strange feature in this whole Lucerne movement is the impudence of the men in undertaking to meddle, under any pretext, in the Catholic affairs of America. . . . All American Catholics will treasure up the affront for future action. . . . The inspiration of the work in Europe comes, . . . from a clique in America. . . . I am quite sure I am right when I bring home to this [Deutsch-Amerikanischer Priester] Verein the whole promptings of the Lucerne proceedings. . . . The great mass of German-speaking Catholics, laymen and priests, are totally opposed to all plans and intrigues and are most heartily in sympathy with everything that is American. . . . The promoters of German foreignism in America are certain journalists whose trade is gone if the German language loses its hold, and certain priests who, on coming to America in advanced years, never learn much English and scarcely know that there is in America a country outside the German village or quarter surrounding their parsonage.[41]

The archbishop enlarged upon these ideas with equal frankness in a second interview granted to an AP correspondent on June 4.[42] He explicitly accepted as true press dispatches cabled from Rome as to

[40] June 1, 1891.

[41] New York *Herald*, June 1, 1891; *Catholic Review*, XXXIX (June 13, 1891), 370.

[42] New York *Times*, June 5, 1891; *Catholic Review*, XXXIX (June 20, 1891, 388.

the interest taken in the success of the memorial by the Prussian ambassador to the Holy See, Herr von Schloeser.

This interpretation by a member of the hierarchy differed radically from that given by the most outstanding Catholic lay editor of the day, John Gilmary Shea. In his paper, the *Catholic News* of New York, Shea scoffed at the thought of Cahensly and Schloeser acting on behalf of any German-American group.[43]

There were certainly some Germans in the United States who were most sincerely perturbed by the Lucerne Memorial. Victor Dworzak, editor of the New York *Katholisches Volksblatt,* when asked to comment on a report that Cahensly was to visit the United States, said that the New York Germans would have nothing to do with him.[44] As the polemical dispute developed in the Catholic and secular press, both English and German, the theme most discussed was that of "conspiracy." Very early in the proceedings, Father William Faerber, corresponding secretary of the Priester-Verein, issued a formal categorical denial that his organization had been in any way responsible for the memorial. Archbishop Katzer, newly-appointed incumbent of the See of Milwaukee, denied all knowledge of the existence of a "clique" as described by his ecclesiastical neighbor in St. Paul, as well as any previous knowledge of the action of the European St. Raphael's Society.[45] Both the Priester-Verein and Katzer noticeably refrained from any expression of opinion upon the demands of the memorial itself.

While these discussions were getting under way in the United States, European developments were also taking place. If we may believe Cahensly's own account, and there seems no reason to doubt its accuracy, the Papal Secretary of State, Cardinal Rampolla, wrote to Cahensly shortly after receipt of the Lucerne Memorial asking for a fuller explanation of the reasons for the requests contained therein. Volpe-Landi and Cahensly obliged by sending to Rampolla a second and longer memorial. This second document, Cahensly is careful

[43] May 31, 1891.

[44] New York *Sun,* May 31, 1891; *Catholic Review,* XXXIX (June 13, 1891), 370.

[45] *Catholic Review,* XXXIX (June 13, 1891), 369; (June 20, 1891), 388. Cf. *ibid.,* pp. 370, 376, 377.

to indicate, was sent on the personal responsibility of its two signatories, and did not constitute an official communication from the St. Raphael's Societies.[46] It dealt in greater detail with reasons for the earlier requests, and again revised the figures of losses to the Catholic faith resulting from American neglect of the immigrant. The new statistics claimed to prove that "Catholicity . . . has sustained a net loss of sixteen millions" in the United States. The proposals with regard to the episcopate were made more precise to indicate that what was desired was the establishment of an approximate equal ratio between the size of immigrant groups and national representation in the American hierarchy.[47]

The first hint of the existence of a second memorial reached the United States in an Associated Press dispatch from Berlin dated June 13 reporting an interview with Cahensly. The author of the memorials struck out at his American critics. He denied that he or the St. Raphael's Societies wished to interfere with Church administration in the United States, but stated that "It is a well-known fact that the Irish in America try to obtain all the bishoprics possible for themselves."[48] Not until July 1 did the New York *Herald* give the text of the memorial itself to the public.

Before that date, however, the controversy had developed to a considerable degree. On June 17, the American Catholic Clerical Union adopted a set of resolutions denouncing the Lucerne Memorial as unwarranted foreign interference, denying the accuracy of its claims of losses, and praising the American hierarchy for its care of the immigrants.[49] Viewing the controversy with, perhaps, greater ob-

---

[46] Cahensly, *Charitas-Schriften, op. cit.,* pp. 40-43.

[47] Part of the German text of this memorial is in *ibid.,* pp. 42-43. Fairly complete English summaries were printed in the New York *Herald,* July 1, 1891; *Catholic Review,* XL (July 11, 1891), 19; *The Tablet* (London), LXXVIII (July 25, 1891), 145-146. The complete and unabridged text appeared in the *Catholic Review,* XXXIX (June 27, 1891), 402.

[48] New York *Times,* New York *Herald,* New York *Tribune,* June 14, 1891; *Catholic Review,* XL (July 25, 1891), 50-51.

[49] The text of these resolutions appeared in a number of journals, among them the Milwaukee *Sentinel,* June 20, 1891; and the *Catholic Review,* XL (July 11, 1891), 20. Practically every Catholic newspaper which printed the resolutions gave them also some editorial attention.

jectivity than most, John Gilmary Shea lamented in the editorial columns of the *Catholic News:*

> A year ago the Catholic body of the United States . . . was made up of devout men of every nation under heaven. Now dissension, jealousy, a spirit of bickering has been aroused which will not easily be banished or allayed. Archbishops, bishops, priests as associated in societies, or individually disclaim any part or responsibility in the Lucerne action, but the evil has been accomplished. . . . The *Herold des Glaubens* says there are American priests in this country who would rather see several million Germans go to hell than forego the opportunity to convert a few hundred Yankees.[50]

The dissension to which Shea referred had perturbed all members of the American hierarchy. The dean of that body, Cardinal Gibbons of Baltimore, held his peace on the matter, publicly at least, until June 28 when, in an interview, he said: "We cannot view without astonishment and indignation a number of self-constituted and officious gentlemen in Europe complaining of the alleged inattention which is paid to the spiritual wants of the foreign population and to the means of redress which they have thought proper to submit to the Holy See."[51] Gibbons emphasized particularly the great amount of consideration that was given by the Church in this country to the welfare of the immigrants. That some action in the matter was either contemplated or taken by members of the hierarchy is obvious from the text of a letter addressed to Cardinal Gibbons by the Papal Secretary of State under orders from the Pope on June 28. Referring to the Cahensly memorials, Cardinal Rampolla wrote:

> From the news received from America on the subject, it would appear that . . . the Episcopate itself was about to take the matter into consideration by special meetings. . . . The august Head of the Church has no design of accepting any proposition which could give rise to any trouble, so long as it is possible to provide for Catholic emigrants . . . the help of national priests, as has hitherto been the custom.[52]

[50] June 28, 1891. Cf. New York *Herald,* June 18, 28, 1891; *Evening Post,* New York, June 28, 1891.

[51] New York *Herald,* June 29, 1891. Cf. Ibid., June 28, 30, 1891; *Catholic Review,* XL (July 11, 1891), 19, 20, 24.

[52] A German translation of this letter is in Cahensly, *Charitas-Schriften, op. cit.,* pp. 45-46. An English translation is in the *Catholic Review,* XL (August 29, 1891), 130.

When "informed" on July 1 by representatives of the secular press that a papal letter had been sent to him denying any intention of acting on Cahensly's suggestions, the Baltimore cardinal expressed satisfaction.[53] Editorial comment was generally favorable.[54] A few days later, on July 11, Gibbons met President Harrison at Cape May, New Jersey. The President expressed to the cardinal his concern over the Cahensly petitions, and "seemed to be much pleased" at being informed that they had been unequivocally rejected by the Holy See in a letter from Rampolla received that very day.[55]

The Cardinal had in his possession not only the letter from the Holy See, but also the full text of the second memorial, which did not become public property until July 25.[56] This copy had come to him in a letter from Archbishop Ireland dated July 2. The St. Paul prelate asked, with reference to Rampolla's letter to Gibbons: "Are we, however, to stop there?" Referring then to the second memorial he continued:

> Note the calumnies against the whole church of America. Note the insults to the Republic, . . . Then, remember that this document is believed in Rome and received sympathy there. Naught but fear compels them to brush it aside. So I am most positively assured. . . . Ought we not take this opportunity to assert ourselves before Rome and compel her to have in the future some regard for us![57]

Other American prelates, on the contrary, believed and hoped that, Rome having spoken, the affair would be closed. Among those doomed to disappointment in this regard was Archbishop Michael A. Corrigan of New York, honorary president of the St. Raphael's Society of the United States. The Leo House in his episcopal city was the headquarters of that society. Even before the archbishop took action, the officers and board of directors of the American foundation

[53] New York *Herald*, July 2, 1891.

[54] Cf. *Ibid.; Catholic Review*, XL (July 4), 8; (July 11), 19-20; (July 18), 33, 35; (July 25), 50-51, 56, 57; (August 1), 70; Baltimore *Sun*, July 3, 1891; New York *Sun*, July 5, 1891; New York *Tribune*, July 6, 1891; *The Tablet* (London), LXXVIII (August 1), 182.

[55] Will, *op. cit.*, I, 524-525.

[56] Cf. note 47, *supra*.

[57] Reilly, *School Controversy*, pp. 70-71.

wrote a letter of sharp criticism directly to Cahensly. They acknowledged the good intentions of the signers of the Lucerne Memorial, but
they regretted the action that they had taken. "Why has the St. Raphael's Society not addressed its wishes and desires first in a proper
manner to the American Bishops? . . . The demands or requests of
the Memorial are altogether too far reaching. . . . Why . . . should
you ask . . . for ordinances which might be suitable for colonial endeavors in South America or Africa, but will not suit at all for conditions as they exist here?" While they thought the existing American interpretation of the memorial malicious, they admitted the
"probability for such a propaganda," and added that, so interpreted,
the memorial "is an insult to the national pride of Americans, and can
only be detrimental to the foreign-born citizens, as well as to the new
immigrants."[58] The principal signer of this letter was Bishop Wigger
of Newark, president of the American St. Raphael's Society, and a
prominent participant in the disputes which followed after.

Archbishop Corrigan waited to communicate with Cahensly until
he had seen the full text of the second memorial as furnished to him
by the editors of the *Catholic Review*. On July 22, 1891, he dis-
patched a long letter to Cahensly. He spoke of the "profound grief
with which I read your Memorial." He charged Cahensly with a
"total misconception" of American institutions, and he added that were
the memorial adopted, "it would result in incalculable harm to religion." Corrigan then referred to American prejudice against the
Church as a *"foreign institution,"* and referred to the tremendous
difficulties of destroying that prejudice. "You can conceive then with
what grief we would see this prejudice confirmed and strengthened
by one of our own friends." Quoting figures, and applying Cahensly's proposals to his own archdiocese, Corrigan quite effectively exposed the impracticability of the entire plan. "It is no wonder that . . .
Cardinal Simeoni has written to me that he himself from his knowledge of this country felt bound to declare openly to you that your request was impossible of realization." The letter went on to deal
with statistics concerning losses to the faith, and with the understandable reasons for such losses as had occurred. Three and a half

[58] July 1, 1891; NYAA, E—c, Cahensly, 1891.

millions, rather than sixteen millions was the figure he quoted. "In conclusion," he stated sharply, "permit me to express the hope that in future you and your zealous colleagues before presenting to the Holy See any important project regarding the welfare of souls intrusted to our charge, will have the kindness to consult with the Bishops who are their legitimate Pastors."[59]

Hierarchical disapproval was the order of the day where Cahensly was concerned. Even those bishops of German birth or leanings could not approve the method which their European friends had used, although they might sympathise with some of the objectives sought and agree with some of the charges made. From the beginning of July until the latter part of August, 1891, the dissensions over the Cahensly memorials seemed to be dissipating themselves. There were additional rumblings in the press, it is true,[60] but on the whole, the matter seemed to have been concluded by the papal decision of June 28.

Men of good-will felt that the *coup de grâce* had been dealt "Cahenslyism" when they read the words uttered on August 20, 1891, by James Cardinal Gibbons in his sermon at the investiture of Archbishop Katzer as the new ordinary of Milwaukee. Katzer was the acknowledged leader of the German group. The dean of the American hierarchy, in the presence of most of its members, took occasion to refer in unmistakable terms to the nationality difficulties of the preceding years. The cardinal called attention to the assemblage of prelates as evidence of the unity of the American Church, then continued:

> Woe to him, my brethren, who would destroy or impair this blessed harmony that reigns among us! Woe to him who would sow tares of discord in the fair fields of the Church of America! Woe to him who would breed dissension among the leaders of Israel by introducing a spirit of nationalism into the camp of the Lord! Brothers we are,

[59] NYAA, C-18. Italics Corrigan's.

[60] Cf. an interview granted by the Reverend George Zurcher, a Catholic temperance reformer, to the Buffalo *News*, reprinted in the *Catholic Temperance Association News*, Philadelphia, July 7, 1891. Cf. also "Herr Cahensly's Scheme Smacks of Politics," in New York *Herald*, July 12, 1891; Professor O'Gorman's account of the views held in Rome on "Cahenslyism," and the comments thereon, as well as various items and comments on the views of Cardinals Persico and Simeoni, in the *Catholic Review*, XL (August 8, 1891), 88; (August 15, 1891), 96, 98, 105. These were of the nature of "post-mortems."

whatever may be our nationality, and brothers we shall remain — we will prove to our countrymen that the ties formed by grace and faith are stronger than flesh and blood—God and our country! This our watchword—Loyalty to God's Church and to our country!—this our religious and political faith. . . . Let us glory in the title of American citizen. We owe our allegiance to one country, and that country is America. We must be in harmony with our political institutions. It matters not whether this is the land of our birth or the land of our adoption. It is the land of our destiny.[61]

Mere words, even those of a Sovereign Pontiff and of a prince of the Church, were not sufficient to stifle the antagonisms and strains which had developed with such rapidity in a short space of time. German, or Polish, or Bohemian, or French Catholics in America, jealous of their own cultures, overwhelmed to a degree by the blatancy of America in the 1890's, clung to their old ways. Had they not, after all, come here to enjoy freedom? Had not many of them left Europe rather than send their children to state-dominated schools? Did they not consider the privilege of raising their offspring to fear God and love their neighbors in their own way, one of the most sacred rights which America had to offer?

Catholics who were a product of the American environment, on the other hand, felt just as strongly about the necessity of unity in the face of prejudice. They loved America, they believed in her and in all her noisy foibles and idiosyncrasies. For them the future held meaning only if they could once and for all identify themselves and their Church with the society in which they lived. Foreign ways and manners must go, and the sooner the better!

As in every conflict of this sort, there were those on both sides who fought all opposition with the utmost tenacity, while the majority looked on, hoping for moderation and mutual understanding. Such understanding came eventually, but not in August, 1891. Hardly had the echoes of Cardinal Gibbons' moving appeal for unity died out of the Milwaukee cathedral before a new, disturbing issue caused the controversy of the previous year to fade into insignificance. This was the troublesome school question, brought to a head by Archbishop

61 James Cardinal Gibbons, *A Retrospect of Fifty Years* (New York, 1916), II, 148-155.

Ireland of St. Paul. In that noteworthy contest no holds were barred. The national prejudices of each party to the conflict became weapons in the war of words. Nor did the activities of Cahensly and his friends in Europe cease. They seemed rather to take on a new life. The result of it all was that the comparatively united stand of the American episcopacy against what they had considered either ill-chosen or malicious proposals (depending on their point of view) concerning Church administration was shattered. Old allies found themselves to be new enemies. This second chapter of "Cahenslyism" has yet to be written. In many respects it is the most intriguing part of the story. In every respect it is the saddest.

JOHN J. MENG

Queens College

ETHNICITY 8, 1–17 (1981)

The Immigrant Church in Gary, Indiana: Religious Adjustment and Cultural Defense

RAYMOND A. MOHL

Florida Atlantic University

AND

NEIL BETTEN

Florida State University

Recent historical and sociological research has demonstrated the central role of the immigrant church in American ethnic communities. European and other immigrants to the United States had been uprooted from the familiar and traditional customs which gave shape and meaning to their lives. In the new land, naturally, most immigrants sought to preserve as much of their cultural heritage as possible. The confrontation with a new national environment and a dynamic urban-industrial society, however, resulted in gradual adjustments and alterations in traditional immigrant life-styles. Caught between loyalty to the old culture and the demands of the new society, the foreign-born securely moored themselves to the cultural anchor of religion. All else might change, but they hoped to keep their church intact with all of its saints and symbols and forms. Yet even the ethnic churches evolved over time as they assumed new functions such as schooling in the defense of cultural and religious integrity.

A number of recent studies suggest how the immigrant churches served the purposes of cultural defense and religious adjustment. Jay Dolan's book, *The Immigrant Church,* for instance, portrays the ethnic or national parish as a crucial link to the old country. Among 19th-century German Catholic immigrants, Dolan argues, the national parish not only satisfied religious needs but "reinforced group consciousness," helped to preserve culture and traditions, and strengthened the sense of ethnicity. For French-Canadian immigrants in the late 19th century, the ethnic parish had similar functions. Battling for ethnic survival, historian Philip T. Silvia, Jr., writes, the French Canadians "sought to cling tenaciously to their religion which would additionally help to preserve their language and culture." Among Polish and Lithuanian immigrants, according to Victor Greene, the ethnic parish was essential to the development of national consciousness and group awareness. In a study of Italians in New York City, Silvano Tomasi contends that the ethnic parish provided continuity

1

with old country ways: "the old dialects and language, religion, traditions and customs were preserved to protect the immigrant group from social disorganization and the shock of adjustment to the new culture." But Tomasi also demonstrates that the national parish, through its ties to the larger structure of the Catholic Church, served as a way station on the road to assimilation. Finally, in a number of articles Timothy L. Smith has argued that the intense character of the immigrant experience heightened religious commitment and that lay initiative predominated in the ethnic churches in the United States—patterns which made the immigrant churches dynamic and changing institutions. In sum, this research reveals to us immigrants who built new religious lives for themselves in America, who created dynamic and flexible religious institutions designed to preserve the old culture but which also eased the process of adjustment to the new land. As Randall M. Miller has recently written, immigrant religion not only provided continuity to the newcomers but "bridged the Old World and the New World and made adjustment possible and bearable."[1]

The immigrant history of Gary, Indiana, supports these recent findings about the ethnic church and the national parish. In this industrial, working-class city, founded in 1906 by the United States Steel Corporation, virtually all of the ethnic parishes were established by laymen. For Gary's immigrants, the ethnic churches became the center of group and community life. The churches, of course, had religious and spiritual purposes, but these roles were integrated with highly functional cultural and nationalistic goals. In addition, all the congregations—churches and synagogues—established their own schools. These institutions, both full-time Catholic or Protestant parochial schools and part-time Hebrew or Greek Orthodox schools, responded to the needs, interests, and direction of lay communities. The ethnic churches, then, were dynamic and changing institutions, taking on new functions and thus easing the process of immigrant adjustment.

American historians have held more definitive views about Roman Catholic immigrants than any others. Thus, the experience of Gary's immigrant Catholics is best understood in the perspective of the historiography of immigrant Catholicism. Historians, for instance, have often pointed to the rivalry between the more established ethnic groups who controlled the Catholic hierarchy and the new southern and eastern European immigrants who wanted their own ethnic and national parishes. It was a conflict, most historians have agreed, between the Irish hierarchy and priests and the new immigrants. Oscar Handlin, in his study, *The Uprooted*, depicted "a struggle, parish by parish, between the old Catholics and the new, a struggle that involved the nationality of the priest, the language used, the saints' days to be observed, and even the name of the church." He added that the attitude of the Bishop became

critical, and by the 1890s they were almost always Irish. Most other general studies of immigration follow Handlin's lead, and case studies of New York and Chicago also demonstrate the Church's effort to create Catholic unity; hierarchy policy in these cities was designed to undermine ethnic separatism and promote the assimilation of the city's immigrant Catholics. An examination of the immigrant churches in a small industrial city such as Gary, however, provides a considerably different picture.[2]

All of Gary's immigrant Catholic parishes were lay founded and were generally autonomous bodies closely reflecting the needs and the aspirations of their members. Any image of a rigid monolith having a dictatorial Catholic hierarchy and staffed by Irish priests who subverted immigrant traditions is thoroughly divorced from Gary's historical reality. The Polish parishes typified Gary's immigrant experience. The idea of starting a parish originated with laymen Frank Zawadski, Anton Bankles, and Peter Pasarshi. They organized support for a church in the Polish community and raised necessary funds. In July 1908 construction workers completed the first church building, St. Hedwig's. A second structure housing the parochial school was finished 2 years later. Other Roman Catholic Polish churches followed the establishment of St. Hedwig: Sacred Heart in 1913 and Holy Family in 1926. The latter served families that moved in the mid-1920s from the original Polish settlement to the East Ridge Road area—part of the rapidly developing Glen Park section.[3]

Laymen similarly established the first Roman Catholic Croatian Church. In late February 1912 about 30 Croatians decided to estabish a Croatian Catholic parish. Only then did they seek informal clerical aid— advice from a Chicago Croatian priest who provided a list of articles necessary for celebration of the Mass. The Croatian community bought the materials, and a Croatian assistant pastor from another city said Mass in an empty storeroom which served as the first church. Only after they established a parish organization did a delegation inform their diocesan Bishop, Herman J. Alerding, of the Fort Wayne Catholic diocese (which included Gary) and request a permanent pastor.[4] Bishop Alerding sought a Croatian-speaking American priest, but without success. He then wrote Archbishop Posilovic of Zagreb requesting a priest from Europe. The Croatian Archbishop sent Father Luka Terzich to serve the newly formed Church of St. Joseph the Worker. Construction of the church began in 1912 on land donated by U.S. Steel's Gary Land Company.[5]

Holy Trinity Parish, the first major Slovak Roman Catholic church had comparable origins. A committee representing 80 families organized the parish in 1911. The group then petitioned Bishop Alerding to provide a pastor. Alerding agreed but again had difficulty in securing a priest who spoke the immigrants' language. The parish committee thus sought a priest themselves, bringing Father Desiderious Major from Bridgeport,

Connecticut, to Gary in 1911. The parish subsequently rented a building and then purchased a church lot with funds provided partly by U.S. Steel. The Slovak parish established a school and convent as well. Other early Roman Catholic churches in Gary began in similar ways. Sometimes, as in the case of St. Emerics Hungarian Church, the parish went without a resident pastor for several years until one acceptable to the parish was found.[6]

Gary's Lithuanian community proved a partial exception to the pattern of lay-founded Roman Catholic parishes. Like other Catholic groups in Gary, the Lithuanian immigrants themselves organized the first parish—in this case in 1910. The parishioners hired their own priest, but he turned out to be an "independent," as a Lithuanian publication put it, and not a Catholic. The demoralized congregation lost its initiative, depending thereafter upon the Bishop to establish the church. In 1916 the Bishop appointed Reverend C. Ambrozaitus as the Lithuanian pastor. St. Emerics Hungarian Parish permitted the Lithuanians to use their church for Mass. Eventually, after a succession of priests, the Lithuanians built their own church in 1917 and established a cohesive congregation.[7]

An examination of the origins of Gary's Roman Catholic parishes demonstrates the absence of an Irish-dominated Catholic hierarchy imposing its views on a hostile clientele. In fact Bishop Alerding worked with local laymen to find mutually acceptable clerics, as well as teachers for the parochial schools. Because laymen organized the parishes themselves, church institutions and services reflected immigrant desires and needs. Church services and sermons were usually conducted according to old country traditions and in the native language; thus creating cultural continuity for immigrants and relating the cultural heritage of generations to their children.

The parish parochial schools had many functions. W. Lloyd Warner's well-known sociological study of "Yankee City" found that "the Catholic schools . . . inculcate obedience to parental authority—respect for the head of the family." In a society which held those speaking with accents in disdain, church schools promoted parental respect and bolstered family cohesiveness often coming asunder from the strains of immigration. This was true in "Yankee City" and in Gary.[8]

In addition to familial and religious functions, the parochial schools also served as institutions designed to preserve ethnic identities. Each Catholic ethnic parish operated an autonomous school fostering ethnic traditions and language. The largest of the Polish schools, St. Hedwig's, had a typical curriculum. In addition to standard academic subjects, the school offered courses in Polish history and culture. More important, for many years Polish sisters taught classes in Polish, directed school performances given in Polish, and taught prayers and catechism in Polish. Many of the immigrant Catholic parishes had similar programs, although occasionally establishing a parochial school was delayed because of difficulty in finding competent teachers with the necessary language ability. It took, for example, 11 years for the Lithuanian parish to establish its school. The congregation wanted Lithuanian teachers and for a time rejected the educational services of American Catholic nuns. Finally, classes began in 1928 with 115 children; but only some of the teachers spoke Lithuanian. Most other Roman Catholic ethnic parishes had parochial schools, including the Slovaks, Germans, Hungarians, and Croatians. In every case, the parochial schools fostered ethnic identity and promoted positive attitudes, understanding, and knowledge of the old country among the children of the parish.[9]

Several Catholic ethnic groups, particularly the Spaniards, Italians, and Mexicans, neither established parochial schools nor sent children in large numbers to the "American," or English-language parochial schools. All three groups had vague anticlerical traditions, and were courted by local Protestant missionary elements as possible converts. A local International Institute study found that many Spaniards immigrated from Spain because they considered the church oppressive. Most Spaniards arrived in Gary during the dictatorship of General Primo de Rivera (1923–1931). They came, in part, as political refugees who resented the alliance between the Church and the authoritarian Spanish regime. It was not surprising that Gary's Spaniards virtually ignored the Catholic Church. As the International Institute study put it, "no other nationality group in Gary is so largely without church connections as the Spanish colony. Only one or two families attend any church." Those few did not belong to a regular parish, but attended the Gary–Alerding Settlement House Chapel. The report added that "so far as is known no [Spanish] children are enrolled in parochial schools." In addition, local high schools taught Spanish, while the Gary Public Library and two Spanish organizations loaned Spanish-language reading material. This made a language-oriented church program unnecessary for Spanish-speaking groups.[10]

Like the Spaniards, other groups with Roman Catholic backgrounds did not uniformly remain wedded to the traditional church. Mexicans also had an anticlerical tradition. But problems faced by Mexican Catholics in Gary reflected America's racist traditions as well. At times Mexicans were turned away from Catholic churches and at other times could not afford the financial demands made by the church.[11]

Although the vast majority of Gary's Poles remained Roman Catholics and attended their national churches, some did join the Divine Providence Polish National Catholic Church. The Polish National Catholic Church was founded in Scranton, Pennsylvania, in 1897 as an offshoot of the Roman Catholic Church. Demands for greater autonomy and congregational control of parish holdings stimulated this schism. The Gary parish was formed in December of 1939 and totaled about 165 families by 1942. Many parishioners felt that the Roman Catholic churches were "not enough help to immigrants." Another active church member found that the National Church "was truly Polish in every way." Many of the social functions were held "strictly in the Polish way."[12]

The various Christian Orthodox Churches constituted the second major set of immigrant religious institutions in Gary. The Orthodox churches developed much the way the Catholic churches did, but they developed a greater degree of autonomy. Gary's Greek Orthodox community set the pattern. Only a few Greeks had emigrated to Gary by 1916; late in that year they held an organizational meeting and applied to the Holy Synod in Greece for a priest. Until a permanent priest was secured, the first liturgies were performed by clerics from Chicago in rented storefront quarters or in tents. In 1919, the Greek Orthodox parish abandoned these improvised facilities for an elaborate new building. Modeled after Hagia Sophia's in Constantinople, Gary's St. Constantine and Helen Greek Orthodox Church has remained a distinctive architectual site. In 1923 a second Greek parish, the Holy Trinity Greek Orthodox Church, emerged. The establishment of this new church, a rival rather than a supplementary parish church, grew out of political differences within the Greek community. With the republicans in control of the St. Constantine parish, the royalists decided to establish their own congregation. In 1926 Crown Prince Paul of Greece took part in laying the cornerstone for the new structure. The depression of the 1930s, however, forced a consolidation of the Greek religious community. Since the smaller group of royalists could no longer finance Holy Trinity, they rejoined St. Constantine.[13]

A lay group of Gary's Serbs established the St. Sava Parish in 1911. The congregation organized a church school board in February 1912; a Milwaukee Serbian, Pavle Veljkov, was secured as Serbian teacher and eventually pastor. While meeting in temporary structures, the parish began building the new St. Sava Church in 1914. After World War One, Gary's Serbian population grew with increased immigration. A second Serbian parish emerged, while the original St. Sava moved to a larger building on a different site. In 1936 the two Serbian parishes joined in planning a new St. Sava Church to serve Gary's entire Serbian Orthodox community. By the end of 1938 the work was completed—with a $5000 gift from U.S. Steel. The Byzantine structure accommodated about 1300 people (600 in the sanctuary and 700 in the auditorium), had school rooms, refreshment room and bar, and a living area for staff and priest. Dedication of the new church—the largest Serbian Orthodox congregation in the United States—turned into a major national Serbian social affair, attended by Konstantin Fotich, Yugoslavia's ambassador to the U.S., and Peter Cabrich, the Yugoslav consul in Chicago.[14]

The initiative and self-determination of the lay community can also be seen in the development of the Romanian Orthodox parish. Romanian workers arrived during Gary's early years. A religious service, consisting mainly of laymen singing part of their liturgy, was first held in what the parish yearbook called "a shack," actually an empty pool hall and club-room. The establishment of a formal parish organization grew out of the local Romanian mutual benefit society. The Leadership of Tricolor, as it was called, organized the parish in 1908 and 6 months later its officers wrote to Europe asking for a priest. Until Father Theodore Nica arrived—eventually from Canada—a Romanian cleric from nearby Indiana Harbor conducted the service. The actual building of the church structure, first called St. George's but later changed to "The Descension of the Holy Ghost," followed the usual pattern—money raised by the congregation supplemented by a donation of land from a real estate firm—in this case independent of U.S. Steel. The church was first built in 1909 slightly west of the city limits, but its remoteness from the bulk of the community resulted in the building being physically moved to the heart of the city in 1916.[15]

The Russian Orthodox community, alone among the Orthodox in Gary, had a parent national organization in the United States before establishing a church in Gary. Nevertheless the local parish was organized under lay initiative, applying in 1911 for a priest. In 1922 the parish built a new structure for the expanding congregation. In the words of the pastor, Father Benjamin Kedrovsky, "thus did God help good Christians wreste on foreign shores an Alter worthy of His Holy Name, of the honor of the Orthodox Church and the glory of the Russian people."[16]

Gary's Christian Orthodox communities included a small Bulgarian group and a Ruthenian congregation. The Ukranians organized the St. Nicholas American Carpatho-Russian Orthodox Church. Most parishioners had been members of St. Michael's Roman Catholic Church of the Byzantine Rite but left the Roman Catholic Church and affiliated with the Greek Orthodox. The Orthodox churches provided immigrant cultural services analogous to those provided by Roman Catholic congregations. The Russian parish, for example, had clubs for various age groups, a theatrical group, an instrumental music group, and a chorus, in addition to the usual services and charitable supports. The functional differences between Orthodox and Catholic cultural and national supportive services were minor, although the Orthodox churches were congregational and virtually autonomous from European or American hierarchial control.[17]

The immigrant churches, of course, served the spiritual needs of the ethnic communities. In providing traditional services in old country languages, the churches eased the transition to a new land. The church also provided the meeting place for family and friends at weddings, baptisms, and funerals serving social needs as well. Like the Catholic congregations, the Orthodox parishes ran schools, but not as substitutes for public school education. They established instead religious folk schools which served students an hour or so a day after public school classes ended. Sometimes classes were held on weekends, but their programs had little in common with the Protestant Sunday Schools. In Gary, almost every non-Roman Catholic, eastern or southern European ethnic group organized or attempted to organize such auxiliary schools. Curricula differed slightly but concentrated on language and tradition. Building such a school often took precedence over construction of the church itself.

The Serbian Church school was typical. The Serbians organized their school board in February 1912 to educate the community's children in the Serbian Orthodox faith. Classes began in a U.S. Steel-owned shack, while the 20 children in attendance during the first year used desks donated by the municipal government. Teaching materials were difficult to find, but locating a qualified teacher in Gary presented an even greater challenge. John T. Marich, a school board member, finally went to a Serbian convention in Cleveland where he hired Pavle Velkjov as Gary's first teacher of Serbian language and culture. Velkjov became a priest in June 1915, and for a short time he served as both pastor and teacher for his Gary flock. As late as 1942, a large majority of the Serbian youth still attended the day schools, which by this time had multiplied in number, and operated during the summer months as well. Classes in religion were supplemented by those in language, history, music, Serbian and religious drama, and the reading of cyrillic script.[18]

The Greek folk school began in 1923, and became as extensive as the Serbian. Classes were first held for about 175 Greek children at Froebel School, a public institution after regular school hours. Students concentrated on studying Greek language and culture. Eventually the Church school moved to its own quarters, where three teachers taught for 1 hour a day, 5 days a week. Together with the Sunday school, Greek education reached 75% of the parish children.[19]

Other Gary ethnic groups similarly sponsored day school programs. Father Benjamin Kedrovsky of the Russian Orthodox Church believed that "with children educated in church schools, the Orthodox and Russian cause will never die in America." The Russian Orthodox church school held classes four afternoons a week. Besides using church facilities, it utilized additional classroom space at the Gary International Institute and at five private homes during the height of its enrollment in the late 1920s. By 1935, at the depth of the depression, the school reduced its week to 3 days and held classes only in one of the private homes. Student enrollment dropped to 80 out of a possible 1000 parish children. The curriculum, similar to that of other day schools concentrated on language, music, religion, and general cultural heritage. The Romanians also held church-sponsored classes three afternoons a week in which students took courses in religion, Bible, church history, catechism, language, history, geography, and music. The Bulgarian and Assyrian communities held similar classes.[20]

Although Gary was often described as a Catholic town, the Orthodox constituted a larger proportion of the city's residents than that of any other major city in the country. But, several immigrant Protestant and Jewish congregations also developed. Immigrants from the British Isles filtered into conveniently located Protestant parishes, and several Lutheran churches in Gary and outlying areas served Germans and Scandinavians.[21]

St. Johns, a German Lutheran Missouri Synod parish located in the Tolleston section of Gary, had a full-time parochial school. Established Protestant organizations supported the founding of several immigrant parishes. Thus Gary's Episcopal Church supported the local parish of the Polish National Catholic Church. Assyrian and Persian Presbyterians first met in the basement of the First Presbyterian Church, and the Hungarian Evangelical and Reformed Church organized its congregation at the Gary Neighborhood House, a Presbyterian settlement. The Protestant immigrant churches tended to be slightly more Americanized than the Catholic and Orthodox churches in Gary. They all, however, undertook similar cultural and language activities.[22]

Gary had even fewer immigrant Jews than immigrant Protestants. Gary's Jews rarely came directly from Europe. They arrived in Gary from other large cities, most often Chicago, although the vast majority originally came from eastern and southeastern Europe. Cultural heritage was closely related to what was, or seemed to be, their unique Jewishness. A Jew from Russian-controlled Lithuania, was neither a Russian nor a Lithuanian, but a Jew whose family happened to have lived in Lithuania—perhaps for a great many generations. They had no desire to foster the cultural milieu of a usually oppressive European host, but rather desired to preserve Jewish culture closely interrelated to religious tradition. Two separate Jewish congregations were formed, one orthodox and the other reformed. Early Jewish settlers held their first services in September 1907 in a hay loft. Temple Beth-El's first structure, a temporary building, was built a year later and expanded to a permanent building in 1912. Temple Israel was established in 1910. As in other cities, the Orthodox Jews kept services closer to the European style while the Reformed considered their services Americanized. Gary's temples, like the ethnic churches, became community centers providing numerous services to the Jewish residents, such as counseling, meeting rooms, and social activities. Temple Beth-El produced a monthly *Bulletin* which contained articles on Zionism, local Jewish achievements—particularly the academic advances of the community's children—and successes of American Jews in general. The *Bulletin* thus provided information, built ethnic pride, and acted as a defense against excessive adoption of American Protestant ways. As one issue bluntly put it, "Don't drop Jewishness." Both temples placed major emphasis on the Jewish education of their children.

The most important Jewish educational institution in the city, the Hebrew Educational Alliance, received national recognition. It was not only highly effective, but extremely demanding. From the beginning the Alliance attracted most of the community's children. When combined with the Sunday School, virtually all the Jewish children in Gary received some kind of Jewish institutional education. Classes were first held at Beth-El, and when a Jewish Community Center was built the school was the first section completed. By 1928 three teachers taught 100 children in six grades. Students attended 5 days a week after public school hours, taking courses in subjects such as Hebrew, Jewish history, Bible, Ceremonials, and the foundations of Judaism. Dr. Benjamin M. Bassin, chairman of the Alliance Board of Education, briefly summed up the schools' role: "We expect our children really to know the past, respect the present and have confidence in the future." A Temple Beth-El publication described the Alliance function as teaching "the youth of Gary the rich cultural heritage of Judaism," to make the children of the congregation "conscious as Jews in a religious and Jewish-Nationalistic sense." In addition, the Sunday school employed six teachers for its less rigorous program. The Hebrew Educational Alliance provided other services as well. It had a library of over 1000 volumes in Hebrew, English, and Yiddish which remained open daily and evenings. And the Alliance occasionally sponsored picnics and gave prizes and awards to outstanding students.[23]

The Alliance regularly enrolled a greater proportion of the children from the Jewish community than the other ethnic days schools attracted from their communities. Therefore the Alliance may have been more effective in serving as a bridge between the old world and American society. The success of the Hebrew Educational Alliance, despite its long hours and full week, can perhaps be explained by the continued minority consciousness of Gary's Jews, well after they took on most American trappings. In addition the Jewish community had a high degree of entrepreneurial success. Thus Gary's Jews established their school on a sound financial footing with less difficulty than some other segments of the immigrant community.

As time progressed, several developments impeded folk school growth for most creedal groups. Younger members of the immigrant community, particularly those born or raised in the United States, used English more than the old country tongue. The various church language programs served to lessen the communication gap between generations, but for the American-raised generation English became their first language. Thus, a small but growing minority from the Christian Orthodox communities preferred churches with English services and sermons and viewed the folk schools delaying integration into the society. Also, as neighborhoods changed and people moved to other churches, folk school attendance declined. Often the older locations proved inconvenient. The Serbian St. Sava parish attempted to overcome the diffusion of its members by operating schools in three different parts of the city. Such projects, emulated by some of the smaller ethnic parishes, served only as stop-gap measures and were financially costly. Economic problems, indeed, had a significant effect on the folk schools. Attendance dropped during economic crises, particularly in the 1930s, for financial conditions prevented the churches and their schools from keeping pace with the geographical shifts of the immigrant communities. The need for folk schools also declined as the children of Gary's original immigrants reached maturity and sometimes married outside their ethnic group. Ethnic schools had much less meaning for the children of those already Americanized. In addition many second generation immigrants, the American-born children of the newcomers, consciously rejected the language and cultural baggage of the old world. Taught in the public schools that their heritage was inferior to American traditions, embarrassed by the immigrant ways and broken English of their parents, realizing that the most Americanized received job advancements, many from this generation rejected the folk school as both unnecessary and a hindrance.

When folk schools declined, many church leaders hoped to reach large numbers of children through an American style Sunday School. Sunday classes, like the American model, concentrated on Bible discussions and were held in English. The Sunday Schools, however, were not fully satisfactory. In 1939 the Serbs dropped their Sunday School and combined a traditional service with the sermon in English intended for youthful parishioners; the Greeks eliminated their Sunday School and attempted to revitalize week-day classes. Sunday Schools continued to emerge but they remained unsuccessful alternates to the dying folk school. With geographical mobility, Americanization, and economic problems, the folk classes declined noticeably for almost all groups, particularly following World War Two. The Catholic parochial schools and the Hebrew Educational Alliance, however, showed greater tenacity.

The most striking aspect of the immigrant churches in Gary lay in the

similarity of role and function. Although significant theological differences existed, the congregations took analogous roads in confronting an
alien urban society. Religious congregations, one of the first institutions
immigrants established, were organized by the immigrants themselves,
not by clerics from the old country or by those already in the United
States. In Europe, as Timothy Smith has noted, Roman Catholic and
Orthodox priests were tied to their diocese and under the direction of
hierarchical seniors. They simply could not migrate at will. Further, the
insecurity of employment in poor American parishes, the geographical
mobility of immigrant workers, transportation and maintenance costs,
and ecclesiastical conflicts at home kept many bishops from permitting
the migration of priests. Immigrant workers and families organized themselves to establish parishes, and they created churches of every denomination which reflected immigrant needs. Once established, the parish
provided a sense of community; it was a community—often in the physical and always in the social sense. Although each national community
lived among other ethnic groups, the church provided a center around
which some parishioners could cluster their homes. Thus, real estate
firms, U.S. Steel's Gary Land Company included, granted land to various
churches. Once the church grew, realtors could be reasonably certain of
selling land to parishioners.[24]

Churches served primarily as social and religious community centers.
Formal classes occasionally provided information to those who needed
direction in an alien society; pastors and priests helped parishioners deal
with a multitude of personal and social problems. The churches sponsored
ethnic, civic, cultural, literary, benevolent, insurance, and in some cases
political groups. Before American entry into World War One, ethnic
churches often propagandized for whatever alliance its homeland supported. The churches helped celebrate religious holidays and national
festivals with special services. All kinds of ethnic organizations met in
such churches. Although technically independent from the church, fraternal, literary, and cultural associations provided church support and received church services. Such secular church functions were not necessarily new to all the immigrant churches. Many of the immigrants came from
countries under foreign domination in which they constituted a "minority" within the larger empire. Their religion became the symbol of nationality and the church a center of political and cultural activities. Often, as
in the case of the Greek church under the Turks, or the rabbis as in Czarist
Russia, clerics were given secular roles by the official governments. Although the particular functions of the church and pastor often changed in
the new American environment, the activist role was not necessarily new.
The classic Thomas and Znaniecki study of Poles in Europe and America
found that the Polish-American parish was "simply the old primary com-

munity, reorganized and concentrated." This was true, if Gary is any indication, of all the major east and southern European parishes.[25]

Saul D. Alinsky has described the Roman Catholic national churches as a "central anchor of security" linking the new and the old country. This was likewise true for the Catholic and nonCatholic ethnic parishes of Gary—and particularly true in the church services. The priest spoke the native language and performed the liturgy according to old country patterns. The parish often constructed church buildings in the European architectural style—sometimes as near-replicas of a church in the home country. Many Gary churches prized sacred relics brought from Europe, which further provided a spiritual connection with the home left behind.[26]

Although the churches maintained a continuity with the old and familiar, they also interpreted American society to the immigrants and aided integration into the new society. American flags hung in church sanctuaries, church classrooms provided citizenship classes, and children of many parishes joined church-based Boy Scout troops. Church-sponsored interfaith meetings, political clubs, credit unions, and scholarships more subtly prepared the newcomer and his family for American urban life. The churches themselves often took on American ways in order to retain the interest and eventual support of parish children growing up in an American environment. Church leaders, as well, tried to satisfy parishioners who wanted "modern," or American, innovations. Thus English was slowly introduced in Greek, Serbian, and Russian services. The Magyar Synod of the Reformed Church (Hungarian Protestants) as early as 1907 held two Sunday services, one in English and the other in Hungarian. In some churches a layman preached in English every other Sunday; in others, English-language youth sermons or American style Sunday Schools were tried, services shortened, and organs and pews introduced. Many parishes joined the Gary Council of Churches, and introduced the system of regular dues paying by parishioners. All the Christian Orthodox churches, with the sole exception of the Greeks, distinguished between members of the parish—those born into the church—and dues-paying members of the congregation. Although common in the United States, this distinction was unknown among Orthodox Christians in Europe.[27]

Of course, the ethnic parishes provided numerous services not necessarily unique to immigrant churches; but these often took on greater importance among immigrants who were often financially pressed and alien to the surrounding society. The high costs of cemetery lots and funeral services were often moderated by religious associations. The costs of marriages and large family gatherings were made tolerable as women of a parish pooled their labor for a family's great occasions. The churches often provided recreational facilities for both young and old and nursery schools for preschool children. In times of crisis, economic or emotional, the church might help with its meager funds or spiritual counseling. The seemingly simple task of obtaining a reference from a local professional—for a job or scholarship—could usually only be satisfied by the minister in the city's early years. A pastor's visits to the old, sick, and hospitalized took on an added dimension when a patient had difficulty in communicating with American nurses, physicians, and welfare workers.

The ethnic parishes devoted considerable effort to providing a cultural link between the immigrant generation and American-born children. The Catholic church, having long before responded to the Protestantized American educational system, provided a parochial school alternative. Under the direction of ethnic parishes, the parochial schools soon fostered a European cultural milieu as well as a standard education. Other ethnic congregations (Protestant, Christian Orthodox, and Jewish) utilized religious folk schools for similar cultural and language goals.

Both the parochial and the religious folk schools served several functions. At a time when the public schools undermined immigrant culture and helped drive a wedge between children and immigrant parents, religious schools transmitted the language and cultural heritage of generations, perhaps softening the impact of a new land and people. These schools, although attended by children really served the parents by lessening the potentially considerable cultural gap between parent and child. The religious school—both folk and parochial—constituted a form of community control of education when the dominant American community remained alien. It is difficult to measure the success of the folk school's cultural goals. Gary's ethnic communities have still retained some of their native traditions and old world identities. They are still ethnic communities in a very real sense. The churches and schools played a role—both in formal education and in bringing members of the community physically together to foster identifiable mutual goals. Religious and ethnic festivals, celebrated at the school, re-created a bond between generations which had been disrupted by integration into a new society. Finally, the laity had considerable control and responsibility over their schools and church. Democracy and group decision-making—so much a part of the American imagination—were fostered along with the development of leadership qualities. This lay influence not only emerged in the Jewish and Christian Orthodox communities, but in the Catholic as well.

Soon after arriving in Gary, the immigrant communities established their churches. Religion provided a form of security through tradition and a continuation of what was known and respectable in an alien, rough and tumble industrial town. Soon the churches took on other functions, both acting as a cultural defense by attempting to preserve and transmit the immigrant heritage to the next generation, and, at the same time, aiding the immigrant in understanding and accepting a new society. Ironically, any success in this latter function undermined the church's ethnic defense role. As most groups became acculturated—especially as European children grew up as Americans—the old world church and the folk school had less validity. Some ethnic parishes withered; others remain in Gary even today. But such testimony to the efficacy of American pluralism must be tempered, since even the surviving churches have adopted much of the American religious style.

NOTES

¹ J. P. Dolan (1975), *The Immigrant Church: New York's Irish and German Catholics, 1815–1865*, pp. 71, 98, 111. Baltimore, Johns Hopkins Univ. Press; P. T. Silvia, Jr. (1979), The 'Flint affair': French-Canadian struggle for survivance. *Catholic Historical Review* 65 (July), 415–416; V. Greene (1975), *For God and Country: The Rise of Polish and Lithuanian Ethnic Consciousness in America*, pp. 1–13. Madison, State Hist. Soc. Wisc; S. Tomasi (1975), *Piety and Power: The Role of Italian Parishes in the New York Metropolitan Area*, pp. 105, 126, 167. New York, Center for Migration Studies; T. L. Smith (1966), Religious denominations as ethnic communities: A regional case study. *Church History* 35 (June) 207–226; T. L. Smith (1971), Lay initiative in the religious life of American immigrants, 1880–1950, in *Anonymous Americans: Explorations in Nineteenth-Century Social History* (T. K. Hareven, Ed.), pp. 214–249. Englewood Cliffs, N.J., Prentice–Hall; T. L. Smith (1978), Religion and ethnicity in America. *American Historical Review* 83 (December), 1155–1185; R. M. Miller (1977), Preface, in *Immigrants and Religion in Urban America* (R. M. Miller and T. D. Marzik, Eds.), viii. Philadelphia, Temple Univ. Press; See also R. M. Linkh (1975), *American Catholicism and European Immigrants, 1900–1924*. New York, Center for Migration Studies; J. W. Sanders (1977), *The Education of an Urban Minority: Catholics in Chicago, 1833–1965*. New York, Oxford Univ. Press; and M. Stolarik (1972), Lay initiative in American-Slovak parishes, 1880–1930. (American Catholic Historical Society of Philadelphia) *Records* 83 (September–December), 151–158.

² O. Handlin (1951), *The Uprooted*, p. 135. New York, Little; General immigration studies which follow Handlin include M. A. Jones (1960), *American Immigration*, p. 255, Chicago, Univ. of Chicago Press, and P. Taylor (1971), *The Distant Magnet: European Emigration to the U.S.A.*, p. 222, London, Harper & Row. For case studies of Chicago and New York, see Tomasi, *Piety and Power*, and Sanders, *Education of an Urban Minority*.

³ *Poland's Millennium of Christianity: The Polish Americans of Indiana, Their History and Their Jubilee* (Gary, Ind., n.d.), unpaginated pamphlet; *Gary Daily Tribune*, July 21, 1909, June 10, 1911, August 29, October 6, 1913.

⁴ *Gary Daily Tribune*, September 23, October 19, 1912, August 30, 1913; *Gary Post-Tribune*, September 23, 1962.

⁵ *Gary Daily Tribune*, July 16, September 23, 1912.

⁶ *Gary Daily Tribune*, March 10, November 8, 1911, July 1, 1912. See also Clipping File, Church Folder, Indiana Room, Gary Public Library (hereafter cited as GPL). On Gary Slovaks, see *Gary Post-Tribune*, May 20, 1956, Clipping File, GPL; on Gary Bohemians, see *Chicago Herald-Examiner*, June 13, 1934, *ibid.*; on St. Michaels Byzantine Catholic Church, see *Gary Post-Tribune*, November 8, 1969, *ibid.*; on St. Emerics Hungarian Catholic Church, see *Gary Post-Tribune*, May 20, 1951, *ibid.*

⁷ *Historical Sketch of the Lithuanians in Gary, 1916–1931* (Gary, Ind. n.d., circa 1931), 6–7; *Gary Daily Tribune*, March 11, April 25, July 1, 1912, April 3, 1914.

⁸ W. L. Warner and L. Srole (1945), *The Social Systems of American Ethnic Groups*, p. 237. New Haven, Conn., Yale Univ. Press.

⁹ *Historical Sketch of Lithuanians in Gary; Gary Daily Tribune,* July 21, 1909; *Gary Post-Tribune,* September 2, 1927; interview with Mrs. Helen Winter concerning Holy Family Polish Parish (interviews cited in this article were conducted by Lorraine King in April 1969 under the direction of the authors; summations of these interviews are deposited with the Oral History Project, Florida State University); "The Croatians in Gary," International Institute Study, 1933, Gary International Institute Papers (hereafter cited as II Papers); Anna Kuzmitz, "Religion of the Immigrant," WIND Broadcast, July 9, 1936, International Institute Radio Scripts, II Papers. For similar findings in other cities during the same period, see L. Rankin (1939), Detroit nationality groups. *Michigan History* 23 (Spring), 158–159; W. G. Fordyce (1950), Attempts to preserve national cultures in Cleveland. *Ohio Historical Quarterly* 49 (April–June), 135–137. See also M. Lazerson (1977), Understanding American Catholic Educational History. *History of Education Quarterly* 17 (Fall), 297–317; R. D. Cross (1965) Origins of the Catholic parochial schools in America, *American Benedictine Review* 16 (June), 194–209.

¹⁰ "The Spanish People in Gary," International Institute Study, 1933, II Papers.

¹¹ N. Betten and R. A. Mohl (1973), From discrimination to repatriation: Mexican life in Gary, Indiana, during the Great Depression. *Pacific Historical Review,* 42, (August), 370–388.

¹² Interview with Mrs. Namihski; interview with Mrs. Winter; *Gary Post-Tribune,* March 21, May 23, August 8, 1941, Clipping File, GPL. A short-lived Polish National Catholic parish was organized in Gary in 1914. See *Gary Daily Tribune,* April 7, 1914.

¹³ *Gary Daily Tribune,* June 4, 1912, October 31, 1917, September 27, 29, 1919; M. E. Carlson, "A Study of the Eastern Orthodox Churches in Gary, Indiana," pp. 21–23, 84–86. M.A. Thesis, University of Chicago, 1942; R. Meister, "A History of Gary, Indiana, 1930–1940, p. 86. Ph.D. Dissertation, University of Notre Dame, 1966; "The Greeks in Gary," International Institute Study, 1933, II Papers. See also, T. Saloutos (1973), The Greek Orthodox Church in the United States and assimilation. *International Migration Review* 7 (Winter), 395–407.

¹⁴ *Gary Daily Tribune,* February 27, March 30, 1914, March 25, April 17, 1915, January 28, 1916, June 7, 1918; *Gary Evening Post,* March 3, 1914; *Gary Post-Tribune,* January 9, 1943, Clipping File, GPL; St. Sava Serbian Orthodox Church, *Our Religious Heritage: 1914–1964,* pp. 116–119 (Gary, Ind. 1964); Carlson, "Eastern Orthodox Churches in Gary, pp. 11–13; Steven Boljanich (St. Sava Church secretary) and Tommy Kazich (St. Sava Church School supervisor) to authors, November 19, 1971.

¹⁵ *Gary Daily Tribune,* March 21, 30, 1912; *Yearbook of the Rumanian Orthodox Church, Descension of the Holy Ghost* (Gary, Ind. 1936), unpaginated; *Gary Post-Tribune,* September 28, 1968, Clipping File, GPL; Carlson, "Eastern Orthodox Churches in Gary. pp. 8–10. See also Andreiu Moldovan, *Mongrafia* (Gary, Ind. 1939).

¹⁶ *Gary Daily Tribune,* July 1, 1912; *Gary Post-Tribune,* May 20, 1956; Carlson, "Eastern Orthodox Churches in Gary," p. 17; Benjamin Kedrovsky, *Na Nivt' Bozhiel: Istoriia St. Pokdovskoi Pravoslavnoi Russkoi Tserkvi V Gorod Gary, Indiana (On God's Field: Twentieth Anniversary of St. Mary's Russian Orthodox Church of Gary, Indiana)* (Gary, Ind. 1931).

¹⁷ "The Bulgarians of Gary," International Institute Study, 1933, II Papers; *Gary Post-Tribune,* May 20, 1956.

¹⁸ St. Sava Serbian Orthodox Church, *Our Religious Heritage,* pp. 59, 79–80; Carlson, "Eastern Orthodox Churches in Gary," p. 57; Boljanich and Kazich to authors, November 19, 1971.

¹⁹ "The Greeks in Gary," II Papers; Carlson, "Eastern Orthodox Churches in Gary," p. 57.

²⁰ Kedrovsky, *Na Nivt' Bozhiei,* pp. 42–45, 133–145, 171–172; *Gary Daily Tribune,* May 18, 1913, October 2, 1922; Carlson, "Eastern Orthodox Churches in Gary," pp. 19, 50–57;

Moldovan, *Mongrafia*, pp. 65–70; "The Bulgarians of Gary," II Papers; *Gary Post-Tribune*, January 28, 1966, Clipping File, GPL. See also M. Serepka (1973), Chicago's System of Lithuanian Schools (Balzekas Museum of Lithuanian Culture). *Museum Review*. On the ethnic folk schools, see also J. A. Fishman (1966), *Language Loyalty in the United States*, pp. 92–126. The Hague, Humanities Press.

[21] On German Lutherans, see *Gary Daily Tribune*, January 8, 1909, March 26, April 6, August 8, 1910, May 5, 1911, July 5, 26, 1912, April 4, 1914. On German Methodists, see *Gary Daily Tribune*, November 5, 1909. On Swedish Lutherans, see *Gary Daily Tribune*, June 13, November 2, December 9, 1910, February 10, 1911, May 3, 1912, August 22, November 26, 1913, February 16, 1914.

[22] *Gary Daily Tribune*, April 13, 1910, September 16, 1911; *Gary Post-Tribune*, July 19, 1940, June 22, 1945, May 20, 1956.

[23] *Gary Daily Tribune*, May 1, 1913; *Gary Post-Tribune*, May 20, 1950, September 18, 1954, May 20, 1956, Clipping File, GPL; *Temple Beth-El Souvenir Album, 1908–1940*, pp. 7–9 (Gary, Ind. 1940); *Beth-El Bulletin*, March 1925, p. 2; March 1928, p. 1; April 1928, pp. 1–2; June 1928, p. 1; May 1928, p. 3.

[24] Smith, "Lay Initiative," p. 225.

[25] W. I. Thomas and F. Znaniecki (1959), *The Polish Peasant in Europe and America*, Vol. II, p. 1523. New York, Dover.

[26] S. D. Alinsky (1960), The urban immigrant, in *Roman Catholicism and the American Way of Life* (Thomas T. McAvoy, Ed.), p. 144. Notre Dame, Ind., Univ. of Notre Dame Press; Carlson, "Eastern Orthodox Churches in Gary," p. 63; I. J. Quillen, "Industrial City: A History of Gary, Indiana to 1929," p. 446 Ph.D. Dissertation, Yale University, 1942.

[27] *Gary Post-Tribune*, November 13, 1935; M. C. M. King, "The Immigrant and His Adopted Country," Radio Script, June 4, 1936, II Papers; Carlson, "Eastern Orthodox Churches in Gary," pp. 40, 65.

FIG. 1. Cambridge Lutheran Church, Cambridge, Minn., as it appeared in 1978. Courtesy of R. L. Carlson.

THE IMMIGRANT CHURCH AS A SYMBOL OF COMMUNITY AND PLACE IN THE UPPER MIDWEST

ROBERT C. OSTERGREN

There can be little doubt that the church as an institution played a major role in the organization and development of community on nineteenth-century American frontiers, especially in the Middle West. Zealous missionary activity was characteristic of American Protestantism in the nineteenth century, and a good portion of that effort was expended on midwestern frontier populations. Thus the region emerged as a locus of fierce competition between the established American denominations. In addition, the Midwest was fertile ground for the establishment of new denominations. Many who settled the region were immigrants who came directly from Europe. Their uprooting severed ties with the formal churches of Europe and created a need in America that was filled by a variety of ethnic denominations.

Robert C. Ostergren is an assistant professor of geography at the University of Wisconsin-Madison. He is the author of several articles treating the cultural geography of Scandinavian immigration to the United States in the nineteenth century.

The result was a heavily churched landscape, especially in the strongly ethnic band of settlement that stretched across the Upper Midwest from northern Illinois and southern Wisconsin to the eastern parts of the Dakotas and Nebraska. A map of churched population based on county data from the 1890 federal census illustrates this religious intensity.[1] It shows that a high proportion of the population along this band of ethnic settlement was affiliated with religious organizations and that an especially high rate of church membership existed in the German and Scandinavian areas of southern Wisconsin and central Minnesota. Indeed, by the end of the century many church leaders considered the Midwest to be "over-churched" and lamented what they clearly felt had been overly competitive efforts to establish churches in the region.[2]

The competition among denominations in the nineteenth century has attracted the attention of scholars and a sizable literature has emerged on the organized efforts to reach and gather the unchurched souls of pioneer populations. Many of these studies focus on the denomination, chronicling the process of denominational mission work, the struggle to establish the new ethnic denominations, and

225

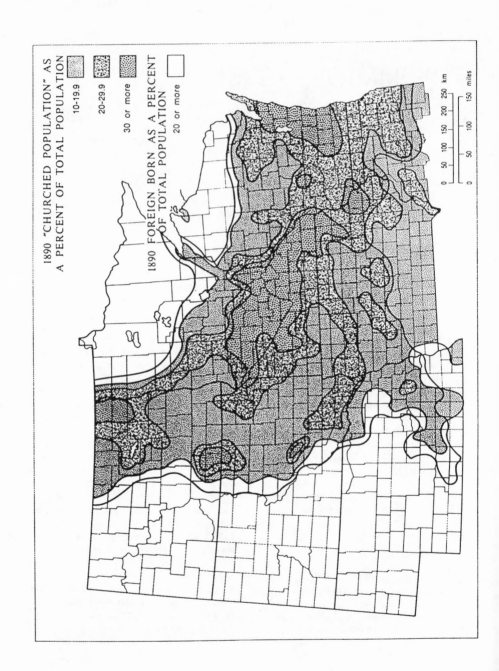

1890 "CHURCHED POPULATION" AS
A PERCENT OF TOTAL POPULATION

10-19.9

20-29.9

30 or more

1890 FOREIGN BORN AS A PERCENT
OF TOTAL POPULATION

20 or more

0   50   100 150 200 250 km

0   50   100   150 miles

the theological issues that made the denominations distinctive and competitive.[3] Less attention has been paid to the role of religious organization at the level of the individual pioneer congregation. Yet it was at this level that the church was most relevant to the new settlers. Whereas the denomination was a structural and purposive organization, dedicated to the preservation and propagation of a theological point of view, the local congregation was a social institution that fulfilled the pioneers' more immediate need for a sense of belonging and for community leadership.

My purpose here is to examine the functional roles of the immigrant church of the Upper Midwest in defining community and in preserving cultural values, with special emphasis on the way in which the physical presence and architectural style of the church may have symbolized these roles. While the functional roles of the immigrant church may be fairly well understood, its place on the cultural landscape has received only passing comment. Historians of American immigration, for instance, generally characterize the church as a symbolic place but do not define the manner in which its symbolism is evident on the landscape. Geographers who make a practice of studying religious landscapes argue that religion can make a substantial impact, particularly under conditions of low diversity. Yet they have done relatively little to demonstrate this in the United States.[4] In his book on American cultural geography, Wilbur Zelinsky noted that the church has been "scandalously neglected" in studies of the American settlement landscape.[5]

The first part of this paper offers some generalizations about these aspects of the immigrant church for the Upper Midwest as a whole. These observations are the by-product of several years of research on immigrant settlement patterns in the region. While they are not based on a systematic investigation, they nonetheless provide a basis for discussion. The balance of the paper examines these generalizations more closely through the specific example of a Swedish Lutheran community in east-central Minnesota.

THE IMMIGRANT CHURCH
IN THE UPPER MIDWEST

The Upper Midwest was a favored destination for European immigrants who hoped to establish themselves on the land. The agricultural frontiers of this region received greater numbers of immigrants than any other region during the nineteenth century. Large groups arrived in the 1830s and again in the late 1840s and early 1850s; the aftermath of the Civil War brought fresh waves of immigrants in the late 1860s and the 1880s. In other words, each forward surge of the frontier was associated with substantial waves of immigration.[6] For the most part the immigrants came from the agricultural regions of northwestern Europe. Migrants from the industrial cities and from southern or eastern Europe were less significant because most of them arrived too late to take advantage of agricultural opportunity on the frontier, except at the western and northern peripheries of the region.

An important characteristic of the settlement pattern was a marked segregation of culture groups. In the migration process people naturally tended to seek out circumstances that were as familiar to them as possible. They relied heavily upon information that recommended settlement frontiers where their own countrymen were settling. Even more valuable was the trusted information that came back to European emigration districts from friends and relatives who had left earlier and were encouraging others to join them. Over time, communication and migration axes developed that connected places in Europe to places in America and over these axes flowed streams of migrants who shared a common cultural heritage. Thus the settlements were typically dominated by immigrants from particular areas in Europe, creating a settlement landscape that resembled an immense patchwork quilt of culturally homogeneous communities.[7]

The immigrants who settled these communities were predominantly Protestant, as might be expected, given their northwest European origins, although the Irish, some of the

Dutch, and many Germans were Roman Catholic.[8] In most cases the church had played a central role in their daily affairs. The state church system in Europe granted the church a virtually unchallenged position in religious life. In addition, the parish, which was the basic administrative unit of the church, served as the basic unit of civil administration in most countries. Therefore the clergy often played a dual role, serving as both spiritual and civil leaders of their flocks.

The question of religious affiliation among new settlers in America was an important and emotionally charged issue. This was due to the emergence of many dissenting religious sects in the nineteenth century, which heightened religious consciousness in many districts, and to the American concept of the separation of church and state, which promoted competitive denominationalism among Protestants.

It is not surprising then that an early and widespread activity among immigrants on the frontier was the founding of churches. Organizational meetings commonly took place in someone's cabin or prairie dugout and were conducted by laymen because in all denominations there was a shortage of clergymen on the frontier. Usually a new congregation's membership grew rapidly, a permanent building was erected, and a call went out for a permanent minister. Typically it was only a short time before most immigrant communities had at least one organized religious establishment in their midst. Competition and schism often produced more than one.

From almost the beginning these churches served a territorial function. The spatial distribution of their membership defined a functional region of which the church was the nodal point. There was, in fact, no other institution on the frontier that could serve this purpose. Townships were arbitrarily defined according to the land survey and had little social significance. Granges, cooperatives, and farmer's associations came much later. Thus, depending on the cultural homogeneity of the local population, the membership field of the church often took on a rather exclusive character,

with well-defined boundaries separating it from other groups and congregations.

Since there was a physical limit to the distance people would travel to worship, given the travel technology of the day, "team-haul spacing" was a common characteristic of church location except where denominational competition or schismatic activity was present. Then competing churches could be placed side by side and the delimitation of boundaries could be less clear. Whether the situation was competitive or not, the church was the center of social activity. Not only was it a place of worship, it was also the site of picnics, socials, and meetings. It was the umbrella organization for a myriad of social and purposive clubs and associations. Even nonmembers in the community were caught up in the social network and looked to the church as the community center.

As the center of community life, the church was charged with the responsibility of upholding values and preserving continuity with the cultural past. Most churches, for instance, made extensive efforts to preserve the language. Services in rural churches across the Upper Midwest were commonly held in the Old World languages well into the early decades of the twentieth century. Church schools were established to instruct the young in the old language and congregations delayed for as long as possible the eventual change to the keeping of official records in English. The church carefully observed the old holidays and customs, singing clubs preserved the traditional music, and women's organizations carried on folk crafts. From the pulpit the clergy warned against the dangers of alcohol, loose morals, and unguarded association with outsiders. The outside world could not be held at arm's length forever, but the church functioned as the first and in some ways the only bulwark against rapid change.

How then was the church a symbolic place and structure on the landscape? Part of the answer is evident to anyone who has traveled the backroads of the region. With the possible exception of the grain elevator, the church is the dominant structure on the rural landscape.

Its presence is visible for miles. In fact, in many parts of the region, the spires of churches serving neighboring communities can be seen from points along their common boundary, which causes one to reflect on the coincidence of "team-haul spacing" and the limits of visibility in open landscapes.

The form is also familiar to the midwestern country traveler. The typical rural church in this region is a white rectangular structure with narrow clapboard siding and a forward bell tower. There are variations, of course. Some have the bell tower on the side. Some have rounded vestries, double doors, and bell cupolas on the roof instead of a bell tower. Building materials vary as well. Stone or brick veneer is not uncommon. Elements of gothic or Greek revival styling frequently adorn structures regardless of size, but the basic form persists.

One might reasonably ask whether variation on the basic form is an indication of ethnic culture. The answer seems to be that generally it is not. By the mid-nineteenth century, variation in building styles in America was more a matter of fashion or fad than an expression of folk culture and, to a large extent, the construction of churches across the Midwest was no exception to this rule. There is evidence that architectural plans and building designs for churches were widely circulated in the latter half of the century. An example is an 1852 pamphlet entitled, *Upjohn's Rural Architecture: Designs, Working Drawings and Specifications for a Wooden Church and other Rural Structures.* The availability of this and numerous publications like it help to explain the structural similarity of churches on the landscape. Upjohn made it quite clear in the preface that his booklet was intended for use in frontier areas:

> My purpose in publishing this book is simply to supply the want which is often felt, especially in the newly settled parts of our country, of designs for cheap but still substantial buildings for the use of parishes, schools, etc.

Upjohn went on to point out that his plans were "plain and practical" and that they included specifications and bills of lumber. He adds, "with these [plans] any intelligent mechanic will be able to carry out the design."[9]

The size of the structure and the choice of building materials reflected the material wealth of the congregation. As congregations grew in membership and wealth they required more spacious quarters and more ostentatious structures. A common event in the history of a congregation was the solicitation of building funds for the purpose of upgrading some aspect of the church building—a new bell tower, pipe organ, or brick veneer exterior. Damage caused by lightning and fire required many congregations to remodel or replace their original buildings. In fact, a congregation that was not forced to rebuild at least once in its history is somewhat rare.

Apparently most congregations went through a series of construction and remodeling phases. The first phase followed the establishment of the congregation and the decision to build a church, ordinarily a rather simple frame structure (sometimes made of logs) with no tower. This structure typically served for only a short time. The second building phase involved its replacement with a larger frame church of the standard variety. Then there was a third phase in which this structure was either replaced, usually because of destruction by fire or storm, or subjected to a series of renovations and redecorations. In many cases a fourth phase occurred around the late 1930s or after World War II in which extensive renovations and additions were undertaken that often radically altered the decor and structure of the building.

Although most churches varied relatively little in their basic structural characteristics and went through the similar building phases, their decoration could be unique and symbolic of a particular past or culture. Consider, for example, the case of the Opdahl church in Hamlin County, South Dakota. This Lutheran church was the focus of a community of Norwegian immigrants, most of whom came from the Trondhjem area of western Norway. Photographs of the Opdahl church taken in the

FIG. 2. *Opdahl Norwegian Lutheran Church, Hamlin County, S.D., in the early twentieth century. Courtesy of Robert Ostergren.*

early part of the twentieth century show a typical midwestern frame structure, but the exterior decoration, especially on the tower, is distinctive. If a frame church in the district of Norway from which these people emigrated is compared to the Opdahl photograph, marked similarities in the decoration of the tower are visible, suggesting that the decorative work on this church was meant to recall a particular past (see Figs. 2 and 3).

It is not surprising that some effort was made to provide a visual link between the new church in America and the mother church in Europe. The parish church, after all, was the richest and most impressive structure known to many emigrants before they left Europe. This linkage was most often accomplished in a minor way on the exterior of the American church and more intensively in the decoration and arrangement of the interior. Traditional craftsmanship, for example, was employed in fashioning altar furnishings, and pulpits and altar paintings were often copies of those that hung in parish churches in the native districts of Europe. Similarly, the painting of ceilings and walls or the location of pulpit

and altar were often reminiscent of another place.

In this way, the church was physically symbolic of its role as the keeper of culture and of continuity with the past. In the mid-twentieth century, however, many of these elements were last in efforts to remodel and refurbish. Intricately frescoed walls and ceilings were covered over with acoustical tile; new furnishings were installed and the old ones consigned to the basement or carted away. Exterior decor disappeared in the interest of easier maintenance. The Opdahl church was no exception to this process. The distinctive decor of the early twentieth century no longer adorns the structure.

FUNCTIONAL ORGANIZATION AND CULTURAL CHANGE

A more detailed illustration of the foregoing generalizations can be achieved through an examination of the organizational and cultural development of a single immigrant church, the Swedish Evangelical Lutheran congregation of Cambridge, Minnesota. It is located in the east-central Minnesota county of Isanti, well

FIG. 3. *Mohult parish church, Trondhjem, Norway. Courtesy of Robert Ostergren.*

within the zone of heavily churched population in the Upper Midwest. Whether its experience is typical of midwestern immigrant churches is difficult to say. It was selected because much detailed information is known about the European origins of the community and about the history of the congregation.[10]

The Cambridge church was organized in a part of Minnesota that received a large and nearly exclusive influx of Swedish settlers. As was often the case, the majority of the immigrants hailed from culturally distinctive districts in Sweden and tended to segregate themselves in the settlement process. One part of this area was settled by immigrants from the province of Dalarna and in particular by people from a single parish known as Rättvik. In 1864, not long after the settlement of the area began, a small group of settlers gathered in the cabin of one of their number and formally organized a Lutheran congregation with the assistance of a clergyman from the neighboring county. Initially the provincial background of the small congregation was mixed, but it was soon dominated by the folk from Rättvik, who began to arrive in large numbers in the summer of 1866.

The Swedish parish of Rättvik is located in the western part of Dalarna, region of large and culturally distinctive parishes. The parish dates from the fourteenth century and is organized around a church located on the shore of the northeastern bay of a large lake known as Siljan. The population, which in the nineteenth century was comprised chiefly of small freeholders, lived in villages scattered along the shores of the lake and along a small valley that leads away from the lake. Everyone was a member of the state church of Sweden, accepting its ministrations and authority in their lives.[11] The parish priest was the spiritual leader of the flock. He was also the king's representative, responsible for keeping civil records of the population, monitoring their movements, and providing guidance in their affairs. The church was in many ways the organizer of society. It administered the parish, providing education, welfare services, and public works.

Services at the parish church were regularly attended. Parishioners who lived in the villages near the shore of the lake were ceremoniously carried to worship in large "church boats" (Fig. 4). Those who lived in the inland villages came down to the church by horse cart. In addition to worship, the Sunday gathering at the church was a social event that lasted all day. The churchyard, after services, was the setting for socializing and informal business. Resplendent in the distinctive parish dress, people stood about and gossiped, discussing weather and crops and perhaps speculating on events in neighboring parishes. Many parishioners maintained small "church stalls" in the churchyard for the purposes of shelter and cooking during the long day.

The parish church in Europe was symbolic of the community and its traditions, and its physical image was carried with the emigrants in their minds as they left for America and remembered long after the journey was over. Its importance is illustrated by the emphasis it received in a poem written for the fortieth anniversary of the founding of the community in America. It begins with these lines:

The service is over in Rättvik's old temple
On the shores of Lake Siljan
But as is the custom all remained to
    visit awhile.
Since there were no newspapers to tell
    of new events
The church yard was the meeting place to
    tell the news.
The stately taciturn men and ladies in
    native dress
Gather together in groups.
Great curiosity is aroused as you hear—
"Have you heard that over in Boda,
Yes, even in our parish
A large group of our people are planning
    to go to America?
Their own native land and beautiful valley,
Their King and Fatherland,
They plan to abandon for a strange and
    foreign country.
The homes that for generations their honorable fathers cherished,
For them have become too small,

FIG. 4. *Rättvik parish church, Sweden, in the late nineteenth century. Courtesy Dalarnas Museum, Falun, Sweden.*

And their homes mean nothing at all.
The graves of their dear ones still green—
Around the church of Lake Siljan.[12]

The early years of the daughter settlement in America were difficult, but the church gradually organized and drew together the Swedish settlers in the area who retained a loyalty to the Lutheran faith. This effort was hampered by the fact that there were Swedish Baptist settlements both to the north and south, which added an element of competition to the religious organization of the region. Initially, the Cambridge church received only token assistance from the ordained ministry of the Swedish Augustana Lutheran Synod. Ministers from congregations in the next county visited the settlement on occasion and theological students were sent to do mission work in the summer, but much of the early preaching and organiza-

tional work was accomplished by laymen. The synod insisted that these persons seek authorization from the synodical president before they preached. It was not until 1869 that the congregation succeeded in calling a permanent pastor to the Cambridge community, and even then he had to be shared with a nearby settlement in the next county.

The area served by the new church was large and communications were poor. These conditions necessitated the maintenance of a number of preaching places during the early years. Later, when better roads made it possible to bring the congregation together on a regular basis, the areas served by the old preaching stations retained some autonomy. Territorial administrative units, called *roten*, or "routes," were instituted that were modeled after the administrative organization of the mother parish.

In fact, the settlers who resided in the various "routes" tended to hail from respective administrative areas in Rättvik, which meant that the new church presided over the transplantation of an old form of local spatial organization.[13] The more distant "routes" to the west and the south insisted for a time on maintaining their own Sunday schools and holding occasional services that were separate from the main church. One of them, the "Isanti route," eventually withdrew from the parish in 1878 in order to form a separate congregation, although its membership was officially recorded in the register of the Cambridge church until 1892.

Each "route" elected members to the parish council, which was modeled after a similar body in the Swedish church. The council concerned itself with the administration of the church and the morality of the parishioners. Substantial portions of the meetings were, in fact, devoted to matters of behavior and the attitude among certain individuals in the community. The councilmen personally confronted offenders about their drinking, use of profane language, frivolous conduct, and conspicuous absence from church. The ultimate action in these cases was excommunication, which occurred with some frequency. An issue of considerable concern in the late 1880s and the 1890s was the "saloon question," which revolved around efforts to ban drinking and gaming houses in the nearby village of Cambridge. The church youth society went so far as to petition the state legislature to vote against saloons in the county.

The church also struggled with the question of preserving the language, an issue that became more significant around the turn of the century as Swedish was less frequently used in second- and third-generation homes. The church gave ground only grudgingly, allowing an English Sunday school division and English services two Sunday evenings a month in 1900, but insisting on the continuation of Swedish services on Sunday mornings, a practice that lasted into the 1920s. The church tried to combat the erosion of language and culture through the maintenance

of a "Swede School" and seriously pursued the goal of full attendance among the young. In his efforts to encourage parents to enroll their children, the pastor wrote in the church notices, "We ought to teach our children the language our fathers and mothers spoke, the first European language that ever re-echoed in the American forest and ever uttered the white man's thoughts in the land of the free."[14]

The church stood against more than the erosion of language. It opposed radical change in general and the influences of the outside world that were becoming more noticeable in the community with the arrival of the railroad in 1899. The 1904 history of the congregation concludes with a comment on the situation:

> The old pietism is not entirely gone. However, since the coming of the railroad we have been troubled by irrelevant and foreign elements. The worldly life of the large cities have invaded our community. It seems as if one is not able to differentiate between good and evil. It is more harmful for us to be thrust into the world arena, because we are not prepared to meet the dangers and temptations. We are too credulous, separated from city life as we have been for so many years.[15]

In spite of the outside influences that may have affected the community, the church remained strong. It continued to have a large and loyal following in the early twentieth century, with more than 60 percent of the local population listed on the membership roles, and it continued to preserve the customs of the past. Men and women, for example, continued to sit on opposite sides of the church as they had done in Rättvik, with the exception of the newlyweds, who ceremoniously appeared together on the first Sunday following the marriage (stata i kyrkan). The deacons of the church were allotted privileged seating in the first pew on the men's side (gubbabanken). Church bells were rung twice before services, one hour before and at the beginning, according to custom. The bells were also used at the traditional "soul-ringing" at funerals, in which the bells were rung once for each year of the

FIG. 5. *Cambridge Swedish Evangelical Lutheran Church, Cambridge, Minn., 1884. Courtesy Isanti County Historical Society, Cambridge, Minn.*

deceased person's life as mourners entered and left the shroud-draped church.

Thus the church strove tenaciously to maintain a cultural continuity with the past throughout the nineteenth and the early twentieth century, even as assimilation with American culture steadily progressed and eventually began to overtake the old ideas and values. The church structure itself, as it passed through building and rebuilding or remodeling phases, symbolized the changing cultural outlook of the community.

CULTURAL CHANGE
AND THE CAMBRIDGE CHURCH

The Cambridge congregation began building its first church structure in 1866 in order to accommodate an organization that was rapidly outgrowing the stage in which services could be held in someone's home. The first church was built under the direction of Jonas Norell, a local resident who was a carpenter by profession, and completed in 1868. It was a plain frame structure, 40 feet by 26 feet, without bell tower or decoration. Like other early churches in the Upper Midwest, the building

was spartan and functional, a reflection of the poor and struggling frontier community it served. In fact, its completion had been delayed for lack of material and the congregation's second permanent minister was reportedly depressed when he first saw it in 1872.

By 1877 the congregation had decided to build a new and more imposing structure. At that time there were more than three hundred communicant members, many of whom had been established in the area long enough to have accumulated some wealth. A building committee was authorized to solicit funds for a church that would be 80 feet long and 56 feet wide, with a bell tower that would rise 101 feet to the top of the cross. Norell, who eventually built several churches in the area, was again commissioned as the chief carpenter and was reimbursed forty dollars for the detailed plan he had drawn. The committee later decided to reduce the size of the building by nearly one-half, the original estimate being a bit too grand. After careful appraisal, they also elected to construct a wooden building, since brick was expensive and not readily available.

The new church, which was completed in 1884, fulfilled all expectations and was a source of pride in the community (Fig. 5). Although some local residents suggest that the church design may have had its origins in Sweden, it is much more similar to other midwestern churches constructed about the same time than it is to the mother church in Rättvik (compare Fig. 4) or to Swedish parish churches in general. While there are many unique features on this church and on other churches built by Norell in the area, the influence of contemporary church design in America is apparent.

The interior, unlike the exterior, was highly symbolic of the cultural past (Fig. 6). The furniture was hand carved by a local craftsman. The walls and ceiling were painted and frescoed in the Swedish style. There was a Swedish verse on the arch over the altar, and the arrangement of altar, vestry doors, and hymnboards resembled the arrangement in the old parish church in Rättvik. On the other

FIG. 6. *Interior of Cambridge Swedish Evangelical Lutheran Church, Cambridge, Minn., circa 1900. Courtesy Isanti County Historical Society, Cambridge, Minn.*

hand, the interior design reveals that a careful effort was made to place some distance between this church and the state church in Sweden, whose theological and liturgical rigidity was not in line with the more pietistic thinking of many of the emigrants. Accordingly, the pulpit was located high above the altar rather than in its traditional position at the side of the nave, with a door leading to it from the vestry behind. In general the contrast between the interior and exterior decoration of the church reflected the outlook of the community—inwardly Swedish and outwardly American.

The 1890s and early 1900s were a time of considerable prosperity and change. With this prosperity came further growth in the size of the congregation and a desire to make decorative changes and renovations. The first of these was a brick veneer covering the exterior of the church, displaying the new affluence of the congregation. At the same time, the one exterior symbol of the past—an old cross with a large sphere at its base similar to the one on the Rättvik church—was replaced by a new "Trinity cross." A photograph taken at the time of this renovation shows workmen erecting the new cross high on top of the spire (Fig. 7). While this photograph celebrates the new,

FIG. 7. *Cambridge Swedish Evangelical Lutheran Church, Cambridge, Minn., during 1892 renovation. Note "church stalls" in lower left-hand corner. Courtesy Isanti County Historical Society, Cambridge, Minn.*

it also captures something of the past. In the lower left-hand corner one can see some of the "church stalls" maintained by parishioners on the grounds of the church, as was the custom in Rättvik. In 1900 the church was wired for electricity, and in 1912 the interior was completely redone. In this remodeling the pulpit was lowered, after much discussion. Apparently the height of the pulpit and the rear entry from the vestry were offensive to some in that this arrangement allowed the pastor to appear on high without having to pass before the assembled congregation. The solution was to install steps leading to the lowered pulpit from either side, in plain view of the parishioners. Many of these changes were the subject of considerable

debate because of their symbolic nature. A youth society meeting in the 1890s, for example, was devoted in all seriousness to the issue, "Which is the most advantageous, to paint or tin panel the church?"

The fourth and longest period of major remodeling and alteration in the church's history began in the thirties. In 1931 a basement was excavated for the purpose of providing central heating, and the north end was remodeled in order to house a new pipe organ and a pastor's study. In 1938 additions were attached to both sides of the tower, and in 1948 the round-arched windows were replaced with windows with Gothic arches. At the same time the interior was drastically altered by the replacement of the plastered vault ceiling with an acoustically tiled, beamed ceiling. A Gothic arch was placed over the chancel. In 1950 the spire was remodeled and covered with asbestos siding. Thus, by the beginning of the 1950s, the appearance of the church, both inside and outside, was substantially different from what it had been at the end of the nineteenth century, like the culture of the community it served (compare Figs. 1 and 7). The centrality of the church, however, endured through all change, and no matter what appearance it projected, it remained the most important source of identity for a transplanted people.

NOTES

1. Federal census materials on religious affiliation are known to have limitations, primarily because the information is based on the response of congregations rather than individuals. For the limited purposes of this map, however, the census figures are sufficiently reliable. For more information on the nature and limitations of census data on religion, see Wilbur Zelinsky, "An Approach to the Religious Geography of the United States: Patterns of Church Membership in 1952," *Annals of the Association of American Geographers* 51 (1961): 141-44. It should be noted that "churched population" percentages of 30 percent or more are extremely high, since most congregations reported only adult communicant membership.

2. This was a major concern of the so-called rural church movement of the early twentieth century, which sought to combat a decline in the vitality of the rural church during this period. See, for example, March Rich, *The Rural Church Movement* (Columbia, Mo.: Juniper Knoll Press, 1957).

3. Good overviews are Sidney E. Mead, "Denominationalism: The Shape of Protestantism in America," *Church History* 23 (1955): 291-320; and L. A. Loetscher, "The Problem of Christian Unity in Early Nineteenth Century America," *Church History* 32 (1963): 3-16.

4. James R. Shortridge, for instance, suggests that the northern plains, with their relatively low religious diversity, are a potentially interesting religious landscape, but are "completely unstudied in this context." See his "Patterns of Religion in the United States," *Geographical Review* 66 (1976): 420-34. A recent exception is Terry G. Jordan, "A Religious Geography of the Hill Country Germans of Texas," in *Ethnicity on the Great Plains*, ed. by Frederick C. Luebke (Lincoln: University of Nebraska Press, 1980), pp. 109-28.

5. Wilbur Zelinsky, *The Cultural Geography of the United States* (Englewood Cliffs, N.J.: Prentice-Hall, 1973), p. 101.

6. For a treatment of settlement advance and the location of culture groups in the Upper Midwest, see Robert C. Ostergren, "Geographic Perspectives on the History of Settlement in the Upper Middle West," *Journal of Upper Midwest History*, forthcoming.

7. These aspects of the settlement process are treated in John G. Rice, *Patterns of Ethnicity in a Minnesota County, 1880-1905*, University of Umeå, Department of Geography, Geographical Reports no. 4 (Umeå, Sweden, 1973); John G. Rice and Robert C. Ostergren, "The Decision to Emigrate: A Study in Diffusion," *Geografiska Annaler* 60B (1978): 1-15; Robert C. Ostergren, "Prairie Bound: Patterns of Migration to a Swedish Settlement on the Dakota Frontier," *Ethnicity on the Great Plains*, ed. by Frederick C. Luebke, pp. 73-91; and Jon Gjerde, "The Effect of Community on Migration: Three Minnesota Townships, 1885-1905," *Journal of Historical Geography* 5 (1979): 403-22.

8. The Roman Catholic church was an important force in the settlement of some groups. For convenience, however, this paper deals exclusively with the more numerous Protestant churches.

9. Upjohn's booklet, which was published in New York in 1852, was actually intended for use in frontier areas of western New York State and the Old Northwest. It was immensely successful, and its influence spread across the country. Another influential booklet of this type was George E. Woodward's *Rural Church Architecture* (New York, 1876).

10. The Cambridge congregation is easily studied because of the remarkably detailed ministerial records kept by the church throughout its history. In addition, there is an excellent

history of the congregation by Jeane Johnson, *The Lighted Spire* (Cambridge, Minn.: Cambridge Lutheran Church Centennial Committee, 1964), and an architectural history of the church by Alan Bergman, *A History of the Cambridge Lutheran Church Building* (Cambridge, Minn.: Archives Committee of the Cambridge Lutheran Church, 1968). Much of the following is based on the church records and these two publications. The assistance of Randolph Johnson of Cambridge, Minnesota, and Marilyn McGriff, who directs the Isanti County Historical Society, is also gratefully acknowledged. For a treatment of the European origins and early development of the American community, see Robert C. Ostergren, "A Community Transplanted: The Formative Experience of a Swedish Immigrant Community in the Upper Middle West," *Journal of Historical Geography* 5 (1979): 189-212.

11. Dissenters were viewed with disfavor in mid-nineteenth-century Sweden, although they had the right to form their own congregations under state control. At the time of the emigration, religious dissension was not prevalent in the parish of Rättvik, but it was present in neighboring parishes.

12. Poem by Alfred Bergin, translated in Johnson, *Lighted Spire*, pp. 34-36.

13. The administrative districts in Rättvik were known as *fjärdingar*. Although they were formed for administrative purposes, they acquired considerable social significance over the centuries, as evidenced by the fact that emigrants from these respective districts tended to settle together in America.

14. Quoted in Johnson, *Lighted Spire*, p. 116.

15. Quoted in Johnson, *Lighted Spire*, pp. 120-21.

The New American Catholic History

MOSES RISCHIN

Even historians and historically minded sociologists with little sense or awareness of the current Roman Catholic scene have been stirred by the precipitous flow of events of the last dozen years to ask questions about the Catholic role in American society. Virtually without warning, the history of American Catholicism has been catapulted from specialized ecclesiastical history of interest to Catholics primarily into an ecumenical history of unprecedented general interest. After hovering backstage for centuries, the Catholic presence has erupted almost simultaneously from the secular and theological wings and burst onto centerstage. A convergence of public events dramatized and personalized for world Catholicism by the papacy of John XXIII and for American Catholicism by the presidency of John F. Kennedy ironically magnified a sense of supreme Catholic crisis and confusion that in its scope and implications dwarfed earlier American Catholic crises, making them appear parochial and intramural by comparison. The elevation to the papacy of the most saintly and humble of priests and the brief presidency of the first Catholic president of the United States turned an aged pope and a young president into symbols of a new public Catholicism, cosmopolitan and courageous in its vision and democratic in its thrust. Vatican II, the ecumenical movement, the race revolution, the general revolt against authority, the new ethnic succession, explosive social and geographic mobility, and the heightened self-consciousness of newer ethnics of European origin and largely Catholic religion, combined with the instant exposure of the mass media, synchronized with an era of American world hegemony and the emergence of an American Catholicism of appropriate dimensions.[1] The implications of such changes for American Catholic history, given the eager search for comparative historical perspectives, the maturing of urban and ethnic history, the universal quest for identity and an upsurge of interest in American religious history, are manifold.

Almost overnight, psychic barriers and feelings of Catholic inferiority that had lingered for generations seemed nearly to dissolve. The Catholic Church as the ready foil of Protestant and post-Protestant America, the symbol and embodiment of the hierarchical, monarchical old order of pre-Reformation and pre-French Revolution Europe, appeared almost as obsolete as the yeoman farmer. Catholics in their delayed and heightened confrontation with the cumulative forces of modernism now seemed analagous to Jews of an earlier era who had experienced a great awakening as their segregated antique civilization sought a new viability in the modern world, and to the succession of Protestant denominations which in the course of almost two centuries had less precipitously encountered secular cultural shock. As a result, those of all religious faiths and none were drawn to share vicariously and at least retrospectively in the Catholic experience.

The discontinuity between past and present that has marked the last decade or so for American Catholics is most vividly illustrated in the two successive editions of *American Catholicism* by its foremost living historian, John Tracy

1. See Philip Gleason, ed., *Contemporary Catholicism in the United States* (Notre Dame, 1969), p. xiii; Sidney E. Ahlstrom, "The Moral and Theological Revolution of the 1960's and Its Implications for American Religious History," in Herbert Bass, ed., *The State of American History* (Chicago, 1970), pp. 108-109.

Mr. Rischin is professor of history in the San Francisco State College, California.

225

Ellis. The interlude between Ellis' original Charles R. Walgreen lectures at the University of Chicago and the publication of the second edition of his book seems to span not fourteen years but a whole new age in the history of religions and most especially in the history of American Catholicism. Clearly the new final chapter, "The Changing Church 1956-1968," over half again as long as the original four chapters surveying four and one-half centuries, is a sequel that excites visions of daring new syntheses and interpretations. Wrote Dr. Ellis:

. . . in the Catholic Church's history of nearly two thousand years one must go back to the third decade of the sixteenth century, when the movement begun by Martin Luther started to spread, to find a parallel to the revolutionary transformation that has taken place since the election in October, 1958, of Pope John XXIII. The change is seen and experienced in every aspect of Catholic life: in the Church's approach to the world, in the style and manner of her apostolate to those outside her fold as well as her own members, in the attitude of those members to the Church itself, and this on virtually every level and in every rank of ecclesiastical and clerical authority . . . as well as in the varied social classes of men and women who constitute the Church's lay membership.[2]

The evidence of revolution on the American scene, in many respects its most active source, was to be found on every hand in the culmination of long-term trends and in the abrupt reversal of long-held postures that call for historical investigation. The decline of the churches of the inner city, the obsolescence of the parish structure, the stubbornness of race prejudice in the face of race revolution, the replacement of Protestant America by the religiously pluralist America, the ecumenical dialogue, the apparent passing of the Irish hegemony, the wholesale reappraisal of education, the crisis of the clergy, the erosion of Catholic identity, and liturgical and architectural innovation are only the more salient expressions of a present that has emerged out of a past demanding redefinition and historical depth and elaboration to which a new generation of Catholic historians has already begun to respond.

Two young scholars especially, David J. O'Brien of Holy Cross College, primarily an intellectual historian, and Philip Gleason of the University of Notre Dame, primarily a social historian, have taken the lead in charting the outlines of a new American Catholic history. The authors of outstanding monographs reflecting the new tendency, they have drawn up an historical balance sheet and prospectus for a new ecclesiological history.[3] Eager to break with hierarchical and juridical habits of thought and defensive institutional reflexes, they are both confident in their Catholic self-criticism and eager to test and reinforce their identities as Catholics and as American historians by identifying the tensions that underlie both.

In a balanced authoritative article on American Catholic historiography, O'Brien leaves no doubt that Catholic denominational history no longer satisfies the intellectual requirements and social needs of a younger generation of historians. O'Brien's analysis takes special account both of the continuities and discontinuities in American Catholic liberal thought that have set the terms of American Catholic historiography and calls for expanded horizons that will not blink at complexity, ambivalence and conflict. Although both Irish and liberal,

2. John Tracy Ellis, *American Catholicism*. Second edition. (Chicago, 1969), pp. 163-164.
3. David J O'Brien, *American Catholics and Social Reform: The New Deal Years* (New York, 1968); Philip Gleason, *Conservative Reformers: German-American Catholics and the Social Order* (Notre Dame, 1968).

he points especially to the one-sided Irish focus in American Catholic history to the neglect of the non-Irish and to the heavy emphasis on liberal Catholicism at the expense of the conservative nineteenth-century bishops. He deplores the total neglect of Catholic thought since World War I, (which his own work on the New Deal years in large part remedies), the lack of interest in the political attitudes and behavior of Catholics, and disregard of the political role of the church.[4]

Like O'Brien, Gleason, in his recently published reader, *Catholicism in America*, breaks fresh ground. In this first tentative and schematic effort to trace out the implications of the new Catholic history based on the available secondary literature, Gleason determinedly avoids the ecclesiological or episcopal synthesis in favor of a larger story that sensitively portrays the interaction between Catholicism and the United States. Except for the opening essay, "The Formation of the Catholic Minority," by the late Thomas T. McAvoy which was published in 1948 and Ellis' landmark essay of 1955, "American Catholics and the Intellectual Life," all the other selections appeared in 1960 or later, most are the work of laymen, and all but one are by Catholics. Arranged in more or less chronological order, the essays focus on general American problems as seen through a Catholic perspective and experience: the distinctive church-state tradition of American Catholicism, the education controversy, the acculturation of the Irish, the nationality problem and German Catholics, woman suffrage, pro-Germanism and American Catholicism during World War I, Catholicism and Americanism in the 1930s, and finally the current crisis of Americanization.[5]

The expanded visions of American Catholic history as projected by O'Brien and Gleason, only sketchily suggested here, hold forth great prospects. But there are additional options and areas which ought not to be overlooked if the new Catholic history is to fulfill its promise.

To a social historian with a major interest in immigration and urban history, it seems apparent that American Catholic historians have not yet settled upon stratagems to incorporate the newer ethnics into their story so as to portray the almost unique cosmopolitan sweep of American Catholicism. The "emotional taxation without representation" of non-Protestant America for which Henry May indicted the nineteenth-century Protestant Anglo-American old order has perhaps been practiced with zealous unawareness by Irish Catholics first at the expense of German Catholics and then at the expense of Italians, Poles, Portuguese, Mexicans and French Canadians.[6]

The diverse European and native American backgrounds that gave texture and character to the immigrant dispersions of the cities ought to be incorporated in detailed definition. Out of phase with one another and the main drift, these Catholicisms have been conditioned by different cultural timetables derived from their areas of origin. Indeed even in the case of the Irish, as Emmet Larkin and his students are demonstrating, the changing social character of Ireland in the nineteenth century, as teaching clergy multiplied, suggests an American Irish mix that has eluded the analyses of even the best historians. Rudolph Vecoli's careful investigation into the distinctive old country religious background of

4. David J. O'Brien, ''American Catholic Historiography,'' *Church History* (March, 1968), 37, pp. 82 ff.
5. Philip Gleason, ed., *Catholicism in America* (New York, 1970), *passim*.
6. See Rudolph J. Vecoli, ''Ethnicity: A Neglected Dimension of American History,'' in Herbert Bass, ed., *The State of American History* (Chicago, 1970), 70 ff.; Henry F. May, *The End of American Innocence* (New York, 1959), p. 122.

Italian immigrants present a striking contrast with the Irish experience, that has yet to be integrated into the American Catholic story. And most recently, Timothy Smith's description of the varied educational experiences of immigrants from eastern Europe and Victor Greene's explanation of the role of the Polish Catholic ghetto as a bridge between Europe and America forcing Poles to discover their own Polish past, need to be phased into the larger story.[7]

Historians will also have to show resourcefulness in employing a variety of research methods to recover the history of the family, a critical institution for registering religious experience, generational conflict and group continuity. Some forty years ago the classic historian of immigration, Marcus Hansen, asked his students at the University of Illinois to research their own family histories as term projects so as to personalize the anonymous histories of most Americans. Upon coming to California in 1962, this hstorian followed Hansen's example (without knowing it at the time) in his own classes with most impressive results. Recently, a number of historians with similar experiences have urged that this method of learning about the history of the family be expanded and that the results be collected and preserved in regional depositories for the use of scholars. Clearly, historians of Catholicism in America could employ this historical stratagem more broadly and effectively than any other in gaining an understanding of the quietly dramatic lives of ordinary people, which somehow has eluded the more formal canons of historical research. In addition, the new social and demographic history, finding its sharpest focus on the urban scene, promises to contribute to our understanding of family patterns and a whole range of institutions where the Catholic experience has been vital. Birth rate, death rate, family size, residential structure, geographical and social mobility, and additional social statistics based on the quantifiable data of census and church and municipal records would no doubt be as illuminating for the American Catholic story as for the colonial New England story that is being rewritten so effectively. "Far from destroying the Irish family, migration into London made family life all the more important as a source of an identity in a new and hostile world,"[8] writes Lynn Lees, in demonstrating statistically the remarkable cohesiveness of the Irish family under stress. What was true for nineteenth-century London merits investigation in American cities, where the Catholic social presence has virtually been ignored by historians, except as political stereotype. Indeed, James P. Walsh, for example, reminds us that during the Progressive years in the wake of the earthquake and fire of 1906, 116,000 of 143,000 San Franciscans reporting church membership were Roman Catholics, most of them Irish, while only 22,000 were Protestants. Yet when a leading historian of Progressivism does not hesitate to

7. Rudolph J. Vecoli, "Prelates and Peasants: Italian Immigrants and the Catholic Church," *Journal of Social History* (Spring, 1969), 2, p. 219; see Humbert S. Nelli, *Italians in Chicago 1880-1930* (New York, 1970), pp. 181 ff.; Emmet Larkin, "Church and State in Ireland in the Nineteenth Century," *Church History* (Fall, 1962), 31, pp. 294 ff.; Timothy Smith, "Immigrant Social Aspirations and American Education," *American Quarterly* (Fall, 1969), 21, pp. 523 ff.; Victor R. Greene, "For God and Country: The Origins of Slavic Catholic Self-Consciousness in America," *Church History* (December, 1966), 25, pp. 13-14. Also see Moses Rischin, "The New Mormon History," *American West* (March, 1969), 6, p. 49, for an introduction to the ferment occurring in the writing of the history of another group.
8. Moses Rischin, "Beyond the Great Divide: Immigration and the Last Frontier," *Journal of American History* (June, 1968), 55, p. 53; Lynn H. Lees, "Patterns of Lower-Class Life: Irish Slum Communities in Nineteenth-Century London," in Stephen Thernstrom and Richard Sennett, eds., *Nineteenth Century Cities: Essays in the New Urban History* (New Haven, 1969), pp. 359, 377.

casually describe San Francisco as a place "where . . . citizens of all shades of skin had shaken off their Puritan heritage and were busy enjoying themselves," it is quite clear that our urban pluralist past has yet to be explored or understood.[9]

Finally, by its very nature Catholic history implies moral commentary both on American Catholics and on the total American scene. Historians of American Catholicism, however cautious and circumspect, will have to risk assessing the influence of Catholicism and of individual Catholics upon the tone and structure of American life at various times and places. Clearly, this will involve some of them in roles as culture critics, roles that ought to prove congenial to Catholic religious sensibilities when disciplined by historical research. It is not fortuitous that William Shannon's iridescent study of *The American Irish* offers a superb criticism both of the Irish and of the United States, or that an entirely different kind of book, *Irish-American Nationalism, 1870-1890* by Thomas N. Brown, superbly illuminates an age in all its complexity by intensely focusing on a single problem.[10]

The danger which the new American Catholic history clearly faces is not the danger of the simplistic, a danger to which, unfortunately, many historians who rediscovered the problem of race in the decade of the *aggiornamento* too easily succumbed. The stories that the historians of American Catholicism or of America's Catholicism have to tell are complex ones that do not lend themselves to a formula. Theirs is clearly a mandate to "approach culture with confidence and charity" as Robert Cross, herald of *aggiornamento*, urged in his memorable book, *The Emergence of Liberal Catholicism in America*, published significantly in 1958.[11] In accepting the risks and the tensions of a cultivated schizophrenia, the price that all men and, above all, historians must pay for the freedom to be complex, the practitioners of the new American Catholic history are assured the greater audience which the story of the American Catholic experience merits.

9. Seamus Breatnac [James P. Walsh], "Should Irish Eyes be Smiling?" *San Francisco* (August, 1970), p. 28; George Mowry, *The California Progressives* (Berkeley, 1951), p. 1; see Jay P. Dolan, "Catholic Minorities in New York City," paper delivered at American Society of Church History session, Boston, December 29, 1970.

10. Philip Gleason, *Contemporary Catholicism*, p. xviii; William V. Shannon, *The American Irish* (New York, 1963); Thomas N. Brown, *Irish-American Nationalism, 1870-1890* (Philadelphia, 1966).

11. Oscar and Mary F. Handlin, "The New History and the Ethnic Factor in American Life," *Perspectives in American History* (1971), 4, p. 22; Robert D. Cross, *The Emergence of Liberal Catholicism in America* (Cambridge, 1958), p. 224.

The Greek Orthodox Church in the United States and Assimilation

By Theodore Saloutos*

The Greek Orthodox Church, or that branch of the Eastern Orthodox Church in the United States that ministers primarily to the spiritual needs of those of Greek birth or ancestry, for the greatest part of her existence resisted assimilation and emphasized the preservation of the Greek national identity. But this turned out to be a more formidable undertaking in a nation of many nationalities and religious denominations such as the United States than in Greece where the population was overwhelmingly Greek, the Church was a state church, and proselytism forbidden.[1] Owing to the unmanageable nature of the assignment, the irresistible pull of the American environment, the slenderness of her resources, differences from within and pressures from without, the Church within recent years has more or less conceded the futility of her earlier efforts.

In coping with this problem the Church has gone through some painful transitional stages: first, that of an uncompromising commitment to the preservation of the Greek national identity; second, that of recognizing that the young were being brought up in the United States and were Greek-Americans; and finally that of acknowledging that as a Church it was difficult to serve two masters at the same time, acknowledging that the Church had become an indigenous one, and admitting that the identity to be preserved was an American rather than a Greek one.

The commitment to the preservation of the Greek national identity was strongest during the years before and immediately after World War I, when immigration was at its peak and thoughts of returning to Greece were still in the minds of many. But the Church had allies in this endeavor, allies whose labors in some cases antedated her own. And these allies included the Greek colonies that emerged in the larger cities, the myriads of local and provincial societies, as well as the Greek American Progressive Association [GAPA] who waged tireless campaigns in behalf of the Greek language, Greek schools, and the Greek faith; the Greek language press whose very existence depended on having enough

---

* Theodore Saloutos, Department of History, University of California, Los Angeles.

[1] *American Hellenic World,* I (April 3, 1926), 4. Especially useful is the pamphlet in Greek by A. A. Iaochim, *The Dangers Facing Hellenism in America* (Boston, 1926), 75 pp. Much, if not most, of this material appeared in one form or another in the *National Herald,* the Greek daily liberal of New York. Walter F. Adeney, *The Greek and Eastern Churches* (New York, 1908), 332-339. See also Nicon D. Patrinacos, "The Greek Orthodox Church in America," *Yearbook 1970,* Greek Orthodox Archdiocese of North and South America (New York, 1970), 90.

Greeks in the country who could read the Greek newspaper; and the irrepressible Greek nationalists who orated long and vociferously on the need for preserving the Greek heritage.[2]

The attempt to discuss the role and influence of the Greek Orthodox Church in resisting assimilation and preserving the Greek national identity calls for a workable definition of both the Greek national identity and assimilation, and some indication of the criteria to be employed. Greek national identity, at least as used in this paper, is associated with the perpetuation of the Greek language, Greek faith, and customs and traditions considered Greek. Assimilation, on the other hand, is defined to include changes in the cultural patterns of Greeks or children of Greeks who came into contact with groups of other ethnic or cultural backgrounds.[3] Such a study, in its ideal setting, would call for numerous case studies relating to the influence of religion, mixed marriages, Greek language schools, naturalization, and the reactions of members of the second and third generations to the idea of preserving the national identity their parents and grandparents bequeathed upon them.

The first Greek immigrants brought with them a strong sense of national identity despite their predominantly peasant origins and inexperience with urban life, and before any Greek churches had been established. Pride in their national identity had been generated by the many years of Greek history that began in the ancient times and came clear down to the present; the folk songs they sang; the folk literature to which they were exposed; the religious and patriotic holidays they observed; and the accounts of oppression told them by their priests, teachers, and village elders. They brought these patriotic sentiments with them and they were reinforced in this country by the establishment of Greek churches, the reading of the Greek language press, the increase in the number of local and provincial societies, and the growth in the number of arrivals from Greece. Contrary to popular belief the history of the Greeks in the mind of the average Greek begins with his illustrious ancient forebears, and not with the outbreak of the Greek Revolution in 1821.[4]

---

[2] Seraphim G. Canoutas, *The New Problem of Hellenism in America* (New York, 1927), 26, in Greek; Mary Hatzidaki, *Our GAPA* (San Francisco, 1952), a pamphlet, in Greek. Two indefatigable champions of the use of the Greek language were Demetrios Callimachos for years the editor of the *National Herald,* and Speros Kotakis, the editor of the less influential *Kathemerini (Daily)* of Chicago. Typical Kotakis appeals for the use of Greek appeared in the Greek *Daily* of August 13, 1926 and April 21, 1931. See also *Loxias* of Chicago, April 16, 1910 and March 2, 1912. Theodore Saloutos, *The Greeks in the United States* (Cambridge, 1964), 96-117.

[3] Milton M. Gordon, *Assimilation in American Life* (New York, 1964), 60-93.

[4] William Miller, *Greek Life in Town and Country* (London, 1905), 42-43. A useful compilation on Greeks, their organizations, churches, and Greek thinking in the United States can be found in the 418-page issue of the *Monthly Illustrated National Herald,* XI (April, 1925), in Greek. Thomas J. Lacey, *Our Greek Immigrants* (New York, 1918), 13-21. *California* (San Francisco), November 10, 1917.

Loss of their Greek identity was a fear that haunted many immigrants before they reached this country, and continued to haunt them years after they arrived. This is what prompted them whenever they settled in certain areas in sufficient numbers to form Greek communities whose primary responsibility was to build churches and schools that would help ensure the perpetuation of their faith and nationality, their customs and traditions. Once the decision to form a church was made these same laymen, who organized the lay communities, petitioned the Patriarchate in Constantinople or the Holy Synod of Greece to assign a priest to them.[5]

The role of the Greek priest in preserving the national identity is clear. Of necessity he was foreign-born and educated in the Old World; he spoke Greek and no English, and was steeped in the customs and traditions of the parishioners. The springing up of Greek colonies, especially in the larger cities, did much to protect the cohesiveness of the group. Greeks, as a rule, also married within the group, especially in the earlier years, which, of course, assisted; but there were notable exceptions that totalled more than many cared to admit.[6]

The determination of the uncoordinated lay communities and churches to maintain the national identity of their members was reinforced by the exhortations of national apostles who came to the United States to plead with their compatriots to remain steadfast to the land of their birth, its customs and traditions; the belief of many, if not most, Greeks that their stay in this country would be brief; the temporary character that most of the churches, schools, and organizations had assumed; the involvement of many laymen and clergymen in the United States with the internal politics of Greece; the formation of feuding royalist and liberal factions; and the fact that the national ambitions of the Greeks had reached fever pitch after World War I.[7]

But exhorting the faithful to preserve their national identity was one thing, to succeed in accomplishing it was another. The internal problems the parishes faced, and the difficulties that the churches of any ethnic group encountered in the formative years were insurmountable. The Church did not have a reigning head until 1922 when the Archdiocese of North and South America was established, or more than thirty years after the first waves of newer Greek immigrants reached our shores. Each community was almost a kingdom unto itself.

[5] *Year Book of St. Constantine and Korais School, 1936* (Chicago, 1936), 1-5; *Greek Star* (Chicago), February 2, 1906; *Ibid.,* November 22, 1907; *Saloniki* (Chicago), December 20, 1913; *Ibid.,* October 10, 1914; *Ibid.,* August 21, 1915; *Ibid.,* December 11, 1915; *Ibid.,* March 18, 1916.

[6] Edward A. Steiner in *American Greek Review,* IV (September, 1926), 10; *California* (San Francisco), March 10, 1919; Ioachim, *The Dangers Facing Hellenism in America,* 7-8.

[7] Saloutos, *The Greeks in the United States,* 104-105 and 184-209; 61st Congress, 3d Session, Senate Document No. 748, Report of the Immigration Commission, IV, *Emigration Conditions in Europe* (Washington, 1911), 391; M. M. Davis, *Immigrant Health and the Community* (New York, 1921), 101-102; Edward S. Forster, *A Short History of Modern Greece,* 1821-1945 (London, 1946), 135-147.

There was no central, coordinating head. Many of the local church heads and warring factions within the community were greatly influenced by the political events in Greece; and what little leadership raised its head was vulnerable to the political winds of change.[8]

By the time a reigning head of the Greek Orthodox Church was designated for the United States in 1922, the Church was in too weak a position to head a drive to maintain the ethnic cohesiveness of her parishioners, and furthermore had to contend with anti-foreignism, intolerance, and isolationist sentiment. Such attitudes were inhospitable to any effort to maintain their group identity, language, customs, and traditions.[9]

The Church furthermore had problems of her own. Apart from her being identified with the political battles of Greece, for which she paid a bitter price, the Church was locked in mortal battle as a result of differences between priests and lay groups, feuding lay factions, hierarchs and parishes. Efforts to centralize the Church aroused the resentment of many who felt that this constituted an encroachment by the clergy on the prerogatives of laymen. The churches were built with the hard-earned monies of the immigrants who established lay communities to finance the building of these churches; and now the bishops and the priests were attempting to strip them of their rights as laymen. These internal divisions within the church and the community drove people away from the church and community.[10]

Relevant to these conflicts was the emergence during the 1920's of the American Hellenic Educational Progressive Association [AHEPA] and the Greek American Progressive Association [GAPA] whose programs went to the heart of the concept of national identity and its preservation. The AHEPA, the bulk of whose members belonged to the Greek Orthodox Church and which believed in soft-pedaling the idea of the Greek national identity, at least for the time being, advocated the naturalization of the unnaturalized Greeks, participation by Greeks in American community affairs, use of the English language in the business affairs of the order, and acceptance into membership anyone who believed in a Supreme Being whether he belonged to the Greek Orthodox Church or not. The GAPA, on the other hand, remained steadfast to the concept of the Greek national identity; it urged strict adherence to the Greek Orthodox Church, the preservation and strengthening of the Greek language schools in the United States, and made Greek its official language.[11]

---

[8] Archbishop Iakovos, "The Fifty Years of Life and Development of the Greek Orthodox Archdiocese of the Americas, 1922-1972," *Yearbook 1972*, Greek Archdiocese of North and South America (New York, 1972), 10-13.

[9] Vasileos I. Chebithes, *Ahepa and the Progress of Hellenism in America* (New York, 1935), 22-25.

[10] *Greek Press* (Chicago), October 26, 1933; *American Hellenic World* (April 3, 1926), 4; *Greek Daily*, April 13, 1928; *Ibid.*, October 10, 1928.

[11] Chebithes, *Ahepa and the Progress of Hellenism . . .*, 26-28; *The Ahepa*, III (November, 1929), 6; *Tribune of GAPA*, XXI (May-June, 1957), 16; Saloutos, *The Greeks in the United States*, 254-257.

The Church, whatever its strengths and weaknesses might have been, faced almost insurmountable difficulties in trying to ward off assimilation and maintain the Hellenic spirit. These included the Immigration Acts of 1921 and especially of 1924, which shut off one of the main wellsprings of Hellenism; the death in the United States of many who did not leave any children; the return to Greece, mainly in the years before and after World War I, of many of the most Greek-oriented immigrants; the pull of the American environment; the shortage of Greek language schools; the distances that separated many from their homes, the Church, and the schools; and the disillusionment and despair that set in following the Greek disaster in Asia Minor in 1922.[12] Eventually all these events had a countereffect and resulted in the waning of the Greek national spirit, and they were beyond the control of the Church.

The consequences of the immigration legislation of 1921 and 1924, which reduced the number of Greeks permitted to enter the country from the thousands they totalled annually to 100 and then to 307, are obvious. A significant source of supply for the perpetuation of Hellenism in the United States had been shut off.[13]

In the beginning the Church viewed the mixed marriage with great horror. For years priests denounced it as a threat to the Greek way of life, and pleaded with the young to remain loyal to the honored traditions of their parents and grandparents. As early as 1926 Bishop Ioachim of Boston estimated that roughly 20 of every 100 Greek families in the United States were involved in mixed marriages. Even if the great majority of the children born of such marriages were baptized in the Greek Orthodox Church and learned some Greek, it would be difficult if not impossible, he maintained, for them to be raised as Greeks because they would learn the language of their non-Greek mother, the children with whom they played on the schoolgrounds, the classroom, and the neighborhood. They were strangers to Hellenism while the father was away; and the disorganized state of the church, and the lack of Sunday schools did not help matters.

Even in the larger cities there were problems such as the distances from the churches and the schools, the time required to get to them, and the moral and physical dangers to which the children were exposed when they travelled too far from their homes. This, according to Bishop Ioachim, affected the lives of about 30 percent of all Greek families living in the larger cities, and the dangers of assimilation were great. He estimated that about 40 percent of the families were on the road to assimilation.

The Greek national identity received another severe jolt from the national disaster that befell the invading armies of Greece in Asia Minor in 1922, the collapse of plans for a "Greater Greece," and the gradual separation of many from Greek community affairs. Especially distressing to the nationalists was the

---

[12] *Year Book of St. Constantine Church and Korais School, 1936*, 47.
[13] *Annual Report of the Commissioner General of Immigration, 1924* (Washington, 1924), 24-25, 27; *Ibid., 1929*, 3; *Ibid., 1930*, 11.

growing number who joined non-Greek organizations and thus compromised with their patriotism, particularly that assortment of "deviates"—the cosmopolitans, members of Jehovah's Witnesses, and the Communists—who disregarded national ideologies.[14]

Chrysostomos, the Metropolitan of Athens who was asked to serve as the first Bishop of North and South America but who declined because he preferred to remain in Greece, had a good understanding of what the United States was doing to the Greeks. He recognized the powerful forces of assimilation at work to remodel them as elements of progress in the new land, but also reminded them that they "can be fine American citizens without ceasing to be Greeks." To maintain this national identity they had to cease their internal quarrels, concentrate on their national culture, and remain united behind the Orthodox Church. Even though they lived in the United States they were considered Greeks. "No force other than the Orthodox church will be able to save them in the ocean of the new world . . ."[15] But his counsel was in vain, as dissension and a medley of other forces were at work.

The bond linking the Church and her parishioners to Hellenism was further weakened by the "Great Depression" which by 1933 had reached alarming proportions. Greek churches in the smaller cities were forced to discontinue services because many parishioners had moved away in search of employment, and the remaining families were unable to support a church and a priest. For a time it appeared that the only parishes likely to survive were the stronger ones in the larger cities.[16] Survival in an economic crisis, in short, had become more of a problem than the preservation of one's ethnic identity.

Even the clergy who were accused of being self-centered and too concerned with their own personal interest to give much thought to the problems of the poor were blamed for the drift away from the Church and Hellenism. "What have the clergy done for the various victims of the depression?" asked one critic. "All other churches and various social organizations have established centers for the care and relief of the poor; only our glorious orthodoxy sleeps under the mandrake and satisfies itself with a few appeals and pompous pretensions. And what shall we say when, as we are told, clergymen are engaging in profitable enterprises, neglecting their high calling to become real estate and stock market manipulators."[17]

The threat to the Greek national identity was stated succinctly by the editor of one of the parish yearbooks when he wrote:

---

[14] Ioachim, *The Dangers Facing Hellenism in America*, 6-10; N. S. Kaltchas, "Philhellenism: Romanticism and Realistic," *The Ahepa*, III (October, 1929), 6-7.

[15] "An Historic Message to the American Greeks," *Illustrated Monthly National Herald*, IX (December, 1923), 23-24.

[16] *Greek Press*, September 28, 1933.

[17] *Proodos* (Chicago), September 30, 1933.

The barring of immigration, mixed marriages, the lack of churches in the small towns, the lack of adequate schools in the big cities, the division of Greeks here and in Greece into two fanatical political factions, the ever increasing complaints against the church and the nation, the utter liberty extended in this country, the so-called cosmopolitans, the students of the Bible, Communism, divorces, the inclination to slander and underestimate the administration of the affairs of the church, and the powers of the environment, are potent factors tending to bring about the destruction of our nationalism.[18]

Beginning with World War II and continuing down to the present the Church attempted simultaneously to revive an interest in things Greek and, especially after 1960, to respond better to the needs of her parishioners in the United States. Although in theory the Church still opposed assimilation and mixed marriages, her leaders started to speak more in terms of preserving the Greek faith, the Greek language, and the building of schools to teach the language, and less in terms of preserving the Greek national identity. But at the same time the Church was urging study of the Greek language, use of English was being encouraged in many of the parishes as a means of retaining some hold on the young and adults who did not understand Greek.

After 1965 and especially after 1968, when the Immigration Act of 1965 went into full effect, the fresh flow of immigrants into the country posed serious problems for the Church which found herself face to face with bewildered newer immigrants who spoke little English and were accustomed to a Church that was Greek, and the members of the second and third generations who were in control and who wanted greater use of the English language in the services and a Church more in harmony with the needs of an American society. Apart from the Greek language and the schools as cultural forces, the Church was stressing her religious role much more than the ethnic.

Perhaps nothing had done more to make the Greeks feel proud of their ancestry and help revive the Greek spirit in the United States than the heroic stand of Greece against the invading forces of Benito Mussolini in late 1940. Many who previously had hidden their Greek identity now came out into the open to say they, too, were Greeks, for Greece in the minds of many had become the Belgium of World War II. The publicity and sympathy showered on the Greeks as a result of their bravery, combined with the fact that Greece found herself on the side of the Allies instead of the Axis Powers brought sighs of relief and a form of recognition never enjoyed previously. This heroic chapter did more to restore ethnic pride and identity than anything that the Church or any other Greek institution could possibly accomplish.

Meanwhile, the Greek Orthodox Church, which had recognized the need for training American-born youth for the priesthood to meet the growing needs of the American parishes, established in 1937 the Holy Cross Greek Orthodox

---

[18] *Year Book of St. Constantine Church and Korais School,* 1936, 47.

Theological School in Pomfret, Connecticut which after World War II was shifted to Brookline, Massachusetts. The first class of Greek Orthodox priests educated in the western hemisphere was gradiated in 1942. Hitherto all the clergy in the 275 churches in the United States had received their theological training in Greece, Turkey or other countries.[19]

The original intentions of the founders of the theological school was a two-year preparatory program whose graduates would complete their training for the priesthood at Halki in Istanbul or at the University of Athens. But World War II made it impossible to send students to Europe for their theological training or to bring priests to the United States from Greece and Turkey as had been the practice. Consequently, the curriculum at Holy Cross was extended to five years and patterned after the theological schools of Europe. But it soon became apparent that the academic traditions of Europe were ill-suited for the needs of candidates who had graduated from American high schools. Hence the curriculum was extended this time to six years, and included a three-year college pretheological preparatory program designed to meet deficiencies in the liberal arts, especially the classics. As of 1965 some 292 students were graduated from the seminary, the bulk of them, 245, ordained as priests.[20] The training of American-born youth for the priesthood was an admission that the Church was responding to the needs of the American environment, as well as to the wanting of a new source of supply.

The ethnic identity of many Greek-Americans further was aroused by the activities of the Greek War Relief Association; the Order of Ahepa; the Marshall Aid program and the various forms of military and technical assistance provided Greece by the United States Government; the increase in the number of Greek-Americans going to Greece as tourists; the appearance of Greek theater, dancing, and singing groups in the United States; and the showing of Greek produced movies and American motion pictures featuring Greek characters and themes. And all this was occurring before the current interest in ethnicity had broken out in the United States during the 1960's.

When Iakovos was enthroned as Archbishop in 1959 the predominant philosophy of the ruling classes within the Church was that the Church in the United States was merely an extension of the Church of Greece, and the spiritual and cultural placement of children born into Greek families was "expected to be none other than that of the youth of the old country. It was . . . inconceivable that the children of Greeks would turn out to be anything but Greeks." Some of the "most avowed Greeks" discovered otherwise. " . . . We did not know— some of us did not want to know—that even in a pluralistic society such as America, the national identity of the young is American even though there was

[19] *San Francisco Chronicle,* June 6, 1942.
[20] *Yearbook, 1965,* Greek Orthodox Archdiocese of North and South America (New York, 1965), 59-60.

ample room for cultural survival to ensure family harmony and religious identification." In short, the Church until the late 1950's had not " . . . and could not assume her rightful leadership in matters pertaining to our identity as a religious and cultural community within the ethnic and cultural panorama of America. The pressures from within and without were too great for her to counteract . . ."[21]

Then things began to change. Beginning with the 1960's the leadership of the Church began to talk about the possible merger of the various Eastern Orthodox Churches in the United States, representing 18 different nationality groups, but it also recognized the formidable barriers that had to be overcome before this could be achieved. As yet no church was prepared "to abandon its own traditions and doctrines or even its own type of worship and accept a new one common to all."[22] This was an unusual pronouncement for a Church that had kept aloof from other Christian bodies and tried to keep "its immigrant flock on the ancient and narrow . . ."[23]

The mixed marriage continued to plague the Church. As late as 1961 the official position of the Church was: "The wish of our Church is that Greek Orthodox Christians be joined in wedlock only with Greek Orthodox. It is the only way possible to secure the perpetuation of our religious and national traditions and also peace and harmony in the Christian family."[24] Statistics bear out that the advice of the Church was not being respected.

MARRIAGES WITHIN THE GREEK ORTHODOX CHURCH, 1963-1971		
Year	Total Marriages	Mixed Marriages
1963[25]	4,025	1,132
1964	4,075	1,190
1965	4,383	1,259
1966[26]	4,393	1,405
1967[27]	4,332	1,640
1968-1969[28]	5,500	1,755
1969-1970[29]	5,101	2,358
1970-1971[30]	5,136	2,473

Although the percentage of mixed marriages performed within the Church increased from slightly more than 28 percent of the total in 1963 to almost 50

[21] Patrinacos, Yearbook, 1970, 90.

[22] New York Times, August 27, 1961.

[23] Newsweek, July 13, 1964, 52.

[24] 1961 Almanac, Greek Orthodox Archdiocese of North and South America (New York, 1961), 180.

[25] Yearbook, 1968 (New York, 1968), 111.

[26] Ibid., 1968, 111; Ibid., 1969, 113.

[27] Ibid., 1969, 113.

[28] Ibid., 1970, 69. The statistics are from September 1, 1968 to August 31, 1969.

[29] Ibid., 1971, 73. The statistics are from September 1, 1969 to August 31, 1970.

[30] Ibid., 1972, 60. The statistics are from September 1, 1970 to August 31, 1971.

percent in 1970-1971, these figures do not indicate the considerable number who married outside the Church. Marriages outside the Church normally were entered into by those whose ties with Greece had weakened and did not have expectations of inheriting property there. Those with close family ties in Greece, on the other hand, largely the more recent arrivals, and with expectations of inheriting property in Greece where the Church was a state church and where being a communicant was required by law to inherit property in the country, were more reluctant to marry outside the Church.

Passage of the Immigration Act of 1965, that went into full effect in 1968, brought roughly 86,000 Greeks into the United States between 1965 and 1971, and thus posed new problems for the Church which again was forced to contend with a growing number of parishioners who were unaccustomed to paying membership dues to the Church in Greece, which was a state-supported church, and who rebelled against what to them appeared to be the dehellenization of the Church.[31] These newcomers joined in with the critics of the older generation who resisted the elimination of Greek from the services, and who claimed that this would only result in the defection of those who did not understand Greek and would undermine the customs and traditions of the Church.

The church authorities mindful of the criticisms that had been levelled at it and in an attempt to strengthen the religious and cultural ties between communicants in Greece and the United States, voted to hold the biennial Congress of the Clergy and Laity in Athens in 1968. This was the first time the highest policy-making body of the Church met outside of the western hemisphere, and it met despite the political unrest in Greece and the travel restrictions being proposed by President Johnson as a means of easing the nation's balance of payments deficit. The Archdiocesan Council characterized the meeting in Athens as "a pilgrimmage . . . to tie the life of the church in America in with the Orthodox of the Old World. It will be a chance for us and our youth delegates to rebaptize ourselves in our tradition." Iakovos furthermore expected the Athens meetings to lend "assistance and support" to the ecumenical policies of the new Primate of the Church in Greece, Archbishop Ieronymos, which, whose predecessor Chrysostomos had opposed.[32]

Efforts to strengthen the ties between the churches in the United States and Greece obviously were not succeeding, and to many it was becoming obvious that the Church in the United States was becoming indigenous. Archbishop Iakovos urged the delegates to the biennial Clergy-Laity Congress in New York in 1970 to reverse a tradition that gradually was being reversed, do as the other Orthodox Churches in the United States had been doing, and switch to an English liturgy. This appeal was made amidst a growing anxiety within the Church over the efforts to maintain both a Greek and an American identity, and the problems

---

[31] Immigration and Naturalization Service, *Annual Report, 1971* (Washington, 1971), 54.
[32] *New York Times,* February 24, 1968.

that had been created for those who did not speak Greek and had entered into mixed marriages.

The American Primate had two recommendations designed to make the Church more relevant to its American surroundings: grant more "de facto autonomy" to the Archdiocese which would enable it to speak out on issues such as abortion, birth control and mixed marriages, something which until then had to be cleared with the Ecumenical Patriarch in Istanbul; and approve of an English translation of the Divine Liturgy and permission to use an abbreviated version of it.

The proposal to permit use of an English version of the Divine Liturgy took on added significance because of the action of the Russian Orthodox Church in Moscow in granting autonomy to a new Orthodox Church of America. The Russians hoped that this would serve as the basis for a single autonomous church of all Orthodox Christian Churches in this country. Iakovos himself had expressed hope of achieving such a unified church through the Standing Conference of Canonical Orthodox Bishops in the Americas which he headed, and originally criticized the Russian move as contrary to canon law.

More autonomy for the Greek Orthodox Archdiocese, it was believed, would facilitate eventual union with other Orthodox Churches, most of which had switched to English; a comparable move by the Greeks would eliminate a point on which their leadership had been challenged by the other Orthodox leaders.[33]

In what must have been the most reformist assembly in the history of the Greek Orthodox Church in the United States, the delegates to the 1970 Clergy-Laity Congress approved the substitution of English and other vernacular tongues for Greek in the liturgy, and endorsed the proposal for more autonomy for the Archdiocese of North and South America. Permission to use the vernacular "as needed" was viewed as "a bow to necessity," and a concession to those who feared that unless this was done, "The pews could be empty in a generation."[34]

Meanwhile the Greek press in Athens was greatly disturbed over what it construed as the "separatist tendencies" of the American Archdiocese. The actions of the New York Congress of the Clergy and Laity was viewed as part of a concerted drive to "de-hellenize" the Church in the New World. Even more disquieting was the move for "de facto" autonomy which was accepted as the first step toward the formation of an "autocephalous" Greek Orthodox Church in the western hemisphere that would be independent of the Ecumenical Patriarchate in Istanbul. Iakovos, however, denied that he was working for a Church independent of the Ecumenical Patriarchate in the foreseeable future.[35]

---

[33] *Ibid.*, June 30, 1970.
[34] *Ibid.*, July 5, 1970.
[35] *Ibid.*, July 4, 1970.

The furor generated by the resolution permitting use of the vernacular in the liturgy came as a surprise, because the English language had been used by an increasing number of parishes, depending on their needs, and was not something decided on the spur of the moment. "There are more than a dozen (translations) now in print, not to mention the fact that over a hundred priests have their own individual translations of the Liturgy as well as of the Sacraments and use them when they deem it necessary. Even during the tenure of the late Archbishop Michael (1949-1958), an English translation of the Liturgy was openly sold by the Archdiocese and . . . used by non-Greek understanding Greek Americans to follow the ritual and, on occasion, by priests for rendering certain parts of the Liturgy. The Archdiocese in the right and duty as the regulatory authority of public worship decided to draft a translation which alone would be authorized for use in appropriate circumstances. This for the purpose of curbing personal initiative which in the case of public worship can prove disastrous."[36]

The 1970 Congress also pledged the Church to deeper involvement in the area of social action. Although the Church had taken public stands on issues prior to this time, none of them came within the activist framework suggested. The increased use of marijuana and the proposed relaxation of the laws to permit its use was deplored. Members were urged to become involved in neighborhood organizations that welcomed minority groups and strove for racial harmony, to avoid violence and extremists of the left and right. Abortion was assailed as being out of harmony "with the life of Christ and a rejection of the most elementary and fundamental principles of faith." War was opposed "in Southeast Asia and in the Middle East, and wherever it may occur." Pornography was denounced, and citizens beseeched to "harness their intellects and energies to reduce to the absolute minimum the defilement of our environment."[37]

The decisions of the 1970 Congress brought sharp reactions from dissidents in the Greek communities of some of the larger cities, especially in New York where Greek was chiefly spoken. The Greek language press reported that the Congress voted to replace the Greek language with English which was a misinterpretation of what actually had occurred. Permission to use the language when needed was not replacing Greek with English. English was to be used in accordance with the needs of the parish, and the approval of the community and the Bishop.[38]

Looking into the future, which was what the Congress of Clergy and Laity attempted in 1970, was a novel experience. "Both clergymen and laymen prefer-

---

[36] Nicon D. Patrinacos, "The Truth About Our Historic 20th Historic Congress," *Orthodox Observer*, XXXVI (September, 1970), 6; *Daily*, April 21, 1931.

[37] *New York Times*, July 5, 1970.

[38] Isaiah Chronopoulos, "The Greek Language Tempest: A Disguised Blessing," *Orthodox Observer*, XXXVI (November, 1970), 10.

red the comfort of undisturbed waters, limiting themselves to sigh away their guilt whenever their conscience bothered them and to leave it all to the coming generation. Our Greek Church has in modern times been very partial to the present but has never had the courage to realize that without the future there is no present . . . ''[39]

In short, the Greek Orthodox Church faced the inevitable and finally conceded that it was unable to resist the forces of assimilation and preserve the Greek national identity as she once thought. And she conceded this very slowly and reluctantly, primarily in the years since World War II and especially since 1960. Throughout the years, however, the Church strove to maintain Greek language schools which in 1972 consisted of 409, 18 Greek-American Day Schools, and 38 Greek Language Classes for Adults.[40] Although they are a far cry from the hopes of the more idealistic, they nevertheless represented a concerted, if not an entirely successful, effort to preserve the Greek language. Despite the protests of dissidents among the older generation and the newer arrivals, the Church had no alternative other than the one it chose if it was to survive.[41] A Greek Orthodox Church more in line with American needs and consistent with the American experience has long been overdue.

---

[39] Patrinacos, *Orthodox Observer*, XXXVI (September, 1970), 4.
[40] *Yearbook, 1972*, Greek Orthodox Archdiocese of North and South America (New York, 1972), 76.
[41] *Washington Post*, September 5, 1970; *New York Times*, January 21, 1973, Section 4.

Religion and Ethnicity in America

TIMOTHY L. SMITH

THAT RELIGION AND ETHNICITY ARE INTERTWINED in modern urban and industrial societies is obvious, but the nature of this relationship and how it developed is not yet clear.[1] Recent studies of the religious aspects of cultural and social systems, particularly by anthropologists, have not yet freed historians from traditional notions about religion and ethnicity. Historians continue to believe that ethnicity is a synonym for nationality and that the religious and ethnic sentiments of immigrant minorities are anachronisms that must give way to the processes of modernization and assimilation.[2]

Although most European languages make it possible to use one word for what in English requires two—"nation" and "people"—ethnicity and nationality are not the same thing. Nationality is established by citizenship. Such varied modern states as Great Britain, Spain, the United States, Brazil, Yugoslavia, the Soviet Union, China, Czechoslovakia, and South Africa have brought under one government several peoples. The sense of peoplehood, moreover, which I take to be the essence of ethnicity, and the social structures that sustain it may flourish without reference to political nationhood at all, as until recently was the case for Jews, Gypsies, Sikhs, and American blacks.[3] In the late nineteenth century many observers expected the sense of nationhood to replace that of peoplehood, either through the "melting pot" as in the

This essay originated as one of six addresses on "The American Experience," delivered at the annual meeting of the American Historical Association in Washington, D.C., December 28-30, 1976 in celebration of the United States bicentennial. Three of these addresses—by Arthur Schlesinger, jr., Robert Kelley, and C. Vann-Woodward—were published previously in the bicentennial issue of the *American Historical Review* in June 1977. THE EDITOR.

[1] Robert Kelley, "Ideology and Political Culture from Jefferson to Nixon," *AHR*, 82 (1977): 531-62. For two beginnings at clarification by sociologists, see Harold J. Abramson, *Ethnic Diversity in Catholic America* (New York, 1973); and Thomas F. O'Dea, *Sociology and the Study of Religion: Theory, Research, Interpretation* (New York, 1970).

[2] For a study that suffers from these faults but deals perceptively with the fallacies of the assimilationist model, see John Higham, *Send These to Me: Jews and Other Immigrants in Urban America* (New York, 1975), 9-20, 202-09, 234-35. But see the essays by Josef Barton, William Galush, and Robert Mirak in Randall Miller and Tom Marzik, eds., *Immigrants and Religion in Urban America* (Philadelphia, 1977), 3-24, 84-102, 138-60.

[3] For an ethnographic survey of old and persisting identities, see John Geipel, *The Europeans: The People, Yesterday and Today—Their Origins and Interrelations* (New York, 1970). Meic Stephens has argued that only since about 1840 did language become "the symbol of nationality"; Stephens, *Linguistic Minorities in Western Europe* (Llandysul, Wales, 1976), xix-xx, passim. But see Pierre L. Van den Berghe, "Ethnic Pluralism in Industrial Societies: A Special Case?" *Ethnicity*, 3 (1976): 242-54.

1155

United States or through the suppression of ethnic loyalties by such policies as Russification, Magyarization, and Germanization. Events have demonstrated, however, that ethnicity is not an anachronism. The mobilization of ethnic groups in modern nations, whether among immigrants such as Finns in the United States or East Indians in Guyana or among peoples who, as the Welsh in Britain or the Georgians in the Soviet Union, are still largely resident in their ancient homelands, has aimed at the future, not at the past.[4] Whether in cities or agricultural regions, near their ancestral villages or in distant lands, modern ethnic movements function chiefly to protect or advance the economic, cultural, or religious interests of persons who, by reason of some combination of actual or supposed common origin, language, or faith, believe they constitute one people.[5] In the process of mobilizing these movements, leaders have often manipulated for immediate purposes the symbols of old national allegiances or invoked the ideology of new ones and thereby made notable contributions to nationalist movements in their homelands. But ethnicity and nationality ought not to be confused. The sense of inherited or acquired identity of the majority people was only one of several sources of the sentiments that sustained nationhood in Europe. The purposes of ethnic organizations in the emigrant *diaspora,* moreover, were far broader than the promotion or protection of an Old World political ideal, even though names such as "Serb National Defense League" or "Polish National Alliance" adorned their office doors.[6]

Following Emile Durkheim and Max Weber, sociologists have long stressed the interrelated functions of religion and ethnicity but, until recently, have also tended to regard both as artifacts of an outmoded past.[7] The title of Milton Gordon's instructive volume on "the role of race, religion, and national origins" in the United States conveyed both a conclusion and a prediction: *Assimilation in American Life.* Much of the point of Nathan Glazer's early contribution to the sociological analysis of ethnicity lay in his surprise—

---

[4] For historical works that make this point, see A. William Hoglund, *Finnish Immigrants in America, 1880–1920* (Madison, Wisc., 1960); and Josef J. Barton, *Peasants and Strangers: Italians, Rumanians, and Slovaks in an American City* (Cambridge, Mass., 1975). Also see David Lowenthal, *West Indian Societies* (New York, 1972), 144–77, 210–11; and Michael Hechter, "The Political Economy of Ethnic Change," *American Journal of Sociology,* 79 (1974): 1152–56, and *Internal Colonialism: The Celtic Fringe in British National Development* (Berkeley and Los Angeles, 1975), esp. 311–40.

[5] See the Introduction to Nathan Glazer and Daniel P. Moynihan, eds., *Ethnicity: Theory and Practice* (Cambridge, Mass., 1975), 18, 25. Paul R. Brass has described North Indian processes of ethnic-group formation out of varied kinds and degrees of shared economic interests, religion, and other cultural resources; Brass, "Ethnicity and Nationality Formation," *Ethnicity,* 3 (1976): 225–31. And Charles F. Keyes has argued that belief in shared descent is a crucial but often contrived aspect of functioning ethnicity; Keyes, "Towards a New Formulation of the Concept Ethnic Group," *Ethnicity,* 3 (1976): 202–06.

[6] Thomas N. Brown, *Irish-American Nationalism, 1870–1890* (Philadelphia, 1966), 85–130; Joseph Rothschild, *East Central Europe between the Two World Wars* (Seattle, 1974), 83–84; Mark Stolarik, "Immigration and Eastern Slovak Nationalism," *Slovakia,* 26 (1976): 13–20; and William Galush, "American Poles and the New Poland: An Example of Change in Ethnic Orientation," *Ethnicity,* 1 (1974): 216–19.

[7] Weber, "Ethnic Groups," in Talcott Parsons *et al.,* eds., *Theories of Society,* 1 (Glencoe, Ill., 1961): 305–09; and Durkheim, *On Morality and Society: Selected Writings,* ed. Robert N. Bellah (Chicago, 1973), ix–x, 222–23. Also see W. Lloyd Warner and Leo Srole, *The Social Systems of American Ethnic Groups* (New Haven, 1945), 156–61, 283–96; and Will Herberg, *Protestant-Catholic-Jew: An Essay in Religious Sociology* (rev. ed., New York, 1960).

shared by the academic community generally—that it had persisted.[8] In the late 1960s a flood of new sociological studies assumed the instrumental and, hence, plastic nature of ethnic affiliation and identity and, in a few cases, analyzed the interweaving of religious ideas, customs, and institutions with the choices and the chances of free persons.[9] Thomas F. O'Dea has recently revived Weber's use of the example of ancient Judaism (in contrast to Durkheim's use of Australian totemism) to demonstrate that systems of religious thought not only may serve to legitimize existing social arrangements but, through prophetic proclamation in a time of crisis, can help break the chains of custom by making new and revolutionary demands, dissolving myths, and declaring a transcendent ethic not identifiable with any existing society or social institution.[10]

The resurgence of ethnicity as a factor in United States politics during the 1960s—involving first blacks, then Chicanos, Puerto Ricans, American Indians, Orientals, and "white ethnics"—was only one manifestation, as British sociologist Michael Hechter put it, of a "resurgence of ethnic political conflict in the most highly differentiated societies." This resurgence challenged the prediction of Max Weber and Talcott Parsons that urbanization and industrialization would gradually erode belief in the sacredness of the "primordial" ethnic sentiments that flourish in "relatively undifferentiated social settings," making way for the formation of political associations by "individuals of similar market orientations." Hechter pointed out that the opposite has been happening: political movements in many advanced societies champion minority languages, promote "national" cultures, and generally seek to "legitimate new cultural forms in the guise of old ones."[11]

Certainly, the worldwide politics of peoplehood helped revive scholarly interest in the history of ethnicity in the United States.[12] My study of a pluralistic society in the Minnesota iron-mining country, begun with Clarke Chambers and Hyman Berman in 1962, yielded results that seemed to contradict prevailing historical dogma in complex ways and led us at first to the

[8] Gordon, *Assimilation in American Life: The Role of Race, Religion, and National Origins* (New York, 1964); Glazer and Daniel P. Moynihan, *Beyond the Melting Pot: The Negroes, Puerto Ricans, Jews, Italians, and Irish of New York City* (Cambridge, Mass., 1963); and Glazer, *American Judaism* (Chicago, 1957), 79–126.

[9] For key essays by many of the sociologists who produced these studies, see Glazer and Moynihan, *Ethnicity: Theory and Practice;* especially see, for the choices of the Chinese in Guyana and Jamaica to convert to the Anglican and Roman Catholic faiths, Donald L. Horowitz, "Ethnic Identity," and Orlando Patterson, "Context and Choice in Ethnic Allegiance: A Theoretical Framework and Caribbean Case Study," in *Ethnicity: Theory and Practice,* 114–18, 305–36. But see Harold J. Abramson, "On the Sociology of Ethnicity and Social Change: A Model of Rootedness and Rootlessness," *Economic and Social Review,* 8 (1976): 43–48.

[10] O'Dea, "Stability and Change and the Dual Role of Religion," in Bernard Barber and Alex Inkeles, eds., *Stability and Social Change* (Boston, 1971), 161–65, 172–77.

[11] Hechter, *Internal Colonialism: The Celtic Fringe in British National Development,* 312–14.

[12] This interest has been evident in the renewed vitality of the Immigration History Society, in the establishment of several university research programs (notably the University of Minnesota's Immigration History Research Center), and in the launching of the journal *Ethnicity.* For additional evidence, see Andrew K. Greeley, *Ethnicity in the United States: A Preliminary Reconnaissance* (New York, 1974); and George Brown Tindall, *The Ethnic Southerners* (Baton Rouge, 1976). Rudolf J. Vecoli has called for more attention to the subject; Vecoli, "Ethnicity: A Neglected Dimension of American History," in Herbert J. Bass, ed., *The State of American History* (Chicago, 1970), 70–89.

notion that developments there might not be typical. Two subsequent research projects and the work of a dozen graduate students have convinced me that the use of churches and synagogues to promote education and upward mobility as well as to define, rationalize, and revitalize ethnoreligious identity was not unusual but rather characteristic of the urbanization of both American blacks and migrating East European villagers, whether in cities near their birthplaces or in Rochester, Cleveland, Chicago, and Minneapolis.[13]

In light of this research America's "urban villagers," to use Herbert Gans's phrase, did not appear as resistant to change as Gans and others thought them to be, either in their new environment or in the village settings from which they came. John Briggs and Josef Barton have now offered persuasive evidence that rural villages in nineteenth-century Sicily, Calabria, and Transylvania underwent those social changes that are often labeled "modernization" or, perhaps less arguably, "urbanization" long before large numbers of their younger residents began to migrate to cities near or far away. With others I have concluded that such modernization also occurred in the Danube basin north of Belgrade, in the Austrian provinces of Slovenia, Galicia, and Bukovina, in Lithuania and Finland, and in that area that is now Eastern Slovakia and the sub-Carpathian Ukraine. Where these changes took place amidst a long-existing cultural diversity, the intertwining of religious feelings with ethnic interests and identities gave both to faith and to the sense of peoplehood a fluid and instrumental quality that was more future-oriented than backward-looking. Emigrants to the United States regrouped on this side of the Atlantic into larger aggregations that both preserved and revised inherited patterns of language, religion, and regional culture. These changes thus demonstrate a dynamic relationship between religion and ethnicity, not the static one that was long the model historians and sociologists followed.[14]

Anthropologists, who came late to the game of modern ethnic studies, seem at the moment to be leading it, in part because they have never discounted the functional significance of religion in culture. True, the first generation, whose

[13] I must here acknowledge my extensive debts to a group of student colleagues who have steadily shared their findings with me for a decade: Josef Barton, John Briggs, William Galush, Mark Stolarik, Matt Susel, Paula Benkart, Arunas Alisauskas, and Frederick Hale; most of their studies are cited below. For a brief report with little reference to the role of religion, to which I subsequently turned, see my "New Approaches to the Study of Immigration in Twentieth-Century America," *AHR*, 71 (1965–66): 1265–79. For my recent review of these issues, see "Native Blacks and Foreign Whites: Varying Responses to Educational Opportunity in America, 1880–1950," *Perspectives in American History*, 6 (1972): 309–36. For recent works—in addition to Barton's *Peasants and Strangers: Italians, Rumanians, and Slovaks in an American City*—that confirm our group's general findings about social mobility and, therefore, diminish the cogency of Stephan Thernstrom's *Poverty and Progress: Social Mobility in a Nineteenth-Century City* (Cambridge, Mass., 1964), see Thernstrom, *The Other Bostonians: Poverty and Progress in the American Metropolis, 1880–1970* (Cambridge, Mass., 1973), 76–176; and Thomas Kessner, *The Golden Door: Italian and Jewish Immigrant Mobility in New York City, 1880–1915* (New York, 1977), esp. 165–70.
[14] For two works that reflect essentially static views of southern Italian peasant culture, see Herbert Gans, *The Urban Villagers* (Glencoe, Ill., 1962); and Rudolf J. Vecoli, "Prelates and Peasants: Italian Immigrants and the Catholic Church," *Journal of Social History*, 2 (1969): 227–33. In comparison, see Barton, *Peasants and Strangers: Italians, Rumanians, and Slovaks in an American City*, 27–47; John Walker Briggs, *An Italian Passage: Immigrants to Three American Cities, 1890–1930* (New Haven, 1978), chaps. 1–3; and Eric R. Wolf, *Peasants* (Englewood Cliffs, N.J., 1966), 83–84. And see my "Lay Initiative in the Religious Life of American Immigrants, 1880–1950," in Tamara K. Hareven, ed., *Anonymous Americans: Explorations in Nineteenth-Century Social History* (Englewood Cliffs, N.J., 1971), 214–49.

works historians know best, was preoccupied with premodern village or "tribal" societies, in which the whole population shared one language and faith. But anthropologists have closely observed the manner in which religious and communal rituals regulated behavior, legitimized power, transformed group memory into ideology, and gave social meaning to each stage in the cycle of individual lives. They have found that pervasive symbols and the recounting or re-enactment of traditional stories drew together the conceptions each people held of the actual and ideal worlds. Yet the preoccupation of anthropologists with such homogenous communities, usually at a given moment in time, provided little impulse to challenge assumptions about the essentially static character of religion in premodern societies.[15]

After World War II the organization of new nations in Africa, Asia, and the Caribbean requiring the political integration of disparate peoples posed questions that prompted a different theoretical approach. Clifford Geertz, who studied Javanese religious cultures, and J. C. Mitchell, who examined the shifting character of tribalism in urban Zaire, have stressed the conflict between such new "integrative" states as Indonesia and what Geertz has called the "enduring structure of primordial identifications" rooted in religious as well as other aspects of primitive societies. Geertz's model and Harold J. Isaacs's development of it in *Idols of the Tribe* have proved attractive to historians and sociologists, in part, perhaps, because Geertz and Isaacs have not seriously disturbed the notion that sentiments that sustain both religion and a sense of unique peoplehood are archaic, even though surprisingly resilient.[16]

Recently, Abner Cohen's studies of African cities—initially of the Hausa community of Muslim cattle merchants in Ibadan, Nigeria—sparked a quantum leap in the sophistication of anthropological inquiry into ethnicity.[17] Following his lead, scholars have examined the pragmatic and often protean uses of ethnicity in widely varying urban settings and have demonstrated that ethnic movements are often a political phenomenon—a mobilization of cultural resources, in which religion is sometimes central, to serve immediate "interests" or goals. These scholars have explicitly rejected the static "primordialist" dogma of Geertz and Isaacs at the very moment when some American historians were finding in it a comprehensive rationale for ethnic

[15] For studies that depart from these assumptions, see Emerick K. Francis, *In Search of Utopia: The Mennonites in Manitoba* (Glencoe, Ill., 1955), 5–7, 15–39; Martin Halpern, *A Serbian Village* (New York, 1958), chaps. 2, 10; and John W. Cole and Eric R. Wolf, *The Hidden Frontier: Ecology and Ethnicity in an Alpine Valley* (New York, 1974). For comparison, see Clifford Geertz, *The Interpretation of Cultures: Selected Essays* (New York, 1973), 87–89, 126–29, 140–41. For a parallel definition of the basis of ethnicity with a psychoanalytic orientation, see Harold R. Isaacs, "Basic Group Identity: The Idols of the Tribe," in Glazer and Moynihan, *Ethnicity: Theory and Practice*, 29–45.

[16] Geertz, "The Integrative Revolution: Primordial Sentiments and Civil Politics in New States," in Geertz, ed., *Old Societies and New States* (New York, 1963), 90–114, esp. 114; Mitchell, *The Kalela Dance: Aspects of Social Relationships among Urban Africans in Northern Rhodesia* (Atlantic Highlands, N.J., 1956); and Isaacs, *Idols of the Tribe: Group Identity and Political Change* (New York, 1975), 38–46, 144, 147–48, 150, 162–65. Also see Edward Shils, "Primordial, Personal, Social, and Civil Ties," *British Journal of Sociology*, 8 (1957): 130–45; and Geertz, *The Religions of Java* (1960; reprint ed., Chicago, 1976), 1–15, 355–81.

[17] Cohen, *Custom and Politics in Urban Africa: A Study of Hausa Migrants in Yoruba Towns* (Berkeley and Los Angeles, 1969), 190–94. For the religious revitalization of 1951–52, see *ibid.*, 149–60.

studies.[18] Even those who found Cohen's stress upon the political functions of ethnicity too narrow for the cases they studied have emphasized that the boundaries of peoplehood were elastic, not fixed, and that a new religious commitment often marked an outsider's incorporation within a group.[19]

Along with these advances in anthropology, sociology, and social history, two other scholarly developments especially pertinent to the American experience prompt me to propose a new beginning. First, historians of Central and Eastern Europe, following the lead of Peter F. Sugar and Donald Treadgold, have elaborated the ethnoreligious diversities that underlay political change in the Habsburg and Russian empires and in the Balkans as Ottoman control receded. The pluralistic and dynamic character of the relationships among the varied peoples of these regions helps explain the easy acceptance of pluralism by their emigrant contingents in the United States.[20]

Second, both Jewish and Christian scholars have promoted a broad renewal of interest in Old Testament theology, partly because of the retrospective impact of the Holocaust upon Jewish thought and partly because of the herculean research of William F. Albright and his students. This theological revival has emphasized Jahweh's covenant to sustain a particular people, formed by their acceptance of his law and lordship, in all the immense challenges of their centuries-long *diaspora*. Recent works such as Emil Fackenheim's *God's Presence in History*, which grounds the culture of Judaism in the Exodus, and Jürgen Moltmann's *Theology of Hope* have underscored the contribution of Jewish messianism and Christian millennialism to the idea of progress. This wide-ranging scholarly effort to make biblical sense of "the reality we all live in," to use Geertz's phrase, has demonstrated afresh that both Judaism and Christianity have aimed to hold together what Geertz calls "ethos," which he defines as a people's view of "right" ideals for life, and "world-view," by which he means their understanding of social reality. Furthermore, both faiths have sought this union of ethos and world-view not simply in the ritualized practices and symbolic behaviors that have pre-

---

[18] Abner Cohen, ed., *Urban Ethnicity* (London, 1974), xii–xv, xxiii; David Parkin, "Congregational and Interpersonal Ideologies in Political Ethnicity," in Cohen, *Urban Ethnicity*, 119–27; and Edward Allworth, "Regeneration in Central Asia," in Allworth, ed., *The Nationality Question in Central Asia* (New York, 1973), 3–5. For the most incisive statement I have read of the political nature of ethnic mobilization, see Immanuel Wallerstein, "The Two Modes of Ethnic Consciousness: Soviet Central Asia in Transition?" in Allworth, *The Nationality Question in Central Asia*, 168–75. But see Judith Nagata, "What Is a Malay? Situational Selection of Ethnic Identity in a Plural Society," *American Ethnologist*, 1 (1974): 331–33, *passim*.

[19] For a discussion of the role of Pentecostal sects in the formation of the "Maragoli" group in rural Uganda, see S. R. Charsley, "The Formation of Ethnic Groups," in Cohen, *Urban Ethnicity*, 338–39, 344–49, *passim*. Also see Shlomo Deshen, "Political Ethnicity and Cultural Ethnicity in Israel during the 1960's," in Cohen, *Urban Ethnicity*, 282–85, 294–97, 302–06; and see Frederik Barth, Introduction, in Barth, ed., *Ethnic Groups and Boundaries* (Boston, 1970), 22–24, *passim*.

[20] Sugar, "The Nature of Non-Germanic Societies under Habsburg Rule," *Slavic Review*, 20 (1963): 16–24; Donald Treadgold, "The Peasant and Religion," in Wayne S. Vucinich, ed., *The Peasant in Nineteenth-Century Russia* (Stanford, Calif., 1965), 72–107; Emanuel Turczynski, "Nationalism and Religion in Eastern Europe," *East European Quarterly*, 5 (1972): 468–86; and Stavrou Skendi, *The Albanian National Awakening, 1878–1912* (Princeton, 1967). For a bibliographical account of recent interpretative trends, see R. V. Burns, *East European History: An Ethnic Approach*, American Historical Association Pamphlets, no. 425 (Washington, 1973).

occupied Geertz but in a set of remarkably persistent and rationally communicated ideas, to which the notion of a pilgrim people is central.[21]

Students of American ethnic history have scarcely begun to see the implications or to sift out and assimilate the results of this recent scholarship. The reconstruction of Jewish and Christian theology in terms of historical process is especially important to an analytical synthesis of the relationship between religion and ethnicity. That synthesis should concentrate upon immigrants from Europe because they came to this country in such numbers as to dominate the history of American ethnic pluralism. Although the injustices suffered by black, Chicano, Oriental, and American Indian minorities justify the multiplication of works on their sociology and history, the result is a growing cultural lag in scholarship. Recent studies of these "racial" minorities routinely analyze aspects of their ethnoreligious systems that sustain emerging social and political objectives, whereas scholars usually treat the religious institutions, cultural forms, and ideologies of immigrant Protestants, Jews, Catholics, and Eastern Orthodox Christians as backward-looking, dysfunctional, or arcane. This essay aims to redress the balance by focusing primarily on the role of religion among groups recently dubbed "white ethnics" and by pointing out resemblances to the way churches have sustained black and Hispanic-American ethnicity.

THE MOBILIZATION OF WHAT BECAME AMERICA'S IMMIGRANT PEOPLES began in most instances in their homelands, amidst a complex rivalry for economic and cultural advantage. Even in the Old World, the developing sense of peoplehood depended heavily upon religious identification, in some cases more so than upon language or myths about common descent. Migration to America, both before and after the United States became a largely urban and industrial society, produced three important alterations in the relationship of faith to ethnic identity: (1) a redefinition, usually in religious terms, of the boundaries of peoplehood, bringing folk memories to bear upon new aspirations; (2) an intensification of the psychic basis of theological reflection and ethnoreligious commitment, due to the emotional consequences of uprooting and repeated resettlement; and (3) a revitalization of the conviction, whether from Jewish messianism or from Christian millennialism, that the goal of history is the creation of a common humanity, a brotherhood of faith and faithfulness. The last two developments made the relationship between religion and ethnicity dialectical. Even while affirming that the unity of all mankind was the goal, intensified religious commitment defined more sharply the boundaries of subcultures and communities. In Western societies, both the confessional

---

[21] Fackenheim, *God's Presence in History: Jewish Affirmations and Philosophical Reflections* (New York, 1970), chaps. 1, 3; and Moltmann, *Theology of Hope, on the Ground of the Implications of a Christian Eschatology* (New York, 1967). Also see Eric Voegelin, *Order and History*, vol. 1: *Israel and Revelation* (Baton Rouge, 1956), ix, xi, 126–27; and Geertz, *Interpretation of Cultures: Selected Essays*, 87–89, 139–41, 126–27. For an opposite argument that rites, not beliefs, are central to a religion's social role, see A. R. Radcliffe-Brown, *Structure and Function in Primitive Society: Essays and Addresses* (New York, 1965), 153–65.

state churches and some of the most intensely pietistic and sectarian groups in
each of the major traditions—Catholic, Orthodox, Jewish, and Protestant—
have played a unifying role, even while ministering to regional, doctrinal, and
ethnic divisions. How this was so in American immigrant communities and
how it fostered that peculiar unity of opposites which John Higham has
recently labeled "pluralistic integration" urgently needs clarification.[22] This
essay seeks to illuminate these three fundamental alterations in the relationship of faith to ethnicity in the United States by illustrating their pervasiveness and significance. Since the alterations began in Europe, I must
begin by summarizing the religious aspects of the changes in culture, society,
and ideology that took place there.

Long before the first substantial migrations of any people occurred, a mobile minority composed of clergymen, peddlers, fishermen, government officials, and soldiers had already sensed that they were part of a cultural
community extending beyond their native villages and valleys. As the agricultural and commercial revolutions spread, moreover, "modern" ideas about
personal success, individual autonomy, work, and risk taking penetrated even
the most isolated European and Near Eastern villages. Conscription to the
armed services took young men to distant places for short periods; agricultural laborers journeyed from the mountains to the plains at harvest time; and
the expansion of trade first encouraged, then undermined, household industry. For decades, peddlers carted the new manufactured products across great
distances. During the nineteenth century the railroads turned this trickle of
goods into a torrent. The construction of railroads by wage labor recruited
from villages where no one had ever seen a steam engine transformed rural
economies and peasant perceptions of time and space. Meanwhile, the population explosion that began in the seventeenth century had prompted the
migration of peoples such as the Scots, Germans, Jews, Rusins, and Rumanians into nearby lands and villages. The resulting conflict and accommodation among groups intensified the sense of uniqueness and sharpened the
psychic boundaries that language, culture, and religion drew among peoples
who lived close together.[23]

Ethnoreligious diversity characterized many of the areas of Western Europe
that first sent peoples to America. Colonial Englishmen were highly conscious
of the religious and other cultural characteristics that distinguished them
from Scottish, Welsh, and Scotch-Irish Protestants and especially from the
Catholic Irish, whose migration to both English and American towns began

---

[22] John Higham, "Hanging Together: Divergent Unities in American History," *JAH*, 41 (1974): 5–28,
foreshadowed in its title a central point in his *Send These to Me: Jews and Other Immigrants in Urban America*,
240–42.
[23] Ian Charles C. Graham, *Colonists from Scotland: Emigration to North America, 1707–1783* (Ithaca, N.Y.,
1956) chaps. 1–3; Mack Walker, *Germany and the Emigration, 1816–1885* (Cambridge, 1965), 1–9; Laurence J.
McCaffrey, *The Irish Diaspora in America* (Bloomington, Ind., 1976), 60–61; Carlile A. Macartney, *Hungary
and Her Successors: The Treaty of Trianon and Its Consequences, 1918–1937* (London, 1937), 83–94, 200–12, 262–75,
356–62, 380–90; Sugar, "Nature of Non-Germanic Societies under Habsburg Rule," 16–24; and Gunther E.
Rothenburg, "The Croatian Military Border and the Rise of Yugoslav Nationalism," *Slavic and Eastern
European Review*, 43 (1964): 35–38, 42.

in the middle of the eighteenth century. Northern Ireland, source of both Catholic and Protestant immigrants, gave colonial America a Scotch-Irish Puritanism quite different from the English variety dominant east of the Hudson River.[24] German-speaking migrants from the Rhineland represented not only various Protestant communions—from Mennonites and Brethren to Lutherans and Reformed Germans—but, as time passed, Catholic and Jewish populations as well. Both of the latter groups came in large numbers from Bavaria in the decades before the Civil War. The Netherlands, whose Protestant and Catholic divisions were reflected in the earliest settlers of New Amsterdam, sent some Quakers and Mennonites and a large Dutch Reformed contingent to the Middle Colonies and, later, both Reformed Dutch and Catholic Belgians to the Midwest.[25] Laplanders—some by language Swedish and others Finnish—were, like the Swede-Finns from certain Baltic islands, Lutheran in religion. In the decades preceding mass migration to America, all of the Scandinavian peoples experienced extensive religious awakenings that heightened their sense of identity as Danes, Norwegians, Swedes, or Finns.[26]

Population expansion, resettlement of peoples, and intensified ethnic rivalry also characterized Central and Eastern Europe in the eighteenth and nineteenth centuries. Rumanians, Orthodox in religion and speaking a language rooted in both Slavic and Latin, spread northward over the Transylvanian plateau, complicating the cultural map of a region long occupied by German-speaking Saxons, Magyars, and an older native population whose ethnic and linguistic identity remains unresolved. Meanwhile, contingents of Carpathian and Galician Jews moved southward into Transylvania, while others fanned out into what is now Slovakia, Hungary, and Yugoslavia. In all of these regions, competition among peasants, tradesmen, and laborers for land and other economic advantages intensified the group loyalties originally defined by religion. Rumanian Orthodox chapels and fortress-like Saxon Lutheran churches still stand in separate sections of hundreds of Transylvanian villages; frequently, the same villages contain Jewish, Rumanian Greek Catholic, and (westward toward Hungary) Magyar Roman Catholic houses of

---

[24] On the general background, see Geipel, *The Europeans: The People, Today and Yesterday.* For Switzerland and Belgium, see William Petersen, "On the Subnations of Western Europe," in Glazer and Moynihan, *Ethnicity: Theory and Practice,* 177–208. R. J. Dickson has demonstrated that economic and not religious considerations provided the chief motive for Scotch-Irish emigration, but he has ignored the role of Presbyterian piety in mobilizing and sustaining their venture; Dickson, *Ulster Emigration to Colonial America, 1718–1775* (London, 1966), 24–25, 33–39. Also see Leonard J. Trinterud, *The Forming of an American Tradition: A Re-examination of Colonial Presbyterianism* (Phildelphia, 1949), 15, 30–31, 34–35, 71–72, 127–30, 137–38, 222–27, 261–64; and L. C. Rudolph, *Hoosier Zion: A Study of Presbyterianism in Indiana to 1850* (New Haven, 1963), 118–29.

[25] For careful essays on Lutheran, Reformed, Mennonite, Moravian, and Brethren immigrants, see F. Ernest Stoeffler, ed., *Continental Pietism and Early American Christianity* (Grand Rapids, 1976). Also see Henry S. Lucas, *Netherlanders in America: Dutch Immigration to the United States and Canada, 1789–1950* (Ann Arbor, 1955); and Eric Hirshler, ed., *Jews from Germany in the United States* (New York, 1955).

[26] Uuras Saarnivaara, *The History of the Laestadian or Apostolic-Lutheran Movement in America* (Ironwood, Mich., 1947); Florence E. Janson, *The Background of Swedish Immigration, 1840–1930* (Philadelphia, 1931). 167–221; and Einar Molland, *Church Life in Norway, 1800–1950,* trans. Harris Kaasa (Minneapolis, 1957), 2–3, 15–19, 35–41, 48–52.

worship. A similar pluralism emerged in the villages and towns of the great basin of the Danube north of Belgrade, called the Banat and the Batchka, and in what is today eastern Slovakia. In the larger Slovak towns, a small German Lutheran population (dating from the seventeenth and eighteenth centuries) profited from the special favor of the Habsburg monarchs. A strong educational program and the impulse to get ahead that migrants generally display enabled them to compete effectively with the far more numerous Slovak Roman Catholics. During the eighteenth and nineteenth centuries a steady stream of Rusin Greek Catholics poured from the Carpathian highlands into the vacant lands around the East Slovak villages; and into the villages and towns came Jews from the same area and Protestant and Roman Catholic Magyars from the south.[27]

Elsewhere in Eastern Europe not only the towns but many of the villages were cockpits of cultural, economic, and political rivalry among ethnoreligious groups long before mass migration to America began. In the Austrian province of Galicia, now southern Poland, Roman Catholic Poles, Greek Catholic or Orthodox Rusins (or Ukrainians, as some of them came to prefer to be called), and Orthodox and Hasidic Jews lived together uneasily in the same towns and villages. In the nineteenth century the government in Vienna counteracted Polish agitation for independence by supporting the communal enterprises of the non-Polish peoples. For similar reasons, the Prussian government usually supported German interests against the Polish population in Posen, Upper Silesia, and the province of West Prussia. Eastward in Bukovina and Lithuania, as in all of the long borderland from the Baltic to the Bosporus, the convergence of Catholic, Orthodox, and Protestant peoples and the rapid expansion of the Jewish population created similar rivalries. The tsarist government, insecure in its control over the western provinces, sought stability through Russification. Along the Dalmatian coast from Trieste to Dubrovnik, Catholic Slovenes and Croats and Orthodox Serbs likewise often lived side by side. Their exposure to Italian and Greek influences through the Adriatic ports as well as their proximity to the large Muslim populations in Bosnia and Herzegovina made the coastal as well as many inland towns and villages arenas of competing cultures. In all of these regions, economic rivalries accentuated the divisions that religion and language defined, as the

---

[27] For relevant sources on village backgrounds, see the citations in my "Lay Initiative in the Religious Life of American Immigrants, 1880-1950," 216-25. For the multi-ethnic character of village life, see Barton, *Peasants and Strangers: Italians, Rumanians, and Slovaks in an American City*, 27-47; Macartney, *Hungary and Her Successors: The Treaty of Trianon and Its Consequences, 1918-1937*, 75-94, 200-11, 251-74, 383-90; Oscar Jászi, *The Dissolution of the Habsburg Empire* (Chicago, 1929), 391-93; Jean Mousset, *Les villes de la Russie subcarpatique (1918-1938): L'effort Tchecoslovaque* (Paris, 1938), 17-26; David Friedmann, *Geschichte der Juden in Humenné vom 13. Jahrhundert bis auf die Gegenwart* (Beregsas, Hungary, 1933), 48-74; Marion Mark Stolarik, "Immigration and Urbanization: The Slovak Experience, 1870-1918" (Ph.D. dissertation, University of Minnesota, 1974), 1-54; and Paula Kaye Benkart, "Religion, Family, and Community among Hungariz..; Migrating to American Cities, 1880-1930" (Ph.D. dissertation, Johns Hopkins University, 1975), 1-58. For the study that supersedes other discussions of the general question, see Turczynski, "Nationalism and Religion in Eastern Europe," 468-71, 475-76, *passim*.

various peoples competed for possession of the soil and for commercial as well as agrarian markets.[28]

The ethnic mobilization of what became America's immigrant peoples began, then, in their homelands amidst complex economic and cultural rivalries. In each case the developing sense of peoplehood depended heavily upon a revitalization of religious faith and commitment. Religious awakenings helped define both the boundaries and the moral ideals of ethnic groups and thrust both townsmen and peasants toward the "modern" goals of autonomy, self-realization, and mobility that were crucial in the decision to migrate. The Irish national awakening, for example, may have helped generate and certainly drew inspiration from the "devotional revolution" which swept through Ireland and its emigrant colonies in England and America in the mid-nineteenth century. John Livingston's revivals, which "Presbyterianized" northern Ireland in the seventeenth century, had an effect upon the Scotch-Irish similar to that of the Wesleyan revival in England and the Pietist movements in Germany in the eighteenth.[29] The awakening of Serbian Orthodoxy—through which Danilo Jakšić, Bishop of Karlovac, marshaled cultural resources for the Serbian resurgence in the Croatian borderlands—roughly paralleled the invigoration of Carpathian Jewry by the intensely personal and communal piety of Hasidism. In the nineteenth century the Haugean and Johnsonian revivals among Norwegian Lutherans, the Ukrainian national movement that the Metropolitans of Lvov helped inspire, and the Slovak Catholic resistance to Magyarization also mobilized religious sentiments to serve ethnic purposes.[30]

Moralism, rooted in biblical teachings but made intensely personal in religious revivals, was an essential ingredient of modernization. The fashioning of "new persons"—involving new perceptions of individual worth, enlarged hopes for both this life and the next, and the internalization of moral

---

[28] For a comprehensive and thoughtful analysis of the ethnoreligious situation in Austrian Galicia and Russian Poland, see Keith Dyrud, "The Rusin Question in Eastern Europe and in America, 1890–World War I" (Ph.D. dissertation, University of Minnesota, 1976), 16–74 (forthcoming, Arno Press). Also see William John Galush, "Forming Polonia: A Study of Four Polish-American Communities, 1890–1940" (Ph.D. dissertation, University of Minnesota, 1975), 1–44; Erich Prokopowitsch, *Die Romanische Nationalbewegung in der Bukowina und der Dako-Romanismus,* Studien zur Geschichte der Österreichisch-Ungarischen Monarchie, no. 3 (Graz, Austria, 1965), 35–110; Ludvik Nemec, "The Ruthenian Uniate Church in Its Historical Perspective," *Church History,* 37 (1969): 371–86; Macartney, *Hungary and Her Successors: The Treaty of Trianon and Its Consequences, 1918–1937,* 356–62; and Smith, "Lay Initiative in the Religious Life of American Immigrants, 1880–1950," 214–49. Arunas Alisauskas has research in progress on Lithuanians in Europe and America.

[29] Emmet Larkin, "The Devotional Revolution in Ireland, 1850–1875," *AHR,* 77 (1972): 636–52; Trinterud, *Colonial Presbyterianism,* 170; Bernard Semmel, *The Methodist Revolution* (New York, 1973), 3–40, 81–108; and Donald F. Durnbaugh, "The Brethren in Early American Church Life," in Stoeffler, *Continental Pietism and Early American Christianity,* 222–32. For an absorbing commentary on the issues Larkin has raised, see David W. Miller, "Irish Catholicism and the Great Famine," *Journal of Social History,* 9 (1975): 81–98.

[30] Turczynski, "Nationalism and Religion in Eastern Europe," 473–76; Gershom Scholem, *Major Trends in Jewish Mysticism* (New York, 1961), 325–50; Molland, *Church Life in Norway, 1800–1950,* 10, 19; Ivan L. Rudnytsky, "The Role of the Ukraine in Modern History," *Slavic Review,* 22 (1963): 203–15; and A. Hlinka, "The Influence of Religion and Catholicism on States and Individuals," in R. W. Seton-Watson, ed., *Slovakia Then and Now: A Political Survey* (London, 1931), 168.

constraints calculated to help converts realize these hopes—seems to have been the primary aim of all religious awakenings. Bernard Semmel has recently argued that John Wesley's lifelong battle against the "antinomian tendencies" of the Reformation doctrines of predestination and of justification "by faith alone" and his immensely complex recasting of Anglican, Arminian, and Moravian teachings stemmed from Wesley's conviction that biblical faith aimed at "holiness"—the moral regeneration of both individuals and societies. Earlier, George M. Stephenson and Einar Molland pointed out that Methodist moralism was critical in early nineteenth-century Swedish and Norwegian revivals, even though Wesley's sect itself won few adherents.[31] The timing and indigenous character of European movements for temperance or total abstinence from alcoholic beverages in the nineteenth century is one clue to the nature of the revitalizations that took place.[32]

Regional religious organizations both sustained and restricted cultural awakenings. In Central and Eastern Europe, for example, long before other agencies of modernization—railroads, newspapers, industrial employment, and the like—began deeply to affect group consciousness in isolated villages, the various religious communities—Roman and Greek Catholic, Lutheran, Reformed, Eastern Orthodox, and Jewish—had fashioned hierarchies of communication or authority that sustained the efforts of pastors, priests, rabbis, and lay leaders to help the members of local congregations find in their faith the moral resources to take advantage of a world of enlarging opportunities. By the nineteenth century, these competitive ethnoreligious structures functioned much like American denominations and were the administrative units with which national or imperial governments dealt. In multi-ethnic regions, a single parish or synagogue often served a half-dozen or more villages, many of which contained sizable populations of other faiths. The pastor or rabbi moved from day to day and week to week across his broad territory, somewhat like an American circuit rider, attending to the needs of groups that in some villages were too small to meet anywhere but in homes. Nineteenth-century Lutheran bishops made regular official visits to Slovak congregations in the northern counties of the old Kingdom of Hungary, for example, as did Reformed bishops from Debrecen to their Magyar congregations in Slovakia and Transylvania. Both were concerned for the preservation of the language as well as the faith of these ethnoreligious communities and for the education as well as the economic advancement of the children. The structure of Jewish life, particularly of Hasidism, was too congregational to allow a formal hierarchy to develop. Yet certain rabbis or zaddikim were most frequently consulted on questions of behavior or belief, and all Jewish congregations

[31] Semmel, *Methodist Revolution*, 93–108, 191–98; and Stephenson, *The Religious Aspects of Swedish Immigration: A Study of Immigrant Churches* (Minneapolis, 1932), 116–17. Molland has noted the work ethic and the moral ideal of holiness in the Haugean reaction against Pietism; *Church Life in Norway, 1800–1950*, 10–19.

[32] Joan Bland has recounted the indigenous origins and convergence during the 1840s of Irish temperance movements in the United States and Ireland; Bland, *Hibernian Crusade: The Story of the Catholic Total Abstinence Union of America* (Washington, 1951), 9–17, 21–24. Also see Janson, *The Background of Swedish Immigration, 1840–1930*, 172–76. For an influential exposition of the term "revitalization," see Anthony F. Wallace, *The Death and Rebirth of the Seneca* (New York, 1969), vii, 239–340.

were preoccupied with the social welfare of their members. As a consequence, in many regions Jewish religious communities became as "denominational" as those of Protestant, Catholic, Orthodox, and Greek Catholic Christians.[33]

Through this variety of cultural awakenings, then, ethnic consciousness fortified by religious faith took hold of the imagination of many Europeans. It affected most the younger people, especially those with the earliest and best opportunities for schooling—precisely the group that provided the majority of emigrants to the United States. By the time they began to consider the possibility of migration, the interweaving of religious and ethnic feelings had become for many a deep-seated habit of mind.[34]

Anticlericalism also flourished in nineteenth-century Europe. Some of the most socially progressive emigrants were hostile to doctrines and rites that they felt impeded progress. But they were a minority. The great majority of Greeks, Slovaks, Swedes, Magyars, Lithuanians, and Rusins that settled in America perceived their pastors, priests, or rabbis as agents of progress.[35] In both the Old World and the New, clergymen provided moral guidance and spiritual comfort to families unable to sustain themselves on the land and dismayed by the manifold adjustments to a commerical or industrial economy. Pastors served as "spiritual advisers" to the many types of mutual benefit societies that spread through nineteenth-century Scandinavia, Germany, Sicily, Calabria, and the Habsburg Empire. They not only legitimized but sometimes, as in the case of the Norwegian moral revivalist Hans Nielsen Hauge, originated plans for the reorganization of economic life. Clergymen were interested in the social welfare of peasants, craftsmen, shopkeepers, and fishermen and served as spokesmen for ethnic interests that the policies of the English, German, Austro-Hungarian, and Russian governments seemed to threaten. As a consequence, many clergymen performed a role in the mobilization of cultural resources that married ethnicity to religion on clearly "modern" terms.[36] Such a role seemed even more appropriate in America,

---

[33] For the "denominational" structure of religious life in eighteenth-century America, see my "Congregation, State, and Denomination: The Forming of the American Religious Structure," *William and Mary Quarterly*, 3d ser., 25 (1968): 168–75. For nineteenth-century developments in Eastern Europe, see my "Lay Initiative in the Religious Life of American Immigrants, 1880–1950," 214–49. Also see Turczynski, "Nationalism and Religion in Eastern Europe," 468–75; and Scholem, *Major Trends in Jewish Mysticism*, 336–37, 344–47.

[34] Abramson has argued that "societal competition" among differing faiths was indispensable to the development of ethnoreligious identity; see *Ethnic Diversity in Catholic America*, 127–52.

[35] Timothy L. Smith, "Religious Denominations as Ethnic Communities: A Regional Case Study," *Church History*, 35 (1966): 207–26; Mary B. Trendley, "Formal Organization and the Americanization Process, with Special Reference to the Greeks of Boston," *American Sociological Review*, 14 (1949): 44–53; and Dyrud, "The Rusin Question in Eastern Europe and in the United States, 1890–World War I," 1833–89.

[36] Their role in mobilizing ethnic groups seems to fit exactly what Glazer and Moynihan have posited as probably the most vital function of ethnic leadership; "Introduction," *Ethnicity: Theory and Practice*, 18, 25. For a description of a comparable development in Ceylon in the 1950s, see Geertz, "Integrative Revolution: Primordial Sentiments and Civil Politics in New States," 122. For pastoral examples in Europe, see Bland, *Hibernian Crusade: The Story of the Catholic Total Abstinence Union of America*, 22–23; Walter J. Kukkonen, "The Influence of the Revival Movements of Finland on the Finnish Lutheran Churches in America," in Ralph J. Jalkanen, ed., *The Faith of the Finns: Historical Perspectives on the Finnish Lutheran Church in America* (East Lansing, Mich., 1972), 82–93; Stephenson, *Religious Aspects of Swedish Immigration*, 74–132, esp. 103–05; Molland, *Church Life in Norway, 1800–1950*, 10, 15–16; and Wilhelm Austerlitz, *Leben und Werken von Weitland Rabbi Dr.* [Mayer] *Austerlitz . . .* (Prešov, Slovakia, 1928), 8, 13, 15–16.

and the laymen who founded congregations here expected the clergymen whom they brought from Europe to perform it.[37]

THUS, THE THREE MAJOR ALTERATIONS in the relationship between ethnicity and religion that took place in America extended and intensified what had begun in Europe. The first of these, to which I now turn, was the redefinition of ethnic boundaries in religious terms. This involved a broadening of the geographic and linguistic backgrounds of persons deemed suitable for inclusion and frequently a decisive narrowing of religious ones.

That this nation's ethnic groups, viewed structurally, were made in America by the voluntary association of newcomers has long been evident.[38] Less clear is the fact that the models for this development had emerged earlier in the multi-ethnic arenas of Europe. What in premodern societies had been the experience of wandering tradesmen, scholars, soldiers, government officials, and religious pilgrims—discovering far from their home villages persons similar to themselves in language, cult, or custom and accepting them as "brothers and sisters" of presumed common descent—became routine among migrants to America. Ethnic organizations coalesced out of both economic and psychic need and found meanings for personal and communal life in the cultural symbols and the religious ideas that their leaders believed were marks of a shared inheritance and, hence, of a common peoplehood. Both the structure and the culture of these emerging ethnoreligious groups helped participants compete more advantageously with members of other groups. And, once established, each group constituted—in Milton Gordon's classic terms—a social system in which the members could satisfy all of their needs for structured human relationships from the cradle to the grave.[39] The Ameri-

---

[37] For a penetrating revision of long-held views, see Josef J. Barton, "Religion and Cultural Change in Czech Immigrant Communities," in Miller and Marzik, *Immigrants and Religion in Urban America*, 9-10, 14-15, 17. For other examples demonstrating that the transfer to America was often direct, see Arthur J. Goren, *New York Jews and the Quest for Community* (New York, 1970), 76-85; Stephenson, *Religious Aspects of Swedish Immigration*, 264-77, 384-94; Jay P. Dolan, *The Immigrant Church: New York's Irish and German Catholics, 1815-1865* (Baltimore, 1975), 64-66, 81-84, and *Catholic Revivalism in the United States, 1830-1900* (South Bend, Ind., 1978), 21-23, 35-36, 189-93; Bernard Coleman and Verona LaBud, *Masinaigans—The Little Book: A Biography of Monsignor Joseph F. Buh, Slovenian Missionary in America, 1864-1922* (St. Paul, 1972), 130-31, 184-87; Arlow W. Anderson, *The Norwegian-Americans* (Boston, 1975), 13-15, 95-98, 102-08; Gillian L. Gollin, *Moravians in Two Worlds: A Study of Changing Communities* (New York, 1967), 9-24, 165-216; Vladimir Kaye, *Early Ukrainian Settlements in Canada, 1895-1900: Dr. Joseph Oeskew's Role in the Settlement of the Canadian Northwest* (Toronto, 1964); and John Walker Briggs, "Church Building in America: Divergent and Convergent Interests of Priests and Lay People in Italian-American Communities," paper read at the Hopkins-Harwichport Seminar in American Religious History, 1975.

[38] See William I. Thomas and Florjan Znaniecki, *The Polish Peasant in Europe and America* (Chicago, 1918); Oscar Handlin, *Boston's Immigrants: A Study in Acculturation* (Cambridge, Mass., 1941); Hoglund, *Finnish Immigrants in America, 1800-1920*; and Philip Gleason, *The Conservative Reformers: German-American Catholics and the Social Order* (Notre Dame, Ind., 1968). Also see Theodore C. Blegen, *Norwegian Migration to America: The American Transition* (Northfield, Minn., 1940); Theodore Saloutos, *The Greeks in the United States* (Cambridge, Mass., 1964); and Rudolph J. Vecoli, "European Americans: From Immigrants to Ethnics," in William H. Cartwright and Richard L. Watson, Jr., eds., *The Reinterpretation of American History and Culture* (Washington, 1973), 81-112.

[39] Gordon, *Assimilation in American Life*, 34-51. For Gordon's more recent thinking, see his "Toward a General Theory of Racial and Ethnic Group Relations," in Glazer and Moynihan, *Ethnicity: Theory and Practice*, 84-110.

can communities were not simply transplantings of Old World political and religious loyalties but reasoned efforts to deal with new challenges. That the national movements in Slovakia, Lithuania, and Poland drew heavily for inspiration, leadership, and funds upon their countrymen in the United States ought not to distort our understanding of the differing cultural, economic, and political purposes of the organizations that the immigrants founded here.[40]

Formal affiliation, however, turned on personal choice. Ethnic association—here defined as residence in a boarding house or tenement, membership in a local or national mutual benefit society, or participation in a musical, dramatic, or recreational club—was determined largely by the immigrant's identification with a particular religious tradition.[41] The appeal of common language, national feeling, and belief in a common descent was sufficient in only a few minor cases to outweigh the attraction of religious affiliation as an organizing impulse.[42] Two problems of perception have obscured this fact: the preoccupation of historians and sociologists with the secular aspects of ethnicity and nationality;[43] and the unexamined assumption that the experiences of linguistic groups among whom no substantial religious divisions existed (Greeks, Poles, Italians, Slovenes, French-Canadians, Scots, and Chicanos) were typical of all groups. Scholars and journalists have written about a major religious segment of the German, Czech, Slovak, Hungarian, Arab, or Russian populations in America under the assumption that ethnic identity was defined by language, while largely ignoring another branch or branches of the same linguistic group whose ethnic life revolved around a different religious affiliation.[44]

[40] Stolarik, "Immigration and Urbanization: The Slovak Experience, 1870–1918"; Galush, "Polish-American Communities, 1890–1940"; Dyrud, "The Rusin Question in Eastern Europe and in America, 1890–World War I"; Arunas Alisauskas, "Religion, Ethnicity, and the Emergence of a Lithuanian Subculture in the United States, 1870–1900," paper read at the Hopkins-Harwichport Seminar in American Religious History, August 1974; and Timothy L. Smith, "Immigrant Social Aspirations and American Education, 1880–1930," *American Quarterly*, 21 (1969): 539–42. Also see Victor Greene, *For God and Country: The Rise of Polish and Lithuanian Ethnic Consciousness in America, 1860–1910* (Madison, Wisc., 1975), 85–99, 143–53.

[41] Several groups of graduate students and I have closely examined the marriage records of numerous immigrant congregations and the personnel records of the mutual benefit societies that supported them. We found that members of local ethnic communities almost invariably came from a wide variety of villages and usually from two or more regions in their homelands. Also see Vilho Niitemaa, "Emigration Research in Finland," in Michael G. Karni, Matti E. Kaups, and Douglas J. Ollila, Jr., eds., *The Finnish Experience in the Western Great Lakes Region: New Perspectives* (Turku, Finland, 1975), 31–33; Dolan, *Immigrant Church: New York's Irish and German Catholics, 1815–1865*, 72–73; and Walter O. Forster, *Zion on the Mississippi: The Settlement of the Saxon Lutherans in Missouri, 1839–1841* (St. Louis, 1953), 150.

[42] For the rich variety of ethnoreligious organizations of Arabic-speaking Americans, see Barbara C. Aswad, ed., *Arabic-Speaking Communities in American Cities* (New York, 1974). For other examples in which language and ethnicity are not correlated, see Keyes, "Towards a New Formulation of the Concept Ethnic Group," 202–04; and Petersen, "Subnations of Western Europe," 177–79. Also see Dell H. Hymes, "Linguistic Problems in Defining the Concept of Tribe," in J. Helm, ed., *Essays on the Problem of Tribe* (Seattle, 1968), 23–48. For a theoretical reconstruction of the whole problem, see Dell H. Hymes, *Foundations in Sociolinguistics* (New York, 1974), 18–19, 30–32, 45–53, 102–05.

[43] This preoccupation is especially obvious in the essays in Glazer and Moynihan, *Ethnicity: Theory and Practice* and in the papers presented at the Schouler Lectures and Symposium on Ethnic Leadership at Johns Hopkins University in February 1976. Oscar and Mary F. Handlin and Thomas Handlin have, moreover, virtually ignored religion; Handlin and Handlin, "The New History and the Ethnic Factor in American Life," *Perspectives in American History*, 4 (1970): 21–23; and Kessner, *The Golden Door: Italian and Jewish Immigrant Mobility in New York City, 1880–1915*.

[44] For one of the finer recent studies, see Kathleen Conzen, *Immigrant Milwaukee, 1836–1860: Accommoda-*

By its policy since 1920 of recording the "mother tongue" of the population, the federal Census Bureau has encouraged the notion that language was the bench mark of ethnicity. For their own reasons, the editors of foreign language newspapers have for decades declared this to be the case. Yet they, at least, knew that Norwegian and Danish were scarcely two languages, that Croatian and Serbian were closely related South Slavic dialects, that literary Ukrainian and Slovak were created in the nineteenth century in order politically to unite regional groups with diverse dialects, and that the dialects of northern and southern Italians were at least as dissimilar as Swedish and Norwegian.[45]

Consider, for example, the role of religion among Germans in America. Those who settled in colonial Pennsylvania were divided between the "church" party (Lutheran or Reformed), whose congregations also attracted settlers of those persuasions hailing from Switzerland or the Low Countries, and the "sectarian" groups which had Anabaptist or Pietist backgrounds. So sharp were the distinctions between these two general alignments and so insistent were the Mennonites, Moravians, and Dunkers upon their particular separateness that, if we stay with Gordon's functional definition, colonial Pennsylvania was the home of a half-dozen German ethnic groups. In the nineteenth century, large-scale immigration from Germany produced several new ethnoreligious communities: a Protestant one, bounded by the Missouri and Wisconsin Lutheran Synods; a Jewish community, the leadership of which soon passed to the Reform rabbis; a small but influential community of freethinkers, united in the *Turnvereine*; and the German Catholics. The organizational center of the last was not a separate church because Roman Catholic doctrine and structure forbade sectarian divisions; so the numerous local and national German Catholic mutual aid societies and their umbrella organization, the *Central-Verein*, provided a surrogate church and nurtured their sense of separate peoplehood.[46] Although in the twentieth century all of the German ethnic groups responded in similar ways to the political crises that the two world wars created in their relationship to other Americans, their segregation in separate parishes, clubs, and neighborhoods as well as the separate paths they took toward accommodation with non-German Protestants, Catholics, and Jews made the notion of a common German "nationality" important only

---

tion and Community in a Frontier City (Cambridge, Mass., 1976). In the chapter on religious developments, Conzen has dealt with both Protestant and Catholic Germans, but not with Jews. The same is true of Carl Wittke's chapter on Germans which also emphasizes free thinkers; Wittke, *We Who Built America: The Saga of the Immigrant* (rev. ed., Cleveland, 1964), 186–256.

[45] Meic Stephens has covered some of these differences from the point of view of a Welsh nationalist who considers all Gaelic speakers as one people; see *Linguistic Minorities in Western Europe,* xix–xx, 1–5, 479–552.

[46] For the early years, see Julius F. Sachse, *The German Pietists of Provincial Pennsylvania, 1694–1708* (Philadelphia, 1895). and *The German Sectarians of Pennsylvania,* 2 vols. (Philadelphia, 1899–1900). For splendid summaries, see John R. Weinlick on Moravians, Donald Durnbaugh on the Brethren or Dunkers, and James R. Tanis on Reformed Pietism in Stoeffler, *Continental Pietism and Early American Christianity,* 123–63, 222–65, 34–73. For the nineteenth century, see Conzen, *Immigrant Milwaukee, 1836–1860,* 158–67; Carl E. Schneider, *The German Church on the American Frontier* (St. Louis, 1939); Colman J. Barry, *The Catholic Church and the German-Americans* (Milwaukee, 1953), and "German Catholics and the Nationality Controversy," in Philip Gleason, ed., *Catholicism in America* (New York, 1970), 68–78; Gleason, *Conservative Reformers: German-American Catholics and the Social Order,* 14–68, 145–58; and Glazer, *American Judaism,* 22–42.

in the politics of foreign policy. By the 1920s the resistance of the separate German religious communities helped to abort plans for a German-American bloc in national elections.[47] The unity which Bismarck imposed on a religiously plural Germany turned out in the American setting to be neither socially nor politically feasible.

A similar sharpening of the religious boundaries of ethnic association took place among Magyar immigrants, whom other Americans often labeled, inaccurately, "Hungarians." After 1867 the Kingdom of Hungary conferred special privileges on minorities that accepted Magyarization in language and political loyalty, as did most of the Jews in the kingdom and scattered groups of Greek Catholic Rusins and Lutheran Germans. After 1903 the Hungarian prime minister extended this policy to Magyars and Rusins in the United States, secretly subsidizing congregations and newspapers whose leaders agreed to resist Americanization and to help keep their followers loyal to both the government and the religious organizations of their homeland. But the subsidies merely helped the Magyars in the United States do more conveniently what immigrants from other nations did on their own: develop increasingly separate ethnic communities—Catholic, Reformed, Lutheran, and Jewish—each sustained by a broad array of congregations, mutual benefit societies, and cultural associations. Until the 1930s, "Hungarian" synagogues stood aloof from both Reform and Orthodox rabbinical organizations; eventually, however, they did what some Magyar Catholics perceived at the outset was inevitable and became an ethnic subcommunity within a major religious tradition. Magyar Lutherans, most of whom joined the Missouri Synod, and the majority of the Reformed congregations, which accepted membership (and subsidies) from either the Presbyterian or Evangelical and Reformed denominations, followed a similar course.[48]

The Rusins, often called Ukrainians or Ruthenians, illustrate particularly well the role of religion in setting new ethnic boundaries. For decades the First Greek Catholic Union and its affiliated organizations defined the ethnic identity of persons of that faith so completely that Slovaks who had been Greek Catholics in Europe became Ruthenians in the United States. During the 1890s wholesale conversions of Greek Catholic Rusins to Orthodoxy in Minnesota, Pennsylvania, and Ohio produced virtually all the "Russians" who lived outside California before 1920, a situation only slightly altered by the arrival after both world wars of refugees more accurately labeled "Rus-

---

[47] Frederick Luebke, "Leadership among German Americans between the World Wars," paper read at the Schouler Lectures and Symposium, Johns Hopkins University, February, 1976, pp. 6–8, 23–25.
[48] Benkart, "Religion, Family, and Community among Hungarians Migrating to American Cities, 1880–1930," 59–101; *The Jewish Review and Observer* (Cleveland), October 17 and 31, 1913, p. 5, p. 3; Louis A. Kalassy, "The Educational and Religious History of the Hungarian Reformed Church in the United States" (Ph.D. dissertation, University of Pittsburgh, 1939), 23–26, 65–72, 132; Dyrud, "The Rusin Question in Europe and in America, 1890–World War I," 227–74; and records in the office of the Hungarian Lutheran Church, Cleveland. I differ with Herberg about the outcome of this process; see his *Protestant-Catholic-Jew: An Essay in Religious Sociology*, 72–98, 254–81. It did not constitute a prostitution of religious values to Americanism but in some ways was a fulfillment of their character and promise. Also see Harold J. Abramson, "The Religio-Ethnic Factor and the American Experience: Another Look at the Three-Generations Hypothesis," *Ethnicity*, 2 (1975): 163–77.

sian."[49] One of the few exceptions to the rule that faith defined ethnic boundaries in America was a third contingent of Rusins—those of both Greek Catholic and Orthodox affiliation—whose political aspirations were so powerful in both the Old World and the New that they, their prelates, and their priests were swept into the Ukrainian national movement.[50]

The consolidation of New World ethnicity and Old World nationalism in Boston's Albanian Orthodox community is almost a caricature of the prevailing pattern. Albania was originally Catholic in the north and Orthodox— under Greek bishops—in the south, but central Albania became Muslim as a result of the Ottoman conquest. In the 1890s nationalists in the south began pressing the Greek hierarchs for priests and a liturgy in their own language and for the early establishment of an independent (in Orthodox terminology, "autocephalous") church. Albanians living outside the country in Bucharest, London, Cairo, and particularly America soon accomplished what the ecclesiastical authorities refused to allow in the home country. In 1903 Fan S. Noli, a native of Thrace who had lived for a time in Athens, moved to Egypt, where he met Orthodox nationalists. Three years later they sent him to Buffalo, New York to assist in the development of an Albanian mutual benefit society. The next year a Greek priest in Hudson, Massachusetts refused to allow a funeral liturgy for a young Albanian nationalist on the grounds that all such persons were automatically excommunicated. The members of the Boston community were outraged, and they persuaded Noli, in order to have him become their pastor, to accept ordination at the hands of the Russian archbishop in New York. Consecrated archbishop, Noli made the Albanian Orthodox Church, formally declared autocephalous in 1919, the center of the Albanian national movement. He translated and published for worldwide distribution an Albanian liturgy, printed textbooks in the native language for use in homeland and American schools, and influenced Catholic and Muslim leaders in the New World to use the pulpit as a forum to promote both Albanian nationalism and the ethnic advancement of their countrymen who had settled in America. When the end of the First World War brought independence to Albania, Noli returned to a land that had never been his home to become one of its first prime ministers.[51]

Much additional evidence of the overriding influence of religion upon identity-formation among other ethnic groups does not need recounting here. I have written elsewhere of the duality of communities, one Christian and the

---

[49] Andrew J. Shipman, "Greek Catholics in America," *Catholic Encyclopedia*, 15 vols. (New York, 1907–12), 6: 745–49, and "Our Russian Catholics: The Greek Ruthenian Church in America," *The* [Russian Orthodox] *Messenger*, 42 (November, 1912): 664–67; Stephen E. Gulovich, *Windows Westward: Rome, Russia, Reunion* (New York, 1947), 124–35; Walter C. Warzewski, "Religion and National Consciousness in the History of the Rusins of Carpatho-Ruthenia and the Byzantine Rite Pittsburgh Exarchate" (Ph.D. dissertation, University of Pittsburgh, 1964), 118–39; Alex Simirenko, *Pilgrims, Colonists, and Frontiersmen: An Ethnic Community in Transition* (Minneapolis, 1964), 37–54; Dimitry Gregorieff, "The Historical Background of Orthodoxy in America," *St. Vladimir's Seminary Quarterly*, 5 (1961): 9–12, 41; and Dyrud, "The Rusin Question in Eastern Europe and in America, 1890–World War I," 136–69, 211–12.

[50] Ukrainian National Association, *Jubilee Book: In Commemoration of the Fortieth Anniversary* (Jersey City, N.J., 1933), 194–98, *passim*.

[51] Skendi, *Albanian National Awakening, 1878–1912*, 6–13, 158–63, 296–303.

other anticlerical or socialist, that emerged around 1900 among Catholic Slovenes and Lutheran Finns. A brief effort to unite all South Slavs in America on the basis of their common descent—as nationalists dreamed of doing in the old country—ran afoul of the Slovenes' belief that they were culturally superior to their fellow Catholic Croatians and the Orthodoxy of the Serbs. Meanwhile, Montenegrin immigrants and those Orthodox Macedonians whose language was Serbo-Croatian became Serbs in America. Slovaks of Catholic, Lutheran, Greek Catholic, and Presbyterian backgrounds managed to unite for a decade or so after 1890 in the National Slovak Society, whose strongly political ideology was conditioned by long resistance to Magyarization in the old country; but congregations and mutual benefit societies soon formed separate national religious brotherhoods that proved to be the decisive catalysts of ethnicity and, eventually, the major avenues of accommodation to a wider American identity.[52]

The very recent emergence of working unity among Catholic Hispanic-Americans illustrates the continuing role of religious affiliation in the evolution of the boundaries of ethnicity. To those Chicanos whose roots lay deep in the soil of the Rio Grande and lower Colorado valleys and in the southern California coastlands, the Anglos were the immigrants—but immigrants who held all the economic and political aces. The twentieth-century movements for social justice among Catholics, however, eventually produced in the American Southwest a band of nuns, teaching brothers, priests, and auxiliary bishops committed to promoting the welfare of Chicanos and of recent Mexican immigrants, whether in that region or in the shanty-towns that housed migratory agricultural workers from the Gulf states to Canada. This development roughly coincided with the emergence in eastern cities of a community of economic and political interests among groups of Catholics from Puerto Rico, Cuba, and other Latin American countries.[53] During the 1970s liberation theology and the quest of Cesar Chavez and others for political clout in the large states of California, Texas, Florida, and New York brought Chicanos and urban Hispanics together. They built their unity, however, within the scaffolding of relationships, beliefs, and social aspirations that they shared as Catholics. In October 1976 a Hispanic-American caucus exercised immense, though unpublicized, influence at the United States Bishops' Conference on Liberty and Justice for All, the first representative assembly of American Catholic clergy and laity held in the twentieth century. On the heels of that achievement, the Hispanic-American members of the United States Congress announced success in the long-frustrated effort to form a congressional caucus. If, as I believe, these developments affirm the mobilization of an enlarged

[52] Smith, "Religious Denominations as Ethnic Communities: A Regional Case Study," 210–24; and Mark Stolarik, "Building Slovak Communities in America," paper read at the Hopkins-Harwichport Seminar in American Religious History, August 1974.

[53] Joseph Fitzpatrick, *Puerto Rican Americans* (Englewood Cliffs, N.J., 1971); Leo Grebler, J. W. Moore, and R. C. Guyman, *The Mexican-American People: The Nation's Second Largest Minority* (New York, 1970), 453–57, 463–68; and Manuel P. Servin, ed., *The Mexican-Americans: An Awakening Minority* (Beverly Hills, Calif., 1970), 176–78, 188–92, 232–33.

and powerful ethnic entity, its political as well as its economic significance reflects the successful linking of ethnic interests to religious idealism in broad strategies that are as much Catholic as Hispanic.[54]

THE CUSTOMS AND BELIEFS of particular varieties of faith and the traditions of loyalty to them seem, then, to have been the decisive determinants of ethnic affiliation in America. The availability of religious structures whose rituals were rooted in the past but whose doctrines sustained expansive hopes for the future does not, however, fully explain the changing relationship of faith to ethnicity in the United States. A second important alteration in that relationship was the intensification of the psychic basis of religious commitment that the acts of uprooting, migration, and repeated resettlement produced in the minds of new Americans. The most important of the several enduring contributions of Oscar Handlin in *The Uprooted* is his evocation of the anxieties, both personal and social, that resulted from forsaking an old home and searching for a new community. An intense interest in the religious meaning of their break with the past lay behind the preoccupation of both clergy and lay emigrants with religious organizations; and this interest stemmed from formidable psychic challenges.[55]

The individual's sense of responsibility for the decision to migrate was primary here. Loneliness, the romanticizing of memories, the guilt for imagined desertion of parents and other relatives, and the search for community and identity in a world of strangers all began the moment the nearest range of hills shut out the view of the emigrant's native valley. Longing for a past that could not be recovered intensified the emotional satisfaction of daring to hope for a better future. Separation from both personal and physical associations of one's childhood community drew emotional strings taut. Friendships, however, were often fleeting; and the lonely vigils—when sickness, unemployment, or personal rejection set individuals apart—produced deep crises of the spirit. At such moments, the concrete symbols of order or hope that the village church and priest and the annual round of religious observances had once provided seemed far away; yet the mysteries of individual existence as well as the confusing agonies of anomie cried out for religious explanation.[56] For this

---

[54] This development is contrary to what Andrew Greeley expected only five years ago; see his *Ethnicity in the United States: A Preliminary Reconnaissance*, 295. My account is based on interviews with officers of the Mexican American Cultural Center in San Antonio. As a consultant to the Bishops' Conference on Liberty and Justice for All, I witnessed the immense influence exercised by the Hispanic-American caucus. Also see Jacques E. Levy, *Cesar Chavez: Autobiography of La Causa* (New York, 1975), 453–62; and Francis P. Firenza, "Latin American Liberation Theology," *Interpretation*, 28 (1974): 441–57. For eschatological, ecumenical, and biblical perspectives, see Juan Luis Segundo, S. J., *Liberation of Theology*, trans. John Drury (New York, 1976), 138–51, 228–37.

[55] Handlin, *The Uprooted: The Epic Story of the Great Migrations that Made the American People* (Boston, 1951). Harold Isaacs has seen the psychic intensity but not the theological implications of uprooting and migration; "Basic Group Identity: Idols of the Tribe," 34, *passim*. But such theological implications gave ideological and emotional stamina to ethnoreligious groups; see Timothy L. Smith, "Refugee Orthodox Congregations in Western Europe, 1945–1948," *Church History*, 38 (1969): 320–26; and Stanford E. Marovitz, "The Lonely New Americans of Abraham Cahan," *American Quarterly*, 20 (1968): 197. For comparison, see John A. Jackson, *The Irish in Britain* (London, 1963), xi–xii, 137, 142–44.

[56] For my brief discussion of this matter, see "Congregation, State, and Denomination: The Forming of

reason, I shall argue, migration was often a theologizing experience—just as it had been when Abraham left the land of his fathers, when the people of the Exodus followed Moses into the wilderness, and when Jeremiah urged the exiles who wept by the rivers of Babylon to make the God of their past the hope of their future.

Preoccupation with the ethical dimension of faith was one outcome of such uprooting. Once in America, immigrants uniformly felt that learning new patterns of correct behavior was crucial to their sense of well-being. Everything was new: the shape and detail of houses, stairways, windows, and stoves; the whir of engines, trolleys, furnaces, and machines; the language, facial expressions, dress, table manners, and forms of both public and private courtesy; and, most important of all, freedom from the moral constraints that village culture had imposed in matters monetary, recreational, occupational, alcoholic, educational, and sexual. Each immigrant had to determine how to act in these new circumstances by reference not simply to a dominant "host" culture but to a dozen competing subcultures, all of which were in the process of adjustment to the materialism and the pragmatism that stemmed from the rush of both newcomers and oldtimers to get ahead.[67] This complex challenge to choose among competing patterns of behavior affected immigrants in all periods of American history; and they persisted in dealing with it on religious terms. At the turn of the twentieth century, Father Paul Tymkevitch declared that the greatest need of young Rusin Greek Catholics was to acquire "habits"—patterns of behavior ratified by both conscience and example and imprinted by repetition, patterns that would make each person his or her own monitor.[68]

But which cultural home should a young man choose? The tradition-oriented group that had preceded him here from the old country and presented itself as guardian of a past he sensed must disappear? The value system of the Americanizing culture-brokers living on the fringes of his own community? The culture of what he perceived to be a "successful" immigrant group that

an American Religious Structure," 156–60. For examples from several settings of such sentiments, see Francis Asbury, *Journal and Letters*, ed. J. Manning Potts *et al.*, 1 (Nashville, 1958): 1, 8, 39–40, 72, 77, 123–25; Donald F. Durnbaugh, ed., *The Brethren in Colonial America: A Source Book on the Transplantation and Development of the Church of the Brethren in the Eighteenth Century* (Elgin, Ill., 1967), 229–31; Charlotte J. Erickson, *Invisible Immigrants: The Adaptation of English and Scottish Emigrants in Nineteenth-Century America* (Coral Gables, Fla., 1972), 73–74, 112, 127–28, 182; Alexander S. Salley, Jr., ed., *Narratives of Early Carolina, 1650–1708* (New York, 1911), 175–76; James W. C. Pennington, *The Fugitive Blacksmith; or, Events in the History of James W. C. Pennington, Pastor of a Presbyterian Church, New York, Formerly a Slave* . . . (London, 1850), 67, 77–78; and Levy, *Chavez*, 23–27, 35–39. Also see Herbert G. Gutman, *The Black Family in Slavery and Freedom, 1750–1925* (New York, 1976), 265–67.

[67] For my development of this point, see "A General Theory of Inter-Ethnic Relations among Peoples Migrating from the Old World to the New," paper read at the Hopkins-Harwichport Seminar in American Religious History, August 1974. Milton Gordon, in contrast with Victor Greene, has remained preoccupied with majority-minority issues; see Gordon, "Toward a General Theory of Racial and Group Relations," 101–05; and Greene, *For God and Country: The Rise of Polish and Lithuanian Consciousness in America, 1860–1910*, chaps. 4, 5, 8.

[68] For the Tymkevitch story, see Emily Greene Balch, "A Shepherd of Immigrants," *Charities*, 13 (1904): 193–94. Also see Gollin, *Moravians in Two Worlds*, 16; and Robert Mirak, "On New Soil: The Armenian Orthodox and Armenian Protestant Churches in the New World to 1915," in Miller and Marzik, *Immigrants and Religion in Urban America*, 139–40, 150–54, esp. 153.

settled here earlier than his own? One or another of the "native" American subcultures shared by persons of his religious faith? Or the secular and hence nonethnic culture of the wider "urban community," which he identified with mass communications, politics, popular entertainment, and a soulless economic order? When one personal crisis or another prompted fears of the dissolution of the person the young immigrant thought he had been, ordinary questions of behavior led into more profound ethical ones, setting the terms by which the religion of his forbears had to respond. Occasionally, the response was a radically perfectionist one.[59]

What Marcus Lee Hansen has called "immigrant Puritanism" owed virtually nothing to colonial New England. It was, rather, a predictable reaction to the ethical or behavioral disorientation that affected most immigrants, whatever the place or the century of their arrival. The surprising attraction of the nineteenth-century total abstinence movement to Irish, German, and Slovenian Catholics, as well as to Finnish Lutherans in Minnesota and Massachusetts, illustrates the force of that reaction.[60] Europeans sometimes complain that American religion is too much concerned with ethical behavior and too little with theological reflection. But to a nation composed of so many migrating peoples, action—right action—was the name of the game. The immigrant's religion needed both rule and the reformation of rules, both the law and the prophets.[61]

Once conceptions of identity and proper behavior had been wrenched loose from the past, the theological interest of new settlers moved naturally to a deep fascination with the future. From its colonial beginnings, the migration of bonded groups or the formation of such groups in the new land made the biblical imagery of the Exodus seem a metaphor for the American experience, not only for English Puritans and Russian Jews, but for Christian villagers of Catholic, Protestant, and Orthodox persuasions from all parts of Europe. If the last great wave did not find urban America to be the promised land, the

[59] Insofar as religious perfectionism has been pervasive in American religious life, its major social impulse lies here. For a discussion of this subject in a somewhat narrower framework, see my *Revivalism and Social Reform in Mid-Nineteenth-Century America* (Nashville, 1957), 103–47. For immigrant perfectionist responses, see Arlow W. Anderson, *The Salt of the Earth: A History of Norwegian-Danish Methodism in America* (Nashville, 1962), 12–17, 28–32; and Solomon Schechter, *Seminary Addresses & Other Papers* (New York, 1915), 42–43, 196–97. For Catholic examples, see Frederic W. Faber, *Growth in Holiness; or, The Progress of the Spiritual Life* (Baltimore, 1855), 1, 15, 34, 130–47; Dolan, *Catholic Revivalism in the United States, 1830–1900*, 178–79, 182; and Coleman and LaBud, *Monsignor Joseph F. Buh, Slovenian Missionary in America, 1864–1922*, 130–31.

[60] Marcus Lee Hansen, *The Immigrant in American History* (Cambridge, Mass., 1940), 97–128; Coleman and LaBud, *Monsignor Joseph F. Buh, Slovenian Missionary in America, 1864–1922*, 166–99, 226–27; James E. Brady, "Father George Zurcher: Prohibitionist Priest," *Catholic Historical Review*, 52 (1976): 426–29; Dolan, *Catholic Revivalism in the United States, 1830–1900*, chap. 6; "Temperance and Temperance Movements," *Catholic Encyclopedia*, 14: 482–93; and Smith, "Religious Denominations as Ethnic Communities: A Regional Case Study," 210–12. Also see the passage on "Moralism in American Jewish Life" in Joseph L. Blau, *Judaism in America: From Curiosity to Third Faith* (Chicago, 1975), 69–72; and Martin E. Marty, *A Nation of Behavers* (Chicago, 1976), 33–51, 158–79.

[61] For a discussion of the moral preachments of the *maggid* in late nineteenth-century London Jewry, see Lloyd P. Gartner, *The Jewish Immigrant in England, 1870–1914* (London, 1960), 189–91; and, for perceptive comments on the relationship of peasant society to an emerging "ecumenical" moral order geared to the "technical order" of urban civilization, see Robert Redfield, *Human Nature and the Study of Society: The Papers of Robert Redfield*, ed. Margaret P. Redfield, 1 (Chicago, 1962): 282–94.

vision of what William Ellery Channing called, in millennial and Protestant terms, "a Better Day" remained pervasive among them. Charismatic leaders in all ethnic groups were messianic and anticipated something like a New Jerusalem. Linking the American future with the Kingdom of God was not, therefore, an exclusively Yankee obsession, nor the Social Gospel a Protestant preserve. Jews of both Reform and Orthodox faith, radical Irish as well as Chicano Catholics, and Mormon converts from Europe (whose trek to the Great Basin Kingdom seemed at first a flight away from civilization rather than a pilgrimage toward a better one) have also been people of the dream.[62]

Out of this pervasive social idealism emerged a conviction among both Jewish and Christian groups that theirs were pilgrim peoples, who had by their own choice responded to a divine call and made a covenant to walk with God. Covenant theology, which Perry Miller has demonstrated was central to the Puritan "errand in the wilderness," turns up at least occasionally in the faith of almost every American ethnic group.[63] We are not surprised, of course, to find Dutch Reformed, Scottish and Scotch-Irish Presbyterians, French Huguenots, and Reformed Magyars voicing this theme; their heritage in the Genevan Reformation, whether filtered through the Westminster Assembly of Divines or not, is obvious. But when Mennonites and Pietist Moravians sing about it in colonial Pennsylvania and pioneer Baptists, German Lutherans, and Scandinavian free-churchmen in the Ohio Valley pick up the refrain, we must stop to listen. We hear echoes of the same conviction in the appeals of nineteenth-century Irish, German, and French Catholic missionaries to the Midwest and, later, in the pastoral addresses of Eastern Orthodox bishops. The doctrine of a people in covenant with God attracted individuals who in the American mazeway bonded themselves in faith with persons whom they would have regarded as strangers in their homelands.[64] Only in the last few decades have students of the ancient Near East discovered evidence that belonging in ancient Israel may have rested less on descent from

[62] Ernest Lee Tuveson, *Redeemer Nation: The Idea of America's Millennial Role* (Chicago, 1968); William Ellery Channing, *The Perfect Life* (1873; reprint ed., Boston, 1901), 116–19, 194–96, *passim*; and Coleman and LaBud, *Monsignor Joseph F. Buh, Slovenian Missionary in America, 1864–1922*, 186. Also see Max Vorspan and Lloyd P. Gartner, *History of the Jews of Los Angeles* (San Marino, Calif., 1970), 157; Francis, *In Search of Utopia: The Mennonites of Manitoba*, 5, 35–39, 81–86; William Mulder, *Homeward to Zion: The Mormon Migration from Scandinavia* (Minneapolis, 1957), 137–45, 149, 154–55, 163, 178; and Forster, *Zion on the Mississippi: The Settlement of the Saxon Lutherans in Missouri, 1839–1841*, 87, 134–36, 151–52.

[63] Miller, "The Marrow of Puritan Divinity," in *Errand into the Wilderness* (Cambridge, Mass., 1956), 48–98. But George H. Williams has suggested that immigrant congregations were not preoccupied with the future, but looked either backward or upward; Williams, "The Wilderness and Paradise in the History of the Church," *Church History*, 28 (1959): 6–7.

[64] Robert Friedmann, "The Doctrine of the Two Worlds," in Guy F. Hershberger, ed., *The Recovery of the Anabaptist Vision* (Scottdale, Pa., 1962), 110–13, 116–17; Gollin, *Moravians in Two Worlds*, 13–19; John F. Cody, *The Origin and Development of the Missionary Baptist Church in Indiana* (Franklin, Ind., 1942), 30, *passim*; Forster, *Zion on the Mississippi: The Settlement of the Saxon Lutherans in Missouri, 1839–1841*, 87, 134–36, 151–52; Armas K. Holmio, "The Beginnings of Finnish Church Life in America," in Ralph J. Kalkanen, ed., *The Faith of the Finns: Historical Perspectives on the Finnish Church in America* (East Lansing, Mich., 1972), 127–28; Simirenko, *Introduction to Pilgrims, Colonists, Frontiersmen: An Ethnic Community in Transition*; Henry Zwaanstra, *Reformed Thought and Experience in a New World: A Study of the Christian Reformed Church and Its American Environment, 1890–1918* (The Hague, 1973), 91–93; and George Dolak, *A History of the Slovak Evangelical Lutheran Church in the United States of America, 1902–1927* (St. Louis, 1955), "Epilog," 163. Also see Max Weber, "Ethnic Groups," 305–08.

Jacob than upon an act of commitment—that is, on the willingness of a
company of former slaves from Egypt and of persons who became their
confederates in the land of Canaan to own the Covenant of Righteousness and
call themselves Jahweh's people.[65]

Accompanying this fascination with a covenanted future was an extensive
personalizing of religious faith—a process frequently confused with making it
private or individualistic. True, the experience of uprooting and resettlement
was a remarkably solitary one, and the traumatic aspects of it affected each
person individually. The result, however, was not to make individual experience the measure of faith but to enlarge the sense of personal involvement in
one's religious community and in its systems of belief and prescriptions for
behavior. Immigrant congregations served diverse family, group, and individual interests. They were not transplants of traditional institutions but communities of commitment and, therefore, arenas of change.[66] Often founded by
lay persons and always dependent on voluntary support, their structures,
leadership, and liturgy had to be shaped to meet pressing human needs.[67] The
same was true of the regional and national ethnic denominations or sub-
communities which emerged in America. They had to justify themselves by
nurturing those morally transforming experiences that the whole membership
perceived to be "saving."[68]

Pastors, rabbis, and lay officers responded to this challenge to make religion
more personal by reinterpreting scriptures and creeds to allow ancient observances to serve new purposes. The nineteenth-century Protestant custom of a
weekly "social meeting" for prayer, testimony, and mutual encouragement
was not the creation of native-born Baptist or Methodist enthusiasts. Nor was
it a popularization of John Wesley's "class meeting." Drawing upon the
German tradition of Pietist conventicles, an immigrant pastor, Philip William

[65] For a summary of the scholarship of the preceding twenty years, see Edward F. Campbell, "Moses
and the Foundation of Israel," *Interpretation*, 29 (1975): 141–54.

[66] William Warren Sweet taught a generation of historians that revivalism made religion more individ-
ualistic; Sweet, *Revivalism in America* (New York, 1945), xi–xiv, *passim*. Also see William G. McLoughlin, ed.,
Introduction to *The American Evangelicals, 1800–1900* (New York, 1968); Marty, *A Nation of Behavers*, 15, 34.
But see Kukkonen, "The Influence of the Revival Movements of Finland on the Finnish Lutheran
Churches in America," 132. W. Clark Roof has argued that substantive commitment, not organizational
affiliation, should be the central conceptual concern in analyzing religious congregations; Roof, "The
Local-Cosmopolite Orientation and Traditional Religious Commitment," *Sociological Analysis*, 33 (1972): 1–
3.

[67] This is a key point in my "Congregation, State, and Denomination: The Forming of the American
Religious Structure." Also see Dolan, *The Immigrant Church: New York's Irish and German Catholics, 1815–1865*,
53–84; Briggs, "Church Building in America: Divergent and Convergent Interests of Priests and Lay People
in Italian-American Communities"; Daniel S. Buczek, *Immigrant Pastor: The Life of the Right Reverend
Monsignor Lucyan Bójnowski of New Britain, Connecticut* (Waterbury, Conn., 1974), 13–16, 18, 39–52, 63; and
Maxwell Whiteman, "Philadelphia's Jewish Neighborhoods," in Allen F. Davis and Mark F. Haller, eds.,
The Peoples of Philadelphia: A History of Ethnic Groups and Lower-Class Life, 1790–1940 (Philadelphia, 1973), 232–
37.

[68] Conzen, *Immigrant Milwaukee, 1836–1860*, 159–68; Vorspan and Gartner, *History of the Jews of Los Angeles*,
55–58, 154–64; Dolan, *The Immigrant Church: New York's Irish and German Catholics, 1815–1865*, 64–66, 75–77;
and Larkin, "The Devotional Revolution in Ireland, 1850–1875," 649–52. Also see Gotthardt D. Bernheim,
heim, *History of the German Settlements and of the Lutheran Church in North and South Carolina . . .* (Philadelphia,
1872), 205–24, *passim*.

Otterbein, fashioned the new institution on the eve of the Revolutionary War in order to cultivate "inward Christianity" among his parishioners. Two examples of shifting emphases in Jewish rituals stand out. The steady elaboration of the ceremony of bar mitzvah reflected communal anxieties about growing up in a pluralistic society that did not recognize the norms of the subculture. And the intensified observance of kaddish (prayers for the dead) testified less to the strength of tradition than to the deepening sense of the significance of individual life in a world of relentless change.[69] The many forms of religious revivalism, I have argued elsewhere, were not "individualistic" in the usual sense that term suggests; though they made faith a profoundly personal experience, their aim and outcome was to bind individuals to new communities of belief and action.[70]

Notions of pilgrimage and expectations of personal and cultural change magnified concern for a basis of moral and religious authority that could provide a sense of permanence to those adapting themselves to shifting social realities. Catholic and Jewish concepts of the authority of tradition, which in theory made the interpretation of biblical truth adaptive, gave place steadily to reliance upon the Bible itself. The result, however, was not to throttle but to enhance the freedom of immigrant pastors and rabbis to adjust faith and practice to new situations. True, the doctrine of papal infallibility—proclaimed, as chance would have it, in the period of greatest Catholic migration—attempted to freeze out innovative appeals to the Scriptures by asserting the ultimate authority of those traditions ratified by Rome.[71] During the same era Protestant fundamentalists, in a doubly ironic development, employed a largely new conception of the Bible's verbal inerrancy to promote innovations in millenarian doctrines as well as to protect other, older doctrines from the rise of scientism and religious modernism.[72] Immigrant congregations, however, were in the vortex of change and found custom and tradition—whether rabbinical, denominational, or pontifical—insufficient to chart their path through a world that seemed increasingly like Alice's moral Wonderland.

[69] For an incisive summary of the new—"modern"—meanings Czech peasants attached to old rituals, ceremonies, and festivals, see Barton, "Religion and Cultural Change in Czech Immigrant Communities," 10–11, 15. Also see Miller, "Irish Catholicism and the Great Famine," 87–93; and O'Dea, "Stability and Change and the Dual Role of Religion," 161–65, 171–72. For the Otterbein story, see Tanis, "Reformed Pietism in Colonial America," 70–72. My interpretation of Jewish rituals is based on a conversation with Lloyd P. Gartner in November 1976. For Irish resistance to the efforts of their priests to curb extensive wakes, see Dolan, *The Immigrant Church: New York's Irish and German Catholics, 1815–1865*, 60–62, 92.

[70] Smith, "Congregation, State, and Denomination: The Forming of the American Religious Structure," 174–75, and *Revivalism and Social Reform in Mid-Nineteenth-Century America*, 80–88. Also see Donald Mathews, "The Second Great Awakening as an Organizing Movement," *American Quarterly*, 21 (1969): 23–43; and Rhys Isaac, "Preachers and Patriots: Popular Culture and the Revolution in Virginia," in Alfred E. Young, ed., *The American Revolution: Explorations in the History of American Radicalism* (DeKalb, Ill., 1976), 138–40.

[71] For a wise review of the "progressive" view of scriptural authority which papal action suppressed, see James T. Burtchaell, *Catholic Theories of Biblical Inspiration since 1810: A Review and Critique* (London, 1969), 282–305.

[72] Ernest R. Sandeen, *The Roots of Fundamentalism: British and American Millenarianism, 1800–1930* (Chicago, 1970), 103–31.

As in the cases of migrating Quakers and Mennonites in colonial Pennsylvania, growing attachment of nineteenth-century ethnic denominations to the authority of the Bible stemmed from expanding perceptions of the relevance of its central principles to new situations.[73] Leaders of the Christian Reformed Church, composed of Dutch Calvinists who emigrated to the upper Midwest after the American Civil War, explicitly disavowed both Old World social customs and their own formal commitment to a literal interpretation of Scripture when they supported the prohibition movement. The broader biblical principle of love for one's neighbor and of responsibility to bear his burdens, they said, was in this case binding. For two decades Swedish Mission Covenant congregations in America were able to cooperate with the Congregationalists at Chicago Theological Seminary because Paul P. Waldenström, their spiritual leader in Scandinavia, had taught them to use the Bible to cast off Lutheran scholasticism. His progressive use of scriptural authority—which exactly paralleled that of America's mid-nineteenth-century social reformers—held back his emigrant coreligionists from fundamentalism, even though they were committed to preserving the "fundamental" doctrines of Christian faith.[74]

Major spokesmen for Judaism also displayed growing attachment to scriptural as against traditional authority. Isaac M. Wise, in a series of essays and addresses in support of Reform Judaism, appealed to the biblical prophets and to modern rational judgment in declaring that the Ten Commandments were the essence of the Torah. The "Law of Moses," comprising the body of the Pentateuch, "reduces to practice the fundamental concept of the Decalogue," he said, "and expounds and expands its doctrines"; but the detailed provisions of Mosaic law were binding only upon Jews residing in the Land of Promise. The Ten Commandments are, however, "eternal law and doctrine," Wise declared. Progressive and law-abiding Jews must decide in the light of both conscience and reason which of their traditional rules and customs would fulfill those principles in the lands of their wandering and lead them to "salvation by righteousness." Solomon Schechter declared at the dedication

---

[73] C. Norman Kraus, "American Mennonites and the Bible, 1750-1950," *Mennonite Quarterly Review*, 41 (1971): 320-23. Forster has recounted the crisis of discredited allegiances amidst which the Lutheran Missouri Synod's biblicism emerged; *Zion on the Mississippi: The Settlement of the Saxon Lutherans in Missouri, 1839-1841*, 75, 82, 173, 279, 464-66, 520. But see Milton L. Rudnick, *Fundamentalism & the Missouri Synod: A Historical Study of Their Interaction and Mutual Influence* (St. Louis, 1966), 68, 75-84. Armas Holmio and Walter Kukkonen have stressed the socially adaptive aspects of revivalist biblicism in Finland, but they have shown the potential for a rigid defense of the objective "word" that developed in one of the three branches of Finnish Lutherans in the United States; Holmio, "The Beginnings of Finnish Church Life in America," 112-17; and Kukkonen, "The Influence of the Revival Movements of Finland on the Finnish Lutheran Churches in America," 122-27.

[74] Zwaanstra, *Reformed Thought and Experience in a New World: A Study of the Christian Reformed Church and Its American Environment, 1890-1918*, esp. 220-23; and, for other evidences of a progressive adaptation of religious views, see ibid., 49-58, 239-50; Frederick A. Hale, "Trans-Atlantic Conservative Protestantism in the Evangelical Free and Mission Covenant Traditions" (Ph.D. dissertation, Johns Hopkins University, 1977), 143-53, 294-97; and Stephenson, *Religious Aspects of Swedish Immigration*, 106-09. For progressive implications of Scandinavian free-church migration, see Anderson, *Norwegian-Americans*, 95-108; and Blegen, *Norwegian Migration to America: The American Transition*, 131-52. For German Catholic progressivism, see Gleason, *Conservative Reformers: German-American Catholics and the Social Order*, 116-44. Also see Forster, *Zion on the Mississippi: The Settlement of Saxon Lutherans in Missouri, 1839-184'*, 53.

of the Jewish Theological Seminary of America in 1903 that "this country is, as everybody knows, a creation of the Bible, particularly of the Old Testament." And the Bible is "still holding its own," he continued, despite the rising influence of higher criticism, which Schechter called "Higher Anti-Semitism."[75]

Uprooted persons seeking a new community needed both a principle of authority and a dynamic and essentially "progressive" use of it. Their way of relying on Scriptures placed them in what had become the mainstream of American evangelical thought.[76] Even in the colonial period America was not settled by persons with radical religious views; either they were progressives or became so here. They were restrained from radicalism by the value they placed on their past and from reaction by their faith in a better future. In *Herzog* Saul Bellow expressed precisely one dimension of this American mood: "Personal responsibility for history, a trait of Western culture, rooted in the Testaments, Old and New, the idea of the continual improvement of human life on earth. What else explained Herzog's ridiculous intensity?"[77]

In such ways the acts of uprooting, migration, resettlement, and community-building became for the participants a theologizing experience, not the secularizing process that some historians have pictured. If George Gallup's pollsters are even remotely accurate in their recent finding that Americans are second only to citizens of India in the pervasiveness and intensity of their religious beliefs and practices, the myths of wholesale secularization are no longer tenable.[78] Migration into modernity may have finished off the hilltop gods of village, tribe, and monastic retreat; but it neither dethroned in Jewish minds the God of Israel nor destroyed in Christian understanding the lordship of Jesus over history. The folk theology and religious piety that flourished in immigrant churches from the beginnings of American settlement were not merely traditional but progressive. Belief and devotion were powerful impulses to accommodation and innovation; and both helped legitimate the behavior, the perceptions, and the structures of association that sustained the processes of change.[79]

[75] Isaac M. Wise, *Essays and Addresses* (1901; reprint ed., New York, 1969), 133–34, 151–52, 157, 159–63; and Schechter, *Seminary Addresses & Other Papers*, 36–37, 48–49. The ethical emphases in Wise's sermon on the character of Moses exactly parallel those of William Ellery Channing's sermon, preached forty years earlier, on "Jesus Christ, the Brother, Friend, and Saviour." For the text of the latter, see Channing, *The Perfect Life*, 238–40. For the importance of the Bible to Swedish Methodists, see Stephenson, *Religious Aspects of Swedish Immigration*, 118; and, for the centrality of biblical authority in Protestant social radicalism, see George D. Herron, *Social Meanings of Religious Experiences* (1896; reprint ed., New York, 1969), xiii–xxiv, passim.
[76] George M. Marsden, *The Evangelical Mind and the New School Presbyterian Experience* (New Haven, 1970), 99–100, 111–16, 142–50, 169–74; and Smith, *Revivalism and Social Reform in Mid-Nineteenth-Century America*, 101, 144, 147, 216–20. Jerry Wayne Brown has provided evidence that the most sophisticated and "progressive" biblical scholarship in New England emanated from evangelical Andover, though the structure of his book argues a Unitarian pre-eminence; see *The Rise of Biblical Criticism in America, 1800–1870: The New England Scholars* (Middletown, Conn., 1969), 46–63.
[77] Bellow, *Herzog* (1976), chap. 11.
[78] Peter C. Wagner, "How Christian Is America?" *Christianity Today*, 21 (1976): 12–16.
[79] See Seymour Martin Lipset, *The First New Nation: The United States in Historical and Comparative Perspective* (London, 1963), 140–41, 158–69. The religious impulse to innovation was, I think, one basis for the working-class political progressivism described by J. Joseph Huthmacher; see his "Urban Liberalism and the Age of Reform," *Mississippi Valley Historical Review*, 49 (1962): 234–39.

The role of Protestant evangelicalism among American blacks confirms that religion contributed in this progressive way both to the formation and to the ideology of ethnic groups. The situation of blacks differed dramatically from that of Europeans, Asians, and Hispanic-Americans, whose forebears came to this country by choice. Such memories as persisted of their African religious traditions were fragmented and suppressed as slaveowners denied them the freedom to choose their neighbors and companions and to follow their own ways and times of religious observance. Partly as a consequence of this imposed disorientation, the psychic and the organizational bases of the sense of peoplehood matured only in the nineteenth century, after generations of enslavement.[60] Emancipation rather than migration, therefore, was the watershed that separated their "new world" from the old. By the time of emancipation, however, their vanguard was explicitly committed to constructing a future out of materials borrowed from white Protestants, particularly from the evangelical Methodists and Baptists, who had secured their conversion and sanctioned, though sometimes reluctantly, their desire for separate congregations. Consequently, for decades Protestant blacks in America made their churches the center of their social life and of their efforts at ethnic—blacks called it "racial"—progress.[61]

But consider the ideas that black preachers, once free, made central to their exposition of biblical faith: the doctrine of God's providential rule over history; close identification with the exodus of a liberated people who they understood were chosen for service, not sovereignty, and by grace, not merit; the conviction that internalized moral law, a covenant of righteousness, was the only sure basis for social order; and the biblical—especially the New Testament—affirmation of human worth and personal identity in this world and the next.[62] Whether these elements in the theology of nineteenth-century blacks were in any part reconstitutions of ideas that had prevailed earlier in Islamic or other African religions is not, from the point of view of this essay, a crucial question. They were, in fact, aspects of the Hebrew and Christian faiths that most American immigrants also believed gave divine sanction and direction to their long pilgrimage toward a more just, happy, and humane tomorrow.

[60] Eugene Genovese, *Roll, Jordan, Roll: The World the Slaves Made* (New York, 1974), 16:-284. Herbert Gutman has pushed a fine point too far in positing a cultural system among slaves—or a racial element in their bi-culturation—that rested exclusively on the ties of family and kinship. He has, however, convincingly demonstrated that these ties were present and powerful. See Gutman, *The Black Family in Slavery and Freedom*, 260-64.

[61] For their ambivalence, see Leon F. Litwack, "Free at Last," in Hareven, *Anonymous Americans: Explorations in Nineteenth-Century Social History*, 142-51, 158-66. Also see E. Franklin Frazier, *The Negro in the United States* (rev. ed., New York, 1957), 338-53; Theodore Hershberger, "Free Blacks in Antebellum Philadelphia," in Davis and Haller, *The Peoples of Philadelphia*, 120-21; James W. St. G. Walker, "The Establishment of a Free Black Community in Nova Scotia, 1783-1840," in Martin L. Kilson and Robert I. Rotberg, eds., *The African Diaspora: Interpretative Essays* (Cambridge, Mass., 1976), 205-07, 214-19; and David M. Tucker, *Black Pastors and Leaders: Memphis, 1819-1972* (Memphis, 1975), 41-54, *passim*.

[62] See my "Slavery and Theology: The Emergence of Black Christian Consciousness in Nineteenth-Century America," *Church History*, 41 (1972): 497-512. For a sophisticated updating of the idea of the Exodus in black theology, see James Cone, "Biblical Revelation and Social Existence," *Interpretation*, 28 (1974): 422-40.

MIGRATION AND RESETTLEMENT, then, altered the relationship between faith and ethnic identity by redefining the boundaries of peoplehood and by intensifying religious reflection and commitment. But it also breathed new life into messianic and millennialist hopes for the unity of all mankind and consequently prevented the cementing of the new patterns of belonging into a permanent American mosaic. In a new nation faced from its beginnings with the problems of unity and diversity, the revitalization of religious convictions accentuated the claim of both Judaism and Christianity to universality and renewed the impulse, largely suppressed among Jews since the first century of the Christian era, to recruit all human beings into a common circle of faith and fellowship.

The idea of a common humanity stands at the center of all major Western religions, and each of the ethnosectarian versions of Jewish and Christian faith in America affirms it. The countercurrents were formidable, to be sure, and on many occasions proved the stronger. But from the beginning—recall Count Zinzendorf's dream of establishing in colonial Pennsylvania an ecumenical "congregation of God in the Spirit"—the conviction that ethnic religiosity is not enough, that biblical faith is both incisive and inclusive and celebrates both particular and universal values has been an important support to the integrative pluralism John Higham has recently described in more secular terms. The ethnic springs of modern American religiosity have given the national culture not a backwater of static dogmas and rituals but a many-channeled stream of conviction that mankind must become one people.[83]

A few illustrations, drawn from both dominant and marginal groups in each faith, must suffice. Reform rabbis in America revived the ecumenical view of monotheism, which in the Book of Genesis was associated with a migratory and pilgrim family, and linked it to reason, science, and progressive democracy. Isaac Wise unashamedly called their conception of the future identical to the Social Gospel's "Kingdom of God."[84] At an opposite pole, the most marginal Jewish sectarians, the *Hasidim*, revived mystical and messianic visions that, in their expectations of the future as well as their search for righteousness through spiritual devotion, likewise broke out of the constraints that rabbinical Judaism sought everywhere to maintain. Thus, in both Reform Judaism and Hasidism, universalism sprang not from the denial of themes that had long been integral to Jewish religious thought but from an enlarged emphasis upon them.[85]

Originally, Christianity was a Jewish sect. Jesus' "good news" was to fulfill

---

[83] David J. O'Brien has stressed the ideal of universal human brotherhood, as opposed to class or national interests, in Dorothy Day's Catholic Worker movement; O'Brien, *American Catholics and Social Reform: The New Deal Years* (New York, 1968), 201–04, 221–27. On Zinzendorf, see Gollin, *Moravians in Two Worlds*, 18–19; and Jacob John Sessler, *Communal Pietism among Early American Moravians* (New York, 1933), 20–71.

[84] Wise, *Essays and Addresses*, 218–20.

[85] Gershom Scholem, *The Messianic Idea in Judaism, and Other Essays in Jewish Spirituality* (New York, 1971), 194–95, 200–01. For a sober re-evaluation of Martin Buber's interpretation of Hasidism, see *ibid.*, 238–48. Also see Scholem, *Major Trends in Jewish Mysticism*, 337–44; and Fackenheim, *God's Presence in History: Jewish Affirmations and Philosophical Reflections*, 8–19, *passim*.

God's promise that in Abraham's seed the gentiles would also share the blessings of the covenant. St. Paul's insistence that in Christ there was neither Jew nor Greek wove together strands common to the theology of both faiths. In Western Christendom thereafter the resistance to sectarianism by the established churches rested on claims to universality that lie at the heart of the New Testament and, in the apostolic reinterpretation of it, of the Old Testament as well. We ought not to be surprised, therefore, to find the idea of catholicity as prominent in the teachings of eighteenth-century Quakers as in those of the Anglican Society for the Propagation of the Gospel in Foreign Parts. John Wesley's inclusive notion of a world parish served his followers as well in the eighteenth century, when they were dissenting Anglicans, as in the nineteenth, when Methodists became the largest Protestant denomination in the United States.[86] During the latter century also, Rome's "missionary" bishops in America appealed to the idea of catholicity in resisting the formation of ethnic parishes and dioceses. These separate units were demanded— first by German priests and then by Polish, Italian, Czech, Slovak, French Canadian, Slovenian, Portuguese, and Spanish-American ones—on alternative "ecumenical" grounds: God was not interested in Americanization but in Christianization. Francis Hodur, who left the Roman communion, stood for catholic Polishness, while his countrymen who remained loyal to the existing structure stood for Polish Catholicism in a pluralistic church.[87]

Similarly, the ethnic Greeks, the dominant group among the Eastern Orthodox, supported the universalist policies of the Ecumenical Patriarch of Constantinople. Though always Greek, the patriarchs were committed by their struggles for the leadership of Orthodoxy outside Eastern Europe to the ancient doctrine of "one city, one bishop" against the intentions of American Serbs, Rumanians, "Russians," Syrians, or Bulgarians to acknowledge only ethnic bishops who were loyal to the patriarchs of Belgrade, Bucharest, Moscow, Antioch, or Sofia. But in their devotion to the notion of ecumenicity the American Greeks were far behind the band of exiled Russian priests led by Georges Florovsky and his protégés, Alexander Schmemann and John Meyendorff. Between the two world wars Florovsky made the tiny Paris hilltop where Saint Sergius Seminary and Nicholas Berdyaev were housed the intellectual and spiritual center for the theological revival of ecumenical Orthodoxy in Western Europe. After World War II Schmemann and Meyendorff accomplished the same for Saint Vladimir's Seminary in Yonkers, New York.[88]

With these illustrations in mind, the declarations of the religious leaders of American blacks, compounded of affirmations and renunciations of their

[86] Semmel, *Methodist Revolution*, 90, 97, 152–57; and Albert C. Outler, *John Wesley*, Library of Protestant Thought (Oxford, 1964), 20–21.

[87] Buczek, *Immigrant Pastor: The Life of the Right Reverend Lucyan Bójnowski*, 13, 15–16, 62–63; and William Galush, "The Polish National Catholic Church: A Survey of Its Origin, Development, and Missions," *Records of the American Catholic Historical Society of Philadelphia*, 83 (1972): 137–38, *passim*.

[88] For this story in more detail, see my "Refugee Orthodox Congregations in Western Europe, 1945–1948," 316–17, 321. Also see George H. Williams, "George Vasilievich Florovsky: His American Career (1938–1965)," *Greek Orthodox Theological Review*, 11 (1965): 9–12, 23–33, 100–06. On the "catholic" ideal in Uniate faith, see Nemec, "Ruthenian Uniate Church," 386–87.

oneness with white Christians, reflect both their reaction to racism and their awareness of the biblical teaching of a common humanity. The African Methodist Episcopal Church, which for generations followed both biblical and Methodist prescriptions in proclaiming the unity of the human race, was in this respect not one step ahead of the Church of God and Bible Prophecy or of Father Divine.[89]

THIS EXTENDED SUMMARY OF THE RELATIONSHIP between religion and ethnicity in America demonstrates that we have now come to the point where anthropological, sociological, psychological, and historical perspectives on ethnicity can coalesce.[90] The volume recently edited by sociologists Nathan Glazer and Daniel P. Moynihan and the recent work of numerous anthropologists reveal the enrichment and diversification of theory and empirical analysis that has come from the comparative study of worldwide ethnic group relationships. Meanwhile, Josef Barton's *Peasants and Strangers* has signaled the growing preoccupation of younger historians of ethnicity with complexity, ambivalence, contradiction, and what I call—in conscious rejection of the metaphors of both melting pot and mosaic—kaleidoscopic change. Scholars in all of these fields should abandon the notion that a set of fixed primordial realities lies behind the changing ethnoreligious relationships we are able to observe and analyze. That Heraclitus should replace Thales as our mentor will please those who find Alfred North Whitehead a modern culture hero. Perhaps also some may be pleased to discover that Moses, Jesus, and Paul were also prophets of process theology—men who called us away from simplistic notions of order, virtue, or psychic health and demanded that we deal with the real and mysteriously complex world of change in terms less doctrinaire and more compassionate than either religious or intellectual dogmatists have recently employed.

[89] Richard Allen, *The Life, Experience, and Gospel Labors of the Rt. Rev. Richard Allen, To Which Is Annexed the Rise and Progress of the African Methodist Episcopal Church* . . . (New York, 1960), 15–41, 70–71; and Benjamin T. Tanner, *An Apology for African Methodism* (Baltimore, 1867), 195.
[90] Edward Shils, "On the Comparative Study of the New States," in Geertz, *Old Societies and New States*, 12–15.

RELIGIOUS DENOMINATIONS AS ETHNIC COMMUNITIES: A REGIONAL CASE STUDY

Timothy L. Smith, *Professor of History,*
University of Minnesota

Recent studies of the history of ethnic groups in America have produced a growing awareness that the relationships between religious institutions and ethnic identity are more complex than was earlier believed. Three factors, it seems to me, are now hindering our efforts to understand these relationships. One is the absence of analyses of the wide functional differences between congregations and denominations, the two kinds of institutions which serve the religious needs of modern democratic societies. Another is the concentration of most historical research in immigrant religion upon one ethnic group. And the third is the emphasis upon the history of either rural frontiers or large cities. In this paper, I wish to present the results of a study of the religious life of the Lake Superior copper and iron mining country, a region in which immigrants from Eastern and Southern Europe are predominant, yet one in which the newcomers of each nationality were spread widely through small towns and villages.

The scattered settlement is crucial to the story, for it made necessary the cooperative relationships among congregations which were the basis of the denominational structures. Of the fourteen towns incorporated in the mining region of northern Minnesota in 1910, for example, four—Virginia, Hibbing, Chisholm, and Eveleth—contained between seven and eleven thousand inhabitants; the remaining ten numbered between one and four thousand. A great many of the immigrants, however, lived not in such towns at all, but in neighboring mining locations. In the seventy-odd such villages which existed at one time or another on the Minnesota Ranges, nationalities were mixed, and organized congregations were rare; generally, if the villagers went to church, they had to get into town.[1] Locations and towns were alike, however, in the fact that, by contrast with the great cities in which most twentieth-century immigrants settled, they were small enough for relationships to be personal. The families along the street might be Finnish, Italian, Croatian, and Swede, but they were real persons, not strangers. Hence the church congregation, even when composed exclusively of one ethnic group, could never be coterminous with the full range of primary, face-to-face relationships which governed the immigrant family's adjustment to its new life.[2]

---

1. U.S. Thirteenth Census (1910), *Abstract. . .with Supplement for Minnesota* (Washington: 1913), 590-591, 595-598.
2. See, for examples, Minnesota State Census, 1895, ms. schedules for St. Louis County, pp. 119-122, showing ten nationalities among the twenty-five heads of households in McKinley; lists of petitioners for sidewalk and sewerage improvements in Eveleth City Council, ''Minute Book'' for 1913 and 1914; and addresses of heads of families of the

The dominant class in these mining towns were Yankees, English-Canadians, and skilled English miners from Cornwall. From their ranks came the captains, foremen, and mining engineers, the doctors, lawyers, and school teachers, and the owners of larger commercial enterprises. Skilled underground miners were principally Scandinavians and Finns, the latter of whom, after 1880, were the most numerous single nationality in the region. As years went by, new arrivals from Slovenia, Croatia, Bohemia, Poland, and Italy filled up the ranks of miners and unskilled laborers. The proportions of such Eastern and Southern European immigrants increased as operations moved westward into Minnesota. There Germans and Scandinavians generally moved upward into foremen's positions or out of mining altogether, while Serbians, Montenegrins, Ukrainians, and Russians crowded into the unskilled jobs at the bottom of the ladder, especially after 1905. Labor turn-over was high. Of the 12,018 men employed by the Oliver Iron Mining Company in 1907, 84.4% were foreign-born, and half of these had resided in the United States less than two years. The census of 1910 showed that two-thirds of the foreign-born population of St. Louis County outside Duluth were from Eastern and Southern Europe, with Finns and South Slavs constituting the largest single groups.[3]

Here, then, was a region of small towns whose population was as polyglot as Chicago, and whose economic life, like that of the great cities of America, depended entirely on giant business organizations. Its religious traditions included all major segments of Protestant, Roman Catholic, Orthodox and Jewish faith, along with some which, like the Uniate Croatians, were almost unknown. For a time the Lake Superior region came as near as any I know to being a microcosm of twentieth century America. The story of the emergence of religious congregations in these communities, and of the denominational super-organizations which proved so necessary to their nurture, offers some important insights, I believe, into the relationship of religion and ethnic community throughout the nation.

A visitor to Calumet, Michigan, at the turn of the century might

Russian Orthodox congregation in Chisholm in 1922 in M. H. Godfrey, September 21, 1922, to John H. McLean (in Oliver Iron Mining Company, Executive Files, folder headed "Contributions, Orthodox Catholic Churches," Minnesota Historical Society). The last record shows that, of nine families living at Glen location, only two were next-door neighbors; of eight at Sawmill location, only two were neighbors; and only two families were neighbors among others scattered through the town.

3. Thirteenth Census, Abstract, 624-628; George O. Virtue, The Minnesota Iron Ranges (U. S. Bureau of Labor, Bulletin No. 84; Washington, D. C.: Government Printing Office, 1909), 350-353; Ely, Minnesota, 70th Anniversary Celebration (pamphlet, composed chiefly of items clipped from Ely newspapers; Ely, 1958), lists Finnish families, pp. 45, 52-53; Iron Home (Ely), August 20, 1889, described Tower population; J. M. Trunk, Ameriški in Amerikanci [Americans in America] (Celovec [Yugoslavia], 1912), 498-499. John Syrjamaki, "Mesabi Communities: A Study of Their Development," unpublished Ph.D. dissertation, Yale University, 1940, 203-215, discusses the phenomenon of ethnic succession.

have attended worship at Trinity Lutheran Church without realizing that the edifice was so named not in honor of the Holy Trinity, but in recognition of the three groups of Lutherans—Finnish, Norwegian, and Swedish—who had united to erect the building in 1876. The Norwegian pastor of a mixed "Scandinavian" parish in nearby Quincy had first served the Lutherans of Calumet, without regard to their national background. His successor, another Norwegian, excommunicated large numbers of Finns, however, apparently because of their devotion to the beliefs of Lars Levi Laestadius, leader during the earlier part of the century of a laymen's revival movement in Finland. But in 1876, Alfred Backman, a Finnish Lutheran pastor, came to serve the church. He formed separate congregations for each of the three nationalities, then directed the construction of the building in which they were to conduct their separate services for many years.[4]

By the time mining operations began in Minnesota a decade later, the three national groups of Lutherans had become sufficiently self-conscious to forbid experiments in united congregations. The only exception were the Swede-speaking Finns, who were ethnically not really at home with either nationality. They eventually followed the dictates of both language and desire for status, and joined the Swedish Lutheran congregations. By 1890, moreover, it had become clear to Swedish and Norwegian newcomers that they did not have to carry the heavy burdens of church-building alone. The several Scandinavian denominations already well-established in the upper Mississippi Valley moved rapidly to supply them with the pastors, publications, schools, and mission funds which they required. The Finnish congregations, by contrast, were generally independent organizations. Their founders were often laymen, and their doctrines were usually Laestadian, an event which owed as much to the necessity of lay leadership in a country where clergymen were scarce as to the fact that many of the immigrants had come from northern Finland where that doctrine had been strong. The transfer of both religious and agricultural customs was an easy one, for both had originated under frontier conditions in Finland, as landless peasants spread northward toward the Arctic Ocean.[5]

4. S. V. Autere, "Calumet in Betlehem Seurakunnan Historian Pääpiirteitä 50 Vuoden in Ajalta" ["A Summary of the History of the Calumet Bethany Congregation"], in *Kirkollinen Kalenteri . . . 1927* (Hancock, Michigan: Finnish Lutheran Book Concern, 1927), 46. U. Saarnivaara, *Amerikan Laestadiolaisuuden eli Apostolis-luterilaisuuden Historia [American Laestadian or Apostolic Lutheran History]* (Ironwood, Michigan: National Publishing Company, 1947), an English summary of which appeared the following year, gives the details on Laestadianism.
I have been assisted in both research and translation of Finnish materials by Professor Douglas Ollila, of Thiel College, whose unpublished dissertation on the Suomi Synod Lutheran Churches, done at Boston University, is the best introduction to theological phases of the subject.
5. Akseli Järnefelt, *Suomalaiset Amerikassa [The Finns in America]* (Helsinki: Kustannusosakeyhtiö Otava, 1899), 144; William Rautanen, *Amerikan Suomalainen Kirkko [The Finnish American Church]* (Hancock: Finnish Lutheran Book Concern, 1911).

The voluntary and independent character of these early congregations is especially evident from their close association with Finnish temperance societies. In the oldest Minnesota mining towns, temperance societies and congregations were founded together. At Ely after some years, a large segment of the membership became discontented with the Laestadian teachings and withdrew to form a new congregation. They worshipped in the temperance hall for twenty-five years, as, for a time, did a third, formed in 1901 among those who wished to associate themselves with the Suomi Synod. In the towns of the Mesabi Range, however, temperance societies uniformly preceded the organization of Finnish congregations. At places like Eveleth, Mountain Iron, Chisholm, Buhl, and Hibbing, the churches met for many years in the temperance halls, and meanwhile relied upon these organizations to conduct Sunday schools, summer schools, and dramatic and social events. An Old World visitor to Ely in 1899 found the temperance hall, called the Finnish Opera House, a center for all manner of cultural activities: a lending library, a band, a dramatic club, and both Saturday and summer schools for young people.[6]

As with congregations, however, so with temperance societies: frequent divisions within local groups prevented these organizations from becoming centers of the entire local community of Finns. At Hibbing, for example, nineteen men formed the first temperance society in 1895, and launched a full program of weekly activities which included plays, speeches and debates, and the issue of a hand-written news sheet called "Star of the Wilderness." They associated themselves at once with the National Finnish Temperance Brotherhood. Controversy soon broke out, however, over religion and rules of discipline. The national society required members to be Christians, directed their meetings be opened with prayer, and forbade dancing and gambling at cards. Debates over these issues at the national convention in 1896 prompted many local units, including the society at Hibbing, to reconstitute themselves as independent groups. Strangely, however, the new by-laws adopted at Hibbing declared that the organization was to continue on a "Christian foundation"; dancing was still forbidden, and meetings both opened and closed with prayer. Nevertheless, a minority of the members set up another society, designed to continue their association with the national brotherhood. Both local groups used the same hall for many years, and both carried on an extensive program of musical, dramatic, and educational activities. The two united with the Workers Club in 1901 to form a Finnish Library, whose holdings later on became the nucleus of the

6. Rautanen, 241-247; Järnefelt, 141-145; Trustees of the Finnish Evangelical Lutheran Congregation, Ely, December 15, 1922, to Captain Charles Trezona (O. I. M. Co., Executive Files, folder, "Contributions, Immigrant Churches, Protestant"); *Eveleth News*, November 21, 1935, p. 1.

Hibbing Public Library.[7]

As time passed, no less than four competing national organizations of Finnish temperance societies emerged. They gave a permanent institutional form, and hence a certain sectarian character, to the local divisions. The functions which they performed in assisting and guiding the activities of local units were precisely the same as those which denominations performed for local church congregations. Each gave steady and increasing emphasis to Finnishness.[8] In 1904 the Walon Lahde Temperance Society in Eveleth initiated a regional celebration on the twenty-fourth of June, traditionally "Mid-Summer Day" in Finland. Delegates of temperance societies from most of the Minnesota Iron Range towns laid the plans, which included a vast picnic with speeches by prominent Finnish laymen and ministers, and "one or two good American public speakers." Three thousand people appeared for the day. Proceeds of the gathering went into a fund to establish a Finnish summer school at which children attending the public schools could be taught the language and history of their father's country.[9] Thereafter, indeed, the preoccupation of both national and local societies with "education," not only in temperance but in Finnishness, was the most important aspect of their activities in any year. "You shouldn't imagine yourselves as Americans, since you are not that," Abraham Ollila told the youth of the Hibbing Temperance Societies in 1909. "You should devote yourselves to national ideals more than you have up to now. . . . Let the flame of nationalism burn, and let minds and hearts be enlightened and warmed."[10]

Against this background, we can better understand the emergence of the several religious denominations serving Finnish Lutherans. The Laestadians, whose congregation organized at Calumet in 1872 soon adopted the name "Finnish Apostolic Lutheran Church," spread through Michigan, Minnesota, Massachusetts, and Oregon. A direct carry-over from the homeland, the chief difference in American Laestadianism was simply that the members were not, as in Finland, nominally part of a national church. What had been a movement within the church there became an independent denomination here—just as had happened to Congregationalists, Presbyterians, and Pietists long before. Such has been, in every decade, the consequence

7. Edith Koivisto, Lupaus: Hibbingin Suomalaisen Raittiusdukkeen Historia vv. 1895-1957 [The Pledge: A History of the Finnish Temperance Movement of Hibbing from 1895 to 1957], unpublished typescript, in the possession of the author, pp. 5-28, 35-38, contains detailed summaries of minutes and of news accounts of activities. Cf. Järnefelt, 144; Eveleth News, September 5, 1903, p. 1.
8. Rautanen, 327-328; Eveleth News, July 21, 1906, p. 3, and January 6, 1909, p. 1, record local meetings of national and regional organizations.
9. Eveleth News, April 15, 1904, p. 1, June 17, 1904, p. 1, and June 24, 1904, p. 1, gives full details. See the same, June 25, 1914, p. 1, by which time the event was a permanent institution.
10. See Koivisto, 122, and, for discussion of local and national educational activities, pp. 52-55, 97-98.

of religious diversity and the separation of church and state. The bonds of union which Laestadians forged in the new land, moreover, were the same as in the old—traveling ministers, the annual "Big Meeting," and a devotional periodical. What was new was that Finnishness now became a commitment, rather than an inheritance, a matter of conscious choice in a land where public schools and close association with diverse peoples in small towns threatened to destroy ethnic identity.[11]

The Suomi Synod of Evangelical Lutherans was the second denomination to appear. J. K. Nikander, pastor at Hancock, Michigan, was the leader of a group of mining-region ministers who set out in 1889 to unite the congregations under their care in a national organization. At a mission meeting in Hancock that year, Nikander's sermon on "The Kingdom of God on This Earth" called for an inclusive body, not a "pure" church, one which would serve all Finnish Lutherans in America without regard to their doctrinal differences, just as did the national church of Finland. The pastors organized a consistory and drew up articles of incorporation which they filed with the county clerk of Houghton County. At that point Ino Ekman, editor of *Kansan Lehti* [*The People's Journal*], a newspaper published in Red Jacket, discovered that the articles had ignored the Michigan law requiring congregations themselves to adopt a declaration of purpose before they could be incorporated into a denominational body. Ekman then attacked the proceeding publicly, charging that the pastors wished to establish an episcopal government and to preserve in the New World the legal guarantee of their salaries which had been so much hated in Finland. Bitter public arguments ensued at the congregational meetings which the law required. In Calumet, Pastor J. W. Eloheimo had to excommunicate five hundred members before the "righteous remnant" of 200 which remained could vote for incorporation. Those excommunicated formed the "Evangelical Lutheran National Congregation of Calumet," known at first as the "People's" church, possibly in part because of the name of Ekman's journal, but perhaps more because of the similarity of the two words in Finnish meaning "national" and "peoples."[12]

Thus the initial effort to create an inclusive fellowship of Finnish Lutheran churches produced not one but two rival organizations. The People's Church movement spread through the mining towns, gathering to itself all those who protested the episcopal tendencies of the Suomi Synod. Eloheimo moved from Calumet to Ironwood, Michigan. There, however, he fell into difficulties with his

11. Saarnivaara, 273-281; Fred R. Mott, Virginia, February 19, 1923, to W. J. Olcott (O. I. M. Co., Executive Files, "Contributions, Immigrant Churches, Protestant").
12. Ollila, 166-187, is an excellent discussion, based on all the contemporary sources, and is the best historical passage in the dissertation.

congregation, wrote a strange prophetic book, and was maneuvered out of the Suomi consistory. He then sought to organize yet another movement, the "Episcopal Fenno-American Church," but wound up in 1896 back in Calumet, pastor of the "People's" congregation whose charter members he had excommunicated six years before! Thereafter Eloheimo took the lead in the incorporation of the Finnish Evangelical Lutheran National Church. The response of local congregations to the opportunity of affiliating with one or the other of two competing denominations was, as in the case of so much of the history of denomination-founding in America, an ambivalent one. Many, as at Ely and Hibbing in Minnesota, stood aloof from formal association, but relied upon one or the other of the two organized bodies to supply preachers for them. Some who did vote to affiliate with one suffered secession by a minority intent on either preserving their independence or joining the other.[13]

Competition served to increase the attention which leaders of the two denominations paid to ethnic identity. The Suomi Synod seemed to be acting out of loyalty to Nikander's inclusive "folk-church" principle, but the National church moved in the same direction without benefit of the rationale. From their two headquarters at Hancock and Ironwood, each published a growing body of literature aimed at the indoctrination of the young not only in religious principles but in that respect for Finnish culture which both denominations came to realize must be preserved or each would perish. The national organizations inspired programs for the training of teachers, provided guidance and encouragement to local groups when enthusiasm for summer and Sunday schools lagged, and sent missionary preachers to organize congregations in Finnish settlements where none existed before. And most important, each established a combined academy and seminary for the training of lay and clerical leaders.[14]

The story of the two colleges deserves a separate word, for it illustrates the service which education has rendered to sectarianism in American history. J. K. Nikander's plan to form a school was set in motion immediately after the incorporation of the Suomi Synod in

13. *Ibid.*, 208-225; G. A. Aho and J. E. Nopola, *Evangelis-Luterilainen Kansalliskirkko.* . . [*Evangelical Lutheran National Church.* . .] (Ironwood, Michigan: National Publishing Company, 1949), 1-45, *passim.*
14. Ollila, 242-252, describes the great range of Suomi Synod publications, including the newspaper *Amerikan Suometar* [*The American Finn*] (Hancock, Michigan, from 1899), and a farm and home journal, *Aura* [*The Plow*] (Hancock, 1914-1923), edited by his grandfather. See, for stages of development of ethnically conscious education, articles in *Kirkollinen Kalenteri* . . . *1904*, 64-65, 72-87; Announcement of plans for a parochial summer school at Eveleth in *Eveleth News*, April 24, 1909, p. 1; John Wargelin's appeal to parents in *Kirkollinen Kalenteri* . . . *1911*, 93-97; Rautanen, 325, 337, 347, for summary and interpretation of Sunday School and summer school work; and the same author's much more blatant appeal to avoid the ''suicide of a nationality'' in William Rautanen, ''Miksi Suomi-Opistoa Muutamat Vastustavat'' [''Why Some Oppose Suomi College''] in *Kirkollinen Kalenteri* . . . *1911*, 102-107; and typical description of expanding youth and educational programs in a thoroughly sectarian, foreign-language setting, in Reverend V. Kuusisto, Virginia, October 24, 1923, to Fred R. Mott (O. I. M. Co., Executive Files, ''Contributions, Immigrant Churches, Protestant'').

1890. Proposals to locate it in St. Paul, Superior, and elsewhere proved unsatisfactory and Nikander finally opened what was called the Suomi College and Seminary at Hancock, Michigan, in the fall of 1896. The original curriculum resembled that of a progressive American high school, save for the inclusion of religion and Finnish. The first class of ministers graduated in 1906. An early emphasis upon business education, however, flourished alongside the theological program during the following decades. Finnish Americans had come to the new land in order to get ahead, and they expected the education which their church provided to give their children the tools to do so.[15]

Similarily, the Finnish Evangelical National Church in 1900 began discussions of a school which would serve both the denomination and independent congregations. The Brooklyn, New York, newspaper, *American Kaiku* [*American Echo*] campaigned actively for the proposal, suggesting a curriculum patterned after the *Realikouluia* [Practical Schools] which were then popular in Finland. A group of 19 pastors and 16 laymen published an appeal of similar import in April, 1903. The annual convention authorized the opening of the school that fall and named it "The Finnish People's College and Theological Seminary." All students were to take two years of fundamental instruction at the high school level. Those planning for the ministry were to spend another two years in theological study, while others gave a like period to business training. The board in charge purchased a campus and a rambling building at Smithville, near Duluth, and in January, 1904, launched the sale of 50,000 shares of stock at $1.00 each to finance the venture.

Almost at once, however, members of Socialistic worker's clubs in the mining region began purchasing shares in large quantities. Four years later they took control of the institution in the name of "revolutionary Marxism" and renamed it "The Work People's College." Ironically, however, the services which the college thereafter performed for the socialists differed not one whit from those rendered earlier to the Christians: indoctrination in both faith and Finnishness, and practical business education for young people eager to get ahead in a capitalist society![16]

The growth of Finnish socialism, indeed, illustrates another facet of the immigrant's quest for ethnic identity. The movement reached the Lake Superior region in 1899 when Antero Tanner and other Marxist lecturers began appearing at workers' halls and temperance

15. Ollila, 259-268; *Suomi Opiston Albumi, 1896-1906 The Suomi College Album, 1896-1906*] (Hancock: Finnish Lutheran Book Concern, 1906), 25-26; Suomi College and Theological Seminary, *Catalog . . . 1918-1919*, 48-58, describes the business course and lists graduates prominent in mining-region firms.
16. *Sosialisti* [newspaper organ of the syndicalist or I.W.W. wing of Finnish socialists], September 1 and September 3, 1914; S. Ilmonen, *Amerikan Suomalaisten Sivistyshistoria* [*American Finnish Cultural History*] (2 vols; Hancock: Finnish Lutheran Book Concern, 1930), I, 162-166. The papers and records of the Work Peoples College have recently been acquired by the University of Minnesota.

gatherings. When members of the temperance societies became socialists, they often sought to divert the common property to their new purposes. In Eveleth, for example, while the middle-class members of one temperance club were off on a summer's jaunt to Finland, the minority left behind voted to reconstitute themselves a socialist society and to transfer the property to the new organization.[17] The bitter experience at the People's College in Duluth was but the climactic example of such maneuvers. Thereafter, the radicals developed their own program of hall socialism, with a full range of such cultural activities as dramatics, discussion groups, music societies, and Saturday and summer schools for children and young people. Rituals for the naming of infants and the burial of the dead made the institutional substitution for the congregation complete.[18] Even more striking, however, was the development of competing national sects of Finnish socialists, each fielding its own team of itinerant evangelists, and each armed with complete publishing, educational, and promotional programs, designed to secure the allegiance of the local workers' clubs. Their story cannot be told in this paper, save to say that by the time World War I broke out, these organizations, too, like the religious denominations, had come to stress Finnishness quite as much as socialism, in their effort to attract and hold the loyalty of their members.[19]

In the long struggle among the church Finns, temperance Finns, and socialist Finns during these years, local divisions within each ideological camp increasingly mirrored the rivalry of the competing national organizations. Lines were by no means always clear, however. Matti Lehtonen, for example, served both as a socialist lecturer and as pastor of the Finnish Methodist Church at Nashwauk, Minnesota. He helped organize a half-dozen such congregations, with the full support of the Minnesota Conference of Methodists.[20] Elsewhere,

17. John I. Kolehmainen, *Sow the Golden Seed* (Fitchburg, Massachusetts: The Raivaaja Publishing Company, 1955), 16-22, tells the story of the coming of Marxism to the workingmen's clubs. On conflicts over property, see Koivisto, 46-50; and Elis Sulkanen, *Amerikan Suomalaisen Työväenliikkeen Historia* [*History of the Finnish American Labor Movement*] (Fitchburg, Massachusetts: The Raivaaja Publishing Company, 1951), 458; and Matt Lahti, interview with the writer, August, 1962.
18. See "Naswaukin S. S. Osaston Ompeluseuran Pöytäkirja ["The Minutes of the Finnish Sewing Circle of Nashwauk] October 1, 1908 - May 25, 1909," ms., now in the Minnesota Historical Society, entries for October and November, 1908; "Nashwaukin S. S. Osaston Huvtomikunnan Pöytäkirja ["Secretarial Record of the Entertainment Committee of the Nashwauk Finnish Socialist Party] 1909-1912," minutes for March 6, 8, and 24, 1911, and February 16, 1912, detailing temperance discussions; *Työmies* [organ of democratic socialism], January 4, 1910, and February 1, 1910, p. 3, noting ritual of naming new-born child; *Sosialisti*, September 7, 1914, p. 1, an early description of a Finnish socialist funeral; and, *Ibid.*, December 18, 1916, p. 1, and December 23, 1916, p. 2. on Christmas celebrations.
19. See summaries in *Sosialisti*, December 11, 1914, p. 3; Kolehmainen, 18-28, 44-52; Ollila, 304-309. On the itinerants, see also *Sosialisti*, June 13, 1914, p. 4, and June 22, 1914, p. 3; and on education, A. B. Makela, ed., *Aakkosia Sosialistien Lapsille* [*A Primer for Socialist Children*] (Hancock: Finnish Publishing Co., n.d.), 39-48.
20. Sulkanen, 63, 87; Rautanen, 230-242; Charles N. Pace, *Our Fathers Build; A Century of Minnesota Methodism* [Minneapolis, 1952?], 132-134; and Methodist Piispallinen Kirkon Suomalisen Lähetyksen Pöytäkirjat, 1911-1931 [Minutes of the Methodist Episcopal Church, Finnish Mission] (ms. at Suomi College and Seminary), *passim*.

Suomi Synod pastors wrestled with the competing claims of their working-class and middle-class members, usually siding with the latter as a means of freeing their national group from identification with labor radicalism, so they maintained.[21] William Rautanen, pastor at Calumet, Michigan, regretted the absence of an organized movement of Christian Socialism among American Finns, and defended the right of individual members to join unions and battle for workingmen's rights. But the common meeting-ground upon which he thought churchmen and socialists might one day stand appeared to the more doctrinaire leaders in both camps a land of never never.[22]

Under such circumstances, the quest of an inclusive ethnic unity among American Finns, either at local or national levels, was a hopeless cause indeed. One university professor reared in a Finnish socialist home at Chisholm in the 1920's remembers having no intimate contacts at all with church Finns, whether preachers or laymen.[23] The Suomi Synod, which clung stubbornly to the theory that it was an inclusive communion, deferred and, by negligence, finally rejected a proposal to merge with the National church on the eve of World War I.[24] The "folk church" concept seems, in retrospect, to have been only the vehicle by which this particular organization rationalized its steady cultivation of ethnic consciousness.[25] Even the temperance societies became suspect to the Suomi Synod, although Rautanen was not sure whether the estrangement was due to their growing broadmindedness on such matters as dancing and card playing or to their increasingly rational philosophy. I suspect it stemmed as much from mere organizational rivalry.[26] Certainly, the competitive and sectarian structure of the temperance groups, like that of other national organizations, dictated policies of isolation.

The most obvious generalization which this sketch of the organization of the spiritual life of American Finns reinforces is that the congregation is the primary institution in American religion. A child of both the chances and the choices of uprooted men, it is oriented to

21. Ollila, 312-315, summarizes much material from newspapers.
22. Rautanen, 330-331; discussion of labor problems by the same writer in *Kirkollinen Kalenteri* . . . *1914*, 59-64; *Työmies*, December 14, 1909, p. 3
23. John Sirjamaki, interview with writer, August, 1962.
24. Ollila, 280-297.
25. Rautanen, 328-329, notes close alliance of Suomi Synod with Kaleva societies. See also, J. W. Lähde, "Säilyttäkäämme Nourisomme Suomalaisena Siveelisenä ja Raittina" ["Let Us Keep Our Youth Finns, Moral and Temperate"] in *Raittiuskalenteri* [*Temperance Almanac*] . . .*1913* (Hancock: Finnish National Brothers Temperance Society, 1912), 137-132. M. N. Westerback, *Erimielisyydet Kansalliskirkossa, Niiten Syyt Ja Seuraukset* [*Differences of Opinion in the National Church, Their Reasons and Consequences*] (Ironwood, Mich: National Publishing Co., 1926), 3-16, deals with early stages of discussion of merger with Missouri Synod Lutheranism. Alfred Haapanen, ed., *Kirkhomme Tyovainiolta, Suomi-Synodin 40 Vuotismuistojulkaisa, 1890-1930* [*From the Workfields of Our Church: The Fortieth Anniversary Publication of the Suomi Synod, 1890-1930*] (Hancock, Mich: Finnish Lutheran Book Concern, 1930), 44, 51, 125, discusses the preservation of the "Finnish cause" in the church.
26. Rautanen, 327-328; "The Temperance Work of our Church People," *Kirkollinen Kalenteri*. . . *1916*, 106-110, urges greater participation.

the future—dedicated to the attainment of objectives which both sermon and song may rationalize. Yet it looks backward also, providing a spiritual substitute for the kin-group left behind. Compounded thus of both hope and memory, the congregation acts to preserve as well as to refashion an ancient faith. When mobility is intensified, whether geographic or social, its usefulness in fulfilling the need for belonging, for personal identity, and for guidance in the adjustment of old customs to new conditions, become very great indeed. This was no more true in Red Jacket, Michigan, in 1890, than it is in suburban New Jersey in 1960.

The religious denomination appears clearly in this story as a structural super-organization designed to give guidance, support, and discipline to local congregations. It was born of social necessity, quite without reference to the high doctrine of "denominationalism" which Professors Sidney Mead and Winthrop Hudson have taught us. The fulfillment of its functions required, however, a specific rationale, a permanent structure, and a leadership dedicated not only to serving the congregations but to perpetuating both the larger institution and their own place in it. Such an organization by its very nature resists sharp changes either in structure or in philosophy, and encourages an exclusive loyalty in its local units. The immigrant denomination, thus conceived, is an ethnic sect; its activities contributed to a sharpened sense of isolation from other organizations competing for the allegiance of members of the same national group; and educational programs, so frequently regarded as broadening, contribute to this sectarian isolation.

Finally, the story of the Finnish Lutherans suggests that small town congregations may be different from those in large cities precisely in the fact that they are less "sectarian" than the denominations of which they are a part. The reasons seem clear: members of the congregation are involved in a host of communal face-to-face relations not only with members of their own ethnic group who belong to other denominations, but with persons belonging to other ethnic and religious groups. To illustrate the "strife of sects" in small towns, as has often been done, may simply obscure a more important source of sectarianism: the competition of national organizations for the loyalty of people whose social or ethnic backgrounds make them the prime prospects for the denomination's growth.

The immense variety of relationships between religious and ethnic identity in America becomes clearer when we turn our attention to the history of the role of the Slovenians in the Roman Catholic parishes in Lake Superior communities. In several important ways their situation contrasted sharply with that of the Lutheran Finns. Instead of one people among several communions, Catholic immigrants to the iron-mining country were many peoples in one: Slovenians, Croatians, and Italians, chiefly, with lesser numbers of Germans, Hungarians, Czechs, Poles, and, from the New World, French Canadians. Even in their homelands, moreover, the consciousness of nationality among all these but the French and the Poles was a recent and uncertain achievement. And in literacy and vocational skills, they all ranged along the bottom of the scale for immigrants in these decades.[27] On the other hand, unlike both Finnish Lutherans and Eastern Orthodox Slavs, the Roman Catholics found an efficient and cohesive religious organization ready to serve them on their arrival in the New World. An adequate force of clergymen, operating under a carefully centralized authority, seemed determined that no migrating believer should be long out of touch with his faith.

Moreover, the Church in this region was committed to a clear-cut philosophy of Americanization. Archbishop John Ireland of St. Paul stood at the head of the group of liberal Irish prelates who during these years sought to befriend labor, cooperate with the public schools, and promote social justice. In 1889, he placed one of his most loyal and tolerant priests, James McGolrick, in charge of the new Diocese of Duluth. McGolrick promptly made Father Joseph Buh, a Slovenian missionary to the Indians who had recently become pastor at the mining town of Tower, Minnesota, chancellor and vicar-general of his diocese.[28] The move was but the first instance of the skillful and persistent policy by which these two bishops sought to bring the new immigrant into the fellowship of the Church. In every town they could count on the support of a nucleus of second-generation Irish and German settlers, many of them in business as saloon-keepers, professional men, or merchants. However willing the bishops were to compromise for a time with ethnic sentiments, their long-range goal was to make the newcomers Americans—on an Irish model, of course. Their policy appears in retrospect to have become the dominant theme of American Roman Catholic history during the first half of this century: a melting-pot church in a mosaic culture.

Finally the Slovenians, unlike any other ethnic group in American history, were preceded into the New World by priests of their own nationality. Frederick Baraga came to Lake Superior as a missionary to the Chippewa Indians in 1831. Later, as bishop of the Diocese of Marquette, he recruited pastors who welcomed French Canadian, Slavic, and Irish newcomers with a sympathy which only immigrant priests could achieve. Meanwhile, his countryman Fran Pirc carried on the Indian missions in Minnesota. Pirc returned to

27. U.S. Commissioner-General of Immigration, *Annual Reports, 1899-1914*, contain an annual summary of literary and work skills.
28. "In Memoriam — Right Reverend James McGolrick," *Acta et Dicta*, V (July, 1918), 153-169; Matija Sava, "Monsignor Fran Jožef Buh," *Ave Maria Koledar*, X (1923), 60-72 [English tr. by Mrs. Mary Molek, in Immigrant Archives, Walter Library, University of Minnesota, as is true of all items from the Slovene referred to hereafter in this article].

Slovenia in 1864 and brought back Buh, already an ordained priest, and 15 students, whom he enrolled, under Buh's care, in St. Paul Seminary. In later years Buh returned to recruit similar groups of students. Already competent in German as well as in their native Slovenian, many of these men learned Czech and Polish as well, along with the Chippewa language, so as to be able to minister to the scattered enclaves of Slavic immigrants appearing along the frontier near their Indian missions.[29]

When, therefore, the earliest Roman Catholic congregations emerged in northern Minnesota their priests were often Slovenians, even though the parishioners were of many nationalities. Riding the spreading network of mining region railroads from his base at Tower, Father Buh said Masses regularly in schoolhouses and town halls as new communities appeared on the Mesabi Range to the south. And he supervised closely the work of the young priests who were assigned to establish parishes there. Matija Šavs, then a divinity student in St. Paul, later remembered that the first service in Biwabik was conducted in a hut thrown together in a few days. Buh preached in English, Slovenian, and French, then in Chippewa, for a few Indians had squatted in the front row.[30] At the larger towns of Virginia and Hibbing the Irish, Germans, Italians, Poles, French Canadians, and others were together far more numerous than the South Slavs. Thus Father Mathias Bilban, ablest of the younger Slovenians, was pastor at Virginia until 1903, but gave way to an Irishman then, James Hogan. At Hibbing a Frenchman, Father C. B. Gamache, was pastor from 1895 until Hogan replaced him in 1911. In Tower and Ely, however, and thereafter in Mesabi towns such as Aurora, Eveleth, Chisholm, and Gilbert, Slovenians and Croatians comprised a majority within the parishes.[31]

As the population of the Range towns grew, dissatisfaction with melting-pot parishes produced desultory attempts to establish national ones. While still at Virginia, Bilban erected the Holy Family Church for his parishioners at nearby Eveleth, where Slovenians were in the majority. When Hogan took charge of the larger parish, he built St. Patrick's Church at Eveleth "for English-speaking Catholics." Both chapels soon became independent of the Virginia church. The Italians at Eveleth, greatly outnumbered in the Holy Family parish, later took steps to establish a congregation of their own. Poles and other groups too small to hope for a national parish then had no

29. *Ibid.*, 60-61; Patrick Lydon, "Notes on the History of the Diocese of Duluth," *Acta et Dicta*, V, 242-245; Trunk, 592-593, 604, contains sketches of younger Slovenian priests.
30. Savs, *loc. cit.*, 62-64.
31. Trunk, 494-498, 547-548, 584; *Ave Maria Koledar* IV (1917), 165. See the list of 38 children confirmed at Tower in *Amerikanski Slovenec*, September 27, 1895, p. 1, of whom 13 were South Slavs, 16 were Irish, 2 were French, 1 Italian, and the remainder English or German.

choice but to move to St. Patrick's and learn English.[32] Meanwhile, at Hibbing, Father John Zarrilli arrived from Italy late in October, 1905: Armed with Bishop McGolrick's blessing and endowed with promotional skills worthy of a Chamber of Commerce secretary, he awakened the first real religious enthusiasm among the Italians in that large town and its sprawling complex of neighboring locations. An Italian congregation also appeared in northside Virginia. Later on the "Polish-Slovenian" Church at Virginia proved an unsuccessful experiment in cooperation.[33]

In smaller towns, a single mixed parish remained the rule, though the nationality of the priest often determined the current state of loyalty among the constituency. Thus Irish Father Joseph Quillin, pastor of St. John the Baptist Church in Biwabik, wrote the Oliver Iron Mining Company in 1919 that he had thirty-six "American" and one hundred and twenty "Austrian" families in his parish, but desperately needed a donation because he "received no help from the Austrians." In a similar appeal four years later the new pastor, John Jershe, a Slovenian, was able to report a much healthier situation, though it is not clear whether the "American" families shared his optimism.[34]

Since Roman Catholic congregations could not under these circumstances serve as exclusive ethnic centers, the Slovenians fashioned a spiritual home by voluntary association in mutual benefit lodges. At Calumet, Michigan, Lodge St. Joseph, founded in 1882, preceded the organization of a separate Slovenian parish by seven years. It eventually became the nucleus of a national organization known as the "Slovene-Croatian Union," though for a long time the Croatians maintained their own associations. At Tower, Buh encouraged the organization of a Slovenian lodge shortly after he arrived there.[35] Meanwhile the Slovenian students at St. Paul Seminary, reacting like typical undergraduates to their minority status, conceived the idea of a national association of church-related lodges, apparently borrowing it from the Czechs, with whose parishes they were well acquainted. The students read eagerly the first issues of the Slovenian newspaper which

32. *Jubilejna Spominska Knjiga . . . Tridesetletnice K.S.K.J. . . . [Jubilee Memorial Book . . . Thirtieth Anniversary . . . Grand Carhiolian-Slovenian Catholic Union of the U. S. A.]* (Cleveland: Ameriska Domovina, 1924), 184-185, sketches the life of Bilban. See also Walter Van Brunt, ed., *Duluth and St. Louis County, Minnesota* (3 vols.; Chicago: American Historical Society, 1921), II, 520-521; and R. J. Mitchell, Eveleth, Minnesota, June 24, 1919, to W. J. Olcott (O. I. M. Co., Exec. Files, ''Contributions, Roman Catholic Churches'').

33. *Hibbing Daily News*, October 21, 1921 [an historical issue], p. 6, quotes contemporary accounts.

34. Joseph S. Quillin, Biwabik, Minnesota, September 26, 1919, to W. J. Olcott; and Charles Grabowsky, Eveleth, Minnesota, October 6, 1923, to W. J. Olcott (O. I. M. Co., Exec. Files, ''Contributions, Roman Catholic Churches'')

35. Ivan Molek, ''Over Hill and Dale; Autobiographical Sketches,'' (unpublished ms., tr. Mary Molek, Immigrant Archives, University of Minnesota), 175-176, 199; *Jubilejna. . . K.S.K.J.*, 186-187.

Father Buh began publishing at Tower in 1891. Embarrassed by its antiquated grammar and careless typesetting, they volunteered to spend summers with him, helping out both with the parish and the publication of the paper, and recruiting members for Slovenian lodges there and at other mining towns. Father Buh, mindful of his non-Slavic parishioners and of his duties to the diocese, stood officially aloof from the latter effort, but privately he encouraged them and they were successful.

Two years later, delegates from several such lodges met in Joliet, Illinois and formed a national organization, the Grand Carniolian Catholic Union, usually known as K.S.K.J., the initials of the title in Slovenian.[36] St. Joseph's Church at Joliet was a Slovenian national parish—the only one then in existence. The pastor there, Francis S. Šušteršič, was thus free openly to support the movement and to accept the presidency of the national body; Matija Šavs, leader of the student group, was elected secretary. Local units sprang up rapidly throughout the Lake Superior region then. The sense of ethnic identity which the Church could not nurture on either local or regional levels had thus created a national association—in the sociological sense of the word, perhaps, a denomination—to fulfill the same purpose. K.S.K.J. was intended "for the propagation of the faith and benefit to the Slovenian nationality." Centralization, one of the seminary students wrote, "would insure the person who moves from one locality to another, or one state to another, of affiliation with the same kind of group among his own people."[37]

From that day forward, the affairs of lodge and church in Slovenian settlements were closely intertwined. In the national parishes which emerged at Calumet, Eveleth, Chicago, and Cleveland, an array of local lodges were responsible for virtually the whole of the congregation's social and lay activities. In mixed congregations where Slovenians were the majority, the official parish social program was at best a limited one. Where they were a minority, the opposite sometimes happened, and some members of the lodges became so estranged from the parish as to fall an easy prey to anti-clerical or socialist agitation.

Curbing radicalism was almost from the beginning one of the justifications which Slovenian priests gave for their participation in the national organization of K.S.K.J.[38] But the longing for belong-

36. *Ibid.*, 11. 59, and, on formation of individual lodges, 180-181; Šavs, *loc. cit.*, 66-69.
37. Contemporary discussions containing the quotations appear in *Amerikanski Slovenec* [Fr. Buh's weekly, Tower, Minn., 1891-1899, and Joliet, Ill., 1899-1915], October 27, 1893, November 10, 1893 [both reprinted in *Glasilo K.S.K.J.*, official organ after 1915, April 7, 1915, p. 10], and a salute from the young seminarians, April 20, 1894, p. 2. Cf. Šavs, *loc. cit.*, 69-70; sketch of the life of Šušteršič in *Sixtieth Anniversary, Grand Carniolian Slovenian Catholic Union . . .* (Joliet: K.S.K. J., 1954), 11
38. See the series of letters by Matija Šavs attacking the socialist printer, M. Sakser, under the pseudonym "Prairie Farmer," *Amerikanski Slovenec,* March 30, 1894, p. 2, April 20, 1894, p. 2, and April 27, 1894, p. 1.

ing was no doubt the greater force at work. The official organ, Buh's newspaper, carried from the beginning letters from individuals and local societies in widely scattered communities, as well as reports of parish activities in the larger centers. Lay leaders in local parishes, like Anton Nemanec, saloonkeeper, merchant, and undertaker at Joliet who succeeded Šušteršič as national president, became pillars of a self-conscious ethnic community in which priests appeared as both lords and servants. Annual conventions, at Tower, Calumet, Eveleth, and Joliet, brought lay delegates and priests together for fun, business, and fellowship, with music provided in the early years by a chorus of Slovenian divinity students from St. Paul.[39] Buh's press issued a Slovene-English dictionary, a catechism, and, beginning in 1897, an annual almanac of Slovenian affairs which, like the newspaper, contained instructions in both citizenship and religion which were designed to ease the immigrant's adjustment to his life in the New World.[40] But, as in the case of the Finns, denominational organization in the long run encouraged rather than restrained ethnic exclusiveness. The Slovenian Catholic group became a national sect.

Being voluntary associations, moreover, such national organizations were, as with Finnish denominations, subject to voluntary division and further sectarian development. In 1898, disagreements over the high rate of insurance claims from mining regions prompted a minority of aggrieved lodges to organize the rival "South Slovenic Catholic Union," known as J.S.K.J., with permanent headquarters at Ely.[41] Michigan Slovenians, meanwhile, went their own way into the S.H.Z., as we have seen. More serious, however, was the threat of anti-clericalism and socialism. Young liberals from the Old Country appeared in America as early as 1894 and were making substantial inroads in the Slovenian Catholic community by the turn of the century. At the national meeting of J.S.K.J. at Omaha in 1903, arguments over the religious requirements for membership produced a secession movement. An anti-clerical monthly began publication, first in Pueblo, Colorado, but soon after in Chicago. A Socialist, Jose Zavertnik, who had recently arrived from Slovenia, became editor in 1904. He took charge of the movement to form a national association of anti-clerical lodges, the Slovene National Benefit Society,

39. *Ibid.*, June 28, 1895, is given over almost completely to the convention at Tower.
40. *Ibid.*, March 30, 1894, p. 3; April, 1894, containing a serial printing of the U. S. Constitution in Slovene; and September 27, 1895, p. 1, advertising the dictionary, a copy of which is in the Immigrant Archives, University of Minnesota, along with a catechism, the annual almanacs after 1897, etc. Cf. F. S. Šušteršič, *Poduk Rajakom Slovencem ki so hočejo naseliti v Ameriki* [*Instructions to Slovene Countrymen Who Desire to Emigrate to America*] (Joliet, Illinois: *Amerikanski Slovenec*, 1903), 21.
41. Joe Zavertnik, *Amerikanski Slovenski. . .* [*American Slovenes. . .*] (Chicago: Slovene National Benefit Society, 1925), 375; Frank Tomsich, Ely, Minnesota [Supreme Secretary, J. S. K. J.], interview with writer, May 30, 1963.

known by the initials S.N.P.J.[42] Spread of this movement in the Lake Superior mining region was very slow, however, until the strike of 1907 created a open rupture in the parishes there. By that time, Socialists had pretty well taken over the anti-clerical movement, partly through the help of a separate organization, the Yugoslav Socialist Federation.[43]

Bitter conflicts between K.S.K.J. and J.S.K.J. lodges and their anti-clerical rivals characterized the following years. Competition at both local and national levels required each group to expand its mutual benefit insurance program, and to develop a full range of Slovenian cultural, social, and recreational activities. This was especially so in the case of the Socialists, who had to divorce their members from the Church and its supporting lodges if they were to succeed. Library associations, singing societies, dramatic clubs, and youth organizations, much in a pattern learned from the Finns, became customary in larger centers, with their printed materials supplied, precisely as in the case of religious denominations, by the publishers of the official newspaper organ.[44] By World War I, the sectarianization of the two national communities of American Slovenians, one church-related and the other socialist, was so great that in the decades which followed communication between the two groups on a personal level almost disappeared.

Two by-products of the competition seem significant. Both priests and lay leaders of the church-related Slovenian lodges were prompted to maintain a pro-labor position, in order to make their opposition to Socialism effective.[45] They had followed this policy for twenty-five years, before the mining companies discovered, at the time of the strike of 1917, that the church-related lodges might become, if properly cultivated, their allies. Scanty evidence leaves the picture confused, and the deep hostility of Slovenian workingmen to

42. Zavertnik, 1-25, and *passim*, is a poorly-organized summary. A complete file of *Glas Svobode* [Monthly and weekly, Pueblo and Chicago, 1902-1908] is on microfilm at the Immigrant Archives, University of Minnesota; see especially, in the issue of February 21, 1906, p. 2, ''Klerikalizem, Liberalizem, Socialna, Demokracija,'' as well as the translations into Slovene of passages from William T. Brown's *Appeal to Reason*, beginning as early as December 25, 1903, p. 1. Molek, 199-200, records the impact upon one freethinker of this paper.

43. *Glas Svobode*, issues for 1904-1906, show only one local lodge in Minnesota, at Ely, *Ameriski Družinski Koledar* [*American Family Almanac*], XI (Chicago: S.N.P.J., 1935), 141-142, attempts an explanation of the continued weakness of Slovene socialist activities in the iron-mining regions.

44. Zavertnik, 376-380, is a rambling account. Trunk, 497, counted in 1911 twelve Slovene lodges serving the 1600 Slovenes of Ely. Molek, 370-371, describes the publications of church Slovenes, but does not do justice to the variety of literature to be seen in the St. Mary's seminary library, Lemont, Illinois. Cf., on origins of Slovene Library Clubs of Chisholm and Ely, *Eveleth News*, April 27, 1916, p. 1; *Proletarec* [weekly organ of Yugoslav Socialist Federation, Chicago, 1907-1948, on microfilm at Immigrant Archives], March 12, 1912, p. 3, and May 7, 1912, p. 3; and Slovene Library Club, Ely, Minnesota, ''Minute Books'' (ms. on microfilm at the Minnesota Historical Society), entries for the year 1913.

45. *Amerikanski Slovenec*, December 22, 1899, pp, 1-5, carries a statement of policy on the move to Joliet.

the great industrial concerns which had dominated their lives made such an outcome in fact improbable. Even after 1917, when company support for Roman Catholic church building programs began for the first time to approach the level which Protestants had enjoyed from the beginning, Slovenian congregations remained on short rations. In some cases, certainly, as at Virginia in the years between 1917 and 1921, both mining captains and Irish priests came to look upon the mixed parishes as agents of a kind of "Americanization" which differed substantially from the liberal aims which Buh and Archbishop Ireland had espoused.[46]

Space does not permit in this paper a detailed discussion of the evidence pertaining to the Italian parishes and their affiliated clubs, nor of a half-dozen other Roman Catholic nationalities. Nor does it allow more than a word about two other ethnic groups which illustrate variant patterns: the Orthodox Serbians and the Jews. The Serbians, whose homes were scattered through a half-dozen Mesabi towns, were able to establish only one parish church, at Chisholm; but by the time they were well settled in the region railroad, street-car and automobile transportation were so efficient that on sacred days the great majority of families could appear. The warmth of fellowship which they experienced with their own kind bound the community together even in the first years, when women were scarce, and when no resident priest was available. None of them doubted that to be a Serbian was to be a member of the Serbian Orthodox Church.[47] Jewish congregations, at Virginia, Eveleth, and Hibbing were Orthodox in practice, as befitted immigrants chiefly from Lithuania. But the scarcity of rabbis and their great distance from centers of American Jewry required them in the earliest years to develop a regional association of synagogues for mutual aid and comfort. Orthodox scruples rapidly gave way to what were in form, though not yet in theory, the customs of Reformed Jews.[48]

As for the several non-Lutheran Protestant denominations, suffice to say here that Presbyterians and Methodists, thanks to the skill and zeal of their home mission agencies, were the most flourishing. For a decade the Presbyterians, under William Bell, sought to establish a "greater Range Parish," designed to minister to the spiritual needs of immigrants in smaller towns and mining locations without

46. O. I. M. Co., Executive Files, "Contributions, Roman Catholic Churches" records fully the shift; see esp. W. J. West, Virginia, Minnesota, November 6, 1918, to W. J. Olcott, one of a series seeking generous support of Our Lady of Lourdes Church, Virginia, whose pastor, West writes, "has always been a friend of ours and most of the membership seem especially well disposed."

47. St. Vasilje of Ostrog Serbian Eastern Orthodox Church, Chisholm, Minnesota, *Golden Jubilee Souvenir Book* (Chisholm, 1960), *passim;* Serbian Benevolent Society, Eveleth, January 18, 1927, to William J. Bell (in William Bell papers, now in Minnesota Historical Society); and William Bell, interview with writer, July 15, 1963.

48. Congregation B'Nai Abraham, Virginia, Minnesota, "Minute Book. 1917-1954" (ms. in possession of the congregation) chronicles the story fully.

demanding their conversion. Pastors of established Presbyterian congregations varied in their response to Bell's evangelism; one in Virginia cultivated an inter-ethnic fellowship. Meanwhile, the organization of Finnish Methodist churches and of the Swedish Methodist Conference testified to that denomination's readiness to fit programs to social conditions. The English-language Methodist congregations, like those of the Protestant Episcopal communion, served a strong complement of Cornish captain's families; they seem on cursory observation to have developed a feeling of identity which was almost an ethnic one as well, if we define that term broadly.[49]

In general, neither melting-pot parishes nor melting-pot denominations seem to have been as successful as the more exclusively ethnic ones in firing the deep emotions to kinship and belonging which enabled them to mold and shape the life of the immigrant in the New World. Moreover, the experience of the Finns was repeated as other groups developed denominational organization above the level of local fellowship; these institutions, not only in their spiritual but in their cultural and educational programs as well, nurtured sectarianism. The religious and emotional weakness of the melting-pot congregation on one hand, and the long-run irrelevance of sectarianism on the other, combined to leave religious institutions at last on the fringes of the real life which the immigrant's children embraced. Instead, they placed their hopes in education and in economic ambition, found their pleasure in the round of athletic, recreational, and social events which the towns sponsored, and adopted as their own the passion for identification with American culture which became the hallmark of the region.[50]

To American church historians, the story told here offers three challenges of much broader significance, I think, than merely the religious history of the mining communities. The first is to study the history of both congregations and denominations in America in reference to social and institutional necessity. Was sectarianism in other communions also a by-product of denominational structures originally devised to give material and spiritual nurture to struggling congregations? If so, were the activities so often thought of as "churchly"—education, youth programs, uniform ritual, and the like—as much divisive as harmonizing influences in American Protestantism? The familiar concept of a straight-line evolution of "sects" into "churches" could scarcely survive such a discovery.

49. The William Bell papers contain numerous contemporary evaluations of the religious life of Range towns during the years 1913-1927; see especially W. P. Shriver, "The Mesabi and Vermillion Ore Ranges of Minnesota," typescript, 1914. A survey of city directories for the second decade of the century showed non-immigrant Protestant churches weak in numbers, and understaffed, far more than immigrant churches.

50. See my essay, "School and Community: The Quest of Equal Opportunity in Iron Mining Towns," multilith in the University of Minnesota Library, esp. pp. 35-42.

Secondly, much work lies ahead for those willing to search out the inner complexities — sociological, religious, and institutional — which characterized Roman Catholic life in twentieth-century America. Despite continuing improvement in the level of scholarship among Roman Catholic no less than Protestant church historians, we know little, yet, about anything other than the deeds and policies of the Irish leaders of the Church. When the stories of the various ethnic sub-communities within Roman Catholicism in America are fully told, with due reference to parish institutions on one hand and national organizations on the other, I suspect that our image of modern American Catholic history will resemble much more closely that of Protestantism. The single and exceedingly important difference will be the continued pressure of a powerfully organized hierarchy, exerted year by year upon every part of the Church, for the creation of one American Catholic faith.

The third challenge is to redefine the concept of ethnic community in American religious history in terms of social psychology, rather than national tradition. In the cases surveyed here, the Finns, Slovenians, and Croatians were divided into several different "ethnic" communities. Each one of these was made in America, and each witnessed the rapid development of a national organization, whether called a Socialist Federation, a mutual benefit society, or a denomination, which contributed heavily to its sense of exclusive identity. Such a redefinition might enable us to understand better the cohesive and persistent force of American religious movements whose membership, being composed chiefly of native-born white Protestants, does not seem at first glance to suggest an ethnic identity. Perhaps the migration of Southern Baptists to northern cities where, one suspects, not just soundness of doctrine, but the sound of the doctrine was crucial to new commitments, is an obvious case in point. I have seen dimly, and tried to record in my history of the Church of the Nazarene, similar developments among rural Wesleyans moving to the city. But much more needs to be done, I should think, before we can understand the social forces which, no less than religious belief or spiritual quest, condition the life of religion in modern industrial societies.

ETHNICITY 2, 204–224 (1975)

Ethnicity: The Vital Center
of Religion in America

HARRY S. STOUT

University of Connecticut

Historians and sociologists have long recognized the interrelationship of religion and ethnicity throughout the course of American history.[1] Unfortunately, in spite of their mutual concern, the two disciplines have gone their separate ways and any substantive examination of the interworkings of religion and ethnicity has remained largely neglected. Although a wide array of descriptive literature has emerged on the subject of ethnic and religious groups in America, there is no synthetic scholarship pulling the works together into a coherent framework. The burgeoning literature has, if anything, obfuscated rather than clarified the complexities involved in the analysis of ethnicity and religion in America.[2] The following interpretation of ethnicity and religion in America is therefore guided by two questions: What was the nature of the interrelationship between ethnicity and religion? and what role does this connection play in the development of American society?

I

Common to the growing body of literature on both the religious and ethnic groups in America is the effort to isolate a unifying theme or comprehensive approach that adequately characterizes the American experience. In religious history, the attempt to epitomize American church history has given rise to varying interpretations summarizing American ecclesiastical developments. William Warren Sweet, for example, found the wellspring of American Christianity in the frontier experience,[3] while later scholars increasingly focused on the growing urbanization of the churches.[4] Pluralism caught the eye of many historians who elevated it to a general principle based primarily on voluntary Protestant denominations and the absence of a state-church.[5] Other disagreed, maintaining, with Will Herberg, that denominations became but individual species of the genus Protestantism–Catholicism–Judaism.[6] In yet another direction, American historians led by H. Richard Niebuhr built on the models of Emile Durkheim, Max Weber, and Ernst Troeltsch, to discover the social sources of religion in America.[7]

With Will Herberg and the sociological analyses of religion, scholars with diverse concerns have become singularly aware of the ethnic im-

204

pact on American religion. Like church historians, ethnic historians are also noting the interrelationship of ethnicity and religion. Most notable are the historians of American politics who, in pointing to "ethno*cultural*" factors in American political behavior, focus primarily on eth*noreligious* factors.[8] But even with the aid of the sophisticated empirical techniques presently available to these scholars, they are often plagued by a rigid framework that examines patterns around simplistic and sometimes artificial dichotomies, such as "melting-pot," or "pluralism," "pietistic," or "liturgical."[9] In short, no one has explained what was the nature of the interrelationship between ethnicity and religion in America and, more importantly, why the two were so closely linked. Perhaps, as Martin Marty suggests, ethnicity is so close to American religion that historians have been reluctant to explore its deepest implications.[10]

Although failing to provide final answers, the increasing amount of work by historians and sociologists has served the admirable purpose of supplying a precise foundation for constructing conceptual frameworks in which existing information and new studies can be placed. Consequently, I hope in this essay to suggest a framework or model that delineates the relationship of ethnicity and religion in America as it has developed in time. The purpose here is not definitive documentation; rather, I will merely offer some random, familiar illustrations at various points along the way.

Prior to the actual presentation of the model, some clarification of the terms "ethnicity" and "religion" is essential. (Whether the terms can adequately support the descriptive and explanatory power ascribed to them is an issue that I shall return to later.) Of the two terms, ethnicity poses a lesser problem and, for our purposes here, Milton Gordon's definition of ethnicity in terms of "peoplehood" serves as a concise foundation. "Within the ethnic group," Gordon explains, "there develops a network of organizations and informal social relationships which permits and encourages the members of the ethnic group to remain within the confines of the group for all of their primary relationships and some of their secondary relationships throughout all the stages of the life cycle."[11] This sense of "peoplehood" or "belongingness" may be narrowly constituted to include only a subgroup within a heterogeneous society or it may become progressively expanded to include other subgroups, a nation, or even the entire human race. The potential expansion of ethnic group identities is, as we shall see, crucial to understanding the evolution of ethnic and religious groups in America. Regardless of the expanse, the ethnic group functions as the primary matrix of associations, supplying identity and meaning (or lack of identity and meaning) to the individual within the ethnic group.

The meaning of "religion" on the other hand is so strewn with semantic

and conceptual obstacles that many scholars settle for an intuitive definition of the term and do not bother to articulate precisely what they
mean. For those who do define the term, religion often is defined institutionally in terms of churches, sects, denominations, or "faiths" oriented
around a shared belief in a deity. In common parlance, the "religious"
individual is the one who attends church and believes in a supreme
being. Such a definition provides for the easy dichotomy between the
"religious" and "nonreligious" individual, "religious" and "secular"
institutions, or the "sacred" and "profane" society.[12] From a sociological perspective, religion has been more broadly defined in group
terms. In Gerhard Lenski's words, religion is "a system of beliefs about
the nature of the force(s) ultimately shaping a man's destiny, and the
practices associated therewith, shared by the members of a group."[13]

Perhaps the most progress in clarifying the meaning of religion in society emerges from the works of scholars engaged in the comparative
study of religious groups. These scholars are rapidly growing skeptical
toward traditional concepts of religion and insist that the term represents
an inadequate concept in need of reformulation. Reacting against the
inherent ideologization of religious phenomena that plagues studies of
religious groups, Wilfred Cantwell Smith argues that the term "religion"
should be dropped from usage. Similarly, Clifford Geertz concludes,
"Our problem, and it grows worse by the day, is not to define religion
but to find it." Geertz goes on to define the "religious perspective" as
"the conviction that the values one holds are grounded in the inherent
structure of reality, that between the way one ought to live and the way
things really are there is an unbreakable inner connection."[14]

But, if it is neither possible nor prudent to seek an empirical definition
of the "essence" of religious experience, it is possible, and indeed necessary, to describe the various expressions of religious experience in historical, sociological, and ideological perspective. Beyond description, it
is equally important to discern the ways in which religious ideas, socio-
cultural traditions, and institutions tend to reinforce or inhibit the religious faith. There are two dimensions operating in tandem here, the
one personal, the other social: it is the commonly shared personal perception of reality and sense of ultimate allegiance that supplies coherence and community on a group level. It is in this context, that personal
religious allegiance and socio-cultural expression interact and reinforce
one another. The particular form that this reinforcement takes in the
American experience represents the subject-matter of this essay.

Part of the reason the subject of religion and ethnicity is so complex is
that the two are seen as separate compartments in a comparative context. Scholars have approached these subjects by seeking to discover the
factors religious and ethnic groups share in common. However, a more

fruitful approach would be to seek out contrasts between the two groups: ways in which the structure, goals, or allegiances of the groups differ. When viewed from this perspective, there are often no fundamental differences, and what is involved here is more than a mere parallelism of cultural and structural institutions; it is two identical expressions of the same phenomenom such that one's ethnicity becomes, in fact, his religion (labeled here "ethnoreligion").

If ethnoreligious faith is an expression of ultimate allegiance, and the "church" represents an institution conceived to maintain and perpetuate that allegiance, then the churches, sects, and denominations become as important as symbols óf ethnic allegiance as they are for themselves. And here it is important not to confuse traditional religious symbols from what is, in fact, symbolized. Seen in such a light, the immigrant churches served the allegiance of the ethnic group at the expense of a prophetic message aimed at all sectors of society. The church service became a symbolic rite of affirmation to one's ethnic association and a vehicle for preserving the ethnic language. Schools were established under the aegis of the church and efforts were made to inculcate the group with ethnic values and faith in the ethnic heritage.

By broadly conceptualizing the meaning of religion and ethnicity, the terms can be used interchangeably because they manifest identical faiths (or allegiances). Ethnicity and belief in the ethnic group, regardless of the group's scope, generate the culture faith or "religion" that constitutes a basic, and often underestimated, force in American history. Both the volume and diversity of ethnic groups in America distinguished them from other societies. Obviously, the sense of "peoplehood" characteristic of the ethnic group existed in some sense among the immigrants prior to their arrival in America. But it was an ethnicity that functioned in an essentially homogenous environment and quite unlike the consciousness-raising ethnic demands imposed upon American immigrants arriving in a hostile environment that included a multitude of disparate and contending ethnic groups. To avoid the sense of alienation that threatened to subsume all immigrant groups, ethnic allegiance assumed both the function and authority of religion among the individual groups.

To say that American religion has generally embodied an ethnic allegiance, however, is not to say that it is a static religion lacking any internal dynamic. To the contrary, it is the thesis of this article that American ethnic religion developes in three successive stages or phases, each of which expands its membership from the former. While religion remains ethnic in content through all three stages, the internal constitution of the ethnic group constantly broadens. The first stage in this model represents the "immigrant" phase in which the ethnic group centered around an amalgam of ecclesiastical and national origins. Thus, for example, the ethnic units of the first stage were the German Catholics, German Lutherans, English Anglican, English Congregational, German Jews or Russian Jews. The second stage represents the integration of the immigrant units into what could roughly be labeled a Protestant-Catholic-Jewish-Black ethnoreligion. In this stage the ethnic group expands on the basis of broad religious faiths and on the basis of race. Thus, for example, white English, Welsh, Scottish, Scotch-Irish, Swedish, Norwegians, Danes, Finns, Germans, and Dutch identified in the ethnic group "white Protestant," as opposed to Blacks, Catholics, or Jews. Finally, in the third stage, Protestants, Catholics, Jews, and Blacks identify as Americans and their ethnoreligion becomes oriented around a national identification with "The American Way of Life."

Having sketched the basic parameters of the ethnoreligion model, it is important to stress that no one individual or ethnic group necessarily corresponds exactly to the model, which I am presenting as a constructed "type" in Max Weber's sense. Neither do the stages follow an exact chronological sequence that can (at this point) be specifically traced through time. This is not to say, however, that the model is wholly removed from any time sequence in the American experience. Rather, it is a "dated and localized" typology in which the dimensions of time and space are roughly apparent but do not conform exactly to any specific empirical instance.[15] Needless to say, at any one point in time or in any one group, a congeries of patterns exist to which the model is only intended as a rough scale or tentative generalization.

II

As early as the first settlements in North America the phenomenom of ethnoreligion, centered around the immigrant church, finds clear expression. A brief look at the New England settlements will illustrate the pattern of American ethnoreligion in the first stage. Like other immigrants,[16] the New England colonists established institutions in the New World that served to perpetuate the strength and vitality of the particular group. One of the primary motives in the migration of English Separating Congregationalists from Leyden to Plymouth Colony, for example, was the fear that their national identity would become submerged in an alien culture.[17] Upon arrival in New England, the settlers demonstrated the sense of "peoplehood" characterizing the ethnic group. At the center of the ethnic group was the church, which supplied the cohesion and insularity necessary for retaining a distinct ethnic community.[18] That the New England holy experiment was insular and intolerant to all outsiders hardly needs documentation. Group consciousness and activity flowed from the church, which did not exist primarily to spread evangelical Christianity to the world, but rather, to preserve the ethnic solidarity of the group. Crucial to retaining this solidarity was the collective conversion experience of the New England towns binding the group into a self-sustaining covenental community.[19] As with subsequent immigrant groups, the Puritans were not practicing a transcendent faith calling for the brotherhood of all the saints; they were practicing a culture faith oriented around nurturing an ethnic community of feeling and aspiration, which looked inward toward preserving the integrity of the group.

As self-contained communities oriented around their particular ethnic group, the Puritan church assumed the dual function of supplying both community and association to its members.[20] That is, the church was a network of primary relationships whose function was to mold the membership into a united community with a strong ethnic identity. Periodically, "revivals" of religion emerged to renew the covenant holding the community together.[21] In Daniel Boorstin's words, "The Puritan beacon for misguided mankind was to be neither a book nor a theory. It was to be the community itself."[22]

The ethnic character of Puritan religion is nowhere more clearly reflected than in Puritan relations with outsiders, notably the American Indians and the Quakers. Bernard Bailyn clearly sees the ethnic significance of Puritan religion in the abject failure of their attempts to transcend ethnic boundaries and evangelize the Indians. The Puritans "enterprise," Bailyn argues, "aimed no longer at unifying society but only at aiding one group to survive in a world of different groups."[23] Similarly, Neil Emerson Salisbury concludes from an extensive examination of Puritan settlers and missionaries that:

> the Puritans created an elitist, tribalistic structure of thought, society, and church that served to widen the gap between themselves and the world. While the "errand into the wilderness" included conversion of the heathen, the tendency toward ingrown exclusiveness in Puritanism worked against the evangelicalism required for such an effort.[24]

Besides the Indian missions debacle, the nature of Puritan religion can also be seen in the general concern of the Puritans with themselves and their families rather than Christian evangelism. The dominating motive in the "half-way covenant" was the fear that the children and the grandchildren of the community would fall by the wayside. Consequently the church had to alter its formation to accomodate itself to a new and broader ethnicity.[25] Persecution of outsiders, notably Quakers,[26] remains the most glaring example of the ethnocentrism that defined the New England religious experiment. Those among the Puritan group who favored toleration were soon isolated and left with the option of leaving either voluntarily or through expulsion.[27]

The Puritans have been discussed here merely for illustrative purposes. All subsequent immigrant groups in America reflected the same
patterns that are associated with the first stage of American ethnoreligion. American Catholics, to cite another example, faced the two-
fold task of preserving the faith of the "old country" while adopting the
nonessential aspects of the faith to the new American culture. The
church functioned as a defense mechanism that protected Catholic immigrants against the dissolvent power of assimilation, against discour-
agement, and that sustained its claims on the individuals in the group. In
his classic description of (largely Catholic) peasant immigrants, Oscar
Handlin observes, "Their [the church's] claim to men's allegiance
rested on a solid basis of authority. It was not an individual choice that
was involved in the process of belonging, but conformity."[28]
Among every major immigrant group the central institution was the
church, which served the function of organizing allegiance around the
ethnic group. Characteristic of all such immigrant churches was the
functioning of the church as a community, the centrality of the pastor in
affirming group solidarity, and the replacement of an evangelical vision
by ethnic insularity.[29] The failure to transcend ethnic boundaries was not
only apparent between diverse nationalities and ecclesiastical affiliations, but also within groups claiming the same ecclesiastical and national heritage, but arriving at different times. Thus, for example, the
"Old" German Lutherans that arrived in the mid-nineteenth century
were rejected by those German Lutherans who arrived earlier (and were
in the second stage). Speaking of these "Old" Lutherans, one observor
clearly described the ethnic focus when he argued, "The Germans [i.e.,
recent arrivals] almost all belong to some church, and are strongly attached to what they call their faith. Hence we have to preach their
religion out of their heads in order to preach Bible religion into their
hearts."[30] The "religion" that had to be replaced was not Luthern Christianity or transcendent faith, but was an ultimate commitment to the
ethnic group that superceded all other claims. Similar patterns as those
above prevailed in virtually every immigrant group in America. If Old
German Lutherans could not worship with German-American Lutherans because they represented two different ethnoreligious stages, neither
could German Catholics commune with German Lutherns, German
Catholics with Irish Catholics, German Jews with Russian Jews, and so
on.[31] In all cases, the spoken transcendent faith was subsumed by culture faiths and the constituency was defined horizontally with the ethnic
group rather than vertically in terms of a shared human-divine encounter.
Although usually not considered immigrants, Black Americans also
constitute an ethnic group whose religion is oriented around supplying

ethnic identity. Like the white immigrant groups, the church lay at the hub of the Black community. Rejected and persecuted by the other white Americans, the Blacks established their own ethnoreligion, which supplied identity for the group. The Black church became an institution that, in William Clebsch's words,

> served as a site for worship and education, recreation and social protests, relief of suffering and redress of grievances. In it, usually only in it, he could be himself among his own, expressing his feelings as he saw fit by the skills of his choice. As Baptist or Methodist, Catholic or Pentecostalist, his denomination gave him a name and identity shared and respected by other citizens.[32]

In terms of group leadership in the Black community, the minister functioned at the center, as the representative of his people.[33] The Black church dignified the Black man, and provided the community and identity necessary to survive in a society of hostile, white ethnoreligions.

III

Just as ethnicity functioned as the religion of the immigrant church, it also functions in the second stage, although in a different form. Here the "triple melting pot" model of Will Herberg—if it is broadly construed to include race and is not seen as a final stage—offers a valid insight. In this stage, the allegiance is no longer introverted and centered around the immigrant group, but it expands to embrace various groups into an ethnoreligion characterized by Herberg as Protestant-Catholic-Jew (and one should add-Black). "The old-line ethnic group, with its foreign language and culture, was not for them," Herberg explains: "They were Americans. But the old family religion, the old ethnic religion, could serve where language and culture could not; the religion of the immigrants—with certain necessary modifications, such as the replacement of the ethnic language by English—was accorded a place in the American scheme of things that made it once both genuinely American and a familiar principle of group identification."[34] Individual ethnic communities began looking outward and sought to contribute to a larger ethnic norm summarized by the label "Protestant," "Catholic," or "Jew." Once again the religion was ethnicity, as the major faiths sought to assert their solidarity and dominance. Furthermore, like the first stage, ethnicity offered the group both association and, to a lesser degree, community.

Because Protestantism was the first dominant faith in the second stage and because its lines of demarcation are so well charted, we shall focus primary attention upon trends among the Protestant denominations. The emergence of denominations and the fragmentation of Protestantism has rightfully assumed a central role in American historiography.[35] What is significant about these denominations, it seems to me, is the affiliation of each denomination with an ethnic group.[36] Equally as significant as their ethnic origins was their gradual "Americanization" and united effort to create a "Righteous Empire" in America.[37] Although the Herbergian stage did not generally emerge until the post-World War II period—and then only temporarily—its roots can be traced to nineteenth century Protestant America. In this context, the rise of Protestant denominations is not primarily one of origins, but rather, one of development and process into a benevolent empire. To understand that process, attention must be focused on the ethnic identifications as they progressively expanded and became more comprehensive.

The dissolution of a state church in America and the emergence of volunteeristic denominations reflected the diversity of ethnoreligions that flourished in the United States with increasing immigration.[38] The growing Protestant ethnic consensus defined the new ethnoreligion of the second stage and, in distinguishing itself from the "others," encouraged the subsequent consolidation of Catholics and Jews.[39] The device first employed by Protestants to present a unified front in America was the revival. Unlike the revivals of the Great Awakening, the series of revivals dating from the late eighteenth century onward was not directed at awakening communities toward "owning" a pre-existent covenant; rather, the revivals sought to revive *individuals* toward reforming their society.[40] The objective of the later revivals was not the community, but those outside the group; the means to effect such an outreach were a series of revivals and benevolent societies.[41] Recognizing the growing number of "outsiders," Protestants expanded their ethnic consciousness from a denominationalism to a pan-Protestant religious association that, through voluntary persuasion, would remain dominant. Protestant ethnoreligion emerged so that, in Lyman Beecher's words, "these men [nonwhite Protestants] do not steal a march on us, and that the rising opposition may meet them early, before they have gathered strength."[42]

The revivals and reform societies were no longer an errand to the godly (ethnic) community, but an errand by the new Protestant empire to the pagan Rome of the aliens.[43] The emergence of revivalism and reform (of aliens) can only be understood by bearing in mind that they were not merely a theological innovation, status-minded reaction, or frontier phenomenom. Their form and causes were fundamentally shaped by the dynamic factor of American ethnoreligion. The very term "revival of *religion*" that came to characterize the Protestants' efforts is instructive here; it reveals that the basic orientation was not around a revival of Christ but was a revival and reinforcement of a new, expanded ethnoreligion of white Protestantism. Nowhere is the non-Christian religion of many American Protestants more clearly reflected than in the secularization of the redemption act through reform societies. Viewed through the "kingdom" motif of H. Richard Niebuhr, American Protestantism continued its negation of the gospel motif through its attempt to inaugurate a divine kingdom on earth directed by white Protestants.[44]

Perhaps the clearest expression of the non-Christian, Protestant ethnoreligion appears in the millenariansim that was intimately laced with the revivals and reform societies.[45] A case in point was the intensely millenarian impulse that permeated the temperance crusade. An illustrative passage that captures the intellectual climate of social reform appeared in an essay entitled "The Temperance Reform A Harbinger of the Millenium," which feverently proclaimed:

> Christians, is it not part of almost every prayer you offer, that God will soon open upon the world the millenial day? Are you acting in consistency with your prayers, by lending your influence to help forward this glorius cause of moral improvement, which must prevail ere the millenium shall fully come?[46]

Endemic to the millenarianism of American Protestantism (both in the reform movements and the later Social Gospel movement) was a belief in the central role of human agencies in introducing the Kingdom of God on earth. The emphasis was placed on man and, more particularly, white Protestants such that "Millenarianism thus institutionalized God's sovereignty. . . . It blunted the inciseveness of God's sovereign presence. In fact, whether God was present or not and whether he was sovereign or not made no difference under an immanental optimism."[47] Beneath the rhetoric of revival, reform, and millenarianism lay the belief and affirmation in Protestant ethnoreligion. Revivalism and reform represented one tool through which the new ethnic consciousness and identity would be forged.

The other primary device for forging the dominant Protestant ethnoreligion was the public school.[48] The public schools were to be at once "nonsectarian" yet dispensers of a common religious heritage drawn from the American experience of white Protestants. Horace Mann, the leading architect of the common school crusade in New England, envisioned a union of education and Protestantism such that the public school:

> welcomes the Bible, and therefore welcomes all the doctrines which the Bible really contains, and that it listens to these doctrines so reverently, that, for the time being, it will not suffer any rash mortal to thrust in his interpolations of their message, or overlay the text with any of the "many inventions" which the heart of man has sought out.[49]

The public school movement soon became a Protestant mission in which patriotism and Protestant religion found clear institutional expression. In short, the public school represented the panacea for white Protestants increasingly facing a society of alien and threatening faces.

One of the darker notes in American history is that white Protestant ethnoreligion resorted not only to persuasion and education but also to persecution of outsiders. Christianity calls for the brotherhood of man, ethnoreligion calls for ultimate allegiance to the ethnic group and rejection of all outsiders. The often chronicled pages of nativism in American history represent the most chilling description of American ethnoreligion in the second stage.[50] The white Protestant mission to pagan Rome realized a literal implementation with the formation of the American Protective Association in 1887.[51] White Protestants were clearly "American;" Catholics, Jews, and Blacks remained outside of the ethnic fold and were un-American. Needless to say, not only Catholics, but all other ethnic associations fell under the wrath of Protestant ethnoreligion.[52] No longer immigrant communities, the second stage of ethnoreligion witnessed an amalgamation of ethnic units and informal union designed to protect themselves from "outsiders."

The focus has been on nineteenth century Protestantism simply because it represented the initial stream in the second stage and, for a long time, was the dominant faith; but similar patterns can be discerned among Catholics, Jews, and Blacks.[53] Among white Catholics, for example, informal union appeared especially in the cities through the parish missions, which sought to unite Irish, German, Italian, and Polish Americans into the inclusive Catholic fold.[54] The religion of ethnicity gradually expanded on all fronts, and ethnic identity was increasingly oriented around the labels Protestant, Catholic, Jew, and Black.

IV

As a typological process rather than an empirical *fait accompli,* America has not yet, nor may ever, entirely reach the third stage of ethnoreligion, labeled "culture" or "civil" religion. In this stage, the religious associations continue to expand their boundaries until a national consensus is reached and the emerging ethnic religion becomes "The American Way of Life." The term "culture religion" has enjoyed such a current vogue with a variety of meanings, that here I will suggest four dimensions integral to American culture religion: individual pragmatism, materialism, faith in progress through technology, and nationalism.

The first constituent in American culture religion and the American Way of Life is its individual pragmatism. Richard Hofstadter refers to this dimension as the "cult of religious practicality," in which the dignity of the individual and the process of self-improvement become a supreme value.[55] The American Way of Life is intensely pragmatic and optimistic; witness for example, the enormous influence and popularity of Norman Vincent Peale in American society.[56]

In terms of self-improvement, the pragmatic mentality is closely allied with the second dimension of American culture religion, namely its materialism. The dominance of pragmatism in American culture religion is possible, as Richard Hofstadter further notes, "wherever the passion for personal advancement has become so intense that the difference between this motive and religious faith has been obscured."[57] The phenomenal growth of a new corporation based entirely on self-initiative attests to the amalgamation of pragmatism and materialism in America. Not surprisingly, that corporation is named "Amway." The great economic abundance and sense of giveness in America permeated American ethnoreligion as the groups encouraged "getting ahead" in society, often to the point of equating "success" with "faith." In American culture religion, not only are both God and Mammon served, but they actually enjoy a healthy rapport! As the ethnic identities of Protestants, Catholics, Jews, and Blacks gradually merges into one imperceptible "American" ethnicity, the materialism remains part and parcel of the ethos.

Closely related to materialism and pragmatism in American culture, religion is faith in progress through the tools of science and technology.[58] From the beginning, Americans have demonstrated a profound optimism and faith in progress, but the advent of technology has produced special pressures on this faith in progress. Progress does not come cheaply because, as Sydney E. Ahlstrom warns, technology "now threatens or has utterly disrupted primordial styles of life the world over. . . . It is gradually making 'organization men' out of every member of the human race."[59] In a word, technology has become an institution, in the sense described by Robert A. Nisbet as "an autonomous pattern of ends, functions, authorities, and allegiances."[60]

The final component of American culture religion is its nationalism. "America" becomes the label for the new ethnoreligion, which asserts itself against all foreign aliens. Protestants, Catholics, and Jews are grafted onto a common American stock that demands their highest allegiance. In short, the American Way is becoming the third stage of American ethnoreligion.[61] This stage is not so much a triple melting pot as it is a new America, where ethnic identities are rooted primarily in the American Way of Life; where ethnic and denominational ties are contentless labels and faint memories. The subservience of Protestantism, Catholicism, and Judaism to the new Americanism is described by Will Herberg when he observes of the three faiths that:

they are three diverse representations of the *same* "spiritual values," the "spiritual values" American democracy is presumed to stand for (the fatherhood of God and brotherhood of man, the dignity of the individual human being, etc.). That is, at bottom, why no one is expected to change his religion as he becomes American; since each of the religions is *equally and authentically American*. . . (italics mine).[62]

In summary, the third stage of American culture religion represents the culmination of a process in which Protestants, Catholics, Jews, and Blacks have merged into identification with Americanism. A state of consensual pluralism is reached in which nominal religious faiths affirm a transcendent association but, in practice, travel to the beat of the American drum.[63] An intricate religious montage emerges in which plurality and consensus are simultaneously visible in the American Way. The previously disparate ethnoreligions exist in a state of mutual toleration in the third stage precisely because they have been replaced by the American culture religion; a national ethnoreligion is the final product.

Ironically, as the churches reconcile themselves to the American Way, they lose their voice and position as the dynamic center of the group. Churches and religious associations are no longer communities sharing primary ties but are associations and passive audiences. The religion of the American Way leads to a religious syncretism so pervasive that all challengers of it are seditious aliens and pluralistic dialogue becomes "confrontation."

V

Given the three stage model of American ethnoreligion, what is the state of ethnoreligion in America today? Evidence from a variety of empirical and impressionistic sources indicates that America seems to be moving rapidly into the third stage. The following illustrations are only included to represent a sampling of current studies. In his examination of Detroit completed in 1961, Gerhard Lenski discovered that Detroit Protestants were moving rapidly toward American culture religion and that the other major faiths were lagging somewhat behind.[64] Such a conclusion is understandable when it is remembered that American Protestantism was, for a long time, the dominant ethnoreligion representing, in pristine form, many of the later characteristics of American ethnoreligion.[65]

Evidence that non-Protestant Americans are similarly moving toward culture religion appears most convincingly in the work of Rodney Stark and Charles Y. Glock completed in 1967. Based on extensive surveys, Stark and Glock asked the question "Are We Entering a Post-Christian Era?" and they concluded that, since the watershed point of World War II, Americans have moved away from "traditional religion," and the "religious beliefs which have been the bedrocks of Christian faith for nearly two millennia are on their way out; this may very well be the dawn of a post-Christian era."[66] Stark and Glock go on to describe a distinct movement in American religion toward a theological "modernism" that eschews all notions, literal or symbolic, of a Christ-centered or deistic religion.[67] In a related vein, J. Milton Yinger discovered that intermarriage among religious faiths has markedly risen, and argues:

> In the United States, the "American Way of Life" has become the operative faith to a substantial degree. Those who wish to relate the national faith to one of the traditional religions are free to do so, provided they do not challenge any of the basic premises of Americanism.[68]

Finally, Nathan Glazer and Daniel P. Moynihan concluded from their study of New York that "religion as a primary identity for Americans has weakened. Particularly in the case of Catholics, confusion and uncertainty have entered what was only a few years ago a very firm and clear identity."[69]

In addition to empirical studies, there is additional evidence that American culture religion is rapidly gaining adherents. Witness for example, the extraordinary popularity of books such as Bishop Robinson's *Honest to God*, Pierre Berton's *The Comfortable Pew*, Harvey Cox's *The Secular City*, or popular individuals cutting across the major faiths such as Billy Graham, Norman Vincent Peale, Malcolm Boyd, or Bishop Sheen. In his controversial and often misunderstood book *The Death of God: The Culture of Our Post-Christian Era*, Gabriel Vahanian reminds us that "religiosity is not faith. . . . It may be that our age still is religious. But it is certainly post-Christian."[70] The particular nature of American religion, in Vahanian's opinion, becomes clearer when he subsequently argues that:

> Religiosity is the cunning by which secularism triumphs over faith in God and, instead, sets up faith—faith in anything—as an end in itself. Such religiosity fulfills civic ends: today it is socially fashionable to be religious.[71]

Other observers of the American scene, from a variety of perspectives, have reached similar conclusions. To the foreign observer, the distinctive flavor of American culture religion is readily apparent. Thus Bryan Wilson concludes:

> If religion in America was to be closely involved in the sense of national identity which the country obviously found so imperative in the years of immigration, it could become effectively involved only as religious differences were themselves eroded, so that all faiths might serve the same end, and become more similar to each other in doing so. Religious commitment and church allegiance *have become* elements in the American value system, accepted parts of the "American Way of Life."[72]

From the historical perspective, both Franklin Littell and Will Herberg speak of the emergence of American culture religion in terms similar to Wilson.[73]

Like the first two stages of American ethnoreligion, American culture religion is "religious," but lacking a transcendent and prophetic faith. The distinctive immigrant experience fostered a religious experience as did the subsequent American experience, but in none of these stages was the experience a Christian, Jewish, or Islamic experience. In this sense, America has never been, nor does it appear to be moving toward a "Christian nation." True there are numerous instances in American history that evidence a real commitment to a transcendent faith, but these are the outstanding exceptions—the strain of dissent in the prevailing American ethnic religious tradition. Seldom have American religious institutions transcended the ethnic community (organized narrowly or nationally) and shunned their own interests, conflicts, and prejudices, to bow in total subjection to the deity they confess. Established on a horizontally based authority, how could they do otherwise? How can a transcendent God survive when he becomes the handmaiden and accessory of a culture faith? The third stage of American culture religion represents the natural outgrowth of an ethnoreligion, whose source of strength and message is derived from allegiance to the ever-expanding ethnoreligious group.

But if American culture religion is the natural extension of American ethnoreligion, it is also a highly problematical and explosive extention. American culture religion is ethnoreligion with one important distinction from the preceeding two stages. The communal involvement and primary relationships present in the first and second stages of American ethnoreligion are conspicuously absent in the third. With the disintegration (through integration) of immigrant and religious faith subcommunities, the sense of identity has also disintegrated, depriving the individual of any reference point from which to relate to the mass society. American culture religion represents an anamalous situation where both laymen *and clergy* doubt, if not overtly deny, the theological basis they affirm in their creeds and rituals. Religion becomes part and parcel of the "giveness" associated with America.[74] As a *given,* rather than something to be achieved, the individual is relegated to a spectator's role in American culture religion, lacking any impulse to *achieve* a community.

Because American culture religion presents only a nation-wide association sharing belief in a culture god, what is the source of individual identity and community? Gabriel Vahanian is useful here as he reminds us that "Togetherness is a substitute sense of community, a counterfeit communion."[75] The society of the American Way supplies nothing more than mere camaraderie, in which the concept of community as other-directed (vertically or horizontally) has been replaced by the mystique of conformity, conformity to ideals that, upon close examination, reveal themselves to be spurious, self-serving credos.

Through the three stage paradigm set forth here, the present situation in American religion comes into clearer focus. It is possible to see the major thread of American history through the various ethnoreligions that have appeared in the nation. The problems emerging from ethnoreligion have not disappeared with the end of overt nativism in the first and second stages but have been metamorphosized into a problem of even greater proportions in the third stage. In the third stage, it is not *groups* alienated from each other, but *individuals* who are totally estranged from their society with no sense of community.

The intolerableness of this situation is, I believe, reflected in negative responses to the American Way, especially through an increasing ethnic consciousness. Spurred by the Black civil rights movement,[76] which not coincidentally established a new first stage ethnoreligion through Black Muslims, some Americans are increasingly seeking solace in a pluralistic past that provides identities and sources of community. The revival of interest in ethnicity bespeaks, in some cases, a return full circle to the first stage of immigrant solidarity. Thus the ethnoreligion pattern has generally prevailed but not yet congealed in the third stage, as the internal components increasingly (but perhaps temporarily) resist the full implimentation of the third stage national ethnoreligion. The extent to which the ethnic "minority" demands for a pluralistic society represent a new ethnic configuration or merely represent the dying gasp of vestigial "immigrant" group consciousness remains open to debate, and lies beyond the purview of this essay.[77]

VI

In conclusion, I would reiterate the basic premise of this article that, in variant forms, religion and ethnicity in America realized identical expression. The development of American ethnoreligion can be roughly ordered around three stages, representing a dynamic process in which the forms are constantly changing through the introduction and maturation of diverse ethnic groups in American history. Needless to say, there are prominent exceptions to the model in the American past; and here I would only suggest that such exceptions were generally the sects, societies, and individuals who failed to thrive among a compelling and dominant ethnic religion in America. In Daniel Boorstin's words, the groups and individuals that transcended American ethnoreligion were drawn from those who "concern for their own purity overshadowed their desire to improve their community."[78]

The paradigm presented here in brief form does not presume to be exhaustive but rather to suggest a tentative typology of religiosity in America as it historically developed.[79] As a process that is not yet completed, the model rejects simplistic generalizations ordered around concepts of assimilation or pluralism because both dimensions are present in the ethnic process in different phases. In the same sense, the history of American churches cannot be described solely in terms of the frontier, urbanization, or denominations but must recognize the centrality of ethnicity in American religious life.

Of course, the validation of the hypothesis put forth in this essay depends upon many more empirically based studies of ethnicity and religion in America. Applying the tri-stage conception with rigor requires us to lay aside the larger generic labels we have customarily attached to the different religious groupings in America, and do more refined studies of ethnoreligious groups. Central to the task of verification will be the application of both historical and sociological techniques to an agreed upon set of procedures and rules on how to proceed. The efforts of the Cambridge Group for the History of Population and Social Structure provides an excellent example of the standardization and unity of method and definition that is necessary for individual studies to be meaningfully synthesized.[80] Hopefully this article will contribute to the conceptual framework necessary for any further understanding of the interrelationships of ethnicity and religion in America.

NOTES

[1] Among the more recent associations of ethnicity and religion see e.g.: Harold J. Abramson, Ethnic diversity within Catholicism: A comparative analysis of contemporary and historical religion. *Journal of Social History* 4, 359–388 (1970–71); Jay P. Dolan, Immigrants in the city: New York's Irish and German Catholics. *Church History* 41, 354–68 (1972); Martin E. Marty, "Ethnicity; The skeleton of religion in America." *Church History* 41, 5–21 (1972); "Pluralism an American challenge." *The Reformed Journal* 23, 11–29 (April, 1973); James Henry Powell, The concept of cultural pluralism in American social thought, 1915–1965, (unpublish. Ph.D. dissertation, University of Notre Dame, 1971); Robert T. Handy, *A Christian America Protestant Hopes and Historical Realities* New York, 1971. pp. 73–79; Martin E. Marty, *Righteous Empire The Protestant Experience in America*, p. 123, New York, 1970; or Franklin H. Littell, *From State Church to Pluralism A Protestant Interpretation of Religion in American History*, p. 49, Chicago, 1962.

[2] See Timothy L. Smith, "Religious denominations as ethnic communities: A regional case study." *Church History* 35, 207 (1966).

[3] William Warren Sweet, *Religion in the Development of American Culture, 1765–1840* New York, 1952. See also Franklin H. Littell, *From State Church to Pluralism* pp. 3–5, 103–07; Whitney Rogers Cross, *The Burned-Over District, the Social and Intellectual History of Enthusiastic Religion in Western New York, 1800–1850* Ithaca, 1950; Alice Felt Tyler, *Freedom's Ferment: Phases of American Social History to 1860* Minneapolis 1944; or Bernard A. Weisberger, *They Gathered At The River The Story of the Great Revivalists and Their Impact upon Religion in America* Boston, 1958.

[4] A transitional figure here is Timothy L. Smith's *Revivalism and Social Reform in Mid-Nineteenth-Century America* New York, 1957, in which social reform represented the half-way point between the frontier revival impulse and the urban Social Gospel movement. On urbanization and religion see especially Charles Howard Hopkins, *The Rise of the Social Gospel in American Protestantism, 1865–1915* New Haven, 1940; Aaron I. Abell, *The Urban Impact on American Protestantism, 1865–1900* Cambridge, 1943; or Paul A. Carter, *The Decline and Revival of the Social Gospel* Ithaca, 1954.

[5] On growing voluntaryism see especially Franklin H. Littell, *From State Church to Pluralism.* On the denominational basis of American religion see Sidney E. Mead, "Denominationalism: The shape of Protestantism in America." *Church History* 23, 291–320 (1954); and Winthrop S. Hudson, "Denominationalism as a Basis for Ecumenicity: A Seventeenth-Century Conception," *Church History* 24, 32–50, (1955).

[6] Will Herberg, *Protestant-Catholic-Jew An Essay in American Religious Sociology,* Garden City, 1955.

[7] See H. Richard Niebuhr, *The Social Sources of Denominationalism,* New York, 1929. More recently, the "case study" sociological approach has taken to test the generalizations of Niebuhr *et al.* See especially Gerhard Lenski's *The Religious Factor A Sociological Study of Religion's Impact on Politics, Economics , and Family Life* Garden City, 1961; and Rodney Stark and Charles Y. Glock, *American Piety: The Nature of Religious Commitment,* Berkeley, 1968.

[8] For an historiographical overview see Robert P. Swierenga, Ethnocultural political analysis: A new approach to American ethnic studies. *American Studies* 5, 59–79 (1970).

[9] The parallel developments in ethnicity and religion are most carefully delineated by Will Herberg in *Protestant-Catholic-Jew.* For a concise summary of the ethnic debate see Milton M. Gordon, *Assimilation in American Life The Role of Race, Religion, and National Origins,* New York, 1964, especially Chapters 4–6.

[10] Martin E. Marty, "Ethnicity: The Skeleton of Religion in America."

[11] Milton M. Gordon, "Assimilation in America: theory and reality, *Daedalus,* 90, 280 Spring, 1961. Similarly, Rudolph Vecoli defines ethnicity as the "group consciousness based on a sense of common origin. . . ." See his Ethnicity: A neglected dimension of American history, *in The State of American History* (Herbert J. Bass, ed.), p. 70, Chicago, 1970.

[12] See e.g., William A. Clebsch, *From Sacred to Profane America: The Role of Religion in American History,* New York, 1968.

[13] Gerhard Lenski, *The Religious Factor,* pp. 298–299.

[14] Wilfred Cantwell Smith, *The Meaning and End of Religion: A New Approach To The Religious Traditions of Mankind,* New York, 1962, p. 50; Clifford Geertz, *Islam Observed: Religious Development in Morocco and Indonesia,* pp. 1, 97, New Haven, 1968.

[15] The use of historical typology is clearly discussed *in Contemporary Social Theory* (Harry Elmer Barnes *et al.,* eds.), pp. 28–29, New York, 1940.

[16] A recent effort that examines the early English as an ethnic group is Charles H. Anderson's, *White Protestant Americans From National Origins to Religious Group,* New Jersey, 1970.

[17] See Thomas Perry, New Plymouth and Old England: A suggestion. *William and Mary Quarterly,* 18, 253 (1961); and Keith L. Sprunger, Other pilgrims in Leiden: Hugh Goodyear and the English Reformed Church. *Church History* 41, 46–60 (1972).

[18] The clearest expression of the Puritan community ideal and the central role of the church is found in Kenneth A. Lockridge, *A New England Town The First Hundred Years,* pp. 1–78, New York, 1970.

[19] Timothy L. Smith, Congregation, state, and denomination: The forming of the American religious structure. *William and Mary Quarterly,* 25, 155–62 (1968).

[20] For a discussion of "community" and "association" as used in this article see Gerhard Lenski, *The Religious Factor* pp. 21–22.

[21] Martin E. Marty, *The New Shape of American Religion*, p. 22, New York, 1958.

[22] Daniel J. Boorstin, *The Americans The Colonial Experience*, p. 4, New York, 1958. Although Boorstin has recently been heavily criticized for his "natural" approach to American history (see e.g., John P. Diggins, The perils of naturalism: Some reflections on Daniel J. Boorstin's approach to American history. *American Quarterly*, 23, 153–81 May, 1971.) I find myself in basic agreement as to the evolution of American society; disagreeing more on the *evaluation* of this development.

[23] Bernard Bailyn, *Education in the Forming of American Society Needs and Opportunities for Study*, pp. 38–41, North Carolina, 1960.

[24] Neil Emerson Salisbury, "Conquest of the 'savage': Puritans, Puritan missionaries, and Indians, 1620–1680." unpublished Ph.D. dissertation, University of California, Los Angeles, 1972. p. 63. In a similar vein see Franklin H. Littell, *From State Church to Pluralism*, pp. 7–11; Martin E. Marty, *Righteous Empire*, pp. 5–13; and William A. Clebsch, *From Sacred to Profane America*, pp. 98–103.

[25] Edmund S. Morgan, *Visible Saints The History of a Puritan Idea*, pp. 120–24, New York, 1963.

[26] Daniel J. Boorstin, *The Colonial Experience*, pp. 35–40.

[27] Harry S. Stout (1974) University men in New England, 1620–1660; A demographic analysis. *Journal of Interdisciplinary History*, 4, 375–400.

[28] Oscar Handlin, *The Uprooted: The Epic Story of the Great Migrants That Made the American People*, p. 119, New York, 1951.

[29] On the immigrant church see esp. H. Richard Niebuhr, *The Social Sources of Denominationalism:* and Will Herberg, *Protestant-Catholic-Jew*, pp. 23–28.

[30] Quoted in Martin E. Marty, *Righteous Empire*, p. 126.

[31] The literature on this subject is expansive; for representative works illustrating the inability of the "immigrant" churches to work together as members of a universal faith see e.g.: Jay P. Dolan, Immigrants in the city, pp. 359–360, 362; Harold J. Abramson, "Ethnic diversity within Catholicism, p. 361; Timothy L. Smith, Religious Denominations as ethnic communities, pp. 217, 225; Rudolph J. Vecoli, "Prelates and peasants Italian immigrants and the Catholic Church. *Journal of Social History* 3, 217–269 (1969); Philip Gleason, *The Conservative Reformers German-American Catholics and the Social Order*, Notre Dame, 1968; Robert D. Cross, *The Emergence of Liberal Catholicism in America*, Cambridge, 1958; Coleman J. Barry, *The Catholic Church and German Americans*, Indiana, 1953; Marshall Sklare, *Conservative Judaism: An American Religious Movement*, Illinois, 1955; Moses Rishin, *The Promised City: New York's Jews 1870–1914*, Cambridge, 1962; and Nathan Glazer, *American Judaism*, Chicago, 1957.

[32] William A. Clebsch, *From Sacred to Profane America*, pp. 97–98. Additional insights into the subject of Black religion in America can be gained from: David M. Reimers, *White Protestantism and the Negro*, New York, 1965; Joseph R. Washington, Jr., *Black Religion:The Negro and Christianity in the United States*, Boston, 1964; Hart M. Nelson, *et al.*, *The Black Church in America* New York, 1971; H. Shelton Smith, *In His Image, But . . . Racism in Southern Religion, 1780–1910*, Durham, 1972; and Joseph C. Hough, Jr., *Black Power and White Protestants A Christian Response to the New Negro Pluralism*, New York, 1968.

[33] Leon Litwack, *North of Slavery The Negro in the Free States, 1790–1860*, Chicago, 1961, p. 187.

[34] Will Herberg, *Protestant-Catholic-Jew*, p. 44.

[35] See above, Note 5.

[36] Charles H. Anderson, *White Protestant Americans*, p. XIV; Martin E. Marty, *Righteous Empire*, p. 121.

[37] See Martin E. Marty, *Righteous Empire;* and Robert T. Handy, *Christian America.*

[38] Sidney E. Mead, From coercion to persuasion: Another look at the rise of religious liberty and the emergence of denominationalism. *Church History* 25, 317–337 (1956).

[39] Will Herberg's *Protestant–Catholic–Jew* discusses this theme extensively.

[40] See especially Timothy L. Smith, *Revivalism and Social Reform.*

[41] Franklin H. Littell, *From State Church to Pluralism*, p. 30.

[42] Lyman Beecher, *The Autobiography of Lyman Beecher* 2 vols., Cambridge, 1961, I, 188.

[43] Martin E. Marty, *The New Shape of American Religion,* p. 10.

[44] H. Richard Niebuhr, *The Kingdom of God in America*, New York, 1959.

[45] On millenarianism see Ira V. Brown, Watchers for the second coming: The millenarian tradition in America, *Mississippi Valley Historical Review,* 44, 451–458 (1952); Whitney R. Cross, *The Burned-Over District,* p. 211–212; and, most importantly, Ernest Tuveson, *Redeemer Nation,* Chicago, 1968.

[46] *Temperance Recorder,* New York State Temperance Society, 1832, Vol. I, p. 5. John L. Thomas similarly discerns the centrality of millennial concerns in the anti-slavery movement. See his, "Antislavery and utopia," in *The Antislavery Vanguard: New Essays on the Abolitionists* (Martin Duberman, ed.), Princeton, 1965, pp. 240–70.

[47] Gabriel Vahanian, *The Death of God: The Culture of Our Post-Christian Era,* p. 67, New York, 1957.

[48] See David Tyack, The kingdom of God and the common school, *The Harvard Educational Review,* 36, 447–469 (1966); and Timothy L. Smith, Protestant schooling and American nationality, 1800–1850, *Journal of American History,* 53, 679–696 (1966–1967). For an incisive overview of education and assimilation see Thomas F. Green, *Education and Pluralism: Ideal and Reality,* Syracuse, 1966.

[49] Lawrence A. Cremin (ed.), *The Republic and the School: Horace Mann on The Education of Free Men,* p. 111, New York, 1957.

[50] On American nativism in the nineteenth and twentieth centuries see Ray Allen Billington, *The Protestant Crusade 1800–1860: A Study of the Origins of American Nativism,* New York, 1938; and John Higham, *Strangers in the Land: Patterns of American Nativism 1860–1925,* New Brunswick, 1955.

[51] Donald L. Kinzer, *An Episode in Anti-Catholicism: The American Protective Association,* Seattle, 1964.

[52] See e.g., Martin E. Marty, *Righteous Empire,* pp. 71–72; and John Higham, Antisemitism in the gilded age: A reinterpretation, *Mississippi Valley Historical Review,* 53, 559–78 (1957).

[53] Will Herberg, *Protestant–Catholic–Jew,* pp. 127–29, 150–227.

[54] See e.g., Jay P. Dolan, Immigrants in the city, 366–368.

[55] Richard Hofstadter, *Anti-Intellectualism in American Life,* p. 264, New York, 1966.

[56] For the historical antecedents of American pragmatism see Daniel P. Boorstin, *The Genius of American Politics,* Chicago, 1958; and *The Americans.*

[57] Richard Hofstadter, *Anti-Intellectualism in American Life,* p. 265.

[58] David M. Potter, *People of Plenty Economic Abundance and the American Character;* Daniel P. Boorstin, *The Genius of American Politics,* especially Chapter 1.

[59] Sidney E. Ahlstrom, The moral and theological revolution of the 1960s and its implications for American religious history. in *The State of American History,* (Herbert J. Bass, ed.), p. 105. See also, Theodore Roszak, *The Making of a Counter Culture: Reflections on The Technocratic Society and Its Youthful Opposition,* New York, 1969; and Jaques Ellul, *The Technological Society,* New York, 1964.

[60] Robert A. Nisbet, The impact of technology on ethical decision-making, in *Religion and Social Conflict* (Robert Lee and Martin E. Marty, eds.), p. 11, New York, 1964.

[61] See: Martin E. Marty, *Righteous Empire,* pp. 258–59; Robert T. Handy, *A Christian*

America, pp. 110–16; and John E. Smylie, "National Ethos and the Church," *Theology Today* 20, 313–21 (1963).

⁶² Will Herberg, *Protestant–Catholic–Jew*, p. 52.

⁶³ William A. Clebsch describes the phenomenom that I have labeled "consensual pluralism," as a mixture of "distinct but ultimately concordant parts." *From Sacred to Profane America*, p. 215.

⁶⁴ Gerhard Lenski, *The Religious Factor*, p. 54.

⁶⁵ *The Religious Factor*, p. 59. Lenski here uses the term "Protestant-dominated secular culture."

⁶⁶ Rodney Stark and Charles Y. Glock, *American Piety*, p. 205.

⁶⁷ *American Piety*, pp. 207–207.

⁶⁸ J. Milton Yinger, "Pluralism, religion, and secularism." *Journal For the Scientific Study of Religion*, 6, 26 (1967).

⁶⁹ Nathan Glazer and Daniel Patrick Moynihan, *Beyond the Melting Pot: The Negroes, Puerto Ricans, Jews, Italians, and Irish of New York City*, p. XXXVI, revised edition, Cambridge, 1970.

⁷⁰ Gabriel Vahanian, *The Death of God*, p. XXXIII, 4.

⁷¹ *The Death of God*, p. 50.

⁷² Bryan R. Wilson, *Religion In Secular Society: A Sociological Comment*, pp. 97–98, London, 1966.

⁷³ Franklin H. Littell, *From State Church to Pluralism*, pp. 73, 125–28, 145, 163–64; Will Herberg, *Protestant–Catholic–Jew*, pp. 88–94, 276–87.

⁷⁴ See above, Note 58.

⁷⁵ Gabriel Vahanian, *The Death of God*, p. 5. See also, William Appleman Williams, *The Contours of American History*, pp. 6–9, revised edition, Chicago, 1966; Rodney Stark and Charles Y. Glock, *American Piety*, p. 210; and J. Milton Yinger, Pluralism, religion, and secularism, p. 25.

⁷⁶ On the Black Church see E. Franklin Frazier, *The Negro Church in America*, New York, 1964; C. Eric Lincoln, *Black Muslims in America*, Boston, 1961; Vincent Harding, "The religion of Black Power," in *The Religious Situation: 1968*, Boston, 1968; and E. V. Ession-Udom, *Black Nationalism: A Search for an Identity in America*, Chicago, 1962.

⁷⁷ For the clearest articulation (and defense) of America's pluralistic composition, see Rudolph Vecoli's Ethnicity: A neglected dimension in American historiography. See also, Nathan Glazer and Daniel P. Moynihan, *Beyond the Melting-Pot;* Milton M. Gordon, *Assimilation in American Life;* Robert P. Swierenga, "Ethnocultural Political Analysis,"; and Martin E. Marty, "Ethnicity: The Skeleton of Religion in America."

⁷⁸ Daniel J. Boorstin, *The Colonial Experience*, p. 68.

⁷⁹ The extent to which this model can be applied to other societies is a subject for further study.

⁸⁰ The Cambridge Group format is outlined in E.A. Wrigley, Family reconstruction, in *An Introduction to English Historical Demography From the Sixteenth to the Nineteenth Century* (D. E. C. Eversley *et al.*), New York, 1966, p. 96–160.

Religion and Immigration Patterns: A Comparative Analysis of Dutch Protestants and Catholics, 1835-1880

ROBERT P. SWIERENGA

IN HISTORICAL scholarship ethnoreligious factors have become salient behavioral variables.[1] The ethnocultural school has swept the field in American political history with the finding that ethnicity rather than class explains voting behavior.[2] Religious scholars are claiming that ethnicity is the vital center of religion in America.[3] Ethnoreligious identity even affected farmers' cropping and livestock patterns in the nineteenth century, according to recent studies.[4] Religion also strongly influenced the process of immigration and subsequent acculturation of the immigrants.[5] It is a challenge, however, to sort out the effects of religion from the equally strong force of national identity.

This article offers one possible approach, that of studying a single nationality group in which differing religious sub-groups participated in the emigration. Dutch emigration in the mid-nineteenth century provides such a research opportunity. Nearly sixty-two thousand Hollanders emigrated in the years 1835-1880 and for each family or single adult who departed, the official records compiled by the Netherlands government specify religion or denominational affiliation. Additionally, the emigration records report more than a dozen other personal facts about the household, including age, sex, and occupation of the family head or single adult; family composition; social class; tax status; presumed reason for emigrating; intended destination; place of last residence; and year of departure.[6]

All of the extant Netherlands emigration records in the years from 1835 through 1880 have been converted into computer files, which contain the name and full information on each registered emigrant household or single adult.[7] These emigration records form the basis of this paper but they have also been augmented by United States population census records of Dutch-born nationals in 1850, 1860, and 1870.[8] Finally, by the process of record-linkage, the Netherlands and United States record series were merged to create a third comprehensive file containing pre- and post-migration biographical information. These three individual-level files permit one to compare the emigration and adjustment patterns of Catholics and Protestants within the same nationality group. This may enable us to assess the role of religion, as distinct from nationality (or ethnicity), in shaping the total immigration experience.

DUTCH EMIGRATION PATTERNS

The Netherlands was never a high emigration country, such as Ireland or Norway. It ranked near the bottom, along with France and Belgium, having an average emigration rate of only 70 per 100,000 population in the century from 1820 to 1920.[9] Total emigration in this period was less than 300,000, of which Catholics numbered approximately 60,000 or 20 percent.[10] Prior to the 1890s, over 90 percent of all Dutch overseas emigrants settled in the United States, with the other 10 percent going to the Dutch colonies in southeast Asia, South America, or the former Dutch colony of South Africa. This American proportion would have been even higher had not the financial panic of 1857 and ensuing Civil War diverted the emigration flow elsewhere for six to seven years. Despite the "America-centeredness" of the Dutch immigrants, they ranked a lowly seventeenth among foreign-born groups in 1900.[11]

The cycles of Dutch emigration closely paralleled the general northern European pattern, with the first high point in 1846-1857, a trough during the American Civil War, a second peak in 1865-1873, followed by a low during the economic crisis of the mid-1870s, and then another high point in the 1880s. Thus, during the period of this study, 1835-1880, there were two complete up and down cycles and the beginning of a third up cycle.[12]

The first emigration era began in the mid-1840s in conjunction with a widespread agricultural crisis caused primarily by the failure of the potato crop for several years. In addition to the food problem, religious dissension in the 1830s within the privileged *Hervormde* (Reformed) church, which had been accompanied by police suppression of dissenters and seceders, strengthened the emigration mentality already strong among rural peasants who had long suffered from poverty and overcrowding.[13] Cheap lands in America and improved means of transportation to reach there provided an irresistible lure. Beginning in 1846, some twenty thousand persons emigrated within a decade. Among both Calvinists and Catholics, families and religious groups emigrated in large numbers, led by their preachers and priests. This group migration was primarily a reflection of harsh religious and economic conditions in the 1840s. After the 1857-1865 hiatus, a "chain migration" continued from the original emigration fields, but new areas became affected as well.

Dutch emigration was primarily rural to rural, with 83 percent originating in rural municipalities in the Netherlands and 60 percent of the American-bound settling in rural areas in the United States. The major emigration sites in the nineteenth century were the North Sea coastal region of clay soils in the northern and southwestern parts of the country (the provinces of Groningen, Friesland, and Zeeland), and the inland sandy-soil region (the provinces of Gelderland, Noord Brabant, and Limburg). For the period 1835-1880, over half (55 percent) of all emigrants originated in the rich clay-soil regions with their highly commercialized and mechanized cultivation of export grains, a third (31 percent) hailed from the thin sandy-soil areas of mixed, small-scale farming, and only 14 percent came from the stable and prosperous dairy regions where the propensity to emigrate was almost nil.[14]

DUTCH CATHOLIC AND PROTESTANT EMIGRANTS COMPARED

Dutch Catholic emigrants resembled their Calvinist compatriots more than they differed from them, although there were some noticeable contrasts, especially in the adaptive process in America.[15] First, Catholics and Protestants had differing emigration locales. Catholics originated in the inland sandy-soil region and Calvinists came mainly from the northern and southwestern coastal regions and, to a lesser extent, from the eastern sandy-soil region, especially the Achterhoek region of Gelderland Province. This regional difference, of course, is simply a reflection of the historic religious geography of the Netherlands in which Catholics primarily inhabited the area south of the Rhine River and Protestants the area to the north. Thus, two-thirds of the Catholics hailed from three southeastern provinces (in order): Noord Brabant, Gelderland, and Limburg; three-fourths of the Reformed emigrants came from four provinces (in order): Zeeland, Gelderland, Zuid Holland, and Groningen; two-thirds of the Seceders emigrated from four provinces (in order): Groningen, Gelderland, Zeeland, and Overijssel (see table 1). The isolated rural province of Drenthe had a comparatively small emigration, but 57.8 percent of its emigrants were Seceders. Only in the traditional Catholic provinces of Noord Brabant and Limburg did Catholic emigrants predominate, with 84.7 and 98.1 percent respectively. In all of the other provinces, the proportion of Catholic emigrants was below 15 percent,

TABLE 1
Religion by Province, Total Netherlands Emigrants, 1835-1880

Province	Reformed	Seceder	Religion Catholic	Jewish	Other	Totals
Drenthe	438 28.6% (1.1%)	885 57.8% (7.8%)	192 12.5% (1.8%)	1 0.0% (0.2%)	16 1.0% (1.5%)	1,532 (2.5%)
Friesland	2,534 65.7 (6.6)	953 24.7 (8.4)	156 4.0 (1.4)	18 0.5 (3.1)	193 5.0 (18.3)	3,854 (6.2)
Gelderland	7,736 62.1 (20.2)	2,136 17.1 (18.7)	2,478 19.9 (23.1)	20 0.2 (3.4)	89 0.7 (8.4)	12,459 (20.1)
Groningen	5,048 58.0 (13.2)	2,998 34.5 (26.3)	527 6.1 (4.9)	40 0.4 (6.9)	86 1.0 (8.2)	8,699 (14.0)
Limburg	23 1.2 (0.1)	1 0.1 (0.0)	1,859 98.1 (17.3)	4 0.2 (0.7)	8 0.4 (0.8)	1,895 (3.0)
Noord Brabant	327 10.2 (0.8)	152 4.8 (1.3)	2,078 84.7 (25.3)	2 0.0 (0.3)	9 0.3 (0.9)	3,198 (5.2)
Noord Holland	2,564 58.1 (6.7)	575 13.0 (5.0)	588 13.3 (5.5)	393 8.9 (67.8)	290 6.6 (27.5)	4,410 (7.1)
Overijssel	1,185 40.6 (3.1)	1,094 37.4 (9.6)	581 19.9 (5.5)	14 0.5 (2.4)	47 1.6 (4.5)	2,921 (4.7)
Utrecht	661 56.5 (1.7)	283 24.2 (2.5)	134 11.4 (1.2)	5 0.4 (0.9)	87 7.4 (8.3)	1,170 (1.9)
Zeeland	11,490 80.4 (30.1)	1,491 10.4 (13.1)	1,241 8.7 (11.6)	2 0.0 (0.3)	71 0.5 (6.7)	14,295 (23.1)
Zuid Holland	6,215 82.5 (16.3)	826 11.0 (7.2)	251 3.3 (2.3)	81 1.1 (14.0)	157 2.1 (14.9)	7,530 (12.2)
Totals	38,221 61.7	11,394 18.4	10,715 17.3	580 0.9	1,053 1.7	61,963

Source: Robert P. Swierenga, Dutch Emigrants to the United States, South Africa, South America, and Southeast Asia, 1835-1880: An Alphabetical Listing by Household Heads and Independent Persons (Wilmington, Del, 1983).

except in the eastern provinces of Gelderland and Overijssel where Catholics comprised 19.9 percent of the emigrants.

More important, Catholics were not as prone to emigrate as were Protestants, because of regional differences and cultural and clerical pressures against it.[16] One of the earliest brochures that warned against emigrating came from the pen of "Catholic citizen" and was published in 1846 in the Catholic center of 's Hertogenbosch. The pamphlet's inflammatory title, "Think Before you Start! A cordial word to my Countrymen concerning the illness in our Fatherland called 'Emigration,'" is sufficient to indicate the strident nature of the text. The desire to emigrate, said the writer, is a "strange disease" that afflicts "a blind crowd," who in the mistaken hope of getting away from "cares and troubles" will instead find a hard, lonely, and despised life in the United States.[17] Catholics comprised 38.3 percent of the Dutch population in 1849 but made up only 17.3 percent of the total emigrants in the years through 1880 (see table 2). Hence, to match their share of the population, over twice as many Catholics should have emigrated. Seceders, on the other hand, were heavily over-represented, particularly in the first wave, which followed on the heels of bitter government repression in the 1830s. Seceders comprised 48.7 percent of all Dutch emigrants in the years 1845-1849, yet they formed only 1.3 percent of the total population in 1849. The new liberal constitution of 1848 sharply reduced the Seceder propensity to emigrate. Nevertheless, through 1880 Seceders numbered 18.4 percent of the emigrants, but they claimed only 3 percent of the Dutch populace in 1869. Thus six times as many Seceders departed the Fatherland as their share of the total population. Reformed (*Hervormde*) church members were also over-represented but by only 7 points. They numbered 54.8 percent of the population in 1849 but comprised 61.7 percent of all emigrants.

As Figure 1 displays, Calvinists overshot and Catholics undershot their proportion of the population in every province except Drenthe, where the pattern was reversed. But Drenthe had an insignificant number of emigrants and can safely be ignored.[18] Interestingly, Calvinist emigrants were most over-represented in the provinces with the largest proportion of Catholics (Noord Brabant, Limburg, and Gelderland) and in the three western urban provinces (Noord and Zuid Holland and Utrecht). This suggests that, for whatever reasons, Calvinists living in the predominantly Catholic areas or in the western conurbation were more eager to emigrate than their compatriots in the rural Protestant hinterland of Friesland, Groningen, and Overijssel.

Catholic emigrants, on the other hand, were heavily under-represented

TABLE 2
Religion by Year, Total Netherlands Emigrants, 1835-1880

YEAR	REFORMED			SECEDER			CATHOLIC			JEWISH			OTHER		
1835	0			6			17			0			0		
1836	0			3			10			0			0		
1837	0			1			0			0			0		
1838	1			0			0			0			0		
1839	9			0			0			0			0		
1840	1			0			1			0			0		
1841	0			5			0			0			0		
1842	8			7			8			0			0		
1843	35			7			32			0			0		
1844	98	152	44.8%	65	94	27.7%	25	93	27.4%	0		0.0%	0		0.0%
1845	221	(0.4%)		178	(0.8%)		110	(0.9%)		0	(0.0%)		6	(0.0%)	
1846	371			744			195			0			14		
1847	871			2297			339			26			19		
1848	880			779			450			21			46		
1849	1023	3366	34.8	711	4709	48.7	330	1424	14.7	18	65	0.7	19	104	1.1
1850	348	(8.8)		77	(41.3)		327	(13.3)		27	(11.2)		10	(9.9)	
1851	580			118			492			11			13		
1852	765			60			283			56			15		
1853	812			152			565			18			78		
1854	2459	4964	58.8	402	809	9.6	642	2309	27.3	68	180	2.1	67	183	2.2
1855	1389	(13.0)		342	(7.1)		300	(21.5)		21	(31.0)		11	(17.4)	
1856	1300			311			263			5			28		
1857	1198			142			244			50			21		
1858	778			28			294			12			25		
1859	303	4968	68.7	11	834	11.5	87	1188	16.4	28	116	1.6	44	129	1.8
1860	772	(13.0)		9	(7.3)		47	(11.1)		6	(20.0)		24	(12.2)	
1861	460			37			127			2			7		
1862	330			21			338			10			17		
1863	327			8			668			0			13		
1864	486	2375	60.1	46	121	3.1	169	1349	34.2	1	19	0.5	25	86	2.2
1865	1218	(6.2)		167	(1.1)		164	(12.6)		14	(3.3)		31	(8.2)	
1866	2502			273			375			16			42		
1867	2740			827			513			25			74		
1868	1931			488			475			16			48		
1869	2320	10711	69.7	505	2260	14.7	518	2045	13.3	15	86	0.6	70	265	1.7
1870	1194	(28.0)		191	(19.8)		366	(19.1)		7	(14.8)		24	(25.2)	
1871	1189			279			330			50			37		
1872	2435			542			439			26			30		
1873	2667			636			555			23			59		
1874	807	8292	68.1	128	1776	14.6	125	1815	14.9	2	108	0.9	38	188	1.5
1875	471	(21.7)		52	(15.6)		116	(16.9)		2	(18.6)		22	(17.8)	
1876	225			22			75			0			30		
1877	172			10			45			3			17		
1878	203			7			20			0			4		
1879	635			61			65			1			4		
1880	1687	3393	71.0	639	791	16.6	169	490	10.2	0	6	0.1	21	98	2.1
		(8.9)			(6.9)			(4.6)			(1.0)			(9.3)	
Total	38,221		61.7	11,394		18.4	10,713		17.3	580		0.9	1053		1.7

N. A. = 611

Source: Same as table 1

---

in the three urban provinces, which indicates that urban Catholics were less prone to emigrate than rural ones. In the traditional Catholic provinces of Noord Brabant and Limburg, Catholic emigrants were under-represented by only 5 percent and 1 percent, respectively. These regional differences in the propensity to emigrate are worthy of further study, but the salient fact remains that Calvinists were more willing than Catholics to leave the Fatherland.

FIGURE 1
Provinces of the Netherlands, Showing the Percentage of Emigration by
Religion, 1835-1880, and the Percentage Over- or Under-represented
According to the 1849 Census

Source: table 1; 1849 Census (Volkstelling) of the Netherlands.

This Catholic-Seceder disparity in emigration raises the question of causation. Both were religious minorities in the society as a whole, although Catholics were in the vast majority in their southern region. Yet, Catholics were far more reluctant to emigrate. What factors might explain this pattern? The Dutch Catholics were the most traditional cultural group in the country. They had the largest families, were least likely to move away from ancestral lands, and were most willing to obey religious leaders. Significantly, Catholic clerics generally discouraged emigration because it threatened to disrupt religious supervision and instruction and might lead to the loss of social control. Only one cleric, Father Theodore Van den Broek, actively recruited emigrants and this was done under the cloak of promoting missionary enterprise. Van den Broek had already established a mission outpost among the Mennominie Indians near Green Bay, Wisconsin, and he sought to build a Christian community there. A Catholic Colonization Society eventually was founded at Nijmegen but it was led by laymen. By contrast, Seceders organized to emigrate at the congregational level, often led by their dominies. In numerous instances, large parts of the congregations emigrated together with their pastors.

The cultural and institutional forces discouraging Catholic emigration were reinforced by economic developments. The Catholic Netherlands was in the upland sandy-soil region where traditional small-scale farming remained the norm. The introduction of commercial fertilizers and land reclamation projects in this region enabled fathers to subdivide their farms among their sons or to open new ones on reclaimed lands. However, in the diluvial sea clay regions of the Protestant north and southwest, a different farming pattern developed. There the cash grain farmers mechanized their operations, consolidated their holdings in the quest for efficient large-scale production, and cut their labor costs by laying off farm workers. These excess laborers had few alternatives but to leave farming and move to the large cities or emigrate to America where cheap land beckoned.

Another economic factor in the low Catholic emigration rate was that the sandy-soil farmers were heavily engaged in the home production of textiles as part of the textile industry centered in the region.[19] Home industry augmented their farm income and provided a greater measure of stability against fluctuating food prices. After 1865, when the textile industry modernized by shifting production from farm cottages to urban factory centers such as Eindhoven, Tilburg, Geldrop, and Helmond, sons and daughters of farmers could go to the nearby towns and cities for work and still remain within a predominantly Catholic culture. Catholic peasants thus had more attractive economic alternatives than did Protestant farm workers in the north and west.

In brief, the emerging industrial growth in the textile centers of southeastern Noord Brabant and Limburg in the third quarter of the nineteenth century served as urban magnets to attract families and single workers from the surrounding rural areas. The only major emigration from Noord Brabant, therefore, originated in the northeastern part of the province that was farthest removed from the textile centers.

The timing of Protestant and Catholic emigration also differed (see table 2 above). Both Catholic and Seceder emigration was heavier in the first wave from 1846 through 1856 and fell off in the decades after 1856. The pattern of the Reformed (*Hervormde*) emigration was the reverse—low in the early phase but gaining momentum over the decades, until the second half of the 1870s when 71.0 percent of all emigrants were Reformed, whereas they numbered 55 percent of the Dutch population.

The Seceders began to depart in large numbers in 1846, one year earlier than did the Catholics, and over 4,800 Seceders left by 1849, 41 percent of the whole. Once the Catholic outflow started in earnest in 1847, they too departed steadily, with the heaviest outflow in 1850-1854 and 1865-1870. These mainly originated in the provinces of Noord Brabant and Gelderland. In the interim years of 1857 to 1865, the adjoining province of Limburg first began contributing emigrants, sending out more than half of all Catholic emigrants during the Civil War era. In the post-bellum decades (1865-1880), the overall Catholic proportion declined to about 14 percent. Improved economic conditions at home and job opportunities across the border in Germany dampened the enthusiasm to emigrate. Thus, Catholic emigration was more important before 1865 than in the post-war decade.[20]

When one compares the Protestant and Catholic emigrants according to occupation, social class, regional background, type and size of sending communities, and family composition, numerous variations are found, but all within an overarching commonality (see table 3). Occupationally, blue collar workers predominated, but the Roman Catholic emigrants were *over*represented among white collar workers, farmers, and skilled craftsmen, such as carpenters and shoemakers. Catholics were heavily *under*represented among farm laborers and unskilled day laborers. Less than a third (29.8 percent) of the Catholics were unskilled laborers, compared to 49.0 percent of the Reformed emigrants and 37.7 percent of the Seceders. Dutch Catholic emigrants thus consistently ranked higher on the occupational prestige scale than did the Protestants. Not surprisingly, because of this, more Catholics were well-to-do (by 2.8 points) and fewer (by 5.6 points) were needy (i.e., on the public dole) than were the Reformed.[21] The Seceders, however, had the lowest percentage classified as needy (17.0 percent) and almost the same percentage of well-to-do as the Catholics (13.9 percent).

The occupational and status differences are partially the result of economic structural differences in the regions of origin. The Catholic areas with mixed farming and protoindustries had a more diverse labor force than the Protestant areas. But more than 80 percent of the emigrants from all three religious groups came from small rural municipalities (below ten thousand population) in their respective regions. Thus, the rural nature of the sending communities was not the source of the occupational differences. Another factor is that more Catholics emigrated singly than did the Reformed. The spread was 22 points—57 percent singles among the Catholics, 46.5 percent among the Reformed, but only 34.8 percent among the Seceders. Single adults without the burden of raising a family would likely have achieved a higher economic standing and entered the white collar class or the coveted blue collar ranks of master craftsmen.

Despite the higher occupational and social status level among Catholic emigrants, when the "last job" in the Netherlands is compared with the "first job" in America, both Catholics and Protestants had identical rates of job changes: 35 percent climbed to a higher job status level and 16 percent skidded to a lower position (see table 4).[22] Both groups, therefore, greatly benefitted from emigration to exactly the same extent, at least in the short-run.

Another difference is that a higher proportion of Catholic emigrants settled in the United States than did the majority of Protestants, many of whom—all non-Seceders—went to Dutch colonies in Southeast Asia and South America, or to South Africa. The Seceders, however, had the highest rate of America-centeredness, averaging 98.6 percent, while 90.4 percent of the Catholic emigrants also went to the United States, compared to 88.9 percent of the Reformed (see table 3 above). Seceders and Catholics, the former a new religious minority and the latter a traditional minority, had suffered sufficiently as second class citizens to dissuade them from emigrating *within* the empire, if equal opportunities beckoned elsewhere.

Another reason that Reformed (*Hervormde*) church members went to the Dutch colonies in greater numbers is that upper-class Protestants traditionally filled the ranks of the civil service and military officials. Among well-to-do Reformed emigrants, there was a stronger likelihood of

TABLE 3

Behavioral Characteristics of Reformed, Seceder, and Roman Catholic Emigrant Family Heads and Single Adults, 1835-1880

Behavioral Category	Reformed %	Seceder %	Catholic %
Occupation in Netherlands			
White Collar	9.3	8.0	10.8
Farmer	11.8	20.5	22.9
Skilled Worker	21.4	25.9	31.7
Unskilled Worker	49.0	37.7	29.8
Farm Laborer	8.5	7.9	4.8
	N=11,318	N=2,863	N=3,695

N.A.=3,900   C=.23 tau-b -.13 gamma = -.21

Social Class			
Well-to-do	11.2	13.9	14.0
Middling	64.3	69.1	67.1
Needy	24.5	17.0	18.9
	N=12,606	N=2.752	N=3,973

N.A.=2,445   C=.08 tau-b= -.06   gamma = -.12

Farming Region			
Dairy (meadows)	10.6	10.3	8.8
Mixed (sandy soil)	25.0	36.1	58.1
Grain (clay soil)	64.4	53.6	33.1
	N=13,079	N=3,250	N=4,079

N.A. = 1,315   C=.34 tau-b = -.21   gamma = -.36

Type of Municipality			
Urban	17.3	11.6	18.2
Rural	82.7	88.4	81.8
	N=13,079	N=3,250	N=4,079

N.A. = 1,315 C=.21   tau- = -.03 gamma = -.09

Size of Municipality			
Over 10,000	13.6	8.7	14.0
Under 10;000	86.4	91.3	86.0
	N=13,079	N=3,250	N=4,079

N.A. = 1,315   C=.23 tau-b = -.04   gamma = -.10

Household Type			
Single	46.5	34.5	57.0
Couple with children	38.7	49.1	31.3
Couple without children	7.2	8.5	5.9
Single parent family	7.7	7.7	5.8
	N=13,090	N=3,253	N=4,118

N.A. = 1,315   C=.14   tau-b = -.04 gamma = -.07

Destination			
U.S.A.	88.9	98.6	90.4
Non-U.S.A.	11.1	1.4	9.6
	N=12,784	N=3,124	N=4,026

N.A. = 1,812   C=.12   tau-b = .06   gamma = -.23

Source: Same as table 1

TABLE 4
Occupational Mobility of Protestants and Catholics from Last to First Job,
Nine Years or Less Since Immigrating: Dutch Male Households and
Single Adults, 1841-1870

	LEVEL OF "FIRST" JOB								Percent Un-changed	Percent climbing	Percent skidding	Total Person/ranks climbing	Total Person/ranks skidding	Total Person/ranks gain
Protestants Level of "last" job	High White Collar	Low White Collar	Farmer	Skilled	Un-skilled	Farm Laborer	Job-less	N						
High White Collar	15	2	10	10	7	0	1	45	33	—	67	—	86	-86
Low White Collar	11	10	54	23	52	0	1	651	7	7	86	11	261	-250
Farmer	2	5	431	20	140	0	2	600	72	1	27	9	308	-299
Skilled	3	15	166	308	136	1	2	631	49	29	22	205	144	61
Unskilled	3	16	363	205	697	3	3	1290	54	45	1	991	9	982
Farm Laborer	0	2	58	36	90	0	0	186	0	100	0	344	--	344
Jobless	0	4	33	9	17	0	0	64	2	98	--	213	--	213
TOTALS	34	54	1115	611	1139	4	10	2967	49	35	16	773	808	965

N.A.=182   C=.55   tau-b=.24   gamma=.33

Catholics Level of "last" job	High White Collar	Low White Collar	Farmer	Skilled	Un-skilled	Farm Laborer	Job-less	N	Percent Un-changed	Percent climbing	Percent skidding	Total Person/ranks climbing	Total Person/ranks skidding	Total Person/ranks gain
High White Collar	0	1	2	0	1	0	0	13	4	0	100	—	7	-9
Low White Collar	1	1	3	3	5	0	0	13	8	8	84	1	24	-23
Farmer	0	2	84	7	22	0	0	115	73	2	25	2	51	-49
Skilled	2	3	33	45	12	1	1	97	46	39	14	45	17	28
Unskilled	1	3	44	14	45	0	0	107	42	58	--	115	--	115
Farm Laborer	0	1	2	2	5	0	0	11	--	100	--	22	--	22
Jobless	3	3	2	3	2	0	0	13	--	100	--	54	--	54
TOTALS	7	14	171	74	92	1	1	360	49	35	16	239	101	138

N.A.=7   C=.55   tau-b=.13   gamma=.18

Source: R.P. Swierenga, Netherlands Emigration—U.S. Census Linked File

TABLE 5
Destination by Religion and Social Class per five periods, Family Heads and
Single Adults, 1835-1880 (in percent)

Social Class	Destination by Religion								
	Reformed			Seceder			Catholic		
Well-to-do	USA	Other	N	USA	Other	N	USA	Other	N
1835–49	96.4	3.6	84	98.6	1.4	147	98.9	1.1	89
1850–59	66.8	33.2	268	94.8	5.2	77	90.8	9.2	130
1860–64	11.3	88.7	213	50.0	50.0	10	45.5	54.5	110
1865–75	69.0	31.0	696	99.2	0.8	132	65.0	35.9	203
1876–80	42.9	57.1	126	100.0	0.0	7	43.8	56.2	16
1835–80	59.0	41.0	1387	96.8	3.2	373	72.1	27.9	548
Middling									
1835–49	98.8	1.2	418	98.2	1.5	508	97.8	2.2	313
1850–59	91.5	8.5	1905	98.0	2.0	293	95.4	4.6	863
1860–64	16.8	33.2	419	80.1	19.9	21	92.5	7.5	227
1865–75	96.8	3.2	4471	99.4	0.6	884	95.7	4.3	1106
1876–80	92.8	7.8	677	99.3	0.7	138	91.5	8.5	94
1835–80	93.7	6.3	7890	98.6	1.4	1844	95.4	4.6	2603
Needy									
1835–49	92.4	7.6	132	100.0	0.0	160	98.2	1.8	56
1850–59	87.2	12.8	1004	100.0	0.0	73	87.8	12.2	286
1860–64	53.2	46.8	218	75.0	25.0	4	78.9	21.1	71
1865–76	94.0	6.0	1461	99.4	0.6	173	81.9	18.1	287
1876–80	96.8	3.2	190	100.0	0.0	47	93.9	6.1	33
1835–80	88.9	11.1	3005	99.6	0.4	457	85.7	14.3	733

Source: Same as table 1.

settling in the Dutch colonies, beginning in the 1850s (see table 5). Between 1835 and 1880, over 4 out of 10 (41.0 percent) upper-class Reformed emigrants went elsewhere than to North America. Middle and lower-class Reformed emigrants, however, continued to opt for the United States by a 10 to 1 margin. Even well-to-do Catholics after 1860 began to avoid the United States. In 1860-1864 over half (54.5 percent) of the wealthy Catholic emigrants departed for Asia and South America. In the post-war decade, 1865-1875, this non-United States proportion dropped to one-third (35.9 percent), which is still high, considering that only 4.6 percent of middle-class Catholics and 14.3 percent of lower-class Catholics did not go to the United States. Clearly, class status strongly influenced destination choices, regardless of religion, among Reformed and even Catholic emigrants. But Seceders again were different. All went to the United States, including upper-class members. Only 12 upper-class and 28

middle and lower-class Seceder families and single adults did not go to the
United States in the entire forty-five year period.

Just as the emigration patterns differed between Protestants and Catholics, so did the settlement behavior in the United States.[23] The Dutch
Catholics established very few immigrant colonies, in distinction from the
Calvinists, and especially the Seceders, who formed ethnic enclaves wherever they settled, whether in rural areas or major cities. Also, over one-
third of the Catholic emigrants settled in cities and towns (above five
thousand population), compared to only one-quarter of the Seceders.
Thus, the Dutch Catholics and Calvinists in America distanced themselves from one another.

The only lasting Dutch Catholic colony of the mid-nineteenth century
was in the Green Bay area, especially southward along the Fox River
Valley at Little Chute and Hollandtown.[24] Dominican missionary Father
Van den Broek instigated this colony when he returned to the
Netherlands on a furlough in 1847. Many Dutch Catholic immigrants,
however, went to the larger cities along the established transportation
routes to the Midwest: Cincinnati and Saint Louis from the South, and
from the East coast Rochester, Buffalo, Cleveland, Detroit, Bay City, Chicago, Milwaukee, and Green Bay. In these places, all Catholic centers with
institutional infrastructures in place, Dutch Catholics readily worshipped
and intermarried with Catholics of other nationalities, especially Germans, Belgians, and Irish. As historian Henry L. Lucas says:

> The common bonds of faith made it possible for them to live happily
> with people who were not Dutch. . . . Dutch Catholics did not tend so
> markedly to settle in Dutch communities, but scattered, were speedily
> assimilated, and so left few distinctive traces.[25]

Cincinnati, Chicago, and Grand Rapids were notable exceptions. The
Dutch Catholics in Cincinnati, four-hundred strong, had by 1854 established their own parish with a Dutch-speaking priest, Father Johannes
Van De Luijtelaar. In Chicago's Kensington district on the far southside,
the only Dutch parish in the city, Saint Willebrord, was organized in the
early 1890s and totaled two hundred families in the era of the First World
War, when a Dutch-born cleric, Father J. A. Van Heertum O. P., pastored
the parish. Saint Joseph's Parish on the near southwest side of Grand
Rapids was founded in 1887 to serve some seventy Dutch families in the
Furniture City. Under the leadership of the Dutch-speaking priest, Henry
Frencken of 's Hertogenbosch, who served the parish from 1887 to 1906,
the church grew to one hundred twenty families by 1915. Dutch language

services ceased in 1906, however, when Father Frencken returned to the Netherlands, and the parish gradually lost its ethnic solidarity. These Dutch Catholic urban churches were three of only twenty-five congregations that were primarily Dutch, according to historian Jacob Van Hinte, but they had no mutual connections and all were short-lived. By contrast, there were five hundred Dutch Calvinist congregations in the 1920s and most continue to the present day.[26] Even the concentrated Fox River Valley (Catholic) settlements failed to maintain a Dutch ethnic flavor after the First World War, except for the two small villages of Hollandtown and Little Chute that still celebrate their annual "Schut" (shooting) festival, which is of Brabantine origin. In short, according to Lucas, "religion encouraged dispersal" for Dutch Catholics, but cemented together Dutch Calvinists.[27]

Calvinists, especially Seceders, in contrast to Catholics, preferred settling in isolated rural colonies or forming Dutch neighborhoods in major cities. Most of the Calvinists settled in southwestern Michigan, southeastern Wisconsin, northern Illinois, central Iowa, western New York, and northern New Jersey. Urban concentrations could be found in Grand Rapids, Kalamazoo, Chicago, Milwaukee, Rochester, Buffalo, Albany, and Paterson. As of 1850, more than three-fourths of the Protestants lived in colonies, whereas less than a third of the Catholics did so. Twenty years later, in 1870, after further emigration as well as internal migration, the proportions remained virtually unchanged.[28]

The geographical distribution by state of Dutch immigrants illustrates these patterns (see table 6).[29] Catholic Dutch comprised over 95 percent of the Dutch-born in Missouri (in Saint Louis City and Bollinger County), over 70 percent in Ohio (in Cincinnati, Cleveland, and Toledo) and Minnesota (widely scattered but mainly in and around Minneapolis-Saint Paul [in Carver County] and in Saint Cloud [Benton County]), and around 40 percent in New York (New York City and Brooklyn, Rochester, Buffalo, Auburn, Albany, Troy) and Wisconsin (Green Bay and environs, Racine and Milwaukee).

Protestants predominated by over 95 percent in Michigan (the southwest sector) and New Jersey (Passaic County [Paterson] and Bergen County [Lodi]), over 90 percent in Iowa (Pella and the Mississippi River cities), Illinois (Chicago area), Kansas (Ottawa County), and Nebraska (Lancaster County). In Indiana (northern part) Protestants made up nearly 75 percent of Dutch-born. In Wisconsin, Protestants ranged over 55 percent (in Sheboygan, Milwaukee, and Southeastern sector generally)

TABLE 6
Religion* by State, 1850, 1860, 1870: Dutch Immigrants and Their Children

State	Protestant 1850 N	%	1860 N	%	1870 N	%	1850-70 N	%	Catholic 1850 N	%	1860 N	%	1870 N	%	1850-70 N	%
IL	204	100.0	884	100.0	2881	92.3	3969	94.3	0	0.0	0	0.0	239	7.7	239	5.7
IN	28	100.0	382	67.8	745	76.6	1155	73.9	0	0.0	181	32.2	227	23.4	408	26.1
IA	1053	93.9	3372	93.4	5598	92.2	10023	92.8	68	6.1	237	6.6	473	7.8	778	7.2
KA	0	0.0	0	0.0	22	0.0	22	100.0	0	0.0	0	0.0	0	0.0	0	0.0
MI	3325	98.7	8882	97.6	17278	98.0	29485	98.0	42	1.3	221	2.4	342	2.0	605	2.0
MN	0	0.0	224	36.4	551	25.4	775	27.8	0	0.0	392	63.6	1622	74.6	2014	72.2
MO	0	0.0	30	3.4	78	4.9	108	4.0	202	100.0	849	96.6	1515	95.1	2566	96.0
NE	0	0.0	0	0.0	110	100.0	110	100.0	0	0.0	0	0.0	0	0.0	0	0.0
NJ	312	100.0	1311	95.3	3833	98.0	5456	97.4	0	0.0	64	4.7	79	2.0	143	2.6
NY	1281	46.5	3956	52.8	5567	74.7	10804	61.0	1473	53.5	3530	47.2	1889	25.3	6892	38.9
OH	81	22.3	580	29.6	787	26.9	1448	27.6	283	77.7	1378	70.4	2137	73.1	3798	72.4
WI	904	54.2	3966	57.7	5730	57.3	10600	57.2	763	45.8	2904	42.3	4274	42.7	7941	42.8
	7188	71.7	23587	70.7	43180	77.8	73955	74.4	2831	28.3	9756	29.3	12797	22.2	25384	25.6

Source: Robert P. Svierenga (compiler), Dutch Immigrants in U.S. Population Censuses, 1850, 1860, and 1870: An Alphabetical Listing by Household Heads of First and Second Generation Immigrants (Wilmington, Del.: forthcoming 1986).

* See note 29 for a description of the method for determining religion.

and in New York State, Protestant Dutch were over 60 percent (in New York City and along the Erie Canal route).

In general, both Protestant and Catholic Dutch favored the Great Lakes region, but the Protestants did so the most (63.5 percent), while 21.8 percent of the Protestants stayed in the East and 28.2 percent of the Catholics went west of the Mississippi River into Missouri and Minnesota (see table 7).

In terms of the size and type of settlement areas, Protestant and Catholic Dutch also favored rural communities, but the Seceders, who had the highest rate of family migration, were most rural with 73.4 percent (see table 8). Catholics were next in selecting rural locations (65.3 percent), and the Reformed (*Hervormde*) were the least rural (59.1 percent). Catholics had the highest propensity to settle in large cities (over twenty-five thousand) at 17.3 percent, with Reformed a close second at 16.9 percent, whereas only 9.4 percent of Seceders resided in large cities. Reformed emigrants had the highest proportion living in medium and small cities (24.0 percent). These figures are averages for the thirty-five year period 1835-1870.

The reasons for these settlement patterns in the first plantings of the mid-nineteenth century are many, but they can be classified as idiosyncratic, cultural, and structural. Individuals often directed immigrants to particular places for their own economic, religious, or cultural reasons. Pioneer immigrants sent America-letters to attract their countrymen. Dutch Catholics went to the Green Bay area because a Dutch priest had

TABLE 7
Religion by Geographic Region, Protestant and Catholic Dutch, 1870

Religion	Great Lakes[a]		Midwest[b]		East[c]	
Protestant	27,421	63.5%	6,359	14.7%	9,400	21.8%
Catholic	7,219	56.4	3,610	28.2	1,968	15.4

Source: Same as table 6.

Note: See note 29 for a description of the method for determining religion.

[a]Great Lakes=IL, IN, MI, OH, WI
[b]Midwest=IO, KA, MO, MN, NE
[c]East=NJ, NY

TABLE 8
Settlement Locale by Religion, Family Heads and Single Adults, 1835-1870

Religion	Settlement Locale		
	Large City	Medium-Small City	Rural
Reformed	532 16.9 (67.4%)	756 24.0 (63.3%)	1,861 59.1 (56.6%)
Seceder	113 9.4 (14.3)	207 17.2 (18.7)	885 73.4 (26.9)
Catholic	144 17.3 (18.3)	144 17.3 (13.0)	543 65.3 (16.5)

Source: Netherlands Emigration Lists and U.S. Census Lists linked file.

begun an Indian mission station there. Other Catholic Dutch settled in large cities that had social and religious institutions in place. Seceders followed their dominies to sparcely settled regions in order to establish homogeneous colonies. Reformed (*Hervormde*) Dutch sometimes sought out descendants of the Old Dutch in New York and New Jersey or they settled among those who had followed the frontier westward to the Great Lakes.

Given the historic Protestant-Catholic division in the Netherlands, it was to be expected that Protestants deliberately avoided Catholic-dominated areas such as northern Wisconsin and cities like Cincinnati and Saint Louis. But apart from the religious consideration, most Dutch in the mid-nineteenth century avoided hot climates and open prairies (both unknown in the Netherlands). The major exception was the Pella, Iowa, colony of the maverick Seceder cleric, Hendrik P. Scholte, who led some nine hundred followers to the Iowa prairies. Pella subsequently founded many other prairie settlements further to the west. The Dutch newcomers also generally sought to locate near major waterways and markets (both common and necessary in the Netherlands), and they desired areas such as forest lands with exploitable natural resources for the cash-hungry settlers.

Structural factors such as social class, family type, and occupation of the immigrants had an effect. Although most of the Dutch chose rural settlement areas, the well-to-do emigrants, whether Reformed, Seceder, or Catholic, all had a greater tendency to settle in rural areas. Conversely, needy emigrants of all religions had a preference for large cities (over

TABLE 9
Non-Dutch Spouse by Religion and Year, Married Dutch Immigrants in the
United States, 1850, 1860, and 1870 (in percent)

Religion	1850	1860	1870
Protestant	5.2	9.9	13.2
Catholic	32.1	43.7	45.6

Source: Same as table 6.

twenty-five thousand) and emigrants of a middling background had a higher rate of settlement in medium and small cities. Similarly, single emigrants, especially Catholics, had a higher likelihood of settling in large cities. Emigrants who had held white collar or unskilled jobs in the Old Country had the highest rate of city residence, whereas skilled workers and farmers had the greatest propensity for rural settlements.

The geographical and institutional differences had a significant impact on marital assimilation. Already in the initial immigrant population (i.e., 1840-1870), Dutch Catholics had a higher intermarriage rate than did Protestants (see table 9). The difference is apparent as early as 1850, within a few years after emigrating, which indicates that some Catholics had married non-Dutch spouses even before emigrating. These were mainly neighboring Flemish Belgians, plus a few German Catholics. In 1850, 32.1 percent of married Dutch-born Catholics had non-Dutch spouses, compared to only 5.2 percent among Protestant Dutch. In 1860, the Catholic outmarriage rate had risen to 43.7 percent and in 1870 to 45.6 percent, whereas Protestant intermarriage rates were 9.9 percent in 1860 and 13.2 percent in 1870. On average, the Dutch Catholics in the United States were four to five times as likely as Protestants to have non-Dutch spouses.

An even more dramatic picture of Catholic outmarriage emerges when the 1870 census figures are separated generationally into couples married before immigration or before the first census enumeration after immigration, and couples married after being reported as single in the first census enumeration after immigration. The latter are mainly Dutch-born children of Dutch parents who were minors at the time of immigration. Among Protestants, 9.8 percent of first generation couples had outmarried by 1870, compared to 24.3 percent of the next generation. But among Catholics, 37.0 percent of first generation couples had married non-

TABLE 10
Nativity of Non-Dutch Spouse by Religion, Dutch-born Households in the
United States, 1850, 1860, and 1870 (in percent)

Religion	Nativity of Non-Dutch Spouse	
	U.S. born	Foreign-born
1850		
Protestant	40	60
Catholic	21	79
1860		
Protestant	28	72
Catholic	12	88
1870		
Protestant	50	50
Catholic	18	82

Source: Same as table 6.

Dutch spouses and an overwhelming 69.9 percent of their unmarried children had selected non-Dutch spouses. Clearly, the less isolated Catholic communities and the international nature of the Roman church broke down the ethnic identity of Dutch Catholics more rapidly than Protestants.

When Dutch Catholics and Protestants did outmarry, the nativity of their choices again differed dramatically. As table 10 shows, over 80 percent of the Catholic non-Dutch marriage partners were foreign-born (in order, German, Belgian, Irish, and French), whereas Protestants intermarried with native-born Americans half the time by 1870 Most of the native-born were children of Dutch-born parents, so the Protestant rate of outgroup marriages was actually lower in 1870 than the 13 percent reported in table 9. When Dutch Protestants married non-Dutch, they were often fellow religionists, German Calvinists from the Dutch border regions of Hanover and Ost Friesland.

CONCLUSION

These findings indicate that religious affiliation significantly influenced the entire resettlement process—the decision to emigrate, the direction of the emigrant stream, and the subsequent adjustment and adaptation in the new homeland. But religious forces operated within a common context. Economic and social forces primarily spurred emigration among the lower and middle classes of all religious communities in the Netherlands. Both Catholic and Protestant Dutch overwhelmingly chose the United States as their destination. Both groups migrated in family chains to communities where relatives and friends had already settled, and both equally experienced upward social mobility. Dutch Catholic emigrants likely experienced a greater uprooting than did the Protestants, but they also assimilated more readily. The international character of the Roman Catholic church weakened their national identity and ethnicity, at the same time that the nationalistic Calvinists maintained their language and institutions, and carved out new daughter colonies when expansion became necessary in the 1870s and 1880s.[30] In short, ethnicity and faith were the vital centers for Dutch Calvinists but the church was the vital center for Dutch Catholics.

NOTES

1. See, for example, C. Y. Gloch and R. Stark, *Religion and Society in Tension* (Chicago, 1965); H. J. Abramson, *Ethnic Diversity in Catholic America* (New York, 1973); Thomas F. O'Dea, *Sociology and the Study of Religion* (New York, 1978); all issues of the *Journal for the Scientific Study of Religion*.

2. The major studies are described in Robert P. Swierenga, "Ethnocultural Political Analysis: A New Approach in American Ethnic Studies," *Journal of American Studies*, 5 (1970): 59-79.

3. Timothy L. Smith, "Religion and Ethnicity in America," *American Historical Review*, 83 (1978): 1155-1185; Martin E. Marty, "Ethnicity: The Skeleton of Religion in America," *Church History*, 41 (1972): 5-21; Harry S. Stout, "Ethnicity: The Vital Center of Religion in America," *Ethnicity*, 2 (1975): 202-224; Jay P. Dolan, "Immigrants in the City: New York's Irish and German Catholics," *Church History*, 41 (1972): 354-368.

4. The literature is summarized in Robert P. Swierenga, "Ethnicity and American Agriculture," *Ohio History*, 89 (1980): 323-344.

5. Joseph M. White, "Religion and Community: Cincinnati Germans, 1814-1870," (Ph.D. diss., University of Notre Dame, 1980); idem, "Historiography of Catholic Immigrants and Religion," *Immigration History Newsletter*, 14 (November 1982): 5-11; Michael G. Karni, "Immigrants and Religion: The Persistence of Ethnic Diversity," *Spectrum*, 1 (1975): 1-8; Smith, "Religion and Ethnicity in America"; Nora Faires, "The Evolution and Significance of Religious Diversity in an Immigrant Community," paper presented to the Social Science History Association meeting, Rochester, N.Y., 1980.

6. A thorough description of this source is in Robert P. Swierenga and Harry S. Stout, "Dutch Immigration in the Nineteenth Century, 1820-1877: A Quantitative Overview," *Indiana Social Studies Quarterly*, 28 (1975): 7-34.

7. Robert P. Swierenga (compiler), *Dutch Emigrants to the United States, South Africa, South America, and Southeast Asia, 1835-1880: An Alphabetical Listing by Household Heads and Independent Persons* (Wilmington, Del., 1983).

8. Robert P. Swierenga (compiler), *Dutch Immigrants in U.S. Population Censuses,*

1850, 1860, and 1870: An Alphabetical Listing by Household Heads of First and Second Generation Immigrants (Wilmington, Del.: forthcoming, 1986).

9. Robert P. Swierenga, "Exodus Netherlands, Promised Land America: Dutch Immigration and Settlement in the United States," in *A Bilateral Bicentennial: A History of Dutch-American Relations*, eds. J. W. Schulte Nordholt and Robert P. Swierenga (New York and Amsterdam, 1982), pp. 127-147, esp. Table 2, p. 131.

10. Jacob Van Hinte, *Netherlanders in America: A Study of Emigration and Settlement in the 19th and 20th Centuries in the United States of America*, trans. Adriaan de Wit (Grand Rapids, Mich., 1985), p. 856, gives the low estimate of forty thousand Catholic emigrants, but this is certainly too low by half. Swierenga, "Exodus Netherlands," pp. 129-130. Henry S. Lucas, *Netherlanders in America: Dutch Immigration to the United States and Canada, 1789-1950* (Ann Arbor, Mich., 1955), follows Van Hinte (pp. 32, 213, 444, 458).

11. For more details on Dutch immigration, see Robert P. Swierenga, "Dutch," in *Harvard Encyclopedia of American Ethnic Groups*, ed., Stephan Thernstrom (Cambridge, Mass., 1980), pp. 284-295.

12. Robert P. Swierenga, "Dutch Immigration Patterns in the Nineteenth and Twentieth Centuries," in *The Dutch in America: Immigration, Settlement, and Cultural Change*, ed. Robert P. Swierenga (New Brunswick, N.J., 1985), pp. 27-32.

13. Robert P. Swierenga, "Local-Cosmopolitan Theory and Immigrant Religion: The Social Bases of the Antebellum Dutch Reformed Schism," *Journal of Social History*, 14 (1980): 113-135.

14. The economic structure of Dutch emigration is analyzed in Robert P. Swierenga, "Dutch International Labour Migration to North America in the Nineteenth Century," in *Dutch Immigration to North America*, eds. Herman Ganzevoort and Mark Boekelman (Toronto, 1983), pp. 1-34.

15. The data on this section on Roman Catholic emigration is described in greater detail in Robert P. Swierenga and Yda Saueressig-Schreuder, "Catholic and Protestant Emigration from the Netherlands in the 19th century: A Comparative Social Structural Analysis," *Tijdschrift voor Economische en Sociale Geografie*, 74 (1983): 25-40.

16. H. Blink. "Immigratie in Amerika en Emigratie uit Europe in Verband met de Economische Toestanden," *Vragen Van Den Dag*, 30 (1910):630; Henry van Stekelenburg, "Tracing the Dutch Roman Catholic Emigrants to North America in the Nineteenth and Twentieth Centuries," in *Dutch Immigration to America*, p. 66. Lucas, *Netherlanders in America*, p. 213, contests this point unconvincingly and also greatly overestimates Catholic emigration.

17. *Verzint eer gij begint! Een hartelijk woord aan mijne landgenooten, over de in ons Vaderland heerschende ziekte genaamd: Landverhuizing* ('s Hertogenbosch, 1846).

18. The few Drenthe Catholics emigrated from the isolated Catholic region of Nieuw-Schoonebeek immediately adjacent to the German border.

19. Yda Saueressig-Schreuder, "Emigration, Settlement, and Assimilation of Dutch Roman Catholic Immigrants in Wisconsin, 1850-1905," (Ph.D. diss., University of Wisconsin, 1982). See also by the same author "Emigration and the Decline of Traditional Industries in mid-nineteenth-century Europe," *Immigration History Newsletter*, 17 (May 1985): 8-10, and "Dutch Catholic emigration in the mid-nineteenth century: Noord-Brabant, 1847-1871," *Journal of Historical Geography*, 11 (1985): 48-69.

20. Yda Saueressig-Schreuder and Robert P. Swierenga, "Catholic Emigration from the Southern Provinces of the Netherlands in the Nineteenth Century," Working Paper no. 27, Netherlands Interuniversity Demographic Institute (Voorburg, 1982), pp. 15-17, 46.

21. Ibid., pp. 18-48.

22. Robert P. Swierenga, "Dutch International Migration and Occupational Change:

A Structural Analysis of Multinational Linked Files," in *History Models and Methods in Migration Research*, ed. Ira A. Glazier (New York, forthcoming 1986).

23. H. A. V. M. van Stekelenburg, "Rooms Katholieke landverhuizers naar de Vereenigde Staten," *Spiegel Historiael*, 12 (1977): 681-689; idem, "Dutch Roman Catholics in the United States," in *Dutch in America*, ed. Swierenga, pp. 64-75; Lucas, *Netherlanders in America*, pp. 213-225, 444-459; Van Hinte, *Netherlanders in America*, pp. 555-557. Irene Hecht, Kinship and Migration: The Making of an Oregon Isolate Community," *Journal of Interdiciplinary History*, 8 (Summer 1977); 45-67.

24. The role of family networks in the founding of Little Chute is documented in Yda Saueressig-Schreuder, "Dutch Catholic Immigrant Settlement in Wisconsin, 1850-1870," in *Dutch in America*, ed. Swierenga, pp. 105-124. For the role of the Dominican Order at Amsterdam in this settlement, see Sister Mary Gilbert Kelly, *Catholic Immigrant Colonization Projects in the United States, 1815-1860* (United States Catholic Historical Society Monograph Series 17) (New York, 1939), pp. 183-185. 270-272; and Frans H. Doppen, "Theodoor J. Van den Broek: Missionary and Emigration Leader. The History of the Dutch Catholic Settlement at Little Chute, Wisconsin," *U.S. Catholic Historian*, 3 (1983): 202-225.

25. Lucas, *Netherlanders in America*, p. 214. See also Van Stekelenburg, "Dutch Roman Catholics in the United States," pp. 73-74.

26. Van Stekelenburg, "Dutch Roman Catholics in the United States," p. 72; Van Hinte, *Netherlanders in America*, pp. 856-857. The information on Saint Joseph's Parish was provided by Fr. Dennis W. Morrow of the Grand Rapids Diocesan Archives.

27. Lucas, *Netherlanders in America*, p. 459.

28. This estimate is derived from *Dutch Immigrants in U.S. Population Censuses.*

29. The religious variable in tables 6, 7, 9, and 10 is determined by classifying each township and city ward in the United States census file as to the "primary religious orientation" of its Dutch immigrant population, according to one of five categories: Protestant, Catholic, Jewish, mixed, and unknown. The designation is based on several factors. The most reliable is the religion in the Netherlands of all families and individuals in the United States census that were linked with the Netherlands Emigration records. Secondary evidence was the family and given names common in the locality, the presence of ministers or priests, the nationality of marriage partners, occupation, and other social and cultural clues. The tables only include the first two categories, Protestant and Catholic.

30. This is also the conclusion of a study of the differential process of assimilation of Dutch Calvinists and Catholics in Canada in the twentieth century. See Joe Graumans, "The Role of Ethno-Religious Organizations in the Assimilation Process of Dutch Christian Reformed and Catholic Immigrants in South Western Ontario" (M.A. thesis, University of Windsor, 1973). Graumans found that "Calvinists built their own Church and Church related structures in Canada, whereas the Catholics join existing Canadian-Catholic organizations" (p. ii). Unfortunately, Graumans did not investigate intermarriage rates by nativity or ethnicity between the two populations. He did, however, find that 88 percent of the Calvinists and 77 percent of Catholics preferred a marriage partner of the same religion for their children, so we can assume that the Calvinists would marry Dutch Reformed while the Catholics, as a minority group, would be unlikely to do so (p. 71).

Who Is the Church? Conflict in a Polish Immigrant Parish in Late Nineteenth-Century Detroit

LESLIE WOODCOCK TENTLER

University of Michigan—Dearborn

Early on the cold morning of Wednesday, December 2, 1885, a crowd began to gather in the forecourt of a handsome brick church on the outskirts of Detroit. The church, only recently blessed, was the Polish Roman Catholic church of Saint Albertus; the crowd, eventually numbering perhaps eight hundred, were Polish immigrants. Most of them were women. Shortly after 6:00, seven policemen marched into the convent opposite the church and soon emerged escorting two Polish priests. The group moved toward the church, but at the church steps the crowd—"the women," according to witnesses— began to jeer at and jostle the priests, and even pelted them with gravel. The police responded vigorously, but they and the priests were pushed from the door several times before they were finally able to enter.[1]

There were too few officers to bar the crowd from the church; the pews filled rapidly with agitated parishioners. And when a priest vested for mass appeared at the altar, the sanctuary rang with cries of anger and denunciation. The mass proceeded, but as the police began to remove the loudest protestors, the din intensified. Women clung to the pews and to each other and even struck policemen in their efforts to remain in the church. The service was hurried to its conclusion, at which most of the crowd left to mill outside. Then at 7:30, the two priests reappeared at the altar to say a second scheduled mass.

The police, by now well reinforced, tried to limit the number entering the church, but women already inside unlocked a side door and a large crowd swarmed into the sanctuary. Several women surged toward the altar. They

I wish to acknowledge, with thanks, the assistance of my colleagues Peter Amann, Jonathan Marwil, Thomas Tentler, and Olivier Zunz, of Father Leonard Blair of the Archives of the Archdiocese of Detroit, and of Father Bohdan Kosicki, until recently the pastor of Sweetest Heart of Mary parish in Detroit. A University of Michigan–Dearborn summer stipend in 1979 helped to support my research.

[1] The narrative here and in the next three paragraphs is drawn from *Detroit Evening News*, 2 December 1885, 1:4–5; *Detroit Evening Journal*, 2 December 1885, 1:1–2; *Detroit Free Press*, 3 December 1885, 5:2–3; *Detroit Tribune*, 3 December 1885, 1:2–3.

0010-4175/83/2186-0426 $2.50 © 1983 Society for Comparative Study of Society and History

were restrained by the police, but soon "an excited crowd was leaning over the communion rail, yelling and brandishing fists." The assisting priest moved forward to reason with the crowd, but could not be heard. As he reached the communion rail, "a dozen hands grabbed his habit and tore it nearly off."[2]

Evidently the priests abandoned the service soon after, but before they had left the sanctuary a woman ascended the altar steps, raised her arms and called for prayer—not for forgiveness but for redress. The protestors responded, falling to their knees. The peace was short-lived. As the two priests, surrounded by a large crowd of police, moved through the churchyard toward the convent, the angry crowd from the church showered them with clods of frozen mud.

Detroit newspapermen were present to record these events—in what was ordinarily a little-visited quarter of the city—because the violence of December 2 was not the first evidence of trouble at Saint Albertus. Cnly the day before, a large crowd, again mainly women, had forcibly ejected a priest from the church as he tried to say early mass. Nor did the violence of December 2 end discord in the parish. On six occasions during the next eighteen months, parishioners battled with police or each other. Many were injured and one man was killed. And on each of these occasions women were prominently involved.[3]

The violence, which caused the Bishop of Detroit to place Saint Albertus church under interdict for nineteen months, bitterly divided the local Polish community. The angriest dissidents eventually seceded from the parish and, notwithstanding their poverty, built a church even grander than Saint Albertus and only two blocks away. To those who remained loyal to Saint Albertus these dissidents were schismatics: they had cut themselves off from the Roman Catholic Church and from salvation. The dissidents, however, always insisted that despite their acknowledged defiance of the Bishop of Detroit, they remained good Roman Catholics. In February 1894, nine years after the troubles began, their confidence was rewarded: by order of the Apostolic Delegate in Washington, the rebellious parish and its priest were formally reconciled with the local bishop.

* * *

Do these curious events, exceptional even in immigrant parishes, contribute significantly to our understanding of the history of American Catholicism? I think they do. The American Church in the nineteenth century became at once more authoritarian and more heterogeneous; this peculiar pattern of develop-

---

[2] *Detroit Evening News*, 2 December 1885, 1:4–5.
[3] *Detroit Evening News*, 1 December 1885, 4:1; *Detroit Evening Journal*, 1 December 1885, 1:3; *Detroit Free Press*, 2 December 1885, 5:2–3; *Detroit Tribune*, 2 December 1885, 2:5.

ment caused serious tensions and a fair degree of conflict between bishops and the laity, bishops and priests, and priests and their congregations. One can surely argue, as many historians do, that the success of the American Church in integrating vast heterogeneous populations into what became a remarkably uniform community was an immense triumph of social control. But the eventual triumph should not blind us to the conflict that troubled the nineteenth-century Church or to the many parishes besides Saint Albertus where dissent erupted into violence.

The emphasis on disciplined conformity in many Church histories usually reflects an excessive preoccupation with the ideas and behavior of the clergy, particularly the bishops. The laity in the parish, difficult to study, are correspondingly slighted. But a focus on the clergy means a limited and often misleading view of the Church. Indeed, Timothy Smith has suggested that a fuller understanding of ethnic Catholicism in the parish may lead to a dramatic revision of the history of the American Church, to a history that "will resemble much more closely that of Protestantism." The important work of Jay Dolan and William Galush amply supports him.[4]

But if a focus on parishioners is a necessary corrective to the clerical bias of much Church history, greater attention to the parish in conflict is necessary to temper the tendency to describe American Church history as an inexorable process of discipline, homogenization, and consolidation. We are most of us too prone to see in the Catholic Church an institution peerlessly capable of inducing conformity within its ranks. The quarrel at Saint Albertus church in late nineteenth-century Detroit challenges our assumptions, and shows us a largely uneducated laity in serious dispute about the nature of Church authority. Their dispute is evidence important to a full understanding of American Church history. And the events in their parish suggest that a revised history of the American Church will include a reassessment of the place of women in this formally patriarchal institution. Recent parish studies have not explored the ways in which lay women understood Church authority and exerted their own authority in the parish.

Poles were not the only Catholics in the nineteenth century to quarrel with Church authority. There were disputes of varying severity between local bishops and congregations with Irish, German, Italian, Slavic, and French

---

4 Timothy L. Smith, "Religious Denominations as Ethnic Communities: A Regional Case Study," *Church History*, 35:2 (June 1966), 226; Jay P. Dolan, *The Immigrant Church: New York's Irish and German Catholics, 1815–1865* (Baltimore: The Johns Hopkins University Press, 1975); William Galush, "Faith and Fatherland: Dimensions of Polish-American Ethnoreligion, 1875–1925," in *Immigrants and Religion in Urban America*, Randall Miller and Thomas Marzik, eds. (Philadelphia: Temple University Press, 1977); *idem*, "Forming Polonia: A Study of Four Polish-American Communities, 1890–1914" (Ph.D. diss., University of Minnesota, 1975). See also Timothy L. Smith, "Lay Initiative in the Religious Life of American Immigrants, 1880–1950," in *Anonymous Americans*, Tamara Hareven, ed. (Englewood Cliffs, N.J.: Prentice-Hall, 1971).

Canadian majorities.[5] But Polish parishes in the late nineteenth century were more prone than others to serious conflict and their conflict more likely to erupt into violence. Most major centers of Polish settlement experienced at least one disruptive parish dispute in the 1880s and 1890s. Buffalo, Cleveland, and Chicago, like Detroit, witnessed the violent birth of secessionist Polish parishes. And in many smaller communities, parish factionalism among Poles led to destruction of property, arrests, injury, and even death.[6] The Detroit papers, alert to the phenomenon in the wake of the troubles at Saint Albertus, reported between 1886 and 1898 violent disputes in Milwaukee, Toledo, Manistee (Michigan), Bay City (Michigan), Posen (Michigan), Plymouth (Pennsylvania), Mill Creek (Pennsylvania), and Depew (New York). In a number of these conflicts women were reported to have been remarkably violent participants.[7]

[5] Patrick Carey, "The Laity's Understanding of the Trustee System, 1785–1855," *The Catholic Historical Review*, 64:3 (July 1978), 357–76; Dolan, *Immigrant Church*, 87–98; Galush, "Forming Polonia," 58–59; James Hennesey, S. J., *American Catholics: A History of the Roman Catholic Community in the United States* (New York: Oxford University Press, 1981), 93–100; Richard M. Linkh, *American Catholicism and European Immigrants, 1900–1924* (Staten Island: Center for Migration Studies, 1976), 106–7; Thomas T. McAvoy, *A History of the Catholic Church in the United States* (Notre Dame: University of Notre Dame Press, 1969), 92–125; Robert F. McNamara, "Trusteeism in the Atlantic States, 1785–1863," *Catholic Historical Review*, 30 (July 1944), 135–54; Alfred G. Stritch, "Trusteeism in the Old Northwest, 1800–1850," *Catholic Historical Review*, 30 (July 1944), 155–164; Silvano M. Tomasi, *Piety and Power: The Role of the Italian Parishes in the New York Metropolitan Area, 1880–1930* (Staten Island: Center for Migration Studies, 1975), 148–53. For late nineteenth-century conflicts in a German and in a French-Canadian parish in Detroit, see *Detroit Evening News*, 10 December 1885, 1:1; *Detroit Sunday News*, 17 April 1892, 3:3; *Detroit Evening News*, 21 April 1892, 5:3–4; 29 October 1892, 7:3; 16 January 1893, 4:4; 18 January 1893, 5:3; 24 July 1893, 4:6; *Detroit Free Press*, 11 December 1885, 5:4.

[6] Daniel S. Buczek, "Polish-Americans and the Roman Catholic Church," *The Polish Review*, 21:3 (1976), 47–49; Galush, "Faith and Fatherland," 90; Victor R. Greene, *For God and Country: The Rise of Polish and Lithuanian Ethnic Consciousness in America* (Madison: State Historical Society of Wisconsin, 1975), 100–121; Edward R. Kantowicz, "Polish Chicago: Survival through Solidarity," in *The Ethnic Frontier*, Melvin G. Holli and Peter d'A Jones, eds. (Grand Rapids, Michigan: William B. Eerdmans Publishing Company, 1977), 194–95; Laurence Orzell, "A Minority within a Minority: The Polish National Catholic Church, 1896–1907," *Polish-American Studies*, 36:1 (Spring 1979), 9–15; Edward Adam Skendzel, *The Kolasinski Story* (Grand Rapids, Michigan: Littleshield Press, 1979), 41–42; W. I. Thomas and Florian Znaniecki, *The Polish Peasant in Europe and America* (New York: Dover Publications, 1958), II, 1528–30, 1551–53. See also *Detroit Sunday News*, 26 January 1890, 1:6; *Detroit Evening News*, 3 February 1890, 2:3; 15 June 1892, 2:3; *Detroit Sunday News*, 19 June 1892, 2:6; *Detroit Evening News*, 22 June 1894, 3:1; 20 August 1894, 3:1.

[7] *Detroit Evening News*, 11 January 1886, 3:5; 4 May 1889, 1:4; 6 May 1889, 1:1; 13 May 1889, 1:5; 23 October 1889, 1:3; 25 March 1890, 2:3; *Detroit Sunday News-Tribune*, 4 October 1896, 8:4; *Detroit Evening News*, 24 November 1896, 4:1; 25 November 1896, 4:3; 4 January 1897, 4:3; 5 January 1897, 6:5; 8 January 1897, 4:4; 9 January 1897, 4:4; *Detroit Sunday News-Tribune*, 10 January 1897, 8:3; *Detroit Evening News*, 11 January 1897, 4:8; *Detroit Sunday News-Tribune*, 17 January 1897, 8:4; *Detroit Evening News*, 20 January 1897, 3:3; 21 January 1897, 4:2; 22 January 1897, 4:3; 25 January 1897, 4:1; 2 February 1897, 4:5; *Detroit Sunday News-Tribune*, 7 February 1897, 8:3; *Detroit Evening News*, 8 February 1897, 4:2; *Detroit*

The Poles, moreover, were the only Catholic group in the United States to generate a large and enduring schismatic church: the Polish National Catholic Church, identifiably Roman Catholic in much of its theology but independent of Rome, was formally organized in 1898. By 1914 it had at least twenty-five parishes, and it enjoyed a healthy growth in the 1920s, a period of concerted assimilationist pressure on immigrant parishes by the American hierarchy. The apparent decline in the twentieth century in the violence generated by Polish parish disputes is at least partly due to the alternative that the Polish National Catholic Church offered to the most bitterly disaffected of the Polish laity. Even so, bitter quarrels within Polish parishes that remained Roman Catholic continued into the twentieth century.[8]

In nearly all Polish parish disputes, principal grievances concerned the desire of the congregation to control parish finances or even hold title to parish property, and to determine or help determine who the pastor would be.[9] One could say, as their clerical critics did, that Polish dissidents insisted on a Protestant model of the church, with congregations functioning virtually autonomously, acknowledging the hierarchy as authority only in matters of doctrine. The most recalcitrant Polish layperson, however, would not have recognized his desires as "Protestant." A Protestant identity was culturally alien to him. And his unwavering commitment to a sacramental theology meant that his dissenting vision of the Church differed in important ways from the understanding common to most Protestant denominations, as we shall see.

Ironically, the group that earlier in the century had caused the most difficulty for their bishops were the Irish, and their difficulties had turned on just those issues that informed later disputes in Polish parishes.[10] The average Irish Catholic was no more disposed than his Polish counterpart to consider himself a covert Protestant, or to join a Protestant church in pursuit of his desire for congregational autonomy. Indeed, considering the degree of support for Catholic institutions and the infrequency of conversion to Protestantism, no ethnic groups were more intensely Catholic than the Poles and the Irish. And yet these groups generated, each in turn, more pressure than any others for a degree of parish autonomy and lay participation in church government always unacceptable to the hierarchy.

It does not appear that either the Poles or the Irish were accustomed in their

Sunday News-Tribune, 21 February 1897, 8:4; *Detroit Evening News*, 22 February 1897, 4:1; 2 March 1897, 4:1; 3 March 1897, 4:5; 29 March 1897, 6:4; 3 April 1897, 4:3; 12 April 1897, 8:1; 7 January 1898, 6:2; 21 February 1898, 4:1.

[8] Galush, "Forming Polonia," 65–68; Orzell, "Minority within a Minority," 5–32.

[9] Galush, "Faith and Fatherland," 90–91; Greene, *For God and Country*, 100–101; Kantowicz, "Polish Chicago," 192–95.

[10] Thomas J. Curran, "The Immigrant Influence on the Roman Catholic Church: New York, a Test Case," in *An American Church: Essays on the Americanization of the Catholic Church*, David J. Alvarez, ed. (Moraga, Calif.: St. Mary's College of California, 1979), 125–128; Dolan, *Immigrant Church*, 89, 92–93; Hennesey, *American Catholics*, 97–100.

homelands to challenge episcopal authority as they did in the United States. [11] There was no strong anticlerical tradition in the popular religion of either nation. Rather, a loyalty to one's priests and bishop was often a defiant statement of support for one's culture and national identity, because in Ireland and in parts of partitioned Poland, Catholicism had been a persecuted religion and a source of resistance to foreign domination. A powerful fusion of national and religious identity inclined Polish and Irish immigrants in the United States to a particularly tenacious defense of traditional religious life against control by outsiders. And like all Catholic immigrants, the Poles and the Irish could be disposed to congregational assertiveness by the heady American experience of parish founding and church building.

It was not without cause, moreover, that many immigrant Catholics felt vulnerable to potentially unsympathetic episcopal authority. As the American hierarchy in the nineteenth century expanded, became more confident and more able effectively to exert authority, parish life was brought increasingly under centralized diocesan control. This control was necessarily administered by a bishop and advisors who were "foreigners" in the eyes of many immigrant Catholics, and who were likely to be proponents of uniformity in the American Church and of swift assimilation for its communicants. Not surprisingly, the pattern of ethnic conflict in the nineteenth-century Church was largely determined by how and when strong episcopal authority was established in the various American dioceses.

The move toward greatly strengthened episcopal authority began in the East. It was here that the growing number of bishops, presiding over dioceses that were increasingly of manageable size, moved decisively during and after the 1820s to secure, in fact as well as in law, episcopal control over parish property, parish financial affairs, and appointment of the clergy. And they met resistance: before the Civil War, the largest number and the bitterest of disputes between individual parishes and the various bishops occurred in the East. By the later nineteenth century, however, the bishops' battle in the East was largely won, with the Irish neatly compensated for their loss of parish autonomy by Irish domination of the hierarchy. [12]

The Church in the Midwest during the antebellum period was not seriously afflicted with struggles over parish rights, and the disputes that did occur there were notably less prolonged and bitter than many in the East. Many midwestern parishes had been founded and were at least partially governed by

---

[11] William Galush has worked in Polish archives with an eye to locating parish disputes in Poland similar to those which occurred in Polish parishes in the United States. The single example he reports, in Galicia in 1914, was in some important respects different from the typical parish quarrel in the American setting. He does find in Galicia, where the clergy were closely allied with the state, the beginnings of an anticlericalism among elements of the peasantry that sometimes led to demands for greater lay control of parish life. Galush, "Forming Polonia," 27, 43.

[12] McNamara, "Trusteeism," 135–54.

strong boards of trustees, and the relative weakness of the region's bishops, caused by the vastness of their territories and the dispersed Catholic population, meant that the trustees' authority was often not directly challenged.[13]

By the later nineteenth century, however, burgeoning midwestern parishes were increasingly subject to strict diocesan discipline. In Detroit, for example, lenient episcopal administration had until 1870 allowed parishes to grow and build with few external controls. But the arrival in the city of Bishop Caspar Borgess in 1870 signaled the beginning of a more centralized, authoritarian administration. Borgess quickly asserted his right to make independent decisions about the founding of new parishes and the expansion of existing ones, to regulate parish fund raising and expenditure, and to appoint and remove priests without congregational interference. He was a bishop with the bureaucratic background common in the hierarchy of the modern Church; his career had been spent largely in the Chancery at Cincinnati. His predecessor, by contrast, had come to the episcopate from a mission pastorate.[14]

The consolidation of episcopal authority before the Civil War seems to have threatened the Irish more immediately than any other group, although German parishes too offered resistance to the bishops. In the later nineteenth century, and particularly in the Midwest, consolidation of episcopal authority most directly threatened the Poles, by then one of the largest and perhaps the most psychologically vulnerable of immigrant Catholic populations. Probably the majority of Poles settled in dioceses whose bishops were in the late nineteenth century only then establishing direct control over parish affairs; these bishops may have been unusually sensitive to challenges to episcopal authority and often liable to deal less than tactfully with troublesome immigrant congregations. But the fears of Polish newcomers often made them hostile to episcopal authority even in old established dioceses. The spread of strong diocesan administration throughout most of the country by the end of the nineteenth century meant simply that sensitive minorities had fewer and fewer opportunities to develop their parishes under mostly nominal outside control. That is why immigrants continued to cause conflict in the Church.

The violence at Saint Albertus, then, exemplifies tensions that affected many Catholic parishes. At issue in this dispute and others like it were two conflicting visions of the Church and Church authority. The clerical vision, forcefully argued in this case by Bishop Borgess and his more tactful but equally resolute successor Bishop John Foley, demanded of the faithful obedience to the clergy not only in matters of faith and morals, but in all aspects of Church life. The American Church might grow and thrive in a democracy,

---

[13] Stritch, "Trusteeism," 155–64.

[14] George Pare, *The Catholic Church in Detroit, 1701–1888* (Detroit: Gabriel Richard Press, 1951), 527–61; Joseph Swastek, *Detroit's Oldest Polish Parish: St. Albertus, Detroit, Michigan, 1872–1972* (n.p., n.p., n.d.), 41–44; *Detroit Evening News*, 3 May 1887, 4:1–3; 30 April 1890, 7:1, 8:2; *Detroit Free Press*, 3 May 1887, 1:5–7.

but it could not be a democratic institution. The Church was of God, and an ordained clergy, as His representatives, necessarily possessed immense authority. Priests were under an imperative obligation to serve the laity selflessly. But they might not, according to Church law and the logic of most Catholic theology, permit the laity a significant share of decision-making power in Church life.

Most clergy and many lay Catholics readily assented to this vision of the Church, although in parishes relatively free of conflict most laypersons probably worried little about the nature of Church authority. But situations of sustained conflict, like that at Saint Albertus, permit us to see, primarily in the behavior of a portion of the laity, the existence of an alternative vision of Church authority, one that is obviously more democratic. Those laypersons at Saint Albertus who resisted the counsels of their priests and their bishops believed firmly that their behavior was justified and that they never ceased to be full communicants of the Roman Catholic Church. If we can understand what notion of right informed their behavior and sustained them as a rebellious congregation, we can understand their vision of the Church and of the authority that governs it.

It is necessary, in this endeavor, to infer a good deal from people's reported behavior. The dissident parishioners from Saint Albertus bequeathed to posterity no disquisitions on the nature of Church authority. But their behavior and the justifications their leaders offered in statements to the local press give evidence of a surprisingly sophisticated vision. While they willingly granted recognition and honor to hierarchical authority, the dissidents reserved to the immediate community an important degree of autonomy. While they embraced a sacramental theology and an ordained priesthood, they identified the Church with the entire worshipping community. And while they sanctioned exclusively male hierarchical authority and male leadership in the parish, they recognized the legitimacy of women's active defense of parish rights.[15]

---

[15] Aside from occasional single editions, no copies of Detroit's Polish-language newspapers survive from the nineteenth century. There is, therefore, no adequate substitute, as a principal source of my narrative, for local English-language newspapers, though I am aware of the weaknesses of such sources. Fortunately, there were in the late 1880s and 1890s four English-language dailies in Detroit, and each covered the dispute at Saint Albertus and its lengthy aftermath attentively. For nearly all important public events in the history of the long dispute there were, then, at least four eyewitnesses who recorded their perceptions, and if they were individually not wholly satisfactory witnesses, each testimony can be checked against that of the others to good effect. I have not reported incidents that were not attested to by at least two newspaper sources, and usually more than two. Fortunately too, the English-language dailies were used by leaders on both sides of the dispute to present their positions to a larger city audience.

Lawrence D. Orton's recent study, *Polish Detroit and the Kolasinski Affair* (Detroit: Wayne State University Press, 1981), provides a narrative of Kolasinski's career between 1882 and 1898. Orton's concerns in his book are substantially different from mine here, and our conclusions differ as well. "The Kolasinski affair," he writes, "was essentially the story of one man's struggle to vindicate himself and triumph at all costs. Although there can be no doubt that Kolasinski cared deeply for the welfare of his congregation, circumstances made them pawns in

* * *

The immediate cause of the violence at Saint Albertus in December 1885 was the dismissal of the pastor, Father Dominic Kolasinski, by the Bishop of Detroit. The Galician-born Kolasinski had come to Saint Albertus in March 1882 from Cracow when he was forty-three years old, a robust, floridly handsome man. Described by contemporaries as an eloquent preacher and charismatic leader, he had successfully exhorted his immigrant flock to replace their modest wooden church with a stately brick one, elaborately decorated and seating 2,500. At its completion in the summer of 1885, the new Saint Albertus was the largest Catholic church in the city.[16]

Kolasinski was a popular priest, but he had influential opponents in his congregation, particularly among the parish trustees, who had in February 1883 petitioned the bishop to overrule their pastor's decisions on the location and cost of the new church. Bishop Borgess, wary of lay assertiveness, upheld Father Kolasinski. His ruling did not, however, quell the tensions between the priest and certain trustees, and in November 1885 complaints against Kolasinski were again lodged with the bishop by certain trustees. This time they accused the priest of financial mismanagement, of charging arbitrary and sometimes excessive fees for services to parishioners, and of sexual immorality. The bishop demanded from Kolasinski the immediate surrender of all parish financial records, which the priest refused, requesting time to make additional entries and corrections. On November 28, without an ecclesiastical hearing, the bishop dismissed him from his pastorate.[17]

the struggle between their stubborn pastor and two strong-willed bishops" (p. 157). I find the parishioners considerably more important as independent actors in the Kolasinski drama than Orton does.

For the history of the initial dispute and subsequent formation of an "independent" parish from the point of view of the children and grandchildren of the disputants, see "50cio Letnia Rocznica Parafii Najsłodszego Serca Marii Panny, 1890–1940" (Detroit: n.p., ca. 1940); "Pamiętnik Diamentowego Jubileuszu Parafji Najsłodszego Serca Marji, Detroit, Michigan, 1890–1965" (Detroit: n.p., ca. 1965).

[16] Skendzel, *Kolasinski Story*, 4–6; Swastek, *Detroit's Oldest Polish Parish*, 65, 67; *Detroit Evening News*, 4 July 1885, 1:8; *Detroit Free Press*, 5 July 1885, 5:4.

[17] Father Kolasinski's guilt or innocence is, happily, not an issue that requires resolution here. Needless to say, the question sparked passionate debate in Detroit's Polish community for many decades after the actual events. Much, though not all, of the correspondence that passed between Bishop Borgess and Kolasinski and Kolasinski's accusers and his defenders can be found in the archives of the Archdiocese of Detroit. One could not, I think, prove the case for or against the priest based on the evidence there, but it is clear that both his accusers and his supporters believed fervently that their version of events was the correct one. The accusations of sexual misconduct, never proved and disbelieved even by some of Kolasinski's foes, probably largely explain the inflexibility of Bishop Borgess and his successor with regard to Kolasinski. Bishop Borgess, who had few sources of information within the Polish community and who relied principally on Father Joseph Dombrowski, a local Kolasinski rival, for guidance in the Kolasinski matter, evidently believed that the priest was guilty of a series of sexual affairs with women and girls in his congregation. He detailed his suspicions in a letter to Archbishop William Henry Elder in Cincinnati. (Bishop Caspar Borgess to Archbishop William Henry Elder, 21 March 1886, Bishop Foley papers, Correspondence, Rev. Kolasinski, "Exhib-

Kolasinski said a farewell mass at Saint Albertus on Sunday, November 29. He preached an emotional sermon, denying all charges, denouncing his accusers, and appealing to the congregation to attend a meeting in his defense to be held after vespers. The late afternoon meeting, which many women attended, was tense. Supporters and opponents of the priest argued hotly, and someone fearing violence called in the police. Many of those present signed, or had signed for them, a petition addressed to Bishop Borgess expressing confidence in Father Kolasinski; it was the first of several pro-Kolasinski petitions sent to the bishop, all of them apparently widely supported. Notwithstanding, Bishop Borgess on November 30 assigned temporary charge of the parish to Father Joseph Dombrowski, the Polish-born chaplain of the nearby convent of the Felician Sisters. Father Kolasinski, however, refused to vacate the Saint Albertus rectory.[18]

It was Father Dombrowski's attempt to function as head of the parish that sparked the violence of December 1 and 2. The crowds of angry women who disrupted mass were determined to uphold Father Kolasinski's claims to his pastorate. On December 3, the assembled women forced the closing of the parish school. And on December 4, in response to the violence, Bishop Borgess ordered Saint Albertus church closed for an indefinite period. Father Dombrowski, however, continued to say mass for an apparently small number of parishioners in the chapel of the Felician convent until he left Detroit some sixteen months later.[19]

its," Archives of the Archdiocese of Detroit (hereafter cited as AAD).) Shortly thereafter, Father Dombrowski attested to Kolasinski's immorality in a report to the Congregation of the Propaganda in Rome. ("Report of the Rev. Joseph Dombrowski to the Propaganda in July, 1886," Bishop Borgess papers, Box 3, File 4, AAD.) When the Detroit Chancery late in 1893 forwarded charges against Kolasinski to Rome at the request of the Propaganda, those charges included the same bill of sexual particulars that Bishop Borgess had sent to Archbishop Elder in 1886. ("In Materia Applicationis Reverendi D. Kolasinski in Quantam ad Nos Aliquo Modo Pertineat," Bishop Foley papers, Correspondence, Rev. Kolasinski, undated, 1892–1893, AAD.) Probably the extravagance of the original accusations of immorality and the embarrassing publicity that attended them caused not only Bishop Borgess but his successor to insist—and to believe—that the accusations were true. And it is likely that the 1885 decision to dismiss Kolasinski without a hearing was precipitated by Bishop Borgess's angry conviction that Kolasinski was an immoral man. The abrupt dismissal led to a series of violent events, each of which increased for Bishop Borgess the need to believe that he had judged Kolasinski rightly. (Bishop Caspar Borgess to Archbishop William Henry Elder, 1 April 1886, Bishop Foley papers, Correspondence, Rev. Kolasinski, "Exhibits," AAD.) Bishop Foley in turn inherited the burden.

See also Skendzel, *Kolasinski Story*, 6–7, 104B–104G; Swaktek, *Detroit's Oldest Polish Parish*, 66–67, 72–73; *Detroit Evening News*, 24 November 1885, 4:1; *Detroit Evening Journal*, 27 November 1885, 1:3.

[18] Skendzel, *Kolasinski Story*, 7; Swastek, *Detroit's Oldest Polish Parish*, 73; *Detroit Evening News*, 30 November 1885, 4:3; *Detroit Evening Journal*, 30 November 1885, 1:1; *Detroit Free Press*, 1 December 1885, 3:3; *Detroit Tribune*, 1 December 1885, 2:5.

[19] Skendzel, *Kolasinski Story*, 7; *Detroit Evening News*, 1 December 1885, 4:1; 3 December 1885, 3:3; *Detroit Sunday News*, 6 December 1885, 4:1; *Detroit Evening Journal*, 1 December 1885, 1:3; 3 December 1885, 4:1; *Detroit Free Press*, 2 December 1885, 5:2–3; 4 December 1885, 3:4–5; 5 December 1885, 4:6; *Detroit Tribune*, 2 December 1885, 2:5; 4 December 1885, 2:6.

The steps of the locked church were the site in early December of several prayer vigils by Father Kolasinski's female supporters. But the intensity of the anger generated by Kolasinski's dismissal and the closing of the church were not again publicly evident until Christmas Day. Early Christmas morning, a large crowd estimated variously at 3,000 to 5,000 persons marched some two miles to the bishop's residence to request the opening of Saint Albertus church for Christmas services. Men, women, and children, dressed in traditional holiday costumes, kept a chilly vigil in the street before the residence for more than two hours, while a six-man delegation tried in vain to see the bishop.[20]

Disappointed, the parishioners vented their frustrations in their own neighborhood. A particular target of verbal abuse throughout the rest of Christmas Day was the shuttered store and house of John Lemke, a leader of the anti-Kolasinski trustees. In the late afternoon, someone fired shots from within the store into an apparently threatening crowd outside, and a young man fell dead. The shooting outraged Kolasinski's supporters, and on December 26 a crowd stoned the store of Thomas Zoltowski, another of Kolasinski's chief opponents. Kolasinski himself still remained in the Saint Albertus rectory, guarded by an armed contingent from the Kosciusko Guard, a military company composed of parish youths.[21]

A heavy police presence enforced an uneasy calm on December 27, and there were no further outbreaks of serious violence until August 16, 1886, some four months after Kolasinski had left Detroit. On that day a large crowd, again primarily women, threw stones at a priest as he left the convent and attacked a second priest when he went to visit a dying parishioner. On August 17 a group of women hired by the diocese to clean the long-empty church were driven from the doors by a largely female crowd whose members "all had either brickbats or lumps of mud in their hands." In the evening the crowd, now reinforced by husbands and sons, threw stones at the police and at the convent. These disturbances were evidently occasioned by rumors that the church would soon be reopened for worship. Kolasinski's followers were determined that no other priest should hold his pastorate.[22]

The same determination sparked conflict with the police seven months later. On March 20, 1887, rumors of the imminent reopening of Saint Albertus caused a crowd to gather at the church for a day-long vigil, and in the

[20] *Detroit Sunday News*, 6 December 1885, 4:1; *Detroit Evening News*, 7 December 1885, 2:1; 25 December 1885, 1:1–2; *Detroit Evening Journal*, 25 December 1885, 1:1–2; *Detroit Free Press*, 26 December 1885, 1:5–6; *Detroit Tribune*, 26 December 1885, 1:5.

[21] *Detroit Evening News*, 26 December 1885, 1:1–4; *Detroit Sunday News*, 27 December 1885, 1:1–4; *Detroit Evening Journal*, 26 December 1885, 1:1–3; *Detroit Free Press*, 26 December 1885, 1:5–6; 28 December 1885, 3:1–4; *Detroit Tribune*, 26 December 1885, 1:5; 27 December 1885, 2:1.

[22] *Detroit Evening News*, 28 December 1885, 4:2–3; 17 August 1886, 4:2; *Detroit Evening Journal*, 28 December 1885, 4:1; 17 August 1886, 4:3; *Detroit Free Press*, 18 August 1886, 5:5; *Detroit Tribune*, 28 December 1885, 4:1–2; 17 August 1886, 4:4; 18 August 1886, 2:5.

evening Kolasinski's supporters attacked the police as they tried to clear the street. Twenty were arrested. And on May 19, 1887—Ascension Day—Kolasinski's supporters tried to take possession of the parish rectory. They were thwarted by the police, who were joined by a sizeable contingent of Saint Albertans who hoped for the reopening of their church and were most anxious that violence not jeopardize this. No further crowd violence disturbed the neighborhood, although the community remained bitterly divided even after Father Kolasinski's eventual reconciliation with the bishop.[23]

But what determined which members of the parish, which numbered at least 7,000 in 1885, were willing to defend Kolasinski with force? Only a minority was prepared to do so: the angry crowds of early December were generally estimated at about 1,000 persons, though we can assume that many of the women spoke for aggrieved family members as well as for themselves. Opponents of Father Kolasinski claimed that most of his ardent supporters were recently arrived Galicians, blindly loyal to their countryman and too ignorant of American customs to understand that one should not slavishly venerate one's priest. The most influential of Kolasinski's opponents were Prussian Poles, who had lived in Detroit for many years. The parish quarrel, they argued, was simply a reflection of ancient regional antagonisms, exacerbated by the unfamiliarity of the new immigrants with their adopted country.[24]

Regional rivalries, however, could not have been a principal cause of the conflict, for both supporters and opponents of Father Kolasinski were mostly of German birth. The records of the secessionist parish that emerged from the dispute—the parish of the Sweetest Heart of Mary—do not provide information on the birthplace of parishioners. But county marriage records for 1889 and 1890, the first two years of Kolasinski's pastorate at the dissident congregation, show that about 87 percent of those marrying at Saint Albertus were born in Germany or Prussia, compared to about 82 percent of those married by Father Kolasinski. An Austrian-born minority existed in Kolasinski's congregation: 8.5 percent of those marrying there in 1889 and 1890 were of Austrian birth, while fewer than 1 percent of the persons married at Saint Albertus were from Austria. We can assume, then, that the small minority of Austrian-born Poles living in the local Polish community in the mid-1880s were largely loyal to Father Kolasinski, perhaps simply because he too was of Austrian birth. But Kolasinski's compelling personality transcended regional loyalties in its appeal, and many in his congregation

[23] *Detroit Evening News,* 21 March 1887, 4:1–2; 20 May 1887, 4:1; *Detroit Evening Journal,* 21 March 1887, 4:3; 20 May 1887, 4:3; *Detroit Free Press,* 21 March 1887, 1:6–7; 20 May 1887, 4:7.

[24] Swastek, *Detroit's Oldest Polish Parish,* 73, 75, 83–84. *Detroit Evening News,* 10 December 1885, 2:3; 5 April 1886, 4:2; *Detroit Free Press,* 4 December 1885, 3:4–5.

were evidently able to understand themselves as Poles, members of a larger community than the region of Poland in which they had been born.[25]

It is possible, even likely, that the anti-Kolasinski leaders hoped to discredit the movement in support of the priest by identifying it with the poor, low-status Galician minority in the community. Certainly the anti-Kolasinski leaders were visibly wealthier and of higher status than their opponents. Kolasinski's most prominent supporters were, by the standards of the community, relatively well-to-do, but they were mostly skilled workers, not entrepreneurs, and their prosperity was more tenuous than that of their leading opponents, who included a contractor, a wealthy grocer, and several saloonkeepers. Few of Kolasinski's leading defenders had previously been trustees at Saint Albertus. Most of them probably found in his cause a welcome first opportunity to exercise church leadership.[26]

Perhaps, then, the dispute at Saint Albertus was fueled essentially by the accumulated grievances of the poorer parishioners against the parish—and community—elite. There is evidence to suggest this. The Saint Albertus loyalists were probably a wealthier group than the pro-Kolasinski dissidents. Again, county marriage records for 1889 and 1890 allow us to compare certain members of the two congregations, although the occupations of young men in their twenties, as most of the bridegrooms were, may not represent the diversity of occupation in a parish as accurately as would a sample of men in their thirties and forties. Still, we could expect that relatively secure fathers would often try to establish marriageable sons as something other than unskilled laborers.

Laborers, however, were far and away the most populous occupational group in both parishes: 51 percent of the bridegrooms at Saint Albertus and 60 percent of those at Sweetest Heart of Mary worked as laborers. Skilled workers were a distinct minority: about 21 percent of the Saint Albertus bridegrooms were skilled or craft workers, compared to 12.5 percent of those at Sweetest Heart of Mary. And entrepreneurs were few: 5.5 percent (nine) of the men at Saint Albertus, less than 1.5 percent (two) at Sweetest Heart of Mary. Both parishes, then, had poor, working-class majorities, but Kolasinski's congregation probably had a larger representation of unskilled workers and fewer members who could claim high status in the community because of wealth or business achievement. Young women's work patterns also support this hypothesis. About 26 percent of the brides at Saint Albertus in 1889 and 1890 reported being employed, mainly as servants and factory workers, but nearly 50 percent of the brides from Kolasinski's congregation

25 Register of Marriages, Wayne County, Michigan, 1889–90. See also Peter A. Ostafin, "The Polish Peasant in Transition: A Study of Group Interaction as a Function of Symbiosis and Common Definition" (Ph.D. diss., University of Michigan, 1948), 251.
26 Polk's *Directory of Detroit*, 1886, 1887, 1888.

claimed to be working for wages. In this parochial and isolated community, the working daughter was often a sign of family poverty. Greater prosperity, at least in these years, meant that women could stay properly at home.[27]

The Kolasinski dispute, then, was not simply a revolt of the poor against the secure. Too many loyal members of Saint Albertus parish lived in poverty. But the evidently greater prosperity of those antagonistic to Kolasinski suggests that the choice for or against the priest did have a dimension related to economics and social standing. Perhaps the dispute was nourished by conflicting world views that both reflected and affected economic status. Those who supported Kolasinski may have identified with him strongly because his vulnerability to outside attack underscored the tenuous nature of immigrant success in America. Their own hard lives and fear of the future helped to make Kolasinski for them an evocative figure. Those who opposed the priest, or refused to defy the bishop on his behalf, may have been generally less anxious about their vulnerability as mostly poor immigrants in a strange country. They chose to respect the authority of long-established community leadership, and evidently did not see in Bishop Borgess a potent threat to the integrity of the Polish community.

That Kolasinski's supporters were unusually apprehensive of the world beyond the community is well illustrated by their attitudes toward Father Dombrowski, Kolasinski's successor at Saint Albertus and a target of the December 1885 disturbances. Father Dombrowski, as founder of the Polish Seminary in Detroit, was an ardent proponent of a distinctively Polish Roman Catholicism. He was also a rival to Father Kolasinski for leadership in the local community. But Kolasinski's supporters saw in Father Dombrowski more than a successful rival to their deposed priest; he was for them a man uncritically, even dangerously, loyal to a hostile bishop. Despite his demonstrated commitment to preserving Polish culture in the United States, many Kolasinski adherents believed that Dombrowski had betrayed the ethnic group to serve personal ambition. Their fears, and to some extent their support of Father Kolasinski, were probably rooted in a sharp sense of economic and cultural vulnerability, and a concomitant dread of change.

Nothing in this discussion begins to explain the prominent role of women in the demonstrations unless it be that employed women are more likely to be assertive than those who stay at home. The most aggressive of Kolasinski's

---

[27] Register of Marriages, Wayne County, Michigan, 1889–90. On the economic status of Poles in late nineteenth-century Detroit, see also Sister Mary Remigia Napolska, "The Polish Immigrant in Detroit to 1914," *Annals of the Polish Roman Catholic Union Archives and Museum*, 10 (1946), Chicago, 34–36; Ostafin, "Polish Peasant in Transition," 371–72; Olivier Zunz, "Detroit's Ethnic Neighborhoods at the End of the Nineteenth Century," Center for Research on Social Organization, Working Paper no. 161 (Ann Arbor: University of Michigan, February 1978), 70.

female supporters, however, were long-married and mothers of many children, women unlikely to work outside the home. Their prominence as Kolasinski supporters was, at least initially, a matter of circumstance. Most of the early demonstrations occurred at short notice on weekday mornings. With husbands and sons at work for long hours away from the neighborhood, homebound women were necessarily the first line of Kolasinski's defense at what they deemed critical moments in the campaign.

But these women evidently believed, or quickly came to believe, that violent behavior on their part was justified by something more than necessity; even in battles where many men were present, women were still aggressive participants. Evidently, too, their husbands and children endorsed this clearly unconventional female behavior, although the willingness of the women to confront the police made them de facto the principal strategists of the campaign to retain Kolasinski. And those who petitioned the bishop on Christmas Day to open Saint Albertus Church—not all of them ardent supporters of Kolasinski—did not find the behavior of the women in early December so unjustifiable as to warrant an interdict.[28]

There was, then, considerable support among the dissidents and even their less committed sympathizers for women who actively sought to affect clerical decision making. But in the meetings of the dissident group and in the eventual organization of a secessionist parish, men alone assumed leadership. The extent to which and the ways in which the dissident community permitted women to exercize authority will be discussed more fully later. It can be said here that the community was evidently not troubled by what might appear to be inconsistencies in its expectations of women.

* * *

Whatever the wellsprings of rebellion, support for Father Kolasinski was initially understood by the dissidents purely in terms of personal loyalty. The first wave of resistance to the bishop was not, to all appearances, occasioned by commitment to any theory of congregational rights. But the extremity of their behavior in defense of the priest soon required of Kolasinski's adherents a more disinterested justification of their resistance to episcopal authority. So did their increasing isolation. Kolasinski left Detroit in April 1886; during his thirty-two month absence his supporters functioned as a congregation without a priest. In April 1887 Bishop Borgess, angered by the recurrent violence which prevented the reopening of Saint Albertus for worship, issued a decree

[28] *Detroit Evening News*, 19 March 1887, 1:3; 21 March 1887, 4:1–2; 20 May 1887, 4:1; 7 December 1888, 4:1; *Detroit Evening Journal*, 25 December 1885, 1:1–2; 26 December 1885, 1:1–3; 28 December 1885, 4:1; 17 August 1886, 4:3; 21 March 1887, 4:3; *Detroit Free Press*, 28 December 1885, 3:1–4; 21 March 1887, 1:6–7; 27 June 1887, 2:2; *Detroit Tribune*, 17 August 1886, 4:4; 18 August 1886, 2:5.

of excommunication against those active on Kolasinski's behalf.[29] In June 1887 the interdict on Saint Albertus was finally lifted, and that parish resumed its normal, vigorous life. Many who initially protested Bishop Borgess's abrupt removal of Kolasinski by signing petitions or by refusing to attend Father Dombrowski's convent masses returned to Saint Albertus under the ministrations of a new priest, Father Vincent Bronikowski. In such demoralizing circumstances, those still loyal to Kolasinski needed more than their loyalty to him to justify and sustain themselves as a dissident community.

Lay leaders of the Kolasinski faction early in the dispute articulated a principled defense of their defiance of episcopal authority. The bishop, they argued, had dismissed Father Kolasinski without a hearing, thus denying the priest's right to due process. Although Kolasinski's rights were unclear under the canon law governing the American Church in 1885, Kolasinski's supporters insisted that both the claim to due process and lay defense of this claim were legitimate. Here, clearly, they departed from the vision of the Church found in canon law. A priest's right to trial before removal for cause by his bishop was in fact established for the American Church by the Congregation of the Propaganda in 1887, and an eminent Michigan canonist argued in 1893 that Kolasinski's removal had been arbitrary. But no canonist or bishop was prepared to recognize the laity as legitimate definers and defenders of clerical rights.[30]

Kolasinski's supporters also raised in their defense an American interpretation of the ancient right of patronage. In many European communities, and certainly in Poland, wealthy individuals or families held the right to nominate the parish priest, because the patron or his forebears had given the money to build the church. But in the United States, donors to the church fund might

---

[29] *Detroit Evening News*, 3 May 1887, 4:1–3; *Detroit Free Press*, 3 May 1887 1:5–7. Such a decree of excommunication would certainly be questionable in the eyes of many canon lawyers. Bishop Foley, successor to Bishop Borgess, obliquely acknowledged the considerable difficulties of excommunication in these circumstances when he declared in January 1889 that all who participated in services at which Father Kolasinski officiated would incur automatic excommunication. See *Detroit Evening News*, 25 January 1889, 1:4; *Detroit Tribune*, 26 January 1889, 5:2.

[30] *The Catholic Encyclopedia* (New York: Robert Appleton Company, 1911), XI, 502, 538; *Detroit Evening News*, 4 December 1885, 4:1; 6 December 1885, 4:1; *Detroit Sunday News*, 27 December 1885, 1:1–4; *Detroit Evening News*, 30 December 1893, 5:4–5; *Detroit Evening Journal*, 7 December 1888, 1:1; *Detroit Free Press*, 2 December 1885, 5:2–3; 3 December 1885, 5:2–3; 28 December 1885, 3:1–4; 8 June 1888, 8:5.

In 1890, the trustees of Sweetest Heart of Mary issued a statement in which they compared Kolasinski's situation to that of Father Edward McGlynn, who was suspended as a priest in the diocese of New York and eventually excommunicated for his refusal to cease speaking on behalf of Henry George and the single tax movement. McGlynn was eventually reinstated, but not until December 1892. That Kolasinski's trustees were aware of the McGlynn case and able in 1890 to consider him still a priest because his superiors had dealt with him unjustly demonstrates that their defense of themselves was broad and principled. They could endorse a priest of another nationality, in a distant city, whose disobedience had occurred in a very different context from that of Father Kolasinski. See *Detroit Sunday News*, 28 September 1890, 2:1.

include most of the congregation. This was usually true in Polish immigrant parishes. As builders of the church, argued Kolasinski's aggrieved supporters, they possessed the right to name the pastor. The staunchly anti-Kolasinski congregation at Saint Albertus made the same argument in 1891 when they withheld their annual pew rents to force the bishop to remove a priest who they claimed spoke inadequate Polish.[31]

The conviction that generous support of the parish entitled a congregation to certain decision-making rights informed most disputes over parish rights between ethnic Catholics and their American bishops. And new immigrant congregations, not surprisingly, were the most likely to assert their purported rights as patrons. Not only did they make considerable sacrifices to support the parish, but their contributions produced schools, churches, convents—all the result of congregational effort and powerful stimuli to strong feelings of ownership. It was the immigrant generation, moreover, who as parish founders were forced to cede title to parish property to the bishop, a requirement which made more than usually evident authority relations in the Church and which occasionally provoked outright resistance. It was the immigrant generation that needed priests who spoke their language and upheld group traditions; their children and grandchildren generally had fewer reasons to fear the independent selection of pastors by a bishop. And the immigrant generation, especially among the Poles, normally found in the parish a primary focus of social, cultural, and emotional life. For their children and grandchildren, the parish was more likely to be one focus among many.[32]

Thus the experiences and needs of the immigrant laity sustained them in their arguments for parish autonomy, and in disputes over parish rights the invocation of Church law by the bishop was rarely persuasive. The First Provisional Synod of the American Church had in 1829 expressly prohibited the right of patronage in the United States, and the American hierarchy, with full papal support, steadfastly denied that congregations or boards of trustees were empowered to make independent decisions about church finances or the parish priest. The Third Plenary Council, meeting in Baltimore in 1884, ruled that trustees were the creatures of the bishop, and that their selection, should they exist at all, was to be by nomination of the pastor to the bishop, who might remove them at his pleasure. That many immigrant congregations continued, often until World War I, to elect their trustees indicates that many

---

[31] Galush, "Faith and Fatherland," 85–86; idem, "Forming Polonia," 27, 58–59; Swastek, *Detroit's Oldest Polish Parish*, 54, 83; *Detroit Evening News*, 17 August 1886, 4:2; 21 March 1887, 4:1–2; 7 December 1888, 4:1; 10 December 1888, 2:3; *Detroit Sunday News*, 28 September 1890, 2:1; *Detroit Evening News*, 11 June 1891, 1:3; 12 June 1891, 1:5; 13 June 1891, 1:3; 15 June 1891, 1:2; 16 June 1891, 1:2, 2:3; 17 June 1891, 1:4; 18 June 1891, 1:3; 20 June 1891, 1:1; *Detroit Sunday News*, 21 June 1891, 2:8; *Detroit Evening News*, 26 June 1891, 1:5; 13 July 1891, 1:1; 16 July 1891, 5:1 *Detroit Sunday News*, 19 July 1891, 2:5; *Detroit Free Press*, 5 April 1886, 4:4; 14 June 1891, 18:3; *Detroit Tribune*, 10 December 1888, 4:4; 10 June 1889, 4:3.

[32] Galush, "Faith and Fatherland," 89; Linkh, *American Catholicism*, 106; Thomas and Znaniecki, *Polish Peasant*, 1523–28, 1545–47.

laypersons postulated a very different model of church authority from that embodied in canon law.[33]

What the laity proposed when they claimed the right, as patrons, to choose the pastor was a contractual relationship between priest and people. They recognized their obligation to support the pastor, but believed that that support obliged the pastor to serve the congregation to its own satisfaction. Those who called a priest might dismiss him, or they might, as Kolasinski's congregation eventually did, alter the terms of his service or compensation. Such contractual notions could imply an assumption that priest and people are social equals, but Kolasinski's parishioners, and many other immigrant Catholics, did not behave as though they believed that this was true. Kolasinski's congregation supported him generously; he lived comfortably, dressed fashionably, and kept an expensive carriage and team—a gift from his parishioners.

Certainly many in the parish were pleased to subsidize a priest who represented them so handsomely in a city where Poles were often regarded with contempt. But they also believed that the pastor, by virtue of his ordination to a sacramental priesthood, stood apart from the people spiritually as well as socially. Kolasinski's supporters thus acted on an understanding of the relationship between clergy and laity that incorporated both democratic and hierarchic ideas, recognizing the uniqueness and sacredness of the priesthood but demanding that the priest respond to congregational wishes in his administration of the parish. Church law, of course, posited a very different relationship between priest and people: congregations were obliged to support their priests, but priests were to remain independent of congregational control. The priest's obligation to his flock was defined solely by his pastoral commission.[34]

Finally, Kolasinski's defenders invoked the specter of a contractual relationship between the laity and the bishop by arguing that Bishop Borgess had forfeited his right to their obedience. Not only had he dealt unjustly with Father Kolasinski, he had failed in his pastoral obligation: when he gave Father Dombrowski, a prominent rival to Kolasinski, the pastorate at Saint Albertus, argued the dissidents, the bishop had made it emotionally impossible for them to baptize their children, marry the young, comfort the dying, and properly bury the dead. Subsequently, the bishop had—unjustly, in their view—formally barred them from the sacraments. To what extent Kolasinski's adherents actually did without the sacraments is impossible to determine; certainly there were priests near the area of Polish settlement who ministered

---

[33] *Catholic Encyclopedia*, XV, 71; Galush, "Forming Polonia," 87, 92–93, 218–20, 258–61; McNamara, "Trusteeism," 146; *Detroit Sunday News*, 19 July 1891, 2:5.

[34] Edward A. Chmielewski, "Minneapolis' Polish Priests, 1886–1914," *Polish-American Studies*, 19:1 (January–June 1962), 31–32; Galush, "Forming Polonia," 221; *Detroit Sunday News*, 9 June 1889, 2:4; *Detroit Evening News*, 8 July 1889, 3:3; 4 January 1898, 1:5, 6:5; *Detroit Free Press*, 31 October 1889, 5:1.

to them in his absence. And the bishop might properly have responded that a priest's personality was not sufficient cause for a Catholic to abstain from the sacraments.[35]

But Kolasinski's advocates believed firmly that they had been unjustifiably denied pastoral care, and this was evidently an important theme in the appeals lodged by Kolasinski and his leading lay supporters with Archbishop William Henry Elder at Cincinnati, with Bishop-designate Foley, with the Apostolic Delegate at Washington, and with the Congregation of the Propaganda at Rome. A higher authority, Kolasinski's spokesmen asserted throughout the life of the rebellious parish, would eventually uphold their actions, and this certainty permitted them to consider themselves good Roman Catholics. Again, a dissident laity finds persuasive a view of church authority that includes elements both of democratic and hierarchical theory. An appeal to the Vatican will surely force the local bishop to respond to the desires of his constituents. Happily, Kolasinski's congregation was never confronted with a definitive denial of redress from Rome.[36]

The lay leaders of Kolasinski's rebellious parish were understandably anxious to justify what many of their neighbors saw as apostasy. But did the ordinary parishioner—a recent immigrant, possibly illiterate, living in poverty—really concern himself with the legitimacy of his priest? Perhaps he was attracted to the parish by Father Kolasinski's eloquent preaching. Perhaps he came to the parish because his kin had chosen to do so.

Most parishioners, however, would have known that the choice was not risk-free. Both Bishops Borgess and Foley had it widely announced in the Polish community that Kolasinski's adherents had excommunicated themselves. The local Polish-language weekly, fiercely anti-Kolasinski, constantly reminded the community that the priest's supporters had cut themselves off from the Church. There was, therefore, considerable incentive for even the most casual member of the rebellious parish to find grounds on which the bishops' pronouncements might be disallowed. And throughout the history of the rebellious parish a preoccupation with legitimacy was continuous and apparently widely held. Kolasinski's sermons dealt with the issue, as did his statements to the press; defectors trying to promote disaffection among his followers argued on the grounds of Kolasinski's illegitimacy as a priest in rebellion; the congregation was adamant that a bishop must bless the cornerstone of their new church because an episcopal blessing was the norm for

[35] *Detroit Sunday News*, 25 November 1888, 8:1; *Detroit Evening News*, 5 July 1890, 1:3; *Detroit Sunday News*, 28 September 1890, 2:1; *Detroit Evening News*, 16 October 1893, 5:3–7; *Detroit Tribune*, 10 June 1889, 4:3.
[36] *Detroit Evening News*, 21 March 1887, 4:1–2; *Detroit Sunday News*, 25 November 1888, 8:1; *Detroit Evening News*, 26 January 1889, 1:5; *Detroit Sunday News*, 29 September 1889, 13:1; *Detroit Evening News*, 24 September 1890, 1:1; 20 July 1891, 5:3; 2 December 1893, 6:3; *Detroit Evening Journal*, 26 January 1889, 1:3; *Detroit Free Press*, 1 December 1888, 8:3; *Michigan Catholic*, 3 October 1889, 4:4–5.

such ceremonies and would give the community an assurance of regularity. The spiritual and social consequences of apostasy in a Polish immigrant community were likely sufficient to make a political philosopher of the most untutored member of a rebellious parish.[37]

* * *

Kolasinski finally surrendered the Saint Albertus rectory and left Detroit in April 1886. Soon after his departure he was granted an exeat by Bishop Borgess, evidently on the intercession of the Archbishop at Cincinnati. He then proceeded to a small Polish settlement in the Dakota Territory, where he remained as pastor until December 1888. In Detroit, news of Kolasinski's new pastorate angered his supporters, who saw in it a tacit acknowledgment by Bishop Borgess that the priest had been innocent of serious wrongdoing. And the news also gave rise to expectations that the priest might soon return as pastor to those who remained loyal in his absence. "We wait each Sunday for our pastoral Father," wrote a fervent Detroit supporter to the initially pro-Kolasinski *Wiarus* in Winona, Minnesota, and look forward to the day when "the Heavenly Father returns him to us as He returned the crucified Jesus to the Sorrowing Mother of God."[38]

In this intoxicating climate of indignation and expectation, an undetermined number of Kolasinski's supporters in his absence organized themselves as a congregation. They also established a school, which was under the direction of Anton Dlugi, a recent immigrant who may have been a blacksmith in Poland but who became schoolmaster and principal lay leader of the new congregation. The earliest extant mention of the new school is a letter from Dlugi to the *Wiarus* in August 1886; he had, he wrote, about two hundred pupils. The school had certainly been organized by the time the letter was written; later testimony, not unimpeachable, claimed that the school was founded in March of that year. No records survive from this period in the history of the new parish, but it is certain that the new school continued under Dlugi's control, meeting in a large frame house near Saint Albertus church, until Kolasinski returned in December 1888. Dlugi left the congregation shortly thereafter, but the school survived and by June 1889 was housed in considerably more substantial quarters.[39]

[37] *Detroit Evening News*, 2 June 1890, 1:3; 10 June 1890, 1:1–2; 2 July 1890, 1:1; 4 July 1890, 1:1; 24 July 1890, 1:2; 24 September 1890, 1:1; 25 September 1890, 1:3; 29 September 1890, 1:1–2; 16 June 1891, 1:1–2; 16 July 1891, 5:1; 25 July 1891, 1:2; 3 September 1891, 2:1; *Detroit Sunday News*, 5 June 1892, 1:8; *Detroit Evening News*, 2 December 1893, 6:3; *Detroit Sunday News-Tribune*, 24 December 1893, 1:2–3; *Detroit Free Press*, 6 June 1892, 5:2–3; 25 December 1893, 1:6–7; *Detroit Tribune*, 6 June 1892, 5:2–4.

[38] *Wiarus*, 20 May 1886, 3:2; 27 May 1886, 1:6. Bishop Caspar H. Borgess to Rt. Rev. Dr. Marty, 3 April 1886 (appended to Chancery brief, "To the Congregation De Propaganda Fide, in re Diocese of Detroit vs. Rev. Dominic Kolasinski," undated, but late 1893), Bishop Foley papers, Rev. Kolasinski, transcripts, folder 2, AAD.

[39] *Wiarus*, 19 August 1886, 2:4; *Detroit Evening News*, 30 November 1888, 1:3; 12 May 1889, 2:1; *Detroit Evening Journal*, 3 January 1889, 1:5; *Detroit Tribune*, 8 June 1888, 5:5–6.

The frame schoolhouse also served the congregation as a meeting house and place of worship during Kolasinski's absence. Regular Sunday services were held there. Mass could not be celebrated, but evidently the group sang hymns, prayed, and recited the rosary. "There was singing and prayer," noted one observer, "and a sort of exercise in which responsive murmurs were made by the people to their leader's intonations." Polish Catholics brought to the United States a rich liturgical tradition; the mass might provide the most intense spiritual experience for most, but they were familiar with a number of nonsacramental devotions. In this sense immigrant Catholics were rather better prepared than Catholics today to sustain a congregation without a priest.[40]

A priest was necessary, however, if parishioners were to fulfill their minimum obligations as Catholics to confess and receive communion during the Easter season, if they were to contract canonically valid marriages, if they were to have the comfort of absolution and anointment at the point of death. In emergencies, laypersons might baptize, but the scrupulous among Kolasinski's supporters might have worried that their situation was not the sort of emergency that, according to Catholic teaching, justified lay baptism. What, then, did the Kolasinski loyalists do? Their leaders claimed that most of the congregation had no access to the sacraments, that as many as eight hundred infants were unbaptized at the time of Kolasinski's return, that the young had been unable to marry in the Church, that the dead had been denied Christian burial—although it was not said that any died unconfessed. If these assertions are true, then perhaps in their priestless years Kolasinski's supporters began to develop an understanding of their religion that was largely nonsacramental. This would represent a major theological reorientation, developing without anyone's intent from defiance of a particular act of ecclesiastical authority.[41]

Extant evidence, however, belies most of the leaders' claims. Perhaps they made extravagant charges to pressure diocesan authorities into allowing Father Kolasinski to return to Detroit. Perhaps their claims expressed anger and anguish at having to receive the sacraments in parishes that were not their own, and sometimes only at the cost of concealing their identities as Kolasinski loyalists. Perhaps they wished to justify their own irregularity by

[40] *Detroit Evening News*, 10 December 1888, 2:3; *Detroit Evening Journal*, 8 December 1888, 5:1; 10 December 1888, 4:3; 12 December 1888, 1:2; *Detroit Free Press*, 10 December 1888, 4:2; *Detroit Tribune*, 8 June 1888, 5:5–6; 9 June 1888, 5:3; 10 December 1888, 4:4.
[41] *Detroit Sunday News*, 18 November 1888, 2:1; *Detroit Evening News*, 7 December 1888, 4:1; 20 February 1889, 1:4; *Detroit Sunday News*, 28 September 1890, 2:1; *Detroit Evening News*, 16 October 1893, 5:3–7; 30 December 1893, 5:4–5. Kolasinski himself variously claimed to have baptized 680 children within three months of his return, and also "more than a thousand." (Fr. Dominic Kolasinski to Fr. Peter, 30 May 1890, Bishop Foley papers, Correspondence, Rev. Kolasinski, undated, 1889–1892, AAD; Petition, Rev. Dominic Kolasinski to Archbishop Satolli, 19 January 1893, Bishop Foley papers, Correspondence, Rev. Kolasinski, 1893–1894, folder 2, AAD.) And he claimed as well that, on his return, "very many were living in marriages [considered] illicit by the Church" (*ibid.*).

reminding the world yet again that Bishop Borgess had failed them in his pastoral ministry. But whatever their leaders' motives, it is not the case that most members of the dissident congregation were denied the sacraments in Kolasinski's absence. This is especially clear with regard to marriage and baptism.

The surviving marriage register at Sweetest Heart of Mary church dates from February 1890 and provides no information about the number of marriages previously performed in the parish. But county marriage records show that Father Kolasinski married thirty-one couples in early 1889. This is an unusually large number for a period of less than two and a half months, but not large enough to suggest a three-year moratorium on weddings in the congregation. Kolasinski married an additional thirty-one couples during the remainder of 1889 and seventy-two couples in 1890. Perhaps a few couples had indeed waited through the long uncertain months of Kolasinski's absence for their weddings. But more probably the majority of those marrying in early 1889 were taking advantage of the interval between Advent and Lent—seasons when marriages were not normally performed in Polish parishes—and making January and February normally busy for their pastor. (Kolasinski married twenty-one couples in January and February of 1890.) Possibly too some couples postponed November weddings in 1888 in anticipation of Kolasinski's rumored return. And perhaps the euphoria that marked his return even prompted a few hesitant courting pairs to marry.[42]

How, then, did members of the dissident congregation marry in their priest's absence? Did they resort to civil ceremonies? There would naturally be great reluctance among persons who considered themselves Catholics to sanction marriages which the Church did not regard as valid. And in fact county marriage records show that very few, if any, of Kolasinski's supporters were married by civil authorities. There were twenty-three civil marriages in Detroit between persons of German, Prussian, Austrian, Russian, or Polish birth in 1888, compared to fifteen such marriages in 1889 and seventeen in 1890. (These figures do not include couples with identifiably Jewish names.) Possibly the larger 1888 total included couples from Kolasinski's parish. But none of those 1888 couples who might plausibly have been from his congregation, given certain information about occupation and residence, appears subsequently as parents in the parish baptismal register. We must conclude that most if not all marriages that took place among Kolasinski's supporters were performed by priests.[43]

Just which priests were willing to marry persons who were by many considered excommunicate cannot be fully determined. Betrothed couples probably turned to priests at neighboring German parishes. They may sometimes have

[42] Register of Marriages, Wayne County, Michigan, 1888, 1889, 1890.
[43] Ibid.

concealed their ties to the dissident congregation and claimed membership in the priest's parish as fellow German-speakers, for many of the German-born Poles spoke some German, and some were fluent in the language. But probably some local priests, reluctant to drive young Kolasinski supporters further into error, married them knowing full well who they were. Father Charles Reilly, the liberal pastor of the Irish-American Saint Patrick parish, in February 1888 married a couple who appeared in 1890 as parents in the Sweetest Heart of Mary baptismal register. Other priests may have believed with Father Reilly that pastoral concern must sometimes mitigate Church discipline. A church survives and grows because it accommodates, even encourages, this kind of flexibility.[44]

Baptism by a priest was certainly deferred in Kolasinski's absence by a number of parents among his supporters. The parish baptismal register records seventy-eight obviously late baptisms in January and February of 1889; eleven more were recorded by August 31 of that year. Kolasinski was, moreover, a notoriously poor recordkeeper, and there may well have been more baptisms of children well beyond early infancy. But it seems most unlikely that hundreds of unbaptized children awaited Kolasinski's return, and it may be that those who were waiting had already been baptized by laymembers of the parish. Catholic theology clearly taught that unbaptized infants had no hope of heaven. The infant death rate in Detroit's Polish community was tragically high: of 233 deaths recorded in the Sweetest Heart of Mary register between April 3, 1898, and November 6, 1899—the earliest surviving death records—113 were those of children under the age of one year, and a further 34 were those of children aged one to five. If most parents in Kolasinski's absence contrived to have their children baptized by a priest, their concern indicated not a lack of loyalty to him but the seriousness with which they regarded the sacrament.[45]

It is probable that many from the dissident congregation regularly attended Sunday mass at various local churches. In April 1888 one Kolasinski loyalist admitted as much to a reporter. By that time, indeed, members of the congregation had on at least two occasions assembled in force during Saturday masses at highly visible downtown churches. Their presence—inspired perhaps in part by the apparent diffusion of diocesan authority after the resignation of Bishop Borgess in April 1887—asserted their stubborn conviction that nothing had occurred which might legitimately exclude them from the worshipping community.[46]

---

[44] Register of Marriages, Wayne County, Michigan, 1888; Baptismal Register, Sweetest Heart of Mary Church, Detroit.

[45] Baptismal Register, Sweetest Heart of Mary Church, Detroit; Death Register, Sweetest Heart of Mary Church, Detroit.

[46] *Detroit Evening News,* 14 April 1888, 4:3.

Whether Kolasinski's adherents in his absence received communion and were confessed at local churches is less clear. But there were opportunities for many of them to do so. Before the reopening of Saint Albertus church in June 1887 other local churches were apparently expected to serve those parishioners loyal to the bishop. Their priests would hardly know who among the Poles approaching the communion rail was loyal to Kolasinski, and the confessional assured anonymity. Kolasinski's leading defenders also acknowledged that Father Reilly at Saint Patrick church permitted at least some of their number to receive the sacraments there. And in November 1888 a reporter spoke to a young girl who claimed that, while she attended Dlugi's school, her mother still went to mass and confession at Saint Albertus, although the mother was a supporter of Kolasinski. The Saint Albertus congregation was very large, and perhaps its overworked priests did not know by sight all who had ties to the dissident community. The Polish faithful, moreover, although regular church-goers, apparently received communion infrequently, which limited the ability of priests to discipline through exclusion from the sacrament.[47]

The period during which the rebellious congregation was priestless, though not leaderless, illustrates again the subtle combination of democratic values and respect for hierarchy that informed the parishioners' understanding of the Church. On the one hand, they were as capable as the most radical Protestant sect of sustaining themselves as a community of worshippers under lay leadership. But at the same time, they understood the sacraments, administered by an ordained priesthood, as necessary to their salvation, and many of them evidently had at least occasional recourse to local priests in order to receive them. Despite their anomalous situation as a congregation without a priest, Kolasinski's supporters obviously considered themselves Catholics in good standing, able to participate in the sacraments. Indeed, the months of conflict with the bishop may have intensified for these immigrant men and women a sense that their identity as Catholics was centered in the sacraments rather than in a particular set of authority relations.

The congregation lived without a priest of its own until December 1888, when Kolasinski returned permanently to Detroit. (He had, the previous summer, paid a three-day visit to the city.) Kolasinski's December return was prompted both by optimism and by apprehension. The appointment in November 1888 of Bishop John Foley to the long-vacant see at Detroit raised hopes in the dissident community—and the hopes of Father Kolasinski—that he would soon be reinstated as a priest in Detroit. Several delegations from the congregation met with the new bishop to plead his case. But Bishop Foley was unyielding; he was determined to end the dispute, but on terms he himself

---

[47] *Detroit Evening News*, 7 December 1885, 2:1; 29 November 1886, 1:1; 16 October 1893, 5:3–7; 16 December 1893, 8:2–3; *Detroit Evening Journal*, 27 June 1887, 4:3; *Detroit Free Press*, 1 December 1888, 8:3.

found acceptable. His near success in doing so brought Father Kolasinski to Detroit in December.[48]

Bishop Foley evidently hoped to end the dispute by appealing personally, and sympathetically, to individual dissidents. In late November and early December he paid two visits to the east-side Polish community, accompanied by Father Dombrowski as interpreter, and called on a number of Kolasinski's followers. He reaffirmed to them Kolasinski's permanent dismissal from the diocese, urged their return to Saint Albertus, but offered himself to baptize any unbaptized children from the dissident community. Despite his unwitting error in appearing with Father Dombrowski, Kolasinski's supporters greeted the bishop emotionally: they knelt for his blessing, kissed his ring, and many apparently promised obedience. But they did not subsequently bring their unbaptized children to him. One local paper mentioned the bishop's baptizing a two-year-old from the dissident congregation in early December, but there are no records of any such baptisms in the bishop's private sacramental records, at Saint Albertus or at the church attached to the Chancery.[49]

Had Father Kolasinski not sent word at this point of his imminent return, it is possible that his Detroit congregation would have lost critically large numbers. Kolasinski's supporters were clearly moved by the bishop's willingness to come to them as a pastor, and his pastoral concern strengthened, in their eyes, his claims to their obedience. They responded as well to the power of his office. Despite their efforts to limit episcopal control of parish life, the Kolasinski loyalists had never challenged the legitimacy of episcopal authority. But Kolasinski's arrival in Detroit on December 8 revived the issue of congregational rights, and forced the wavering parishioners to choose sides. They did not hesitate. Insisting that they remained loyal to a hierarchical church, they argued again that a bishop who violated their rights as laypersons forfeited his claims to their obedience. Bishop Foley further justified them in this course, they believed, by refusing a personal appeal from Father Kolasinski for his own reinstatement.[50]

[48] *Detroit Evening News*, 7 June 1888, 1:5; 11 June 1888, 4:2; *Detroit Sunday News*, 18 November 1888, 2:1; 25 November 1888, 8:1; *Detroit Evening News*, 30 November 1888, 1:3; 7 December 1888, 4:1; *Detroit Sunday News*, 9 December 1888, 2:1; *Detroit Evening Journal*, 1 December 1888, 5:1; 10 December 1888, 4:3; *Detroit Free Press*, 8 June 1888, 8:5; 11 June 1888, 2:5; 8 December 1888, 8:2; 9 December 1888, 19:5; *Detroit Tribune*, 8 June 1888, 5:5–6; 9 June 1888, 5:3; 10 June 1888, 5:1; 6 December 1888, 5:5; 7 December 1888, 4:5; 9 December 1888, 5:3.

[49] *Detroit Evening News*, 1 December 1888, 1:3; *Detroit Sunday News*, 2 December 1888, 2:7; *Detroit Evening Journal*, 29 November 1888, 1:5; 3 December 1888, 2:4; *Detroit Free Press*, 1 December 1888, 8:3; 2 December 1888, 18:3; *Detroit Tribune*, 8 December 1888, 5:1; Baptismal Register, St. Albertus Church, Detroit, Michigan (entries for November and December, 1888); Baptismal Register, St. Aloysius Church, Detroit, Michigan (entries for November and December, 1888); Bishops' Private Sacramental Records, AAD.

[50] *Detroit Sunday News*, 9 December 1888, 2:1; *Detroit Evening News*, 10 December 1888, 2:3; *Detroit Sunday News*, 16 December 1888, 1:4; *Detroit Evening Journal*, 10 December 1888, 4:3; 17 December 1888, 2:3; *Detroit Free Press*, 9 December 1888, 19:5; 10 December 1888, 4:2; *Detroit Tribune*, 10 December 1888, 4:4; 18 December 1888, 5:4.

Kolasinski appears to have been reluctant, even after this rebuff, to defy the bishop openly; he did not say mass publicly until January 23. But already in mid-December a committee from his congregation was negotiating to buy a large plot of land two blocks west of Saint Albertus. The first installment was paid on December 28, and in late January plans were announced for a school-house and for the eventual construction of an enormous church, the cost of which was placed at $100,000. A parish spokesman explained that the construction would be financed by a $50 gift from each of the congregation's 2,000 families. Doubtless he exaggerated—the congregation was mostly poor and its numbers probably fewer than claimed. He spoke in the hyperbolic mode of nineteenth-century parish rivalry, and expressed as well the emotions that sustained the group in the face of the new bishop's opposition.[51]

A lay committee of eighteen men drew up formal articles of association for the new parish in early February 1889, stipulating a largely lay-controlled mode of parish government. The three years of conflict—and experience as a priestless congregation—bore fruit in this clear statement of congregational prerogatives. Seven male trustees, at least twenty-one years of age, were to manage the "temporal affairs" of the parish. The trustees were to be elected annually by the congregation—presumably its adult male members, although the articles of association mention no age or sex requirements for voter eligi-bility. The pastor was to be an ex-officio member of the board of trustees, party to the deliberations of the board, but without a vote of his own. And the pastor—to whom the "spiritual affairs" of the parish were "left entirely"—was to be chosen by the trustees, who might elect a candidate "for one or more years in their discretion." (Father Kolasinski was apparently elected pastor for the full thirty-year legal life of the corporation, granted the status and security his people believed was his due but within the context of ex-plicitly defined congregational rights.) Few founding documents can have been further from the letter and spirit of the canon law governing American parishes in the nineteenth century, but the signators were secure in their Roman Catholic identity: "every person who believes in the Roman Catholic faith and performs their Easter duties shall be eligible for membership in said corporation."[52]

---

[51] *Detroit Evening News,* 24 January 1889, 1:2; 26 January 1889, 1:5; *Detroit Evening Journal,* 15 December 1888, 5:3; 29 December 1888, 8:2; 23 January 1889, 1:3; 24 January 1889, 1:2; *Detroit Tribune,* 27 January 1889, 5:4. Sweetest Heart of Mary parish claimed 2,000 families in 1898, the first year for which the Diocese of Detroit recorded annual statistics for this parish. There is good evidence that parish membership grew considerably between 1889 and 1898. (Account Book 15: Parish Statistics and Accounts, 1894–1916, p. 11, AAD.) Late in 1893, however, Father Baart of Marshall, Michigan, a sympathetic but relatively dispassionate observer of the Kolasinski affair, argued that "Polish priests who have charge of other parishes, not friendly to him, state he has from 1800 to 3000 families, ie, from 9000 to 15000 souls, who recognize his pastorate over them." (Rev. P. A. Baart to Rev. Charles P. Grannan, 4 November 1893, Bishop Foley papers, Correspondence, Rev. Kolasinski, folder 2, AAD.)

[52] Articles of Association of the Roman Catholic Parish of the Sacred Heart of St. Mary of the

That the congregation so established was large and dedicated is demonstrated by the rapid completion of the parish school, which was blessed in June 1889. Said to have cost some $20,000, the school was a three-story brick building, with classrooms and the priest's quarters on the upper stories and a church that could seat nearly 1,000 on the ground floor. The spirit and size of the parish were evident at the building's dedication: two bands led a procession of 3,000 persons, including members of the Kosciusko Guard and four parish fraternities. Father Kolasinski, assisted by eighteen acolytes, blessed the exterior of the building and the interior of the church. Massive crowds—parishioners and the curious—flooded the church grounds. While high mass was sung, from noon until 2:00 o'clock, "the thousands on the outside were seen to kneel, some in the mud and others on pieces of stone, slate and boards. A lively little shower came down about 12:30 o'clock, but the rain had no terror for those outside as they devoutly knelt with bared heads." An hour after the conclusion of the mass, a large crowd attended vespers.[53]

The fervor of the worshippers, marvelous to middle-class witnesses on this and other occasions, merits a brief discussion here. Particularly for cohesive ethnic groups, worship is an important source of communal emotion and identity, and a key to understanding how individuals view themselves, their place in the worshipping community, and their relationship to the larger society. It is not possible here to consider the ways in which liturgy and communal identity were linked for Polish immigrants. But we can consider how the experience of the liturgy affected immigrant perceptions of Church authority in the American setting.

It is evident that participation in the liturgy was an intensely emotional experience for many of the immigrant faithful at the Sweetest Heart of Mary church, and at other Polish churches in Detroit. In part this was because the traditional liturgy evoked strong memories of Poland. More important, the traditional Polish liturgy invited the congregation to participate fully, drawing individuals into the drama of the service in active affirmation of their culture and their faith. The mass, of course, was said in Latin, and the essentials of the rite were priest-centered. But the congregation sang and chanted responses, and were a responsive audience for the long, emotional sermon. Father Kolasinski could move his hearers to tears and exclamations as effectively as a revivalist preacher, and his gifts were widely admired in the Polish community. Vespers, popular in his and other Polish parishes, were genuinely

City of Detroit of the State of Michigan, 9 February 1889. (Bishop Borgess papers, Box 3, file 4, AAD.) The name of the new parish, for many years mistranslated into English as the Sacred Heart of Mary, is readily identifiable as Roman Catholic. This may well have been a factor in the choice. And the Virgin may have represented for many in the parish the accepting, nurturant aspects of their faith as opposed to the harsh discipline they had come to associate with the local Chancery.

53 *Detroit Evening News,* 9 June 1889, 2:4; 10 June 1889, 4:1; 5 September 1891, 1:1–2; *Detroit Free Press,* 10 June 1889, 4:3; *Detroit Tribune,* 10 June 1889, 4:3.

congregational worship. Parishioners usually sang hymns and psalms in Polish, then knelt for the Benediction of the Blessed Sacrament.[54]

The liturgical year in the Polish Church, moreover, was marked by celebrations that embraced the whole community. Public processions, at Corpus Christi and the Marian devotions in May and often on other occasions as well, were dramatic affirmations of community solidarity and religious faith. A distinctively Polish liturgy at major feasts accomplished the powerful fusion of cultural identity and religious belief. Certain ceremonies, such as the initialing of the doors of the home at Epiphany, the blessing of the candles on the feast of Candlemas, the blessing of the Easter food on Holy Saturday, dignified the family as a worshipping group. The traditional liturgy, in short, engaged the individual as a member of the congregation, of the community, and of the family, and gave him the means to respond actively in each of these roles.[55]

But the vitality of congregational worship among Poles and other Catholic groups was in the United States relatively short-lived. With assimilation, traditional liturgies fell increasingly into disuse among all ethnic groups, and by the time of the Second Vatican Council the nonparticipation of the congregation in the liturgy was considered by many Catholics an aspect of church life in serious need of reform. We know already that assimilation also meant that Catholics were increasingly unlikely to claim patronage rights in the parish. What is the relationship between these two phenomena?

The passing of traditional liturgies did not in itself cause a waning sense of congregational patronage, nor can the reverse be true. But since participation in a traditional liturgy strengthens communal identity, it makes the worshipper in a multiethnic society sharply aware of the cultural divisions which can permeate a church that is uniform in terms of theology and law. The impulse to identify "church" with "congregation" is strengthened, as is the tendency to see church authority beyond the parish as unsympathetic or even hostile. Beyond questions of ethnic identity, and more fundamental, full participation in the liturgy enables individuals to understand the church as a worshipping community to which the people are no less essential than the priest or leader.

Thus, in the right circumstances, as for example where the congregation are the builders of the church and fear that ecclesiastical authority threatens their

[54] Swastek, *Detroit's Oldest Polish Parish*, 114, 154; *Detroit Evening News*, 4 July 1890, 1:1; 29 September 1890, 1:1–2; 23 December 1893, 1:1–2; *Detroit Free Press*, 25 June 1887, 5:2; 10 June 1889, 4:3; 6 June 1892, 5:2–3; 19 February 1894, 1:5–6, 3:4–5; *Detroit Tribune*, 19 February 1894, 1:2–3, 3:6–7; 9 July 1894, 5:6; *Michigan Catholic*, 31 January 1889, 8:4. On preaching in nineteenth-century American Catholicism, see Jay Dolan, *Catholic Revivalism: the American Experience, 1830–1900* (Notre Dame: University of Notre Dame Press, 1978).

[55] Galush, "Forming Polonia," 156; Napolska, "Polish Immigrant in Detroit," 64–66; Swastek, *Detroit's Oldest Polish Parish*, 114; Peter Roberts, *Anthracite Coal Communities* (New York: Macmillan Company, 1904), 215; *Detroit Evening News*, 25 December 1897, 5:3–4; *Detroit Free Press*, 25 June 1887, 5:2.

cultural integrity, the liturgy may provide important support for an emerging ethic of lay participation in church government. And when a people surrenders its traditions of congregational worship, one element of support for lay activism disappears. Significantly, the reforms of the 1960s revived for the American Church not only a more genuinely congregational liturgy but active lay involvement in parish government.

*   *   *

Kolasinski's congregation continued to grow during the early 1890s, although another Polish church was opened in 1890 just five blocks west of the Sweetest Heart of Mary. Most of the new members of Kolasinski's parish were probably immigrants recently arrived in Detroit. Some of them may not have been fully aware of Kolasinski's irregular status: the newcomers had not experienced the initial troubles, the liturgy and social life of the parish were conventional, and Kolasinski himself frequently assured his flock that they were good Roman Catholics. Bitter jealousy, moreover, characterized relations between some Polish priests in the United States, and some new parishioners might have assumed that accusations against Father Kolasinski were merely spiteful propaganda. There would then be no need to think about what defined legitimacy in the Church.[56]

Nonetheless, some members of the congregation were sufficiently anxious about the status of the parish to insist that a bishop bless the cornerstone of the proposed church, and their numbers were sufficiently large that their unease delayed for a time the collection of funds and excavation of the site, the latter task done principally by the men in the congregation. Ground was finally broken in July 1890 but the cornerstone was not blessed until June 1892. The June ceremonies were even more elaborate than those which marked the blessing of the schoolhouse, and the congregation now supported eight societies in addition to the Kosciusko Guard. The bishop imported for the occasion was identified only as a visitor from Russian Poland; he was evidently an irregular Polish priest who had lived for some time in the United States. The ruse was effective, however, in stilling most congregational doubt, and the church was substantially completed by December 1893. It was blessed on December 24, the officiating bishop a Frenchman who claimed to have been consecrated by the Old Catholics in Utrecht and hence in the apostolic succession.[57]

[56] *Detroit Evening News*, 14 September 1891, 1:5; 7 January 1892, 5:4; 23 January 1893, 1:1.

[57] *Detroit Evening News*, 27 May 1890, 2:3; 26 July 1890, 1:5; 26 September 1890, 1:5; *Detroit Sunday News*, 14 December 1890, 1:7–8; *Detroit Evening News*, 16 July 1891, 5:1; 20 July 1891, 5:3; 3 September 1891, 2:1; 5 September 1891, 1:1; *Detroit Sunday News*, 5 June 1892, 1:8; *Detroit Evening News*, 6 June 1892, 4:4–5; 4 July 1892, 1:1–2; 23 December 1893, 1:1–2; 25 December 1893, 1:1–6, 6:3; 26 December 1893, 5:4–5; *Detroit Free Press*, 6 June 1892, 5:2–3; 25 December 1893, 1:6–7; *Detroit Tribune*, 6 June 1892, 5:2–4; 25 December 1893, 1:2–3. (Continued on next page.)

The new church, seating 2,500 and larger than Saint Albertus, was an awesome building, at least in its setting of modest frame cottages and dusty streets. Its two massive bell towers soared 226 feet, dominating the eastside skyline, and the interior was elaborate, with high Gothic arches, a star-studded vault, and carved altars. The transept was lit by enormous stained-glass windows. The church was said to have cost in excess of $120,000, and, while this figure may have been inflated for public consumption, there is no doubt that this church was immensely expensive. The money came almost exclusively from parishioners; sixteen families were said to have mortgaged their homes to make long-term loans to the church fund. The parish was deeply in debt by December 1893, and a gathering depression was already evident in Detroit. But December 24 was a day of triumph and hope. Twelve church societies, two parish military companies, and thousands of gaily dressed spectators provided vivid testimony to the spiritual health of the young parish.[58]

The great and growing number in Kolasinski's congregation, variously estimated at 10,000 to 15,000, provided compelling reason for the Apostolic Delegate in Washington to seek to effect a reconciliation between the priest and his bishop. Kolasinski himself was anxious for reconciliation, although only on certain terms, and his case was strengthened by a recent liberalization of procedures governing the dismissal of priests in the American Church, procedures which, although not in effect in 1885, lent a certain support to Kolasinski's claims that his own dismissal without a hearing had been excessively arbitrary. The Apostolic Delegate, moreover, had arrived in Washington in 1892 expressly to impose discipline and uniform procedures on bishops too often in conflict with one another and their priests. Kolasinski's reinstatement was first discussed not long after the Delegate reinstated Father Edward McGlynn, who had been suspended for his political activities by New York's conservative Archbishop Michael Corrigan. Negotiations in the Kolasinski case lasted for more than a year, and eventually involved the Congregation of the Propaganda at Rome. Bishop Foley was most reluctant to have Kolasinski as a priest in his diocese, while Kolasinski refused to be

---

Descriptions of the event and speculation about the identity of Kolasinski's imported "bishop" can also be found in the reports of a Detroit detective agency, hired by diocesan authorities to infiltrate the crowds around the church and to send confidential reports directly to Bishop Foley. The reports cover the activities around the church during December 23–26, 1893. Only one agency operative spoke Polish, however, and two hapless agents were arrested on December 24 for suspicious loitering. They spent most of the day at the local police station. Given the circumstances, the confidential reports offered the Bishop little he could not have read in the local papers. See Bishop Foley papers, Correspondence, Rev. Kolasinski, 1893–1894, folders 5 and 6, AAD.

[58] *Detroit Evening News*, 26 July 1890, 1:5; 16 October 1893, 5:3–7; 23 December 1893, 1:1–2; *Detroit Sunday News-Tribune*, 24 December 1893, 1:2–3; *Detroit Free Press*, 25 December 1893, 1:6–7; *Detroit Tribune*, 25 December 1893, 1:2–3.

moved from his pastorate. There was also bitter opposition among many Detroit priests to a reconciliation.[59]

Eventually, however, agreement was achieved and on February 18, 1894, an immense crowd filled Sweetest Heart of Mary church to witness Father Kolasinski's reconciliation with his superiors. The priest was allowed to preach before having to read—in English, German, and Polish—a prescribed retraction of his acts and statements in defiance of episcopal authority. Evidently his sermon was masterful; his rich voice filled the church and he moved many in the vast crowd to tears. His theme was the sufferings of his congregation in exile. But when, at the close of the sermon, he began to read his confession, his voice dropped to a whisper. In vain, Monsignor Donato Sbarretti, the representative of the Apostolic Delegate, ordered him to speak more loudly. Few in the congregation heard the retraction, and observers believed that most in the parish thought that Father Kolasinski had never been in error. He was simply being granted, by a benevolent higher authority, the recognition unfairly denied him by the bishop.[60]

The conditions of Kolasinski's readmission to the Church were not ungenerous. Besides the public retraction and a public profession of faith, he had been required to spend a week of penitent meditation in a Chicago monastery. The church itself was blessed by Monsignor Sbarretti, the earlier blessing thus publicly declared invalid. Kolasinski was not made the permanent rector of his church, and he was to dismiss his assistant priests, with future assistants to be appointed by the bishop. But he was to remain the pastor of his congregation, and that congregation was to hold title to its property until it was free of debt. This latter provision, almost certainly stemming from the bishop's fear that the congregation could not meet its debts, was seen as a victory in the parish. The negotiations, from the pa-

---

[59] McAvoy, *History*, 277, 303–4, 309; *Detroit Evening News*, 12 August 1891, 5:5; 5 September 1891, 1:1; 23 January 1893, 1:1; 24 January 1893, 1:1; 26 January 1893, 1:3; 28 January 1893, 5:2; 16 October 1893, 5:3–7; 2 December 1893, 6:3; 16 December 1893, 8:2–3; 22 December 1893 1:1; 23 December 1893, 1:1–2; 30 December 1893, 5:4–5; 5 January 1894, 1:5, 4:6–7; 10 January 1894, 1:1, 6:3–4; 12 January 1894, 1:5; 7 February 1894, 5:3; *Detroit Sunday News-Tribune*, 11 February 1894, 1:8; *Detroit Evening News*, 12 February 1894, 6:4; *Detroit Sunday News-Tribune*, 18 February 1894, 8:3; *Detroit Free Press*, 7 February 1894, 4:5; 12 February 1894, 5:4; *Michigan Catholic*, 15 February 1894, 4:2. Extensive correspondence concerning the negotiations involving Archbishop Satolli, Bishop Foley, and Father Kolasinski can be found in the Bishop Foley papers for the years 1893 and 1894. The Foley papers also include six petitions from priests in the diocese objecting to Kolasinski's reinstatement (Correspondence, Rev. Kolasinski, 1893–1894, folder 1, AAD).

[60] *Detroit Evening News*, 19 February 1894, 5:2–4; *Detroit Free Press*, 19 February 1894, 1:5–6, 3:4–5; *Detroit Tribune*, 19 February 1894, 1:2–3, 3:6–7; *Michigan Catholic*, 22 February 1894, 4:2. See also "Draft of Agreement between Bishop John Foley and Rev. Dominic Kolasinski," Bishop Foley papers, Correspondence, Rev. Kolasinski, 1893–1894, folder 3, AAD; "Form of Retraction to be Read in Public by Rev. Dominic Kolasinski on the Occasion of his Reconciliation with the Church," Bishop Foley papers, Correspondence, Rev. Kolasinski, 1893–1894, folder 3, AAD. Both the agreement and the form of retraction were reported accurately in the newspaper accounts.

rishioners' point of view, had granted them the rights their rebellion had defended. They had chosen their pastor and they alone would make decisions about parish finances.[61]

Those decisions proved over the next few years to be difficult ones. The depression of the mid-1890s seriously affected Detroit's Poles, dependent as they were on unskilled factory work and day labor. It was evident by late 1894 that the parish could not meet all of its considerable debts, and on February 1, 1897, the church property was placed at auction by order of a city court. The property was sold in early March, to the grief and anger of the congregation. Without the protection of ownership, one parishioner told a reporter, the parish would be completely under control of the bishop, "our stepfather." Unlike Kolasinski, "our real father," he explained, the bishop cared not for the needs of the parishioners but only for their money. He gave voice to the anxieties that seem to a latter-day observer so important a source of the "Kolasinski crisis."[62]

In mid-April, however, the congregation, through its board of trustees, secured a loan from a Canadian bank which enabled them to repurchase the church property. But the financial situation remained precarious, and eventually occasioned Father Kolasinski's only serious defeat in parish politics. Although he had to work with his board of trustees, who were elected annually by the congregation, Kolasinski evidently exerted considerable leverage on financial decision making and accounted only vaguely for the many fees he received above his $700 yearly salary. The trustees, however, were determined to enforce strict economies in parish administration despite Kolasinski's extravagant style, and by December 1897 the priest and trustees were in open conflict. Kolasinski publicly urged the congregation to repudiate the board at its next election. But on January 3, 1898, the annual parish meeting not only reelected the trustees, but stripped the priest of all authority in financial matters and regulated the amounts of the fees he was entitled to receive.[63]

Kolasinski died only four months later, on April 11, 1898. The frenzied scenes of grief at the bier and at the funeral, which an estimated 20,000 attended, caused observers to muse on the extraordinary power this charismat-

---

[61] *Detroit Evening News*, 5 September 1891, 1:1; 7 February 1894, 5:3; 11 February 1894, 1:8; 17 February 1894, 1:5; *Detroit Free Press*, 19 February 1894, 1:5-6, 3:4-5; *Detroit Tribune*, 19 February 1894, 1:2-3, 3:6-7.

[62] *Detroit Evening News*, 10 August 1893, 4:5; *Detroit Sunday News-Tribune*, 18 November 1894, 8:2; 2 December 1894, 8:2; *Detroit Evening News*, 1 February 1897, 6:2; 2 February 1897, 6:2; 4 March 1897, 5:2; 5 March 1897, 5:3-5; 17 March 1897, 5:6; *Detroit Free Press*, 2 February 1897, 7:3; 3 February 1897, 5:5; 5 March 1897, 5:4; 6 March 1897, 10:2.

[63] *Detroit Evening News*, 20 April 1897, 1:5; 13 December 1897, 1:1; 4 January 1898, 1:5, 6:5; 5 January 1898, 6:4; 10 January 1898, 6:1; 15 January 1898, 1:6; *Detroit Free Press*, 21 April 1897, 3:5; 5 January 1898, 7:1; *Detroit Tribune*, 4 January 1898, 5:3; 5 January 1898, 8:4; 6 January 1898, 8:4; 7 January 1898, 8:3.

ic priest had exercized over his people. But the largely forgotten parish meeting in January indicates a more complex relationship. Kolasinski was passionately loved and revered by many in his congregation, and nearly all seemed willing to support him handsomely. But despite his honored and privileged status, he was not above congregational control in matters of parish administration. Authority in the Church, his parishioners' behavior said, could legitimately command deference and loyalty beyond that appropriate to secular authority. But it was not beyond a measure of popular control.[64]

* * *

The events discussed in this article were unusual, even in Polish–American parishes at the end of the nineteenth century. They were not, however, so rare that historians can afford to ignore them. They are events which broaden our understanding of the history of the Catholic Church in the United States. The view from the pew is not the view from the pulpit, which in turn differs from the view from the episcopal residence. All three perspectives are necessary for an adequate understanding of Church history. These events should also prompt us to examine the parish in times of conflict as well as times of peace. For it is in times of conflict that individuals are forced to ask themselves difficult questions about what the Church is and what authorities legitimately govern it. And in times of conflict we can see, in peoples' statements and behavior, how they choose to answer these questions.

The particular conflict discussed in these pages cannot be evidence for conclusions about the whole of the American Church in the late nineteenth century. But this single parish narrative does suggest that historians of American Catholicism should in their studies consider the following hypotheses. First, the history of Catholicism in the United States includes a good deal more lay initiative at the parish level than has generally been reported. Many immigrant parishes in particular were in their early years as substantially lay controlled as many Protestant congregations. And second, the defense of lay authority, when it was challenged, included important democratic elements. Many Catholics, it seems, even without the benefit of liberal education, could not accept without significant modification the extreme hierarchicalism of nineteenth- and early-twentieth-century Catholic teaching. Still, as we have seen, popular Catholic understanding of Church authority differed from that held by many Protestants, for most Catholics did not fundamentally challenge the legitimacy of hierarchical authority. They did not both for theological reasons and because the reality of a strong hierarchy was an effective limitation on the scope of debate within the Church.

[64] *Detroit Evening News,* 11 April 1898, 5:1–3; 12 April 1898, 8:1; 13 April 1898, 6:1–2; *Detroit Free Press,* 12 April 1898, 10:6; 14 April 1898, 10:2; *Detroit Tribune,* 12 April 1898, 5:2–3; 13 April 1898, 8:2; 14 April 1898, 5:5–6.

In their years of conflict with their bishops, Kolasinski's parishioners articulated a view of the Church and its authority that, ironically, anticipated
several significant reforms of the Second Vatican Council. Their arguments
were predicated on an understanding of the Church as the community of all
the faithful. They understood their parish to have been born in the years of
Kolasinski's absence, when they constituted a community of faith and worship but were without a priest. The Constitution on the Church of the Second
Vatican Council affirms the understanding of Church as community, though it
does not justify defiance of episcopal authority. Kolasinski's parishioners
argued for a measure of congregational autonomy in order to preserve ethnic
traditions within a universal Church. The Second Vatican Council encouraged
the support of cultural diversity within the Roman Church, gently repudiating
an older policy of absolute conformity to certain European traditions. And
Kolasinski's congregation achieved the vital parish life regarded as essential
to Church renewal by progressives and moderates at Vatican II. A vital parish
life cannot flourish if the laity are not given broad opportunities to participate
in parish government as well as congregational worship, as these same Council delegates recognized.[65]

Like the reformers of Vatican II, however, Kolasinski's parishioners articulated a view of the Church that contained important ambiguities. Both groups
endorsed a greater role for the laity in Church affairs, but both invested a
hierarchy of ordained priests with immense powers over the spiritual and
temporal life of the Church. Clearly, there are many occasions on which lay
initiative and clerical authority will conflict. For Kolasinski's parishioners,
and for Kolasinski himself, a definitive declaration from Rome that they were
schismatics would have created an agonizing crisis, one resolved by some
American Poles by joining the Polish National Catholic Church, which guaranteed considerable autonomy to its congregations. But since trained theologians have not succeeded in articulating a consistent theory that enables the
Church to be both democratic and hierarchical, we can hardly fault the
Kolasinskians for their failure.

The roles which women might legitimately play in parish decision making
were also defined by Kolasinski's parishioners in a manner delicately poised
between democratic norms and patriarchal tradition. Women, the parishioners' behavior says, might defend basic parish rights but they were not
formally to govern the parish. They could make and enforce decisions as
members of demonstrations, but not as parish trustees. The former role, for all
its aggressiveness, was a defensive role as well as an informal one, and in
their unconventional incarnation as street combatants, women were fighting

---

[65] Austin P. Flannery, ed., *Documents of Vatican II* (Grand Rapids, Mich.: William P.
Eerdmans Company, 1975), esp. "The Constitution on the Sacred Liturgy," "Decree on the
Catholic Eastern Churches," "Decree on the Apostolate of Lay People," "Lumen Gentium,"
"Gaudium et Spes."

to maintain the community's traditions. The position of trustee, on the other hand, formally conferred power to control and even change the community; it was an assertive and not simply a reactive role, and thus appropriate only to men. And while the women of the parish were remarkably aggressive in street battles, as women were reported to be in other, similar conflicts, there is no evidence that they regarded their exclusion from parish leadership positions as wrong. Indeed, the day-to-day organizational life of the parish was largely segregated according to sex.

The women of the parish had, in fact, a considerable stake in the maintenance of traditional ways, and this helps to explain their militancy as defenders of Kolasinski's cause. Their lives were much more circumscribed than those of their husbands and sons. Wives in Detroit's Polish community rarely worked outside the home, many could speak no English, and many were illiterate or semiliterate. A high birth rate meant that their lives were centered on the family and on the oppressively crowded house. A high infant death rate infused the weariness of daily life with periodic sorrow.[66] For these women, traditional religious observances gave color and meaning to life, and it was their good fortune to inherit a rich celebratory tradition. Traditional Polish Catholicism, moreover, emphasized the importance of home and family against the attractions of the outside world, and enhanced the status of women as keepers of the home and guardians of traditional culture. When Kolasinski's female supporters took to the streets, they were defending not only a revered priest but a closed and traditional community against the interference of critical outsiders.

It is also clear that women regarded themselves as patrons of the parish, and thus entitled to a voice in its affairs. Women did not work outside the home, but their labor in the home was essential to family survival, and their gardening and fuel gathering were wealth-producing activities. Any contributions to the church were obviously the result of family labor and not simply the work of men. Thus, there was ample reason for women as well as men to say that "we built the church." But their commitment to tradition was sufficiently strong that a sense of patronage did not translate into a demand to share parish government with men.

One wonders, certainly, whether women who had literally fought for their parish were not changed by the experience, whether they did not regard authority in the parish—of male clergy and male trustees—with the critical eyes of idled veterans. And this may be true. But the typical Polish parish was so rich in sex-segregated voluntary groups—Sweetest Heart of Mary had fourteen associations and three military companies by 1898—that the energies of the most ambitious lay men and women could probably find adequate channels. These groups played important roles in the devotional life of the

[66] Zunz, "Detroit's Ethnic Neighborhoods", 54, 57, 63–64, 67–68.

parish and in its day-to-day administration; in the large parish, particularly, and in certain areas of parish life, lay associations might come to rival the authority of the clergy and the trustees. A woman who accepted her formally subordinate role in the parish could if she wished find socially legitimate ways of asserting herself, and in this sense the sexual politics of the parish mirrored the sexual politics of the family. In both institutions, patriarchal values were at once accepted and subtly undermined by very traditional women.

A discussion of nineteenth-century immigrant Catholicism that draws parallels to the Second Vatican Council can appropriately conclude with a word about the recent history of the American Church. That recent history must also be examined from the perspective of the congregation as well as the hierarchy. In some respects, this is comparatively easy to do. A well-educated laity now voice opinions in print on a wide variety of church-related issues. The contemporary clergy is unprecedentedly supportive of discussions of the nature of the Church and ecclesiastical authority.

But in one important respect the historian of the recent Church faces a more difficult task than the historian of immigrant Catholicism: the issues that are today most likely to prompt Catholics to reflection on the nature of Church authority are not the ownership of parish property or the selection of the priest, but issues of sexual morality, specifically birth control, divorce, and abortion. Issues relating to parish rights are public and generally defended collectively. Issues of sexual morality are private and resolved individually. Catholics who practice birth control do not issue public statements in their own defense. And yet, because many who call themselves Catholics do practice birth control, we must assume that their vision of the Church and its authority encompasses this apparent contradiction. I suspect that for these Catholics, as for Kolasinski's parishioners, Catholicism is most importantly both a valued cultural inheritance and a body of sacrament and liturgy that gives meaning to life. It is much less essentially a matter of strict obedience to hierarchical authority.

RUDOLPH J. VECOLI

PRELATES AND PEASANTS

Italian Immigrants and the Catholic Church

Has the immigrant kept the faith? Gerald Shaughnessy gave an affirmative answer to this question in his book published in 1925.[1] Marshalling impressive statistical evidence, the future Bishop of Seattle laid to rest this issue which had been the source of heated controversy for half a century. Had a "leakage" of tens of millions of souls from the vessel of Faith taken place? Or had the Church successfully preserved "its own" from the snares and pitfalls awaiting them in this religious wilderness? The Shaughnessy thesis provided reassuring proof that American Catholicism had indeed met and surmounted the challenge of assimilating the polyglot immigrant masses into "a flourishing, closely knit, firmly welded Church." By doing so it confirmed the benevolent view of immigration as a providential ("almost miraculous") force in the growth of the Catholic Church in America.[2]

Several years earlier, Edmund M. Dunne, Bishop of Peoria, in an essay on "The Church and the Immigrant," had expounded a similar proposition with regard to the assimilative power of the Church. Dunne went on to define the dual mission of American Catholicism. The immigrant must be kept faithful to his religion and he must be made a good American citizen. The Church, according to Dunne, was the essential vehicle for the Americanization of foreigners: "She is the best qualified to weld into one democratic brotherhood, one great American citizenship the children of vari-

---

RUDOLPH J. VECOLI is in the history department of the University of Minnesota. An earlier version of this paper was read at the American Historical Association meetings, San Francisco, December, 1965.

[1] *Has The Immigrant Kept the Faith?* (New York, 1925).

[2] *Ibid.,* 221-222, 268-269. Shaughnessy concluded that no leakage had taken place "beyond that defection of Catholics which ordinarily takes place among any population due to the weakness of human nature and the usual manifestations of the same."

ous climes, temperaments, and conditions."[3] Others developed
the corollary theme that the Catholic Church was "the one great
conservative influence among the immigrant classes of our cities";
her discipline checked the spread of radical tendencies which
threatened the stability of the social order.[4]

Almost a half century after these assertions were formulated,
they remain the accepted, though largely unexamined, generalizations of the historiography of American Catholicism. The Church,
it is said, was highly successful in retaining the loyalty of the
Catholic immigrants.[5] In the process it served as "a 'melting pot'
for the millions of its faithful" and encouraged the newcomers "to
love and to understand American political and civic ideals."[6]
Catholic historians are fond of quoting Henry Steele Commager's
statement which has reference to the years after 1880: "It might,
indeed, be maintained that the Catholic Church was, during this
period, one of the most effective of all agencies for democracy
and Americanization."[7] The conservative role of the Church in its
relation to the immigrant proletariat has been reaffirmed recently
with the claim that its teachings "closed [the immigrants'] ears
to siren-songs of radicalism or revolt."[8]

---

[3] "The Church and the Immigrant," in C. E. McQuire, ed., *Catholic Builders of
the Nation* (5 vols., Boston, 1923), II, 1-15. Dunne had previously expressed
his concept of the Americanizing role of the Church in his work, *Memoirs of
"Zi Pre"* (St. Louis, Mo., 1914), 20.

[4] *The New World*, Feb. 29, 1908. This was the official organ of the Archdiocese of Chicago. This view of the Church as an instrument of social control
was also expressed in the *Official Guide and Program* of the First American
Catholic Missionary Congress held in Chicago, November 15-18, 1908: "Through
the growth of Socialism and demonstrations of anarchy, the inability of the
State to assimilate properly to American standards the hundreds of thousands
of foreigners flocking to our shores has been shown. This function . . . must be
performed by a persistent agency, which teaches respect for human regulation
as an expression of Divine Will." (164).

[5] John Tracy Ellis, *American Catholicism* (New York, 1965), 122; Henry J.
Browne, "Catholicism in the United States," in James Ward Smith and A. Leland
Jamison, eds., *The Shaping of America: Religion* (4 vols., Princeton, 1961), I,
93; Colman J. Barry, *The Catholic Church and German Americans* (Milwaukee,
1953), 262-263. Although regarding Shaughnessy's work as "the best authority
on the subject," Monsignor Ellis takes the prudent position that "in the final
analysis . . . the exact extent of the leakage among American Catholics is known
only to the recording angel. . . ."

[6] Barry, *Catholic Church and German Americans*, viii, 276-277.

[7] Ellis, *American Catholicism*, 102; Vincent De Santis, "The American Historian Looks at the Catholic Immigrant," in Thomas T. McAvoy, ed., *Roman
Catholicism and the American Way of Life* (Notre Dame, 1960), 234. The quote
is from *The American Mind* (New Haven, 1950), 193.

[8] Browne, "Catholicism in the United States," 103.

These generalizations, however, must be regarded at best as tentative hypotheses, since we lack studies of the interaction between the American Church and many of the Catholic ethnic groups. That this should be especially true for the Eastern and Southern Europeans is a cause for puzzlement, for, as John Tracy Ellis has pointed out, "for no national institution was the so-called 'New Immigration' . . . more a living reality."[9] It is a curious fact that the historians of the "Church of the Immigrants" have neglected the study of many of the peoples who today constitute major elements in the American Catholic population. One may speculate that this was a consequence of the apologetic perspective which long dominated American Catholic historiography. The American character of the Church, not its foreign origins, provided the central theme of Catholic historical writings.[10]

Yet the impact of the immigrants upon the Church, as well as the influence of the Church upon the immigrants, has clearly been a central feature of American Catholic history. The clash and accommodation of variant Catholic traditions, the conflicts between American and foreign clergy, the controversy over the Americanizing role of the Church, the institutional responses of the Church to the needs of the poor and exploited, and the struggles between Catholics and Protestants for the fealty of the children of the immigrants—such phenomena expressed the ethnic diversity which has been fundamental to the shaping of American Catholicism. Although historians have certainly not entirely neglected these topics, the literature of American Catholic history has been largely and strangely silent with respect to major ethnic groups. There are not as yet satisfactory treatments of the relations between the Church and Bohemians, Croats, Italians, Lithuanians, Magyars, Poles, Ruthenians, Slovaks, or Slovenes.[11] This article is in the nature of

---

[9] Ellis, *American Catholicism*, 101. Monsignor Ellis and other Catholic historians have recognized and lamented this deficiency. *Ibid.*, 181; see also McAvoy, *Roman Catholicism*, 139, 225.

[10] John Paul Cadden, *The Historiography of the American Catholic Church: 1785-1943* (Washington, D.C., 1944), *passim*.

[11] A notable exception is the excellent *History of the Archdiocese of Boston* (3 vols., New York, 1944) by R.H. Lord, *et al.*, which has a section on the "Newer Catholic Races" in Volume III. Certain of these groups are briefly discussed by John L. Thomas, "Nationalities and American Catholicism," in *The Catholic Church, U.S.A.*, edited by Louis J. Putz (Chicago, 1956), 155-176; McAvoy, *Roman Catholicism*, Part II: "Immigration and American Catholicism," 131-234. Joseph Cada, *Czech-American Catholics, 1850-1920* (Chicago, 1964)

an initial reconnaissance into the history of the Italian immigration
in its relations to the American Catholic Church.[12]

Over the course of a century (1820-1920), the Catholic immigration from Italy was second only to that from Ireland.[13] Coming
from the seat of the Church, one might have expected that the
countrymen of the Pope would have been received with open arms
as a precious increment to the ranks of American Catholics. From
the point of view of the Church in the United States, however, the
Italian influx soon took on a threatening and even sinister aspect.
What became known as the "Italian Problem" developed into a
major source of concern and controversy which involved prelates
and clergy in Italy and the United States, including the Supreme
Pontiff himself.[14] Millions of Italian immigrants and their children,
it was thought, were succumbing to religious indifference and even
apostasy, deserting to the camp of the enemies of the true faith.
What were the causes of this massive "leakage"? Where did the
responsibility for it lie? What measures would be most effective in
repairing this spiritual loss? These questions were long and hotly
debated, sometimes in a spirit of rancor, in ecclesiastical councils,
in public forums, and in print by American and Italian churchmen.
   The American Catholic Church had a pronounced Hibernian
cast during the period of Italian immigration. Despite the presence
of a large German minority, the Irish predominated in the hierarchy,
clergy, and laity, particularly in those areas of the country where

is a useful but brief history, while Victor R. Greene, "For God and Country:
the Origins of Slavic Catholic Self-Consciousness in America," *Church History*,
XXXV (Dec., 1966), 1-15, is a suggestive probe of the subject.
   [12] This study is based on the published record and the few manuscript sources
accessible to me. The complete story of the religious aspect of the Italian immigration will not be known until the archives of archdioceses, dioceses, and
religious orders in the United States and Italy are opened to the scholar.
   [13] The net Catholic immigration from Italy was 1,640,533, while that from
Ireland was 2,383,791. Barry, *Catholic Church and German Americans*, 6. This
statistic is based on the assumption that Italy was almost entirely Catholic (97
percent Catholic is the proportion Shaughnessy accepts; *Has the Immigrant Kept
the Faith?*, 112); this is itself a questionable assumption.
   [14] A thorough discussion of the initial phase of the "Italian Problem," primarily
from the point-of-view of the American hierarchy, is Henry J. Browne, "The
'Italian Problem' in the Catholic Church of the United States, 1880-1900," *United
States Catholic Historical Society, Historical Records and Studies*, XXXV (New
York, 1946), 46-72. Two contemporary studies still useful are Aurelio Palmieri,
Il grave problema religioso italiano negli Stati Uniti (Firenze, 1921) and
Christopher Perrotta, "Catholic Care of the Italian Immigrant in the United
States" (unpublished master's thesis, Catholic University of America, 1925).

the Italians settled most densely. The fact that the Irish Catholics nourished an intense prejudice toward the King of Italy and his subjects was to have a pronounced influence upon the religious adjustment of the Italians. The source of this animosity was the encroachment upon the temporal authority and domain of the Papacy resulting from the unification of Italy. During the *risorgimento*, the American Irish led by Archbishop John Hughes of New York raised Zouaves, funds, and prayers for the defense of the Holy See. From the pulpit, anathemas were hurled at Garibaldi, Victor Emmanuel, and their followers as despoilers of the patrimony of the Church.[15]

Among the few thousand Italians in mid-nineteenth century America were many political exiles, who had participated in the ill-fated revolutionary uprisings of the 1830's and 1840's.[16] Through organizations, publications, and public meetings, these Italian patriots agitated vociferously in behalf of the unification of Italy. Their strongest invective was reserved for the Papal power which they regarded as the chief obstacle to the realization of their aspirations. Pius IX himself was attacked in *L'Unione Italiana* of Chicago:

The Grand Tyrant, the butcher of liberty, the Father of the Faithful, the Heir of St. Peter, who invokes the aid of bayonets in apparent defense of a religion by no one threatened, and who has his foundation not in the blood of martyrs, but in the greed for temporal dominion and hatred against the unity and liberty of Italy.[17]

The anti-Papal propaganda reached a fever pitch with the arrival of Father Alessandro Gavazzi, the "priest-hero" of the revolution of 1848, whose lectures touched off anti-Catholic riots. Gavazzi and the Italian nationalists launched bitter attacks upon Monsignor Gaetano Bedini during his visit to the United States in 1854. They denounced the papal nuncio as the "Bloody Butcher of Bologna" who had committed atrocities against the revolutionaries. The announced intention of Italians and others to burn Bedini in effigy in front of the residence of Archbishop Hughes brought out hundreds of armed Irishmen to defend their prelate. The turmoil which ac-

---

15 Howard R. Marraro, *American Opinion on the Unification of Italy, 1846-1861* (New York, 1932), 241-304.

16 *Ibid.*, 165-185; see also the articles by Marraro, "Italians in New York during the First Half of the Nineteenth Century," *New York History*, XXVI (July, 1945), 278-306, and "Italians in New York in the Eighteen Fifties," *id.*, XXX (April, July, 1949), 181-203; 276-303.

17 *L'Unione Italiana* (Chicago), Feb. 26, 1868.

companied Bedini's visit led the editor of the *Irish American* to comment that the mission of the Italian in America was aimed at exciting Protestant animosity against the Irish Catholics.[18] For their part, the Italians were convinced that the Irish who succored the Pope with money and men were religious fanatics and sworn enemies of *la patria*.[19]

The occupation of Rome by Italian troops on September 20, 1870, joyfully celebrated by the Italians in America, was to the American Catholics the act of supreme sacrilege.[20] Pius IX and his successors refused to recognize the new Kingdom of Italy, forbade Catholic participation in political life, and styled themselves "prisoners of the Vatican." This conflict between Church and State in Italy had severe repercussions for the Italian immigrants. For the American Irish, the "Roman Question" was a perennial source of hostility toward Italy and Italians. From the pulpit, they were taught that Victor Emmanuel and Garibaldi were brigands who had stolen the Papal domain. Many believed that the Pope was literally a prisoner in chains, sleeping on straw and living on crusts of bread. When the Italians appeared on the scene, it was to be expected that the Irish would greet the jailers of the Holy Father with brickbats rather than bouquets.[21] Nor was the demeanor of the newcomers such as to persuade the Irish that they were devout sons of the Mother Church.

Unlike the Irish or Poles whose Catholicism was an integral part of their national identity, it was difficult to be both an Italian patriot and a faithful Catholic. An aggressive anticlericalism became a powerful force in late nineteenth-century Italy as nationalist, liberal, and socialist views prevailed. Such was particularly true of

---

18 Marraro, *American Opinion*, 138-145, 170; Ray Allen Billington, *The Protestant Crusade 1800-1860* (Chicago, 1964), 300-304. Among Gavazzi's lectures were "The Papal System and its Intolerance" and "Romanism and Paganism are the Same." *The Lectures Complete of Father Gavazzi* (New York, 1854).

19 *L'Unione Italiana*, Dec. 4, 11, 25, 1867; Feb. 26, March 25, April 29, May 6, 1868.

20 *Chicago Times*, Oct. 3, 5, 1870; *The New World*, Oct. 7, 1893; Sept. 14, 1895; Feb. 25, March 4, 1911.

21 Giovanni Schiavo, *Italian American History*, Vol. II: *The Italian Contribution to the Catholic Church in America* (2 vols., New York, 1949), 531-533; Luigi Carnovale, *Il Giornalismo degli emigrati italiani nel Nord America* (Chicago, 1909), 136-139; *La Parola dei Socialisti* (Chicago), March 5, 1908. Although the German Catholics were strong defenders of the temporal power, there is no evidence that this resulted in hostility against the Italian immigrants. Without exception the Italians held the Irish responsible for their grievances.

the educated classes, among whom, as Luigi Villari observed, "The rarest thing in the world is to meet a Clerical."[22] Taking part in the mass migration of these years was an intellectual proletariat of doctors, teachers, journalists, and scholars. Although a small minority, they occupied a strategic position in the political and cultural life of the Italian colonies. While many regarded themselves as Catholics, they agreed almost to a man that the Papacy was the enemy of liberty and progress. Through their publications and free-thought societies, they carried on an anti-clerical propaganda among their countrymen in America.[23] Although a few Catholic newspapers were published, the colonial press by and large championed the cause of united Italy and heaped abuse on the Pope and his minions. These polemics sometimes took extreme rhetorical forms, as when *L'Italia* of Chicago exclaimed: "When Leo XIII kneels before Christ, He should let him have a blow which would knock him head over heels into hell!!!"[24] The Italian radicals were the most extreme *mangiapreti* (literally "priest-eaters"); through journals such as *Il Proletario* and *La Parola dei Socialisti*, they waged an unrelenting warfare against the Church and all its works.[25] In addition, anti-clerical publications from Italy were available in the Italian colonies. Of *L'Asino*, of Rome, the Rev. Pietro Pisani declared:

We cannot estimate how much evil that infamous sheet has done and still does among the mass, in great part illiterate, of our emigrants to

---

[22] Luigi Villari, *Italian Life in Town and Country* (New York, 1902), 147, 152; Denis Mack Smith, *Italy* (Ann Arbor, Michigan, 1959), 89-98, 139, 222; F.C. Capozzi, *Protestantism and the Latin Soul* (Philadelphia, 1918), 37, 145-147. Capozzi was rector of St. Mary's Episcopal Church in Wind Gap, Pennsylvania.
[23] *Chicago Record-Herald*, March 1, 1908; Carnovale, *Giornalismo*, 108-112, 136-139; "Lettere da Chicago di un Missionario Bonomelliano (1912-1913)," *Studi Emigrazione* (Rome), 1 (Oct., 1964), 70. Riccardo Cordiferro, a well known journalist and poet, presented a lecture on "The Priest Through History" before Italian audiences in many American cities. It began: "I hate proud and vainglorious men, liars, hypocrites, impostors; and every species of villain found in large numbers all over the world; but the men that I hate the most, and those whom I abhor and despise above the rest—are the priests. This fierce hatred of mine has no end, this contempt which I bear for the most dishonorable and immoral men that have ever disgraced humanity, has been firmly implanted in my nature." "The Priest Through History," typescript; Riccardo Cordiferro Papers (Immigrant Archives, University of Minnesota Library).
[24] *L'Italia* (Chicago), June 18, 1887; see also Feb. 26, 1887, Sept. 22, 1888.
[25] Mario De Ciampis, "Storia del Movimento Socialista Rivoluzionario Italiano," *La Parola del Popolo, Cinquantesimo Anniversario, 1908-1958*, 9 (Dec., 1958-Jan., 1959), 136-163. See also any issue of *Il Proletario* or *La Parola dei Socialisti*.

which it speaks the language of hatred and vice with vignettes and caricatures which are themselves the triumph of audacity and depravity.[26]

An American priest indignantly reported: "Italian news-shops of Chicago are ablaze with vile anti-clerical literature, and display in the street windows gross caricatures of the Pope and Bishops of the Church."[27]

The Italian nationalists boldly celebrated the anniversary of the seizure of Rome with parades and dinners. They raised statues in the public parks to Garibaldi and commemorated the martyrdom of Giordano Bruno, the symbol of clerical intolerance.[28] These provocative observances did not go unnoticed by the ecclesiastical authorities. Bishops and priests fulminated against the "robbery of the pontifical states," prohibited Italians from taking part in nationalist manifestations, denounced Bruno as a renegade monk, condemned Garibaldi and Mazzini as enemies of the Church, and even prohibited the carrying of the Italian flag into Catholic churches. The anticlericalism of the Italians scandalized the American Irish, who were distinguished by reverence and respect for their priests. By contrast, the Italian gained the reputation of excelling all others for "irreverence, hostility and blasphemy."[29]

It was in Chicago that the confrontation between the Italian anti-clericals and the American hierarchy came to a head. For several years, Alessandro Mastrovalerio, anti-clerical journalist, and the Reverend Edmund Dunne, then pastor of the Italian Church of the Guardian Angel, had been exchanging compliments in the pages of La Tribuna Italiana and the Catholic New World. A proposal to name a public school after Garibaldi raised the controversy to a new level of intensity. Despite petitions by Italian organizations, the Board of Education under pressure from the Church rejected the suggestion. Dunne declared that the naming of a school after "an

[26] Pietro Pisani, L' Emigrazione Avvertimenti e Consigli agli emigranti (Firenze, 1907), 23. See also The New World, August 22, 1903, June 11, 1904, Nov. 30, 1907.

[27] W. H. Agnew, "Pastoral Care of Italian Children in America," The Ecclesiastical Review, 48 (March, 1913), 260.

[28] L'Italia, Sept. 15, 1888; Sept. 20, 1890; Sept. 28-29, 1895; Carnovale, Giornalismo, 160-185; Il XX settembre Discorso Commemorativo detto dal Cav. Dott. A. LAGORIO sotto gli auspici del'Circolo Dante Alighieri (Chicago, 1904).

[29] The New World, Sept. 14, 1895; August 22, 1903; April 25, 1908; Feb. 25, March 4, 1911; March 6, 1914; La Tribuna Italiana (Chicago), Sept. 10, 1904; Chicago Record-Herald, March 1, 1908; Carnovale, Giornalismo, 110-112.

ignorant bushwhacker notorious for desecrating and looting churches and monasteries" would have been an insult to the Catholics of Chicago. He would just as soon have had the school named after Beelzebub, Bob Ingersol or Judas Iscariot.[30] Such denigration of Garibaldi infuriated the patriotic Italians. Mastrovalerio attributed the Board's action to the "ignorant, intolerant fanaticism of the Irish." Noting that three Chicago schools had been named after Irish saloon keepers, *L'Italia* commented bitterly: "If the Italians wished to name the school in Polk Street after some fishvendor from Naples or Sicilian ragpicker, oh, that would be different, but the name of Garibaldi is a truly risky thing."[31]

This affront to their national pride rankled in the breast of the Italian intelligensia who responded by forming the "Circolo Giordano Bruno." The "Circolo," which was composed of professional and businessmen, had as its objective the liberation of the Italian workers from "superstition and ignorance," i.e., from clerical domination. Its primary targets, however, were the Irish priests and principally Dunne, who had been elevated to Chancellor of the Archdiocese of Chicago.[32]

Then on February 23, 1908 an Italian immigrant shot and killed a priest while he was serving holy communion in Denver, Colorado. The nation was horror-stricken by the act and responded with a hue and cry against Italian anarchists. In Chicago, Dunne charged that the assassin had been inspired to commit the deed by the "Circolo Giordano Bruno." He added: "There is no denying lives of Chicago priests are endangered by recent anti-clerical agitation." A thrill of terror swept the city as priests said mass under police protection, especially in the Italian churches.[33] Seeing an opportunity to scotch the anti-clerical movement which had been a thorn in its side, the Church unleashed a witch-hunt against the "Circolo." The organ of the Archdiocese, *The New World*, granting that the Italians were "in the mass a law-abiding and deeply religious people," declared that "amongst them are to be found coteries of evil minded and foul hearted men who are banded together for the

---

30 Dunne, *Memoirs*, 51; *The New World*, April 30, June 11, 25, 1904.
31 *La Tribuna Italiana*, June 11, 18, 25, 1904; *L'Italia*, June 11, July 2, 1904.
32 *Chicago Record-Herald*, Feb. 28, March 1, 1908. The membership list of the "Circolo" was published in the Feb. 29, 1908 issue of *The New World*.
33 *The New World*, Feb. 29, 1908; *Chicago Record-Herald*, Feb. 24–March 2, 1908. In all the Catholic Churches of Chicago, the sermons on March 1 were devoted to attacks on anarchism and anticlericalism.

purpose of disseminating principles that make for social and religious unrest . . . and that not seldom goad unfortunates like Alio
to terrible crimes." The "Circolo" was "a menace to public welfare
. . . an evil thing that city police would do well to kill." *The New
World* warned that American Catholics were not possessed of the
lamb-like meekness of Catholic Italy:

The men who rose at the call of the saintly Archbishop Hughes to
defend the Church of New York against the intrigues of know-nothingism
are as able and as willing in Chicago today—were the call made upon
them—to drive this imported Italian radical anti-clericalism like a rat
back to its lair.[34]

Since the "Circolo" had been meeting at Hull House, *The New
World* extended its attack to "Mother Jane Addams, the professional
humanitarian and patron saint of anti-Catholic bigotry in this city."
Miss Addams sought to refute the charge that the "Circolo" harbored anarchists, pointing out that anti-clericalism was quite a different thing from anarchism. This distinction, however, escaped
the *Chicago Inter-Ocean* which found between the anti-church
anarchists and the anti-state anarchists as much difference as between rattlesnakes and copperheads.[35]

Despite the storm of abuse which broke about their heads, the
Giordano Bruno members were not intimidated. At a public meeting, they denied that they espoused violence and charged Dunne
with defaming the Italians because of hatred for "our race." *La
Parola dei Socialisti* charged that Dunne was seeking to silence
the "Circolo" because it was teaching the people:

No money to the priests, no public parades, no fasts to merit the prize
from God. . . . Because he has no arguments to refute ours, because we

[34] *The New World*, Feb. 29, 1908. As a matter of record, repressive measures
by immigration agents, post office officials, and the Chicago police did follow
the assassination.
[35] A lengthy interview with Jane Addams concerning the nature of Italian
anticlericalism was published in *Chicago Record-Herald*, March 1, 1908. See also
her *Twenty Years at Hull-House* (New York, 1961), 292. This was one of a
number of savage attacks on Jane Addams in the archdiocesan organ; see *The
New World* Feb. 29, March 7, April 25, 1908; Feb. 22, 1913; Feb. 27, March 6,
1914. *The New World* denounced social settlements generally as "mere roosting-
places for frowsy anarchists, fierce-eyed socialists, professed anti-clericals and
a coterie of long-haired sociologists intent upon probing the moonshine with pale
fingers." Editorial: "As to Social Settlements," April 25, 1908.

are opening the eyes of the people, he uses the occasion to call upon the gallows. The vile liar affirms that the Circolo Giordano Bruno of Chicago, with its anti-religious propaganda armed the unfortunate of Denver, and calls upon the police to defend the paunchy reverends.[36]

In a spirit of defiance, the "Circolo" presented a drama depicting the life of Giordano Bruno. *The New World* commented: "Isn't this a nice way to instruct Italian immigrants and their children? Isn't it an excellent way in which to grow up a fine crop of priest-hating anarchists? Is it any wonder that some Italians are losing their faith, in this country?" Despite the declaration that "anti-clericalism has no place in America," the campaign of the Italian freethinkers and socialists against the Church continued unabated.[37] Although they did not always take such dramatic form, conflicts between American Catholicism and Italian anticlericalism were common occurrences. The widespread antipathy the Italian immigrants encountered, particularly among the Irish, stemmed in good measure from this clash of religious cultures. The Chicago delegation to the First Congress of Italians Abroad understood this well:

We Italians are not religious enthusiasts; we are sincere, strong anti-clericals opposed to the temporal power of the Church. For this reason we are not well regarded in this country in which the power of the Church is reaching dangerous proportions, especially by the Irish element which is in the great majority in the United States and which has made itself the defender of the Papacy and the Church.[38]

Anticlericalism may have been the most notorious aspect of the "Italian Problem," but it was not its most significant dimension. The great majority of the immigrants from Italy were not free thinkers or socialists; rather they were *contadini* (peasants) from the *Mezzogiorno*.[39] Modern notions of nationalism and radicalism

---

[36] *Chicago Record-Herald*, March 2, 1908; *La Parola dei Socialisti*, Feb. 25, March 5, 1908. The socialist journal declared that Dunne was "an Irishman, who belongs to that race of most intolerant Catholic fanatics whose priests teach them that we Italians keep the pope prisoner and make him sleep on a lurid straw cot. . . . From this stems, the inveterate hatred nourished by the priests of the Irish towards the Italians."

[37] *La Parola dei Socialisti*, March, 5, 1908; May 10, 1913; *The New World*, April 25, 1908; Feb. 27, March 6, 1914.

[38] Comitato Locale di Chicago, *Primo Congresso degli Italiani all' estero sotto l'atto patronato di S.M. Vittorio Emanuele III* (Chicago, 1908).

[39] These generalizations are ventured with regard to the religious culture of the peasants of Southern Italy with the necessary qualification that there were

had not penetrated the isolated villages of southern Italy. In their religion as in all else, the peasants were intensely parochial and traditional. While nominally Roman Catholics, theirs was a folk religion, a fusion of Christian and pre-Christian elements, of animism, polytheism, and sorcery with the sacraments of the Church. "Even the ceremonies of the Church," Carlo Levi observed, "become pagan rites, celebrating the existence of inanimate things, which the peasants endow with a soul, and the innumerable earthly divinities of the Village."[40] Dominated by a sense of awe, fear, and reverence for the supernatural, the peasants were profoundly religious. However, their beliefs and practices did not conform to the doctrines and liturgy of the Church.

The religion of the *contadini* was enclosed within the spirit of *campanilismo*.[41] Each village had its own array of madonnas, saints, and assorted spirits to be venerated, propitiated, or exorcised. There was no turn of fortune, for good or for ill, that was not due to the benevolence or malevolence of these supernatural beings. God, like the King, was a distant, unapproachable figure, but the local saints and madonnas, like the landlords, were real personages whose favor was of vital importance. With a mixture of piety and shrewdness, the supplicants bargained with their patrons, offering gifts, sacrifices, and praise, if their petitions were granted.[42] The feast day of the patron saint or madonna was the highpoint in the

---

significant differences not only among the various regions, but as between provinces and even villages. The ensuing discussion is based upon both sources contemporary with the period of emigration and more recent anthropological and literary studies. Cultural change has come slowly to the *Mezzogiorno* as a recent article suggests: Ann Cornelisen, "Prophecies, Witches, and Spells," *The Atlantic Monthly*, CCXXII (August, 1968), 56-66. Among the works found useful were the following: Edward C. Banfield, *The Moral Basis of a Backward Society* (Glencoe, Ill., 1958); Richard Bagot, *The Italians of Today* (Chicago, 1913); Leonard W. Moss and Stephen C. Cappannari, "Folklore and Medicine in an Italian Village," *Journal of American Folklore*, LXXIII (April, 1960), 85-102; Pascal D'Angelo, *Son of Italy* (New York, 1924); Pietro di Donato, *Three Circles of Light* (New York, 1960); Carlo Levi, *Christ Stopped at Eboli* (New York, 1947); Jerre Mangione, *Mount Allegro* (New York, 1963); Villari, *Italian Life*; Phyllis H. Williams, *South Italian Folkways in Europe and America* (New Haven, 1938).

[40] Levi, *Christ Stopped* (New York, 1947), 117; cf., Cornelisen, "Prophecies," 64.

[41] *Campanilismo* was a figure of speech suggesting that the world of the peasantry was confined within earshot of the village belfrey.

[42] If the saint, however, failed to produce the desired result, his statue stood in danger of being cast out of church. Moss, "Folklore," 100; Williams, *South Italian Folkways*, 137; Mangione, *Mount Allegro*, 72.

life of the village. With panegyrics, processions, brass bands, and fireworks, these communal celebrations exalted the miraculous powers of the patron and invoked his protection upon the village. Since to *fa bella figura* was assumed to be a common aspiration of spiritual as well as human beings, the statue of the saint clothed in fine robes and adorned with jewels was paraded through the streets followed by the throng of admirers.[43]

Among the spirits of the villages were some not to be found in the calendar of the Church. The *contadini* lived in dire fear of the evil eye (*malocchio* or *jettatura*). Spells cast by witches could destroy crops, bring sickness and death, or arouse forbidden passions. To combat these malevolent forces, the peasants had recourse to sorcerers (*mago* or *strega*) to break spells, exorcise spirits, and divine the future. These black arts were an essential element in the folk religion of Southern Italy. Particularly for the peasantry, amulets, potions, and magical rites were at least as important as the sacraments of the Church in coping with the terrors of the supernatural.[44]

For the Church as an institution the South Italian peasants had little sense of reverence. Historically it had been allied with the landowning aristrocracy and had shown little sympathy for the misery of the *contadini*. Although surrounded by a multitude of clergy, the people by and large were not instructed in the fundamental doctrines of the Catholic faith. Toward their village priests, whom they regarded as parasites living off their labors, the peasants often displayed attitudes of familiar contempt. Clerical immorality and greed figured largely in the folk humor of Italy. The parish priest appeared to be regarded as a functionary who performed the necessary rites of baptisms, marriages, and funerals. Other than on these occasions and feast days, the *contadini*, especially the men, seldom set foot in church. The fact that the priests rarely accompanied their parishioners to America reflected the lack of reciprocal affection between the clergy and people.[45]

---

43 Cornelisen, "Prophecies," 65-66; Levi, *Christ Stopped*, 117-118; Williams, *South Italian Folkways*, 138-140.

44 D'Angelo, *Son of Italy*, 24-43; Levi, *Christ Stopped, passim;* Moss, "Folklore," 95-102; Williams, *South Italian Folkways*, 135-159.

45 Bagot, *Italians*, 42-44, 102-107; Banfield, *Moral Basis*, 17-18, 129-132; Levi, *Christ Stopped*, 39-41, 89-94, 110-117; Villari, *Italian Life*, 156-158. Regarding the anticlericalism of the *contadini* see the novel about Sicilians in the West End of Boston by Joseph Caruso, *The Priest* (New York, 1956). "In Sicily, on Sundays

The Italian peasants, to be sure, thought of themselves as *cristiani*; not to be a Christian was to be a Turk, a racial memory of the Saracens. Their brand of Christianity, however, had little in common with American Catholicism. An observer noted in 1888: "The fact is that the Catholic Church in America is to the mass of the Italians almost like a new religion."[46] Those Italians who ventured into Irish or German churches found them as alien as Protestant chapels. The coldly rational atmosphere, the discipline, the attentive congregation, were foreign to the Italians who were used to behaving in church as they would in their own house. Nor did the poorly dressed, sometimes unwashed, Italians find a ready welcome in the churches of other nationalities. Often they were turned away or seated in the rear with Negroes. Sometimes they heard themselves denounced as "Dagos" from the pulpit and told that they were not wanted.[47]

The temporary and unsettled character of much of the Italian immigration was itself not conducive to religious regularity. A stock answer of the immigrants was: "We did not come to America

and holy days, while the men played cards in the village squares in open contempt of the archpriests behind the church doors, the women would file into church and attend Mass. But they would walk out without giving any money to the Church. God doesn't want money, they would say; He wants love, and that is all we can give Him, Love. The men would say: 'God is a tool of the landlords. The landlords and the Italian investors pay Him; He is on their side.' Secretly, though, they were religious. The Lord had suffered for them at the hands of the wealthy landlords, too; He had made the world, had put fish in the sea; His Bleeding Heart was a sign of His love of the poor. The men did not attend the churches, but on feast days they paraded. And they attended funerals, had their children baptized, confirmed, and married by the Church. Priests are no good, they said; it is a shame that the only place you can reach God is in their Church." *The Priest,* 21.

[46] Bernard J. Lynch, "The Italians in New York," *The Catholic World,* XLVII (April, 1888), 72; Walter Persegati, "I Missionari Scalabriniani negli Stati Uniti d'America," *Cinquantesimo: Numero Speciale de "L'Emigratio Italiano,"* XLIX (May-June, 1953), 46; Padre V.D., *L'Apostolo degli emigrati nelle Americhe ossia Mons. Scalabrini e L'Istituto de'suoi missionari* (Piacenza, 1909), 12.

[47] One of the first Italian missionaries, Father Antonio Demo, attributed the estrangement of many of the immigrants from the Church to such experiences: "Only too often the poor Italian was driven away even from the door of the church. People despised him for two reasons: he had no money to dispose of, and they looked on him as excommunicated because he kept the Pope a prisoner." *America,* XII (Nov. 28, 1914), 169. Another Italian priest recalled the vulgar epithets which were launched against his countrymen from the pulpits of certain Irish churches: "Our old emigrants of Philadelphia still remember with bitterness the anti-Italian rages of an Irish pastor of the church of St. Paul who for twenty years occupied himself in flagellating the Italians in his Sunday sermons and warning them not to set foot in his church." Aurelio Palmieri, "Il clero italiano negli Stati Uniti," *La Vita Italiana,* VIII (Feb. 15, 1920), 125. See also Palmieri, *Il grave problema,* 34.

to attend church but to work, make some money and go back home. When we return to Italy, there we will attend mass."[48] Great numbers of Italians were employed in gangs on railroads and public works far from any church and often laboring on Sundays. Yet as permanent Italian settlements did emerge, there was a conspicuous lag in the erection of churches, particularly in comparison with other Catholic immigrants of the day, such as the Poles.[49] The lack of priests and churches of their own did not appear to trouble the Italians greatly. The lag in forming Italian parishes was, however, not entirely a matter of religious indifference. It also reflected the deficiency in community-building capability among the immigrants. Intense particularlistic loyalties to family and village prevented the Italians from acting in concert for secular as well as religious purposes.[50]

In the *spirito di campanile*, the peasants clung, as Jane Addams put it, to the "local sanctities" of their villages. Although reluctant to contribute to a church building fund, the *paesani* (townsmen) sent their hard-earned savings to finance the *festa* at home or spent hundreds of dollars for an exact replica of the statue of "La Madonna del Carmine" or of "San Rocco." When they did build a church, it must have a campanile and an altar identical to those in the *paese*. If several groups of townsmen participated, heated controversy over which patron saint was to be honored in the naming of the church was sure to erupt.[51] The mutual aid societies formed by the South Italians also bore the names of the patron saints of their respective villages. The proliferation of these pious-sounding organizations, however, was not an indication of devotion to the Church. Often the members attended mass only on the feast day of their patron, which was also an occasion for carousing and merrymaking.[52]

The primary function of these societies was to sponsor the *festa*

---

[48] Angelo di Domenica, *Protestant Witness of a New American* (Chicago, 1956), 42; *America*, XII (Dec. 19, 1914), 243.

[49] According to the religious census of 1916, for example, there were 466 Catholic Churches in which Polish alone was used and 149 in which Italian alone was used. Shaughnessy, *Has the Immigrant Kept the Faith?*, 218.

[50] For a discussion of the particularistic loyalties of the Italian immigrants see: Rudolph J. Vecoli, "*Contadini* in Chicago: A Critique of *The Uprooted*," *The Journal of American History*, LI (Dec. 1964), 404-417.

[51] Addams, *Twenty Years*, 176; Olindo Marzulli, *Gl'Italiani di Essex* (Newark, N.J., 1911), 29; *Venticinque anni di Missione fra gl'Immigrati Italiani di Boston, Mass. 1888-1913* (Milano, 1913), 45, 260; G. Sofia, ed., *Missioni Scalabriniane in America* (Rome, 1939), 106; *L'Italia*, June 16, 1894.

[52] Dunne, *Memoirs*, 18, 28; Agnew, "Pastoral Care," 260-261; Marzuilli, *Gl'Italiani*, 29.

of the saint or madonna as the religious confraternity had in the village. The *festa* was the most authentic expression of South Italian culture transplanted to the New World. No effort or expense was spared in the effort to recreate the feast in every detail. "The solemn choreographic processions of our villages," an Italian journalist observed, "are exactly reproduced, except for the greater effort due to the greater economic prosperity."[53] During the *festa*, the streets of the Italian quarter took on the aspect of a village fair: streets and houses were decorated with banners, flags, and lanterns, while streets were lined with shrines and booths. Delicacies to titillate the Southern Italian palate were dispensed from sidewalk stands, as were religious objects and amulets against the evil eye. Meanwhile brass bands played arias from the well-loved operas of Verdi. Everything was contrived to create the illusion of being once more in the Old Country:

The crowd in the thronged streets, the cries of the vendors, the shouts of the children, the laughter bursting forth like the bottles of soda and beer which wash down the nuts and castagne; the red slices of watermelon and the pasteries and ice cream; the explosions of petards; the burst of the rockets in luminous and prodigious flowers in the vast sky; the procession; the fervent prayers offered to the Madonna smiling among the gifts of sparkling jewels; these things caused me to relive for awhile the *vita paesana*.[54]

The culmination of the *festa* came on Sunday. A high mass was celebrated with a panegyric of the saint and an invocation of his protection upon the members of the society from every imaginable evil. At the moment the host was raised, a salvo of torpedoes was exploded outside the church. The statue of the saint was then carried through the streets followed by the society in full regalia, bands, and the retinue of the devout. In the fulfillment of vows, many walked barefoot, carrying huge candles, others bore wax offerings in the shape of afflicted parts of the body, while some crawled on their hands and knees. Every few hundred feet the procession halted so that the faithful might pin money and jewels to the vestments of the saint. During the summer months, any Sunday witnessed these medieval pageants wending their way through the "Little Italies"

---

[53] Marzuili, *GI'Italiani*, 29.
[54] *L'Italia*, July 13, 26, 1901; "Old World Customs Continued in Chicago," *By Archer Road* (Chicago), I (Sept., 1907); Di Donato, *Three Circles*, 112.

of American cities. In the lives of the *contadini*, in America as in Italy, the *festa* was the one truly social occasion of the year, a release from the cycle of toil and self-denial, a time of emotional and material extravagance. The magnificent display of fireworks with which every feast ended was the final act of prodigality: "Last of all rockets shot upward into the dark, more 'bombe' were exploded and the lanterns were put out—the 'festa' was over, the morrow at hand, when labor would begin once more."[55]

Within their homes, the immigrants also clung tenaciously to their "sacred, ancestral traditions." Religious images adorned the walls; votive lamps burned before shrines to the saints and madonnas. Saints' days were observed with special foods and prayers, and few homes lacked a *presèpio* (manger scene) at Christmas. Nor had the ocean crossing diminished their dread of the *malocchio*. Amulets were worn and rituals performed to ward off the evil spirits. Sorcerers continued to practice their black arts in the Italian settlements of New York and Chicago even as they had in Calabria and Sicily.[56] Thus it was not the lack of religious sentiment on the part of the Italians which aroused the concern of American Catholics; rather it appears that the folk religion of the *contadini* did not accord with the standards of religious conduct prescribed by the Church in the United States. "These ethnic survivals," Amy Bernardy observed, "cause us to be laughed at, even disdained, exposed to sarcasm of the Americans, but taken together they reflect the image of the race and scheme of the *paese* from which they have emigrated."[57]

Americans, Catholics and Protestants alike, came to regard the Italian immigrants as little better than pagans and idolators. Protestant missionaries thought them "just as ignorant of the true Christ and of the [Christian] way of life as any heathen in darkest Africa." The *feste* were "nothing more than sensual orgies with music and

---

[55] Dunne, *Memoirs*, 17; G. A. Bica, "Account of North Side Sicilian Colony," Chicago Community Inventory; "Special Graces and Favors Attesting the Devotion to St. M.M. De Pazzi in Philadelphia," in Antonio Isoleri, *Souvenir and Bouquet* (Philadelphia, 1911), 76-84; "Celebrating a Feast Day," *By Archer Road*, III (Sept., 1909); Williams, *South Italian Folkways*, 149-152; Anna Zaloha, "A Study of the Persistence of Italian Customs Among 143 Families of Italian Descent" (Master's thesis, Northwestern University, 1937), 96-102.

[56] Alice Hamilton, "Witchcraft in West Polk Street," *American Mercury*, X (Jan., 1927), 71-75; Magione, *Mount Allegro*, 70-120; Williams, *South Italian Folkways*, 152-159; Zahola, "Persistence of Italian Customs," 74, 90-94, 158-163; *L'Italia*, Nov. 23, 1901; Oct. 3, 1903; *Chicago Tribune*, Jan. 19, 1900.

[57] Amy A. Bernardy, *Italia randagia attraverso gli Stati Uniti* (Torino, 1913), 42-45.

fireworks."[58] Although such attacks were protested as "an outrage on Catholic sentiment," American Catholics voiced quite similar criticisms of the Italians. The Southern Italians were said to demonstrate "very little love of the faith, and very little knowledge of it." "Their religion, what there is of it," one critic asserted, "is exterior." The indictment of the religious culture of the Italians was summed up in the Jesuit journal, *America*:

Piety does not consist in processions or carrying candles, in prostrations before a statue of the Madonna, in processions in honor of patron saints of villages, but true piety consists in the daily fulfillment of the religious duties exacted of us by God Almighty and His Church and it consists in a love for that Church and her ministers. In these points, no matter how numerous be the Italian processions, no matter how heavy the candles, no matter how many lights they carry, the Italian immigrant seems very deficient.[59]

Educated Italians joined in the chorus of criticism of "this humiliating religious display, this theatrical vulgarity" of the *feste* of the *contadini*. The anticlericals condemned the festivals for exposing the Italians to ridicule, but most of all because they exalted the saints above the national heroes:

Why do not our countrymen instead of spending so much money in useless illuminations, processions, and festivals, now for a saint, again for a madonna, demonstrate their patriotism by commemorating the great men . . . who fought for the holy cause of liberty for the people? Up, Countrymen, first be patriots and then religious.[60]

Certain Italian clergymen also found the *feste* as celebrated in America objectionable. They charged that the proceeds of the feasts flowed into the coffers of the society or of the promoters rather than

[58] Lucy Rider Meyer, "The Italians of Chicago—their Religious Susceptibility," *The Northwestern Christian Advocate* (Chicago), XXXIX (July 29, 1891), 2; *The "Black Hole" or the missionary experiences of a girl in the slums of Chicago, 1891-1892* (n.p., n.d.), *passim.;* "Religion of Lucky Pieces, Witches, and the Evil Eye," *World Outlook*, III (Oct., 1917), 24-25, 28; *La Fiamma* (Chicago), August 1, 1923 (Chicago Omnibus Project, The Chicago Foreign Language Press Survey, W.P.A.; hereafter cited W.P.A.).

[59] *America*, XII (Dec. 19, 1914), 244-245; *id.*, XII (Oct. 31, 1914) 66; John Gilmary Shea, "The Progress of the Church in the United States," *The American Catholic Quarterly Review*, IX (July, 1884), 496; Lynch, "Italians in New York," 69; *The New World*, Sept. 17, 1904; Oct. 5, 1907.

[60] *L'Italia*, Oct. 16-17, 23-24, 1897; August 25, 1906; *La Tribuna Italiana*, August 13, 1907. W.P.A.

of the Church. Don Luigi Guanella asserted that "these sacred–profane *feste*, where the profit motive is mixed with that of material entertainment" should be prohibited.[61] Condemnation from whatever quarter, however, appeared to have little effect upon the immigrants. When the Church did prohibit certain feasts, the societies proceeded to hold them without benefit of clergy or even with the services of a defrocked priest. Whatever the abuses associated with them, the observance of the feast-days was too deeply ingrained in the Southern Italian culture to be easily eradicated.[62]

Discussions of the "Italian Problem" usually concluded that the solution lay in the provision of zealous Italian priests who would dedicate themselves to the spiritual care of their countrymen in America. Italian churchmen had played a noteworthy role in nineteenth-century American Catholicism; as bishops, college presidents, teachers, missionaries, and parish priests, more than three hundred of them had contributed to the building of the Church.[63] It was thus not simply that the Italian clergy loved "too well the sunny skies of Italy to venture into the missionary field," which explained why the immigrants were bereft of pastoral care. True, it was uncommon for a parish priest to accompany his flock to America; but even those Italian clerics who were here shunned rather than sought out their compatriots. One reason was the indifference if not outright hostility with which they could expect to be received. "What distresses our priests very much who work among the Italians," commented a missionary, "is the small gratitude which these feel toward the work of the priest and the little respect which they display toward the person of the priest himself."[64] Thus many Italian clergymen preferred to serve other nationalities who treated their pastors with reverence and generosity.

The priest who ventured into an Italian settlement was uncertain

---

61 Lorenzo Sterlocchi, *Cenni Biografici di Monsignor Giov. Battista Scalabrini Vescovo di Piacenza con appendice sulle opere di Don Luigi Guanella ed il suo viaggio in America* (2nd ed., Como, 1913), 119.

62 Dunne, *Memoirs*, 86; *Chicago Tribune*, August 14, 1903; Antonio Mangano, *Sons of Italy* (New York, 1917), 16. Mangano was the director of the Italian Department of Colgate Theological Seminary.

63 For a comprehensive account of the role of Italians in the nineteenth-century American church see: Schiavo, *Italian American History*, II, 111-405.

64 "Lettere da Chicago," 71; John T. McNicholas, "The Need of American Priests for the Italian Missions," *The Ecclesiastical Review*, XXXIX (Dec., 1908), 681.

of the reception he would receive. Among northern Italians, who tended to be extremely anticlerical, he might be greeted with verbal abuse and even physical violence. Two priests arriving in Chicopee, Kansas, were received by the coal-miners with a volley of rocks and rotten vegetables. The stoneworkers of Barre, Vermont, drove the Italian priest out of town. But even in southern Italian settlements the missionary might be advised: "We have no need of priests here, it would be better if you returned from whence you came."[65] The manifesto of the Italian socialists of Chicago Heights expressed the sentiment of many of their countrymen:

We who turned out of our country by this misery, came in this land sacred to liberty to look for a morsel of bread for our children, and instead we see here the Italian priest who followed us as far as here, insinuating himself among the ignorant people to suck them in the name of God—the biggest part of that hard earned bread, destined to the hungry children. We believe that it is our right and our duty to tell our credulous countrymen to distrust these blood-suckers, to unyoke themselves from their religious ideas. We say to the people: If there is a God, Heaven certainly will be a reward for those honest men who work and suffer, without the need of buying it, maintaining priest in laziness.[66]

In colonies where such views prevailed, the immigrants "*boicottano* (it is the word used) the Churches, prohibiting attendance to the women and children, renouncing the baptism of their children, declaring war on the priests, who are marked as the enemy of the workers, the natural ally of the *padroni*, the protector of the rich, the accomplice in sum of the exploiters."[67]

In America, Amy Bernardy noted, "the Catholic Church is a business and must sustain itself."[68] It was precisely as business ventures that the Italian churches were the most dismal failures. Many churches established for the Italians were abandoned after a short time, because of lack of financial support. This was regarded as a cardinal failing, if not sin, of the Italians. Bishop Richard Gilmour of Cleveland declared: "They do not understand, or do not wish to understand, that in America the Churches and the schools

[65] Schiavo, *Italian American History*, II, 495; Luigi Villari, *Gli Stati Uniti d'America e L'emigrazione italiana* (Milano, 1912), 228; *L'Italia*, Oct. 11, 1890; Mangano, *Sons of Italy*, 30; Sofia, *Missioni Scalabriniane*, 122.

[66] *La Parola dei Socialisti*, March 12, 1908. The original text is in English.

[67] Pisani, *L'Emigrazione*, 10; Persegati, "I Missionari Scalabriniani," 60-61.

[68] Bernardy, *Italia randagia*, 38.

must be maintained by the spontaneous offerings of the faithful. This defect is born of their indifference toward the religion."[69]

The Italians suffered in this respect from comparison with the Irish; John Gilmary Shea, the Catholic historian, drew the invidious contrast: "Far different from the humble Irish who years ago, laboring on the great public works, always welcomed a priest, and helped to erect churches as they moved along, the Italians neither frequent the churches now accessible to them, nor exert themselves to erect others where they can hear the words of truth in their own tongue."[70] In Italy, the clergy and religious institutions were financed by governmental subventions. Hence, there was no tradition of voluntary support; rather the peasants looked to the Church for charity. Motivated by the single-minded purpose of financial accumulation, the immigrants were untouched by exhortations to build churches and schools. Of the Italian, one critic commented: "acquisition is the first law of his energies, and his real economies usually begin with the Church."[71] The practice of collecting "admission" at the church door particularly scandalized the immigrants. "Is the Church then a theatre?" one asked. For the poor and frugal Italians, the ten or fifteen cents was often an insuperable obstacle.[72]

The niggardliness of the Italians toward the Church was encouraged by the anticlericals who urged them not to patronize the *sacre botteghe* (holy shops). Mastrovalerio, for example, accused the Italian priests of milking the immigrants to pay for churches which remained the property of the Archbishop. To which Reverend Dunne replied:

[69] Pacifico Capitani, *La Questione Italiana negli Stati Uniti D'America* (Cleveland, 1891), 4, 11-12. Father Nicolo Odone, pastor of the Italian Church of the Holy Redeemer of St. Paul, told his congregation that in the United States it was necessary to contribute to the support of the pastor and church under danger of mortal sin. "Libro degli Annunzi dell '8 Maggio 1906 all' 8 Marzo 1908 fatti nella Chiesa Italiana del Ss. Redentore in St. Paul, Minnesota." Papers of Father Nicolo Carlo Odone (Immigrant Archives, University of Minnesota Library).

[70] Shea, "Progress of the Church," 496. It is interesting to compare this statement with that made a generation earlier by Bishop James R. Bayley regarding the Irish immigrants: "There are many demoralized by herding in our large cities, who, though they may be called Catholics, never practice any duty of their religion—who do not come near our churches—and are, in fact, entirely beyond our control." Quoted in Sister Hildegarde Yeager, *Life of James R. Bayley* (Washington, D.C., 1947), 132.

[71] *America*, XII (Dec. 5, 1914), 194; Padre V.D., *L'Apostolo*, 17-18; Palmieri, *Grave Problema*, 42; Aurelio Palmieri, "The Contribution of the Italian Catholic Clergy to the United States," in McGuire, ed., *Catholic Builders*, II, 144.

[72] Capitani, *Questione Italiana*, 11; Bernardy, *Italia Randagia*, 38; Palmieri, *Grave Problema*, 34.

One familiar with the scanty income derived from the average Italian parish must be amused at his mendacious insinuation that we are laboring among his compatriots for the sake of filthy lucre. To borrow his barnyard metaphor, let me assure him, from seven years' personal experience among his patriotic countrymen, that it has been indeed dry milking.[73]

Comparing the generosity of certain nationalities with the parsimony of his countrymen, Monsignor Aloysius Pozzi lamented: "Why wasn't I born in Belfast, Dublin, Limerick or Kilkenny!"[74] Don Luigi Valetto, a missionary in Chicago, calculated the annual contributions to the Church per 10,000 population of various ethnic groups as follows: Poles, $65,000; Irish, $40,000; Germans, $30,000; Italians, $3,000. Since the Poles were at this time roughly on an equal footing with the Italians, economics were obviously not the prime determinant of the level of giving.[75]

Lack of financial support from their compatriots placed the Italian priests in a humiliating role of dependency before the American clergy. This relationship of inferiority was symbolized by the system of annex parishes, whereby the basement of a church was assigned to the Italians for worship. However, this arrangement was not thought to be insulting, for as an American Irish writer declared: "The Italians as a body are not humiliated by humiliation."[76] When the Reverend Nicolo Odone accepted an invitation from Archbishop John Ireland to form an Italian parish in St. Paul, he found his "church" to be the dark and dirty crypt of the Cathedral. For ten years Odone celebrated mass in the *Basamento*, as it was popularly known among the Italians. Seeking to raise funds for a church building, Odone appealed to the Italians' sense of pride by affirming the necessity of terminating the dependence "dall Chiesa d'sopra."

[73] *La Parola dei Socialisti*, Feb. 25, March 5, 1908; *La Tribuna Italiana*, Jan. 14, 1905; *The New World*, Dec. 26, 1906; Dunne, *Memoirs*, 22-23. At the dedication of the new Italian church in Philadelphia, the Reverend Antonio Isoleri recalled bitterly: "We were humiliated in collecting and selling tickets by the jests and mockeries of those, unfortunates! who more than their Religion, love 25 cents and a glass of beer." Isoleri, *Souvenir*, 119.

[74] Aloysius Pozzi, *For Faith and Country* (Trenton, N.J., 1907), 30. Quoted in Perrotta, "Catholic Care," 25. Pozzi who was pastor of an Italian church in Trenton also sighed: "Why were we not persecuted as the Irish and the Poles for our Faith?"

[75] "Lettere da Chicago," 71. Collections at the Church of the Holy Redeemer in St. Paul averaged less than $2 a mass in 1906, "Libro di Sacristia, Entrate ed Uscite—Chiesa Ss. Redentore," Odone Papers.

[76] Lynch, "Italians in New York," 72; Browne, "Italian Problem," 67-68.

What a humiliation [he added], for us, here, numerous as we are . . .
to have to come here in this low and humid hall placed under the
feet of a dissimilar people which sometimes looks down on us, in more
than one case where dependence on the humor of others, and more than
once we must of necessity swallow the bitter and hard-to-swallow pill,
Oh let us reawaken in us the national pride, we are Italians and let us
remember we are children of Dante Allighieri. . . .[77]

In his efforts to build an Italian Church, however, Odone ran
afoul of the spirit of regionalism which plagued priests elsewhere as
well. The fact that the immigrants did not think of themselves first
as Italians, but rather as Genoese, Sicilians, or Tuscans, made for
jealousies and rivalries within congregations. Odone, himself from
Liguria, felt it necessary to reassure his congregation that he did not
harbor regional prejudices:

They are welcome in this church the Italians of the Neapolitan Provinces,
those of the Sicilian Provinces, of the Tuscan Provinces, of the Ligurian
Provinces, of the Lombard Provinces, Veneto, Piedmont, in sum of all
the provinces of the Italian nation. I do not make distinctions among
Italians. Be they of the north or of the south, from *alta* or *bassa Italia,*
that is not important.[78]

Nonetheless, regional animosities contributed to the failure of his
campaign to raise funds for an Italian church.

The fact that most of the Italian missionaries were from the
northern regions, while the mass of the immigrants were from the
Mezzogiorno, exacerbated regional feelings. Between such priests
and the people there was a gulf of cultural and linguistic differences.
A young priest from Tuscany arriving in a Sicilian parish exclaimed: "Is it possible that these are Italians?" The clergymen
from *alta Italia* tended to look down upon the southern Italians,
while the latter regarded the priests as foreigners. During World
War I, a priest from Trentino with a Teutonic name was accused
of being a German and driven out of his parish. Critics of the
Italian clergy pointed to these antagonisms as evidence that there

---

[77] "Libro degli Annunzi," Odone Papers.

[78] *Ibid.* On regional antagonisms as they affected this particular church see:
"Memorie raccolte per servire a scriver la Storia della Missione e Parrocchia
Italiana in St. Paul, Minnesota, S.U. d'America. Memorie compilate dal primo
Pastore di detta Parrocchia Italiana Rev. Nicolo Odone, 1908" and "Raggualio
del Movimento per la Chiesa Italiana in St. Paul, Minn.," Odone Papers.

existed "hardly any bond of sympathy" between the priests and the mass of immigrants.[79]

The Italian priest was also exposed to malicious gossip and slander inspired by anticlerical sources. Attacks such as the following were not uncommon in the radical press:

Last summer when you were absent some weeks some gossipers said you were ill with a malady commonly call *mal francese,* but do not bother with this gossip and continue to fill your suitcase with money, so that soon you will become fat and rotund, but I advise you to be cautious with the young maidens because one of those might become plump, etc.[80]

Suspicions of sexual misconduct on the part of clergymen appear to have been endemic in the Italian colonies. One Italian priest felt compelled to publish a public defense against charges that he had seduced a young woman.[81] Such allegations were, however, not without some basis in fact. The quality of some of the Italian clergy who came to America left something to be desired. Not a few left Italy because of some indiscretion or scandal. In 1884, Archbishop Corrigan reported that of twelve Italian priests in his archdiocese, ten had been expelled from Italy because of crimes *contra sextum.*[82] The protests against the behavior of clergymen caused Leo XIII to issue a circular in 1890 which prohibited the emigration of a priest unless he had the consent of his ordinary, of the Congregation of the Council, and had been accepted by an American bishop. Despite increasingly severe restrictions, the exodus of priests of dubious character continued.[83] Before an audience of Italian prelates in 1906, Father Francesco Beccherini, pastor of the Church of St. Francis in Detroit, appealed for closer surveillance of the clerical emigration:

---

[79] McNicholas, "Need of American Priests," 681-682; Perrotta, "Catholic Care," 35; interviews.

[80] *La Parola dei Socialisti,* Feb. 17, 1908.

[81] Ernesto D'Acquila, *Il Trionfo dell'Innocenza* (Newark, N.J., 1899). Reverend D'Acquila was rector of the Italian Church of Our Lady of Mt. Carmel of Newark.

[82] Frederick J. Zwierlein, *The Life and Letters of Bishop McQuaid* (3 vols., Rochester, N.Y. 1926), II, 334.

[83] Browne, "Italian Problem," 68-69; Perrotta, "Catholic Care," 33-35; Joseph E. Ciesluk, *National Parishes in the United States* (Catholic University of America Canon Law Studies No. 190; Washington, D.C., 1944), 34-35, 145. The problem was not peculiar to the Italian clergy. In the mid-nineteenth century, the first and second Plenary Councils had warned against the immigration of priests who came "more for material gain than for the zeal of souls." *Ibid.,* 33.

For the honor of the Italian clergy, for the salvation of souls, and for the good of the Church, it is necessary to close the entrance to a vertible stream of a certain clergy which goes over there, which is simply the bilge of every diocese of Italy and which smirches our reputation and honor in general.[84]

American bishops, Beccherini noted, believed that religious superiors in Italy were not above providing misleading letters and passage to rid themselves of troublesome subjects.

Of the regular clergy who came to America, it was said that for the most part they came *a cercare una messa* (in search of a mass), just as the other emigrants came in search of work. Such priests gave to the Italian clergy generally a reputation of seeking their "pecuniary interests" rather than the salvation of souls. Occasional incidents of exorbitant fees for dispensing the sacraments and of misappropriation of church funds confirmed the worst suspicions of the immigrants. Even the worthy priest fell under the blighting shadow of the mistrust engendered.[85]

Confidence in the Italian clergy was further undermined by the large number of apostate priests who became Protestant ministers. More than half of the some 450 Italian evangelical missionaries in 1918 were reported to be former priests.[86] While some were sincere converts, it was widely believed that many had made "an opportune conversion, exploiting then converters and converts." Such "renegade" priests tended to be strongly disliked by the Italians.

Defrocked priests were also responsible for the establishment of a number of "Independent Italian Catholic Churches." In 1899, the "Reverend" Antonio D'Andrea, who was later to emerge as a powerful figure in the Chicago underworld, founded the "Chiesa di S. Antonio di Padova" with the benediction of the Bishop of the Polish National Catholic Church.[87] In Hackensack, New Jersey, a suspended priest, Antiono Giulio Lenzi, established an independent church for the Italians who had been vainly requesting their own

[84] Francesco Beccherini, *Il Fenomeno dell'Emigrazione negli Stati Uniti d'America* (Sansepolcro, 1906), 22-23.

[85] Bernardy, *Italia randagia*, 38; Villari, *Gli Stati Uniti*, 286; Perrotta, "Catholic Care," 29-30; *Venticinque Anni*, 110-111; "Raggualio," 44-45, 59; "Book of Peace and of Information," V, 103, Odone Papers.

[86] Enrico C. Sartorio, *Social and Religious Life of Italians in America* (Boston, 1918), 114; Bernardy, *Italia Randagia*, 41; Perrotta, "Catholic Care," 40; Francis D. De Bilio, "Protestant Mission Work Among Italians in Boston," (doctoral dissertation, Boston University, 1949), 203.

[87] *L'Italia*, May 27, June 24, August 19, Sept. 9, 1899; Virgil W. Peterson, *Barbarians in Our Midst* (Boston, 1952), 115-116.

parish for several years. The Bishop of the Polish National Catholic Church, within which Lenzi styled himself "Vicar General of the Italian Independent Churches," on one occasion confirmed 1700 children in this church. Two other suspended priests organized an "Independent Italian Church" in Marlboro, Massachusetts, in 1919.[88] Although the movement for an independent Catholic church never achieved the proportions among the Italians that it did among the Poles, these incidents expressed a rebelliousness on the part of both priests and people against the American hierarchy.

Accustomed to the deference of Irish Catholics, the American prelates were exasperated by the insubordinate attitude of the Italians. It seemed the height of impudence that a people unwilling to support their churches yet presumed to dictate who would be their pastors. In Trenton, for example, the refusal of the Bishop to appoint an Italian priest for the Church of St. Joachim resulted in a schism which lasted for several years. A large segment of the Italian colony seceded *en masse* to the Protestant mission which had an Italian minister. Under the motto "Italian school; Italian pastor; Italian sisters," the Trenton Italians formed a committee which collected thousands of dollars and thousands of signatures on a petition. Following the accession of a new Bishop, these demands were met and the Italians returned to the fold.[89]

The Italians of the North End of Boston had for some years attended a church of the Italian Franciscans. However, the majority of the parishoners were Irish, and the Italians felt that they were placed in "a condition of humliating inferiority." Determined to have a church exclusively for the Italians, they formed the Society of San Marco which raised funds and purchased a Baptist meeting-house. However, before turning the church over to the Archbishop, the Society insisted that its representative have control over receipts and expenditures as in the manner of the Italian trustee system. The Archbishop rejected this condition and refused to give his benediction to the church. He regarded the San Marco members as "malcontents, rebels against legitimate authority, and champions of the dangerous trustee system." Not to be cowed, the Society obtained the good offices of several Italian eccelesiastics to intercede on its behalf at the Vatican. Meanwhile the members of the San Marco

---

[88] Palmieri, *Grave Problema*, 60; Lord, *Archdiocese of Boston*, III, 735-736.
[89] Scilla De Glauco, *Un Inno di Fede Immortale* (New York, 1943), 70, 89-93.

after attending mass at an American church gathered in their chapel for religious devotions. After this state of affairs had continued for several years, an Italian missionary, Father Francesco Zaboglio, arrived in Boston to intercede on behalf of the San Marco Society. Finally in 1890, Archbishop John J. Williams authorized the opening of the church under the name Sacred Heart.[90] Similar challenges to ecclesiastical authority took place elsewhere, though usually with a less successful outcome.

While the existence of an "Italian Problem" was generally acknowledged, there was considerable disagreement among churchmen with regard to causes and remedies. The subject was first brought before the American hierarchy at the Third Plenary Council of Baltimore in 1884. The Prefect of the Congregation of the Propaganda, Cardinal Giovanni Simeoni, requested that legislation on the issue of Italian immigration be prepared. Archbishop James Gibbons assigned the task to Archbishop William H. Elder of Cincinnati, assuring him: "There is little to be said about it, and its study involves very little labor." However, when the chapter "Of Italian Immigrants" was presented to the Council it encountered vigorous opposition. Archibishop Michael A. Corrigan of New York declared that the report failed to emphasize sufficiently the religious ignorance and indifference of the Italians. "The Bishops and priests of New York City and vicinity," he asserted, "have made every effort to make provision for the Italians so that they can have sermons in their own tongue and assist at Mass, but everything has been in vain." Bishop Bernard J. McQuaid of Rochester saw no reason why the Church should express special solicitude for the immigrants from Italy. The outcome of the debate was a rewriting of the chapter under the title "Of Colonists and Immigrants." With regard to the Italians, the Council recommended only that societies to assist the emigrants be established and that priests "conspicuous in morals and learning, and consumed with zeal for souls" accompany the emigrants abroad.[91] The American bishops pessimistically

---

[90] *Venticinque Anni*, 61-88, provides a documented account from the point of view of the San Marco Society, while Lord, *Archdiocese of Boston*, III, 224-226, presents the affair in a somewhat different light. The account in Remo Rizzato, *Figure di Missionari Scalabriniani* (New York, 1948?), 40-43, attributes the opening of the church to the intercession of the Pope himself.

[91] Barry, *Catholic Church*, 56-58; Browne, "Italian Problem," 55-60; Zwierlein, *Bishop McQuaid*, 333-335.

reported to Rome that the Italians "suffered greater spiritual destitution than any other immigrants." However, the prelates were restrained in expressing their sentiments, for as the secretary of the Council wrote to Gibbons:

It is a very delicate matter to tell the Sovereign Pontiff how utterly faithless the specimens of his country coming here really are. Ignorance of their religion and a depth of vice little known to us yet, are the prominent characteristics.[92]

In effect, the American hierarchy viewed the problem as one originating in Italy and one to be solved by the Church in Italy.

A work published in 1886 by Monsignor Gennaro de Concilio confirmed the sorry religious state of the Italian immigrants. De Concilio, professor of theology at Seton Hall University and pastor of an Italian church in Jersey City, lamented that half a million of his countrymen were living "without any religious help or comfort, and do not practice any religious duty; they do not hear mass; they do not, for years and years, use the sacraments; they do not listen to the word of God." Many had succumbed to the Protestant missions which employed "vile and infamous apostates" or to the Masonic sects which instilled a hatred of everything Catholic. The remedy, De Concilio urged, was in the provision of national parishes entrusted to good Italian priests.[93]

De Concilio's tract reportedly inspired Pope Leo XIII's letter of December 10, 1888 to the American bishops on the Italian immigration. Deploring the material and spiritual evils besetting the immigrants, Leo expressed his grave concern for the decay of Christain morality among them and stressed the need to provide them "with the saving care of ministers of God familiar with the Italian language." He hailed the establishment of an Apostolic College of Priests in Piacenza the previous year to train a "ministry of Christ

---

[92] Quoted in Browne, "Italian Problem," 59. Cf. Orestes A. Brownson's statement made in 1849: "Nobody can deny that in external decorum and the ordinary moral and social virtues the Irish Catholics are the most deficient class of our community." Quoted in Arthur M. Schlesinger, Jr., *A Pilgrim's Progress: Orestes A. Brownson* (Boston and Toronto, 1966), 214, n.49.

[93] Gennaro de Concilio, *Sullo stato religioso degl'italiani negli Stati Uniti d'America* (Newark, N.J., 1886). A copy of this work has not been located; however, portions of its text were reprinted in: Raffaele Ballerini, "Delle condizioni relgiose degli emigrati italiani negli Stati Uniti d'America," *Civilta Cattolica*, series XIII, 11 (1888), 641-653.

for the scattered Italians." Upon the American bishops Leo laid the charge of providing the necessary facilities for those missionaries who came to labor in their dioceses.[94]

The cause of the Italian immigrants was also taken up by the Reverend Pacifico N. Capitani, pastor of the first Italian church in Cleveland. In a series of articles on the "Italian Question" which appeared in the *Freeman's Journal* in 1889, Capitani rose to the defense of his countrymen whom he believed had been slandered in a work published in New York the previous year entitled *Fiat Lux*.[95] Its anonymous author had asserted that the Italian Catholics "are nothing less than a public scandal, a disgrace to Italy and to the Religion which they profess." Their children were Catholic only in name, while in fact they were Protestants or pagans. Capitani responded, if the Italians were indeed degraded as pictured, who was to blame? What had been done for the spiritual well-being of the Italians in America before the voice of Leo XIII was heard? Had their miserable state ever been taken into consideration in the Episcopal Curias? Had recourse even been taken to the Congregation of the Propaganda as had been done for other nationalities? Had anyone ever risen to their defense? The answer to all of these questions, Capitani declared, was No![96]

Capitani proposed the establishment of an Italo-American College in the United States for the preparation of missionaries for the Italians. Such an institution would train English-speaking Italian priests; this, Capitani thought, was absolutely essential if the American-born generation was to be saved. The College would recruit its students from among the sons of immigrants as well as from Italy. The American bishops, argued Capitani, would receive more favorably these American-trained priests who would be under their sole jurisdiction rather than missionaries subject to a superior in Italy.[97] Although the plan for an Italo-American College was endorsed by various prelates, including Cardinal Gibbons, nothing

---

[94] The English text is in John Tracy Ellis, ed., *Documents of American Catholic History* (Milwaukee, 1962), 462-466. *The American Ecclesiastical Review*, I (Feb., 1889), carried the Latin text and commented: "If the thought has obtruded itself at times that Rome was deaf to the representations of existing evils because their recognition wounded national pride, it has proved a rash judgement in the case of Leo XIII." *Ibid.*, 44.

[95] Capitani believed that the anonymous author of *Fiat Lux* was an Italian priest, *Questione Italiana*, 10.

[96] *Ibid.*, 8-15.

[97] *Ibid.*, 25-39.

came of it. One reason may have been the lack of support among the Italian immigrants themselves. The anticlericals regarded the project with suspicion:

Do you promoters of the College recognize the government of the Patria or do you repudiate it like the Italian missionaires in Japan and China? Would you teach the pupils to love our glorious sovereign? Would you teach that Rome is the capital of Italy? Or will you preach from the pulpit hatred of Italy?[98]

Although the Italian immigration increased greatly from the 1890's on, the number of Italian priests in America did not rise proportionately. This was the brunt of H. J. Desmond's tract, *The Neglected Italians A Memorial to the Italian Hieracy* [*sic!*] published in 1899.[99] Desmond, editor of the *Catholic Citizen* of Milwaukee, charged the Italian clergy with indifference to the fate of their emigrating countrymen. Pointing out that all of the other immigrants brought their priests with them he chided the Italian priest who "loves too well the sunny skies of fair Italy to venture into the missionary field." While in Italy there was one priest to every 370 souls, there were not more than sixty Italian priests laboring among their countrymen in America, a ratio of one to every 12,000. Desmond declared that he was using the adjective "neglected" in an accusatory as well as descriptive sense: "Catholic Italy, with her rich church endowments, her surplus of priests and her virtual control of the revenues of the Catholic world, should at least look after her own children."[100]

While some found the tone of Desmond's polemic insolent, all agreed that he had laid bare the central fact of the "Italian Problem," i.e., the failure of the Italian priests to accompany their parishioners

---

[98] *L'Italia,* Sept. 13, Oct. 11, 1890. Yet another reason for the failure of the project may have been the sparsity of religious vocations among the sons of the immigrants. Not until quite recently has the number of Italian-Americans entering the priesthood become relatively siginificant. See Persegati, "Missionari Scalabriniani," 52.

[99] (Milwaukee, 1899). The pamphlet was evidently intended for the eyes of the Roman Curia, since the text was both in English and an atrocious Italian. Aside from a genuine concern for the Italians, Desmond used the issue to express his annoyance at the Congregation of the Propaganda for meddling in American affairs: "The children of the Pope's countrymen in America are going en masse to the American public schools, while in Rome the Propaganda is concerning itself over the religious condition of Irish-American children." *Ibid.,* 9.

[100] *Ibid.,* 8.

to America. As Father Beccherini told an audience of distinguished clerics in Italy, this was a reproach which was always and everywhere thrown in one's face, but a merited reproach, he added, "for our pastors who allow the flock to leave and indifferently remain to guard the sheep fold." The American episcopacy, according to Beccherini, regarded the priests of Italy as directly and absolutely responsible for the great losses of Italians to the Church. Beccherini closed with an eloquent appeal to the Italian clergy to respond to the voices of Jesus Christ, His Church, and *la patria* which called them to serve their countrymen abroad.[101]

Speaking before the Congress of the American Federation of Catholic Societies in 1913, Reverend Salvatore Cianci, pastor of the Italian Church of Grand Rapids, declared: "Above all we have need of Italian priests; this is the general lament." But he suggested that the American hierarchy might do more than it had to remedy this deficiency. Rome, he believed, was not yet completely informed of the needs of the Italian immigration. The bishops should report the number of Italians in each diocese and request the number of priests necessary. Noting that many dioceses were without a single Italian priest, Cianci proposed that each diocese have at least one missionary to travel among the scattered settlements of Italians.[102]

In 1913, the *Catholic Citizen* termed the fate of the Italian immigrants "Our biggest Catholic question."[103] During these peak years of the immigration from Italy, concern over this issue reached new heights. This concern erupted in a heated controversy in the pages of *America*. For several months during 1914, the critics and defenders of the Italians exchanged angry retorts. The apologists (for the most part Italian priests) asserted that by and large the Italian people were good, practicing Catholics, disoriented perhaps by the experience of immigration, but loyal to their ancestral faith.[104] They further intimated that what estrangement had taken place was in large part due to the prejudice the Italians had en-

---

101 Beccherini, *Fenomeno dell'Emigrazione*, 16-23.
102 Salvatore Cianci, *Il Lavoro Sociale in Mezzo agli italiani* (n.p., n.d.), 18-19.
103 D. Lynch, "The Religious Condition of Italians in New York," *America*, X (March 21, 1914), 558-559; "Catholic Italian Losses," *The Literary Digest*, XLVII (Oct. 11, 1913), 636. The *Catholic Citizen* estimated that nearly a million Italian immigrants had been lost to the Church.
104 In the ranks of the defenders was Edmund M. Dunne, now Bishop of Peoria. *America*, XII (Nov. 21, 1914), 144. He asserted that seven years as a pastor of an Italian church had taught him to appreciate the high grade of morality among the poor immigrants.

countered among American Catholics. Most of the correspondents, however, agreed with the contention that the immigrants came "insufficiently instructed in their Faith, and not infrequently with a hatred of the Church and the priesthood in their hearts."[105] The Italians, it was said, entered readily into Freemasonry and other anti-Christian societies and fell easy victims to the Protestant proselytizer. Herbert Hadley, the main protagonist in the polemic, summed up for the prosecution:

The question at issue is what is the collective result produced in this country among the millions of Italians after well nigh thirty years of labor and the expenditure of a large sum of American money. Is then the collective spiritual result among the Italians commensurate with the vast expense and the toil bestowed upon them? My contention is, and I think it is borne out by most priests familiar with the subject, no.[106]

Indeed, three decades after the Council of Baltimore had collectively shaken its head in dismay over the "spiritual destitution" of the Italians, the pessimistic estimate of these immigrants had hardly changed at all. The "Italian Problem" appeared to be impervious to all solutions.

Whatever their attitude toward the immigrants, all agreed that the Church had a vital stake in the American-born generations. Even if the adult Italians were incorrigible, the challenge remained of the "bright-eyed, laughter-loving, industrious and intelligent Italian children who are going to be our fellow-citizens." As the Bishop of Trenton put it: "If we cannot get the adults, let us try to get the children."[107] Exposed to an irreligious home enviornment, the corrupting influences of city life, and the wiles of Protestant proselytizers, the young Italians were thought to be in dire peril of spiritual and moral corruption. The duty of the Church was twofold,

---

[105] *Id.,* XII (Oct. 31, 1914), 66; (Nov. 7, 1914), 93; (Dec. 19. 1914), 245.

[106] *Id.,* XII (Dec. 19, 1914), 243. Hadley attributed the condition of the immigrants to the defective character of the Italian clergy: "Why did not the Italian priests accompany their countrymen in the early days of their immigration as did the priests of other nationalities? How is it that so many today in this country do not wish to labor among their own countrymen? Why is it that Pius X undertook the reform of the seminaries in southern Italy? Why the stringent regulations with regard to the immigration into this country of the Italian clergy?"

[107] Walter T. Leahy, *The Catholic Church of the Diocese of Trenton, New Jersey* (Princeton, c. 1906), 201; *America,* XII (Dec. 19, 1914), 246.

to make good Catholics and good citizens of them. This dual mission was well-defined by the Reverend Dunne:

Is it no concern of ours whether a notable portion of our Catholic brethren remain faithful to their religion or apostasize or drift into infidelity? Shall we step aside in order to let well-meaning non-Catholic philanthropists wrest from the Church's bosom a considerable number of those who belong to her by birth? As loyal Americans, can we remain indifferent while in the most congested neighborhood of Chicago, children are growing up in the gutter like social weeds, to become afterward a menace to our Garden City? Charity begins at home, and we have here in the Italian colony of Chicago a vast missionary field to cultivate, a variegated collection of sickly plants, both physical and moral, that need our special attention.[108]

From the Catholic point of view, the parochial school was to be the chief agency for the salvation, civic as well as spiritual, of the Italian children. Dr. Francis C. Kelley, president of the Catholic Church Extension Society declared: "The Italian religious problem can be settled only in one way and that is through [parochial] schools."[109] In accordance with this prescription, the motto in certain dioceses was: "Build the School First!" The support of schools in Italian parishes, however, was no easy matter. "Experience has amply proved that the Italians will not send their children to the parochial schools, if they have to pay for them there," was the common complaint of the clergy.[110] Without a tradition of confessional education, the frugal peasants could not understand why they should pay to send their children to church schools when free public schools were available. In addition to the economic objection, the anticlericals opposed religious education. *La Tribune Italiana* urged the parents: "Italians, send your children to public schools. Religion should be taught in the sanctuary of the family."[111]

The aversion to parochial schools was strengthened by the preju-

---

108 *The New World*, March 18, 1899; Agnew, "Pastoral Care," 259-263.
109 *The New World*, Oct. 1, 1915; *America*, XII (Dec. 19, 1914), 244.
110 Perrotta, "Catholic Care," 79; *The New World*, June 17, 1899.
111 *La Tribuna Italiana*, Sept. 9, 1906, W.P.A.; Cianci, *Lavoro Sociale*, 15-16; Palmieri, "Contribution of Italian Catholic Clergy," 135-136. At the dedication of a parochial school in Bayonne, N.J., the Italian pastor remarked: "But is this a feast day of joy and thanksgiving for all our countrymen of Bayonne? Alas! Sowers of discord scream that in the Catholic schools directed by the clergy and sisters, one learns only the Pater Noster and nothing else!" De Glauco, *Un Inno*, 212.

dice which the Italian children sometimes encountered among the American sisters and pupils. Because the Irish resented the invasion of their schools by the "poorly-clad, unclean, Italian children," it was suggested that the latter be segregated in separate classrooms "until such time as no objection could be made to having them mingle with our children." On occasion, the Italian children were seated in the last row of the classroom or exposed to other humiliating treatment. In the classroom as well as on the playground, they were the objects of taunts against their nationality.[112] For this reason among others, the Italian priests argued that Italian sisters were best suited to teach the children of the immigrants. Their presence in the schools would reassure the parents that their sons and daughters would not be mistreated because they were Italian. The bilingual parochial school, they contended, which preserved the mother tongue, would also induce the Italians to send their children there. Since the immigrants proved themselves reluctant to support even such schools, parochial education for the Italians relied largely on the benevolence of the American episcopacy. While some remained indifferent, others like Bishop Thomas J. Walsh of Trenton generously provided both schools and Italian nuns. Walsh believed that the bilingual school was the means to "save all the Italian children of America, and through all these children all the Italian people."[113]

The introduction of Italian sisters into the parochial schools, however, was vigorously opposed by the American teaching orders. Efforts were even made to replace Italian nuns with American sisters. These efforts had the support of the aggressive Americanizers such as the Reverend John T. McNicholas, who maintained: "Certainly we should try to make Americans of the Italians, and that as quickly as possible." The presence of foreign teachers in the parochial schools, it was charged, tended to perpetuate "foreign

---

[112] McNicholas, "Need of American Priests," 680-681; Lynch, "Italians in New York," 72; Rosa Cassettari, "The Story of an Italian Neighbor (as told to Marie Hall Ets)," 338, MS. However, Italians of one region sometimes refused to have their children attend a school frequented by children from another region of Italy. De Glauco, *Un Inno*, 66.

[113] Palmieri, "Contribution of Italian Catholic Clergy," 131; Rev. J. Zarrilli, *A Prayerful Appeal to the American Hierarchy in behalf of the Italian Catholic Cause in the United States* (Two Harbors, Minn., 1924), 14; Zarrilli, "Some More Light on the Italian Problem," *The Ecclesiastical Review*, LXXIX (Sept., 1928), 268-269; Miles Muredach, "An Experiment in City Home Missions," *Extension Magazine* (April, 1923), reprinted in Zarrilli, *Prayerful Appeal*, 19-26.

national aspirations to the lessening of sympathy with American ideals."[114] Rather than recruiting members of Italian teaching orders it was proposed that American sisters be sent to Italy to study the language and customs as preparation for teaching the children of the immigrants. These attitudes help to explain why of the 649 sisters teaching in Italian parochial schools in 1918, only 125 were Italian.[115]

Despite the strenuous efforts to bring the Italian children into parochial schools, only a small minority of them ever received a Catholic education. The crux of the matter was, as one missionary observed: "The Italians do not want to make sacrifices to found and sustain parochial schools as do all the Catholics of the other nationalities."[116] Thus as late as 1924 there was only one school for every six Italian churches. But even where "free parochial schools" were provided for the Italians, they seemed to prefer a public education for their children. The estimate made in 1899 that nine-tenths of the Italian children were either in "godless public schools" or on the streets does not appear to have changed much in succeeding decades.[117]

If the public schools were thought to be destructive of the true faith, so much more was this the case with the Protestant missions. The Italians and especially their children were thought to be the chosen prey of a vast missionary effort on the part of the evangelical churches. *The New World* observed:

Designing societies with deluding names are forth to proselyte. Sinister social settlements abound and are laying foundations broad and deep

---

114 McNicholas, "Need of American Priests," 680; "Pastoral Care of Foreign Catholics in America," *The Ecclesiastical Review*, LXX (Feb., 1924), 178; De Glauco, *Un Inno*, 85-86.

115 Palmieri, *Grave Problema*, 55.

116 "Lettere da Chicago," 70.

117 Perrotta, "Catholic Care," 78. Perrotta estimated that half a million Italian children were growing up without any religious training. Desmond, *Neglected Italians*, 8-9; Sister M. Agnes Gertrude, "Italian Immigration into Philadelphia," *Records of the American Catholic Historical Society of Philadelphia*, LVIII (Sept., 1947), 200. In Chicago, where Archbishop Quigley made a vigorous effort to bring the Italian children into the parochial schools, only eleven percent of the Italian children were receiving a Catholic education in 1917. Frank O. Beck, "The Italian in Chicago," *Bulletin of the Chicago Department of Public Welfare*, II (Feb., 1919), 20. In 1914, there were twenty-three Polish, twenty-two German, and only three Italian parochial schools in Chicago. Edith Abbot and S.P. Breckinridge, *Truancy and Non-Attendance in the Chicago Public Schools* (Chicago, 1917), 279. *The New World*, June 7, 1913; Oct. 1, 1915.

for a decay of faith. Specious rescue societies and sectarian home-missions are incessantly active. Everywhere nets are spread for the unwary.[118]

The "misguided soul-chasers," as the Protestant missionaries were labeled, were accused of using material inducements to bring the Italians into their chapels and schools. Families were offered clothing, food, and jobs, while children were given candy and toys if they attended Protestant services. In the "sectarian dens of these human spiders," Dunne declared, English language classes, sewing instruction, nurseries, musical bands, and other welfare and social programs were used to detach the immigrants from the Mother Church. Nor, it was said, did the Italians have any scruples about taking advantage of these facilities.[119]

To combat the Protestant inroads, the Church felt compelled to adopt the techniques of its competitors in its own work among the Italians. The First American Catholic Missionary Congress which met in Chicago in 1908 had for its watchword: "Save Our Own; Save the Children of the Immigrants." Commenting on the vigorous home-missions of the evangelical churches, the Official Program of the Congress asserted: "We will do well to look closely into this work of proselytizing which is going on in every corner of the country . . . we can learn something from the methods of our adversaries."[120] Noting the effective use of volunteers by the Protestant missions, the Catholic clergy called for a lay apostolate to come to the rescue of the Italian children. In Chicago, Boston, and elsewhere, Sunday School Associations of well-to-do Americans were formed to teach catechism and conduct social activities among the young people of the "Little Italies." Copying Protestant strategy, gifts were given to the children who attended classes, while social centers with billiard and reading rooms, singing and dramatic clubs, employment bureaus and health clinics, were used to attract the young adults. Catholic social settlements such as St. Rose's Settlement in New York City, the Madonna House in Philadelphia, and the Guardian Angel Center of Chicago, offered a variety of educational

---

[118] August 20, 1904. Desmond commented: "Every Protestant Church in America has its missions among the Italian immigrants seeking to gather them in, and especially seeking to proselyte their children." *Neglected Italians*, 6.

[119] Dunne, *Memoirs*, 19-20, 84; Agnew, "Pastoral Care," 261-262; Bernardy, *Italia Randagia*, 40; Shea, "Progress of the Church," 496.

[120] First American Catholic Missionary Congress, *Official Guide*, 110.

and recreational programs to keep the Italian young people in the fold.[121]

These activities were also intended to teach the children "real American patriotism and American loyalty to the Church."[122] Meanwhile the Society of St. Vincent De Paul in the various dioceses sought to provide assistance to the Italian poor who might otherwise turn to the Protestant charities. "By such corporal works of mercy," observed *The New World*, "the allegiance of the Italians is won."[123] While it might be an exaggeration to claim that Catholic welfare activities were the direct result of Protestant example,[124] the Church did in fact adopt the strategy of social service in response to the challenge of proselytization among the Italians.

The abandonment of its emigrating children was the grievous charge brought against the Church of Italy by its critics. While there was much justice in the accusation, the heroic efforts of those Italian priests and sisters who did take up the cause of the immigrants were not generally acknowledged. In the face of extraordinary obstacles, zealous missionaries did dedicate themselves to the spiritual and physical advancement of their countrymen. Members of various Italian religious orders, Jesuits, Franciscans, Servites, and Conventuals, established the earliest churches for the immigrants.[125] However, it was not until 1887 that Monsignor Giovanni Batista Scalabrini, Bishop of Piacenza, founded the Apostolic College of Priests (to which Leo XIII referred in his encyclical) to train priests for the apostolate among the Italians abroad.[126]

---

121 Marie A. Dunne, "In Little Italy," *The New World*, Nov. 26, 1909; Lynch, "Religious Condition," 559; Agnew, "Pastoral Care," 264-267; Gertrude, "Italian Immigration," 203; Laurence Franklin, "The Italian in America," *The Catholic World*, LXXI (April 1900), 67-70.

122 McNicholas, "Need of American Priests," 678-680, 687; *The New World*, Oct. 8, 22, 1915. When World War I broke out, the Guardian Angel Social Center of Chicago intensified its efforts to make the Italians "loyal American citizens inspired by the sacrificial ideals of Catholicism." *The New World*, Dec. 10, 1915.

123 Nov. 29, 1913; Palmieri, "Contribution of Italian Catholic Clergy," 141; *Venticinque Anni*, 179-186.

124 Mangano claimed that Catholic welfare programs were the "direct result of the example of Protestant work." *Sons of Italy*, 151.

125 Schiavo, *Italian American History*, II, 481-502.

126 Two recent publications supersede previous writings about Bishop Scalabrini and the order he founded, the Pious Society of St. Charles Borromeo: Marco Caliaro and Mario Francesconi, *L'Apostolo degli emigranti Giovanni Battista*

Distressed by the plight of the immigrants, Scalabrini called attention to the abuses from which they suffered and proposed measures for their protection. His pamphlet, *L'emigrazione italiana in America* (1887), stimulated among religious and secular authorities alike a greater concern for their dispersed countrymen.[127] With the blessings of the Holy See, Scalabrini established the "Congregazione dei Missionari per gli Emigrati" dedicated to "keeping alive in the hearts of our emigrating countrymen the Catholic faith and of procuring, insofar as possible, their moral, civil, and economic well-being."[128] When news of this reached Archbishop Corrigan, he wrote to Scalabrini:

Now I breathe more easily. There is hope that we can do something for these dear souls who are being lost by the thousand. Until now I could find no way to secure their salvation. Now I am tranquil and content. In the meantime I commend to you my abandoned Italians. If it would be possible I would wish two missionaries as soon as possible.[129]

In response to this urgent request, the first Scalabrini Fathers arrived in New York City on July 20, 1888 to begin their mission among the Italians.

In the decades which followed, hundreds of missionaries went forth from the mother house in Piacenza to labor among their countrymen in South and North America. They established mission centers, churches, schools, orphanages, hospitals, and other institutions to serve the immigrants. By 1905, there were twenty Scalabrini parishes in the United States alone. The missionaries of St. Charles also organized branches of the St. Raphael Society for the Protection of Italian Immigrants in New York (1891) and Boston (1902). Through its agents, the St. Raphael sought to protect the newcomers from the "merchants in human flesh," and to provide material and spiritual assistance to those in need.[130] Such

---

Scalabrini (Milan, 1968) and Antonio Perotti, "La società italiana di fronte alle prime migrazioni di massa," *Studi Emigrazione,* V (Feb.-June, 1968). This article was substantially completed before these volumes came to hand.

[127] The text of this pamphlet and other writings of Bishop Scalabrini and his missionaries are reprinted in: Perotti, "La Società italiana," 199-506.

[128] Padre V.D., *L'Apostolo,* 24-27; Caliaro, *L'Apostolo,* 256-260.

[129] Quoted in Padre Costantino Sassi, *Parrocchia della Madonna di Pompei in New York Notizie Storiche dei Primi Cinquant'Anni dalla Sua Foundazione: 1892-1942* (Rome, 1946), 17.

[130] Persegati, "Missionari Scalabriniani," 45-53; Padre V.D., *L'Apostolo,* 27-36; Caliaro, *L'Apostolo,* 261-270, 313-315. On learning that Archbishop Corrigan

were the fruits of these labors that when Bishop Scalabrini visited the United States in 1901 he was warmly greeted as the "Father of the Immigrants." The Archbishop of Cincinnati told him:

Before your Priests came, we believed that the Italians were no better than animals, refractory to whatever preachment of good, and thus we abandoned them to themselves: today we must admit that the Italian colony is better than all the others.[131]

Scalabrini heard but one complaint with regard to his missionaries: "There are not enough of them. All the bishops who have Italians in their dioceses clamor for them."[132] With the whole of the Western Hemisphere as its missionary field, the Society of St. Charles simply lacked resources adequate to the task.

Other Italian religious orders also labored in the vineyard of immigration. By 1918, some twenty-six, including Franciscans, Jesuits, Augustinians, Dominicans, Pallotines, Stigmatines, Servites, and Salesians were active in the United States, administering parishes, schools, and charitable institutions for the immigrants.[133] As Don Luigi Guanella observed in 1913:

There are not by now Italian religious orders or congregations which do not in some measure send their children to the United States to alleviate the miseries of our countrymen who are crying, of our compatriots staggering in the whirlpools of the great cities.[134]

The Italian religious were thought to be more successful than the secular priests in attracting and holding the immigrants. This was attributed to their more vigorous defense of their right to provide spiritual care for their countrymen against the pretensions of the American clergy. The American priests who presided over territorial parishes, of course, resisted the erection of national parishes which they regarded as encroachments on their domain. The work of the religious orders, if zealous, was severely limited by an inade-

---

had approved the establishment of a St. Raphael Society in New York, Cardinal Simeoni, prefect of the Propaganda, commented: "He will probably have all the other Irish Bishops down on him in consequence." Quoted in Barry, *Catholic Church and German Americans*, 166.

131 Quoted in Sterlocchi, *Cenni Biografici*, 56.

132 Icilio Felici, *Father to the Immigrants*, trans. by Carol della Chiesa (New York, 1955), 92.

133 Palmieri, "Clero Italiano," 118; *Grave Problema*, 49.

134 Sterlocchi, *Cenni Biografici*, 113.

quate number of hands. In 1918, of the 710 Italian parish priests in
the United States only 223 were religious.[135] This meant that most
Italian churches were ministered by secular clergy who, by and
large, were not distinguished by ability or zeal. Mindful of this
situation, Pius X decreed in 1914 that a college be established in
Rome to prepare young diocesan priests who would devote themselves to the care of the Italians in America. Although the war
delayed the erection of the college, Benedict XV announced his
intention to proceed with this plan. In 1920, he established an
ordinariate for chaplains for the Italian emigrants with Bishop
Michele Cerrati at its head. Shortly thereafter a Pontifical College
of the Immigration was established in Rome. However, this came
too late to have much of an impact upon the "Italian Problem."[136]

In the missions to the immigrants, the Italian sisters were the
"right hands of the pastors." They cared for the sick, helped the
poor, and educated the children. Sometimes the nuns could enter
houses whose doors were closed to the priest.[137] Among the religious orders of women, the primacy belonged to the Missionary
Sisters of the Sacred Heart. It was Bishop Scalabrini who first suggested to Mother Francesca Xavier Cabrini that she devote her
efforts in behalf of the Italians in the Americas. Upon the invitation
of Archbishop Corrigan, Mother Cabrini and six of her Sisters
arrived in New York City in 1889. From these modest beginnings
were to come a large number of colleges, schools, orphanages,
hospitals, and day nursuries. At the time of Mother Cabrini's death
in Chicago in 1917, the Sisters of the Sacred Heart had grown to
2300 nuns who administered sixty-seven institutions in six countries.[138] Other orders of Italian sisters also exercised their ministry

[135] Palmieri, "Clero Italiano," 117; *Grave Problema*, 47-49; Perrotta, "Catholic Care," 64.

[136] Ciesluk, *National Parishes*, 34; *The New World*, April 24, 1914; Palmieri,
Grave Problema, 65; Perrotta, "Catholic Care," 74-75; "Circular Letter of S.
Consistorial Congregation to the Most Rev. Ordinaries of America Concerning
the Care of Italian Emigrants," *The Ecclesiastical Review Year Book for Priests
1917* (Philadelphia, 1916), 65-66. The Consistorial Congregation alluding to the
potential loss of many Italians to the Church declared: "To avert so great an evil
the sole remedy is to increase the number of priests who, burning with zeal and
piety, and skilled in the Italian language and, if needs be, in the vernacular
speech, may devote themselves to the care of the Italian emigrants."

[137] Palmieri, "Contribution of Italian Catholic Clergy," 131-133.

[138] Felici, *Father*, 215-219; Palmieri, *Grave Problema*, 51-53; James J. Walsh,
"An Apostle of the Italians," *The Catholic World*, CVIII (April, 1918), 64-71;
Emilia de Sanctis Rosmini, *Santa Francesca Saverio Cabrini* (Rome, 1946); *The
New World*, April 10, 1914.

of teaching, nursing, and charity on behalf of the immigrants. Among these were the Pallottine Sisters, the Missionary Zelatrices of the Sacred Heart, and the Religious Teachers Filippini. The Italian nuns were not always well regarded by American priests. As the Reverend Aurelio Palmieri commented: "Their heroism approached at times sublime heights, especially in the Italian parishes directed by members of the Hibernian-American clergy."[139]

If this missionary enterprise was in response to the cry of the emigrants, it was also an expression of the growing spirit of Christain democracy in Italy. Even as Catholic reformers in the spirit of Leo XIII's encyclical, *Rerum Novarum*, sought to alleviate injustice and suffering in Italy (and to counteract the appeal of socialism) by organizing trade unions, cooperatives, and welfare agencies, they addressed themselves to the related problems of emigration. Bishop Scalabrini embodied these dual concerns in his own career, as did his good friend, Bishop Geremia Bonomelli of Cremona.[140] The "Societá di San Raffaele per La Protezione degli emigranti," founded in 1889 at the urging of Scalabrini, had committees in the major Italian ports to assist and protect the emigrants.[141] In 1906 with the approval of Pius X, the Chaplains of Emigration was established by Monsignor G. Coccolo to provide spiritual care during the ocean crossing. "Italica Gens," founded in 1909 by a federation of Italian clergy, sought to assist Italians resident overseas. Under its auspices, a "Segretariato del Popolo" was opened in a number of American cities to help the immigrants find jobs, secure welfare services, provide financial aid, etc. "Italica Gens" also

---

139 Palmieri, "Clero italiano," 118. For a detailed account of the Religious Teachers Filippini which illustrates this point see: De Glauco, *Un Inno, passim.*
140 Caliaro, *L'Apostolo,* 19-22, and *passim.*; Smith, *Italy,* 224; Pisani, *L'Emigrazione,* 20-21. Bishop Bonomelli's "Opera di Assistenza" sought to aid the Italian immigrants in Europe and the Levant as the Society of St. Charles did in the Americas.
141 The Italian organization which was initially known as the "Associazione di patronato per l'emigrazione" was patterned after the German St. Raphaels-verein. Bishop Scalabrini and Peter Paul Cahensly were close friends and associates. In fact, the Lucerne Memorial which touched off the Cahenslyism controversy was authored by Marchese G.B. Volpe-Landi, president of the Italian society, with the approval of Scalabrini. The Italians were taken to task for their role in this affair by the Rev. Henry A. Brann in *The Catholic World*: "We say to the Marchese Landi that until he and his countrymen free Leo XIII from the chains which they have permitted to be fastened around the feet of his authority, they are in no position to criticize the Catholicity of other nations." Barry, *Catholic Church and German Americans,* 131-182; Caliaro, *L'Apostolo,* 300-324; Perotti, "La società italiana," 54-78.

promoted the agricultural colonization of the Italians, but with little success. The American branches of the St. Raphael Society engaged in a variety of social services. The New York branch opened a House of Refuge in 1900 as a shelter for the weary, sick and lost among the new arrivals. Newspapers, tracts, and guides were published to counteract the propaganda of the "sowers of hate." Nurseries, evening schools, sewing classes, theatre groups, reading rooms, hospitals, orphanages, and employment offices, were established under the auspices of the Italian religious orders.[142]

Through such forms of assistance the Italian priests sought not only to offset the material inducements offered by the Protestant missions, but to refute the socialist charge that they were "the natural allies of the *padroni*." Rather than being enemies of the proletariat, the priests sought to persuade the workers that they were the "disinterested friends of the working class."[143] The best way to do so according to the Reverend Cianci was to expose and combat the atrocious exploitation to which the laborers were subjected by the "bosses" and "banchisti." "Let us help the Italian workers in their temporal needs," he asserted, "and we will have gained them for the Church."[144] Such a course of action, however, was a perilous one for the Italian priest since it brought him into conflict with the "prominenti," i.e., the most influential individuals in the Italian colonies. Yet there were courageous missionaries who did wage effective campaigns against the system of "bossismo."[145]

Given the antagonistic relations between church and state in Italy, it might appear curious that the priests should be exponents of Italian patriotism. However, the rationale of the national parish was the assumption of a collective identity based on nationality. The absence of a strong sense of nationalism among the immigrants caused some to question the need for an Italian clergy. On the other hand, the anticlericals suspected the priests of being traitors to the *patria*. The burden of proof rested upon the Italian missionaires both to demonstrate their patriotism and its relevance to their

---

[142] *Venticinque Anni,* 153-357; Palmieri, "Contribution of Italian Catholic Clergy," 141-143; "Lettere da Chicago," 68-74; Pisani, *L'Emigrazione,* 30; *The New World,* Oct. 9, 1909; George J. Hoffman, "Catholic Immigrant Aid Societies in New York City from 1880 to 1920," (doctoral dissertation, St. John's University, 1947), 55-99.

[143] *Venticinque Anni,* 233; Pisani, *L'Emigrazione,* 20-21.

[144] Cianci, *Lavoro Sociale,* 12-17.

[145] *Venticinque Anni,* 205-221; Perotti, "La società italiana," 96-116.

religious function. Thus the ministers of the gospel were often unabashed apostles of *italianità*. Rather than Catholicism and patriotism being in conflict, they were proclaimed to be inseparable:

Take away from our emigrant people its faith, and you have taken from it the *patria;* take away its Catholic character and you will have at the same time taken away that of being Italian, and on the contrary leave them Catholic and rest assured, they will remain Italian.[146]

From the pulpit, the priests tried to awaken a spirit of national pride by invoking the figures of Dante Allighieri and Cristoforo Colombo. They exhorted the Italians to honor the ideals of Religion, *Patria*, and Family. The immigrants were urged not to bring shame on the Italian name by failing to support their churches and schools as did other nationalities. The Italian clergy thought of themselves as the guardians of Italian culture. Hence, they placed great stress on the teaching of the Italian language and history in the schools so that the children might learn to love both God and *patria*. The priests saw themselves as the defenders of true patriotism, "of the *italianità* and of the Catholicism of the sons of Italy."[147]

The Libyan War provided an opportunity for the Italian clergy to demonstrate its loyalty. *Il Progresso Italo-Americano* observed:

It is noble and comforting to see how the Italian clergy in America, in this difficult, but glorious hour, which Italy is crossing at this moment, competes in works of charity, animated by a high sense of patriotism. They have demonstrated how the sentiment of the *patria* and the sentiment of religion can not and must not be disjoined, but must constitute an harmonious whole.[148]

As long as the "Roman Question" remained an issue, however, the anticlericals were not persuaded by such avowals of patriotism. They viewed any governmental patronage of religious institutions as sinister. When the Italian consul in Chicago entrusted the administration of a shelter for poor immigrants to the Sisters of the

---

146 Beccherini, *Fenomeno dell'Emigrazione*, 14.

147 Cianci, *Lavoro Sociale*, 20; *Venticinque Anni*, 169; Sterlocchi, *Cenni Biografici*, 54, 113; Rev. Antonio Isoleri, *Un Ricordo delle Feste Colombiane celebrate in Philadelphia, Stati Uniti d'America, nell'Ottobre del 1892* (Philadelphia, 1892); "Libro degli Annunzi," June 10, 1906, Odone Papers; Pisani, *L'Emigrazione*, 19.

148 Quoted in: *Venticinque Anni*, 253.

Sacred Heart, the socialists protested that "Catholic propaganda will be fed through the medium of a bowl of soup."[149] For the same reason, the Italian parochial schools were not subsidized by the Italian government. Between the Italian missionaries and the representatives of the Italian government there was often mutual suspicion and hostility. The tension between loyalty to the Church and loyalty to the *patria* was not to be entirely resolved until the Lateran Treaties of 1929 settled the outstanding issues between the Kingdom of Italy and the Vatican.[150]

The attitude of the American hierarchy was of decisive influence in determining the response of the Church to the immigrants from Italy. As the Reverend John Zarrilli declared: "The whole destiny and future of the Italians in America is, to a great extent, in the hands of the American Bishops."[151] With a number of notable exceptions, these prelates seemed to feel that little could or ought to be done for the Italians. The problem was one for the Italian hierarchy or the Congregation of the Propaganda. As late as the 1920's there were large cities and entire dioceses with significant numbers of Italians which did not have a single Italian priest. In certain dioceses it was reported that not only was no effort made to secure Italian clergymen, but that they were actually excluded.[152] Such a course was openly advocated by the Reverend John T. McNicholas, himself pastor of an Italian church for some years and later Bishop of Duluth. He contended that the Italian priests, religious as well as secular, were not suited by character and training to care for their countrymen in America. McNicholas held that American priests with some knowledge of the Italian language and customs were best equipped both to sanctify and to Americanize the Italian immigrants.[153]

---

[149] *La Parola dei Socialisti*, Jan. 3, 17, May 23, 1914 (W.P.A.); *The Survey*, XXXI (Jan. 17, 1914), 457.

[150] Cianci, *Lavoro Sociale*, 11, 15; *Venticinque Anni*, 213; Diary, March 24, 1917, Odone Papers; Theodore Abel, *Protestant Home Missions to Catholic Immigrants* (New York, 1933), 48-49. Abel reported that following news of the agreement between Mussolini and the Vatican there were several instances of Italian youths stoning Protestant mission centers.

[151] Zarrilli, *Prayerful Appeal*, 2.

[152] *Ibid.*, 18-19; Palmieri, *Grave Problema*, 27; Diary, Dec. 26, 1928, Odone Papers.

[153] McNicholas, "Need of American Priests," 681-682.

Certain American bishops sent students to seminaries in Italy to prepare them for the Italian missions. Although this was justified by the lack of Italian clergy, when a priest from Italy did present himself before a bishop he not infrequently received a cool reception. "The Italian priests," declared the Reverend Palmieri, "must suffer the hardest humiliations . . . before receiving the *scrap of paper* which authorizes them with infinite and fastidious restrictions and with an empty purse to assume the spiritual care of their compatriots."[154] A bitter attack was launched against the American hierarchy by a schismatic priest, Antonio Giulio Lenzi, who accused it of waging war against the Italian clergy, of unjustly suspending them, of denying them facilities while Italian colonies were crying for priests of their nationality. All these wrongs, Lenzi attributed to domination of the Church in America by the Irish.[155]

Those who wished to refute such accusations cited the generosity and affection manifested by certain prelates toward the Italians. Recognizing the inability of these immigrants to build their own churches and schools, they provided buildings, priests, and sisters out of Church resources. Within a decade, for example, Archbishop James Edward Quigley established a dozen Italian parishes in Chicago; in Buffalo, Bishop Carl Henry Colton founded seventeen churches for the Italians; while in Trenton, Bishop Thomas J. Walsh supplied them with schools staffed by Italian sisters. The early concern shown by Archbishop Corrigan of New York for the Italians was continued by his successor, Cardinal John Farley, who is reported to have said: "I have more Italians in New York than the Pope has in Rome." Farley erected twenty-one churches and schools and provided priests and nuns for them.[156] He also established a diocesan bureau in 1912 for the special care of the Italians. An "Apostolato italiano" under the direction of the Reverend Roberto Biasotti was organized to give missions in the Italian parishes. The Archbishop also called his Italian priests together several times a year to confer on common problems. This procedure was said to increase confidence on the part of the clergy and the people in their ecclesiastical superiors; it was recommended "if the

---

154 Palmieri, "Clero Italiano," 122; Rizzato, *Figure*, 40-43.
155 Palmieri, *Grave Problema*, 61-62.
156 *Ibid.*, 63; Perrotta, "Catholic Care," 68-74; Muredach, "Experiment in City Home Missions," 19-26; Beccherini, *Fenomeno dell'Emigrazione*, 18.

immigrant is not to become a prey to socialist agitation and a
danger to the liberties and peace of Church and State."[157] Other
bishops also busied themselves more or less effectively to do something for their Italians, but their activity does not appear to have
aroused the majority of the episcopacy from its mood of fatalism
with respect to the "Italian Problem." If, as Palmieri asserts, the
American hierarchy was not in general responsible for the religious
neglect of the Italian immigrants,[158] yet it was not without blame.

That the Roman Catholic Church in the United States should
be almost equally concerned with the Americanization of the
Italians as with the salvation of their souls might appear to be
paradoxical. Yet such was the natural consequence of the anxiety
on the part of certain ecclesiastics that the Church lose its foreign
character. These liberal prelates believed that rather than being in
conflict Catholicism and Americanism were in basic harmony.
Striving to persuade their fellow citizens of the unqualified and un-
divided loyalty of Catholics in the United States, they opposed any
policy which tended to perpetuate the "foreign" element in the
Church. In the Cahenslyism controversy of the 1890's, the Ameri-
canists led by Archbishop John Ireland repelled what they regarded
as an effort to create a permanent German Catholic party within
the Church. Committed to the proposition that it was the duty of
the Church to bring about a rapid assimilation of the Catholic immigrants, the liberals in the hierarchy viewed with disapproval the
efforts of Eastern and Southern Europeans to transplant their
religious cultures to America.[159]

Among the various elements of the "Italian Problem," this policy
of coercive Americanization was not the least significant, particularly since to the Italians what presented itself in the guise of
American Catholicism had pronounced Hibernian lineaments. Al-

---

[157] "Diocesan Bureaux for the Care of Italian, Slav, Ruthenian, and Asiatic
Catholics in America," *The Ecclesiastical Review*, LXVIII (Feb., 1913), 221-222.
[158] Palmieri, *Grave Problema*, 62.
[159] Robert Cross, *The Emergence of Liberal Catholicism in America* (Chicago,
1968), 29-39, 88-94; Barry, *Catholic Church and German Americans*, *passim*.
Barry, however, contends that following Leo XIII's apostolic brief, *Testem benevolentiae*, of 1899, which rejected certain opinions under the heading of "Americanism," the American bishops were more responsive to the rights and needs of
various national groups. Such does not appear to have been true on the whole for
the Italians or for other groups as well. In 1920, the Poles appealed to the Holy
See against their neglect in the United States, their lack of representation in the
hierarchy, and the policy of Americanization. *Ibid.*, 251-254, 275n.

though the protests against Irish clerical aggression were many, the case was most cogently presented by the Reverend Aurelio Palmieri. A learned Augustinian who had spent many years in America, Palmieri was probably the most astute commentator on the religious situation of the Italian immigrants. While freely admitting the spiritual deficiencies of his countrymen, Palmieri identified the arrogance and antipathy which the American Irish clergy expressed toward the Italians as contributing largely to their estrangement from the Church.[160]

Agreeing that Catholicism in the United States must in time become "perfectly American," Palmieri declared that Americanization ought not to mean a monopoly of the Church for the benefit of a particular race. While the Italians might wish to become Americans, they did not intend in religion to become the helots of yet another race of immigrants. "It would be folly," Palmieri asserted, "to expect that the immigrant debarked on these shores be immediately . . . torn from his pastors who have educated his religious infancy, forced to renounce his *feste*, his traditions, his manifestations of piety, his saints, and to transform himself not yet into an American Catholic, but into a Catholic of another race."[161] The substitution of Irish or German priests for Italians in the care of the immigrants Palmieri thought an absurdity. Particularly the Irish, he thought, were repelled by the anticlericalism and irreligiousness of the Italians. "The apostolate accompanied by disgust," he warned, "is easily sterile." The practical apostasy of large members of immigrants Palmieri attributed to this aversion they sensed among the American clergy:

Is it any wonder that our emigrants turn their backs to a church which reserves for them insults and disgust, which segregates their children from associating with Catholic children of other nationalities, and which sprays in their face the gall of slander?[162]

The Italians had concluded that the Church in America was a wicked stepmother.

---

[160] Commenting on the attitudes of American Irish priests toward the Italians, Palmieri observed: "It explains why our immigrants, even those who were practicing Catholics in Italy, disembarked in America, stay as far away as they can from the Irish churches and clergy, and prefer, when lacking Italian churches, to have recourse to German priests rather than to scorners of their race." "Clero Italiano," 124; *Grave Problema*, 34-35.

[161] "Clero Italiano," 114-115.

[162] *Ibid.*, 125; *Grave Problema*, 32.

Suggesting that the Irish clergy devote their apostolic zeal to their Celtic brethren, ravaged by alcoholism and apostasy, Palmieri declared that they were the most ill-suited for the task of keeping the Italians bound to Catholicism. They lacked understanding and sympathy for the noisy, imaginative piety, the religious psychology, the customs, needs, and defects of the *contadini*. What was needed were priests who understood the dialects and the religious traditions of the immigrants, especially the cults of the patron saints and feasts of southern Italy. Only the Italian priests who were not preoccupied with a "reformatory puritanism," according to Palmieri, could reawaken in their hearts remembrances of their ancestral faith.[163] Recognizing the failure of the Italian clergy to accompany the emigrants, Palmieri added his voice to those calling for an apostolate of Italian priests in behalf of their abandoned countrymen. He also noted that while many bishops of the American church were born and educated abroad, the Italians lacked "a pastor of our race." As long as they were treated as outcasts, Palmieri believed that the work of religious Americanization among the Italians would have only negative results.[164]

The Reverend John Zarrilli, longtime pastor of Italian parishes in Minnesota, also gave long and careful thought to the "Italian Problem." In a series of articles in the 1920's, he proposed several measures based on the proposition that "the salvation of the Italians must come, in the first place and mainly, from the Italians themselves."[165] Like Palmieri, he insisted on the necessity for priests who

[163] *Ibid.*, 29-30, 36-37, 40-41. Palmieri commented that just as the American Catholics refused to celebrate the "obscure feasts of unknown saints" of the Italians so the latter were not inclined toward devotions to St. Patrick and St. Lorenzo O'Toole.

[164] "Clero Italiano," 127; *Grave Problema*, 29, 35. Palmieri noted that 35 of the bishops and cardinals of the American church were born and educated in Ireland. Although two Italians served as bishops in the United States in the nineteenth century (Joseph Rosati of St. Louis and Ignazio Persico of Savannah), none achieved episcopal office again until after 1940. The sees presided over by Italian ordinaries since then have included Alexandria, La.; Amarillo, Texas; Camden, N.J.; Natchez, Miss.; and Steubenville, Ohio. It was not until 1968 that an Italian–American became head of a major diocese; Francis John Mugavero, son of Sicilian immigrants, was named Bishop of the Diocese of Brooklyn. *The New York Times*, July 18, 1968, 30; Joseph Bernard Code, *Dictionary of the American Hierarchy 1789-1940* (New York, 1940); *The Official Catholic Directory* (New York, 1968).

[165] When an article of his was rejected by *The Ecclesiastical Review* on the grounds that it was "too aggressive," Zarrilli published his views in a pamphlet, *A Prayerful Appeal to the American Hierarchy in behalf of the Italian Catholic Cause in the United States* (Two Harbors, Minn., 1924).

understood the dialects, the customs, "the very souls," of the immigrants and who loved them. But Zarrilli added, such priests ought to be thoroughly Americanized in their attitudes and methods. An Italo-American Catholic Center should be established to provide the necessary indoctrination for Italian priests before they assumed pastoral duties. Zarrilli also envisioned the Center "as a clearing house for Italian Catholic thought and movements in the United States." It might publish an Italian Catholic periodical, sponsor an annual congress of Italian clergymen, and serve as headquarters for a national organization of laymen. Zarrilli suggested that the Holy See appoint an Italian with episcopal authority to direct the Center. In addition, he urged that several bishops of Italian nationality be added to the American hierarchy. "I do not believe," he commented,

that it is so unreasonable a desire to have, of over one hundred Bishops in the United States, three of four of Italian nationality with a population of about four million Italians, (almost one-fifth of the Catholics of the country), or about one Bishop to each million people.[166]

Zarrilli's proposals came under intense fire from American churchmen. They were denounced on the grounds that they would tend to perpetuate "foreign national aspirations to the lessening of sympathy with American ideals"; a critic asserted:

Priests of foreign birth and training feel bound and bent on perpetuating the foreign spirit and traditions through language teaching, newspapers, schools and foreign organizations. Since they do not hope to be recognized on a level with the native American priest in the appointment to English-speaking congregations, they feel that they must foster and perpetuate the exclusive separatist spirit among their own nationals.[167]

Rather than a Center as Zarrilli had suggested, a Propaganda College was proposed where foreign priests "would be naturalized and educated in those things required of the citizen and ecclesiastic

---

166 *Ibid.*, 3-10, 16. In reply to the argument that the Italians did not deserve bishops of their nationality because they did not support the Church, Zarrilli countered that perhaps they would do better if given recognition according to the American principle of "no taxation without representation."

167 "Pastoral Care of Foreign Catholics in America," *The Ecclesiastical Review*, LXX (Feb., 1924), 178-179. Zarrilli suspected his anonymous critic of being "a certain Irish clergyman who pretends to be a specialist on the Italian question." *Prayerful Appeal*, 15.

before being put in position of authority over prospective or actual American citizens of his own race or nationality." Likewise the idea of Italian bishops was attacked as promoting nationalism and hindering Americanization.[168] To these objections, Zarrilli replied that he had no intention of encouraging a separatist spirit, but he added:

> Americanization, which is a kind of civil conversion, like the conversion to the faith, should be gradual, spontaneous and be brought about through education, persuasion, not through violent methods and the destruction of what good the immigrant may have, his language included.[169]

Judging from the response, the proposals of Palmieri and Zarrilli raised the spectre of an Italian Cahensylism before the clerical Americanizers. Whether for this reason or not, nothing concrete appears to have come of them.

Writing in 1921, Palmieri concluded that the gravity of the "Italian Problem" had not diminished since Desmond had called attention to the neglected Italians two decades earlier.[170] All that had been done was grossly inadequate to meet the religious needs of the immigrants. In 1918, according to *The Catholic Directory*, there were 710 Italian priests to care for over three million persons of Italian stock, a ratio of one priest for every 5600 Italians. Italian Catholicism, Palmieri grieved, was undergoing a systematic massacre in America.[171] Other students of the subject estimated that from one half to two thirds of the Italians were not practicing Catholics.[172]

---

[168] "Pastoral Care of Foreign Catholics," 179-180.

[169] Zarrilli, *Prayerful Appeal*, 15. Some decades later, Reverend Colman J. Barry pondered whether "too hasty Americanization" might have had a blighting effect upon Catholic cultural and intellectual life. Reflecting upon the impoverishment in America of Catholic traditions in forms of worship and liturgy, in the arts and crafts, Barry suggested "that such aspects of a Christian culture could have developed and received real impetus from immigrant groups like the Germans if they were not up-rooted and shorn of their true identities so rapidly and completely." "The German Catholic Immigrant," in McAvoy, *Roman Catholicism*, 202-203. ,

[170] *Grave Problema*, 22.

[171] *Ibid.*, 35, 49. According to the Census of Religious Bodies of 1916, 149 Catholic Churches used Italian exclusively while 327 used Italian and English. Presumably there were many non-Italians in the combined membership of 1,515,-818. Shaughnessy, *Has the Immigrant Kept the Faith?*, 218.

[172] Mangano, *Sons of Italy*, 150; Sartorio, *Social and Religious Life*, 104; Perrotta, "Catholic Care," 43. Such estimates were at best educated guesses. As Shaughnessy pointed out, there had never been an accurate census taken of the

Because of their estrangement from the Catholic Church it did not follow that the Italians were embracing Protestantism. The widespread opinion that an "impressive minority" of the Italians were going over to the evangelical sects was in error.[173] Despite an enormous investment of zeal and money, the gains of the Protestant denominations among the immigrants were minimal. The Reverend Enrico Chieri, a veteran of the Protestant missions, sorrowfully admitted: "Fifty years of painful efforts of Protestant proselytism among Italians have ended with a complete failure."[174] Two other Protestant missionaries, Enrico C. Sartorio and Antonio Mangano, agreed that the total membership of the Italian Protestant Churches was not much more than 25,000.[175] A judgment expressed in 1933 with regard to Protestant missions was certainly valid for the Italians:

The unimpressive results of fifty years of formal church work among immigrants clearly show that it has failed to fulfill the expectations of serving as an adequate means of evangelizing the masses of Catholic immigrants.[176]

After a half century of missionary labors by *both* Catholics and

---

Catholics in the United States. The Church relied on estimates made by pastors and bishops, while the federal census did not report on religious affiliation. The statistics on religious bodies collected by the government were derived from estimates made by clergymen rather than a true census. *Has the Immigrant Kept the Faith?*, 33.

173 The term is that of Robert F. Foerster, *The Italian Emigration of Our Times* (Cambridge, Mass., 1919), 398.

174 Quoted in Perrotta, "Catholic Care," 42. See also Aurelio Palmieri, "Italian Protestantism in the United States," *The Catholic World*, XVII (May, 1918), 177-189.

175 Mangano, *Sons of Italy*, 175; Sartorio, *Social and Religious Life*, 110-113. According to the Census of Religious Bodies of 1916, there were a total of 202 Italian Protestant churches using Italian alone or Italian and English with 53,073 members. Shaughnessy, *Has the Immigrant Kept the Faith?*, 220. Even these modest claims were challenged by Palmieri who contended that the statistics were inflated and included Italian Waldensians as well. He concluded that the "whole gain of American Protestant propaganda may be computed at something like 6,000." "Contribution of Italian Catholic Clergy," 140.

176 Abel, *Protestant Home Missions*, 38. Abel calculated the total membership of the Protestant missions in the early 1930's at between fifty and sixty thousand. Of these, half were thought to be converts from Catholicism; they included Slavs, Magyars, and Mexicans, as well as Italians. *Ibid.*, 33-34. The history of Italian Protestantism in the United States has yet to be written; for an introduction to the subject see: John B. Bisceglia, *Italian Evangelical Pioneers* (Kansas City, Mo., 1948); De Bilio, "Protestant Mission Work Among Italians in Boston"; Di Domenica, *Protestant Witness of a New American*; George B. Watts, *The Waldenses in the New World* (Durham, N.C., 1941).

Protestants, the majority of the Italian immigrants remained either nominal Roman Catholics or without church ties of any kind. Neither American Catholicism nor American Protestantism succeeded in remaking the Italian peasants in its own image. While the freethinkers and socialists remained aggressively anticlerical, for the majority religion continued to be what it had been in their *paesi*: a belief in the efficacy of magic and devotions to their saints and madonnas coupled with a basic indifference to and distrust of the institutional church.

The case of the Italians casts grave doubt on the validity of the Shaughnessy–Dunne–Commager thesis with regard to the assimilative role of the Catholic Church in the United States. Rather than serving as a primary agency for integrating the immigrants into American society, it is evident that the American Church, in part because of its own definite ethnic character, had a limited capacity to absorb the Italians who came from very different cultural backgrounds. Neither is there any convincing evidence that the Church served as an effective means of social control with regard to the Italians. Since anticlericalism was a basic tenet of Italian socialism, the strong influence exerted by the American Church in secular matters served to exacerbate rather than allay this radical tendency among the immigrants. The "Italian Problem" was many things to many people, but to the Italian immigrants themselves it may have been that the Church in the United States was more American and Irish than Catholic.

ACKNOWLEDGMENTS

Harold J. Abramson, "Ethnic Diversity Within Catholicism: A Comparative Analysis of Contemporary and Historical Religion," *Journal of Social History*, 4:4 (Summer 1971), 359–388. Reprinted with the permission of *Journal of Social History*. Courtesy of Yale University Library.

Daniel S. Buczek, "Polish-Americans and the Roman Catholic Church," *Polish Review*, 21:3 (1976), 39–61. Reprinted with the permission of the *Polish Review*. Courtesy of the *Polish Review*.

John J. Bukowczyk, "Mary the Messiah: Polish Immigrant Heresy and the Malleable Ideology of the Roman Catholic Church, 1880–1930," *Journal of American Ethnic History*, 4:2 (Spring 1985), 5–32. Reprinted with the permission of *Journal of American Ethnic History*. Courtesy of George E. Pozzetta.

John J. Bukowczyk, "The Transforming Power of the Machine: Popular Religion, Ideology, and Secularization Among Polish Immigrant Workers in the United States, 1880–1940," *International Labor and Working-Class History*, 34 (Fall 1988), 22–38. Reprinted with the permission of *International Labor and Working-Class History*. Courtesy of the Library of Congress.

Jay P. Dolan, "The Immigrants and Their Gods: A New Perspective in American Religious History," *Church History*, 57:1 (March 1988), 61–72. Reprinted with the permission of *Church History*. Courtesy of Yale University Library.

Jay P. Dolan, "Immigrants in the City: New York's Irish and German Catholics," *Church History*, 41:3 (September 1972), 354–368. Reprinted with the permission of *Church History*. Courtesy of Yale University Library.

William Galush, "Both Polish and Catholic: Immigrant Clergy in the American Church," *Catholic Historical Review*, 70:3 (July 1984), 407–427. Reprinted with the permission of *Catholic Historical Review*. Courtesy of *Catholic Historical Review*.

David A. Gerber, "Modernity in the Service of Tradition: Catholic Lay Trustees at Buffalo's St. Louis Church and the Transformation of European Communal Traditions, 1829–1855," *Journal of Social History*, 15 (Summer 1982), 655–684. Reprinted with the permission of *Journal of Social History*. Courtesy of Yale University Library.

Jon Gjerde, "Conflict and Community: A Case Study of the Immigrant Church in the United States," *Journal of Social History*, 19 (1986), 681–697. Reprinted with the permission of *Journal of Social History*. Courtesy of George E. Pozzetta.

Robert F. Harney, "Religion and Ethnocultural Communities," *Polyphony*, I (Summer 1978), 1–10. Reprinted with the permission of *Poliphony*. Courtesy of George E. Pozzetta.

Frederick C. Luebke, "German Immigrants and Churches in Nebraska, 1889–1915," *Mid-America*, 50:2 (April 1968), 116–130. Reprinted with the permission of *Mid-America*. Courtesy of *Mid-America*.

Martin E. Marty, "Ethnicity: The Skeleton of Religion in America," *Church History*, 41:1 (March 1972), 5–21. Reprinted with the permission of *Church History*. Courtesy of Yale University Library.

John J. Meng, "Cahenslyism: The First Stage, 1883–1891," *Catholic Historical Review*, XXXI:4 (January 1946), 389–413. Reprinted with the permission of *Catholic Historical Review*. Courtesy of Yale University Library.

Raymond A. Mohl and Neil Betten, "The Immigrant Church in Gary, Indiana: Religious Adjustment and Cultural Defense," *Ethnicity*, 8:1 (March 1981), 1–17. Reprinted with the permission of *Ethnicity*. Courtesy of George E. Pozzetta.

Robert C. Ostergren, "The Immigrant Church as a Symbol of Community and Place in the Upper Midwest," *Great Plains Quarterly*, 1:4 (Fall 1981), 225–238. Reprinted with the permission of *Great Plains Quarterly*. Courtesy of Yale University Library.

Moses Rischin, "The New American Catholic History," *Church History*, 41:2 (June 1972), 225–229. Reprinted with the permission of *Church History*. Courtesy of Yale University Library.

Theodore Saloutos, "The Greek Orthodox Church in the United States and Assimilation," *International Migration Review*, 7:4 (Winter 1973), 395–407. Reprinted with the permission of *International Migration Review*. Courtesy of *International Migration Review*.

Timothy L. Smith, "Religion and Ethnicity in America," *American Historical Review*, 83 (December 1978), 1155–1185. Courtesy of George E. Pozzetta.

Timothy L. Smith, "Religious Denominations as Ethnic Communities: A Regional Case Study," *Church History*, 35:2 (June 1966), 207–226. Reprinted with the permission of *Church History*. Courtesy of Yale University Library.

Robert P. Swierenga, "Religion and Immigration Patterns: A Comparative Analysis of Dutch Protestants and Catholics, 1835–1880," *Journal of American Ethnic History*, 5:2 (Spring 1986), 23–45. Reprinted with the permission of *Journal of American Ethnic History*. Courtesy of Yale Univerity Library.

Leslie Woodcock Tentler, "Who Is the Church? Conflict in a Polish Immigrant Parish in Late Nineteenth-Century Detroit," *Comparative Studies in Society and History*, 25:2 (April 1983), 241–276. Reprinted with the permission of Cambridge University Press. Courtesy of Yale University Library.

Rudolph J. Vecoli, "Prelates and Peasants: Italian Immigrants and the Catholic Church," *Journal of Social History*, 2:3 (Spring 1969), 217–268. Reprinted with the permission of *Journal of Social History*. Courtesy of Yale University Library.

DATE DUE

FEB 24 1998			